C Mathematical Function Handbook

More Books of Interest for Scientists and Engineers

0-07-003358-7	Baker	*More C Tools for Scientists and Engineers*
0-07-003355-2	Baker	*C Tools for Scientists and Engineers*
0-07-008845-4	Buerger	*LATEX: For Scientists and Engineers*
0-07-026001-X	Hancock, Krieger	*C Primer, Third Edition*
0-07-045001-3	McGilton, Morgan	*Introducing the UNIX System*
0-07-043152-3	Morgan, McGilton	*Introducing the UNIX System V*
0-07-031697-X	Parrette, ITDC	*UNIX: For Application Developers*
0-07-031700-3		
0-07-059180-6	Smith	*C++: For Scientists and Engineers*
0-07-058708-6	Smith	*Advanced Turbo C*
0-07-058707-8		
0-07-062879-5	Tare	*UNIX Utilities*
0-07-062884-X		
0-07-062885-8	Tare	*Data Processing in UNIX*

C Mathematical Function Handbook

Louis Baker

McGraw-Hill, Inc.

New York St. Louis San Francisco Auckland Bogotá
Caracas Lisbon London Madrid Mexico Milan
Montreal New Delhi Paris San Juan São Paulo
Singapore Sydney Tokyo Toronto

Library of Congress Cataloging-in-Publication Data

Baker, Louis.
C mathematical function handbook / Louis Baker.
p. cm.
Includes bibliographical references and index.
ISBN 0-07-911158-0
1. Functions, Special—Computer programs. 2. C (Computer program language) I. Title.
QA351.B17 1991
515'.5'02855262—dc20 91-30926
CIP

1 2 3 4 5 6 7 8 9 0 DOC/DOC 9 7 6 5 4 3 2 1

P/N 003459-1
PART OF
ISBN 0-07-911158-0

The sponsoring editor for this book was Jeanne Glasser, the editing supervisor was Jim Halston, and the production supervisor was Pamela A. Pelton.

Printed and bound by R. R. Donnelley & Sons Company.

To Jennie

Contents

Preface: What's in It (This Book) for You

This book is intended to provide a collection of tested algorithms that compute all of the functions in Abramowitz and Stegun's classic *Handbook of Mathematical Functions*—and more. (For the lawyers out there, it does not include the tables of constants in the first two chapters, the number theoretic results of Chapter 24, the numerical analysis aids of and "scales of notation tables" of Chapters 25 and 28, or the Laplace transforms of Chapter 29. It also does not include explicit methods for determining zeros or other special values of some functions—these may be found using the functions contained herein with a Newton-Raphson or other root finder, such a discussed in my book, *C Tools for Scientists and Engineers*.)

All of the methods used are explained and documented. Users do not have to take the author's word that the method presented is valid; they will be given the information to use it intelligently and knowledgably. Much of "computer science" is still an art. Therefore, it is desirable that readers understand what programs are doing in order to avoid any possible pitfalls. Users should not only run the test problems to convince themselves the programs are working as they should; users should also critically examine their working runs to be sure the results are reasonable.

How to Use This Book

There are a number of ways to use this book. One is to lift a program bodily, run the test case, and then apply it to the problem at hand. The Chapters are ordered to conform to that of Abramowitz and Stegun. I do encourage readers to read the discussion and understand the methods discussed. This will help to avoid embarrassments later. As the source is presented, ROM-able code for embedded applications can be produced, for example. Another use for this book would be as a set of examples of working C and C++ code. Readers uncomfortable with pointer variables, for example, will see many applications of them and could learn how to use them from seeing them in action. The numerical methods used could be a useful supplement to texts on numerical analysis, and the non-numerical algorithms should be of interest to programmers. The statistical methods will be of interest to statisticians, social scientists, or students in such courses. Similarly, engineers and physical scientists, researchers, and students should all be able to find useful programs in this book.

One thing I find annoying about Abramowitz and Stegun's book is that they tabulate, for instance, not the complex exponential integral $E_1(z)$ but $z\, e^z E_1(z)$. When z is a complex number, this is particularly frustrating to convert into the desired function. This is perhaps the worst case, but fairly common functions such as those for Bessel functions, etc., often have values scaled by e^x or some other factor, forcing the reader to calculate instead of merely looking up the desired answer! With the routines in this book, you can now tabulate the functions you want without scaling factors.

To keep the size (and cost!) of this book reasonable, redundancy has been kept to a minimum. It is assumed that you will read the code listings, and that information contained in these (such as required arguments, calling conventions, etc.) need not be repeated in the text.

C for Scientists and Engineers

This book is written in C for a number of reasons. This language is rapidly becoming the *lingua franca* of the computer world. It is on machines from microcomputers to supercomputers, PCs to Crays, thanks in no small part to the ubiquity of the UNIX operating system. It is a structured, high-level language. Algorithms written in C should be very portable, and easily converted with reasonable readiness into other high-level languages. Just about every FORTRAN compiler has an interface to a C compiler (examples on the IBM-PC family include Microsoft FORTRAN and C, NDP FORTRAN and Metaware High C), but many popular C compilers cannot call FORTRAN routines (e.g., Turbo C/C++). It is now common to have common code generators and optimizers for a family of compilers, so the optimization of code is independent of the language.

What This Book Contains

Rarely is one algorithm better than all others for all cases. For this reason, alternative methods for the various cases that may appear are discussed where appropriate. While every effort has been expended to use methods that are "state-of-the-art," computer science changes at a rapid pace, and it is possible that improvements will be discovered. I would appreciate hearing from readers with improvements, corrections, better algorithms for some problems, etc.

It is my sincere hope that readers will save themselves much grief by being able to use the routines presented here with a minimum of effort. I also hope that students and others will take the opportunity to learn from the methods presented here. They are not perfect, but most derive from a long series of efforts by workers in the fields of programming and numerical analysis. They, therefore, represent the distilled effort of many people. I apologize to those workers whose contributions I fail to adequately cite, through ignorance or error. Readers of this book might justly feel that they are standing on the shoulders of many giants when they use some of the methods contained herein; they will almost certainly "see" further by doing so than by relying on only their own legs.

Acknowledgments

I'd like to thank many colleagues for their help, especially B. S. Newberger for contributing FORTRAN programs they had written, and A. Giancola for much critical advice. The book was typeset with Ventura publisher (excluding program listings), the figures scanned with a Princeton LS-300, and camera-ready copy was produced with a PS Jet + .

Words to the Wise

The table of content's of the *LINPACK User's Guide* by J. J. Dongarra et al. (Philadelphia: SIAM 1979), contains the quotation: "R.T.F.M." Anonymous. That advice applies here as well. Don't run codes you don't understand, or you won't understand the answers (even if you think you do).

While every effort has been made to test and ensure the correctness of the methods presented here, final responsibility rests with the user for assuring their results are correct. All of the references, codes, and tables I have used to prepare this book either have extensive lists of errata (such as Abramowitz and Stegun) or have had errors I have noted, or both. I do not have the *hubris* to presume this book is the first flawless work on the subject. The programs presented here are without warranty, and no liability shall be incurred by the author or the publisher for any loss or damage caused directly or indirectly by the programs or algorithms described in this book. (Please read the full disclaimer which appears on the copyright page.) Please check all programs and results carefully. In addition to running the test problems contained in this book, generate your own to confirm that you fully understand the calling conventions and data formats. To paraphrase John Philpot Curran, the condition upon which freedom from errors depends is eternal vigilance.

Louis Baker

C
Mathematical Function Handbook

Chapter 1

Special Functions and Numerical Analysis

In this chapter, we briefly review the elements of numerical analysis and IEEE-STD-754 of relevance to this book. Consult the references at the end of this chapter for more information.

Correspondence with Abramowitz and Stegun

The first two chapters of Abramowitz and Stegun are on physical and mathematical constants. In their place, this chapter and the next discuss numerical analysis and the C language. The remaining chapters in this book present functions and programs which correspond to the results in the corresponding chapters of Abramowitz and Stegun.

Numerical Analysis

There are many good texts on numerical analysis. For discussions with particular regard to C, see the next chapter and the books *C Tools for Scientists and Engineers* (hereafter called *C Tools*) and *More C Tools for Scientists and Engineers* (hereafter called *More C Tools*). The former contains brief discussions of error analysis, finite-precision arithmetic, and complexity analysis, a chapter on C (including debugging tips), and a variety of programs such as LU decomposition, the Fast Fourier Transform, and others. The latter contains a discussion of continued fractions and rational approximation techniques in its presentation of the Complex Error function and various statistical functions, and random number generators. These functions are contained in this package, but the full discussion is not reproduced. The references in those books will also be of interest.

The IEEE-754 Standard

In order to make computation less sensitive to the idiosyncracies of different hardware architectures, the IEEE promulgated a standard in 1985. It is not adhered to universally; in fact, many architectures that claim to adhere to it do not do so perfectly (see Dewar and Smosna's comments). One sore point is the requirement for gradual underflow, in which numbers too small for normal representation become *denormal* numbers. Because it is computationally expensive to deal with such numbers, some manufacturers prefer sudden underflow, in which the underflowed value is set to zero.

The standard provides for two principal types of precision, single and double (a third, extended, is intended for processor use and is not normally accessible to the user, especially from high-level languages). These are shown in Table 1.1. (More precise values should be found in your compiler's **float.h** header file, if it exists. In Turbo C 2.0, the value for **DBL_MAX** is defined as an external variable **_huge_dble**, and you must run a program to find that it is roughly 1.7979693e+308. Similarly, the maximum values for single precision and extended are found to be 3.402823e+38 and 1.189731e+4932 . The header contains the usual IEE-754 values for minimum representable numbers and precision, i.e., the difference between 1.0 and the next representable number.) The type **float** in C generally corresponds to single precision while type **double** to double precision as defined in the standard. While the smallest type **double** normal number is approximately 2.225e-308, the smallest denormal is approximately 4.94e-324.

Table 1.1
IEEE Standard 754 Floating-Point Types

Type	Exponent		Mantissa	
	Size (Bits)	Max. Digits (Decimal)	Size (Bits)	Precision (Decimal Digits)
Single	8	≈ 37	23	≈ 7
Double	11	≈ 308	52	≈ 16

Note that single and double precision differ in both the range of allowed exponents as well as in the number of digits of precision in the mantissa. The precision of floating-point numbers on MIL-STD-1750A processors is the same as single precision in the IEEE standard. The behavior, as regards underflow, for example, is different. Also, the 1750A has extended precision floating-point numbers occupying 48 bits (same exponent range), and there is no analog of IEEE double precision.

Double precision will be required when the magnitude of the numbers of interest are in the range of 10^{37}, or when numbers smaller than 10^{-37} must be dealt with. This can often happen when porting codes from environments in which larger ranges are supported. Double precision will also be required when numerical round-off error is important, such as solving large systems of simultaneous equations. Older C compilers did all floating-point calculations, and passed all function arguments, using type **double**. In general, the behavior of numerical co-processors is such that the cost of double precision calculations is similar to that of single precision. Benchmark results suggest double precision computation, including the costs of memory transfers, is 10-15% more costly than single precision. The major difference in computational cost is in moving twice as many data bytes. The Intel i860 appears to be equally fast at either precision. In general, this book treats floating-point numbers as type **double**. This is probably a good rule, and should only be violated if very large arrays of data must be handled. Even then, it may be useful to do calculations in double precision. A common example is calculating a dot product of two vectors, which can be accumulated in double precision even if each vector is of type **float**.

Many of the functions here do not produce the full 16 decimal digits of precision for the functions calculated. Generally, such precision is not needed. If it is, there is probably another routine in this book that will, at greater computational expense, produce the required accuracy. Thus, instead of using a rapid Hasting's approximation to the exponential integral of Chapter five, the more general routines may be used with appropriate tolerences as necessary.

The standard provides for signed infinite numbers, and both quiet and signaling NaN's (Not a Number). For example, taking the logarithm of zero will result in a negative infinite being returned, while that of a negative number will generally be a quiet NaN. Most operations on erroneous arguments produce quiet NaN's. A signaling NaN will cause a trap (interrupt) if used as an argument, while a quiet NaN will generally propagate through without raising an exception condition.

Practical Considerations

In optimizing code, it is necessary to understand the costs of operations. Table 1.2 is designed to compare the costs of multiplication, division, and common function evaluation for the Motorola, Intel, and Cyrix math coprocessors. The latest Intel chips, such as the 486i (or 80486) and the 860i, have an on-board floating-point unit.

Please note that this table is not intended to compare the processors; the timing for a floating-point addition has been normalized to 1.0 for each processor. Note also the disclaimer that this table is based on literature supplied by Cyrix, Intel, and by Motorola. Timings are approximate and depend upon memory access type and, in the case of the 486, cache hit or miss. Finally, each co-processor has an evolving design, with newer versions continuously being designed. In fact, the 68881 has been followed by the 68882. The timing statistics can therefore be expected to change, with the more expensive operations becoming less so relative to addition, and the overall performance improving.

Table 1. 2
Relative Times for Floating-Point Operations
(Time for Add is normalized to 1 for each processor.)

Operation	Motorola 68881	Cyrix	Intel 486i	Intel 386
Add, Subtract	1.0	1.0	1.0	1.0
Multipy	1.4	1.3	1.6	1.7
Divide	2.0	2.0	7.3	3.0
Square Root	2.1	2.0	8.5	4.0
sine	11.4	4.2	24	15.0
cosine	7.7	5.8	24	17.0
sine and cosine	8.8	6.3	29	18.0
tangent	9.3	5.0	24	10.5
arctangent	7.9	5.5	29	13.0
logarithm	11.4	5.8	31	15.4
2^x	-	4.2	24	10.0

Sources: Adapted from Cyrix, Intel, and Motorola literature.

Note that multiplication is not much more expensive than addition, and division only slightly more so, for most processors. Thus, the "strength reduction" optimization of replacing 2.0 * x by $x + x$ saves a bit of time, but trying the same sort of thing with 3.0 * x would not be a good idea. There is a "trick" often suggested for multiplying two complex numbers. It saves on a multiplication at the cost of three additions and subtractions and the storage of two to three intermediate results. This produces a loss, not a savings in time, for these processors. To further complicate matters, RISC processors are now appearing with parallel units for addition and multiplication (such as the i860). It might be desirable on such hardware to attempt to balance the number of multiplies and adds, to keep both units occupied. Strength reduction would slow things down if it queued operations for the addition unit while the multiplier was starved!

The i486 appears to have timing ratios quite different from the other chips. The explanation is that great effort (and probably silicon real estate) has been expended to minimize the time for floating-point addition and multiplication on this chip (addition takes about one-third the number of clock cycles it did on the 387, averaging about 10 on the i486 compared to over 30 on the 387). On the other hand, division and the transcendental operations take only marginally fewer cycles than on the 387.

Another optimization commonly suggested is "unrolling loops." This means rewriting loops such as (in FORTRAN):

```
DO I =1,N
     SUM = SUM + A(I)
ENDDO
```

as something like:

```
DO I =1,N,4
     SUM = SUM + A(I) + A(I+1) + A(I+2) + A(I+3)
ENDDO
```

(The above assumes that **N** is a multiple of four, or that any "excess" locations of **A** are defined to be zero.) Whether this speeds things up or slows things down is hardware and compiler dependent. In some cases, it can halve the time consumed by a loop (Dongarra and Hinds). The behavior may be very different for pipelined and non-pipelined architectures, for example. The unrolling might be necessary to keep the pipeline full. It may also save on overhead of tests. For other architectures, increasing the code within the loop might cause cache misses or page faults, slowing things down.

It might also surprise some people that square roots are so cheap. It should also be clear that logarithms and exponentiation should be avoided if possible. In some circumstances, such as particle simulation codes, cheap, low-precision versions of exponentiation and the Gaussian function are used to save time. There is generally little interest in the "tail" of the Gaussian, and errors here tend to have little influence on the final result. Once a number is very small, it is not important in these cases precisely how small. There are some "dial-a-precision" methods in which the number of terms can be chosen for the degree of precision (see Chapter 4, for example).

The Weitek co-processors typically perform roughly two- to three-times as fast as those listed above for the basic arithmetic operations. They do not support the transcendentals, which must be calculated in software. This means there could be a good deal of variation depending upon the host architecture and software run-time library functions. It is likely that the relative cost of transcendentals will be higher than for the Intel and Cyrix chips, but that the overall speed will be comparable.

Finally, it is worth emphasizing that complexity analysis is more than just counting the number of adds and multiplies. One example might be Strassen's well-known method for matrix multiplication (see, e.g., Baase), which has an operation count as a function of the matrix dimension n which behaves asymptotically like $n^{lg\ 7} \approx n^{2.81}$, apparently better than Gaussian elimination's $O(n^3)$ behavior. In practice, its overhead in subscript arithmetic and memory accesses is such that it is unattractive for all reasonable n.

References

M. Abramowitz and I. Stegun, *Handbook of Mathematical Functions* (Washington, D. C.: National Bureau of Standards, Dept. of Commerce, 1964). Reprinted by Dover Publ., N. Y., in 1965.

S. Baase, *Computer Algorithms*, 2nd ed. (Reading, MA: Addison-Wesley, 1988).

L. Baker, *C Tools for Scientists and Engineers* (N. Y.: McGraw-Hill, 1989).

L. Baker, *More C Tools for Scientists and Engineers* (N. Y.: McGraw-Hill, 1990).

S. D. Conte and C. deBoor, *Elementary Numerical Analysis,* 2nd ed. (N. Y.: McGraw-Hill, 1972).

R. B. K. Dewar & M. Smosna, *Microprocessors: A Programmer's View* (N. Y.: McGraw-Hill, 1990).

J. J. Dongarra and A. R. Hinds, "Unrolling loops in FORTRAN," *Software–Practice and Experience*, **9**,#3, pp.219-226, March 1979.

C. F. Gerald, *Applied Numerical Analysis* (Reading, MA: Addison-Wesley, 1970).

G. E. Forsythe, M. A. Malcon, C. B. Moler, *Computer Methods for Mathematical Computations* (Englewood Cliffs, N. J. : Prentice-Hall, 1977).

R. W. Hamming, *Numerical Methods for Scientists and Engineers* (N. Y.: McGraw-Hill, 1973). Reprinted by Dover Publ., N. Y. in 1986.

T. R. F. Nonweiler, *Computational Mathematics* (West Sussex: Ellis Horwood, 1984).

G. Strang, *Introduction to Applied Mathematics* (Wellesley, MA: Wellesley-Cambridge Press, 1986).

J. H. Wilkinson, *The Algebraic Eigenvalue Problem* (Oxford: Clarendon Press, 1965). [Despite its title, which suggests a narrow focus, this book has an excellent coverage of error analysis in numerics.]

Chapter 2

Special Functions in C and C++

In this chapter, we discuss the specifics of this implementation of mathematical functions in C and C++.

C and C++

Portability, ANSII C, and C++

The "obsolete" style of function definition is:

```
mathfunction(x, result1, result2)
    double x,*result1,*result2;
    {...
    }
```

whereas the preferred ANSI C version would be more like:

```
void mathfunction(doublex,double *result1,double *result2)
    {...
    }
```

The Turbo C 2.0 compiler, for example, will warn you about the obsolete declaration (that is, unless you turn off the warning message). It will correctly compile the code. However, older compilers will not accept the newer declarations, and might stumble over the keyword void. For maximum portability, we have used the "obsolete" style. If the warning messages irk you, turn them off!

As noted in the preface, it would be difficult to find a platform that does not support C. The same cannot be said for C++, however. For that reason, we have generally avoided producing code in C++. Some code was written for less popular functions, such as the Hurwitz zeta function $\zeta(a,s)$, the Lerch Phi transcendent $\Phi(a,s,z)$, the generalized hypergeometric function pFq, Meijer's G function, and a few others. These all required heavy use of complex arithmetic. It did not seem justified to port them to more portable, vanilla C.

Infinite Loops

Often, a loop is executed until convergence, i. e., an unknown number of times. This is often done as:

```
while(1)
    {
    ...
    if(convergence) break;
    }
```

Generally preferable is the form:

```
for(;;)
    {
    ...
    if(convergence) break;
    }
```

which saves the overhead of testing that 1 is not equal to zero on each passage of the loop. In loops where we are certain we cannot get into trouble, we use this form, with a statement in header file **Cmlib.h** of the form:

```
#define infinite_loop
```

to enable us to write:

```
#include "cmlib.h"
...
   infinite_loop
      {
      ...
      if(convergence) break;
      }
```

If there is a possibility of non-convergence, a finite loop with a large limit on the iteration count is used.

There are many indentation styles. I prefer to have corresponding brackets { and } on the same indentation level, so that the matching one may be more easily found. Using "tabs" of three spaces gives the best readability, I have been told.

In testing to determine if a variable is zero, I will often use a statement of the form **if(n==0)** or **if(n!=0)** rather than the more obscure **if(!n)** and **if(n)**. Most optimizers will omit the subtraction of zero, and the code is much more readable.

Header Files COMPLEX.H, CMLIB.H, PROTOM.H

There are three header files included in this collection. File **Complex.h** contains the definition of the complex type, as well as various macro definitions to make computing with complex number less painful. In a later chapter, C++ code will be presented to make complex computation in C almost painless. File **Complex.h** is designed to be fully compatible with the ANSI C standard, which defines a **struct complex** and a function **cabs()**. File **Cmlib.h** contains a number of useful macros, includes the **math.h** header file. Finally, **Protom.h** contains prototypes for the functions of this library. I recommend you compile a library file of these routines, thereby saving the grief of worrying what function is where. Earlier versions of **Complex.h** appear in the *C Tools* and *More C Tools* books and in an article in *C User's Journal* (reference in Chapter 3). The header file **Complex.hpp,** intended for use with C++, is discussed in a later article in the same journal, along with various considerations on using C++. **Complex.h** and **Cmlib.h** are in the next chapter, **Complex.hpp** in Chapter 27, and **Protom.h** in this chapter. **Complex.h** may generate a warning that the function **abs()** has been redefined; in the standard library it takes an integer argument, returns an integer, and is typically out-of-line. Rename **abs()** to **dabs()** everywhere if you need to do so. I have never seen a use for the integer version. **Protom.h** also serves as a catalog of C functions by filename.

Error Handling

There are many philosophies about error handling. There is little or no uninimity, however. For example, the *Borland Turbo C Library Reference Manual* states "**matherr** .. is not compatible with ANSI C. **matherr** might not be supported in future versions..."

The general philosophy employed is that errors such as divisions by zero are tested for and trapped by the library routine, rather than allowing the system error handler to take charge. On my home machine, running Turbo C 2.0, errors such as division by zero or stack corruption (caused by passing an argument of incorrect type to a function), can cause a variety of behaviors including a "hang," an error message with additional garbage on the screen, or other, unpredictable, behavior. Some effort has been made to prevent these happenings with functions from this book, but it is certain that a clever user can find ways to outsmart me.

In keeping with the usual C philosophy, errors that are encountered are usually handled unobtrusively. The code returns with an errorcode, and the user is expected to be vigilantly checking this value and, if it does represent an error, the user takes the proper action. The **Cmlib.h** file contains standard error return values **errorcode** and **ierror**. Currently, these are defined as -10^{60} and –255. **errorcode** was chosen so as to give sensible answers in applications where an infinite value is the result of an invalid function argument. For example, in calculating Clebsh-Gordon coefficients, one sums fractions with denominators involving gamma functions. The gamma function is undefined (infinite) for negative integers and zero. These terms in the sum should be ignored, i. e., set to zero. By returning a very large value in such circumstances, such terms become negligible, and correct results are obtained. This cannot be relied upon in all circumstances, however. For example, if the numerator and denominator both contain "infinite" values, the ratio **errorcode/errorcode** = 1, whereas the correct ratio might be different. Although a single factor of **errorcode** should not cause an overflow, a few could if multiplied in succession. Users can easily modify these values by changing the **#define** statement in the header file. For example, a value such as NaN (Not a Number) of the IEEE-754 standard could be used. In some cases, where merely returning an error indication appears to be insufficient, we write an error message to file **stderr**. This is usually the console unless the user has re-directed it.

If an untrapped **errorcode** value has been returned, a bizarre result such as 5.37×10^{53} might appear in a calculation. As this library does not test every return value for **errorcode**, ingeneous users might find a way to produce such a number.

Pitfalls with Special Functions

Many special functions are defined as the solutions of linear, homogeneous, second order, ordinary differential equations. As a result, there is some ambiguity in their definitions. As such differential equations have two solutions, in general, there may be different ideas as to how to define and separate the two. For the Legendre functions, the branch cut $-1 < x < 1$ on the real axis is one of the areas of most practical interest, but poses problems as to the definition when a treatment valid for complex arguments is used.

The Fresnel integrals $S(x)$ and $C(x)$ are defined three different ways by Abramowitz and Stegun, *Higher Transcendental Functions,* and Spanier and Oldham's *An Atlas of Functions*. Some authors define the digamma function as $\psi(x) = \frac{d}{dx}\Gamma(x)$, others $\psi(x) = \frac{d}{dx}\Gamma(x+1)$.

Another example might be the associated bessel and wedge functions. The usual definition of I_n is $I_n(x) = i^n J_n(ix)$, where $i = \sqrt{-1}$. This is so that it has real values. Just looking at the differential equation, you would have no way of knowing about the normalization factor. This is no problem for the associated Bessel functions, if you use the correct definition. But what about the wedge functions, I_{iv} and K_{iv}, where there are no generally accepted definitions? Using, say, *Mathematica*, you will get complex values for I_{iv}. How is one to proceed here? Or for I_n when n is not an integer? For our choices, see the appropriate chapter. Other authors may make different choices, however.

These examples do not exhaust all the possible variations in function definitions. In short, always be sure the function you are using is the function supplied by the code in this book—don't simply assume it is because the name is right!

Normalization Conventions

If the function $f(x)$ is a solution to a linear differential equation, so is $Af(x)$ where A is any constant. This leads to differences in normalization in functions. There are a number of "standard" normalizations for spheroidal wave functions, for example. The associated Legendre functions have different normalization conventions assigned by different authors. Often, but not always, you can tell which is being used from the notation: $P_{nm}(x)$ or $Pnm(x)$.

Tips and Pitfalls in C

C makes it easy to shoot yourself in the foot, often without realizing it (except for the pain). One example: suppose you have defined a pointer to a type double as

```
double *x;
```

and wish to divide the number y by it:

```
z= y/*x;
```

The compiler will see the /*, assume a comment has begun, and you will probably have a slew of error messages.

Far more worrisome are the errors that occur at run-time. FORTRAN programmers often forget that in C, array subscripts are based at zero and cannot be changed, and that arrays are stored in row-major order. Thus, a[0][0] is the first element of the a array and a[0][1] the second. Another common error ex-FORTRANers are susceptible to is to forget that arguments are passed by value, not by name as in FORTRAN. This means that the argument value, not a pointer (the address of the argument), is pushed onto the stack by the caller. This prevents inadvertent modification of variables by subroutines (as can happen in FORTRAN), but means pointers must be explicitly passed if you want a procedure to return more than a single value. The syntax for this in C is confusing, because it is asymmetric. The call looks like

```
mathfunction(&a,&b,&c,&d);
```

while the function declaration looks like (in ANSI standard style):

```
mathfunction(double *a, double *b, double *c, double *d)
```

Here & evaluates the address, while * is the indirection operator.

There are many ways to corrupt the stack. It's particularly easy to do this with printf(), as this function does not have prototypes which would prevent sending arguments of the wrong type. Similar remarks apply to scanf(). Code such as

```
double x;

printf(" %e ",x);

scanf(" %d ", &x);
```

will produce at best incorrect results, and very possibly a "hung" machine. Note, by the way, that pointers must be supplied to scanf(). For double precision arguments, the format specifier should be %le. The same problems can occur when integers of type **long** are read in or printed out with %d instead of %ld. Finally, as in the latest FORTRAN standards but not in earlier FORTRANs, procedures "forget" values of local variables between calls. To save the value of a variable, it should either be a global ("external" in the terminology of Kernighan and Ritchie), i. e., declared outside of a function, or declared with the keyword **static**. The declaration of an external variable may be preceded by the keyword **static** to prevent it from being visible outside of the file in which it is declared. This can be used to prevent name conflicts between files, or, as with **private** variables in Ada, to prevent unauthorized use.

At least one program in this book (AGM.CPP and friends, Chapter 29) requires more than the default stack size for Turbo C (4K). If you do not have a stack overflow check enabled, the result might seem to you to be bizarre behavior. Therefore, when strange bugs happen, suspect such a problem before blaming the code.

Calling C from C++

Obviously, a book with code in both C and C++ should tell you how to use one with the other. C++ compilers use a technique called "name mangling." This means that the function's name as visible to the compiler is not the name that you gave it, but that name modified to include information about the arguments and return value. This allows function overloading, i. e., functions with the same name (as assigned by the programmer), but different argument types or return values. Because the C compiler does not mangle names, the C++ compiler will not recognize such functions without help.

A declaration of the form:

extern "C" double mathfunction (double x)

is required. Here the keyword extern can be followed by either "C" or "C++", with other language names being ignored.

If you are dealing with complex numbers, I recommend doing the arithmetic using the class complex rather than the struct complex. It will be much easier to write a+b than CADD(ans,a,b); . To avoid naming conflicts, in the C++ program declare:

struct cmplx { double x,y};

at the start of the file, and then use cmplx types to communicate with C functions that expect this structure. You can then easily convert between the two:

struct cmplx old;

complex new;

new = complex(old.x , old.y) ;

old.x = new.real() ; old.y = new.imaginary() ;

References

Higher Transcendental Functions, A. Erdelyi, ed. (Malabar, FL: R. E. Krieger, 1981). (Reprint of original edition published by McGraw-Hill, 1953.)

J. Spanier and K. B. Oldham, *An Atlas of Functions* (N. Y. : Hemisphere, 1987).

```
/*
Cmlib.h
header of useful definitions and include of math.h

from C Mathematical Function Handbook by Louis Baker
Copyright 1991 by Louis Baker. All rights reserved.
*/


#include <math.h>

#define pi 3.14159265358979323846264338327 9
#define  Egamma 0.577215664901532860606512090082402431
#define abs(x) ((x)>0.? (x): -(x))
#define errorcode -1.e60
#define ierrorcode -255
#define infinite_loop for(;;)
```

```
/*
COMPLEX.H header file
 * use for complex arithmetic in C
 * see COMPLEX.C for support functions such as
   csqrt(),clog(),cexp(),argmt(),polarxy()

from Handbook of C tools for Scientists and Engineers by L.
Baker

*/

#ifndef complex

#include <math.h>

#else

double sqrt();
struct complex { double x;
       double y;} ;
#endif

static double TP,T2,T3;/* dummy static so no conflict with
other modules*/

/* for below, X,Y are complex structures, and one is
returned*/

#define CMULTR(X,Y) ((X).x*(Y).x-(X).y*(Y).y)
#define CMULTI(X,Y)  ((X).y*(Y).x+(X).x *(Y).y)
/* CMLT uses 1 fewer multiplication but more adds than
CMULT not generally
recommended */
#define CMLT(Z,X,Y)
{TP=(X.x+X.y)*(Y.x+Y.y);T2=X.x*Y.x;T3=X.y*Y.y;Z.y=TP-T2-
T3;z.X=T2-T3;}

#define CDRN(X,Y)   ((X).x*(Y).x+(Y).y*(X).y)
#define CDIN(X,Y)   ((X).y*(Y).x-(X).x*(Y).y)
#define CNORM(X)  ((X).x*(X).x+(X).y*(X).y)
/*#define CNRM(X)  (X->x*X->x+X->y*X->y)
*/
#define CDIV(z,nu,de)
{TP=CNORM(de);(z).x=CDRN(nu,de)/TP;(z).y=CDIN(nu,de)/TP;}
#define CONJG(z,X) {(z).x=(X).x;(z).y=-(X).y;}
/*#define CONJ(X) {(X).y=-(X).y}
*/
#define CMULT(z,X,Y) {(z).x=CMULTR((X),(Y)); (z).y=CMUL-
TI((X),(Y));}
```

```
#define CADD(z,X,Y) {(z).x=(X).x+(Y).x;(z).y=(X).y+(Y).y;}
#define CSUB(z,X,Y) {(z).x=(X).x-(Y).x;(z).y=(X).y-(Y).y;}
#define CLET(to,from) {(to).x=(from).x;(to).y=(from).y;}
/* For a "bulletproof" form of cabs use
   #define cabs(X) Euclidd((X).x,(X).y)
*/
#ifndef cabs
#define cabs(X) sqrt((X).y*(X).y+(X).x*(X).x)
#endif
#define CMPLX(X,real,imag) {(X).x=(real);(X).y=(imag);}
#define CASSN(to,from) {to.x=from->x;to.y=from->y;}
#define CTREAL(z,X,real)
{(z).x=(X).x*(real);(z).y=(X).y*(real);}
#define CSET(to,from) {to->x=(from).x;to->y=(from).y;}
```

```
/*
Prototypes for C Mathematical Function Handbook
from C Mathematical Function Handbook by Louis Baker
Copyright 1991 by Louis Baker. All rights reserved.
*/
#include "complex.h"

/* Chapter 3: powers and roots file:pr.c*/
double power( double x, double n);
double root(double x,int n);
double square_rt(double x);
double cube_rt(double x);
double Euclidd(double xin, double yin);

/* Chapter 3: roots of polynomial equations file:polyrt.c*/
solvq(struct complex *b,struct complex *c,
   struct complex *ans1, struct complex *ans2);
int cubic(double a,double b,double c,double *r1,double
*r2,double *r3);
int quartic(double a,double b,double c,double d,
  struct complex *r1,struct complex *r2,struct complex *r3,
  struct complex *r4);
ctreal(struct complex *x,double y,struct complex *ans);
cpow(struct complex *x,struct complex *y,
   struct complex *ans );
ccubic( struct complex *a1,struct complex *a2,
struct complex *a3,struct complex *r1,struct complex *r2,
struct complex *r3);
cquartic( struct complex *a1,struct complex *a2,
struct complex *a3,struct complex *a4,
struct complex *r1,struct complex *r2,struct complex
*r3,struct complex *r4);


/* Chapter 4: elementary functions file:elem.c*/
double ln(double x);
double expon(double x);
double sine(double xi);
double arc_tan(double xi);
double arc_sine(double xi);
double hyper_sin(double x);
double hyper_cos(double x);
double hyper_tan(double x);
double arc_hyper_sin(double x);
double arc_hyper_cos(double x);
double arc_hyper_tan(double x);
double cosine(double x);
double arc_cosine(double x);
double tangent(double x);
```

```
double tangnt(double x);
double arc_tangent(double y, double x);

/* Chapter 4: functions for complex analysis file: com-
plex.c*/
double sign(double x);
double argmt(double  x,double y);
double Argmt(double x,double y);
clog( struct complex *x,struct complex *ans);
csqrt(struct complex *z,struct complex *ans);
polarxy(double r, double angle,   double *x, double *y);
cexp( struct complex *x,struct complex *ans);
ctrig( struct complex *z,struct complex *ccos,
struct complex *csin);
csin(struct complex *x,struct complex *ans);
ccos(struct complex *x,struct complex *ans);
ctan(struct complex *x,struct complex *ans);
ccot(struct complex *x,struct complex *ans);
csinh(struct complex *x,struct complex *ans);
ccosh(struct complex *x,struct complex *ans);
casin(struct complex *x,struct complex *ans);
cacos(struct complex *x,struct complex *ans);
catan(struct complex *x,struct complex *ans);
printc(struct complex *z);

/* Chapter 5: exponential integral and relatives file:
expi.c*/
double e1(double x);
double si(double x);
double ci(double x);
/*double en(double x);  en,f,g,eicf,fcf,f01,g01,g2,f2,ceii
not intended for direct user invocation
not made static for special cases where direct call desired
*/
double e1s(double x);
double en(double x, double n);
double eicf(double x);
double e(double x,int n);
double E1(double x);
double Eict(double x);
double Eis(double x);
double eias(double x);
double ei(double x);
double Ei(double x);
double li(double x);
double alpha(double x,int n);
double beta(double x,int n);
double c01(double x);
double s01(double x);
```

```
cei( double x,double y, double k,double toler,
   double *u,double *v,int *n);
ceii( double x,double y, double k,double toler,
   double *u,double *v,int *n);
cexpint(struct complex *z,double k,double toler,
struct complex *ans,int *iter);
double f( double x);
double g( double x);
double f2( double x, double y);
double g2( double x, double y);
double f01( double x);
double g01( double x);
double fcf( double x,int n,  double a[], double b[]);
double c2(double x, double y);
double s2(double x, double y);

/* Chapter 6: Gamma function and relatives file: g.c*/
double gamma(double x);
double loggam(double x);
double P(double a,double x);
double incgam(double a, double x);
double BigGamma(double a, double x);
double Pgamma(double a, double x);
double SmallGamma(double a, double x);
double fac(double x);
double pochhammer(double z, int n);
double gammaqd(double xin);
cgamma(struct complex *zz,struct complex *ans,
struct complex *loggam);
cdigamma(struct complex *x,struct complex *ans);
double polygam(double z,int n);

/* Chapter 6: Digamma function and relatives file: digam.c
*/
double digamma(double x);
double digam(double x);
double pg1(double x);
double pg2(double x);

/* Chapter 7: Error and relate functions. file: pdfs.c*/
cerror( struct complex *a, struct complex *b, double eps);
double erf( double z, double *erfc);
double dawson(double x);
fresnel(double z, double *fci, double *fsi);
pdisp( struct complex *zetai,double eps,
 struct complex *zeeo,struct complex *zeeprimo,int iter);
cfsmall(double eps);/* NOT intended for direct use by
users*/
cfbig(double eps);/* NOT intended for direct use by users*/
```

```
double ritchie( double x);
/* Chapter 7: Complementary error function for complex arg.
file: cerfc.c*/
cerfc( struct complex *z, struct complex *ans);
/* Chapter 7: Error and relate functions. file: ierfc.c*/
double ierfc(double z, int n);
double ierfcf(double x, int n);
ierfctable (double z, int n, double table[]);
/* Chapter 7: Error and relate functions. file: boehmer.c*/
double boehmer( double x, double nu, int type);
double Si(double x);
double Ci(double x);
double Shi(double x);
double Chi(double x);
double Fresnel( double x, int type);
/* ba: asympt. boehmer. not for direct use*/
double ba(double x,double nu, int type);

/* Chapter 8: Legendre Functions file: leg.c*/
double plm( int l,int m, double x);
double pl0(int l,double x);
double ql0(int l, double x);
double qlm(int l,int m,double x);
double pli(int l,double z) ;
double qli(int l,double z);
double legendrea(int m,int n,double x,int real);
qleg(int m,int nmax,double x,int real,double r[] ,
   double q[]);
double qnu(double x,double nu,int real);
double pnu(double x,double nu);
/* Chapter 8: Legendre Functions file: Mehler.c*/
double Mehler(double x,double z,int mm) ;
double Mehler0(double x,double z);
/* Chapter 8: Legendre Functions file: gaut.c*/
leg1(double x,int a,int nmax,double p[]);
leg2(double x,int m,int nmax,int d,double q[]) ;
leg3(double  x,int n,int mmax,int d,double q[]);
legend1(double x,double alpha,int nmax,int d,double p[]);
legend2(double x,double a,int m,int nmax,int d,double p[]);
conical(double x,double tau,int nmax,int d,double p[]);
toroidal(double x,int m,int nmax,int d,double q[]);
double arccosh(double x);
double conicalt(double theta,double tau);
double conicala(double x,double tau);
/* Chapter 8: Legendre Functions file: torp.c*/
double Ptoroidal(int n, double x);

/* Chapter 9: Bessel Functions file: bessr.c*/
double j0(double x);
```

```
double j1(double x);
double y0(double x);
double y1(double x);
double i0(double x);
double i1(double x);
double k0(double x);
double k1(double x);
void ke(double x, double *,double *,double *, double *);
void be(double x, double *, double *, double *, double *);
CTHET(double X, double *PARTR, double *PARTI);
CPHI(double X, double *PARTR, double *PARTI);
/* Chapter 9: Bessel Functions file: besst.c*/
double jn(double x, int n);
double yn(double x, int n);
double in(double x, int n);
double kn(double x, int n);
/* Chapter 9: Bessel Functions file: cbess.c*/
Bessel( int nn,struct complex *z,struct complex *j,
struct complex *y,
   struct complex *h2,struct complex *jprime,
   struct complex *yprime,struct complex *h2prime);
bessel( int nn,struct complex *z,struct complex *j,
   struct complex *y,
   struct complex *h2,struct complex *jprime,
   struct complex *yprime,struct complex *h2prime,
   int *ivalck);
double jint(int n, double z);
ibess(struct complex *z,struct complex *i, int n);
kbess(struct complex *z,struct complex *k,int n);
kelvin(int n,double x,struct complex *be,struct complex
*ke);
forward(struct complex *z,struct complex *ratio
   , int idim, struct complex *r1);
backward(struct complex *z,struct complex *ratio
   , int idim);
cbess(struct complex *z,struct complex *j0,
struct complex *j1,
   struct complex *y0,struct complex *y1,
struct complex *h20,
   struct complex *h21,int *ivchk);
/* Chapter 9: Bessel Function Zeros  file:bessz.c*/
double ti(double y);
double jass(double z,double nu);
besspq(double a, double x,double *pa,double *qa,
double *pa1,double *qa1);
int zerobes(double a,int n, double z[],int d);
/* Chapter 10: spherical Bessel Functions  file:spbn.c*/
double sjn(double x, int n);
double syn(double x, int n);
```

```
double skn(double x, int n);
double sinb(double x, int n);
double si0(double x);
double si1(double x);
double sim1(double x);
double sim2(double x);
double sj0(double x);
double sj1(double x);
double sy0(double x);
double sy1(double x);
double sk0(double x);
double sk1(double x);

/* Chapter 10: Bessel Functions file:abb.c*/
/* bessel functions of order 1/3 and -1/3 */
double jt( double z);
double jmt( double z);
double it( double z);
double imt( double z);
/* bessel functions of real order*/
double jbes( double z, double nu);
double jas( double z, double nu);
double ybes( double z, double nu);
double kbes( double z, double nu);
double ibes( double z, double nu);
/* Airy functions, their derivatives and integrals*/
double smallf(double z);
double smallg(double z);
double ai(double z);
double bi(double z);
double dai(double z);
double dbi(double z);
double bigf(double z);
double bigg(double z);
double IAi(double z);
double IBi(double z);
/* Anger and Weber functions*/
aw( double nu, double z, double *jj, double *e);
/* Chapter 11: Integrals of Bessel Functions file:bessi.c*/
double ji(double x);
double jii(double x);
double jin(double x, int n);
double jiotn(double x, int n);
double ki(double x);
double kii(double x);
double ii0m1t(double x);
double ij0t(double x);
double iy0t(double x);
double ik0t(double x);
```

```
double ii0tas(double x);
double ik0tas(double x);
double y0i( double x);
double i0i( double x);
/* Chapter 11: Integrals of Bessel Functions file:
   bickley.c*/
double bii(double x);/* bii not for user direct call*/
double bickley(double x, double rr);
double Jrn(double x, double r, int n);
/* Chapter 11: Integrals of Bessel Functions file:simp.c*/
double adsimp(double a,double b,double eps,double (*f)());
double simp(double a,double da,
   double fa,double fm,double fb,double area,double est,
   double eps,double (*f)());
/* Chapter 12: Bessel Functions file:struv.c*/
double StruveH(double nu, double x);
double StruveL(double nu, double x);
/* Chapter 12: Bessel Functions file:struvl.c*/
double h0(double x);
double h0a(double x);
double h1(double x);
double h1a(double x);
double l0(double x);
double l0a(double x);
double l1(double x);
double l1a(double x);
/* Chapter 12: Integrals of Struve Bessel Functions
file:struvi.c*/
double ModStruveI( double x);
double StruveI(double x);
double StruveIot(double x);
/* Chapter 12: Bessel Functions file:iaw.c*/
double gamtab(double x);
iaw(int m, struct complex *s, struct complex *ans);

/* Chapter 13: Confluent Hypergeometric Functions file:
chf.c */
Cpow(struct complex *x,struct complex *y,
   struct complex *ans);
c1f1(struct complex  *a,struct complex  *c,
   struct complex  *x
   ,int top,struct complex  *ans);
cu(struct complex  *a,struct complex  *c,struct complex  *x
   ,struct complex  *ans);
/* Chapter 13: Confluent Hypergeometric Functions file:
chfs.c */
Jbessel(struct complex *order,struct complex *arg,struct
complex *ans);
```

```
Ibessel(struct complex *order,struct complex *arg,struct
complex *ans);
Kbessel(struct complex *order,struct complex *arg,struct
complex *ans);
Airy(struct complex *z, struct complex *ans);
BiAiry(struct complex *z, struct complex *ans);
bateman(struct complex *nu,struct complex *arg,
    struct complex *ans);
cunningham(struct complex *n,struct complex *m,
   struct complex *x,struct complex *ans);
toronto(struct complex *m,struct complex *n,
   struct complex *r,struct complex *ans);
charlier(int n,struct complex *nu,struct complex *x,
   struct complex *ans);
Laguerre(struct complex * a,int n,struct complex * x,
   struct complex *ans);
/* Chapter 13: Confluent Hypergeometric Functions file:
chfw.c */
Mwhit(struct complex *k,struct complex *mu,
   struct complex *x,struct complex *ans);
Wwhit(struct complex *k,struct complex *mu,
   struct complex *x,struct complex *ans);
/* Chapter 13: Confluent Hypergeometric Functions file: u.c
*/
double uabx(double a, double b, double x, double eps,
   double *uprime);
/* following not intended for direct user call*/
brec(double a,double b,int k,double *f,double *g,double x);
chu(double a,double b,double x,int kmax,double eps,
   double u[],double *uprime);

/* Chapter 14:  Coulomb Wave Functions file: cwf.c */
/* only coulombf and coulombg are intended for direct user
call*/
double coulombf(double eta,double rho,int l);
double coulombg(double eta,double rho,int l);
double gl(double q);
cwfa(int l, double eta,double rho, double *fl,double *gl,
   double *flp, double *glp);

/* Chapter 15: Hypergeometric and relatives hyperg.c*/
double f21(double a,double b,double c,double x);
double f12(double a,double b,double c,double x);
double F01(double a,double x);
/* Chapter 15: Hypergeometric and relatives f211.c-f213.c*/
cpochhammer(struct complex *x, int n, struct complex *ans);
cf21( struct complex *a,struct complex *b,struct complex *c,
   struct complex *x,struct complex *ans);
```

```
f21big(struct complex *ain,struct complex *bin,
   struct complex *c,
   struct complex *x,struct complex *ans);
f211(struct complex *a,struct complex *b,struct complex *c,
   struct complex *x,struct complex *ans);

/* Chapter 15: Legendre P for complex parameters */
cp(struct complex *z,struct complex *mu,struct complex *nu,
      struct complex *ans);

/* Chapter 15: Legendre Q for complex parameters */
cq(struct complex *z,struct complex *mu,struct complex *nu,
      struct complex *ans);



/* Chapter 16:  Elliptic Functions file: cje.c */
cjef( struct complex *u, double m, struct complex *sn,
   struct complex *cn, struct complex *dn);
double ratmp(double m);
double ratmm(double m);
double solvem(double ratio,double mu,double ml,
double (*ratv)());
double getm(double g2,double g3,int d);
weier(struct complex *z,double g2,double g3,
struct complex *p,
   struct complex *pp,double *mp,double *kp,double *ep,
   double *omegap,double *eta,double *ehp);
ctld(struct complex *v,struct complex *q,struct complex *t1,
   struct complex *t2,struct complex *t3,
   struct complex *t4);
sigma(struct complex *z,struct complex *ans,double k,
   double omega,
   double eta,double m,double g2,double g3);
zetaw(struct complex *z,struct complex *ans,
   double k,double omega,
   double eta,double m,double g2,double g3);
/* Chapter 16:  Elliptic Functions file: ct5.c */
ctheta(struct complex *v,struct complex *q,
   struct complex *ct1,
   struct complex *ct2,struct complex *ct3,
   struct complex *ct4);
double q(double m);
double mq(double q);
emf(struct complex *q,struct complex *m) ;
emft(struct complex *t,struct complex *m) ;
amc(struct complex *x,double m,struct complex *ans) ;
/* Chapter 17:  Elliptic Integrals file: te.c */
tek(int id, double m, double *k, double *e);
```

```
tef(double phi, double m, double sig, double *f, double *e);
double jzeta(double phi, double m);
double am(double u, double m);
jef(double u, double m,double *sn,double *cn,double *dn);
double heuman(double phi,double m);
theta(double v,double m,double *t1,double *t2,
   double *t3,double *t4);
neville(double  u,double m,double *ts,double *tc,
   double *td,double *tn);
/* Chapter 17:  Elliptic Integrals file: E3.c */
double e3(double n,double phi,double m,double sig);
/* Chapter 17:  Elliptic Integrals file: cef.c */
cef(double m,struct complex *z,struct complex *e,
   struct complex *f,double sig);
czeta(double m,struct complex *z,struct complex *ans,
   double sig);
/* Chapter 17:  Elliptic Integrals file: ce.c */
ce(struct complex *u,double m,struct complex *ce);

/* Chapter 18:  Weierstrass Functions file: invw.c*/
invp(double g2,double g3,struct complex *z,
   struct complex *ans);
/* Chapter 18:  Elliptic Functions Brent root finder file:
brent.c */
double brent(double a,double b,double eta,double t,
double (*f)());

/* Chapter 19:  Parabolic Cylinder Functions file:  */
double wpcf(double a, double xx);
double wa(double a, double xx);
double wairy(double a, double xx);
double upcf(double nu, double x);
double vpcf(double nu, double x);
double mwhit(double k, double mu, double z);
double wwhit(double k, double mu, double z);
double m(double a, double b, double z);
double u(double a, double b, double z);

/* Chapter 20:  Mathieu Functions file: mathieu.c */
int matheign(double q, int r, int odd,double *eigenv);
double mathieu(double x,double q, int r,
   double eigenv[],int sol,int fnc, int norm);
int tmofa(double alfa, double *tm, double *dtm);
int coef();
double fj(int n);
double fy(int n);
double dy(int n);
double dj(int n);
double ds(int n);
```

```
double dc(int n);
double dds(int k);
double ddc(int k);
double ps(int k);
double pc(int k);
double dps(int k);
double dpc(int k);
sum(double (*func)());
bessinit(int sol,int n);
int math(double xx,double qq,int r, double cv,
   int sol,int fnc,int norm,double f[],int k[]);
int bounds(int k,double approx,double tola,double *cv,
   int coln);
int mfitr8(double tola,double *cv,double *dcv);
int mfcval(int n,int r,double qq,double *cv,int coln);

/* Chapter 21:  Spheroidal Wave Functions file: spherr.c */
double simb(double x,int n);
double dssph(double c, double s);
double fs(double c, double s);
double es(double c, double s);
double gs(double c, double s);
int ste(double d[],double e[],int n);
int solve(double c,int prolate,int odd,int order,int nmax);
int figi(double above[],double below[],int nmax);
double nmn(int m,int n,int limit);
double rho(int m,int n, int limit);
double betsph(int m,int r);
double gamsph(int m,int r);
double asph(int m,int r);
double bsph(int m,int r);
double csph(int m,int r);
int tridi(double bl[],double diag[],double ab[],
   double c[],int n);
int setd(int mm,int n);
double angular(int mm,int n,int kind,double eta,int imag);
double radswf(int m,int n,int kind,double eta);
double radial(int m,int n,int kind,double xi);
double sphjoin(int m,int n,int kind,int limit);
/* Chapter 22: Legendre Functions file: legp.c*/
legptable(double x, int ntop, int m);

/* Chapter 22:  Orthogonal  file: orthop.c */
/* backp not intended for direct user call*/
double backp(int n,int cc,int typcp,double x);
double Pjacobi(double alpha,double beta,int n,double x) ;
double laguerre(double alpha,int n,double x);
double Cgegenbauer(double alpha,int n,double x);
double Tcheby( int n, double x);
```

```
double Ucheby( int n, double x);
double Plegendre(int n, double x);
double Hermite(int n, double x);

/* Chapter 23: Zeta (real arg.) and relatives */
double zeta( double r);
double bernoulli (int n);
double euler (int n);
double bernpoly ( int n, double x);
double eulerpoly ( int n, double x);
double debye (double x, int n);
double dilog(double x);
double clausen(double theta);
double zeta1( double z);
double zeta2( double z, double a);
double bigphi(double z, double s, double v);
double betacat( double s);
double lambda(double s);
double eta( double s);
double ifermi(double mu, double s);

/* Chapter 24:Stirling Numbers. file: stirl.c */
double stirl1( int m, int n);
double stirl2( int m, int n);
double stirlingf( int m, int n);
/* Chapter 24: Fibonacci numbers. file:fib.c */
double fib( int n);
/* Chapter 24: binomial coefficient. file:binom.c */
double binom(double n, double m);
/* Chapter 25: Numerical Methods: no functions*/

/*Chapter 26: Statistics. file:stath.c*/
/* independent module. No prototypes*/

/*Chapter 26: Statistics. file:random.c*/
/* random variates */
double erlang( int k, double mean);
double expon(double mean);
double cauchy();
double logistic(double a, double k);
int randi(int nvalue, float probd[]);
double uniform(double a, double b);
double normal( double mean, double sd, double *s1,
   double *s2);
double norm(double mean, double sd);
/* random number generators*/
double u32(void);
double u16(void);
double randm(void);
```

```
/* alternative exponential, cauchy, normal */
double ex(void);
double ca(void);
double na(void);

/*Chapter 26: Statistics.  file:dist.c*/
/*distributions*/
double binomial_dist(int x,int n, double p);
double neg_binomial_dist(int x,int y, double p);
double poisson_dist(int x,double lambda);
double hypergeometric_dist(int N, int m, int k, int x);
double erlang_dist(double b,int c,double x);
/* random numbers*/
int binomial(int n, double p);
int neg_binomial(int x, double p);
double chisq(int v);
double extreme (double a, double b);
int geometric(double p);
int hypergeometric(int N, int X, int smalln);
double lognormal(double median, double sigma);/*
sigma=shape parameter*/
double pareto( double c);
int poisson(double lambda);
double weibull(double b, double c);
double binomial_coef(int n, int m);

/*Chapter 27: Misc.
   see also ritchie in pdfs.c,debye in ebznew.c*/
/*Chapter27: sievert integral file:misc.c*/
double sievert( double x, double theta);
/*Chapter27: Clebsh-Gordon coeff. & relatives file:wig-
ner.c*/
int notint(double x);
int nothint( double x);
int triangle( double j1, double j2, double j);
double m1e(double x);
double wigner(double j,double j1,double j2,double m,
   double m1,double m2);
double ClebshGordon(double j1,double m1,double j2,double m2,
   double j,double m);
double wigner3j(double j,double j1,double j2,
double m,double m1,
   double m2);
double delta(double a,double b,double c);
double gammn(double x);
double racah(double a,double b,double c,double d,
   double e,double f);
double wigner6j(double a,double b,double c,double d,
   double e,double f);
```

```
double Wigner6j(double a,double b,double c,double d,
   double e,double f);
double Wigner9j(double a,double b,double c,double d,
   double e,double f
   ,double g,double h,double i);
double X(double a,double b,double c,double d,
   double e,double f
   ,double g,double h,double i);
double V(double a,double b,double c,double A,
   double B,double C);
double CG(double j1,double j2,double j,double m1,
   double m2,double m);
/*Chapter27: dilogarithm function (see also dilog in
ebznew.c)
                  file: dilog.c*/
double Dlog(double x);
/*Chapter27: "Abramowitz" functions file: F123.c*/
double af1s(double x);
double af2s(double x);
double af3s(double x);
double afa(double x,double n);
double af1(double x);
double af2(double x);
double af3(double x);
double af(double x,int n);
/*Chapter27: polylogarithm function file: polylog.c*/
double polylog(double x, double n);
/*Chapter27: Lobashevsky function NOT IN A&S file:Lob.c*/
double Lob(double x);
/*Chapter27: mu, nu and relatives function NOT IN A&Sfile:
nu.c*/
double mu(double x,double ain,double bin);
double nu(double x);
double Nu(double x,double a);
double nui(double t);
/*Chapter 28:Scales no functions*/

/*Chapter 29: C++ no prototypes here*/
```

Chapter 3

Elementary Analytical Methods

With this chapter, we begin presenting C code for producing the results analagous to those in the correspondingly-numbered chapters of Abramowitz and Stegun. This chapter contains code to:

calculate powers and roots

compute with complex numbers

find the roots of quadratic, cubic, and quartic polynomials

Powers and Roots

We use the "Russian Peasant" algorithm to compute the integer x^n (including x^{-n}) powers of numbers. This method will not always use the minimum number of multiplications (for computing x^{27}, it will use eight multiplications, whereas it can be computed using only five). It is generally not too prodigal, however, and the cost of determining the optimal algorithm for general n will generally be such as to make that calculation unattractive. The Russian Peasant method is also simple and produces compact, fast code. The exponent n is written as a binary number. For each one bit in its binary representation, the corresponding factor is multiplied into the accumulated product to form the power. The factor is then squared to produce the power corresponding to the next higher bit in the representation of n. This procedure is efficiently done since n is represented in binary by the computer anyway! Shifts can be used to move through n bit-by-bit, testing the lowest bit by using the AND operator & and masking for the lowest bit. Our implementation of power is general. It uses exponentiation and logarithms for non-integral powers, and computes $1/x^n$ for x^{-n}. The use of floating-point arithmetic may slow things down a bit relative to integer arithmetic, but insures that overflow is not as great a problem.

We use the Newton-Raphson iteration to compute roots. Special functions are provided for square and cube roots, along with a general root finder. Co-processors such as the Intel 80387 have built-in square root functions, which should be used if available. These work in a similar fashion, except that 1) to find the square root of x, they first use a transformation of the form $x = 22n\ y$, where **y** is in some specified range, so that the square root of x is of the form $2n\ sqrt(y)$, 2) they use an initial approximation to *sqrt(y)*, generally a polynomial or rational function. This can be done because y is in a fixed range, e.g., $1 < y < 4$). They apply the Newton-Raphson iteration a small, fixed number of times to achieve the required precision. This suffices because the error in the initial approximation can be made small, the quadratic convergence properties of the Newton-Raphson iteration are well-understood, and saves the overhead of tests in the iteration loop. In the CRAY mathematical library, ***sqrt(z)*** is first transformed into $v\ sqrt(w)$ where $1 \le w \le 2$, and $sqrt(w)$ is found by taking as an initial guess $\frac{33}{32} + \frac{3}{8}(w - \frac{33}{32})$ and applying the Newton-Raphson iteration given in the next paragraph three times.

The Newton-Raphson method is discussed more fully in *C Tools*, particularly the potential pitfalls. Briefly, to solve $f(x_0) = 0$, let iteration proceed from approximation x_n to x_{n+1} with $x_n = x_{n+1} + \delta x$. Use a Taylor series to form $f(x + \delta x) = f(x) + f'(x)\delta x$, which may be easily solved for δx. For determining square roots, use $f(x) = x^2 - A$ to find the square root of A. Thus, $x_{n+1} = \frac{1}{2}[x_n + \frac{A}{x_n}]$. It is easy to find the formula for cube roots, or general roots.

Complex Numbers

The C language does not support complex numbers as FORTRAN does. A header file is presented in *C Tools* which supports the basic arithmetic operations on complex numbers. A modified version of this file is presented in an article in *C User's Journal*. With C++, it is possible to employ operator overloading the permit statements such as *a=b+c*; in which *a*, *b*, and *c* are complex variables. In this chapter, we present a revised version of the C header file, **Complex.h**, which permits the expression of the above calculation via a macro of the form CADD(a,b,c);. See either of the previous publications referenced here for a full discussion. The C++ implementation will be discussed in Chapter 29 on C++ later in this book.

The functions for powers and roots have been "bulletproofed" to a reasonable degree to avoid divisions by zero and similar problems. Note that anything to the 0th power is zero, including zero. This makes good mathematical sense as a limiting case, and conforms to the BSD 4.3 UNIX convention.

The function **hypot(x,y)** is available on many UNIX systems and returns the Euclidean distance, $\sqrt{x^2+y^2}$. It may therefore be used to find the magnitude of a complex number. A "bulletproofed" version is given here. It is not used by the cabs() function in complex.h, as the latter is coded in-line and is therefore more efficient in general. The user can change this if desired. Our version of hypot() relies on the system square root routine or the square root function given here. A fast algorithm developed by Moler and Morrison is given in the referenced work by them. Jon Bentley discusses this problem in his book *More Programming Pearls.*

Roots of Polynomials

The roots of polynomials of fourth degree or less may be found exactly, "by radicals," in a finite number of steps. The roots of quintics may be found in terms of elliptic functions, but this is not numerically efficient. *C Tools* presents a highly robust solver due to Jenkins and Traub for finding the roots of polynomials, and it may be used for higher-order polynomials. Muller's method and the Newton-Raphson method are also discussed in *C Tools* and may be used for polynomials and other nonlinear problems.

Quadratics

The general solution of the quadratic $ax^2+bx+c=0$ is well known to be expressible as

$$x=\frac{-b\pm\sqrt{b^2-4ac}}{2a}$$

and may be found as follows. The leading coefficient may be assumed to be non-zero; otherwise, it is not a quadratic equation. We may then divide thru by it, obtaining $x^2+(b/a)x+c/a=0$. We now "complete the square," writing this as $[(x+\frac{b}{2a})^2-(\frac{b^2}{4a^2})]+c/a=0$. We then solve for the binomial $x+\frac{b}{2a}$, take square roots of both sides, and the result follows.

This formula can develop numerical difficulties for small $|a|$. Numerical errors thwart the cancellation of terms in the numerator, resulting in an absurd value for one of the roots. See *C Tools.*

Cubics

The solution to cubics was first found (ca. 1500-1515) by Scipione del Ferro of Bologna, apparently discovered independently by Fontanna Niccolo ('Tartaglia,' which means stammerer or stutterer in Italian; Leonardo of Pisa is better known as Fibonacci, which means something like block-head, at least according to M. Schroder, although according to another book it means simply "son of Bonacci"; his numbers we shall treat later in this book), told to Geronimo (or Gerolamo) Cardano (Cardan when Latinized) under a sworn oath of secrecy not to reveal it. Cardan published it in his book in 1545 (crediting it to Tartaglia and generalizing it), so it is now known as Cardan's solution.

The simplest derivation of this result that I have seen is in a footnote in a book by James Jeans. Consider the identity $(a-b)^3 = a^3 - 3a^2b + 3ab^2 - b^3$. This may be rewritten as $(a-b)^3 + 3ab(a-b) - (a^3 - b^3) = 0$. Comparing this to the equation $y^3 + py - q = 0$, we see that $a - b$ will be a solution if $p = 3ab$ and $q = a^3 - b^3$. Letting $z = a^3$, we can solve the quadratic $z^2 - qz - \frac{p}{27} = 0$ for a root z. There will then be three values of a, and three corresponding values for b, which will give the three required solutions. These three values of a can be called $a, \omega a, \omega^2 a$, where $\omega = \frac{1}{2} + \frac{\sqrt{3}}{2} i$ is a cube root of 1.

A general cubic may be put into the required form by dividing thru by the leading coefficient, and removing the quadratic term by a transformation of the form $y = x - \frac{b}{3}$, where b is the coefficient of the quadratic term after the division. The code uses slightly different conventions, assuming a solution of the form $y = u^{\frac{1}{3}} + v^{\frac{1}{3}}$ and solving $y + 3hy - g = 0$. (It follows Rietz and Crathorne's treatment with minor differences.)

The reader might want to solve $x^3 - 2x - 5 = 0$, whose real root 2.0944551...was used by Wallis to demonstrate Newton's method, and whose root is known to 4000 digits (see Wells).

Quartics (biquardratics)

Cardan's pupil Ferrari applied the solution of the cubic to the problem of the quartic.

Our treatment follows Rietz and Crathorne's. The quartic $x^4 + a_1x^3 + a_2x^2 + a_3x + a_4 = 0$ is assumed to be convertible to the form

$(x^2 + px + q)^2 = (mx + b)^2$ by the addition of the term seen on the right-hand side to both sides of the equation. It turns out that we need to solve a cubic to determine the value(s) of q that make this possible. Having done this, the necessary values of m and b can be determined. After taking the square roots of both sides of the transformed equation, we have two quadratics to solve, $x^2 + px + q = \pm(mx + b)$, whose four roots are the four roots to our original equation.

Implementation Considerations

Testing of the programs revealed that finite-precision effects can cause it to matter which root is chosen in the cubic and quartic procedures. Therefore, to "bulletproof" the code, we test the first root to see if it really satisfies the required equation. If it does not have a suitably small residual (which can be set by the user via the #define statement for the parameter eps), the program goes back and tries again. If it fails for all three choices, it gives up and returns an errorcode. The code is written to try all nine possibilities for choices of cube roots (three for each), but, at least in the ideal world, either one of the loops is superfluous and at most three tries should succeed. Currently, the code is written to stop and return after one is found which satisfies the residual criterion. If this does not happen, the code returns the roots corresponding to the smallest residual for the first root.

Another pitfall was revealed by tests. In the case of the equation $x^3 + i = 0$, the intermediate variable u should be zero. Round-off caused this to be 3.06e-17. Because a subsequent cube root is taken, $u^{\frac{1}{3}}$ became approximately 3.e-6 instead of 0. This resulted in a residual of 9.3e-6, exceeding the tolerance eps and producing a warning message. This problem was circumvented for this case by setting $u = 0$ if $h = 0$. This loss of precision is always possible, however, when roots are taken or if cancellation is required for the correct answer. Consider yourself warned! The roots obtained by these "exact" solvers can be used as starting values for an iterative solver, such as a Newton-Raphson method, and refined if the error residuals are not satisfactory. (But be careful of double roots!) Or the methods in *C Tools*, such as the Jenkins-Traub solver, can be used.

Each of the root finders for cubics and quartics contains a core procedure, which solves for the roots for general complex coefficents, and a version which calls with real coefficients. For real coefficients, the cubic has at least one real root. In the case of the cubics, it was useful for some applications to have the real root returned as a real number, and the other two roots, which could either be both real or a complex-conjugate pair, in two real numbers. If all roots are real, the three roots are returned along with the return code value of 0. If not, the real and imaginary parts are returned in the other two type double values, with a return code value of 1. A similar procedure, to call the quartic solver for real coefficients and return the complex roots, is also provided.

The polynomial root finders require, for example, the ability to find the cube root of complex numbers. The functions to do this are contained in the next chapter.

Quintics

It was proved by Abel and Galois that quintics and higher degree equations cannot in general be solved in terms of radicals, as discussed above for degree four and lower polynomial equations. Hermite showed that the quintic, after suitable transformation, is generally solvable by the use of elliptic modular functions. These are discussed in Chapter 16. See Davis for a discussion. It is almost certainly better to use iterative methods, such as the Jenkins-Traub method discussed in *C Tools*.

References

L. Baker, "Complex Arithmetic and Matrices in C," *C User's Journal*, May 1990, p. 59.

J. Bentley, *More Programming Pearls* (Reading, M. A.: Addison-Wesley Publishing Co., 1988).

H. T. Davis, *Introduction to Nonlinear Differential and Integral Equations* (N. Y.: Dover, 1960).

J. Jeans, *The Growth of Physical Science* (N. Y.: Fawcett, 1958).

C. Moler and J. Morrison, *IBM J. Research and Development*, **27**, p.577, 1983.

H. L. Rietz & A. R. Crathorne, *College Algebra* (N. Y.: H. Holt & CO., 1909).

M. R. Schroder, *Number Theory in Science and Communication* (N. Y.: Springer, 1984).

D. Wells, *The Penguin Dictionary of Curious and Interesting Numbers* (N. Y.: Penguin, 1986).

```
/*
complex variable auxilliary routines
from C Mathematical Function Handbook by Louis Baker
Copyright 1991 by Louis Baker. All rights reserved.

sign  returns sign of type double argument, i.e. -1,+1, or 0
argmt   argument of complex number (i.e., angle in polar
representation)
      returns angle between -pi to pi
Argmt as above, but returns 0 to 2pi
clog   complex logarithm
csqrt   complex square root
polarxy convert from polar to rectangular
cexp   complex exponential
ctrig   complex cosine and sine
      complex trig functions:
csin   sine
ccos   cosine
ctan  tangent
ccot  cotangent
csinh   sinh
ccosh   cosh
casin arcsine
cacos arccosine
catan arctangent
printc   print a complex number

*/

#include "stdio.h"
#include "stdlib.h"
#include "cmlib.h"
#include "complex.h"
#include "protom.h"
/*   #define DEFATAN2*/

/*static unsigned int btm,top;*/

double sign(x) double x;
{if(x==0.)return 0.;
return (x>=0.)?1.:-1.;
}

double argmt(y,x)
double x,y;
{/* returns answer between -pi to pi, in conformity with
atan2
 and the complex log branch cut along negative real axis.
This way, the logs of complex conjugates are conjugates */
```

```
/* caveat- Aztec C returns 0,not + or -halfpi if x=0., y
nonzero*/
double ans,ratio,/*twopi=6.283185307,*/halfpi=.5*pi;
double atan(),undef=0.0;/* change if desired*/
/* use atan2 if it exists:*/
#ifdef DEFATAN2
printf(" using system atan2\n");
return atan2(y,x);
/*otherwise, hand code it*/
#else
if(y==0.)
   {
   if(x>0.)return 0.;
   else if(x<0.)return pi;
   else return undef;
   }
if (x==0.){if(y>0.) return (halfpi);
      if(y<0.) return(-halfpi);
      /*return (halfpi*sign(y));*/
      return(undef);
     };
ratio=(y/x);ans=atan(ratio);
/*atan returns answer between -halfpi and halfpi*/
if(x>0.) return ans;/* Quadrants I and IV*/
/* x<0.*/
if( y<0.) return ans-pi;/*Quadrant III y/x and ans >0*/
return  ans+pi;/*Quadrant II x<0, y>=0 ans<0*/
#endif
}

double Argmt(y,x)
double x,y;
{/* returns answer between 0 and twopi, as needed in
complex principal argument*/
/* caveat- Aztec C returns 0,not + or -halfpi if x=0., y
nonzero*/
double ans,ratio,twopi=6.283185307,halfpi=1.570796327;
double atan(),undef=0.0;/* change if desired*/
if(y==0.)
   {
   if(x>0.)return 0.;
   else if(x<0.)return pi;
   else return undef;
   }
if (x==0.){if(y>0.) return(halfpi);
      if(y<0.) return(pi+halfpi);
      return(undef);
     };
/* if -pi to pi: if(x==0.)return (halfpi*sign(y));*/
```

```
ratio=(y/x);ans=atan(ratio);
/*atan returns answer between -halfpi and halfpi*/
/* now move to correct quadrant  between -pi and pi*/
if (ratio>0.){/* ratio, ans>0. */
        if (x>0.) return(ans);/* quadrant I*/
      /* else x<0.,y<0. quadrant III*/
      return (pi+ans);
             };
/* else ratio,ans<0.*/
if(x>0.)return(twopi+ans);/*quadrant IV*/
/*else x<0.,y>0., quadrant II*/
return(pi+ans);

/* if answer bwtn -pi and pi desired: if ans<=pi accept ans
unchanged
   else   ans-twopi
   this will affect quadrant III,IV only. change:
      III: pi+ans to ans-pi
       IV: twopi+ans to ans
*/
}

/*------------- complex logarithm function ---------------*/

clog(x,ans) struct complex *x,*ans;
{
double r,argmt(),sqrt(),log(),angle;
r= sqrt( CNORM(*x) );
angle=argmt(x->y,x->x);
ans->x=log(r);
ans->y=angle;
return;
}

/* ----------------- complex square root -------------------
-*/

csqrt(z,ans) struct complex *z,*ans;
{
double x,y,r,sqrt(),argmt(),angle;
r=  sqrt(sqrt( CNORM(*z) ) );
angle=.5*argmt(z->y,z->x);
polarxy(r,angle,&x,&y);
ans->x=x;
ans->y=y;
return;
}
```

```
/* ------- convert from polar to rectangular coordinates----
*/

polarxy(r,angle,x,y) double r,angle,*x,*y;
{double sin(),cos();
*x=r*cos(angle);
*y=r*sin(angle);
return;
}

/* complex exponential function */

cexp( x,ans) struct complex *x,*ans;
{
double y,exp(),sin(),cos();
y = exp ( x->x);
ans->x= y*cos (x->y);
ans->y= y*sin (x->y);
return;
}

/* cosine, sine of complex arguments
 .5(cexp(i*z)+(cexp(-i*z)),etc.*/

ctrig( z,ccos,csin) struct complex *z,*ccos,*csin;
{
double si,co,real,imag,e,ei,sinh,cosh,exp(),sin(),cos();
real=z->x;imag=z->y;
e = exp (imag);ei=1./e;
sinh= .5*(e-ei);
cosh=.5*(e+ei);
co=cos(real);
si=sin(real);
ccos->x=co*cosh;
ccos->y=-si*sinh;
csin->x=si*cosh;
csin->y=co*sinh;
return 0;
}


csin(z,ans) struct complex *z,*ans;
{
double sin(),cos(),sinh(),cosh(),x,y;
x=z->x;y=z->y;
ans->x= sin(x)*cosh(y);ans->y= cos(x)*sinh(y);
return 0;
}
```

```
ccos(z,ans) struct complex *z,*ans;
{
double sin(),cos(),sinh(),cosh(),x,y;
x=z->x;y=z->y;
ans->x= cos(x)*cosh(y);ans->y= -sin(x)*sinh(y);
return 0;
}


ctan( x,ans) struct complex *x,*ans;
{struct complex c,s;
ctrig(x,&c,&s);
if( cabs( c) != 0.)
   {CDIV( (*ans),s,c);return 0;}
CMPLX( *ans, errorcode,errorcode);return 1;
}

ccot(x,ans) struct complex *x,*ans;
   {struct complex ccos,csin;
   ctrig(x,&ccos,&csin);
   CDIV((*ans),ccos,csin);
   return 0;
   }


csinh(x,ans) struct complex *x,*ans;
{struct complex i,y,z; CMPLX(i,0.,1.);
CMULT(y,i,*x);
ctrig(&y,&z,ans);
CMULT(z,*ans,i);CTREAL(*ans,z,-1.);
return 0;
}

ccosh(x,ans) struct complex *x,*ans;
{struct complex i,y,z; CMPLX(i,0.,1.);
CMULT(y,i,*x);ctrig(&y,ans,&z);
return 0;
}

/* asin z= -i log(iz+sqrt(1-z^2))
   acos z= -i log( z+sqrt(z^2-1)) can add any multiple of
twopi*/

casin(x,ans) struct complex *x,*ans;
{
struct complex ci,z2,arg,sum,z;
CLET(z,*x);
CMULT(z2,z,z);
CMPLX(ci,0.,1.);CMPLX(arg,1.,0.);CSUB(arg,arg,z2);
```

```
clog(&arg,&sum);CTREAL(sum,sum,.5);cexp(&sum,&arg);
CMULT(sum,z,ci);CADD(sum,sum,arg);clog(&sum,&arg);
CMULT(sum,arg,ci);CTREAL((*ans),sum,-1.);
return 0;
}

cacos(x,ans) struct complex *x,*ans;
{
struct complex ci,z2,arg,sum,z;
CLET(z,*x);
CMULT(z2,z,z);
CMPLX(ci,0.,1.);CMPLX(arg,1.,0.);CSUB(arg,z2,arg);
clog(&arg,&sum);CTREAL(sum,sum,.5);cexp(&sum,&arg);
CADD(sum,z,arg);clog(&sum,&arg);
CMULT(sum,arg,ci);CTREAL((*ans),sum,-1.);
return 0;
}

catan(x,ans) struct complex *x,*ans;
{struct complex i,n,d,r;CMPLX(i,0.,1.);
CADD(n,i,*x);CSUB(d,i,*x);CDIV(r,n,d); clog(&r,&d);
CMULT(r,i,d); CTREAL(*ans,d, .5);return 0;
}

printc( z) struct complex *z;
{char *s;
if(z->y <0.) s="";
else s="+";
printf(" %le %s %le i ",z->x,s,z->y);
return 0;
}
```

```
/*
powers and roots
from C Mathematical Function Handbook by Louis Baker
Copyright 1991 by Louis Baker. All rights reserved.

power      x^n for x real general n (integers special)
root      x^(1/n)  for integral n
square_rt   square root
cube_rt      cube root
Euclidd      Euclidean distance. hypot() on some systems.
      use in a "bulletproofed" form of cabs()
*/

#define tol 1.e-8
#include "cmlib.h"
#include "protom.h"

double power( double x, double n)
   {
   int k,i;double pow,p;
   if(n==0.)return 1.0;/* return x^0=1 (even if x=0)*/
   if(x==1.)return 1.;
   if(x==0.)
      {if(n>0.)return 0.;
      return errorcode;
      }
   k=n;
   /*non-integral*/
   if( ((double)k-n)!=0.)
      {
      if(x<=0.)return errorcode;
      return expon(n*ln(x));
      }
   pow=1.;
   p=x;if(x<0)p=-p;
   if(k<0){k=-k;i=1;}
   else i=0;
   while(k)
      {
      if( 1 & k)pow*=p;
      p*=p;
      k>>=1;
      }
   if(x<0 && (((int)n)%2))
      {
      if(i) return -1./pow;
      return -pow;
      }
   if(i) return 1./pow;
```

```
   return pow;
   }


double root(xx,ni) double xx;int ni;
   {double mult,a,z,x,b,c,zo;int d,n;
   x=xx;mult=1.;n=abs(ni);
   if(n==0)return 1.0;/* return x^0=1 (even if x=0)*/
   if(x==0.)return 0.0;
   if(x==1.)return 1.;
   if(x<0 && !(n%2))return errorcode;
   if(x<0){x=-x;mult=-1.;}
   a=1./n;b=1.-a;c=a*x;d=n-1;
   z=zo=1.;
   for(;;)
      {
      z= b*z+c/power(z,d);
      if(abs(z-zo)<tol)
         {if(ni>0)return z*mult;
         return mult/z;
         }
      zo=z;
      }
   }


double square_rt(double x)
   {double /*y,*/z,old;
   if(x<0.)return errorcode;
   if(x==0.)return 0.;
   if(x==1.)return 1.;
   z=1.;/*initial guess*/
   infinite_loop
      {
      old=z;
      z= .5*(z+x/z);
      if( abs(old-z)<tol)break;
      }
   return z;
   }

double cube_rt(double x)
   {double /*y,*/z,old,c;
   if(x==0.)return 0.;
   if(x==1.)return 1.;
   c=1./3.;
   z=(x>0.)?1.:-1.;/*initial guess*/
   infinite_loop
      {
```

```
        old=z;
        z= (2.*z+x/(z*z))*c;
        if( abs(old-z)<tol)break;
        }
    return z;
    }

double Euclidd(xin,yin)double xin,yin;
    {
    double x,y,hold;
    x=abs(xin);y=abs(yin);
    if(x<y){hold=x;x=y;y=hold;}
    /* x largest mag. of xin or yin */
    if(x==0.)return 0.;
    if(y==0.) return x;
    hold= y/x;
    return x*sqrt(1.+hold*hold);
    }
```

```
/*
polynomial root finders
from C Mathematical Function Handbook by Louis Baker
Copyright 1991 by Louis Baker. All rights reserved.

solvq   solve quadratic
ctreal   x^n where x is complex and n is real
cpow   x^n where x, n are complex
ccubic   solve cubic with complex coefficient
cubic   solve cubic with real coefficients
cquartic solve quartic with complex coefficients
quartic  solve quartic with real coefficients
*/


#include <stdio.h>
#include <stdlib.h>
#include "cmlib.h"
#include "complex.h"
#include "protom.h"
/*static csqrt(x,y) struct complex *x,*y;
{struct complex z;clog(x,&z);CTREAL(z,z,.5);cexp(&z,y);}*/

solvq(b,c,ans1,ans2) struct complex *b,*c,*ans1,*ans2;
{
struct complex disc,ca;
CMULT(disc,*b,*b);CTREAL(ca,*c,4.);CSUB(disc,disc,ca);
csqrt(&disc,&disc);CTREAL(disc,disc,.5);
CTREAL(ca,*b,-.5);
CADD(*ans1,ca,disc);CSUB(*ans2,ca,disc);
return 0;}

static struct complex disc;

/* x^y where y real, x complex*/

ctreal(x, y, ans) struct complex *x,*ans; double y;
{struct complex z;
if( cabs((*x))==0.){CMPLX((*ans),0.,0.);return 1;}
clog(x,&z);CTREAL(z,z,y);cexp(&z,ans);
return 0;
}

cpow(x, y, ans) struct complex *x,*y,*ans;
{struct complex z,a;
if( cabs((*x))==0.){CMPLX((*ans),0.,0.);return 1;}
clog(x,&z);CMULT(a,z,*y);cexp(&a,ans);
return 0;
}
```

```
/*  could make eps an external (global) variable for con-
trol*/
#define eps 1.e-8
double polyresid;/*residual error for return if of inter-
est*/

ccubic(a1,a2,a3,r1,r2,r3) struct complex
*a1,*a2,*a3,*r1,*r2,*r3;
{struct complex h,g,of-
fset,d1,d2,d3,d4,u,v,w,w2,b1,b2,b3,ut,vt;
double third=1./3.,bestr;
int j,k;
CMPLX(w, -.5, sqrt(3.)*.5);
CONJG(w2,w);
CTREAL(offset,*a1,third);
CMULT(d2,*a1,*a1);CTREAL(d1,*a2,3.);CSUB(d1,d1,d2);
CTREAL(h,d1,third*third);
CMULT(d3,d2,*a1);CTREAL(d3,d3,2./27.);
CMULT(d2,*a1,*a2);CTREAL(d2,d2,third);
CSUB(g,d3,d2);
bestr=cabs(h);
CADD(g,g,(*a3));
CMULT(disc,g,g);CTREAL(g,g,-1.);
CMULT(d1,h,h);CMULT(d2,d1,h);CTREAL(d1,d2,4.);/* d2=h^3
d1=4h^3*/
CADD(disc,disc,d1);
/*printc(&disc);printf("=disc\n");*/
csqrt( &disc, &d1);
/*printc(&d1);printf("=sqrt disc\n");*/
CADD(d4,d1,g);CTREAL(u,d4,.5);
/*CSUB(d3,g,d1);CTREAL(v,d3,.5);*/
if(bestr==0.){CMPLX(u,0.,0.);}
CSUB(v,g,u);
/*printc(&h);printf("=h\n");printc(&g);printf("=g\n");
printc(&u);printf("=u\n");printc(&v);printf("=v\n");*/
/*CDIV(v,d2,u);CTREAL(v,v,-1.); pblm if |u| small */
CMULT(d3,u,v);CADD(d3,d3,d2);
/*printc(&d3);printf(" = uv+H^3 should be zero\n");*/
 bestr=1.e37;
 ctreal(&v,third,&d1);CLET(ut,d1);
 ctreal(&u,third,&d1);CLET(vt,d1);
 for(j=0;j<3;j++)
   {
   for(k=0;k<3;k++)
       {
/*       printc(&ut);printf("=u^third\n");
      printc(&vt);printf("=v^third\n");*/
      CADD( *r1,ut,vt);
```

```
        CMULT(d1,ut,w);CMULT(d2,vt,w2);
        CADD(*r2,d1,d2);
        CMULT(d1,ut,w2);CMULT(d2,vt,w);
        CADD(*r3,d1,d2);
        CSUB(*r1,*r1,offset);
        CSUB(*r2,*r2,offset);
        CSUB(*r3,*r3,offset);
        /* check*/
        CADD(h,*a1,*r1);CMULT(g,h,*r1);CADD(h,g,*a2);
        CMULT(g,h,*r1);CADD(g,g,*a3);
        polyresid=cabs(g);
/*        printc(r1);printf("=r1, resid %le \n",polyresid);*/
        if( polyresid < eps)return 0;
        if(polyresid<bestr)
           {bestr=polyresid;
           CLET(b1,*r1);CLET(b2,*r2);CLET(b3,*r3);
           }
        CMULT(*r1,vt,w);CLET(vt,*r1);
        }
    CMULT(*r1,ut,w);CLET(ut,*r1);
    }
        {
        /*if(bestr>eps)*/
        fprintf(stderr," ccubic: best resid=%le  eps %le\n"
           ,bestr,eps);
        CSET(r1,b1);CSET(r2,b2); CSET(r3,b3);
        polyresid=bestr;
        if(bestr>eps)return 1;
        }
return 0;
}

int cubic(a,b,c,r1,r2,r3) double a,b,c,*r1,*r2,*r3;
{/* solve cubic x^3+ax^2+b^x+c=0.
if 3 real roots, return 0, roots in r1,2,3
if 1 real, two complex. real in r1, r2 is real pt +/-r3*i
return1*/
struct complex a1,a2,a3,cr1,cr2,cr3;
CMPLX(a1,a,0.);
CMPLX(a2,b,0.);
CMPLX(a3,c,0.);
ccubic(&a1,&a2,&a3,&cr1,&cr2,&cr3);
if(  abs(disc.y)> eps)
    {fprintf(stderr," complex cubic discriminant: %le
%le\n",disc.x,disc.y);
    return ierrorcode;
    }
if( disc.x <=0)
    { /* if =0, some roots equal but still all are real*/
```

```
   *r1= cr1.x;
   *r2= cr2.x;
   *r3= cr3.x;
   return 0;
   }
/* one real, two complex conj roots*/
if( abs(cr1.y ) < eps)
   { *r1= cr1.x;
   *r2=cr2.x;
   *r3=cr2.y;
   }
else if( abs(cr2.y ) < eps)
   { *r1= cr2.x;
   *r2=cr1.x;
   *r3=cr1.y;
   }
else
   { *r1= cr3.x;
   *r2=cr2.x;
   *r3=cr2.y;
   }
return 1;
}

cquartic(a1,a2,a3,a4,r1,r2,r3,r4)
struct complex *a1,*a2,*a3,*a4,*r1,*r2,*r3,*r4;
{
struct complex a,b,c,d,q1,q2,q3,m,q,g,h,b1,b2,b3,b4;
int try,sel;double bestr;
CTREAL(a,*a2,-.5);
CMULT(b,*a1,*a3);CTREAL(b,b,.25);CSUB(b,b,*a4);
CMULT(c,*a2,*a4);CTREAL(c,c,4.);CMULT(d,*a3,*a3);CSUB(c,c,d);
CMULT(d,*a1,*a1);CMULT(q1,d,*a4);CSUB(c,c,q1);
CTREAL(c,c,.125);
try=ccubic(&a,&b,&c,&q1,&q2,&q3);
if(try){fprintf(stderr," cquartic bad return
ccubic\n");return 1;}
/*
printf(" q1 %le %le\n",q1.x,q1.y);
printf(" q2 %le %le\n",q2.x,q2.y);
printf(" q3 %le %le\n",q3.x,q3.y);
 */
try=sel=0;bestr=1.e30;
CLET(q,q1);
if( abs(q2.y)/(cabs(q2)+eps) <
abs(q.y)/(cabs(q)+eps)){CLET(q,q2);sel=1;}
if( abs(q3.y)/(cabs(q3)+eps)
<abs(q.y)/(cabs(q)+eps)){CLET(q,q3);sel=2;}
```

```
attempt:
/*printf(" sel=%d try=%d\n",sel,try);*/
CMULT(a,*a1,*a1);CTREAL(a,a,.25);CTREAL(b,q,2.);CADD(a,a,b);
CSUB(a,a,*a2); csqrt(&a,&m);polyresid=cabs(m);
if( polyresid< eps)
   {CMULT(a,q,q);CSUB(a,a,*a4);csqrt(&a,&b);}
else
   {CMULT(b,
q,*a1);CSUB(c,b,*a3);CDIV(b,c,m);CTREAL(b,b,.5);}
/* solve quadratics x^2 +(a1*.5 -m)x +q1 -b  =0
         x^2 +(a1*.5 +m)x +q1 +b =0 */
CTREAL(a,*a1,.5);CSUB(a,a,m);
CSUB(c,q,b);
solvq(&a,&c,r1,r2);
CTREAL(a,*a1,.5);CADD(a,a,m);
CADD(c,q,b);
solvq(&a,&c,r3,r4);
/* check */
CADD(h,*a1,*r1);CMULT(g,h,*r1);CADD(h,g,*a2);
CMULT(g,h,*r1);CADD(g,g,*a3);
CMULT(h,g,*r1);CADD(g,h,*a4);polyresid=cabs(g);
if( polyresid > eps)
   {try++;
   if( polyresid <bestr)

{bestr=polyresid;CLET(b1,*r1);CLET(b2,*r2);CLET(b3,*r3);
CLET(b4,*r4);
      }
   /*printf(" retry as resid=%le\n",polyresid);*/
   if(!sel){CLET(q,q2);sel=1;}
   else{CLET(q,q3);sel=2;}
   if(try<3)goto attempt;
   polyresid=bestr;
   CSET(r1,b1); CSET(r2,b2);   CSET(r3,b3); CSET(r4,b4);
   fprintf(stderr," cquartic: resid=%le  teps=%le\n"
      ,polyresid,eps);
   return 1;
   }
return 0;
}

quartic(a,b,c,d,r1,r2,r3,r4) double a,b,c,d;
struct complex *r1,*r2,*r3,*r4;
{
struct complex a1,a2,a3,a4;int retval;
CMPLX(a1,a,0.);
CMPLX(a2,b,0.);
CMPLX(a3,c,0.);
CMPLX(a4,d,0.);
```

```
/* elementary transcendental functions
from C Mathematical Function Handbook by Louis Baker
Copyright 1991 by Louis Baker. All rights reserved.

ln   natural logarithm
expon   exponential
sine    sine functions
arc_tan   arc tangent
arc_sin   arc sine
   hyperbolic functions:
hyper_sin
hyper_cos
hyper_tan
   arc hyperbolic functions:
arc_hyper_sin
arc_hyper_cos
arc_hyper_tan

cosine
arc_cosine
tangent    tangent= sin/cos
tangnt      tangent by continued fraction method
arc_tangent

cosine
*/
#include "cmlib.h"
#include "protom.h"
#define tol 1.e-9
#define twopi 2.*pi
#define halfpi .5*pi

double ln(double xin)
   {double sum,x,term,/*old,*/y,ys,factor,power,offset;int
i;
   double e=2.718281828459045;
   /*positive x only, please!*/
   x=xin;
   if(x<=0.)return errorcode;
   if(x==1.)return 0.;
   if(x<.5)return -ln(1./x);
   offset=0.;
   power=factor=term=1.;
   sum= 1.;i=3;
   /* unsophisticated range reduction*/
   while( x>e)
      {  x/=e; offset+=1.;
       /*printf("offset now %le x=%le\n",offset,x);*/
      }
```

```
   /* loop won't work well for large |x|, so need the above
*/
   y= (x-1.)/(x+1.);
   ys=y*y;
   infinite_loop
      {
      /*old=term;*/
      factor=1./((double)i);
      power*=ys;
      term=factor*power;
      sum+=term;
      if( abs(term)< tol)break;
      i+=2;
      }
   return 2.*y*sum+offset;
   }

double expon(double x)
   {
   double sum,term/*,old,y*/,factor,power;int i;
   if(x<-65.)return 0.;
   if(x>65.) return -errorcode;
   if(x>=1.)return 1./expon(-x);
   power=factor=term=1.;
   sum= 1.;i=1;
   infinite_loop
      {
      /*old=term;*/
      factor /= ((double)i);
      power*=x;
      term=factor*power;
      sum+=term;
      if( abs(term)< tol)break;
      i++;
      }
   return sum;
   }

double sine(double xi)
   {
   double sum,term,/*old,*/x,y,factor,power,z;/*int i;*/
   x=xi;
   while(x > twopi) x-=twopi;
   while(x < -twopi) x+=twopi;
   if(x==0.)return 0.;
   if(x==twopi)return 0.;
   power=factor=term=1.;
   sum= 1.;z=2.;y=x*x;
   infinite_loop
```

```
        {
        /*old=term;*/
        factor /=(-z*(z+1.));
        power*=y;
        term=factor*power;
        sum+=term;
        if( abs(term)< tol)break;
        z+=2.;
        }
    return sum*x;
    }


double arc_tan(double xi)
    {
    double sum,term,old,x,y,power/*,sign,factor*/,z;int
i/*,big*/;
    x=xi;
    if(x==0.)return 0.;
    /* convergence problems if y=x=1.*/
/*  series  4.4.42 first
    if(x==1.)return pi*.25;
    if(x==-1.)return -pi*.25;
    power=factor=term=1.;
    sum= 1.;z=3.;
    if(abs(x)<1.)big=0;
    else {big=1;x=1./x;}
    y=x*x;          sign=-1.;
    infinite_loop
        {
        factor =(sign/z);
        power*=y;
        term=factor*power;
        sum+=term;
        if( abs(term)< tol)break;
        z+=2.;                  sign=-sign;
        }
    sum=big?pi*.5-sum*x:sum*x;
    if(x>=0.)return sum;
    return -sum;
    */
    if(abs(x)>1.)
        { sum=arc_tan(1./x);
        if(x>0.)return pi*.5-sum;
        else return -pi*.5-sum;
        }
    /* series 4.42.last*/
    y=x*x;old=1./(1.+y);z=y*old;
    sum=1.;i=4;power=z*2./3.;
```

```
   infinite_loop
      {
      term=power;
      sum+=term;
      if( abs(term)< tol)break;
      power*=(z*i/(i+1.));
      i+=2;
      }
   return x*old*sum;
   }

double arc_sine(double xi)
   {
   double sum,term/*,old*/,x,y,factor,power,z,q;/*int i;*/
   x=xi;
   if(x==0.)return 0.;
   if(x==1.)return halfpi;
   if(x==-1.)return -halfpi;
   if(abs(x)>1.)return errorcode;
   if(abs(x)>.7071)
      {
      sum=arc_tan(x/square_rt(1.-x*x));
      return sum;
      }
/*       return halfpi-arc_sine(square_rt(1.-x*x));*/
   power=factor=term=1.;
   sum= 1.;z=2.;y=x*x;
   while(1)
      {
      /*old=term;*/
      q=z-1.;
      factor *=    q*q/(z*(z+1.));
      power*=y;
      term=factor*power;
      sum+=term;
      if( abs(term)< tol)break;
      z+=2.;
      }
   return sum*x;
   }

double hyper_sin(double x)
   {double ex;ex=expon(x); return (ex-1./ex)*.5;}
double hyper_cos(double x)
   {double ex;ex=expon(x); return (ex+1./ex)*.5;}
double hyper_tan(double x)
   {double ex,i;ex=expon(x);
   if(ex!=0.)i=1./ex;
   else return 1.;
```

```
   return (ex-i)/(ex+i);}
double arc_hyper_sin(double x)
   { return ln(x+square_rt(x*x+1.));}
double arc_hyper_cos(double x)
   {
   if(x<1.)return errorcode;
   if(x==1.)return 0.;
   return ln(x+square_rt(x*x-1.));}
double arc_hyper_tan(double x)
   {
   if(abs(x)>1.)return errorcode;
   if(x==1.)return -errorcode;
   if(x==-1.)return errorcode;
   return .5*ln((1.+x)/(1.-x));}

double cosine(double x) { return sine(pi*.5+x);}
double arc_cosine(double x) {return pi*.5-arc_sine(x);}

double tangent(double x)
   {
   double d;d=cosine(x);
   if(d==0.)return errorcode;
   return sine(x)/d;
   }

double tangnt(double x)
   {/*continued fraction method*/
   double z,ao=1.,ae=0.,bo=0.,be=1.,c,a,b,old,new,norm;int
first=1;
   while(x>pi)x-=pi;
   while(x<-pi)x+=pi;
   if(abs(x)==halfpi)return errorcode;
   if(x==0.)return 0.;
   /* tan= z/1- z^2/3- z^/5-*/
   z=x*x;
   c=1.;
   old=0.;
   norm=1.;
   while(1)
      {
      a=first? x:-z;
      b=c;
      ao= b*ae+a*ao;
      bo= b*be+a*bo;
      c+=2.;
      a=-z;b=c;
      ae= b*ao+a*ae;
      be= b*bo+a*be;
      /*printf(" ae be %le %le\n",ae,be);*/
```

```
        if( abs(ae)>10.)
            {norm=1./(ae);
            ae*=norm;be*=norm;
            ao*=norm;bo*=norm;
            }
        c+=2.;
        first=0;
        new= ae/be;
        if(abs(new-old)<tol)break;
        old=new;
        }
    return new;
    }
/*continued fraction method slower than tangnt*/
/*
double Tangnt(double x)
    {
    double z,ao=1.,ae=0.,bo=0.,be=1.,c,a,b,old,new;
    while(x>pi)x-=pi;
    while(x<-pi)x+=pi;
    if(abs(x)==halfpi)return errorcode;
    if(x==0.)return 0.;
    z=x*x;
    c=1.;
    old=0.;
    while(1)
        {
        a=-z;
        b=c;
        ao= b*ae+a*ao;
        bo= b*be+a*bo;
        c+=2.;
        a=-z;b=c;
        ae= b*ao+a*ae;
        be= b*bo+a*be;
        c+=2.;
        new= ae/be;
        if(abs(new-old)<tol)break;
        old=new;
        }
    return -new/x;
    }
*/
double arc_tangent(double y, double x)
    {double at;
    /* returns angle between -pi and pi.  "branch cut" x<0 */
    if(x==0.)
        {if (y==0.)return 0.;/* or errorcode-this is choice
of atan2*/
```

```
        if(y>0.)return halfpi;
        else return  -halfpi;
        }
    at=arc_tan( y/x);/* sign of at is sign of y/x -
pi/2<at<pi/2*/
    /* positive at*/
    if(x>0. )return at;/* quadrant I or 4 -pi/2 to pi/2 */
    if(y<0.)return at-pi;/* or pi+at>pi quadrand III*/
    /* negative at*/
    /* else quadrant II*/
    return at+pi;
    }
```

```
/*  main()
test driver for programs of Chapters 3-4
from C Mathematical Function Handbook by Louis Baker
Copyright 1991 by Louis Baker. All rights reserved.
*/

#include <time.h>
#include <stdio.h>
#include "protom.h"
clock_t a,b,c;
long t1,t2;

#include "cmlib.h"
#include "complex.h"
#include "protom.h"

getcmplx( struct complex *z);


getcmplx(z) struct complex *z;
{double r,i;
scanf("%le%le",&r,&i); (z->x)=r;(z->y)=i;return 0;
}

extern double polyresid;

main()
{double x,y,c,d,e,f,r,s,t;int i;struct complex
cz,cx,cy,cu,n,p;
/*a=clock();
for(i=0;i<10000;i++)
   y=tangnt(.1);
b=clock();
for(i=0;i<10000;i++)
   y=Tangnt(1.1);
c=clock();

printf(" using division(T): %ld  using first(t):%ld\n",c-
b,b-a);
*/
printf(" test of cubic solver for imaginary coef\n");
CMPLX(p,0.,1.);CMPLX(n,0.,0.);ccubic(&n,&n,&p,&cx,&cy,&cz);
printc(&cx);printf("\n");
printc(&cy);printf("\n");printc(&cz);printf("\n");
printf(" test of cubic solver for imaginary coef\n");
CMPLX(p,0.,-1.);CMPLX(n,0.,0.);ccubic(&n,&n,&p,&cx,&cy,&cz);
printc(&cx);printf("\n");
printc(&cy);printf("\n");printc(&cz);
printf("\n test of quartic solver for imaginary coef\n");
```

```
CMPLX(p,0.,1.);CMPLX(n,0.,0.);cquar-
tic(&n,&n,&n,&p,&cx,&cy,&cz,&cu);
printc(&cx);printc(&cy);printf("\n");
printc(&cz);printc(&cu);
printf("\n test of quartic solver for imaginary coef\n");
CMPLX(p,0.,-1.);CMPLX(n,0.,0.);cquar-
tic(&n,&n,&n,&p,&cx,&cy,&cz,&cu);
printc(&cx);printc(&cy);printf("\n");
printc(&cz);printc(&cu);
printf("\n");
infinite_loop
   {printf(" enter real b,c,d cubic\n");
   scanf("%le%le%le",&c,&d,&e);
   if(c==0. && d==0. && e==0.) break;
   i=cubic(c,d,e,&r,&s,&t);
   printf(" ans components: %le %le %le %d resid
%le\n",r,s,t,i,polyresid);
   }
infinite_loop
   {printf(" enter real b,c,d,e quartic\n");
   scanf("%le%le%le%le",&c,&d,&e,&f);
   if(c==0. && d==0. && e==0. && f==0.) break;
   i=quartic(c,d,e,f,&cx,&cy,&cz,&cu);
   printc(&cx);
   printc(&cy);
   printc(&cz);
   printc(&cu);
   printf(" quartic return value=%d
resid=%le\n",i,polyresid);
   }
infinite_loop
   {printf(" power:enter x,y\n");scanf("%le%le",&x,&y);
   if(x>1000.)break;
   printf(" x^n=%le\n",power(x,y));
   i=y;
   printf(" x^(1/(int)n)=%le\n",root(x,i));
   }
infinite_loop
   {printf(" hypot:enter x,y\n");scanf("%le%le",&x,&y);
   if(x>1000.)break;
   printf(" Euclidean distance=%le\n",Euclidd(x,y));
   i=y;
   printf(" x^(1/(int)n)=%le\n",root(x,i));
   }
infinitc_loop
   {printf(" cube rootenter x\n");scanf("%le",&x);
   if(x>1000.)break;
   printf("cbrt=%le\n",cube_rt(x));}
infinite_loop
```

```
   {printf(" tan enter x\n");scanf("%le",&x);if(x>10.)break;
   printf(" tan=%le %le \n",tangnt(x),tangent(x));}
infinite_loop
   {printf(" arc sin/cos enter
x\n");scanf("%le",&x);if(x>1.)break;
   printf("asine=%le
acos=%le\n",arc_sine(x),arc_cosine(x));}
infinite_loop
   {printf(" atan enter
x\n");scanf("%le",&x);if(x==0.)break;
   printf("arc_tan=%le arc_tan-
gent=%le\n",arc_tan(x),arc_tangent(2.*x,2.));}
infinite_loop
   {printf(" enter x\n");scanf("%le",&x);
   if(x==0.)break;
   printf("ln=%le\n",ln(x));}
infinite_loop
   {printf(" exp, hyper enter x\n");scanf("%le",&x);
   if(x>1000.)break;
   printf("exp=%le cosh %le sinh %le tanh %le\n",
      y=expon(x),hyper_cos(x),hyper_sin(x),hyper_tan(x));
   if(y==-errorcode || y==0.)break;
   }
infinite_loop
   {printf(" archyp enter x\n");scanf("%le",&x);
   if(x>1000.)break;
   printf("arc cosh =%le sinh %le tanh %le\n",
      arc_hyper_cos(x),arc_hyper_sin(x),arc_hyper_tan(x));
   if(y==-errorcode || y==0.)break;
   }
infinite_loop
   {printf(" sqrt enter x\n");scanf("%le",&x);
   if(x>1000.)break;
   if(x<0.)break;
   printf("sqrt=%le\n",square_rt(x));}
infinite_loop
   {printf("  enter complex z for clog\n");getcmplx(&cz);
   printc(&cz);
   if(cabs(cz)>100.)break;
   clog(&cz,&cx);
   printc(&cx);}

infinite_loop
   {printf("  enter complex z for ctrig\n");getcmplx(&cz);
   if(cabs(cz)>100.)break;
   ctrig(&cz,&cx,&cy);
   printc(&cx);}

infinite_loop
```

```
    {printf("  enter complex z for cexp\n");getcmplx(&cz);
    if(cabs(cz)>100.)break;
    cexp(&cz,&cx);
    printc(&cx);}
infinite_loop
    {printf("  enter complex z for ccosh\n");getcmplx(&cz);
    if(cabs(cz)>100.)break;
    ccosh(&cz,&cx);
    printc(&cx);}
infinite_loop
    {printf("  enter complex z for csinh\n");getcmplx(&cz);
    if(cabs(cz)>100.)break;
    csinh(&cz,&cx);
    printc(&cx);}
return 0;
}
```

```
retval=cquartic(&a1,&a2,&a3,&a4,r1,r2,r3,r4);
/* could use return value to signal type of roots if ret-
val=0*/
return retval;
}
```

```
Test Output for Chapters 3 and 4
elem
 test of cubic solver for imaginary coef
 8.660254e-01  -5.000000e-01 i
 -1.035955e-16 + 1.000000e+00 i
 -8.660254e-01  -5.000000e-01 i
 test of cubic solver for imaginary coef
 8.660254e-01 + 5.000000e-01 i
 -8.660254e-01 + 5.000000e-01 i
 -1.035955e-16  -1.000000e+00 i
 test of quartic solver for imaginary coef
 9.238795e-01  -3.826834e-01 i  3.826834e-01 + 9.238795e-01
i
 -3.826834e-01  -9.238795e-01 i  -9.238795e-01 + 3.826834e-
01 i
 test of quartic solver for imaginary coef
 9.238795e-01 + 3.826834e-01 i  -3.826834e-01 + 9.238795e-
01 i
 3.826834e-01  -9.238795e-01 i  -9.238795e-01  -3.826834e-
01 i
 enter real b,c,d cubic
-4 6 -4
 ans components: 2.000000e+00 1.000000e+00 1.000000e+00 1
resid 0.000000e+00
 enter real b,c,d cubic
6 -60 -416
 ans components: 8.000000e+00 -7.000000e+00 -1.732051e+00 1
resid 4.547474e-13
 enter real b,c,d cubic
3 -36 36
 ans components: 3.883254e+00 1.153520e+00 -8.036774e+00 0
resid 2.131628e-14
 enter real b,c,d cubic
0 0 1
 ans components: -1.000000e+00 5.000000e-01 8.660254e-01 1
resid 3.994472e-16
 enter real b,c,d cubic
0 0 -1
 ans components: 1.000000e+00 -5.000000e-01 8.660254e-01 1
resid 0.000000e+00
 enter real b,c,d cubic
3 2 1
 ans components: -2.324718e+00 -3.376410e-01 5.622795e-01 1
resid 2.534865e-16
 enter real b,c,d cubic
0 -15 -126
 ans components: 6.000000e+00 -3.000000e+00 -3.464102e+00 1
resid 9.947598e-14
 enter real b,c,d cubic
```

```
0 -981 -11340
 ans components: 3.600000e+01 -1.500000e+01 -2.100000e+01 0
resid 0.000000e+00
 enter real b,c,d cubic
0 0 0
 enter real b,c,d,e quartic
-6 12 -20 -12
 4.449490e+00  -1.677619e-16 i  -4.494897e-01 + 3.992391e-
16 i  1.000000e+00 + 2.236068e+00 i  1.000000e+00  -
2.236068e+00 i  quartic return value=0 resid=6.891556e-14
 enter real b,c,d,e quartic
-1 -21 1 20
 5.000000e+00 + 0.000000e+00 i  -1.000000e+00 + -
0.000000e+00 i  1.000000e+00 + 0.000000e+00 i  -
4.000000e+00 + -0.000000e+00 i  quartic return value=0
resid=0.000000e+00
 enter real b,c,d,e quartic
-3 20 44 54
 2.470639e+00  -4.640533e+00 i  2.470639e+00 + 4.640533e+00
i  -9.706390e-01 + 1.005808e+00 i  -9.706390e-01  -
1.005808e+00 i  quartic return value=0 resid=1.072176e-13
 enter real b,c,d,e quartic
0 0 0 0
 power:enter x,y
2 5
 x^n=3.200000e+01
 x^(1/(int)n)=1.148698e+00
 power:enter x,y
500 5
 x^n=3.125000e+13
 x^(1/(int)n)=3.465724e+00
 power:enter x,y
512 3
 x^n=1.342177e+08
 x^(1/(int)n)=8.000000e+00
 power:enter x,y
2000 0
 cube rootenter x
512
cbrt=8.000000e+00
 cube rootenter x
2
cbrt=1.259921e+00
 cube rootenter x
27
cbrt=3.000000e+00
 cube rootenter x
2000
 tan enter x
```

```
.1
 tan=1.003347e-01 1.003347e-01
 tan enter x
.5
 tan=5.463025e-01 5.463025e-01
 tan enter x
1
 tan=1.557408e+00 1.557408e+00
 tan enter x
10
 tan=6.483608e-01 6.483608e-01
 tan enter x
-.5
 tan=-5.463025e-01 -5.463025e-01
 tan enter x
-1
 tan=-1.557408e+00 -1.557408e+00
 tan enter x
-10
 tan=-6.483608e-01 -6.483608e-01
 tan enter x
0
 tan=0.000000e+00 0.000000e+00
 tan enter x
20000
 arc sin/cos enter x
.5
asine=5.235988e-01 acos=1.047198e+00
 arc sin/cos enter x
. 0
asine=0.000000e+00 acos=1.570796e+00
 arc sin/cos enter x
.001
asine=1.000000e-03 acos=1.569796e+00
 arc sin/cos enter x
.1
asine=1.001674e-01 acos=1.470629e+00
 arc sin/cos enter x
.5
asine=5.235988e-01 acos=1.047198e+00
 arc sin/cos enter x
.7
asine=7.753975e-01 acos=7.953988e-01
 arc sin/cos enter x
.8
asine=9.272952e-01 acos=6.435011e-01
 arc sin/cos enter x
.9
asine=1.119770e+00 acos=4.510268e-01
```

```
 arc sin/cos enter x
.9999
asine=1.563244e+00 acos=7.552048e-03
 arc sin/cos enter x
1
asine=1.570796e+00 acos=0.000000e+00
 arc sin/cos enter x
-.1
asine=-1.001674e-01 acos=1.670964e+00
 arc sin/cos enter x
-.5
asine=-5.235988e-01 acos=2.094395e+00
 arc sin/cos enter x
-.7
asine=-7.753975e-01 acos=2.346194e+00
 arc sin/cos enter x
-.8
asine=-9.272952e-01 acos=2.498092e+00
 arc sin/cos enter x
-.9
asine=-1.119770e+00 acos=2.690566e+00
 arc sin/cos enter x
-.99
asine=-1.429257e+00 acos=3.000053e+00
 arc sin/cos enter x
-1
asine=-1.570796e+00 acos=3.141593e+00
 arc sin/cos enter x
20000
 atan enter x
.1
arc_tan=9.966865e-02 arc_tangent=9.966865e-02
 atan enter x
.5
arc_tan=4.636476e-01 arc_tangent=4.636476e-01
 atan enter x
1
arc_tan=7.853982e-01 arc_tangent=7.853982e-01
 atan enter x
-.5
arc_tan=-4.636476e-01 arc_tangent=-4.636476e-01
 atan enter x
2
arc_tan=1.107149e+00 arc_tangent=1.107149e+00
 atan enter x
-2
arc_tan=-1.107149e+00 arc_tangent=-1.107149e+00
 atan enter x
0
```

```
 enter x
.5
ln=-6.931472e-01
 enter x
2
ln=6.931472e-01
 enter x
1
ln=0.000000e+00
 enter x
2.718281828459045
ln=1.000000e+00
 enter x
10
ln=2.302585e+00
 enter x
100
ln=4.605170e+00
 enter x
0
 exp, hyper enter x
1
exp=2.718282e+00 cosh 1.543081e+00 sinh 1.175201e+00 tanh
7.615942e-01
 exp, hyper enter x
2
exp=7.389056e+00 cosh 3.762196e+00 sinh 3.626860e+00 tanh
9.640276e-01
 exp, hyper enter x
-1
exp=3.678794e-01 cosh 1.543081e+00 sinh -1.175201e+00 tanh -
7.615942e-01
 exp, hyper enter x
.5
exp=1.648721e+00 cosh 1.127626e+00 sinh 5.210953e-01 tanh
4.621172e-01
 exp, hyper enter x
20000
 archyp enter x
.3678794
arc cosh =-1.000000e+60 sinh 3.600496e-01 tanh 3.859684e-01
 archyp enter x
1.543081
arc cosh =1.000000e+00 sinh 1.218425e+00 tanh -1.000000e+60
 archyp enter x
1.175201
arc cosh =5.836291e-01 sinh 9.999999e-01 tanh -1.000000e+60
 archyp enter x
.7615942
```

```
arc cosh =-1.000000e+60 sinh 7.023967e-01 tanh 1.000000e+00
 archyp enter x
-1.175201
arc cosh =-1.000000e+60 sinh -9.999999e-01 tanh -
1.000000e+60
 archyp enter x
0
arc cosh =-1.000000e+60 sinh 0.000000e+00 tanh 0.000000e+00
 archyp enter x
20000
 sqrt enter x
2
sqrt=1.414214e+00
 sqrt enter x
10
sqrt=3.162278e+00
 sqrt enter x
512
sqrt=2.262742e+01
 sqrt enter x
256
sqrt=1.600000e+01
 sqrt enter x
20000
  enter complex z for clog
1 0
 1.000000e+00 + 0.000000e+00 i  0.000000e+00 + 0.000000e+00
i   enter complex z for clog
2 0
 2.000000e+00 + 0.000000e+00 i  6.931472e-01 + 0.000000e+00
i   enter complex z for clog
-2 0
 -2.000000e+00 + 0.000000e+00 i  6.931472e-01 +
3.141593e+00 i   enter complex z for clog
0 -2
 0.000000e+00  -2.000000e+00 i  6.931472e-01  -1.570796e+00
i   enter complex z for clog
0 2
 0.000000e+00 + 2.000000e+00 i  6.931472e-01 + 1.570796e+00
i   enter complex z for clog
1 1
 1.000000e+00 + 1.000000e+00 i  3.465736e-01 + 7.853982e-01
i   enter complex z for clog
1 -1
 1.000000e+00  -1.000000e+00 i  3.465736e-01  -7.853982e-01
i   enter complex z for clog
-1 1
 -1.000000e+00 + 1.000000e+00 i  3.465736e-01 +
2.356194e+00 i   enter complex z for clog
```

```
-1 -1
 -1.000000e+00  -1.000000e+00 i  3.465736e-01  -
2.356194e+00 i   enter complex z for clog
2000 0
 2.000000e+03 + 0.000000e+00 i   enter complex z for ctrig
1 0
 5.403023e-01 + -0.000000e+00 i   enter complex z for ctrig
0 1
 1.543081e+00 + -0.000000e+00 i   enter complex z for ctrig
1 1
 8.337300e-01  -9.888977e-01 i   enter complex z for ctrig
20000 0
  enter complex z for cexp
1 0
 2.718282e+00 + 0.000000e+00 i   enter complex z for cexp
0 1
 5.403023e-01 + 8.414710e-01 i   enter complex z for cexp
-1 0
 3.678794e-01 + 0.000000e+00 i   enter complex z for cexp
0 -1
 5.403023e-01  -8.414710e-01 i   enter complex z for cexp
2000 0
  enter complex z for ccosh
1 0
 1.543081e+00 + -0.000000e+00 i   enter complex z for ccosh
0 1
 5.403023e-01 + 0.000000e+00 i   enter complex z for ccosh
-1 0
 1.543081e+00 + -0.000000e+00 i   enter complex z for ccosh
0 -1
 5.403023e-01 + -0.000000e+00 i   enter complex z for ccosh
20000 0
  enter complex z for csinh
1 0
 1.175201e+00 + -0.000000e+00 i   enter complex z for csinh
0 1
 0.000000e+00 + 8.414710e-01 i   enter complex z for csinh
-1 0
 -1.175201e+00 + 0.000000e+00 i   enter complex z for csinh
0 -1
 -0.000000e+00  -8.414710e-01 i   enter complex z for csinh
2000 0
```

Chapter 4

Elementary Transcendental Functions

In this chapter we present two sets of programs. First, the elementary transcendental functions for real arguments for the exponential, circular, and hyperbolic trigonometric functions, and their inverses. We also present functions for complex arguments.

Elementary Functions

Elementary functions are normally calculated by the math co-processor, or by system routines. If you must use these functions, I strongly urge you to use the hardware or the system library. The routines here are not optimized, as it is not possible to do so for an unknown environment. One problem which might be encountered is that the system routines are not suitable for ROM-able code. They may not be reentrant, and therefore not suitable for a multi-processing environment, or interruptable. (See the article by R. Naro in the references for a discussion of how to work around such problems in Turbo C 2.0.)

In general, all methods to calculate $y = elem(x)$ where *elem()* is some elementary function transform the problem into $y= A*f(z)$, where z is in some limited range. The discussion of how this is done for the *sqrt(x)* function, given in the previous chapter, is an example of this process. There are many choices for computing this function. We list and reference these, so that interested users can use the method optimal to their situation. The hardware characteristics and required precision must be kept in mind while choosing a method.

The methods presented here can give a precision limited only by that of the hardware and of the required tolerance specification. They are not fast, however. Normally, a power series or continued fraction representation is used. See *More C Tools* for a discussion of the use of continued fractions.

The CORDIC method is used by the Intel 80387 for circular functions, and is described in the references by Ruckdeschel and Jarvis. It breaks the angle up into components which may be easily calculated with shifts (instead of general multiplications), and computes the trigonometric functions by successive rotations, i.e., additions of these angles.

Polynomial approximations are used by the Cyrix chip, and are given for arbitrary precision in the papers by Clenshaw, Miller, and Woodger, and Miller. Here an expansion in Chebyshev[1] polynomials is used. This permits the user to tailor the precision of the approximation by simply adding more terms. Once the user has decided on the necessary precision, it would be desirable to use nested evaluation of a simple polynomial, which will halve the number of additions required (see Rice). In some cases, where cancellation is significant, such a conversion is dangerous (again, see Rice).

Rational approximations are given in Abramowitz and Stegun (see Chapter 1 for reference). The CRAY elementary function library routines employ rational approximations. Rational Chebyshev expansions can be developed by the Remez algorithm, which dates from 1934; see the paper by Cody et al. Cody et al., by the way, spell the name Remes (the name is transliterated from the Russian).

The SUN mathematical library **libm.a** uses tables in the computation of exp, log, and atan. Obviously, if memory is not at a premium, this can be a rapid approach. It also provides functions such as **ilogb(x)** to return the base 2 unbiased exponent of a floating-point number, which may be used to facilitate low-level operations on floating-point numbers.

The Cephes library, by S. L. Moshier, contains C code for elementary functions. The comments read "direct inquiries to 30 Frost Street, Cambridge, MA 02140." The library is available as diskette LC609 from Computer Solutions, P. O. Box 354, Mason, MI 48854, and appears to be in the public domain.

The "bible" in this area, although perhaps somewhat dated, is by Cody and Waite.

Complex Elementary Functions

For complex values of the arguments, the elementary functions can be written in terms of elementary functions of real arguments. One question arises as to the location of branch points. For the logarithm, we adopt the usual

1. Following the tradition set by T. E. Lawrence in *Seven Pillars of Wisdom*, no attempt will be made to spell this name consistently. There is at least as much justification here, as there as there are many transliterations to be seen.

convention of putting the branch cut on the negative real axis. This makes the logarithms of complex conjugate arguments complex conjugates. This corrresponds to the natural convention of FORTRAN and C routines such as **atan2(y,x)**, which return an answer between $-\pi$ and π. (In *C Tools*, we used a different convention which returned an angle between 0 and 2π.) Our function, **argmt(y,x)**, corresponds to the new convention, with **Argmt(y,x)** corresponding to the one of the *C Tools* book.

If your compiler is not case-sensitive, delete the latter or rename it. To enable **argmt()** to use the system **atan2()** function, use the **#define** statement near the beginning of the file.

The methods presented have an accuracy limited only by the machine's precision and the tolerances specified. They all transform the arguments and use either series or continued fractions.

Gudermannian

You may encounter the Gudermannian, defined by $u = gd(x) = \arctan(\sinh x)$. It was used primarily to allow calculation of hyperbolic functions given tables of circular trigonometric functions and $gd(x)$.

References

C. W. Clenshaw, G. F. Miller, M. Woodger, *Numerische Mathematik,* **4**, 403-419, 1963.

W. J. Cody, Jr., W. Fraser, J. F. Hart, *Numerische Mathematik*, **12**, 242, 1968.

W. J. Cody, Jr. and W. Waite, *Software Manual for the Elementary Functions* (Englewood Cliffs, N. J.: Prentice Hall, 1980).

P. Jarvis, "Implementing CORDIC Algorithms," *Dr. Dobbs Journal*, Oct. 1990, p. 152.

G. F. Miller, *Numerische Mathematik,* **7**, p. 194-196, 1965.

R. Naro, "Reentrant Floating Point," *Embedded Systems Programming*, April 1990, p. 63.

E. Remez, Comptes Rendes, **199**, 337, 1934.

J. R. Rice, *Numerische Mathematik,* **7**, 426-435, 1965.

F. R. Ruckdeschel, *Basic Scientific Subroutines*, Vol. II (N. Y.: McGraw-Hill, 1981).

Chapter 5

Exponential Integral and Relatives

Exponential and Related Integrals

Functions are presented here for computing the following integrals:

$$E_n(z) = \int_1^{\infty} \frac{e^{-zt}}{t^n} dt \, , \; Ei(x) = P \int_{-\infty}^{x} \frac{e^t}{t} dt$$

$$\alpha_n(z) = \int_1^{\infty} t^n e^{-zt} dt \, , \; \beta_n(z) = \int_{-1}^{1} t^n e^{-zt} dt$$

$$Si(x) = \int_0^x \frac{\sin t}{t} dt, \;\; Ci(x) = \gamma + \ln x + \int_0^x \frac{\cos t - 1}{t} dt = -\int_x^{\infty} \frac{\cos t}{t} dt$$

$$Shi(x) = \int_0^x \frac{\sinh t}{t} dt, \; Chi(x) = \gamma + \ln x + \int_0^x \frac{\cosh t - 1}{t} dt$$

Here the symbol P in the definition of Ei denotes the Cauchy principal value of the integral is to be taken because of the singularity of the integrand at $t = 0$. Note that $E_1(x) = -Ei(-x)$. Various other functions are customarily defined in terms of these integrals, such as $li(x) = \int_0^x \frac{1}{\ln t} dt = Ei(\ln x)$ or $Cin(x)$ defined via $Cin(x) = \gamma + \ln x + Ci(x)$, i.e., $Cin(x) = \int_0^x \frac{\cos t - 1}{t} dt$. The function $li(x)$ is denoted $Li(x)$ by some authors. It is related to the asymptotic distribution of prime numbers. The exponential integrals are important in transport and scattering problems. The sine and cosine integrals are of interest in antenna theory. See Fig. 5-1 for $Shi(x)$ and $Chi(x)$. Finally, in some problems, such as the scattering of electromagnetic waves from wires, it is useful to define iterated functions as follows. Following Einarsson in Bowman et al., ed., denote $T(x) = \int_x^\infty \frac{e^{i(t-x)}}{t} dt = -e^{-ix}(Ci(x) + Si(x) - \frac{1}{2} i \pi)$ and $l_0 = \gamma + \log x - \frac{1}{2} i \pi$.

Then the functions $l_{01}(x) = l_2(x,x) = \int_x^\infty \frac{T(t)}{t} e^{i(t-x)} dt = c_{01}(x) - i\, s_{01}(x)$,

$l_{11}(x) = l_2(0,x) = \int_x^\infty \frac{T(t)}{t} dt = c_{11}(x) - i\, s_{11}(x)$, where

$l_2(x,y) = \int_0^\infty \frac{T(y + t y)}{1 + t} e^{i(t-x)} dt.$ In this chapter, we present some approximations to the c_{01}, s_{01}, c_2 and s_2 integrals, a variety of functions for the integrals listed for real arguments, and the exponential integral for complex arguments. See also Chapter 7 on the Error Function and related integrals for Shi(x), Chi(x), the Boehmer and other related integrals. Here γ is Euler's constant (also called the Euler-Mascheroni number) and is approximately .5772. It is discussed further in the next chapter. It is not known whether this number is irrational or if it is transcendental.

Methods

In general, the approach is similar to that of the last chapter. Series and continued fraction representations are used, as well as rational approximations from the cited source as well as Abramowitz and Stegun. The complex error function is based upon the method of A. Beam. Roland Bulirsch has published Chebyshev approximations similar to those discussed in the previous chapter for the sine, cosine, and Fresnel integrals.

References

A. Beam, *Complex Error Function*, Algorithm 14, *CALGO (Collected Algorithms from ACM).*

R. Bulirsch, *Numerische Mathematik*, **9**, 380-385, 1967.

Electromagnetic and Acoustic Scattering by Simple Shapes, ed. J. J. Bowman, T. B. A. Senior, P. L. E. Uslenghi (N. Y.: Hemisphere Publications, 1987).

Shi(x) and Chi(x)

(Figure next page.)

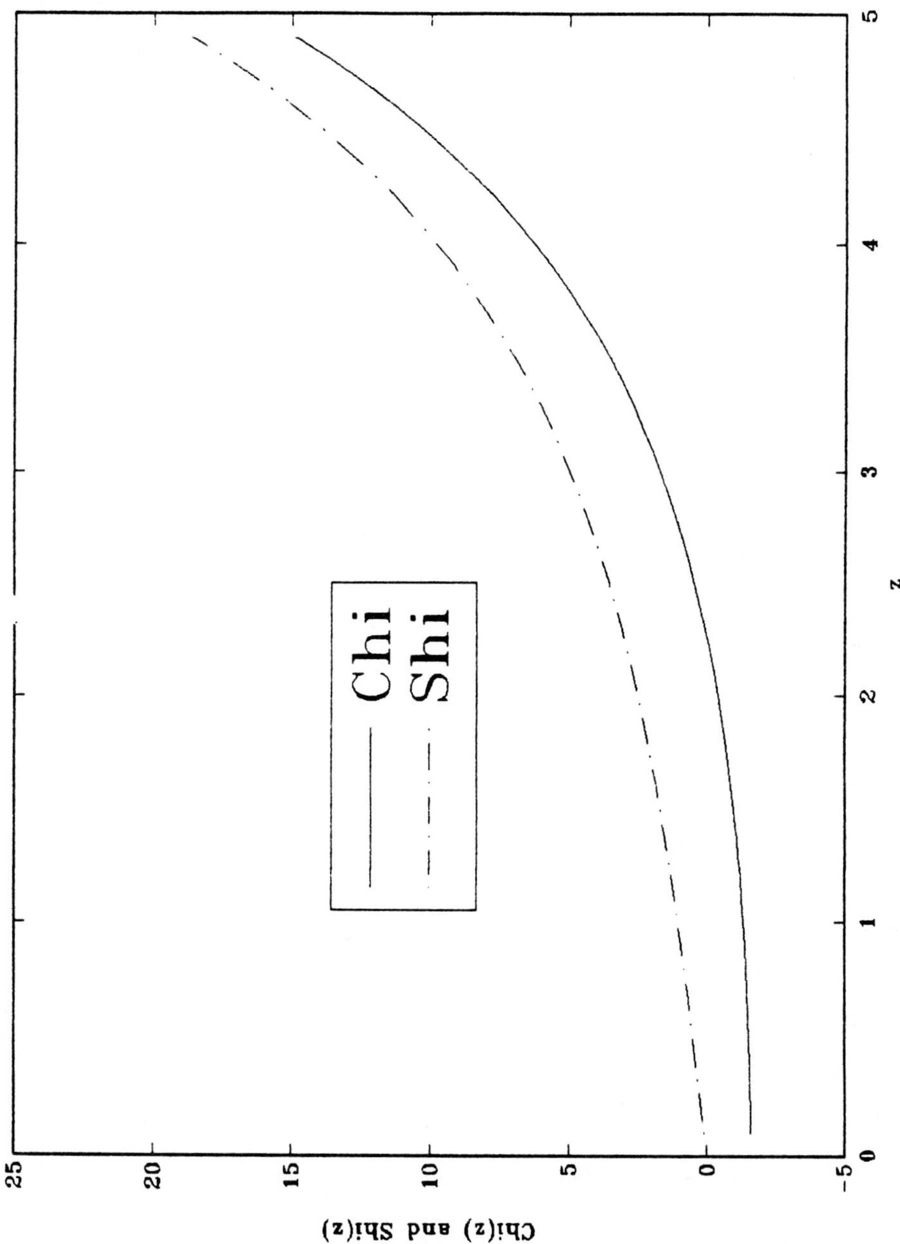

Fig. 5-1: *Chi* and *Shi* functions.

```
/* functions for the evaluation of the
 Exponential  Integral
and the sine and cosine integrals and
   their relatives

from C Mathematical Function Handbook by Louis Baker
Copyright 1991 by Louis Baker. All rights reserved.

e1      E1(x) rational approx.
         error:  < 2x10^-7 0<x<1, < 2x10^-8 1<x<infinity
si,ci   sine and cosine integrals, rational approx.
         error:  < 5x10^-7 0<x<inf
f,g     auxilliary functions for above: not intened for
direct use. static.
en      En exponential integral-continued fraction used.
aux. routine
e1s     E1, series
eicf    Ei(x), continued fraction approx. aux. routine
e       E(x,n) Exponential integral-general
ei      Ei(x) Ei-general
Eict    Ei, moderate and large x, Cody & Thatcher rational
approx.
Eis     Ei, small x, Cody & Thatcher rational approx.
eias    asymptotic approximate fit aux. routine
li      Li(x)
alpha   alpha(x,n)
beta    beta(x,n)  Do not confuse with Beta function!

iterated sine and cosine integrals from Ch12 of Bowman et
al.:
f(),g() are those of Abramowitz & Stegun Ch. 5
c() and s() of Bowman et al. are g, -f respectively.
Note the following relations:
Abramowitz and Stegun:
Si= integral[0 to x] sin(t)/t
Ci= gamma+log(x)+ integral[0 to x] (cos(t)-1)/t
si=Si- pi/2
f= Ci sin - si cos
g= -Ci cos - si sin

Bowman et. al./Einarsson: rational approx. iterated Si,Ci
integrals.
T= c-is   (= g+if in A&S notation)
 = integral[x to infinity] exp i(t-x) /t = -exp ix [Ci+Si-i
pi/2]

l2(x,y)    = integral[0 to infinity] T(y+ty) exp ixt/(1+t)
   = c2-is2
   errors: < 2.e-5 for 2<x, 0<=y<1
```

```
with l2(x,x)= c01-is01
   errors: <  8.e-10 for 0<x<=2, 9.e-9 x>2

cei   complex exponential integral (all double arg)
ceii   scaled complex exponential integral (all double arg)

cexpint complex exponential integral (complex arg)
*/

#include "cmlib.h"
#include "protom.h"
#include <stdio.h>
#define DOFOR(i,to) for(i=0;i<to;i++)

/* make external global double for use elsewhere*/


double e1(x) double x;
{
double log(),exp(),y;
   if(x< 0.)return errorcode;
if(x<1.)
   y=(((((.00107857*x-.00976004)*x+.0551968)*x-.24991055)*x
       +.99999193)*x-Egamma)-log(x);
else
y=(((((x+8.5733287401)*x+18.0590169730)*x+8.6347608925)*x
   +.2677737343))/(((((x+9.5733223454)*x+25.6329561486)*x
     +21.0996530827)*x+3.9584969228)*x)*exp(-x);
     return(y);
}

double si(x) double x;
{
double z,cos(),sin(),f(),g();
if(x<1.)
   {
   z=x*x;
/*   return(x*(1.-z*(.055555555-z*(.00166666666-
z*.0000283446))) );*/
   return(x*(.999999998-z*(.055555480-z*(.001666289-
z*.000027739))) );
   }
else
   return(pi*.5-f(x)*cos(x)-g(x)*sin(x));
/*next for the DeSmet C compiler-others will warn of un-
reachable stmt*/
return(0.);
}
```

```
/*Warning: Name conflict with console input function ci()
in DeSmet C*/
double ci(x) double x;
{
double z,y,f(),g(),log(),cos(),sin();
if(x<1.)
   {
   z=x*x;
/*   y=-z*(.25+z*(z*(.0002314814-z*.0000031001)-
.01041666))*/
   y=-z*(.25+z*(z*(.000231447-z*.000003046)-.01041666))
     + Egamma +log(x);
   }
else
   y=f(x)*sin(x)-g(x)*cos(x);
return(y);
}
/* f, g not for direct user use */

static double f(x) double x;
{ double z;
z=x*x;
return(((((z+38.027264)*z+265.187033)*z+335.67720)*z
     +38.102495))/(((((z+40.021433)*z+322.624911)*z+
     570.236280)*z+157.105423)*x);
}

static double  g(x) double x;
{
double z;
z=x*x;
   return(((((z+42.242855)*z+302.757865)*z+352.018498)*z+

21.821899))/(((((z+48.196927)*z+482.485984)*z+1114.978885
      )*z+449.690326)*z);
}

#define small 1.e-20

int itktg; /* global to report iteration count*/

double en(x,n) double x,n;
{
int i,itmax=50;
double d,c,delta,h,a,tol=1.e-7,exp();
/* continued fraction: not reliable for small x*/
if(x==0.)
   {
   if(n==1.)return(-1.);/*error*/
```

```
   return 1./(n-1.);
   }
h=small;d=0.;c=h;
for (i=0;i<itmax;i++)
   {
   if(!i)a=1.;
   else
      a=i;
   d=x+a*d;
   c=x+a/c;
   if(d==0.)d=small;
   if(c==0.)c=small;
   d=1./d;
   delta=d*c;
   h*=delta;
   a= n + i;
   d=1.+a*d;
   c=1.+a/c;
   if(d==0.)d=small;
   if(c==0.)c=small;
   d=1./d;
   delta=d*c;
   h*=delta;
   if(abs(delta-1.)<tol)break;
   }
return(h*exp(-x));/* return best guess*/
}

double e1s(x) double x;
{/* e1, series*/
int n; double sum,factor,m,tol=1.e-8;
sum=0.;factor=-x;
for(n=1;n<1000;n++)
   {
   sum+=factor;
   if( abs(factor)<tol*abs(sum))break;
   m=n+1.;
   factor *= -x*n/(m*m);
   }
return  -Egamma-log(x)-sum;
}

double eicf(x) double x;
{
int i,itmax=100;
double podd,peven,qodd,qeven,y,z,a,b,tol=1.e-6,zold,exp();
qodd=0.;qeven=1.;
podd=1.;peven=0.;
z=0.;
```

```
/* continued fraction not reliable for small x*/
for (i=0;i<itmax;i++)
   {
   if(!i)a=1.;
   else
      a=-i;
   b=x;
   podd= a*podd+b*peven;
   qodd= a*qodd+b*qeven;
   a= -(1. + i);
   b=1.;
   peven=a*peven+b*podd;
   qeven= a*qeven+b*qodd;
   zold=z;
   z=peven/qeven;
   itktg=i;
   if( (i>0) && abs(z-zold) < tol)
      {printf(" leaving eicf Ei/exp(x)=%e\n",z);
      return z*exp(x);
      }
   /* re norm*/
   if( abs(qodd)>10.)
      {
      y=1./qodd;
      peven*=y;
      podd*=y;
      qeven*=y;
      qodd=1.;
      }
   }
printf(" Ei not converged\n");
return(z*exp(x));/* return best guess*/
}
/*
double eia(x) double x;
{
double y,e1(),exp();
y=1./x;
if(y>.4)return(0.);
return e1(x)*exp(2.*x)*(1.+8.808*y-32.06*y*y+185.633*y*y*y)
   /(1.+6.5418*y-37.207*y*y+130.691*y*y*y);
}
*/

double e(x,n) double x;int n;
{
int k,ncross=2;
/* choose ncross based on timing*/
double y,ee;
```

```
if(!n) return exp(-x)/x;
if(n==1)return e1(x);
if(x>1. && n>ncross)return en(x,(double) n);
y=exp(-x);
ee=e1(x);
for(k=1;k<n;k++)
   {
   ee= (y-x*ee)/k;
   }
return ee;
}


double E1(x) double x;
{double Ei();
if(x<0.)return -Ei(-x);
if(x==0.)return -errorcode;
if(x<=1.)return e1s(x);
/* x>1.*/
return en(x,1.);
}



#define itmax 40

static double fcf(x,n,a,b) double x,a[],b[];int n;
{double value;int i;
value=1.;
for(i=1;i<=n;i++)
   {
   value= b[n-i]/(a[n-i]+x+value);
   }
return value;
}

static double a24[9]={-3.0000000032098126575З,-
5.00006640413131002475,
-7.06810977895039358836,-15.28566236369296368З9,-
7.63147701620253630855,
-27.97985386243053893З0,-18.19496649298689064ЗЗ,-
223.12767077763240955,
175.33880126546597239},   b24[9]={
1.99999999999048104167,-2.99999894040324959612,-
7.99243595776330741065,
-12.01877635471547432З8,70.48318471804246759З8,
117.17922050208645528З,137.79039023657479987ЗЗ,
3.97277109100414518365,39784.597716741472084};
```

```
static double a12[8]={-2.073093182550626,66.81633520851786,
-61.8811145837267426,13.615334713984657547,-
32.460770029937463678,
-8.7163735593963354058,
-17.808311603699779966,-4.088838379362196702},b12[8]={
 .99905385353462753131,.99655264231071911439,
4267.5815993503950849,11.526405585745173857,
688.27350646689188421,27.549295584621895224,
 77.697693140151074176,50.693912820579735193};

static double
a6[8]={5.731167057445080,4.18102422562856622231,
5.886582407532811, -19.41329675144307,
7.8947220929445722122,23.273023383903914,
-36.778311347831145794,-2.4694098344836126512},
b6[8]={ 1.1462525324910161914 3,-199.1496002312351636,
341.36521252437553905,52.316556873455861379,
317.27948925436932786,-8.3876708411896407065 6,
965.40521742928030312,2.6398300731802459334};


#define tol 1.e-6

static double Eict(x)double x;
{
double exp(),y,z;
if(x>24.)
   z=1.+(1.00000000000004855+fcf(x,9,a24,b24))/x;
else if(x<=24. && x>12.)
   z=(1.0000051738331117+fcf(x,8,a12,b12));
else if(x<=12. && x>=6.)
   {
   z=(9.9895766651165517e-01+fcf(x,8,a6,b6));
   }
   y=exp(x)/x;
/*printf(" exp/x=%e other %e ",y,z);*/
   return y*z;
}

double scale;

/* approximate accuracy:
order   digits
3   5
4   7
6   12
9   20
*/
/*#define order 3*/
```

```
/*#define order 4*/
/*#define order 6*/
#define order 9

static double Eis(double x)
   {
   double x0= .372507410781366634461991866580;

/*   double p[4]={-2.2409438e3*.5,-1.832677e2,-9.0053723e1,-
5.6796891};
   double q[4]={-8.5609557e2*.5, 4.097087e2,-
8.3056797e1,6.75};
*/
/*   double
p[5]={3.360281229e4*.5,1.521253684e3,1.540472598e3,
7.554503527e1,6.214595703};
   double q[5]={.5*1.337025876e4,-
6.737936555e3,1.583666607e3,
-1.921193866e2,1.01250e1};
*/
/*   double p[7]={1.45747321743484e7*.5,4.71761893143542e4,
7.84689687508871e5,1.35036011184167e4,
7.35420513947427e3,1.80339138516268e2,7.75745083328328};
   double q[7]={.5* 6.06704887208133e6,
-3.22441109528198e6 , 8.67868680839173e5,
-1.39638471189123e5,1.39851277161255e4,-
8.27775609141545e2,2.278125e1};
  */
double p[10]={-
4.16580813336049942418791e11*.5,1.21776981361995946775800e10,
-2.53018239845990193488558e10,3.19843542352377385110488e8,
-3.53778096944311334848e8,-3.13986608642472658620 5e5,
-1.42998415720916103800064e6,-1.42870725001970057773776e4,
-1.28312206592620678144e3,-1.29637026024748300285 9e1};
double q[10]={-
1.79347498371510097233371e11*.5,9.89009342624817494398 86e10,
-2.89862726965544953426 58e10,5.42296179844729550118 62e9,
-7.01085687742159540653 76e8,6.46988309565764285876 53e7,
-4.26484348121771614054 83e6,1.94184694407598803614 15e5,
-5.56484705433690828468 19e3,7.688671875e1};

   double h,z,y,n,no,noo,d,dold,doo;  int i;
   z=x/6.;y =2.*z-1.;z=2.*y;
   noo=doo=0.; no=p[order];dold=q[order];
   for(i= (order-1);i>0;i--)
      {
      n= z*no-noo+p[i];
      d= z*dold-doo+q[i];
      doo=dold;dold=d;
```

```
        noo=no;no=n;
        }
    n=y*n-noo+p[0];
    d=y*d-doo+q[0];
    h=x-x0;
    return log(1.+h/x0)+(h)*n/d;
    }

double eias(x) double x;
{double term,oterm,sum;
int i;
sum=0; oterm=term=1.;
for(i=1;i<itmax;i++)
    {
    sum+=term;
    oterm=term;
    term*= i/x;
    if(abs(term)>abs(oterm) || abs(term)<tol*abs(sum))break;
    }
/*printf(" sum=%e\n",sum);*/
return exp(x)/x*sum;
}

double Ei(x) double x;
{
int i;
double sum,term,tolr=1.e-7,xcross=25.;
/*"exact"*/
if(x<=0.)return errorcode;
if(x>xcross)return eias(x);
if(x>1.)return eicf(x);
sum= log(x)+ Egamma;
term=x;
for (i=1;i<itmax;i++)
    {
    sum+=term/(i);
    term*=x/(i+1);
    if( abs(term)<tol || abs(term)<abs(sum)*tolr)return sum;
    itktg=i;
    }
printf(" too many iterations\n");
return errorcode;
}

double ei(x) double x;
{
/* next 4 stmts for Rational approx. remove otherwise*/
if(x<=0.)return -e1(-x);
if(x>20.)return eias(x);
```

```
if(x>6.)return Eict(x);
return Eis(x);
}

double li(x) double x;
{
double ei(),log();
if(x<1.)return errorcode;
return ei(log(x));
}

double alpha(x,n) double x; int n;
{
return pow(x, -(double)(n+1))*
   gamma((double)(n+1))*(1.-incgam((double)(n+1),x));

/* first find alpha n=0, then use recurrence:*/
/*currently disabled, might be useful small n,x*/
/*{
z=exp(-x);y=z/x;
if(!n)return y;

for (k=1;k<=n;k++)
   {
   y=(z+k*y)/x;
   }
return y;
}*/
}

double beta(x,n) double x; int n;
{
double realn,exp(),eps=1.e-5,z,y,sinh,sign,bet,log();
int k;
if(x==0.)return 0.;
if(!n)
   { /* beta sub-0(x)=2sinh(x)/x no divide by zero */
   z=exp(-x);y=1./z;return (y-z)/x;
   }
if(x<0. || n< 1)return errorcode;
realn=n;/* n==0 handled above so no log problems*/
if( x<(realn*.368+.821+.184*log(realn)))
   {/*backward recursion*/
printf(" backward\n");
   k=10+n;
   z=exp(-x);y=1./z;
   bet=0.;
   sign= (k%2)?-1.:1.;
   for( ;k>=n;k--)
```

```
        {
        bet= (x*bet+z+sign*y)/(k+1);
        sign=-sign;
        }
    return bet;
    }
/* forward recursion*/
sign=-1.;
if(x<eps)
    {
    x=eps;
    z= exp(-x);y=1./z;
    sinh=.5*(y-z);
    bet=2. *(1.+x*x*.1666666);
    }
else
    {
    z=exp(-x); y=1./z;
    sinh=.5*(y-z);
    bet=sinh*2./x;
    }
if(!n)return bet;
for (k=1;k<=n;k++)
    {
    bet=(y*sign-z+k*bet)/x;
    sign*=-1.;
    }
return bet;
}


double f01(x) double x;
{double log(),y,z;
y=(Egamma+log(x));       z=x*x;
return .5*y*y-pi*pi/24.-z*
(.125+z*(-2.60416632e-3+z*(3.857955e-5+z*(-3.87035e-
7+z*2.61455e-9))));
}
double g01(x) double x;
{double log(),y,z;
y=(Egamma+log(x));       z=x*x;
return -.5*pi*y+x*
(.9999999992+z*(-.0185185136+z*(3.3332344e-4+z*
(-4.0422785e-6+z*3.201246e-8))));
}

double c01(x) double x;
{double sin(),cos(),f01(),g01(),z;
if(x<0.)return errorcode;
```

```
if(x<=2.)return f01(x)*cos(x)+g01(x)*sin(x);
z=x*x;
return -(z*(20.96173922+z*(7.150169966+z*
(.4371420242+z*.005415719186)))-3.85642854)
 /((100.+z*(70.34218899+z*(11.16783932+z*
(.496599058+z*.005415884237))))*z);
}

double s01(x) double x;
{double sin(),cos(),f01(),g01(),z;
if(x<0.)return errorcode;
if(x<=2.)return f01(x)*sin(x)-g01(x)*cos(x);
z=x*x;
return -
(.5423489064+z*(43.88413692+z*(14.246573437+z*(.8460999768+z*
.009972860283))))
 /((100.+z*(60.93657+z*(8.503549177+z*(.3369899234+
z*.003314700857))))*x*z);
}


double g2(x,y)double x,y;
{
double sqrt(),log(),atan(),xs,ys,p,q,r,sum,a,sa,f(),g();
double aa[3]={17.420076,.501312744,3.43966581};
double A[3]={.05299936,.422384803,.241865419};
int i;
xs=x*x;ys=y*y;
p=f(x*.5);q=g(x*.5);                      r=log(2.*y/x);
sum=0.;
for(i=0;i<3;i++)
   {
   a=aa[i];sa=sqrt(a);
   sum+=A[i]/(a+xs)*(.5*x*log((ys+a)/(a+.25*xs))-
sa*atan((2.*y-x)*sa/(x*y+2.*a)));}
return -(p*q)+f(x)*r-.282750417*(r/x)-sum;

}
double f2(x,y)double x,y;
{
double sqrt(),log(),atan(),xs,ys,p,q,r,sum,a,sa,f(),g();
double aa[3]={21.850456,.770345382,1.55715659};
double A[3]={.163725227,.34115997,.428765629};
int i;
xs=x*x;ys=y*y;
p=f(x*.5);q=g(x*.5);                      r=log(2.*y/x);
sum=0.;
for(i=0;i<3;i++)
   {
```

```
   a=aa[i];sa=sqrt(a);
   sum+=A[i]/(a+xs)*(.5*log((ys+a)/(a+.25*xs))+x/sa*
atan((2.*y-x)*sa/(x*y+2.*a)));}
return .5*(q*q-p*p)-g(x)*r+ .066349174*(2.-x/y+r)/xs+sum;
}

double c2(x,y) double x,y;
{double f(),g(),f2();
if(x<2.)return errorcode;
if(1.<=y && y<=x) return f2(x,y);
if(y<1.)return g(y)*g(x-y)-f(y)*f(x-y)-f2(x,x-y);
return errorcode;
}

double s2(x,y) double x,y;
{double f(),g(),g2();
if(x<2.)return errorcode;
if(1.<=y && y<=x) return g2(x,y);
if(y<1.)return -g(y)*f(x-y)-f(y)*g(x-y)-g2(x,x-y);
return errorcode;
}


struct complex ceiscaled;

/* continued fraction approx. from CALGO 14 */
cei(x,y,k,toler,u,v,n) double x,y,k,toler,*u,*v;int *n;
{
struct complex z,ans,e,temp; double d;
z.x=x;z.y=y;
d=cabs(z);
if(d<1.e-20)
   {*n=0;
   if(k>1){*u=1./(k-1.);*v=0.;}
   else {*u=-errorcode;*v=0.;}
   return 0;
   }
ceii(x,y,k,toler,u,v,n);
/*printf(" %e %e scaled zexp(z)E\n",*u,*v);*/
ceiscaled.x=*u;
ceiscaled.y=*v;
/* scale by dividing by z*exp(z)*/
CMPLX(ans,*u,*v);CDIV(temp,ans,z);cexp(&z,&e);
CDIV(ans,temp,e);
*u=ans.x;*v=ans.y;
return 0;
}
```

```
ceii(x,y,k,toler,u,v,n) double x,y,k,toler,*u,*v; int *n;
{/* finds complex 'exponential integral' u+iv= z^kexp(z) in-
tegral z to infinity
(z=x+iy) of exp-t dt/t^k . do not use |z|<.05 as conver-
gence is slow*/
 double M,K,t1,t2,t3,a,b,c,d,g,h,e; int m;
 struct complex  cz,term,sum,power,offset;double fac;
 cz.x=x;cz.y=y;
 fac=cabs(cz);
 if(fac<1.e-20)
   { if(k>1) {*u=0.;*v=0.;/* En=1./(k-1),but scaled
x*exp(x)=0*/
      return;}
     else {*u=-errorcode;*v=0.;return;}
   }
 if(fac<=.05 &&!(y==0.&&x<0))
   {/* use series for small |z| unless arg(z)=pi*/
   if(k==1)
      {CMPLX(offset,-Egamma,0.);
      clog(&cz,&term);CSUB(offset,offset,term);
      }
   else
      {
      clog(&cz,&term);CMPLX(offset,digamma((double)k),0.);
      CSUB(offset,offset,term);
      CTREAL(offset,offset,1./gamma((double)k));
      CTREAL(term,cz,-1.);clog(&term,&sum);
      CTREAL(sum,sum,(double)(k-1));cexp(&sum,&term);
      CMULT(sum,offset,term);CLET(offset,sum);
      }
   CMPLX(sum,0.,0.);
   CTREAL(cz,cz,-1.);
   fac=1.; CMPLX(power,1.,0.);
   for(m=0;m<100;m++)
      {
      if(m) fac*=m;
      if(m==(k-1))continue;
      CTREAL(term,power,1./((m-k+1)*fac));
      CADD(sum,sum,term);
      if(cabs(term)<cabs(sum)*toler)break;
      CMULT(term,power,cz);
      CLET(power,term);
      *n=m;
      }
   CSUB(offset,offset,sum);/* now multiplby by exp(x)*x */
   CMULT(sum,offset,cz);CTREAL(sum,sum,-1.);
   CTREAL(offset,cz,-1.);cexp(&offset,&term);
   CMULT(offset,term,sum);*u=offset.x;*v=offset.y;return;
   }
```

```
 e=tol*tol;
 *u=c=a=1.;*v=d=b=0.;
 *n=1; K=k-1;
 do
 {
 g=*u;h=*v;(*n)++;
/*printf(" n is %d\n",*n);*/
 m=(*n)>>1;
 M=((m<<1)==(*n))? m+K:m;
 t1=x+M*c;t2=y+M*d;
 if(t1==0. && t2==0.){fprintf(stderr," cei:
t1=t2=0\n");return;}
 t3=1./(t1*t1+t2*t2);
 c=(x*t1+y*t2)*t3;
 d=(y*t1-x*t2)*t3;
 t1=c-1;t2=a;
 a=a*t1-d*b;b=d*t2+t1*b;
 *u=g+a;*v=h+b;
 }while( (a*a+b*b)/(*u* *u+*v* *v)>e);
 return;
}

cexpint(z,n,toler,ans,iter) struct complex *z,*ans;double
toler,n;int *iter;
{ cei(z->x,z->y,n,toler,&(ans->x),&(ans->y),iter);
return 0;
}
```

```
/*
test driver exponential integrals and gamma functions
from C Mathematical Function Handbook by Louis Baker
Copyright 1991 by Louis Baker. All rights reserved.
*/

#include <stdio.h>
#include "cmlib.h"
#include "protom.h"
#include <stdio.h>
#include "cmlib.h"
#include "protom.h"

extern struct complex ceiscaled;

main()
{float a,b,kk; int n;
double x,y,k,u,v;
struct complex c,d,e;
infinite_loop{
   printf(" E1: enter x\n");scanf("%le",&x);
   if(x>1000.)break;printf("e1=%le s=%le
cf=%le\n",e1(x),e1s(x),en(x,1.));
   printf(" E1=%le\n",E1(x));
   }
infinite_loop{
   printf(" En: enter x,n\n");scanf("%le%d",&x,&n);
   if(x>1000.)break;
   printf(" En=%le\n",en(x,(double)n));
   }
infinite_loop{
   printf(" Ei: enter x\n");scanf("%le",&x);
   if(x>1000.)break;printf("Ei=%le\n",ei(x));
   }
infinite_loop{
   printf(" enter x,n  for alpha,
beta\n");scanf("%le%d",&x,&n);
   if(x>1000.)break;printf("alpha=%le
beta=%le\n",alpha(x,n),beta(x,n));
   }
infinite_loop{
   printf(" En complex arg:enter x,y k(==0. to end)");
   scanf("%e%e%e",&a,&b,&kk);
   if(kk==0.)break;x=a;y=b;k=kk;
   /* conventional En would have z^k-1 factor so we have ad-
ditional z*/
   cei(x,y,k,1.e-5,&u,&v,&n);
   printf(" iter=%d ans= %e %e \n",n,u,v);
   CMPLX(c,x,y); cexpint(&c,k,1.e-5,&d,&n);
```

```
   printf(" En =");printc(&d);printf("\n");
   printf(" z^nExp(z)En=");printc(&ceiscaled);printf("\n");

   }
infinite_loop{
   printf(" gamma enter x\n");scanf("%le",&x);
   if(x>1000.)break;printf("gamma=%le %le\n",gamma(x),
gammaqd(x));
   printf("digamma=%le %le\n",digamma(x),digam(x));
   printf("polygamma 1 and 2=%le %le\n",pg1(x),pg2(x));
   }
infinite_loop{
   printf(" complex gamma enter x,y\n");
   scanf("%le%le",&x,&y);
   if(x>1000.)break;CMPLX(c,x,y);cgamma(&c,&d,&e);
   printc(&d);printc(&e);
   printf(" gamma, log gamma \n");
   cdigamma(&c,&d);
   printc(&d);printc(&e);
   printf(" gamma, log gamma \n");
   }
infinite_loop{
   printf(" pochhammer enter x,n\n");scanf("%le%d",&x,&n);
   if(x>1000.)break;printf("Pochhammer=%le\n",pochham-
mer(x,n));
   }
return 0;
}
```

```
Test Driver Results: Exponential Integral & Relatives
expi
 E1: enter x
1
e1=2.193839e-01 s=2.193839e-01 cf=2.193839e-01
 E1=2.193839e-01
 E1: enter x
.5
e1=5.597731e-01 s=5.597736e-01 cf=5.597736e-01
 E1=5.597736e-01
 E1: enter x
2
e1=4.890051e-02 s=4.890051e-02 cf=4.890051e-02
 E1=4.890051e-02
 E1: enter x
5
e1=1.148296e-03 s=1.148299e-03 cf=1.148296e-03
 E1=1.148296e-03
 E1: enter x
10
e1=4.156969e-06 s=4.160991e-06 cf=4.156969e-06
 E1=4.156969e-06
 E1: enter x
30
e1=3.021552e-15 s=-2.224349e-06 cf=3.021552e-15
 E1=3.021552e-15
 E1: enter x
20000
 En: enter x,n
.4 20
 En=3.451400e-02
 En: enter x,n
2000 0
 Ei: enter x
.5
Ei=4.542199e-01
 Ei: enter x
1
Ei=1.895118e+00
 Ei: enter x
2
Ei=4.954234e+00
 Ei: enter x
8
Ei=4.406645e+02
 Ei: enter x
12
Ei=1.495976e+04
 Ei: enter x
```

```
30
Ei=3.689727e+11
 Ei: enter x
20000
 enter x,n  for alpha, beta
3 0
alpha=1.659569e-02 beta=6.678583e+00
 enter x,n  for alpha, beta
3 1
alpha=2.212759e-02 beta=-4.485580e+00
 enter x,n  for alpha, beta
3 2
alpha=3.134741e-02 beta=3.688196e+00
 enter x,n  for alpha, beta
.5 0
alpha=1.213061e+00 beta=2.084381e+00
 enter x,n  for alpha, beta
.5 1
 backward
alpha=3.639184e+00 beta=-3.417414e-01
 enter x,n  for alpha, beta
.5 2
 backward
alpha=1.576980e+01 beta=7.174156e-01
 enter x,n  for alpha, beta
2000 0
 enter x,y k(==0. to end)1 1 1
 6.733210e-01 1.478638e-01 scaled zexp(z)E
 iter=34 ans= 2.816130e-04 -1.793245e-01
 6.733210e-01 1.478638e-01 scaled zexp(z)E
 complex arg answer=
 2.816130e-04  -1.793245e-01 i
 enter x,y k(==0. to end)-1 1 1
 8.134859e-01 5.786974e-01 scaled zexp(z)E
 iter=149 ans= -1.764625e+00 -7.538232e-01
 8.134859e-01 5.786974e-01 scaled zexp(z)E
 complex arg answer=
 -1.764625e+00  -7.538232e-01 i
 enter x,y k(==0. to end)0 0 0
 gamma enter x
5
gamma=2.400000e+01 2.400000e+01
digamma=1.506118e+00 1.506118e+00
polygamma 1 and 2=2.213227e-01 -4.718933e-02
 gamma enter x
-1.5
gamma=2.363272e+00 2.363272e+00
digamma=7.031566e-01 7.031545e-01
polygamma 1 and 2=-1.035993e+01 -3.121679e+01
```

```
 gamma enter x
-.5
gamma=-3.544907e+00 -3.544907e+00
digamma=3.648997e-02 3.648997e-02
polygamma 1 and 2=-1.080448e+01 3.017748e+01
 gamma enter x
.5
gamma=1.772454e+00 1.772454e+00
digamma=-1.963510e+00 -1.963510e+00
polygamma 1 and 2=4.934877e+00 -1.682880e+01
 gamma enter x
2000
 complex gamma enter x,y
4 5
 1.496553e-01 + 3.146033e-01 i  -1.054448e+00 +
7.409966e+00 i  gamma, log gamma
 1.808447e+00 + 9.590160e-01 i  -1.054448e+00 +
7.409966e+00 i  gamma, log gamma
 complex gamma enter x,y
4 -5
 1.496553e-01  -3.146033e-01 i  -1.054448e+00  -
7.409966e+00 i  gamma, log gamma
 1.808447e+00  -9.590160e-01 i  -1.054448e+00  -
7.409966e+00 i  gamma, log gamma
 complex gamma enter x,y
1 1
 4.980157e-01  -1.549498e-01 i  -6.509232e-01  -3.016403e-
01 i  gamma, log gamma
 9.465032e-02 + 1.076674e+00 i  -6.509232e-01  -3.016403e-
01 i  gamma, log gamma
 complex gamma enter x,y
1 -1
 4.980157e-01 + 1.549498e-01 i  -6.509232e-01 + 3.016403e-
01 i  gamma, log gamma
 9.465032e-02  -1.076674e+00 i  -6.509232e-01 + 3.016403e-
01 i  gamma, log gamma
 complex gamma enter x,y
2000 0
 pochhammer enter x,n
1 1
Pochhammer=1.000000e+00
 pochhammer enter x,n
1 0
Pochhammer=1.000000e+00
 pochhammer enter x,n
1 2
Pochhammer=2.000000e+00
 pochhammer enter x,n
1 3
```

```
Pochhammer=6.000000e+00
 pochhammer enter x,n
0 0
Pochhammer=1.000000e+00
 pochhammer enter x,n
0 1
Pochhammer=0.000000e+00
 pochhammer enter x,n
0 2
Pochhammer=0.000000e+00
 pochhammer enter x,n
.5 0
Pochhammer=1.000000e+00
 pochhammer enter x,n
.5 1
Pochhammer=5.000000e-01
 pochhammer enter x,n
.5 2
Pochhammer=7.499998e-01
 pochhammer enter x,n
-.5
1
Pochhammer=-5.000001e-01
 pochhammer enter x,n
-.5 2
Pochhammer=-2.500000e-01
 pochhammer enter x,n
-1 0
Pochhammer=1.000000e+00
 pochhammer enter x,n
-1 1
Pochhammer=-1.000000e+00
 pochhammer enter x,n
-1 2
Pochhammer=0.000000e+00
 pochhammer enter x,n
-1 4
Pochhammer=0.000000e+00
 pochhammer enter x,n
-10 0
Pochhammer=1.000000e+00
 pochhammer enter x,n
-10 1
Pochhammer=-1.000000e+01
 pochhammer enter x,n
-10 2
Pochhammer=9.000000e+01
 pochhammer enter x,n
-10 3
```

```
Pochhammer=-7.200000e+02
 pochhammer enter x,n
-10 4
Pochhammer=5.040000e+03
 pochhammer enter x,n
-10 20
Pochhammer=0.000000e+00
 pochhammer enter x,n
2000 0
```

Chapter 6

Gamma Function and Related Integrals

Gamma Function and Relatives

The gamma function is defined by $\Gamma(x) = \int_0^\infty t^{x-1} e^{-t}\, dt$. It is related to the factorial function $n! = \Gamma(n+1)$. One occasionally sees the notation $\Pi(x) = \Gamma(x+1)$, which corresponds to the factorial function, but emphasizes the fact that it is valid for arguments other than just integers. The Pochammer symbol is defined as follows: $(z)_0 = 1, (z)_n = z(z+1)\ldots(z+n-1)$. It can be evaluated as $(z)_n = \dfrac{\Gamma(z+n)}{\Gamma(z)}$ if the denominator is defined. The incomplete gamma function comes in a number of varieties: $P(a,x) = \dfrac{\int_0^a t^{x-1} e^{-t}\, dt}{\Gamma(a)}$, $\gamma(a,z) = P(a,z)\Gamma(a)$, $\gamma^*(a,x) = x^{-a} P(a,x)$ and $\Gamma(a,x) = \Gamma(x) - \gamma(a,x)$. The incomplete gamma functions are of interest in statistics because of their relationship to the chi-square (χ^2) distribution. Also of interest are the derivatives of the gamma function, named the digamma function $\psi(x) = \dfrac{d}{dx} \ln\Gamma(x) = \dfrac{1}{\Gamma(x)} \dfrac{d}{dx}\Gamma(x)$, and the polygamma functions $\psi^{(1)}(x) = \dfrac{d}{dx}\psi(x)$, etc., where $\psi^{(n)}$ is the n-th derivative of ψ. Recall the comments in Chapter 2 as to how some authors, such as Tuma, use the definition $\psi(x) = \dfrac{d}{dx}\Gamma(x+1)$. Euler's gamma, $\gamma = .5772\ldots$, may be defined (and calculated) via $\psi(1) = -\gamma$.

The Pochhammer Symbol

The Pochhammer symbol occurs in numerous series expansions. It is discussed more fully in Chapters 15 and 29 in the discussions of the Hypergeometric function and its generalizations. The complex version of the function is given in Chapter 15. The basic definition of the function is $(x)_0 = 1$, $(x)_1 = x$, $(x)_n = x(x - 1)(x - 2)...(x - n + 1))$. Note that the relationship $(x)_n = \Gamma(x + n)/\Gamma(x)$ may be used unless x is zero or a negative integer. This relationship is often the most efficient means of computation.

Methods

Series, continued fraction, and asymptotic formulae are all used. The continued fraction methods for the incomplete gamma functions are discussed in *More C Tools*, Chapter 5. The rational approximations for the digamma and first two polygamma functions are from Tuma. See also Chapter 26 for the incomplete gamma functions and relatives.

Asymptotic Series

Asymptotic series are used for large argument values. They are semi-converent, i. e., they diverge at some point; the terms in the series first decrease and then increase. The error is generally smaller than the magnitude of the last retained term. It only makes the results less accurate to add more terms to the sum after the minimum term has been used. Therefore, there is a limit to the accuracy obtainable for any given argument value. For the gamma and digamma functions, use of relationships between $\Gamma(x)$ and $\Gamma(x + 1)$ enable us to relate the value of the function for any given x to that of an arbitrarily larger x, thus giving us (in principle) unlimited accuracy. This will not be true for asymptotic series in general, however. The crossover point for argument magnitude, determining that for larger values the asymptotic series is used and for smaller values series, has to be determined by the accuracy requirements.

Reference

J. J. Tuma, *Handbook of Numerical Calcuations in Engineering* (N. Y.: McGraw-Hill, 1989).

```
/*
Gamma Function & Relatives
from C Mathematical Function Handbook by Louis Baker
Copyright 1991 by Louis Baker. All rights reserved.

loggam,gamma   logarithm of gamma, gamma functions all real
x.
P incgam BigGamma lcgam, ucgam
      versions of incomplete gamma function
fac      factorial
pochhammer   pochhammer symbol for real x, integer n
cgamma      gamma, log gamma for complex arguments
gammaqd      compact, "exact" gamma.
cdigamma   digamma for complex arguments
polygam      polygamma function for real arguments
*/

#include <stdio.h>
#include "cmlib.h"
#define DOFOR(I,J) for(I=0;I<J;I++)
#include "complex.h"
#include "protom.h"

#define min(a,b) (((a)<(b))? (a): (b))

int itkt;
int iterp;/* global to return count used*/


double gamma(x) double x;
{
double y,z;
if(x<=0. &&  (((x-(double)((int)x)))==0.) )
   {
   fprintf(stderr," gamma: arg 0 or neg. integer=%le\n",x);
   return errorcode;
   }
y=exp(loggam(x));
if(x>=0.)return(y);
z=  2*(((int)(-x))%2) -1;
return(y*z);
}


double loggam(x) double x;
{
int i;
double z,tmp,ser,log(),sin(),*coeff;
static double logsr2pi=.918938533;
```

```
static double b[9]={.035868343,-.193527818,.482199394,-
.756704078,
.918206857,-.897056937,.988205891,-.577191652,1.0};

/*if( x<0.&& x> -1. )
   {
   return((loggam(1.+x)-log(-x)));
   }
else requires two levels of recursion and  log call,not sin
*/
if (x<-0.) /*was x< -1. when above implemented */
      {/*transform to x>0. will blow up if x integer, as it
should*/
      z=1.-x;/* z>2. */
      return(log(pi/abs(sin(pi*z)))-loggam(z) );
      }
else
   if (x<=1.)/* 0<=x<1 */
      {
      /*z=1.-x*/;/*  0<=z<1*/
      /*return( log(z*pi/sin(pi*z))-loggam(1.+z));*/
      /* Ab& Stegun-takes less than half the time*/
      if(x==0.)return 0.;
      tmp=b[0];
      coeff=&(b[1]);
      for(i=1;i<9;i++)tmp= tmp*x+ *(coeff++);
      return(log(tmp/x));
      }
/* use below for x>1.*/
else
   if(x<=2.)
      {
      tmp=b[0];
      coeff=&(b[1]);
      z=x-1.;
      for(i=1;i<9;i++)tmp= tmp*z+ *(coeff++);
      return(log(tmp));
      }
z=1./x;
tmp=z*z;
ser= (1./12.+tmp*(-1./360.+tmp*(1/1260.-tmp/1680.)    ))*z;
/*ser= (.08333333333333+tmp*(tmp*(0.000793650793-
.000595238095*tmp)
   -.002777777777))*z;*/
return (logsr2pi-x+(x-.5)*log(x)+ser);
}
#define small 1.e-30

double P(a,x) double x,a;
```

```
{/* P incomplete gamma function*/
int i,itmax=100;
double gln,exp(),log(),loggam(),sum,ap,del,fi,start,
tol=3.e-7,c0,d0,ana,offset,mult,delta;
/* error condition return -1 on invalid arguments*/
if( x< 0. || a<0. ) return(-1.);
if(x==0.)return(0.);
gln=loggam(a);
if (x< (a+1.))
   {
   /*series*/
   offset=0.;
   mult=1.;
   ap=a;
   sum=1./a;
   del=sum;
   DOFOR(i,itmax)
      {
      ap++;
      del*=x/ap;
      sum+=del;
      if( abs(del)<abs(sum)*tol) goto fini;
      }
      fprintf(stderr," trouble incomplete gamma series\n");
   }
else
   {
   offset=1.;
   mult=-1.;
   start=small;
   sum=start;/*fictitious should be small but numerical
pblms?*/
   d0=0.;c0=sum;
   DOFOR(i,itmax)
      {
      fi=i;
      if(i)ana=fi;
      else ana=1.;
      d0= (x+d0*ana);
      c0=(x+ana/c0);
      if(d0==0.)d0=small;
      if(c0==0.)c0=small;
      d0=1./d0;
      delta=d0*c0;sum*=delta;
      ana=fi+1.-a;
      d0= (1.+d0*ana);
      c0=(1.+ana/c0);
      if(d0==0.)d0=small;
      if(c0==0.)c0=small;
```

```
        d0=1./d0;
        delta=d0*c0;sum*=delta;
        if( abs(delta-1.)<tol)
           {/*sum-=start;*/ goto fini;}
        }
    fprintf(stderr," trouble incomplete gamma cont.
fract\n");
    }
/*return(-1.);*/
fini:return(offset+mult*sum*exp(-x+a*log(x)-gln));
}
double incgam(a,x) double a,x;
{return P(a,x);}
double lcgam(a,x) double a,x;
{double gamma();return P(a,x)*gamma(a);}
double ucgam(a,x)double a,x;
{double gamma(); return gamma(a)*(1.-P(a,x));}

double BigGamma(a,x) double x,a;
{/* incomplete gamma function*/
int i,itmax=100;
double exp(),log(),gamma(),mult,offset,sum,ap,del,fi,start,
tol=3.e-7,c0,d0,ana,delta;
if( x< 0. || a<0. ) return(errorcode);
if(x==0.)return(0.);
if (x< (a+1.))
    {
    /*series */
    offset=gamma(a);
    mult=-1.;
    ap=a;
    sum=1./a;
    del=sum;
    DOFOR(i,itmax)
        {
        ap++;
        del*=x/ap;
        sum+=del;
        if( abs(del)<abs(sum)*tol) goto fini;
        }
        fprintf(stderr," trouble incomplete gamma series\n");
    }
else
    {
    offset=0.;
    mult=1.;
    start=small;
    sum=start;/*fictitious should be small but numerical
pblms?*/
```

```
   d0=0.;c0=sum;
   DOFOR(i,itmax)
      {
      fi=i;
      if(i)ana=fi;
      else ana=1.;
      d0= (x+d0*ana);
      c0=(x+ana/c0);
      if(d0==0.)d0=small;
      if(c0==0.)c0=small;
      d0=1./d0;
      delta=d0*c0;sum*=delta;
      ana=fi+1.-a;
      d0= (1.+d0*ana);
      c0=(1.+ana/c0);
      if(d0==0.)d0=small;
      if(c0==0.)c0=small;
      d0=1./d0;
      delta=d0*c0;sum*=delta;
      if( abs(delta-1.)<tol)
         {/*sum-=start;*/ goto fini;}
      }
   fprintf(stderr," trouble incomplete gamma cont.
fract\n");
   }
fini:return(offset+mult*sum*exp(-x+a*log(x)));
}

double Pgamma(a,x)double a,x;
{double gamma(); return BigGamma(a,x)/gamma(a);}

double Smallgamma(a,x)double a,x;
{return P(a,x)*gamma(a);}

double fac(x) double x;
{
double gamma();
return gamma(x+1.);
}

double pochhammer(z,n) int n;double z;
{double gamma(),m;int k;
if(!n)return 1.;
k=z;
if( (z-k)!=0. || z>0.)
   return gamma(z+n)/gamma(z);
/* z is a negative integer*/
if(n==1)return z;
m=z;
```

```
for (k=1;k<n;k++)
   {m *=(z+k);if(m==0.)return 0.;}
return m;
}

/* quick & dirty gamma function*/
#define lim 20

double gammaqd( double xin)
{double xi,factor=1.,g,x,sin(),exp(),sqrt(),pow();
/*reflect*/
x=xin;
if(x==0.)return errorcode;
if(x<0.)
   {
   if(abs( x-(int)x)<1.e-10)return errorcode;
   return pi/(gamma(1.-x)*sin(pi*x));
   }
/* may take x>0 at this point*/
while(x< lim){factor=factor/x;x++;}xi=1./x;
g= factor*(exp(-x))*(pow(x,x-.5))*sqrt(2.*pi)*
(1.+xi*(1./(12.)+xi*(1./(288.)-
xi*(139./(51840.)+571./(2488320.*x)))));
return g;
}

/* complex gamma*/


cgamma(zz,ans,loggam) struct complex *zz,*ans,*loggam;
{struct complex z,zm,t,tt,sum,term,den,a,aux;
 double c[12]={1./12.,-1./360.,1./1260.,
-1./1680., 1./1188.,-691./360360.,1./156.,
 -3617./122400.,43867./244188.,-174611./1125400.,
77683./5796.},
  x,y,tol=1.e-7,xdist,log();
 int flip;
 /* best of the bunch- from CALGO 404 Lucas and Terrill */
 /* modified 9/25/90 so that |gamma(x+iy)|=|gamma(x-iy)|
 independently of how argmt() returns answer*/
 int i,m,reflect;
 CLET(z,*zz);flip=0.;
 x=z.x;y=z.y; reflect=0;
 if( x<tol)
   {
   xdist=x- ((int)(x-.5));
   CMPLX(zm,xdist,y);
   if(cabs(zm)<tol)
      {ans->x=errorcode; ans->y=0.;return 0;}
```

```
    if(x<0.)
        {
        reflect=1;x=1.-x;y=-y;CMPLX(z,1.,0.);CSUB(z,z,*zz);
        }
    }
if(y<0.)
    {flip=1;y=-y;z.y=y;}
m=0;
 while(x<10.)
    {
    x+=1.;
    m++;
    }
while( /*abs*/(y)>=x)
    {
    x+=1.;m++;
    }
CMPLX(t,x,y);
CMULT(tt,t,t);CLET(den,t);
CMPLX(aux,.5,0.);CSUB(aux,t,aux);
clog(&t,&zm);CMULT(sum,aux,zm);CSUB(sum,sum,t);
sum.x+= .5*log(2.*pi);
for(i=0;i<11;i++)
    {
    CMPLX(aux,c[i],0.);CDIV(term,aux,den);
    if(abs(term.x)<abs(sum.x)*tol)
        {
        if(y==0. ||(abs(term.y)>=abs(sum.y) ) )break;
        }
    CADD(sum,sum,term);
    CMULT(aux,den,tt);CLET(den,aux);
    }
if(m)
    {for(i=0;i<m;i++)
        {CMPLX(a, (double)i,0.);CADD(a,a,z);
        clog(&a,&aux); CSUB(sum,sum,aux);
        }
    }
if(reflect)
    {
    CMPLX(aux,pi,0.);
    CTREAL(t,z,pi);
    csin(&t,&tt);
    CDIV(den,aux,tt);
    clog(&den,&aux);
    CSUB(sum,aux,sum);
    }
if(flip) {sum.y=-sum.y;}
CSET(loggam,sum);cexp(&sum,ans);
```

```
/*printc(loggam);printc(ans);printf(" before flip\n");*/
/* if(flip) {ans->y=-ans->y;loggam->y=-loggam->y;}*/
 /* flip sign of imaginary part of gamma. as log(x)=|z|+i
arg(z),
 flip sign of imag. part of logarithm*/
 return 0;
 }



extern double digammin;

cdigamma(x,ans) struct complex *ans,*x;
{struct complex q,y,z,sum,rq,one;
if(x->x==1. && x->y==0.){CMPLX(*ans, - Egamma ,0.);return
0;;}
CLET(q,*x);CMPLX(sum,0.,0.);CMPLX(one,1.,0.);
if(q.x < 0.){
   if( abs((int)(q.x)-q.x && q.y==0.) <1.e-8)
      {CMPLX((*ans),errorcode,errorcode);return 1;}
   CSUB(q,one,*x);
   CTREAL(rq,*x,pi);
   ccot(&rq,&sum);
   CTREAL(sum,sum,pi);
   }
   /*note sum subtracted from final result*/
if(digammin<20.)digammin=20.;
while(q.x<digammin)
   {
   if(q.x==0. && q.y==0.){CMPLX((*ans),errorcode,error-
code);return 1;}
   CDIV(rq,one,q);CADD(sum,sum,rq);
   q.x+=1.;
   }
CDIV(y,one,q);/*y=1/q*/;CMULT(z,y,y);clog(&q,&rq);
/* logx-1/2x- sum n=1 to inf of  B[2n]z^-2n/2n*/
CSUB(*ans,rq,sum);CTREAL(rq,y,-.5);CADD(*ans,*ans,rq);
CLET(sum,(z));CTREAL(sum,sum,-1./240.);
sum.x+=1./252.;CMULT(rq,sum,z);rq.x-= 1./120.;
CMULT(sum,rq,z); sum.x+=1./12.;   CMULT(rq,sum,z);
CSUB(*ans,*ans,rq);
return 0;
}

#define itmax 1000

double polygam(z,n) double z; int n;
{/* wrong for n=0. better to use digam, etc. where pos-
sible*/
```

```
double x; int m; m=n+1; x=(double)m;
return ( (n%2)? 1.:-1.) *gamma(x)*zeta2( x,z);
}
```

```
/*
digamma and first 2 polygamma functions
from C Mathematical Function Handbook by Louis Baker
Copyright 1991 by Louis Baker. All rights reserved.

digam   =(d/dx) (log Gamma).
   former rational approx.,latter 'exact'

digamma,pg1,pg2   1st,2nd deriv. of digamma
   based on approx. in Tuma. |error|< 1.e-10

*/

#include "cmlib.h"
#include "protom.h"

double digammin;

double digamma(x) double x;
{double q,y,z,log(),sum,tan();
q=x;    sum=0.;
if(q==0.)return errorcode;
if(digammin<=0.)digammin=30.;
if(q<0.){
   if( abs((int)(q)-q) <1.e-8)return errorcode;
   q=1.-x;sum=pi/tan(pi*x);}/*note sum subtracted from
final result*/
while(q<digammin)
   {
   if(q==0.)return errorcode;
   sum+=1./q;
   q++;
   }
y=1/q;z=y*y;
/* logx-1/2x- sum n=1 to inf of  B[2n]z^-2n/2n*/
return log(q)-sum-.5*y-z*(1./12.-z*(1/120.-z*(1/252.-
z/240.)));
}

double pg1(x) double x;
{
int i;
double sum,z,u,sin(),y;
double b[10]={.4041138064,.1471100206,.0500956643,
.0160671426,.004941886,.0014725602,.0004282353,
.0001221952,.000034347,.0000095387};
if( x<=0. && abs((int)(x)-x) <1.e-8)return errorcode;
u=x-1.;
if(u>0. && u<=.5)
```

```
    {
    sum=b[9];
    y=u*u;
    for(i=8;i>=0;i--)
        {
        sum= sum*y+b[i];
        }
    sum*=u;
    /*printf(" omega=%e\n",sum);*/
    z=1./(u+1.); /* z=1/x */
    sum-=.5*z*z;
    z=1./(1.-u);
    sum+=.5*z*z;
    z=sin(u*pi);
    return  pi*pi*.5/(z*z)-sum-.5/(u*u);
    }
if(x>=2.)
    {
    /*printf(" asymptotic x=%e\n",x);*/
    y=1./x;
    z=y*y;
/*printf(" asymptotic z,y=%e %e\n",y,z);*/
/* desmet blows up on underflow*/
    return(y+z*(.5+y*(1./6.+z*(-1./30./*+z*(1./42.-
z/30.)*/))));
    }
if(x<0.)
    {
    z=sin(pi*x);
    return (-pg1(1.-x)-pi*pi/(z*z));
    }
/*  .5<=x<2.*/
/*if(x>1.)*/
return(pg1(x+1.)+1./(x*x));
}

double pg2(x)double x;
{
int i;
double sum,z,u,y,sin(),cos();
double b[10]={.4041138064,.4431326652,
.250478322,.1124699968,.04476974,
.0161981556,.0055670524,.001832928,.0005839092,.000181222};
if( x<=0. && abs((int)(x)-x) <1.e-8)return errorcode;
u=x-1.;
if(u>0. && u<=.5)
    {
    sum=b[9];
    y=u*u;
```

```
    for(i=8;i>=0;i--)
        {
        sum= sum*y+b[i];
        }
    z=1./(u+1.);
    sum+=z*z*z;
    z=1./(1.-u);
    sum+=z*z*z;
    z=sin(u*pi);
    return  -pi*pi*pi*cos(pi*u)/(z*z*z)-sum+1./(u*u*u);
    }
if(x>=2.)
    {
    y=1./x;
    z=y*y;
    /* prevent underflows for DeSmet*/
    return(-z+z*(-y+z*(.5+z*(1./6./*+z*(-1./6.+z*(.3-
5.*z/6.))*/))));
    }
if(x<0.)
    {
    z=sin(pi*x);
    return (pg2(1.-x)+pi*pi*pi*cos(pi*z)/(z*z*z));
    }
/*  .5<=x<2.*/
/*if(x>1.)*/
return(pg2(x+1.)-2./(x*x*x));
}


double digam(x) double x;
{
/* caveat- Tuma defines ad dlog gamma(x+1)/dx,
A & S d log gamma(x)/dx
*   will conform to A&S*/
double sum,z,y,g,log(),tan();
double b[9]={ Egamma ,.2020569031,.0369277551,
.0083492774,.0020083928,.0004941886,.0001227133,
.0000305882,.0000076372};
double c[11]={0.,0.,.4227843351,.9227843351,1.2561176684,
1.5061176684,1.7061176684,1.8727843351,2.0156417780,
2.1406414780,2.25175258918};
double u;int i;
if( x<=0. && abs((int)(x)-x) <1.e-8)return errorcode;
g= Egamma;
if(x==1.)return -g;
if(x<=10.)
    {i=x; if( abs(x-(double)i)<1.e-8)return c[i];   }
u=x-1.;
```

```
if(u>-0.5 && u<=.5)/*x between .5 and 1.5*/
   {
   sum=b[8];
   y=u*u;
   for(i=7;i>=0;i--)
      {
      sum= sum*y+b[i];
      }
   if(u>0.)
   return 1.+.5/u- 1./((1.+u)*(1.-u))-pi*.5/tan(pi*u)-sum;
   return 1.-.5/u- 1./((1.+u)*(1.-u))+pi*.5/tan(pi*u)-sum;
   }
if(x>2.)
   {
   y=1./x;
   z=y*y;
   return(log(x)-y*.5+z*(z*(1./120.-z/252.)-1./12.));
   }
if(x<-.5)
   return (digam(1.-x)-pi/tan(pi*x));
/*  .5<=x<2.*/
/*if(x>1.)*/
return(digam(x+1.)-1./(x));
/* .0<=x<=.5 also*/
}
```

Chapter 7

Error Function and Relatives

This chapter includes functions for the Error function for real and complex arguments, as well as the Fresnel integrals and Boehmer integrals. The latter are related to the sine and cosine integrals of the previous chapter, and functions for *Shi*(*x*), *Chi*(*x*), *Ci*(*x*), etc., are given here based upon the Boehmer integrals.

Error Function and Relatives

The error function is defined by $erf(z) = \frac{2}{\sqrt{\pi}}\int_0^z e^{-t^2}\,dt$. The complementary error function is given by $erfc(z) = 1 - erf(z)$. These functions are of great interest in statistics and will be encountered again in Chapter 26, where some functions for their calculation will be presented. The auxiliary function $w(z) = e^{-x^2} erfc(-iz)$ is often used (see below). We provide this $w(z)$ function as well as erfc(z) for complex z. Also, Dawson's integral occurs in some Laplace transforms of interest, and is $F(x) = e^{-x^2}\int_0^z e^{t^2}\,dt$. It occurs in the theory of the coupling of an electromagnetic wave with an exponential rise to a horizontal wire over an imperfect ground plane, for example (see Vance). Many other functions of interest in physics are related to these. In particular, the plasma dispersion function is $Z(z) = i\sqrt{\pi}e^{-z^2}(1 + erf(iz)) = \frac{-1}{\sqrt{\pi}}\int_{-\infty}^{\infty}\frac{e^{-x^2}}{z - x}dx$. As you might expect from the name, this function is of interest in the dispersion relations for plasmas with finite temperatures. The finite temperature introduces the Gaussian term. Similarly, the Voight function occurs in the shape of a spectral line due to the finite temperature of the medium, and is the convolution of the Gaussian function with the natural line shape (due to quantum mechanical broadening), the so-called Lorentzian line profile. The Voight function is real, but may be defined for our purposes with $W(x,t) = U(x,t) + iV(x,t)$ as the function U, where $U(x,t) = \frac{1}{\sqrt{4\pi t}} \int_{-\infty}^{\infty} \frac{e^{-(x-y)^2/(4t)}}{1+y^2} dy$, while the imaginary part is $V(x,t) = \frac{1}{\sqrt{4\pi t}} \int_{-\infty}^{\infty} \frac{e^{-(x-y)^2/(4t)}}{1+y^2} y\, dy$. If we split the function w(z) defined above into real and imaginary parts via $w(z) = H(z) + iK(z)$, then $H(a,u) = \frac{1}{a\sqrt{\pi}} U(\frac{u}{a}, \frac{1}{4a^2})$ and similarly for K and V. The "Rocket Flight Functions" $A(x) = \frac{1}{\pi\sqrt{2}} \int_0^{\infty} \frac{e^{-\pi x^2 y/2}}{1+y^2} y^{-1/2} dy$ and $.B(x) = \frac{1}{\pi\sqrt{2}} \int_0^{\infty} \frac{e^{-\pi x^2 y/2}}{1+y^2} y^{1/2} dy$ are given by $A(x) = \frac{1}{2}[H(z,z) + K(z,z)]$, $B(x) = \frac{1}{2}[H(z,z) - K(z,z)]$, with $z = x\sqrt{\pi}/2$. Various other integrals, including the Fresnel integrals and Dawson's integral may be related to H and K (see below).

The repeated integrals of the (complementary) error function are $i^n erfc\, z = \int_z^{\infty} i^{n-1}\, erfc\, t\, dt$ with $i^0 erfc\, z = erfc\, z$, and satisfy the differential equation $\frac{d^2y}{dz^2} + 2z\frac{dy}{dz} - 2ny = 0$. They occur in numerous diffusion problems and are discussed in Carslaw and Jaeger.

The Fresnel integrals are defined in at least three different manners by different authors. Abramowitz and Stegun, whom we follow here, use $S(x) = \int_0^x \sin(\frac{\pi}{2}t^2)\, dt$ and $C(x) = \int_0^x \cos(\frac{\pi}{2}t^2)\, dt$. Other forms differ in the normalization of the argument, and are $S(x) = \sqrt{2/\pi} \int_0^x \sin(t^2)\, dt$ and $S(x) = \frac{1}{\sqrt{2\pi}} \int_0^x \frac{\sin(t)}{\sqrt{t}} dt$. Abramowitz and Stegun denote these as S_1 and S_2, respectively. There are similar analogs of C(x). Note that $S(x) = S_1(\sqrt{\pi/2}\, x) = S_2(\frac{\pi}{2}x^2)$.

The Boehmer integrals $S(x;\nu) = \int_x^\infty t^{\nu-1} \sin t \, dt$ and $C(x;\nu) = \int_x^\infty t^{\nu-1} \cos t \, dt$ are related to both the exponential integrals of Chapter 5 as well as the Fresnel functions. We use the notation of Spanier and Oldham. Note that they define the Fresnel integrals in the form denoted as S_1 and C_1 in Abramowitz and Stegun.

Methods

Recurrence Relations

Because the use of recurrence relations will be important in this and the following chapters, a brief discussion is included here. The recurrence relation 7.2.5 of Abramowitz and Stegun, $i^n \, erfc\, z = -\frac{z}{n} i^{n-1} \, erfc\, z + \frac{1}{2n} i^{n-2} erfc\, z$, may be used to compute the iterated error function for $n = 1, 2, \ldots$ in a number of ways. The obvious method, in which we start with the values of $i^0 erfc\, z$ and $i^1 erfc\, z$ and proceed to higher n, is called forward recursion. There is one potential problem with this method, which afflicts the iterated error function. The recurrence is a second-order difference equation, and behaves like a second-order differential equation in many ways. It has two solutions in general, one increasing with n and the other decreasing. The iterated error function decreases as n increases, so we need to find the decreasing solution. If the starting values were exactly right and there were no roundoff, there would be no problem. But in the real world, our initial values have some error, which may be viewed as a small admixture of the second solution, which grows with n. For large enough n, this component will swamp the other, correct component, resulting in large errors. This is called an instability of the recurrence. The cure is to use backward recurrence. In this method, we start by setting scaled values of the function in an array, say, *ierfc*[N+1] = 0 and *ierfc*[*N*] = 1, where *N* is large compared to *n*, iterating the recurrence back to setting *ierfc*[1]. But we know the correct value of ierfc[1] should be *erfc*(*z*), so we can return as our answer (*erfc*(*z*) / *ierfc*[1]) *ierfc*[n]. Note that scaling will never change 0 to another value, so *N* must be chosen so that *ierfc*[*N*+1] is negligably small. This brings us to another possible difficulty, also illustrated by the iterated error function. For small values of z, *ierfc* decreases very slowly as *n* increases. Thus, *N* would have to be prohibitively large to get reasonable accuracy with backward recursion. The iterated error function is calculated by C code which uses recursion relations. Although backward is always stable, for $x < .9$ forward recursion is used for the reason given above. Gautschi's paper on three-term recurrence relation is the classic work in the field, and has been used in the chapter. G. F Miller, referenced in Chapter 4, played an important role in the development of these computational methods, and backward recursion is sometimes called Miller recursion. It will be called upon a number of times in this book, particularly in relation to the Bessel functions.

C Code

The complex error function, plasma dispersion function, and its relatives are based upon the programs in *More C Tools*. In addition, we provide the complementary error function for complex arguments in a separate file. It uses w(z) as provided in the package from *More C Tools*. Series and asymptotic representations are used for the Boehmer integrals and other functions. Note that a table of i^nerfc can be calculated for $n = 0,1,...$ in one swoop if desired, using ierfctable() instead of ierfc(). Often, when i^{n-} erfc for one value of n is in a formula, so are those for $n - 1,....$

References

H. S. Carslaw and J. C. Jaeger, *The Conduction of Heat in Solids* (Oxford: Clarendon Press, 1959).

W. Gautschi, *SIAM Review*, **9**, 24, 1967.

J. Spanier and K. B. Oldham, *An Atlas of Functions* (N. Y.: Hemisphere, 1987).

E. T. Vance, *Coupling to Shielded Cables* (N. Y: J. Wiley, 1978).

Figure: Dawson's Integral

We plot Dawson's integral as Fig. 7-1, not necessarily because it is a pretty picture but because I have not seen it plotted elsewhere.

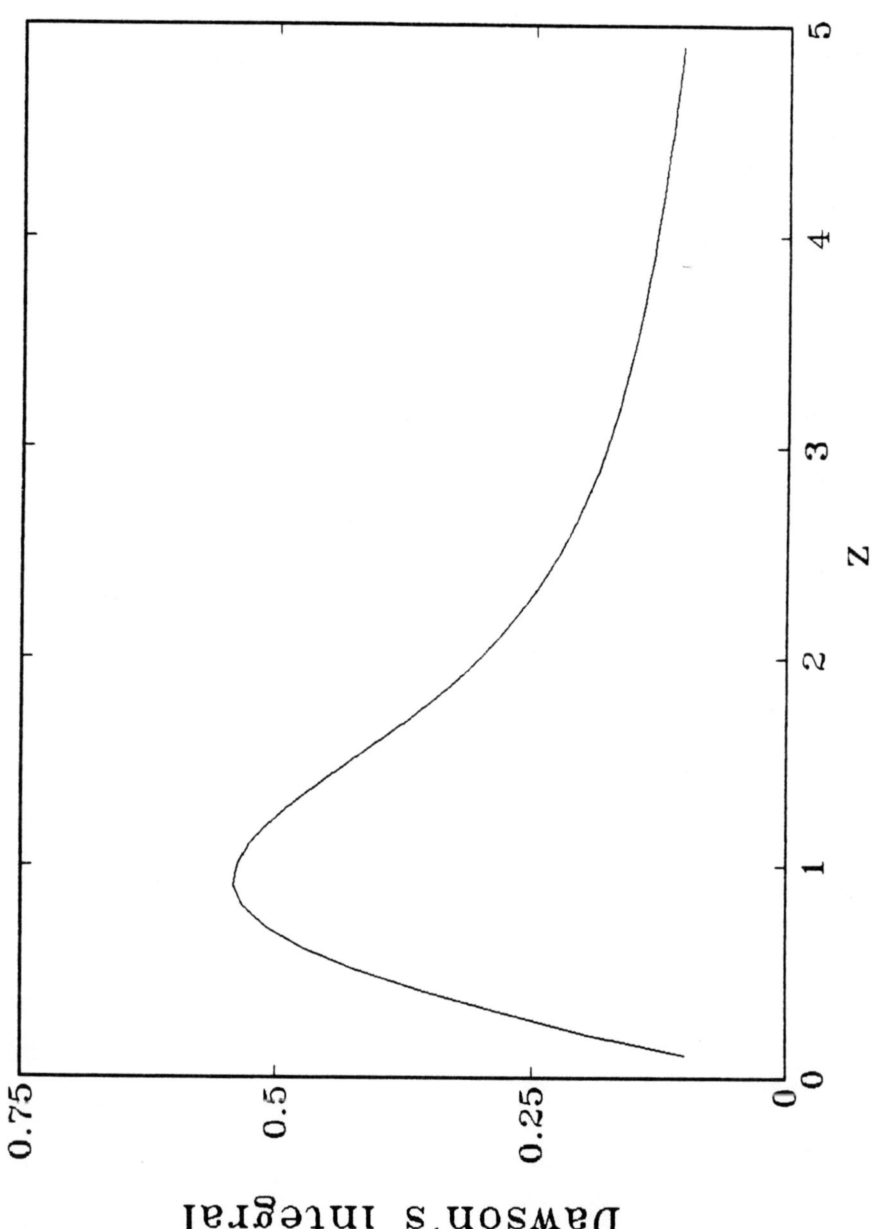

Fig. 7-1: Dawson's Integral.

```
/*
package of routines that compute the
plasma dispersion function
for complex arguments, returning a complex value

allied functions computed are the error function and the
Fresnel integrals

routines for handling complex arithmetic in C are included

from More C tools for scientists and engineers by L. Baker

*/

extern int iterp;/* global to return count used*/
int limit, kt;
/* for below, x,y are complex structures, and one is
returned*/
#include "cmlib.h"
#include "complex.h"
#include "protom.h"
struct complex    c1,c0,o,o2,ir;



cerror(a,b,eps)double eps; struct complex *a,*b;
{
struct complex dummy; double irtpi;
irtpi = 1./sqrt(pi);/*=.564189583*/
pdisp(a,eps,b,&dummy,20);
dummy.x=b->y;/* dummy=-i * b */
dummy.y=-b->x;
CTREAL((*b),dummy,irtpi);
}

double erf(z,erfc)
double *erfc,z;
{
struct complex cz1,cz,c4,czeta,czsp;
int iter;
double erff,exp();
c4.y=.5641895835;
c4.x=0.;
CMPLX(cz,0.,z);
iter=40;
pdisp(&cz,1.e-5,&czeta,&czsp,iter);
/*printf(" erf ");
printc(&czeta);printc(&czsp);printf("\n");*/
CMULT(cz1,c4,czeta);
```

```
erff=1.+cz1.x*exp(-z*z);
*erfc=1.-erff;
return (erff);
}

double dawson(x) double x;
{
double eps=1.e-5;
int iter=30;
struct complex z,ans,derans;
z.x=x;z.y=0;
pdisp(&z,eps,&ans,&derans,iter);
return (-.5*ans.x);
}

/* compute the Fresnel integrals */

fresnel (z,fci,fsi) double z,*fci,*fsi;
{
int iter;
double aa;
struct complex ci,c1,c2,c3,cz,czeta,czp,cdum,cdu1;
aa=.8862269255;
c1.x=aa;
c1.y=aa;
ci.x=0.;ci.y=1.;
c2.x=0.;
c2.y=1.570796327;
c3.x=-.5641895835;
c3.y=c3.x;
CTREAL(cz,c1,z);
iter=20;
pdisp(&cz,1.e-5,&czeta,&czp,iter);
/*printf(" fresnel ");
printc(&czeta);printc(&czp);printf("\n");*/
CTREAL(cdum,c2, (z*z) );
cexp(&cdum,&cdu1);
CMULT(cdum,cdu1,czeta);
CMULT(cdu1,cdum,ci);
CTREAL(cdu1,cdu1,-.5);
cdu1.x=cdu1.x-aa;
CMULT(cdum,cdu1,c3);
*fci=cdum.x;
*fsi=cdum.y;
return;
}
```

```
/* compute the plasma dispersion function and its deriva-
tives
iter is maximum iteration count allowed, eps desired error
zetai is the input argument, zeeo the value of the function
and zeeprimo the first derivative (both output)

*/
int itmax=20,lhpsw;
static struct complex Zeta,zee,zeeprim;
static struct complex w,ww,g1,G2,ofo,z,zetasq,zp,bp,bpp1,bs;
static struct complex crtpi,a1,a2,a3,
b1,b2,b3,t1,t2,u1,u2,v1,v2,cdum,cdu2,cdu3,cdu1;
static double flhp,csw,xi1,ct1,ct2,cp1,app1,dreal;


pdisp(zetai,eps,zeeo,zeeprimo,iter) int iter;double eps;
struct complex *zetai,*zeeprimo,*zeeo;
{
c1.x=1.;
c1.y=0.;
crtpi.x=0.;
crtpi.y=1.772453851;
c0.x=0.;c0.y=0.;
CASSN(Zeta,zetai);
if(iter>0) itmax=iter;
if( Zeta.x< 0.){lhpsw=-
1;CONJG(cdum,Zeta);CSUB(Zeta,c0,cdum);}
   else {lhpsw=1;}
flhp=lhpsw;
if( Zeta.y<0.) csw=-1.;
   else csw=1.;

CMULT(zetasq,Zeta,Zeta);
CMPLX(w, Zeta.x, (csw*Zeta.y));
CMULT(ww,w,w);
/*printf(" pdf w,ww
");printc(&w);printc(&ww);printf("\n");*/
if ( abs(Zeta.y)>=1. || cabs(Zeta)>10.)
{
/* continued fraction approx for  abs( Im(Zeta) ) >1 */
cfbig(eps);
}
else
{/* abs(Zeta)<1*/
cfsmall(eps);
}
if(lhpsw==-1){
      CONJG(cdum,z);
```

```
      CSUB(z,c0,cdum);
        };
CLET(zee,z);
/*printf(" zee=");printc(&zee);printf("\n");*/
if(lhpsw==-1) {
      CONJG(cdum,Zeta);
      CSUB(Zeta,c0,cdum);
         };
CMULT(zetasq,Zeta,Zeta);
if(cabs(Zeta)>10.)
   {
   CLET(cdum,c1);cdum.x=cdum.x-csw;
   CMULT(cdu2,cdum,zetasq);
   CTREAL(cdu2,cdu2,-.5);
   cexp(&cdu2,&cdu3);
   CMULT(cdu1,cdum,cdu3);
   CMULT(zp,cdu1,crtpi);
   CLET(u1,c1);
   CLET(u2,c0);
   cdum.x=3.5;cdum.y=0.;
   CSUB(cdum,cdum,ww);
   cdu2.x=-1.5;cdu2.y=0.;
   CDIV(v1,cdu2,cdum);
   CLET(v2,c0);
   CLET(t1,v1);
   CLET(t2,c0);
   iterp=1;
   while(1==1)
      {
      app1= -(iterp+1)*(iterp+2.5);
      cdum.y=0;
      cdum.x=1.5+2*iterp;
      CSUB(bp,cdum,ww);
      CLET(bpp1,bp);bpp1.x=bpp1.x+2.;
      CMULT(bs,bpp1,bp);
      CTREAL(cdum,u1,app1);
      CADD(cdu2,cdum,bs);
      CDIV(u2,bs,cdu2);
      CSUB(cdum,u2,c1);
      CMULT(v2,v1,cdum);
      CADD(t2,v2,t1);
      CSUB(cdum,t2,t1);
      if(cabs(cdum)<eps || iterp>itmax) break;
      iterp++;
      CLET(u1,u2);
      CLET(t1,t2);
      CLET(v1,v2);
      }
      CMULT(cdum,zp,Zeta);
```

```
        CTREAL(cdum,cdum,-2.);
        CSUB(cdu1,t2,ww);
        cdu2.x=cdu1.x+1.5;
        cdu2.y=cdu1.y *csw;
        CDIV(zeeprim,c1,cdu2);
        CTREAL(zeeprim,zeeprim,-1.);
        CADD(zeeprim,zeeprim,cdum);
if(lhpsw==-1)
        {
        CONJG(cdum,zeeprim);
        CLET(zeeprim,cdum);
        }
/*printf(" zeeprim=");printc(&zeeprim);printf("\n");*/
}
else
    {
    CMULT(cdum,Zeta,z);
    CADD(cdum,c1,cdum);
    CTREAL(zeeprim,cdum,-2.);
    };
CSET(zeeprimo,zeeprim);
CSET(zeeo,zee);
return;
}
cfbig(eps)double eps;
{
iterp=1;
CLET(a1,c1);
CLET(a2,c0);
cdum.x=2.5;cdum.y=0.;
CSUB(cdum,cdum,ww);
cdu2.x=-.5;cdu2.y=0.;
CDIV(b1,cdu2,cdum);
CLET(b2,c0);
CLET(t1,b1);
CLET(t2,c0);/*printf(" big\n");
printc(&a1);printc(&a2);printc(&b1);printc(&b2);
printc(&t1);printc(&t2);*/
while(1)
    {
    app1=-(iterp+1)*(iterp+.5);
    dreal=.5+2*iterp;
    CLET(bp,c0); CSUB(bp,bp,ww);
    bp.x=bp.x+dreal;
    CLET(bpp1,bp);bpp1.x=bpp1.x+2.;
    CMULT(bs,bp,bpp1);
    CTREAL(cdum,a1,app1);
    CADD(cdum,cdum,bs);
    CDIV(a2,bs,cdum);
```

```
    CSUB(cdum,a2,c1);
    CMULT(b2,b1,cdum);
    CADD(t2,t1,b2);
    CSUB(cdum,t2,t1);
/*printc(&a1);printc(&a2);printc(&b1);printc(&b2);
printc(&t1);printc(&t2);
printc(&bp);printc(&bpp1);printc(&bs);printf(" %d\n",iterp);
*/
    if( cabs(cdum) < eps || iterp>itmax) break;
    iterp++;
    CLET(a1,a2);
    CLET(b1,b2);
    CLET(t1,t2);
    }
CLET(cdum,c1);cdum.x=cdum.x-csw;
CTREAL(cdum,cdum,-.5);
CMULT(cdu2,cdum,zetasq);
cexp(&cdu2,&cdu3);
CLET(cdum,c1);cdum.x=cdum.x-csw;
CMULT(cdu2,cdum,cdu3);
CMULT(cdum,cdu2,crtpi);
CSUB(cdu3,t2,ww);
CLET(cdu2,cdu3);
cdu3.x=cdu3.x+.5;
cdu1.x=cdu3.x;
cdu1.y= csw*cdu2.y;
CDIV(cdu3,Zeta,cdu1);
CADD(z,cdum, cdu3);
return 0;
}

cfsmall(eps)double eps;
{
xi1=1.;
CLET(b1,c1);
CLET(a1,c1);
ct1=2.5;
cp1=.5;
cdum.x=ww.x/ct1;cdum.y=ww.y/ct1;
CADD(b2,cdum,c1);
CTREAL(cdum,ww,.6666666666);
CSUB(a2,b2,cdum);
iterp=1;
/*printf(" small");*/
/* recursive calculation of kummer function*/
while(1==1){
    ct2=ct1*ct1;
    CTREAL(cdum,ww,(cp1/(ct2+ct1+ct1)));
    CADD(g1,c1,cdum);
```

```
    CTREAL(cdum,ww,(xi1*(xi1+cp1)/(ct2*(ct2-1.))));
       CMULT(G2,cdum,ww);
    CMULT(cdum,G2,a1);
    CMULT(cdu2,g1,a2);
    CADD(a3,cdum,cdu2);
    CMULT(cdum,G2,b1);
    CMULT(cdu2,g1,b2);
    CADD(b3,cdum,cdu2);
    CDIV(cdu2,a2,b2);
    CDIV(cdu3,a3,b3);
    CSUB(cdum,cdu3,cdu2);
/*printc(&a1);printc(&a2);printc(&a3);
printc(&b1);printc(&b2);printc(&b3);printc(&g1);
printc(&G2);printf("%f %f %f %d\n",ct1,ct2,xi1,iterp);
*/
    if( cabs(cdum) <eps || iterp>itmax)break;
    CLET(a1,a2);
    CLET(b1,b2);
    CLET(a2,a3);
    CLET(b2,b3);
    ct1=ct1+2.;
    xi1=xi1+1.;
    iterp++;
      }
CMPLX(ofo,cdu3.x,(csw*cdu3.y));
CSUB(cdum,c0,zetasq);
cexp(&cdum,&cdu2);
CMULT(cdum,cdu2,crtpi);
CMULT(cdu2,Zeta,ofo);
CTREAL(cdu2,cdu2,2.);
CSUB(z,cdum,cdu2);
/*printf(" ofo,z,iter"); printc(&ofo);printc(&z);printf("
%d\n",iterp);
*/
return 0;
}

double ritchie(x) double x;
{/* integral from 0 to infinity exp(-x*x)/(t+x)*/
double exp(),sqrt(),dawson(),ei(),y;
y=x*x;
return  sqrt(pi)*dawson(x)-.5*ei(y)*exp(-y);
}
```

```
/*
iterated error function
 backward recursion used, as
well as forward for small arguments.

from C Mathematical Function Handbook by Louis Baker
Copyright 1991 by Louis Baker. All rights reserved.
*/

#include <alloc.h>
#include <stdio.h>
#include "cmlib.h"
#include "protom.h"


static double *tierfc=NULL;

double ierfc(z,n) int n; double z;
{/* uses stable backward recursion for large z. this give
poor results for
small z, however*/
int m,i;
double *w,norm,coef,ans,ratio;
if(!n){ norm=erf(z,&coef); if(tierfc)*tierfc=coef; return
coef;}/* erfc*/
if(n==-1) return exp(-z*z)*2./sqrt(pi);
if(z<0. || n<-1)return errorcode;
if(z<.9)return ierfcf(z,n);
m=n+15;
if(z<2.)m+=10;
if(z<1.75) m+=10;
if(z<1.5) m+=10;
if(z<1.)m+=10;
w=(double *)malloc( (m+3)*sizeof(double));
if(w==NULL)
   {
   fprintf(stderr," ierfc could not allocate space for
array");
   return errorcode;/* or 0., as the result is quite small*/
   }
w[m+1]=1.;w[m+2]=0.;
for(i=m;i>=-1;i--)
   {
   norm= 2.*(i+2)*w[i+2]+z*2.*w[i+1];
   /*printf(" w[%d]= %e\n",i,norm);*/
   if (i!=-1) w[i]=norm;
   }
coef=2./sqrt(pi)*exp(-z*z);
/*printf(" coef=%e\n",coef);*/
```

```
ratio=coef/norm;
ans=w[n]*ratio;
if(tierfc)
   {for(i=0;i<=n;i++) tierfc[i]=w[i]*ratio;}
free(w);
return ans;
}


double ierfcf(x,n) double x;int n;
{/* uses forward recursion-can be unstable. not recom-
mended*/
double erf(),y,z,exch;
int k;
y=erf(x,&z);
if(tierfc)*tierfc=z;
if(!n)return z;
y=2./sqrt(pi)*exp(-x*x);
if(n==-1)return y;
if(z<0. || n<-1)return errorcode;
/* y=i^-1,z=i^0*/
for(k=1;1;k++)
   {
   y=(.5*y-x*z)/k;
   if(tierfc)tierfc[k]=y;
   if(k==n)break;
   exch=z;
   z=y;
   y=exch;
   }
return y;
}


/* returns table[k]= i ^k erfc (z) for k=0,...,n*/
ierfctable(z,n,table) int n; double z, table[];
{double dum;
tierfc=table;
dum=ierfc(z,n);
tierfc=NULL;
if(dum==errorcode){table[0]=errorcode;return ierrorcode;}
return 0;
}
```

```
/*
Boehmer (generalized Fresnel) integral
and relatives
from C Mathematical Function Handbook by Louis Baker
Copyright 1991 by Louis Baker. All rights reserved.
Boehmer S/C(x,nu) = integral from x to infinity t^(nu-1)
sin/cos(t)dt

boehmer(x,nu,type)   type= 0 C 1 for S (type-1,-2 used for
Shi,Chi calc)
Si,Ci,Shi,Chi       exponential integral relatives (see A&S)
Fresnel(x,type)       type=0 C 1 for S  Fresnel Integrals
ba(x,nu,type)       used for asymtotic regime.  do not call
directly.

Based on Spanier and Oldham with Shi,Chi from Abramowitz &
Stegun.
Corrected sign error in S&O 39:12:14
*/
#include <stdio.h>
#include "cmlib.h"
#include "protom.h"
#define tol 1.e-8

extern int kt; /* term count. if<0, for asymptotic series
else series*/
extern double limit;/* series-asymptotic crossover argument
for Boehmer*/

/* type = 0  C ;  =1 for S*/

/* aysmptotic formulae for large x*/
double ba(x,nu,typei) int typei;double x,nu;
   {
   double xn,c,s,a,b,term,y,oldterm;int j,type;
   type=typei;
   y=-1./(x*x);
   if(type<0)/* special procedure for Shi,Chi*/
      {y=-y;
      if(type==-1)type=1;
      else type=0;
      c=cosh(x);s=sinh(x);
      }
   else   {c=cos(x);s=sin(x);}
   kt=0;
   for(j=2,a=1.,term=1.;j<1000;j+=2)
      {
      oldterm=term;
      term *= (j-1-nu)*(j-nu)*y;
```

```
        if(abs(term)>abs(oldterm))break;
        a+=term;
        kt--;
        if(abs(term)<tol*abs(a))break;
        }
    for(j=3,b=1.,term=1.;j<1000;j+=2)
        {
        oldterm=term;
        term*= (j-1-nu)*(j-nu)*y;
        if(abs(term)>abs(oldterm))break;
        b+=term;
        kt--;
        if(abs(term)<tol*abs(b))break;
        }
    xn=pow(x,nu-2.);
/*printf(" a, b %le %le c s\n",a,b,c,s);*/
    switch(typei)
        { case 1:  return xn*(x*c*a+(1.-nu)*s*b);/* S ok*/
          case 0:  return -xn*(x*s*a-(1.-nu)*c*b);/*sign
error S&O*/
         case -1:  return -xn*(x*c*a+(1.-nu)*s*b);/* S ok*/
          case -2:  return -xn*(x*s*a+(1.-nu)*c*b);/*sign
error S&O*/
          default:
             fprintf(stderr," badt type to asympt. boeh-
mer\n");
             return errorcode;
        }
    }

double boehmer( x, nu,typei)int typei;double x,nu;
    {
    double y,x0,sum,term,factor,p,q,gamma(),si(),ci();int
j,flag,type;
    type=typei;
    if(limit<=20.) limit=20.;/* default/floor*/
    if(x<0.)return errorcode;
    /* x<0. would require power of negative x */
    /*if(nu>=1.)return errorcode;*/ /* nu>=1 not allowed,
but works?*/
    if(nu==0.)flag=1;
    else flag=0;
    if(nu<0.)
        {/* cannot do gamma(nu) nu=0,-1,-2,...*/
        /* for nu=0 use S= .5*pi-Si, C= -Ci(x)*/
        /*recurrences S(x,nu)=(-C(x,nu+1)-x^nu sin(x))/nu
                      C(x,nu)=(S(x,nu+1)-x^nu cos(x))/nu
        may be used for negative nu to get to positive nu */
/*      if( nu==0.)
```

```
            { return type? .5*pi-si(x):ci(x);}*/
        /*else nu<0.*/
        if(x==0.)return errorcode;
        /* pow(0,nu) for nu<0 infinite*/
        if(type)   return (-boehmer(x,nu+1.,0)-
pow(x,nu)*sin(x))/nu;
        /*else C*/ return ( boehmer(x,nu+1.,1)-
pow(x,nu)*cos(x))/nu;
        }
    /* trap -inf for Ci,Chi(type==0,-2) at x=0, nu=0(flag)*/
    if(flag && ((!type)||(type==-2)) && x==0.)
                        return errorcode;
    if( abs(x) > limit) return ba(x,nu,typei);
    p=nu*pi*.5;
    if(!flag)x0= gamma(nu)*(type? sin(p):cos(p));
    else x0= type? .5*pi : -log(abs(x))- Egamma ;
    y=-x*x;sum=0.;
    if(type<0)/* special procedure for Shi,Chi*/
        {y=-y;
        if(type==-1)type=1;
        else type=0;
        }
    factor= type? 1.+nu:nu;/* first term 1/(1+nu) S or 1/nu
C*/
    sum=flag?(type?1.:0.): 1./factor; term=1.;kt=0;
    /*printf(" sum initialized to %le\n",sum);*/
    for(j=1;j<1000;j++)
        {
        p= type? (j<<1)+1:(j<<1);
        term*= y/((p)*(p-1.));
/*printf(" j=%d p=%le,type=%d sum=%le\n",j,p,type,sum);
printf("term=%le term/(p+nu)=%le p=%le\n",term,
term/(p+nu),p);*/
        sum+=term/(p+nu);
        kt++;
        if(abs(term)<tol*abs(sum))break;
        }
    if(x>0.){q= pow(x,nu);if(type)q*=x;}
    else q=0.;
/*printf(" [SC](0,nu)=%le sum=%le power=%le\n",x0,sum,q);*/
/*   if(flag && type) return .5*pi-x*(sum);*/
    return x0  q*sum;
    }

double Fresnel(x,type)double x; int type;
    {
    /* corrected from Spanier and Oldham- they
        would have argument x*x, without pi/2 */
    return .5-boehmer(x*x*pi*.5,.5,type)/sqrt(2.*pi);
```

```
   }


/*sine and cosine integrals. si(x) is Si(x) not si= Si-
pi/2*/

double Si(x) double x;
   {
   return pi*.5-boehmer(x,0.,1);
   }

double Ci(x) double x;
   {return -boehmer(x,0.,0);
   }
double Shi(x) double x;
   {
   return pi*.5-boehmer(x,0.,-1);
   }

double Chi(x) double x;
   {return -boehmer(x,0.,-2);
   }
```

```
/*
Complementary Error function for complex arguments.
from C Mathematical Function Handbook by Louis Baker
Copyright 1991 by Louis Baker. All rights reserved.
*/

#include <stdio.h>
#include "cmlib.h"
#include "protom.h"

cerfc(z,ans) struct complex *z,*ans;
{/*erfc for complex z*/
struct complex i,x,y,p,q;
x.x= - z->y;x.y= z->x;
cerror(&x, &y,1.e-7);
CMULT(p,*z,*z);CTREAL(p,p,-1.);
cexp(&p,&q);CMULT(*ans,q,y);
return 0;
}
```

```
/*
Test Driver Chapter 7
from C Mathematical Function Handbook by Louis Baker
Copyright 1991 by Louis Baker. All rights reserved.
*/
#include <stdio.h>
#include "cmlib.h"
#include "protom.h"

extern double limit;
extern int kt,iterp;
FILE *fileid,*ploth,*plotd;
main()
   {double x,y,z,nu,table[10]; struct complex arg,ans;
   int i;double erfc,si,ci,q;
   while(1)
      {printf(" enter x, limit for Shi\n");
      scanf("%le%le",&x,&limit);
      if(limit<=0.)break;
      printf(" Shi Chi %le %le\n",Shi(x),Chi(x));
      }
   printf(" enter limit\n");scanf("%le",&limit);
   while(1)
      {printf("enter x,nu\n");scanf("%le%le",&x,&nu);
      if(x> 1000.)break;
      printf(" x nu %le %le\n",x,nu);
      printf(" Si %le Ci %le Shi %le Chi %le\n",
Si(x),Ci(x),Shi(x),Chi(x));
      printf(" %d series S=%le iter \n",kt, boemer(x,nu,1));
      printf(" %d series C=%le iter \n",kt,
boehmer(x,nu,0));
      printf(" %d series FresnelS=%le iter \n",kt,
Fresnel(x,1));
      printf(" %d series FresnelC=%le iter \n",kt,
Fresnel(x,0));
      if(x>5.)
         {
         printf(" %d asymp  S=%le iter \n" ,kt,ba(x,nu,1));
         printf(" %d asymp  C=%le iter \n" ,kt,ba(x,nu,0));
         }
      }
   printf(" ierfc to compare with A&S Ex 5 p. 305\n");
   printf(" %e %e %e \n",
ierfc(1.72,1),ierfc(1.72,2),ierfc(1.72,3));
   ierfctable(1.72,3,table);
   printf(" %e %e %e \n", table[1],table[2],table[3]);
   ierfctable(.5,3,table);
   printf(" %e %e %e \n", table[1],table[2],table[3]);
   fileid=fopen("PLOT.DAT","w");
```

```
   fprintf(fileid," 4 \n");
   ploth=fopen("PLOTH.DAT","w");
   fprintf(ploth," 2 \n");
   plotd=fopen("PLOTD.DAT","w");
   fprintf(plotd," 1 \n");
   q=1/.56418958;
   printf(" FWDierfc %e %e\n",ierfcf(.1,2),ierfcf(.5,2));
   printf(" FWDierfc %e %e\n",ierfcf(.1,4),ierfcf(.5,4));
   printf(" FWDierfc %e %e\n",ierfcf(.1,6),ierfcf(.5,6));
   /* proof backward is BAD for small z*/
   printf(" scaled ierfc %e
%e\n",q*ierfc(.1,1),q*ierfc(.5,1));
   printf(" scaled ierfcf %e
%e\n",q*ierfcf(.1,1),q*ierfcf(.5,1));
   printf(" scaled ierfc %e
%e\n",4.*ierfc(.1,2),4.*ierfc(.5,2));
   printf(" scaled ierfcf %e
%e\n",4.*ierfcf(.1,2),4.*ierfcf(.5,2));
   printf(" scaled ierfc %e
%e\n",32.*ierfc(.1,4),32.*ierfc(.5,4));
   printf(" scaled ierfcf %e
%e\n",32.*ierfcf(.1,4),32.*ierfcf(.5,4));
   /* proof forward is BAD for large z*/
   printf(" scaled ierfc %e
%e\n",384.*ierfc(.1,6),384.*ierfc(.5,6));
   printf(" scaled ierfcf %e
%e\n",384.*ierfcf(.1,6),384.*ierfcf(.5,6));

   printf(" scaled ierfc %e
%e\n",122880.*ierfc(.1,10),122880.*ierfc(.5,10));
   printf(" scaled ierfcf %e
%e\n",122880.*ierfcf(.1,10),122880.*ierfcf(.5,10));

   printf(" scaled ierfc %e
%e\n",32.*ierfc(1.,4),32.*ierfc(5.,4));
   printf(" scaled ierfcf %e
%e\n",32.*ierfcf(1.,4),32.*ierfcf(5.,4));

   printf(" scaled ierfc %e
%e\n",384.*ierfc(1.,6),384.*ierfc(5.,6));
   printf(" scaled ierfcf %e
%e\n",384.*ierfcf(1.,6),384.*ierfcf(5.,6));

   printf(" scaled ierfc %e
%e\n",122880.*ierfc(1.,10),122880.*ierfc(5.,10));
   printf(" scaled ierfcf %e
%e\n",122880.*ierfcf(1.,10),122880.*ierfcf(5.,10));

   infinite_loop
```

```
      {
      printf(" enter x,n for ierfc\n") ;
                     scanf("%le%d",&x,&i);
      if(x>1000.)break;
      printf(" ierf=%le fwd=%le\n", ierfc(x,i),ierfcf(x,i));
      }

   infinite_loop
      {
      printf(" enter x,y for cerror\n");
                     scanf("%le%le",&x,&y);
      if(x>1000.)break; CMPLX(arg,x,y);
                      cerror(&arg,&ans,1.e-6);
      printc(&ans);printf(" = complex error\n");
      if( y<0.)
         {/* note that w(x+iy) is not conj. of w(x-iy)*/
         arg.y=-arg.y;
         cerror(&arg,&ans,1.e-6);
         q= exp( y*y-x*x)*2.;
         ci= cos(2.*x*y)*q;si=-sin(2.*x*y)*q;
         /* remember to conjugate w(x+iy) and that y >0
here*/
         printf(" should be real=%le imag=%le\n" ,    ci-
ans.x,si+ans.y);
         }
      }
   infinite_loop
      {
      printf(" enter x,y for cerfc\n");
                     scanf("%le%le",&x,&y);
      if(x>1000.)break; CMPLX(arg,x,y); cerfc(&arg,&ans);
      printc(&ans);
      printf(" = complex complementary error\n");
      if(y==0.) printf(" erf=%le\n",1.-ans.x);
      }

   for (i=0;i<50;i++)
      {
      x=(i+1)*.1;
      y=erf(x,&erfc);
      fresnel(x,&ci,&si);
      z=dawson(x);
      printf(" x=%f %f %f %f %f %e
%d\n",x,y,erfc,ci,si,z,iterp);
      fprintf(fileid,"%f %le %le %le
%le\n",x,y,erfc,ci,si,Chi(x),Shi(x));
      fprintf(ploth,"%f %le %le\n",x,Chi(x),Shi(x));
      fprintf(plotd,"%f %le\n",x,z);
      };
```

```
return (0);
}
```

```
enter x, limit for Shi 1 20
 Shi Chi 1.057251e+00 -1.310145e+00
 enter x, limit for Shi 0 0
 enter limit
10
enter x,nu
1 1
 x nu 1.000000e+00 1.000000e+00
 Si 9.460831e-01 Ci 3.374039e-01 Shi 1.057251e+00
Chi -1.310145e+00
 6 series S=5.403023e-01 iter
 6 series C=-8.414710e-01 iter
 7 series FresnelS=4.382591e-01 iter
 7 series FresnelC=7.798934e-01 iter
enter x,nu
1 2
 x nu 1.000000e+00 2.000000e+00
 Si 9.460831e-01 Ci 3.374039e-01 Shi 1.057251e+00
Chi -1.310145e+00
 6 series S=-3.011687e-01 iter
 6 series C=-1.381773e+00 iter
 7 series FresnelS=4.382591e-01 iter
 7 series FresnelC=7.798934e-01 iter
enter x,nu
1 0
 x nu 1.000000e+00 0.000000e+00
 Si 9.460831e-01 Ci 3.374039e-01 Shi 1.057251e+00
Chi -1.310145e+00
 6 series S=6.247133e-01 iter
 6 series C=-3.374039e-01 iter
 7 series FresnelS=4.382591e-01 iter
 7 series FresnelC=7.798934e-01 iter
enter x,nu
2000 0
 ierfc to compare with A&S Ex 5 p. 305
 3.487371e-03 7.501542e-04 1.511401e-04
 3.487371e-03 7.501542e-04 1.511401e-04
 1.996412e-01 6.996472e-02 2.161275e-02
 FWDierfc 1.983932e-01 6.996472e-02
 FWDierfc 2.300688e-02 6.043997e-03
 FWDierfc 1.805425e-03 3.739268e-04
 scaled ierfc 8.327380e-01 3.538549e-01
 scaled ierfcf 8.327380e-01 3.538549e-01
 scaled ierfc 7.935727e-01 2.798589e-01
 scaled ierfcf 7.935727e-01 2.798589e-01
 scaled ierfc 7.362202e-01 1.934079e-01
 scaled ierfcf 7.362202e-01 1.934079e-01
 scaled ierfc 6.932831e-01 1.435879e-01
```

```
 scaled ierfcf 6.932831e-01 1.435879e-01
 scaled ierfc 6.289707e-01 8.847439e-02
 scaled ierfcf 6.289707e-01 8.847439e-02
 scaled ierfc 2.764417e-02 3.835917e-15
 scaled ierfcf 2.763841e-02 -1.760696e-14
 scaled ierfc 1.538506e-02 3.703360e-16
 scaled ierfcf 1.537458e-02 -2.517193e-13
 scaled ierfc 5.900652e-03 6.518294e-18
 scaled ierfcf 5.873017e-03 -1.652909e-11
 enter x,n for ierfc
2000 0
 enter x,y for cerror
1 1
 3.047443e-01 + 2.082188e-01 i  = complex error
 enter x,y for cerror
1 -1
 -1.137038e+00 + 2.026814e+00 i  = complex error
 enter x,y for cerror
-1 1
 3.047443e-01  -2.082188e-01 i  = complex error
 enter x,y for cerror
.4 1
 4.038178e-01 + 1.043806e-01 i  = complex error
 enter x,y for cerror
-.4 1
 4.038178e-01  -1.043806e-01 i  = complex error
 enter x,y for cerror
.4 -1
 2.823839e+00 + 3.427700e+00 i  = complex error
 should be real=2.823839e+00 imag=3.427700e+00
 enter x,y for cerror
2000 0
 enter x,y for cerfc
1 0
 1.572992e-01 + -0.000000e+00 i  = complex complementary
error
 erf=8.427008e-01
 enter x,y for cerfc
1.450616 1.880943
 1.000001e+00 + 5.739470e-07 i  = complex complementary
error
 enter x,y for cerfc
5.4521922 5.68883744
 1.000000e+00  -2.005243e-08 i  = complex complementary
error
 enter x,y for cerfc
2000 0
 x=0.100000 0.112463 0.887537 0.099998 0.000524  9.933599e-
02 1
```

```
 x=0.200000 0.222703 0.777297 0.199921 0.004188
1.947510e-01 1
 x=0.300000 0.328627 0.671373 0.299401 0.014117
2.826317e-01 2
 x=0.400000 0.428392 0.571608 0.397481 0.033359
3.599435e-01 2
 x=0.500000 0.520500 0.479500 0.492344 0.064732
4.244364e-01 2
 x=0.600000 0.603856 0.396144 0.581095 0.110540
4.747632e-01 2
 x=0.700000 0.677801 0.322199 0.659652 0.172136
5.105041e-01 2
 x=0.800000 0.742101 0.257899 0.722844 0.249341
5.321017e-01 3
 x=0.900000 0.796908 0.203092 0.764823 0.339776
5.407243e-01 3
 x=1.000000 0.842702 0.157298 0.779893 0.438259
5.380795e-01 3
 x=1.100000 0.880206 0.119794 0.763807 0.536498
5.262067e-01 3
 x=1.200000 0.910314 0.089686 0.715437 0.623401
5.072736e-01 3
 x=1.300000 0.934008 0.065992 0.638550 0.686333
4.833975e-01 4
 x=1.400000 0.952285 0.047715 0.543096 0.713525
4.565072e-01 4
 x=1.500000 0.966105 0.033895 0.445261 0.697505
4.282490e-01 4
 x=1.600000 0.976348 0.023652 0.365462 0.638888
3.999398e-01 4
 x=1.700000 0.983790 0.016210 0.323827 0.549196
3.725591e-01 4
 x=1.800000 0.989091 0.010909 0.333633 0.450939
3.467728e-01 5
 x=1.900000 0.992790 0.007210 0.394471 0.373347
3.229744e-01 5
 x=2.000000 0.995322 0.004678 0.488253 0.343416
3.013405e-01 5
 x=2.100000 0.997021 0.002979 0.581564 0.374273
2.818852e-01 5
 x=2.200000 0.998137 0.001863 0.636286 0.455705
2.645107e-01 6
 x=2.300000 0.998857 0.001143 0.626562 0.553152
2.490529e-01 6
 x=2.400000 0.999311 0.000689 0.554961 0.619690
2.353129e-01 6
 x=2.500000 0.999593 0.000407 0.457413 0.619182
2.230834e-01 6
 x=2.600000 0.999764 0.000236 0.388937 0.549989
```

```
2.121643e-01 6
 x=2.700000 0.999866 0.000134 0.392494 0.452917
2.023746e-01 7
 x=2.800000 0.999925 0.000075 0.467492 0.391528
1.935509e-01 7
 x=2.900000 0.999959 0.000041 0.562376 0.410141
1.855556e-01 7
 x=3.000000 0.999978 0.000022 0.605721 0.496313
1.782718e-01 7
 x=3.100000 0.999988 0.000012 0.561594 0.581816
1.716020e-01 7
 x=3.200000 0.999994 0.000006 0.466320 0.593349
1.654618e-01 8
 x=3.300000 0.999997 0.000003 0.405694 0.519286
1.597881e-01 8
 x=3.400000 0.999998 0.000002 0.438492 0.429649
1.545232e-01 8
 x=3.500000 0.999999 0.000001 0.532572 0.415248
1.496199e-01 8
 x=3.600000 1.000000 0.000000 0.587953 0.492309
1.450387e-01 8
 x=3.700000 1.000000 0.000000 0.541946 0.574980
1.407517e-01 9
 x=3.800000 1.000000 0.000000 0.448095 0.565619
1.367221e-01 9
 x=3.900000 1.000000 0.000000 0.422333 0.475202
1.329290e-01 9
 x=4.000000 1.000000 0.000000 0.498426 0.420516
1.293510e-01 9
 x=4.100000 1.000000 0.000000 0.573696 0.475798
1.259641e-01 10
 x=4.200000 1.000000 0.000000 0.541719 0.563199
1.227598e-01 10
 x=4.300000 1.000000 0.000000 0.449441 0.553996
1.197202e-01 10
 x=4.400000 1.000000 0.000000 0.438333 0.462268
1.168321e-01 10
 x=4.500000 1.000000 0.000000 0.526026 0.434273
1.140837e-01 10
 x=4.600000 1.000000 0.000000 0.567237 0.516192
1.114733e-01 11
 x=4.700000 1.000000 0.000000 0.491426 0.567145
1.089785e-01 11
 x=4.800000 1.000000 0.000000 0.433797 0.496750
1.065964e-01 11
 x=4.900000 1.000000 0.000000 0.500161 0.435067
1.043196e-01 11
 x=5.000000 1.000000 0.000000 0.563631 0.499191
1.021329e-01 12
```

Chapter 8

Legendre Functions

Legendre Functions

The Legendre functions $P_\nu^\mu(z)$ and $Q_\nu^\mu(z)$ are solutions of the differential equation $(1-z^2)\frac{d^2w}{dz^2}-2z\frac{dw}{dz}+[\nu(\nu+1)-\frac{\mu^2}{1-z^2}]\,w=0$. There are singularities at $x = \infty$ and $x = \pm 1$, with a branch cut between the last two along the real axis. For even integer μ, the values above and below this line are slightly different, but for other values they are not. The definitions $P_\nu{}^\mu(z)=\lim_{\varepsilon\to 0}\frac{1}{2}[\,P(z+i\varepsilon)\,e^{i\frac{\pi}{2}\mu}+P(z-i\varepsilon)\;e^{-i\frac{\pi}{2}\mu}]$ and $Q_\nu{}^\mu(z)=\lim_{\varepsilon\to 0}\frac{1}{2}e^{-i\pi\mu}\;[\,Q(z-i\varepsilon)\,e^{i\frac{\pi}{2}\mu}+Q(z+i\varepsilon)\;e^{-i\frac{\pi}{2}\mu}]$ may be used along the cut. The values along this cut are probably those of most interest, as it is for real x between –1 and 1 that are of interest for spherical harmonics. The values for real $|x| > 1$ and imaginary x are of importance in oblate and prolate spheroidal coordinates. Lebedev's book provides a particularly good discussion of the applications of the conical and toroidal functions as well as the fundamental theory. Hochstadt's book was used for some results on the associated Legendre function.

The Legendre functions may be defined in terms of the Hypergeometric function by $P_\nu^\mu(z)=\frac{1}{\Gamma(1-\mu)}[\frac{z+1}{z-1}]^{\frac{\mu}{2}}\;F(-\nu,\nu+1;1-\mu;\frac{1-z}{2})$ and

$$Q_\nu^\mu(z)=e^{i\mu\pi}\,2^{-\nu-1}\sqrt{\pi}\,\frac{\Gamma(\nu+\mu+1)}{\Gamma(\nu+\frac{3}{2})}\,z^{-\nu-\mu-1}\,(z^2-1)^{\frac{\mu}{2}}$$

$$F(1+\frac{\nu}{2}+\frac{\mu}{2},\frac{1}{2}+\frac{\nu}{2}+\frac{\mu}{2};\nu+\frac{3}{2};\frac{1}{z^2})$$

(The factor of $\Gamma(1-\mu)$ in the denominator of the first expression might appear to cause problems for μ a positive integer. This is not the case, due to equation 15.1.2 of Abramowitz and Stegun; see Chapter 15.) There are numerous special cases of interest. The toroidal or ring functions are of interest for real $|x| > 1$, and have half-integral values of mu. They are related to complete elliptic integrals. For integer n and m, the P_n^m are polynomials and the $Q_\nu^\mu(z)$ involve logarithms and rational functions. The Mehler or conical functions have complex $\nu = -\frac{1}{2} + i\lambda$. See Lebedv's book for applications of the torodial and conical functions. Note also that a variety of sign conventions and normalizations are used. Different conventions for functions of an imaginary argument are used by Morse and Feshbach and by Smythe, for example. (We have used the conventions of the latter for the programs **pli()** and **qli()**.)

Because of their importance, we present a suite of routines for calculating many special cases of these functions. We also use the hypergeometric functions for obtaining values in the general case of complex arguments and parameters. The code for such cases is presented in Chapter 15. The function **legptable()** will be used in Chapter 21 on Spheroidal Wave functions.

Derivatives

Derivatives may be computed by using recurrence relation 8.5.2,

$(z^2 - 1)\frac{dP_\nu^\mu}{dz} = (\nu + \mu)(\nu + \mu - 1)(z^2 - 1)P_\nu^{\mu - 1} - \mu z P_\nu^\mu$. (The identical formula applies to Q.)

Applications

The Legendre functions arise as solutions to the non-radial portion of Laplace's equation $\nabla^2 \Phi = 0$ when the equation is solved by separation of variables, that is, when it is assumed that the solution is of the form $\Phi = F(r)G(\theta)H(\varphi)$. The solution is of the form $Y_{lm}\left(\frac{A}{r^{l+1}} + Br^l\right)$, where Y_{lm} are spherical harmonics. The Y_{lm} are proportional to the associated Legendre functions: $Y_{lm} = A\, P_l^m(\cos\theta)\, e^{im\varphi}$ where

$A = \left(\frac{(2n+1)(n-|m|)!}{4\pi(n+|m|)!}\right)^{.5}$ is the cutomary normalization. Note that a variety of normalizations is to be found in the literature. Also note that m and n are integers. Finally, note that for $|m|>n$, the Y_{lm} vanishes. A general solution is formed from a sum of terms of the form shown. Typical problems often require only the P functions and not the Q, which are of course singular at the poles. Some problems do require the Q functions as well.

The solution of the Laplace equation for a conical surface requires the use of the conical functions. Problems involving hyperboloids also can give rise to solutions containing the conical functions. The toroidal functions will occur in problems involving toroids (doughnuts; often called anchor rings in old texts). See Lebedev for examples.

Spheroidal Wave functions, discussed in Chapter 21, involve sums of Legendre functions. Typically, both P and Q are required. For oblate spheroids, imaginary values of the argument are required, while for prolate coordinates, real values are required, with the argument of the Q between –1 and 1 and that of P of magnitude greater than one.

Methods

Typically, recurrence relations are used. The algorithms developed by W. Gautsche are used for the cases of real argument $|x| > 1$. Those of J. R. Hernden are used for purely imaginary arguments and real arguments. Results in Lebedev and Bowman et al. (see Chapter 5) are used for the conical functions. As with the iterated error function of the previous chapter, one often encounters situations in which a table of values for a function with fixed argument by varying n or m. Redundant computation is avoided with a routine that produces such a table, and a number of varieties are provided here and in Chapter 21. For example, the routine legptable() in Chapter 21 produces a table of $P_n^m(z)$ for $n = m$ up to $n = nmax$. Other routines given below also produce an array of values. Note that the routines for imaginary arguments use the sign conventions of Smythe in order to give real answers, and may not agree in sign or reality with values computed from the hypergeometric function. Similar remarks apply to the two programs that use Hernden's algorithms.

References

J. R. Hernden, Algorithms 47 and 62, CALGO (*Collected Algorithms of the ACM*).

W. Gautschi, Algorithm 259, CALGO.

H. Hochstadt, *The Functions of Mathematical Physics* (N. Y.: Dover, 1986).

N. N. Lebedev, *Special Functions and their Applications* (N. Y.: Dover, 1972).

P. M. Morse and H. Feshbach, *Methods of Mathematical Physics* (N. Y.: McGraw-Hill, 1964).

W. R. Smythe, *Static and Dynamic Electricity* (N. Y.: McGraw-Hill, 1968).

```
/*
Legendre and Associated Legendre functions
Copyright 1991 by Louis Baker. All rights reserved.
   real arguments:
double plm(l,m,x) int l,m;double x;
double pl0(l,x) double x;
double ql0(l,x) double x;
double qlm(l,m,x) double x; int l,m;
double pmunu(mu,nu,x) double nu,mu,x;
double qmunu(mu,nu,x) double nu,mu,x;
double pnu(x,nu)double x,nu;
   imaginary arguments:
double pli(l,z) int l; double z;
double qli(l,z) int l; double z;
   real=1 for real arguments, 0 imaginary:
double legendrea(m,n,x,real) int m,n,real;double x;
   return a table in q[] (ratios in r[]) for given m,
n=0,nmax
qleg(m,nmax,x,real,r,q) int m,nmax,real; double x,r[],q[];
double qnu(x,nu,real)int real;double x,nu;

legendrea based upon CALGO 47,qleg CALGO 62 by J. R. Herndon
*/


#include "cmlib.h"
#include "complex.h"
#include "protom.h"
#include <stdio.h>

double plm(l,m,x) int l,m;double x;
{/* m<=l*/
int i;
double pmm,coef,factor,sqrt(),pl0();
/*if(abs(x)>1.)return errorcode;*/
if(m==0 && abs(x)>1.)return pl0(l,x); /* do not use pl0 off
cut*/
if( abs(x)>1.)
   {
   return ((m-1-l)*x*plm(l,m-1,x)-(m+l-1)*plm(l-1,m-
1,x))/sqrt(x*x-1.);
   /* will ultimately get to pl0 call*/
   }
pmm=1.;/* |x|<=1 */
if(m>0)
   {
   coef=sqrt((1.-x)*(1.+x));
   factor=1.;
   for(i=1;i<=m;i++)
```

```
        {
        pmm*=-factor*coef;
        if(pmm==0.)break;/* x=1*/
        factor+=2.;
        }
    }
if(l==m)return pmm;
coef= x*( (m<<1)+1.)*pmm;
if(l==(m+1))return coef;
for(i=m+2;i<=l;i++)
    {factor= (x*((i<<1)-1)*coef-(i+m-1)*pmm)/(i-m);
    pmm=coef;
    coef=factor;
    }
return factor;
}

double pl0(l,x) int l; double x;
{int i;
double old,older,new;
if(l==0)return 1.;
if(l==1)return x;
old=x;older=1.;
for(i=2;i<=l;i++)
    {new=(((i<<1)-1)*x*old-(i-1)*older)/(i);
    older=old;old=new;/*forward recursion-stable for all x
it seems */
    }
return new;
}


double ql0(l,x) double x;
{
int i;
double log(),old,older,new,qlm();
if(abs(x)>1.) return qlm(l,0,x);/* this sum unstable large
x*/
/*sum=0.;twol=l<<1;
for(i=l-1;i>=0;i-=2)
    {
    j=l-i;
    term= (twol-(j))/((double)(l*j));
    sum+= pl0(i,x)*term;
    }
return pl0(l,x)*.5*log(abs((1.+x)/(1.-x)))-sum;*/
older= .5*log(abs((1.+x)/(1.-x)));
if(l==0)return older;
old=older*x-1.;
```

```
if(l==1)return old;
for(i=2;i<=l;i++)
   {new=(((i<<1)-1)*x*old-(i-1)*older)/(i);
   older=old;old=new;/*forward recursion-stable for
abs(x)<1 ? */
   }
return new;
}

double qlm(l,m,x) double x; int l,m;
{         int i;
double sqrt(),ql0(),pow(),gamma(),f21(),term,log();
if(m==0 && x<1. )return ql0(l,x);
if( abs(x)<1. && l>=0 && m>=0)
   {
   return ((m-1-l)*x*qlm(l,m-l,x)-(m+l-1)*qlm(l-1,m-
1,x))/sqrt(1.-x*x);
   /* will ultimately get to ql0 call*/
   }
if(abs(x)==1.)return errorcode;
if(!m)
   {if(l>=0 && l<3)
      {term=.5*log((x+1.)/(x-1.));
      if(!l) return term;
      else if(l==1) return term*x-1.;
      else return term*.5*x*(3.*x-1.)-1.5*x;
      }
   }
/*if(abs(x)>=2.)*/
   {
   term= 1.;
   if(l)for (i=1;i<=l;i++)term*= .5*((i<<1)+1);
   return  pow(2.,(double)(-l))*(m%2?-1.:1.)*
   pow(x*x-1., m*.5)*pow(x,-m-l-1.)*gamma(l+m+1.)/term*
   f21( 1.+.5*(l+m),.5*(1.+l+m),1.5+l, 1/(x*x));
   }
/*else
   {
   term= sqrt(x*x-1.);
   f=f21(.5+m,.5-m,1.5+l, (term-x)/term*.5);
   return f*sqrt(.5*pi)*(m%2?-1.:1.)*
   pow((x-
term),.5+l)*gamma(1.+l+m)/(gamma(1.5+l)*sqrt(term));
   }*/
/*return  pow(2.,-1.-l)*sqrt(pi)*(m%2?-1.:1.)*
pow(x*x-1., m*.5)*pow(x,-m-l-1.)*gamma(l+m+1.)/gamma(1.5+l)*
f21( 1.+.5*(l+m),.5*(1.+l+m),1.5+l, 1/(x*x));*/
}
```

```
double pli(l,z) int l; double z;
{/*omitting factor of -1^(n/2)= i^n*/
double pow(),sum,zz,term,gamma(),coef,twol;
int m,i,j,k;m=l>>1;twol= l<<1;
if(!l)return 1.;
if(z==0.)
    {if(l%2)return 0.;
    term= ((l/2))%2? -1.:1.;
    for(i=1;i<l;i+=2) term*= i/((double)(i+1));
    return term;

    }
sum=gamma(l+1.);
coef= gamma((l<<1)+1.)/(sum*sum); sum=0.;
zz=z*z;term = 1.;k=1;sum=1.;
for(k=1;k<=m;k++)
    {
    j=k<<1;
    term*= (l-k+1.)*(l-j+2.)*(l-j+1.)/(zz*(k)*(twol-
j+2)*(twol-j+1) );
    sum+=term;
    }
return pow(z*.5,(double)l)*sum*coef;
}

#define itmax 50
#define tol 1.e-6

double qli(l,z) int l; double z;
{/*omitting factor of (-i)^n+1        */
double pow(),atan(),sum,zz,term,coef,gamma();int twol,twolp;
int i,j,k;twol= l<<1;twolp=twol+1;
if(!l){if(z==0.)return -pi*.5;return -atan(1/z);}
if(abs(z)<1.e-7)
    {
    if(l%2)
        {if(l==1)return -1.;
        term= ((l+1)/2)%2? -1.:1.;
        for(i=2;i<l;i+=2) term*= i/((double)(i+1));
        return term;
        }
    else{return -pi*.5*pli(l,0.);}

    }
if( abs(z)>1.)
    {
    sum= gamma(l+1.);coef= gamma(twol+2.)/(sum*sum);
```

```
    sum=0.;
    zz=z*z;term = 1.;
    for(k=1;k<=itmax;k++)
        {
        j=k<<1;
        sum+=term;
        if( abs(term)<tol*abs(sum))break;
        term*= -(l+k)*(l+j-
1)*(l+j)/(zz*(k)*(twolp+j)*(twolp+j-1) );
        }
    return sum/(z*pow(z*.5,(double)l)*coef);
    }
else if(z==1.) return 1.e60;
/*else*/
sum=0.;/* Hochstadt p.158 only terms for which l+k odd*/
j= (l%2)?0:1;term=1.;
for(k=j;k<l;k+=2)
    {
    sum+=term*(((k<<1)+1)<<1)*pli(k,z)/((l-k)*(l+k+1));
    term=-term;
    }
/*printf(" sum=%e\n",sum);*/
return pli(l,z)*(pi*.5-atan(z))-sum;
}

/*static int nsmall;*/

double legendrea(m,n,x,real) int m,n,real;double x;
{/* P m,n real=1 real 0 imaginary arg.*/
int i,j,k; double p,z,w,y,gamma[41],sqrt();
k=n-m;
if(k<0)return 0.;
if(!n)return 1.;
w=z=1.;
if(n!=m)for(i=1;i<=k;i++) z*=x;
gamma[0]=1.;
for(i=1;i<=(n+n);i++)
    {
    gamma[i]=w*gamma[i-1];w+=1.;
    }
if(x==0.)
    {
    i=k>>1;
    if((i<<1)!=k)return 0.;
    p= gamma[m+n]/(gamma[i]*gamma[m+i]);
    }
else
    {
        w=1.;y=1./(x*x+1.e-20);
```

```
    if(real){y=-y;w=-w;}
    j=3;p=0.;
    for(i=1;i<=12;i++)
        {
        if( (k+2)/2<i ) break;
        p+=gamma[(n<<1)-(i<<1)+2]*z
            /(gamma[i-1]*gamma[n-i+1]*gamma[k-(i<<1)+j-1]);
        z*=y;
        }
    }
z=1.;
for (i=1;i<=n;i++)z+=z;
p/=z;
if(!real)
    {
    i= n-((n>>2)<<2);/* n-4(n/4) corrected by george from
herndon */
    if(i>1)p=-p;
    }
if(!m)return p;
j=m>>1;z=abs(w+x*x);
if(m!=(j<<1))
    {z=sqrt(z);
    j=m;
    }
for(i=1;i<=j;i++)p*=z;
return p;
}

/* for Qn,m (x) x>=1 returns array for n 0 to nmax R ratios
of q*/

qleg(m,nmax,x,real,r,q) int m,nmax,real; double x,r[],q[];
{double t,q0,s,log(),sqrt(),atan();int i,n;
if(x==1. && real){fprintf(stderr," x==1 out of range for
real qleg\n");
    for(i=0;i<=nmax;i++)q[i]=errorcode;return ;}
if(nmax<=13)n=25;
else n=nmax+7;r[0]=0.;
if(real)
    {
    if(!m) q[0]=.5*log((1.+x)/abs(x-1.));
    else
        {
        t=-1./sqrt(abs(x*x-1.));
        q0=0.;
        q[0]=t;
        for(i=2;i<=m;i++)
            {
```

```
            s=(x+x)*(i-1)*t*q[0]+(3.*i-i*i-2)*q0;
            q0=q[0];q[0]=s;
            }
        }
    if(x==1.)q[0]=1.e60;/*big*/
    r[n+1]=x-sqrt(abs(x*x-1.));
    for (i=n;i>=1;i--)
        {
        r[i]=(i+m)/(((i<<1)+1.)*x+(m-i-1)*r[i+1]);
        }
    goto end;
    }
/* imaginary x*/
if(!m)
    {
    if(x<.5) q[0]=atan(x)-.5*pi;
    else q[0]=-atan(1./x);
    }
else
    {
    t=1./sqrt(x*x+1.);
    q0=0.;
    q[0]=t;
    for(i=2;i<=m;i++)
        {
        s= (x+x)*(i-1)*t*q[0]+(3*i-i*i-2)*q0;
        q0=q[0];q[0]=s;
        }
    }
r[n+1]= x-sqrt(x*x+1.);
for(i=n;i>=1;i--)
    {r[i]= (i+m)/((i-m+1.)*r[i+1]-((i<<1)+1)*x);}
/*   printf(" r[%d]=%e\n",i,r[i]);}*/
for(i=1;i<=nmax;i+=2)
    r[i]=-r[i];
end:
for(i=1;i<=nmax;i++)q[i]=q[i-1]*r[i];
/* for x=0, does not do well on odd order terms*/
if(!m && abs(x)<1.e-8 && nmax>0)
    {/*odd l*/
    if(nmax<1)return;
    q[1]=-1.;if(nmax<=1)return;
    t= 1.;
    for(i=2;i<=nmax;i+=2)
        {
        t*= i/((double)(i+1));
        q[i+1]=t*((i/2)%2?1.:-1.);
        }
    return;
```

```
    }
return;
}

double qnu(x,nu,real)int real;double x,nu;
{
double y,f21(),sqrt(),gamma(),z,pow(),sin(),cos(),f;
if(x>1.)
    {
    z=1./(x*x);
    if(!real)z=-z;f= f21(1.+.5*nu,.5*(nu+1.),nu+1.5,z);
    /*printf(" f21=%e\n",f);*/
    return sqrt(pi)*gamma(nu+1.)/(gamma(nu+1.5)*pow(
2.*x,nu+1.))
        *f;
    }
else if(x==1. || x==-1.)return errorcode;
if(!real)return errorcode;/* this limitation removable com-
plex ans*/
z= x*x;y=pi*nu*.5;
return sqrt(pi)*(gamma(1.+.5*nu)*cos(y)/gamma(.5*(nu+1.))
    *f21(.5-.5*nu,1.+.5*nu,1.5,z)-
gamma(.5*(1.+nu))*sin(y)*.5/gamma(1.+.5*nu)
    *f21(.5*(1.+nu),-.5*nu,.5,z));

}
/* pmunu and qmunu are not intended for direct use and are
not
prototyped in  protom.h */

/* CAVEAT: pmunu NOT FULLY GENERAL- USE COMPLEX VERSION cp
*/
double pmunu(mu,nu,x) double nu,mu,x;
{int n,m;/* -1< x < 2 */
double gamma(),pow(),f21(),z;
n=nu;m=mu;
if( abs(x)<=1. && (double)n==nu && (double)m==mu)return
plm(n,m,x);
z=1.-mu;
if( x==1. || (z-((int)z)==0. && z<=0.)) return errorcode;
if(abs(1.-x)<2.) return f21(-nu,nu+1.,1.-mu,.5*(1.-x))*
    pow(abs((x+1.)/(x-1.)),.5*mu)/gamma(1.-mu);
else
    {
    fprintf(stderr," out of range |1-x| p mu nu\n");
    return errorcode;
    }
}
```

```
/* CAVEAT: qmunu NOT FULLY GENERAL- USE COMPLEX VERSION cq
*/
double qmunu(mu,nu,x) double nu,mu,x;
{int n,m; /* returns Qmn, nu(x) divided by exp(i*pi*mu),
which
will be complex if mu not an integer. Use complex versions
if needed.*/
double gamma(),pow(),f21(),z,y,d1,d2;
n=nu;m=mu;
if(  (double)n==nu && (double)m==mu)return qlm(n,m,x);
z=.5*(1.-x);
/*if(abs(z)<1.)*/
if(mu==m)return errorcode;
d1=1.+nu-mu;
if( (d1==((int)d1)) && d1<=0.)return errorcode;
d2=1.+mu+nu;
if( (d2==((int)d2)) && d2<=0.)return errorcode;
    {
    y=pow(abs((1.+x)/(1.-x)),.5*mu);return
    .5*( f21(-nu,1.+nu,1.+mu,z)/(y*gamma(d1))
    *gamma(-mu)*gamma(d2)
    +gamma(mu)*f21(-nu,1.+nu,1.-mu,z)*y);
    }
/*else
    {
    fprintf(stderr," out of range |1-x| q mu nu x=%le\n",x);
    return errorcode;
    }
*/
}

double pnu(x,nu) double x,nu;
{
double y;
if(abs(x)<1.) return pmunu(0.,nu,x);
y=1./(x*x);
return (gamma(nu+.5)*pow(2.*x,nu)/gamma(nu+1.)
    *f21(.5-.5*nu,-.5*nu,.5-nu,y) +
    gamma(-.5-nu)/gamma(-nu)*pow(2.*x,-nu-1.)
    *f21(.5*nu+1.,.5*(nu+1.),nu+1.5,y)    )/sqrt(pi);
}
```

```
/*
Legendre functions for |x|>1
from C Mathematical Function Handbook by Louis Baker
Copyright 1991 by Louis Baker. All rights reserved.
based upon CALGO 259 by Walter Gautschi
leg1(x,a,nmax,p) double x,p[];int a,nmax;  Pa,n(x) n=0 to
nmax
leg2(x,m,nmax,d,q) double x,q[];int m,nmax,d; Qm,n(x)  n=0
to nmax
leg3( x,n,mmax,d,q) int n,mmax,d; double x,q[]; Qm,n(x) m=0
to mmax
legend1(x,alpha,nmax,d,p)      double x,alpha,p[]; int
d,nmax; Pa,n=0 nmax
legend2(x,a,m,nmax,d,p) double p[],a,x;int m,nmax,d;P a+n,m
n=0 to nmax
conical(x,tau,nmax,d,p) double x,tau,p[];int nmax,d;
toroidal(x,m,nmax,d,q)   int m,d,nmax; double x,q[];

not based upon CALGO 259:
arccosh(x)   arc hyperbolic cosine
double conicalt(theta,tau) double theta,tau;conical for
|x|<1
double conicala(x,tau) double x,tau; asymptotic conical

*/
#include <stdio.h>
#include <alloc.h>
#include "cmlib.h"
#include "protom.h"
/*
   #define malloc farmalloc
   #define free   farfree
*/

leg1(x,a,nmax,p) double x,p[];int a,nmax;
{/* Pa,n(x) n=0 to nmax x>1*/
double *rr, x1,sum,r,s,pow(),sqrt();       int n,nstop;
if( x<1. || a<0 || nmax<0)
   {fprintf(stderr," leg1 bad argument\n");
return ierrorcode;}
if(x==1. ||a==0){p[0]=1.;for(n=1;n<=nmax;n++)p[n]=0.;return
0;}
rr=malloc( (nmax+1)* sizeof(double) );
if(rr==NULL)
   {fprintf(stderr," leg1 memory allocation error\n");
return ierrorcode;}
for(n=a+1;n<=nmax;n++) p[n]=0.;
x1=sqrt(x*x-1.);
sum= pow( (x+x1),(double)a);x1=2.*x/x1;
```

```
r=s=0.;
for(n=a;n>=1;n--)
   {
   r= (a+1-n)/(n*x1+r*(n+a+1));
   s=r*(2.+s);
   if(n<=nmax) rr[n-1]=r;
   }
p[0]=sum/(1.+s);
nstop= (nmax<=a)? nmax-1:a-1;
for(n=0; n<=nstop;n++)p[n+1]=(n+a+1.)*rr[n]*p[n];
free(rr);
return 0;
}


leg2(x,m,nmax,d,q) double x,q[];int m,nmax,d;
{/* qn,m(x) n=0 to nmax x>1*/
int n,nu,p,flag;
double sqrt(),pow(),log(),x1,q0,q1,q2,epsilon,r,*rr,*qap-
prox;
if( x<1. || m<0 || nmax<0)
   {fprintf(stderr," leg2 bad argument\n");
                   return ierrorcode;}
rr=malloc( (nmax+1)* sizeof(double) );
qapprox=malloc( nmax* sizeof(double) );
if(rr==NULL||qapprox==NULL)
   {fprintf(stderr," leg2 memory allocation
error\n");return ierrorcode;}
x1=sqrt(x*x-1.);
q1= .5*log((x+1.)/(x-1.));
if(!m)   q[0]=q1;
else
   {
   q2=-1/x1;x1=2.*x/x1;
   for(n=1;n<m;n++)
      {
      q0=q1;q1=q2;
      q2=-n*x1*q1-n*(n-1)*q0;
      }
   q[0]=q2;
   }
for(n=0;n<=nmax;n++)qapprox[n]=0.;
epsilon=.5*pow(10.,(double)-d);
nu=20+ 1.25*nmax;
while(1)
   {r=0.;
   flag=1;
   for(n=nu; n>=1;n--)
      {
```

```
        r=(n+m)/(((n<<1)+1)*x-(n-m+1.)*r);
        if(n<=nmax)rr[n-1]=r;
        }
    for(n=0;n<nmax;n++)q[n+1]=rr[n]*q[n];
    for(n=0;n<=nmax;n++)
        {
        if( abs(q[n]-qapprox[n])>epsilon*abs(q[n])
){flag=0;break;}
        }
    if(flag)break;
    for(p=0;p<=nmax;p++)qapprox[p]=q[p];
    nu+=10;
    if(nu> 400){fprintf(stderr," leg2 cannot meet tolerence
req.\n");break;}
    }
free(rr);free(qapprox);return 0;
}


leg3( x,n,mmax,d,q) int n,mmax,d; double x,q[];
{/* qn,m m=0 to mmax*/
int m; double x1,*q1,sqrt();
if(n<0 ||x<1. ||mmax<0)
    {fprintf(stderr," leg3 argument error\n");
                    return ierrorcode;}
q1=malloc((n+1)* sizeof(double) );
if(q1==NULL)
    {fprintf(stderr," leg3 memory allocation error\n");
                    return ierrorcode;}
leg2(x,0,n,d,q1); q[0]=q1[n];
x1=2.*x/sqrt(x*x-1.);
if(mmax>0)
    {leg2(x,1,n,d,q1); q[1]=q1[n];}
for(m=1;m<mmax;m++)q[m+1]=-m*x1*q[m]-(m+n)*(m-n-1.)*q[m-1];
free(q1);
return 0;
}


legend1(x,alpha,nmax,d,p)       double x,alpha,p[]; int
d,nmax;
{/* p alpha n n=0 nmax x>1*/
int n,nu,m,flag; double a,epsilon,x1,sum,c,r,s, *papprox,
*rr,pow(),sqrt();
if(x<1. ||nmax<0){
fprintf(stderr, " legend1 argument error\n"); return 0;}
if(x==1.)
    {
    p[0]=1.;for(n=1;n<=nmax;n++)p[n]=0.;return 0;
```

```
   }
rr= malloc ( (nmax+1)* sizeof(double) );
papprox= malloc ( (nmax+1)* sizeof(double) );
if(rr==NULL||papprox==NULL)
   {fprintf(stderr," legend1 memory allocation
error\n");return ierrorcode;}
a=(alpha<.5)? -alpha-1.: alpha;
for(n=0;n<=nmax;n++)papprox[n]=0.;
epsilon=pow(10.,(double) -d)*.5;
x1=sqrt(x*x-1.); sum=pow(x+x1, a);x1=2.*x/x1;
nu=20+
(37.26+.1283*(a+38.26)*x)*nmax/(37.26+.1283*(a+1.)*x);
while(1)
   {
   flag=1;
   r=s=0.;
   for(n=nu;n>=1;n--)
      {
      r=(a+1.-n)/(n*x1+(n+a+1.)*r);s=r*(2.+s);
      if(n<=nmax)rr[n-1]=r;
      }
   p[0]=sum/(1.+s);
   for(n=0;n<nmax;n++)p[n+1]=rr[n]*p[n];
   for(n=0;n<=nmax;n++)
      {
      if(abs(p[n]-papprox[n])>ep-
silon*abs(p[n])){flag=0;break;}

      }
   if(flag)break;
   for(m=0;m<=nmax;m++)papprox[m]=p[m];nu+=10;
   if(nu> 200){fprintf(stderr," legend1 cannot meet
tolerence req.\n");break;}
   }
c=1.;
for(n=1;n<=nmax;n++)
   {c*=(a+n);p[n]*=c;
   }
free(rr);free(papprox);
return 0;
}

legend2(x,a,m,nmax,d,p) double p[],a,x;int m,nmax,d;
{/*p a+n,m n=0 nmax x>1*/
double *p1,denom; int n;
if(m<0 ||x<1. ||nmax<0)
{fprintf(stderr," legend2 argument error\n");
return ierrorcode;}
p1= malloc ((nmax+1) * sizeof(double) );
```

```
if(p1==NULL)
{fprintf(stderr," legend2 memory allocation error\n");
return ierrorcode;}
legend1(x,a,m,d,p1); p[0]=p1[m];
if(nmax>0)
   {
   legend1(x,a+1.,m,d,p1);
   p[1]=p1[m];
   }

for(n=1;n<nmax;n++)
   {
   denom=(n-m+1)+a;
   if(denom==0.)
         {fprintf(stderr,
                  "legend2 zero denominator n=%d\n", n);
         p[n+1]=errorcode;
         return 1;}
   p[n+1]=(((n<<1)+2.*a+1.)*x*p[n]-(n+a+m)*p[n-1])/(denom);
   }
return 0;
}

#define numax 1000

conical(x,tau,nmax,d,p) double x,tau,p[];int nmax,d;
{/* p -.5+i*tau,n (x) n=0 to nmax x>1 */
int n,nu,m,flag;
double epsilon,t,x1,x2,sum,lambda1,lambda2,lambda,r,s,
   *rr,*papprox,pow(),sqrt(),log(),cos(),aux1,aux2,aux3;
if(x<1. || nmax<0){ fprintf(stderr," conical argument
error\n");return 0;}
if(x==1.)
   {p[0]=1.;for(n=1;n<=nmax;n++)p[n]=0.;return 0;}
rr=malloc( (nmax+1)* sizeof(double) );
papprox=malloc( (nmax+1)* sizeof(double) );
if(rr==NULL||papprox==NULL)
   {fprintf(stderr," conical memory allocation
error\n");return 0;}
t=tau*tau;
for(n=0;n<=nmax;n++)papprox[n]=0.;
epsilon=.5*pow(10.,(double)-d);
x1=sqrt(x*x-1.);x2=x+x1;
sum= cos(tau*log(x2))/sqrt(x2); x1=2.*x/x1;
nu=30+ ((1.+(.14+.0246*tau)*(x-1.))*nmax);
while(1)
   {
   flag=1;n=2;
   lambda1=1./(.25+t);
```

```
   lambda2=(3.-4.*t)/((.25+t)*(2.25+t));
   L1:aux2=tau/n; aux1=1.+.5/n;
   lambda= (1.+1./n)*(2.*lambda2-
lambda1)/(aux1*aux1+aux2*aux2);
   if(n<nu)
      {lambda1=lambda2;lambda2=lambda;n++;goto L1;}
   r=s=0.;
   L2:
   aux1= 1.-.5/n;aux2=tau/n;
   aux3=(aux1*aux1+aux2*aux2);
   r=-aux3/(x1+(1.+1./n)*r);
   s=r*(lambda2+s);
   if(n<=nmax) rr[n-1]=r;
   lambda1=lambda2;
   aux1=1.+.5/n;
   lambda2=2.*lambda2-
(aux2*aux2+aux1*aux1)*lambda/(1.+1./n);
   lambda=lambda1;n--;
   if(n>=1)goto L2;
   p[0]=sum/(1.+s);
   for(n=0;n<nmax;n++)p[n+1]=rr[n]*p[n];
   for(n=0;n<=nmax;n++)
      {
      if(abs(p[n]-papprox[n])>ep-
silon*abs(p[n])){flag=0;break;}
      }
   if(flag)break;
   for(m=0;m<=nmax;m++)papprox[m]=p[m];nu+=60;
   if(nu>numax){fprintf(stderr," conical did not meet
tolerence req.\n");break;}
   }

t=1.;
for(n=1;n<=nmax;n++) {t*=n;p[n]*=t;}
free(rr);free(papprox); return 0;
}


toroidal(x,m,nmax,d,q)   int m,d,nmax; double x,q[];
{/* q -.5+n,m x n=0 nmax x>1*/
double *rr,*qapprox,pow(),sqrt(),epsilon,r,s,sum,c,x1;int
flag,n,nu;
if(x<=1. || nmax<0){
fprintf(stderr," toroidal argument error\n");
return ierrorcode;}
rr=malloc( (nmax+1)* sizeof(double) );
qapprox=malloc( (nmax+1)* sizeof(double) );
if(rr==NULL||qapprox==NULL)
   {fprintf(stderr,
```

```
" toroidal memory allocation error\n");
return ierrorcode;}
for(n=0;n<=nmax;n++)qapprox[n]=0.;
epsilon= pow(10.,(double)-d)*.5;
c=2.2214414691;
if(m>=0)
   for(n=0;n<m;n++)c*= -(n+.5);
else
   for(n=0;n>=m+1;n--)c/=(.5-n);
sum=c/sqrt(x-1.);if(m)sum*=pow((x+1.)/(x-1.),.5*m);x1=2.*x;
nu=20+ (1.15+(.0146+.00122*m)/(x-1.))*nmax;
while(1)
   {flag=1;
   r=s=0.;
   for(n=nu;n>=1;n--)
      {
      r=(n+m-.5)/(n*x1-r*(n-m+.5));
      s=r*(2.+s);
      if(n<=nmax)rr[n-1]=r;
      }
   q[0]=sum/(1.+s);
   for(n=0;n<nmax;n++)q[n+1]=q[n]*rr[n];
   for(n=0;n<=nmax;n++)
      {
      if(abs(q[n]-qapprox[n])>ep-
silon*abs(q[n])){flag=0;break;}
      }
   if(flag)break;
   for(n=0;n<=nmax;n++)qapprox[n]=q[n];nu+=10;
   if(nu>numax){
fprintf(stderr," toroidal did not meet tolerence req.\n")
;break;}
   }
free(rr);free(qapprox);return 0;
}

#define itmax 60
#define tol 1.e-9

double conicalt(theta,tau) double theta,tau;
{/* conical for -1<cos(theta)<=1 as argument. series*/
double s,sum,t,term,sin(); int j,i,k;
if(theta<0. || theta>=pi)return errorcode;
s=sin(.5*theta);s*=s;sum=1.;term=1.;t=tau*tau;
for(i=1;i<itmax;i++)
   {
   j=(i<<1);k=j-1;
   term*=(t+.25*k*k)*s/(i*i);
   sum+=term;
```

```
    if(abs(term)<tol*abs(sum))return sum;
    }
fprintf(stderr," no convergence conical x\n");
return sum;
}

double arccosh(x) double x;
{double log(),sqrt();
return  log( x+sqrt(x*x-1.));
}

double conicala(x,tau) double x,tau;
{double b,acos(),sqrt(),exp(),sin(),cos(),sinh();
/* P .5-i*tau (x) for large tau */
if(abs(x)>1.)
    {
    b=arccosh(x);
    return sqrt(2./(pi*tau*sinh(b)))*sin(tau*b+.25*pi);
    }
b=acos(x);
return exp(tau*b)/sqrt(2.*pi*tau*sin(b));
}
```

```
/*
Toroidal P |x|>1
from C Mathematical Function Handbook by Louis Baker
Copyright 1991 by Louis Baker. All rights reserved.

*/
#include <stdio.h>
#include "cmlib.h"
#include "protom.h"
#define tol 1.e-8

double Ptoroidal(n,x) int n;double x;
{/*based on 7.10.8 of Lebedev */
double alpha,sum,fsum,term,factor,trm;int k,nmk;
if(x<0.)return errorcode;
alpha=arccosh(x);
fsum=0.;factor= exp(-2.*alpha);term=1.;
for(k=0;k<n;k++)
    {
    nmk=n-k;
    fsum+= gamma((double)nmk)*gamma(k+.5)
        /(gamma(nmk+.5)*gamma((double)(k+1)))*term;
    term*=factor;
    }
fsum*= exp( alpha*(n-.5))/pi;
trm=1.;
for(k=0,sum=0.;k<1000;k++)
    {
    nmk=n+k;
    term=
gamma(nmk+.5)*gamma(k+.5)/(gamma(k+1.)*gamma(nmk+1.))
        *trm*(2.*alpha+digam(1.+k)-digam(.5+k)
        +digam(nmk+1.)-digam(nmk+.5));
    sum+=term;
    if(abs(term)<tol*abs(sum))goto fini;
    trm*=factor;
    }
fprintf(stderr," Ptoroidal did not meet tolerance\n");
fini:sum*= exp(-alpha*(.5+n))/(pi*pi);
return sum+fsum;
}
```

```
/*
Mehler (Conical Legendre) functions
from C Mathematical Function Handbook by Louis Baker
Copyright 1991 by Louis Baker. All rights reserved.
Mehler(x,z,mm) Mehler conical function P  [ix-.5] (z)
Mehler0(x,z) double x,z;
*/
#include "cmlib.h"
#include "protom.h"
#include <stdio.h>
#define iabs(x) ((x)<0?-(x):(x))
#define tol 1.e-9

double Mehler(x,z,mm) double x,z;int mm;
{/* P ix-1/2(z) */
double y,sum,t,q,term,factor,pow(),kmm,gamma(),tan,kk,power;
int m,k;
/* z=cos theta, y =sin(theta/2)^2*/
if(z==-1.)return errorcode;
y=.5*(1.-z);tan= (1.-z)/(1.+z);
/* k -m,x(z)*/ m=iabs(mm);
sum=1.;t= 4.*x*x;q=1.;term=t+1.;
factor=term/(4.*(1.+m))*y;
for(k=1;k<1000;k++)
   {sum+=factor;
   q+=2.;
   term=t+q*q;
   factor*=term/((k+1.)*4.*(m+1.+k))*y;
   if(abs(factor)<tol*abs(sum))goto fini;
/*printf(" Mehler sum=%e latest term %e\n",sum,factor);*/
   }
fprintf(stderr," Mehler tolerance not achieved\n");
fini:power= m?pow(tan,(double)m):1.;
kmm= (m%2?-1.:1.)/gamma(m+1.)*power*sum;
if(mm<=0)return kmm;
kk=kmm;t*=.25;/*t=x*x*/
for(k=1;k<=(m<<1)-1;k+=2)
   {
   kk*=(t+.25*(k*k));
   }
return kk;
}

double Mehler0(x,z) double x,z;
{/* P ix-1/2(z) */
double y,sum,t,q,term,fac-
tor,pow(),gamma(),tan,cosh(),log(),g,yy,lt,r,ss;
int k;
/* z=cos theta, y =sin(theta/2)^2*/
```

```
y=.5*(1.-z);t=4.*x*x;term=t+1.;q=1.;
/* k m=0,x(z)*/
if(z==-1.)return errorcode;
if(y>.95)
   {/* near log. singularity at theta=pi, cos()=-1,y=1*/
   yy= .5*(1.+z);tan= (1.-z)/(1.+z);lt=log(tan);
   for(g=0.,k=1;k<100;k++)
      {
      q=(k<<1)-1;
      term= (t-q)/(k*(t+q*q));
      g+=term;
      if(abs(term)<tol*abs(g))goto fini;
      }
      fprintf(stderr," Mehler0(y.95 1st) tolerance not
achieved\n");
      fini: g*=2.;
/*printf(" g= %e cos^2 theta/2=%e\n",g,yy);*/
   factor=(t+1.)/(4.*(1.))*yy;sum=0.;
   ss=0.;r=1.;q=1.;
   for(k=1;k<1000;k++)
      {
      ss+=1./r;r+=1.;
      /*printf(" ss=%e\n",ss);*/
      tan=factor*(lt-g+2.*ss);
      sum+=tan;
      /*printf(" sum=%e factor %e latest term %e\n",sum,fac-
tor,tan);*/
      if(abs(tan)<tol*abs(sum))goto fin;
      q+=2.;
      term=t+q*q;
      factor*=term*yy/((k+1.)*4.*(1.+k));
      }
      fprintf(stderr," Mehler0(y.95 2nd) tolerance not
achieved\n");
      fin: return cosh(pi*x)/pi*(lt-g+sum);
   }
sum=1.;t= 4.*x*x;q=1.;term=t+1.;
factor=term/4.*y;
for(k=1;k<1000;k++)
   {sum+=factor;
   if(abs(factor)<tol*abs(sum))goto fin2;
   q+=2.;
   term=t+q*q;
   factor*=term/((k+1.)*4.*(1.+k))*y;
   }
fprintf(stderr," Mehler0 tolerance not achieved\n");
fin2: return sum;
}
```

```
/*
test driver for Legendre functions of chapter 8.
from C Mathematical Function Handbook by Louis Baker
Copyright 1991 by Louis Baker. All rights reserved.
*/
#include <stdio.h>
#include <alloc.h>
#include "cmlib.h"
#include "protom.h"

extern double leg[100];

main()
{
double s2,f21(),q0,q1;
float   x,tau; double z,y,b,p[200]; int
i,l,n,m,d=7,real,rtcode;
double q[200],r[200];

while(1)
   {
   printf(" P: enter nmax, m, x\n");
   scanf("%d%d%le",&n,&m,&z);
   if(n==0 && m==0 && z==0.)break;
   legptable(z,n,m);
   for(i=0;i<=n;i++)printf(" %d %le\n",i,leg[i]);
   }

/* exercise Gaut.c and added routines*/
while(1)
   {
   printf(" P: enter n, mmax, x1 \n");
   scanf("%d%d%e",&n,&m,&x);z=x;
   if(n==0 && m==0 && x==0.)break;
   rtcode=leg1(z,n,m,p);
   if(rtcode)continue;
   for(i=0;i<=m;i++)printf(" %d %le\n",i,p[i]);
   }
while(1)
   {
   printf(" Q:enter nmax, m, x\n");
   scanf("%d%d%e",&n,&m,&x);z=x;
   if(n==0 && m==0 && x==0.)break;
   rtcode=leg2(z,m,n,d,p);
   if(rtcode)continue;
   for(i=0;i<=n;i++)printf(" %d %le\n",i,p[i]);
   }
while(1)
   {
```

```
   printf(" Q:enter n, mmax, x\n");
   scanf("%d%d%e",&n,&m,&x);z=x;
   if(n==0 &&m==0 && x==0.)break;
   rtcode=leg3(z,n,m,d,p);
   if(rtcode)continue;
   for(i=0;i<=m;i++)printf(" %d %le\n",i,p[i]);
   }
while(1)
   {
   printf(" P:enter alpha mmax x\n");
   scanf("%e%d%e",&tau,&m,&x);z=x;y=tau;
   if(tau==0. &&m==0 && x==0.)break;
   rtcode=legend1(z,y,m,d,p);
   if(rtcode)continue;
   for(i=0;i<=m;i++)printf(" %d %le\n",i,p[i]);
   }

while(1)
   {
   printf(" P:enter alpha+nmax m x\n");
   scanf("%e%d%d%e",&tau,&n,&m,&x);z=x;y=tau;
   if(tau==0. && n==0 &&m==0 && x==0.)break;
   rtcode=legend2(z,y,m,n,d,p);
   if(rtcode)continue;
   for(i=0;i<=n;i++)printf(" %d %le\n",i,p[i]);
   }

printf(" toroidal chk Q:\n");
for(i=0;i<10;i++)
   {
   z=1.+(i+1)*.1;
   toroidal(z,0,1,d,p);
   /*y= sqrt((z-1.)/(z+1.));*/
   s2=(2./(z+1.));            y=sqrt(s2);
   tek(0,s2,&q0,&q1);
   q1= z*y*q0-sqrt(2.*(1.+z))*q1;
   printf(
" z %f Q-1/2,Q1/2=%le %le; elliptic I: %le %le \n"
      ,z,p[0],p[1],y*q0,q1);
   }

printf(" toroidal chk\n");
for(i=0;i<10;i++)
   {
   b=1.+(i+1)*.1;
    z= cosh(b);
   toroidal(z,0,1,d,p);
   /*  7.10.1 of Lebedev*/
```

```
   q0= sqrt(pi)*gamma(.5)/gamma(1.)*exp(-
                      .5*b)*f21(.5,.5,1.,exp(-2.*b));
   q1= sqrt(pi)*gamma(1.5)/gamma(2.)*exp(-
1.5*b)*f21(1.5,.5,2.,exp(-2.*b));

   printf(" z %f %le %le Q-1/2,P1/2 ck: %le
%le\n",z,p[0],p[1],q0,q1);
   }

while(1)
   {
   printf(" Q toroidal:enter m nmax x\n");
   scanf("%d%d%e",&m,&n,&x);z=x;y=tau;
   if(m==0 &&n==0 && x==0.)break;
   toroidal(z,m,n,d,p);
   for(i=0;i<=n;i++)printf(" %d %le\n",i,p[i]);
   }
while(1)
   {
   printf(" P toroidal:enter n x\n");
   scanf("%d%e",&n,&x);z=x;
   if(n==0 && x==0.)break;
   printf(" toroidal P=%le\n",Ptoroidal(n,z));
   }

while(1)
   {printf(" enter 1 for  Q(x) 0 Q(ix) -1
stop\n");scanf("%d",&real);
   if(real<0 ) break;
   printf(" enter nu,x for Q\n");scanf("%le%le",&b,&z);
   printf(" x=%f nu=%f %le\n",z,b,qnu(z,b,real));
   }

while(1)
   {
   printf("  conical enter tau, theta\n");
   scanf("%e%e",&tau,&x); z=x;b=tau;
   if(z==0. && b==0.)break;
   printf(" ans=%le theta=%le tau=%le\n",
                      conicalt(z,b),z,b);
   }

printf(" asympt. tau conical ck\n");
for(i=1;i<10;i++)
   {
   /* small ztheta= pi*i/10.;
   z=cos(theta);
   rtcode=conical(z,tau,0,d,p);
   if(rtcode)continue;
```

```
    s2= sin(theta*.5);s2*=s2;
    y= 1. +(4.*tau*tau+1.)/(4.)*s2
     + (4.*tau*tau+1.)*(4.*tau*tau+9.)/(4.*16.)*s2*s2;
    printf(" ans=%le vs %le\n",p[0],y);*/
    b= 2.;
    z=cosh(b);
    tau =10.*i;
    rtcode=conical(z,tau,0,d,p);
    if(rtcode)continue;
    q0=sqrt(2./(pi*tau*sinh(b)))*sin(tau*b+.25*pi);
    printf(" z tau %f %f ans %le %le\n",z,tau,p[0],q0);
    }

while(1)
    {
    printf(" conical:enter tau nmax x\n");
    scanf("%e%d%e",&tau,&n,&x);z=x;y=tau;
    if(tau==0. &&n==0 && x==0.)break;
    rtcode=conical(z,y,n,d,p);
    if(rtcode)continue;
    for(i=0;i<=n;i++)printf(" %d %le\n",i,p[i]);
    }

/* leg.c: Hernden*/
while(1)
    {
    printf(" enter l,m,r=1 real( to quit),x\n");
    scanf("%d%d%d%f",&l,&m,&real,&x);
    if(real<0)break; z=x;
    printf(" %le\n",legendrea(m,l,z,real));
    }
while(1)
    {
    printf(" enter l,m,r=1 real,x0. real to quit\n");
    scanf("%d%d%d%f",&l,&m,&real,&x);
    if(real<0)break; z=x;   qleg(m,l,z,real,r,q);
    for(i=0;i<=l;i++)printf(" %d r=%le q=%le\n",i,r[i],q[i]);
    }
/* leg.c: other */
while(1)
    {
    printf(" plm enter l,m,x real,x\n");
    scanf("%d%d%le",&l,&m,&z);
    if(z>1000.)break;
    printf(" for real x. %le for imag x, m=0:
%le\n",plm(l,m,z),pli(l,z));
    }
while(1)
    {
```

```
   printf(" qlm enter l,m,x real,x\n");
   scanf("%d%d%le",&l,&m,&z);
   if(z>1000.)break;
   printf(" for real x: %le for imag x, m=0:
%le\n",qlm(l,m,z),qli(l,z));
   }
while(1)
   {
   printf(" pmu,nu & qmu,nu: enter mu,nu,x real,x\n");
   scanf("%le%le%le",&y,&b,&z);
   if(z>1000.)break;
   printf(" P,Q: %le %le\n",pmunu(y,b,z),qmunu(y,b,z));
   }

/* Mehler*/
while(1)
   {
   printf(" enter x,z,mm Mehler x1000 to quit\n");
   scanf("%le%le%d",&z,&y,&m);
   if(z>1000.)break;
   printf(" Mehler=%le for z=0: %le\n",Mehler(z,y,m),Meh-
ler0(z,y));
   }

}
```

```
Test Output for Legendre functions
 P: enter nmax, m, x
5 0 3
 0 1.000000e+00
 1 3.000000e+00
 2 1.300000e+01
 3 6.300000e+01
 4 3.210000e+02
 5 1.683000e+03
 P: enter nmax, m, x
5 2 3
 0 2.400000e+01
 1 3.600000e+02
 2 3.720000e+03
 3 3.276000e+04
 4 2.637600e+05
 5 2.004912e+06
 P: enter nmax, m, x
0 0 0 P: enter n, mmax, x1
2 2 3
 0 1.300000e+01
 1 2.545584e+01
 2 2.400000e+01
 P: enter n, mmax, x1
2 1 3
 0 1.300000e+01
 1 2.545584e+01
 P: enter n, mmax, x1
2 0 3
 0 1.300000e+01
 P: enter n, mmax, x1
0 0 0
 Q:enter nmax, m, x
2 2 3
 0 7.500000e-01
 1 2.500000e-01
 2 6.776617e-02
 Q:enter nmax, m, x
0 00 0
 Q:enter n, mmax, x
2 2 3
 0 5.456674e 03
 1 -1.651147e-02
 2 6.776617e-02
 Q:enter n, mmax, x
0 0 0
 P:enter alpha mmax x
2 2 3
 0 1.300000e+01
```

```
 1 2.545584e+01
 2 2.400000e+01
 P:enter alpha mmax x
0 0 0
 P:enter alpha+nmax m x
2 2 2 3
 echo x=3.000000e+00 alpha=2.000000e+00 m=2 n=2
 0 2.400000e+01
 1 3.600000e+02
 2 3.720000e+03
 P:enter alpha+nmax m x
1 2 2 3
 echo x=3.000000e+00 alpha=1.000000e+00 m=2 n=2
 0 0.000000e+00
 1 2.400000e+01
 2 3.600000e+02
 P:enter alpha+nmax m x
0 2 2 3
 echo x=3.000000e+00 alpha=0.000000e+00 m=2 n=2
legend2 zero denominator n=1
 0 0.000000e+00
 1 0.000000e+00
 2 -1.000000e+60
 P:enter alpha+nmax m x
1.e-9 2 2 3
 echo x=3.000000e+00 alpha=1.000000e-09 m=2 n=2
 0 -5.000000e-10
 1 2.500000e-09
 2 2.400000e+01
 P:enter alpha+nmax m x
0 0 0 0
 toroidal chk Q:
 z 1.100000 Q-1/2,Q1/2=2.861193e+00 9.787603e-01;
elliptic I: 2.861193e+00 9.787603e-01
 z 1.200000 Q-1/2,Q1/2=2.500957e+00 6.995548e-01;
elliptic I: 2.500957e+00 6.995548e-01
 z 1.300000 Q-1/2,Q1/2=2.288167e+00 5.536485e-01;
elliptic I: 2.288167e+00 5.536485e-01
 z 1.400000 Q-1/2,Q1/2=2.136572e+00 4.597942e-01;
elliptic I: 2.136572e+00 4.597942e-01
 z 1.500000 Q-1/2,Q1/2=2.018906e+00 3.931751e-01;
elliptic I: 2.018906e+00 3.931751e-01
 z 1.600000 Q-1/2,Q1/2=1.922921e+00 3.430180e-01;
elliptic I: 1.922921e+00 3.430180e-01
 z 1.700000 Q-1/2,Q1/2=1.842030e+00 3.037243e-01;
elliptic I: 1.842030e+00 3.037243e-01
 z 1.800000 Q-1/2,Q1/2=1.772268e+00 2.720402e-01;
elliptic I: 1.772268e+00 2.720402e-01
 z 1.900000 Q-1/2,Q1/2=1.711062e+00 2.459226e-01;
```

```
elliptic I: 1.711062e+00 2.459226e-01
 z 2.000000 Q-1/2,Q1/2=1.656638e+00 2.240143e-01;
elliptic I: 1.656638e+00 2.240143e-01
 toroidal chk
 z 1.668519 1.866143e+00 3.151510e-01 Q-1/2,Q1/2 ck:
1.866143e+00 3.151510e-01
 z 1.810656 1.765376e+00 2.690205e-01 Q-1/2,Q1/2 ck:
1.765376e+00 2.690205e-01
 z 1.970914 1.671850e+00 2.300138e-01 Q-1/2,Q1/2 ck:
1.671850e+00 2.300138e-01
 z 2.150898 1.584633e+00 1.969150e-01 Q-1/2,Q1/2 ck:
1.584633e+00 1.969150e-01
 z 2.352410 1.502990e+00 1.687516e-01 Q-1/2,Q1/2 ck:
1.502990e+00 1.687516e-01
 z 2.577464 1.426333e+00 1.447348e-01 Q-1/2,Q1/2 ck:
1.426333e+00 1.447349e-01
 z 2.828315 1.354182e+00 1.242182e-01 Q-1/2,Q1/2 ck:
1.354182e+00 1.242182e-01
 z 3.107473 1.286138e+00 1.066667e-01 Q-1/2,Q1/2 ck:
1.286138e+00 1.066667e-01
 z 3.417732 1.221865e+00 9.163472e-02 Q-1/2,Q1/2 ck:
1.221865e+00 9.163473e-02
 z 3.762196 1.161075e+00 7.874872e-02 Q-1/2,Q1/2 ck:
1.161075e+00 7.874873e-02
 Q toroidal:enter m nmax x
0 1 2
 0 1.656638e+00
 1 2.240143e-01
 Q toroidal:enter m nmax x
0 0 0
 P toroidal:enter n x
2 3
 toroidal P=6.111339e+00
 P toroidal:enter n x
 P toroidal:enter n x
1 3
 toroidal P=1.597387e+00
 P toroidal:enter n x
0 3
 toroidal P=8.346270e-01
 P toroidal:enter n x
0 2
 toroidal P=9.012864e-01
 P toroidal:enter n x
1 2
 toroidal P=1.329138e+00
 P toroidal:enter n x
3 2 2
 toroidal P=3.243940e+00
```

```
 P toroidal:enter n x
0 0
 enter 1 for  Q(x) 0 Q(ix) -1 stop
1
 enter nu,x for Q
2 3
 x=3.000000 nu=2.000000 5.456674e-03
 enter 1 for  Q(x) 0 Q(ix) -1 stop
2 .5
 enter nu,x for Q
3
 x=3.000000 nu=0.500000 1.128886e-01
 enter 1 for  Q(x) 0 Q(ix) -1 stop
1
 enter nu,x for Q
2 .5
 x=0.500000 nu=2.000000 -1.637326e+00
 enter 1 for  Q(x) 0 Q(ix) -1 stop
0
 enter nu,x for Q
2 .5
 x=0.500000 nu=2.000000 -1.000000e+60
 enter 1 for  Q(x) 0 Q(ix) -1 stop
0
 enter nu,x for Q
2 2
 x=2.000000 nu=2.000000 1.370946e-02
 enter 1 for  Q(x) 0 Q(ix) -1 stop
-1
  conical enter tau, theta
1 1.047197551
 ans=1.392126e+00 theta=1.047198e+00 tau=1.000000e+00
  conical enter tau, theta
0 0
 asympt. tau conical ck
 z tau 3.762196 10.000000 ans 1.243545e-01 1.237575e-01
 z tau 3.762196 20.000000 ans 5.784867e-03 5.178609e-03
 z tau 3.762196 30.000000 ans -6.784803e-02 -6.800041e-02
 z tau 3.762196 40.000000 ans -5.185953e-02 -5.172580e-02
 z tau 3.762196 50.000000 ans 1.476430e-02 1.491309e-02
 z tau 3.762196 60.000000 ans 5.332547e-02 5.334497e-02
 z tau 3.762196 70.000000 ans 2.778192e-02 2.770473e-02
 z tau 3.762196 80.000000 ans -2.498267e-02 -2.504688e-02
 z tau 3.762196 90.000000 ans -4.371557e-02 -4.370652e-02
 conical:enter tau nmax x
10 2 3.762196
 0 1.243544e-01
 1 -5.213910e-01
 2 -1.138484e+01
```

```
 conical:enter tau nmax x
0 0 0
 enter l,m,r=1 real( to quit),x
2 0 1 3
 1.300000e+01
 enter l,m,r=1 real( to quit),x
2 0 1 .5
 -1.250000e-01
 enter l,m,r=1 real( to quit),x
0 0 0 3
 1.000000e+00
 enter l,m,r=1 real( to quit),x
0 2 0 3
 0.000000e+00
 enter l,m,r=1 real( to quit),x
0 0 1 3
 1.000000e+00
 enter l,m,r=1 real( to quit),x
20 0 0 3
 7.713194e+14
 enter l,m,r=1 real( to quit),x
2 0 0 3
 -1.400000e+01
 enter l,m,r=1 real( to quit),x
0 0 -1 0
 enter l,m,r=1 real,x0. real to quit
2 0 1 3
 0 r=0.000000e+00 q=3.465736e-01
 1 r=1.146099e-01 q=3.972077e-02
 2 r=1.373758e-01 q=5.456674e-03
 enter l,m,r=1 real,x0. real to quit
2 0 1 .5
 0 r=0.000000e+00 q=5.493061e-01
 1 r=4.956632e-01 q=2.722708e-01
 2 r=-2.587495e-01 q=-7.044994e-02
 enter l,m,r=1 real,x0. real to quit
2 0 0 3
 0 r=0.000000e+00 q=-3.217506e-01
 1 r=1.079978e-01 q=-3.474834e-02
 2 r=-1.297260e-01 q=4.507762e-03
 enter l,m,r=1 real,x0. real to quit
2 0 0 .5
 0 r=0.000000e+00 q=-1.107149e+00
 1 r=4.032210e-01 q=-4.464256e-01
 2 r=-4.900147e-01 q=2.187551e-01
 enter l,m,r=1 real,x0. real to quit
0 0 -1 0
 plm enter l,m,x real,x
2 0 3
```

```
 for real x: 1.300000e+01 for imag x, m=0: 1.400000e+01
 plm enter l,m,x real,x
2 0 .5
 for real x: -1.250000e-01 for imag x, m=0: 8.750001e-01
 plm enter l,m,x real,x
0 0 2000
 qlm enter l,m,x real,x
2 0 3
 for real x: -3.411169e-01 for imag x, m=0: 4.507762e-03
 qlm enter l,m,x real,x
2 0 .5
 for real x: -8.186633e-01 for imag x, m=0: 2.187552e-01
 qlm enter l,m,x real,x
0 0 2000
 pnu & qnu: enter nu,x real,x
1 3
 gamma: arg 0 or neg. integer=-1.000000e+00
 P,Q: 3.000000e+00 3.972078e-02
 pnu & qnu: enter nu,x real,x
1 .5
 P,Q: 5.000000e-01 -7.253469e-01
 pnu & qnu: enter nu,x real,x
0 3
 gamma: arg 0 or neg. integer=-0.000000e+00
 P,Q: 1.000000e+00 3.465736e-01
 pnu & qnu: enter nu,x real,x
0 .5
 P,Q: 1.000000e+00 1.098612e+00
 pnu & qnu: enter nu,x real,x
0 2000
 enter x,z,mm Mehler x1000 to quit
1 .5 0
 Mehler=1.392126e+00 for m=0: 1.392126e+00
 enter x,z,mm Mehler x1000 to quit
2000 2000 2000
```

Chapter 9

Bessel Functions

Abramowitz and Stegun devote four chapters to Bessel functions, more than any other function. This is in accord with my experience that the Bessel function is the most used function of mathematical physics. We will follow their segregation of programs to chapters, with Chapter 9 for general fuctions, Chapter 10 for those of fractional order, Chapter 11 for integrals of Bessel functions, and Chapter 12 for Struve and Anger-Weber functions. However, it seems appropriate to provide all necessary definitions here, so that reference need be made only to one chapter to determine the most relevant facts.

The Bessel functions may be defined as solutions of a family of differential equations, or by integrals. The Bessel function $J_\nu(z)$ is the solution of the differential equation $z\dfrac{d^2w}{dz^2} + z\dfrac{dw}{dz} + (z^2 - \nu^2)\,w = 0$ which is regular at z = 0. It may also be defined as the integral $J_\nu(z) = \dfrac{1}{\pi}\displaystyle\int_0^\pi \cos(z \sin\theta - \nu\theta)\,d\theta - \dfrac{\sin(\nu\pi)}{\pi}\displaystyle\int_0^\infty e^{-z \sinh t - \nu t}\,dt$. Note that the last term vanishes for integral values of ν, which is called the order of the function. The other solution of the equation is called a Neumann function (or Weber function according to Abramowitz and Stegun) and denoted N_ν or Y_ν. In wave propagation problems, the Hankel functions $H^{(1)} = J + i\,Y$ and $H^{(2)} = J - i\,Y$ often arise.

The related equation $z\dfrac{d^2w}{dz^2} + z\dfrac{dw}{dz} + (z^2 + \nu^2)\,w = 0$ could be written as a Bessel function with imaginary ν. The equation $z\dfrac{d^2w}{dz^2} + z\dfrac{dw}{dz} - (z^2 + \nu^2)\,w = 0$ could be treated as having solutions of the form $J(iz)$ or $N(iz)$. The solutions are usually denoted as $I_\nu(z)$ and

$K_\nu(z)$, and are defined (relative to $J(iz)$ and $N(iz)$) so that they take real values.

The solutions of $z\frac{d^2w}{dz^2}+z\frac{dw}{dz}+(-z^2+\nu^2)\,w=0$ are sometimes called wedge functions, and may be treated as $I_{i\nu}(z)$ or $K_{i\nu}(z)$. The general equation of the form $x^2y''+(1-2a)\,xy'+[b^2c^2x^{2c}+(a^2-c^2p^2)\,]\,y=0$ has as its solution $y=x^a\,[C_1J_p(b\,x^c)+C_2Y_p(b\,x^c)\,]$. (See page 147 of Jahnke and Emde for many more equations solvable by means of Bessel functions.) One special case of interest is $y''-xy=0$ whose solutions are Bessel functions of order one third (a = 1/2, p = 1/3, c = 3/2, b = 2/3). The Airy functions are closely related to these functions (see Chapter 10).

Bessel functions of complex arguments are of interest. The square roots of i are $\pm(1+i)/\sqrt{2}$, and those of $-i$ are $\pm(1-i)/\sqrt{2}$. In electromagnetic problems involving a harmonic or sinusoidal time dependence $e^{i\omega t}$, Bessel functions of arguments of the form of a real number multiplied by the square root of i can arise. A typical example is the diffusion of such an AC current into a resistive wire. The current tends to stay on the surface of the wire—the "skin depth" effect. Such Bessel functions are called Kelvin functions, and are typically written in the form $ber_\nu(x)+i\,bei_\nu(x)$ for $J_\nu(x\,e^{3\pi i/4})$ and $ker_\nu(x)+i\,kei_\nu(x)$ for $e^{-\nu\pi i/2}\,K_\nu(x\,e^{\pi i/4})$. Note that the exponentials within the Bessel function arguments are square roots of the imaginary unit. In applying these functions, there is an important caveat. Some expressions, such as for the impedance of such a wire, involve the derivative of the Bessel function with respect to x. Note that this is not $ber'+i\,bei'$. The impedance is generally a complex number, thereby containing both resistive (real) and reactive (imaginary) terms. This is discussed, for example, in Ramo et al. The impedance of such a wire is $Z=\frac{-T}{2\pi a\sigma}\frac{J_0(Ta)}{J_0'(Ta)}$, where a is the wire radius and $T=i^{-1/2}\frac{\sqrt{2}}{\delta}$ and δ is the skin depth.

Struve Functions

Following Watson, define the operator: $\nabla_\nu=z^2\frac{d^2}{dz^2}+z\frac{d}{dz}+z^2-\nu^2$. Then we can define the Struve function $\mathbf{H}_\nu$ as the inhomogeneous solution to the equation $\nabla_\nu \boldsymbol{H}=4\frac{(z/2)^{\nu+1}}{\Gamma(\nu+\frac{1}{2})\,\Gamma(\frac{1}{2})}$ and the modified Struve function $\mathbf{L}_\nu$ by a similar relationship for imaginary argument, $\boldsymbol{L}_\nu=-i\,e^{-i\pi\nu/2}\boldsymbol{H}_\nu(iz)$. It is not at all obvious from the definition why one might be interested in such functions. The Struve functions are of importance principally in evaluating the integrals of Bessel functions, as will be discussed below, in Chapter 11, and in more detail in Chapter 12.

Anger and Weber Functions

The Anger function $\boldsymbol{J}_\nu$ and Weber function $\boldsymbol{E}_\nu$ (also called the Lommel-Weber function Ω_ν) can be defined via $\nabla_\nu \boldsymbol{J}_\nu = \frac{(z-\nu)}{\pi} \sin\nu\pi$ and $\nabla_\nu \boldsymbol{E}_\nu = -\frac{(z+\nu)}{\pi} - \frac{(z-\nu)}{\pi} \cos\nu\pi$ (see Magnus and Oberhettinger). A more natural definition for these related functions will be given in Chapter 12. Note that when ν is an integer, the sine term vanishes and Anger's function reduces to the Bessel function J_ν. These functions (and their integral) show up, for example, in problems involving loop antennas. See Chapter 12 for more details.

Relationship to Confluent Hypergeometric Function

As will be discussed in Chapter 13, the Bessel functions can be expressed in terms of the Confluent Hypergeometric functions. This will be exploited to provide functions capable of evaluating the Bessel functions for arbitrary complex arguments. This relationship cuts both ways. In a program based upon one of Temme, discussed in Chapter 13, the Confluent Hypergeometric function U can be evaluated in some parameter regimes by evaluating the modified Bessel function K_ν. (I suspect he did this because he had previously developed a program for evaluating the Bessel function.)

Derivatives

As with the Legendre functions of the previous chapter, recurrences may be used to determine derivatives. The formulae are given in Abramowitz and Stegun 9.1.27, and include $F_\nu{}' = .5(F_{\nu-1} - F_{\nu+1})$.

Other Related Functions

There are other functions that might be discussed here, such as the Neumann polynomials $O_n(x)$, or the Lommel functions $U(x,y)$, $S_{\mu,\nu}(x)$ and $s_{\mu,\nu}(x)$. For example, $\nabla_\nu s_{\mu\,\nu} = z^{\mu+1}$. These functions are discussed in a number of books, including Watson and the Bateman manuscript project (Erdelyi et al.). They do not seem to be of much interest, however. For example, Lommel used the U functions in studies of diffraction by a knife edge. Subsequent treatments, such as the analysis by Sommerfeld, have made those studies obsolete.

Zeros of Bessel Functions

When $\nu \geq -1$, the zeros of J_ν are all real. If ν is real, there are an infinite number of zeros for $J_\nu, J_\nu', Y_\nu, Y_\nu'$. Generally, only real roots are of interest for such applications. These zeros are often of use in eigenfunction expansions in terms of Bessel function. We provide a C version of a program, due to Temme, which finds zeros of these four functions. Zeros of other functions, or combinations, may be found by defining a function to evaluate to the quantity whose zero is desired, and using the root-finding methods of *C Tools*, the Newton-Raphson, or Muller methods. In fact, Temme uses a higher-order version of Newton's method specialized for the case of interest.

Applications

F. W. Bessel was in fact concerned with solving the Kepler problem, i. e., the determination of orbits in a graviational field. This involved a series expansion in coefficients which were defined by the integral for J_n for integral n. See Bowman's book for a discussion of this application as well as Watson for a full history.

Most commonly, Bessel functions appear in problems involving the Laplacian operator in cylindrical or spherical coordinates. This includes the Helmholtz version of the wave equation, as well as Poisson's equation for the electrostatic potential. Radial spheroidal wave functions (see Chapter 21) involve series expansions in spherical Bessel functions.

Methods

Bessel functions of orders differing by integers may be found by recurrence relations. This enables tables to be formed of such sequences. A number of programs contained here develop such tables, in an array **double^bessela[100]** which is treated as a global variable similar to the table of Legendre functions developed in the previous chapter. One of these programs will be used in Chapter 21. As discussed in Chapter 5, some care must be used in applying recurrences stably.

The routines for computing Bessel functions with complex arguments and integral orders are based upon **bessel** by R. C. Lindberg.

Chapter 13 contains routines for determining Bessel functions for general complex orders and arguments, and are based upon representing the Bessel functions in terms of the Confluent Hypergeometric function.

Series and asymptotic expansions are used in some functions. For rapid evalution requiring only moderate precision, rational approximations due to Hastings and given in Abramowitz and Stegun are presented.

Due to the intimate relationships between the functions of these four chapters, it was simplest to use a single test driver to exercise all of these functions.

References

F. W. Bowman, *Introduction to Bessel Functions* (N. Y.: Dover, 1965).

Higher Transcendental Functions, (Bateman Manuscript Project) (A. Erdelyi, ed.) (N. Y.: McGraw-Hill, 1953).

E. Janke and F. Emde, *Tables of Functions* (N. Y.: Dover, 1945).

R. C. Lindberg, Math Note 1 of Phillips, Lab, Kirtland AFB, Oct. 15, 1966. (Available through DTIC, the Defense Technical Information Center).

W. Magnus & F. Oberhettinger, *Formulas and Theorems for the Functions of Mathematical Physics* (N. Y.: Chelsea Publishing, 1972).

S. Ramo, J. R. Whinnery, T. van Duzer, *Fields and Waves in Communications Electronics*, 2nd ed. (N. Y.: J. Wiley, 1984).

N. M. Temme, *J. Comp. Physics*, **19**, 324, 1975.

N. M. Temme, *J. Comp. Physics*, **32**, 270, 1979.

G. N. Watson, *Treatise on Bessel Functions* (Cambridge: University Press, 1922).

```
/*
Bessel functions for complex arguments
from C Mathematical Function Handbook by Louis Baker
Copyright 1991 by Louis Baker. All rights reserved.

bessel returns bessel functions and derivatives for complex
arguments,
   integer orders.
jint(int n, double z) Jn(z)
ibess   In(z) complex z integer n
kbess   Kn(z) complex z integer n
kelvin   kelvin functions of order n, real argument

service routines (not intended for direct user call):
forward   forward recursion in order
backward backward recursion in order
cbess   lowest order functions calculated

based upon FORTRAN subroutine BESSEL by R. C. Lindberg
published in Math Note 1 by Air Force Weapons Lab.
Kirtland AFB, NM (now Phillips Lab.)

*/

#include <stdlib.h>
#include <stdio.h>
#include "cmlib.h"
#include "protom.h"

static unsigned int btm,top;

int Bessel( int nn,struct complex *z,struct complex *j,
   struct complex *y,
   struct complex *h2,struct complex *jprime,
   struct complex *yprime,struct complex *h2prime)
{int ivalck,rv;
rv=bessel(nn,z,j,y,h2,jprime,yprime,h2prime,&ivalck);
return ivalck;
}

forward(z,ratio,idim,r1) int idim; struct complex
*z,*ratio,*r1;
{
struct complex p,twooz,two,c1;
int i,imax;
two.x=2.;two.y=0.;
c1.x=1.;c1.y=0.;
imax=idim-1;
CDIV(twooz, two,(*z));
```

```
CASSN((ratio[0]),r1);
for (i=0;i<imax;i++)
   {
/*printf(" i,imax=%d %d\n",i,imax);
if( &(ratio[i])>top)
printf(" femory top %x %x %d\n",ratio[i],top,i);
if( &(ratio[i+1])>top)
printf(" fmem+1 top %x %x %d\n",ratio[i],top,i);
if( &(ratio[i])<btm)
printf(" femory btm %x %x %d\n",ratio[i],btm,i);
if( &(ratio[i+1])<btm)
printf(" fem+1 btm %x %x %d\n",ratio[i],btm,i);
*/
   CMULT(p,(ratio[i]),twooz );
   CTREAL(p,p,(double)(i+1));
   CSUB(p,p,c1);
   CDIV((ratio[i+1]),p,(ratio[i]));
   }
return 0;
}

#define limit 1.e-8
#define big   ( - ( errorcode ) )

backward(z,ratio,idim) int idim; struct complex *z,*ratio;
{
struct complex p,denom,twooz,two,c1;
int j,i;
two.x=2.;two.y=0.;
c1.x=1.;c1.y=0.;
CDIV(twooz, two,(*z) );
for (j=0;j<idim;j++)
   {CMPLX(ratio[j],0.,0.);}
CTREAL(denom,*z,.5/(idim));
CLET((ratio[idim-1]),denom);
for(i=idim-2;i>=0;i--)
   {
/*
printf(" backward: i=%d \n",i);
if( &(ratio[i])>top)
printf(" bemory top %x %x %d\n",ratio[i],top,i);
if( &(ratio[i+1])>top)
printf(" bmem+1 top %x %x %d\n",ratio[i],top,i);
if( &(ratio[i])<btm)
printf(" bemory btm %x %x %d\n",ratio[i],btm,i);
if( &(ratio[i+1])<btm)
printf(" bmem+1 btm %x %x %d\n",ratio[i],btm,i);
*/
   CTREAL(p,twooz, (double)(i+1) );
```

```
   CSUB(denom ,p ,ratio[i+1]);
   if( cabs(denom)>limit)
      {
      CDIV((ratio[i]),c1,denom);
      }
   else
      {
      CMPLX((ratio[i]),big,0. );
      }
   }
return 0;
}

bessel(nn,z,j,y,h2,jprime,yprime,h2prime,ivalck)
struct complex *z,*j,*y,*h2,*jprime,*yprime,*h2prime; int
nn,*ivalck;
{
struct complex
p,q,ci,c1,c0,cb,jz,j1,yz,y1,hz,h1,r1,aux1,aux2;
struct complex *b,*fy,*fh,yzadd,jzadd,hzadd,noverz;
/*struct complex b[1000];*/
int i,iret,check,idim,n;
n=nn;
CMPLX(ci,0.,1.);
CMPLX(c0,0.,0.);
CMPLX(c1,1.,0.);
/*CMPLX(cb,1.e10,0.);*/
CMPLX(cb, abs(errorcode) ,0.);
iret=0; *ivalck=0;
if(n<0)
   {
   n=-n;
   iret=1;
   }
if(n<=1)
   {
   cbess(z,&jz,&j1,&yz,&y1,&hz,&h1,&check);
   if(check)*ivalck=1;
   if(n==1)
      {
      CSET(j,j1);
      CSET(y,y1);
      CSET(h2,h1);
      if(cabs(*z)!=0.)
         {
         CDIV(p,c1,*z);
         CMULT(q,p,j1);
         CSUB(*jprime,jz,q);
         CMULT(q,p,y1);
```

```
          CSUB(*yprime,yz,q);
          CMULT(q,p,h1);
          CSUB(*h2prime,hz,q);
          if(iret)
             {
             if( !(n-((n>>1)<<1)) )return *ivalck;
             CTREAL((*j),(*j),-1.);
             CTREAL((*y),(*y),-1.);
             CTREAL((*h2),(*h2),-1.);
             CTREAL((*jprime),(*jprime),-1.);
             CTREAL((*yprime),(*yprime),-1.);
             CTREAL((*h2prime),(*h2prime),-1.);
             }
          return *ivalck;
          }/* z=0*/
       CMPLX(*jprime,0.,0.);
       CMPLX(*yprime,0.,0.);
       CMPLX(*h2prime,0.,0.);
       return *ivalck;
       }
    /*n=0*/
    CSET(j,jz);
    CSET(y,yz);
    CSET(h2,hz);
    CSUB(*jprime,c0,j1);
    CSUB(*yprime,c0,y1);
    CSUB(*h2prime,c0,h1);
    return *ivalck;
    }
if(cabs(*z)==0.)
    {
    CSET(j,c0);
    CSET(jprime,c0);
    CSET(y,cb);CTREAL(*y,*y,-1.);
    CSET(h2,cb);
    CSET(yprime,cb);
    CSET(h2prime,cb);CTREAL(*h2prime,*h2prime,-1.)
    /* *ivalck=1; default to 0 */
    return *ivalck;
    }
/*else*/
CDIV(p,c1,*z);
CTREAL(noverz,p,((double)n));
cbess(z,&jz,&j1,&yz,&y1,&hz,&h1,&check);
CSET(j,jz);
/* set up via malloc b array of idim length*/
idim=20*n;
b= malloc( sizeof( struct complex) *idim+50*8);
if(!b)
```

```
    {
    fprintf(stderr,
      " bessel: malloc memory error backward\n");
    return (*ivalck=2);
    }
/*
btm=b;
top=btm+idim;
*/
backward(z,b,idim);
for(i=0;i<n;i++)
    {
    CMULT(p,*j,(b[i]));
    CSET(j,p);
    }
CSUB(q,noverz,(b[n]));
CMULT((*jprime),q,(*j));
CDIV(r1,y1,yz);
idim=n+2;
fy= malloc( sizeof(struct complex) *idim+50*8);
/*
btm=fy;
top=btm+idim;
*/
if(!fy)
    {
    fprintf(stderr,
       " bessel: malloc memory error forward\n");
    return (*ivalck=3);
    }
forward(z,fy,idim,&r1);
CLET((*y),yz);
for(i=0;i<n;i++)
    {
    CMULT(p,(*y),(fy[i]));
    CSET(y,p);
    }
CSUB(q,noverz,fy[n]);
CMULT(*yprime,q,*y);
CDIV(r1,y1,yz);
CMULT(jzadd,*j,b[n]);
CMULT(yzadd,*y,fy[n]);
if( (*z).y ==0.)
    {
    CMULT(q,ci,*y);
    CSUB(*h2,*j,q);
    CMULT(q,yz,fy[n]);
    CMULT(aux2,q,ci);
    CMULT(p,jz,b[n]);
```

```
    CSUB(q,p,aux2);
    CMULT(aux1,noverz,*h2);
    CSUB((*h2prime),aux1,q);
    CSUB(hzadd,p,aux2);
    free(b);free(fy);
    }
else
    {
    CDIV(r1,h1,hz);
    idim=n+2;
    fh= malloc( sizeof(struct complex) *idim+8*50);
    if(!fh)
        {
        fprintf(stderr," bessel: memory error forward2\n");
        return (*ivalck=4);
        }
/*
btm=fh;
top=btm+idim;
*/
    forward(z,fh,idim,&r1);
    CSET(h2,hz);
    for(i=0;i<n;i++)
        {
        CMULT(q,*h2,fh[i]);
        CSET(h2,q);
        }
    CMULT(p,noverz,(*h2));
    CMULT(q,(*h2),fh[n]);
    CSUB((*h2prime),p,q);
    CMULT(hzadd,(*h2),fh[n]);
    free(fh);
    if(iret)
        {
        /*printf(" processing for negative n\n");*/
        if( !(n-((n>>1)<<1)) )return 0;
        CTREAL((*j),(*j),-1.);
        CTREAL((*y),(*y),-1.);
        CTREAL((*h2),(*h2),-1.);
        CADD(q,noverz,b[n]);
        CMULT((*jprime),q,(*j));
        CADD(q,noverz,fy[n]);
        CMULT((*yprime),q,(*y));
        CMULT(q,ci,(*yprime));
        CSUB((*h2prime),(*j),q);
        }
/*printf(" fini bessel\n");*/
    }
/* diff eq. chk*/
```

```
return *ivalck;
}

struct complex wronsk;

cbess(z,j0,j1,y0,y1,h20,h21,ivchk)
struct complex *z,*j0,*j1,*y0,*y1,*h20,*h21;int *ivchk;
{
struct complex
p,q,zsq,fact,zfact,j0add,j1add,ez,aux1,aux2,aux,cosp,sinp,
cii,c1,ci;
double skinv, fk,fn,fkfact,fkfi,tol=1.e-8,u,tolz=1.e-
8,tolw=1.e-8;
int phase;
/*printc(z);printf(" = z entered cbess\n");*/
*ivchk=0;
CMPLX(cii,1.,1.);
CMPLX(c1,1.,0.);
CMPLX(ci,0.,1.);
if( cabs(*z)<= 10.)
    {
    CMPLX(*j0,1.,0.);
    CMPLX(*j1,1.,0.);
    CMPLX(*y0,0.,0.);
    CMPLX(*y1,1.,0.);
    CMULT(p,*z,*z);
    CTREAL(zsq,p,-.25);
    fk=1.;
    fkfact=1.;
    CMPLX(zfact,1.,0.);
    skinv=1.;
    do
        {/*series*/
        CMULT(p,zfact,zsq);
        CLET(zfact,p);
        fkfi=1./fkfact;
        CTREAL(fact,zfact,fkfi);
        CTREAL(j0add,fact,fkfi);
        fk+=1.;
        fkfact*=fk;
        fkfi=1./fkfact;
        CTREAL(j1add,fact,fkfi);
        CADD(*j0,*j0,j0add);
        CADD(*j1,*j1,j1add);
        CTREAL(p,j0add,skinv);
        CADD(*y0,*y0,p);
        CTREAL(p,j1add, (skinv+skinv+1./fk));
        CADD(*y1,*y1,p);
        skinv+=1./fk;
```

```
      }while(cabs(j1add)>cabs(*j0)*tol ||
cabs(j1add)>cabs(*j1)*tol);
   CMULT(p,*j1,*z);
   CTREAL(*j1,p,.5);
   /*printc(j0);printc(j1);
    printf(" j0, j1 after series\n");*/
   if(cabs(*z)< tolz)
      {
      CMPLX(*y0,-big,0.)
      CMPLX(*y1,-big,0.);
      CMPLX(*h20,big,0.);
      CMPLX(*h21,big,0.);
      *ivchk=0;
      return 0;
      }

   CTREAL(p,*z,.5);
   clog(&p,&q);q.x+=.5772156649;
   fkfi=1./1.570796326795;
   CMULT(p,q,*j0);
   CSUB(*y0,p,*y0);
   CTREAL(*y0,*y0,fkfi);
   CMULT(p,q,*j1);
   CMULT(aux1,*y1,zsq);
   CSUB(aux2,c1,aux1);
   CDIV(aux1,aux2,*z);
   CSUB(q,p,aux1);
   CTREAL(*y1,q,fkfi);
   CMULT(aux1,ci,*y0);
   CSUB(*h20,*j0,aux1);
   CMULT(aux1,ci,*y1);
   CSUB(*h21,*j1,aux1);

   goto wronskian;
   }
/*else*/
if( abs(z->y)<1.e-9 && z->x < 0.)
   {
   phase=1;
   z->x = -(z->x);
   }
else
   phase=0;
/* above added to handle phase= pi, ie z real <0 */
CTREAL(ez,*z,8.);
CTREAL(fact,*z,pi);
csqrt(&fact,&aux);
CDIV(fact,c1,aux);
ctrig(z,&aux1,&aux2);
```

```
CMULT(cosp,aux1,fact);
CMULT(sinp,aux2,fact);
CMULT(aux1,*z,ci);
CTREAL(aux1,aux1,-1.);
cexp(&aux1,&aux);
CMULT(aux1,aux,fact);
CMULT(zfact,aux1,cii);
u=0.;
retry:
fn=1.;
fk=1.;
CMPLX(p,1.,0.);
CMPLX(aux, (u-1.),0.);
CDIV(q,aux,ez);
CLET(fact,q);
do
   {
   fn+=2.;
   fk+=1.;
   CTREAL(aux,fact, -(u-fn*fn)/fk);
   CDIV(fact,aux,ez);
   CADD(p,p,fact);
   fn+=2.;
   fk+=1.;
   CTREAL(aux,fact, (u-fn*fn)/fk);
   CDIV(fact,aux,ez);
   CADD(q,q,fact);
   }while(fk<21. && cabs(fact)>cabs(q)*tol);
if( u <=0.)
   {
   CADD(aux1,p,q);
   CSUB(aux2,p,q);
   CMULT(aux,aux1,cosp);
   CMULT(fact,aux2,sinp);
   CADD(*j0,aux,fact);
   CMULT(aux,aux1,sinp);
   CMULT(fact,aux2,cosp);
   CSUB(*y0,aux,fact);
   CMULT(aux,ci,q);
   CSUB(aux,p,aux);
   CMULT(*h20,aux,zfact);
   u=4.;
   goto retry;
   }
CADD(aux1,p,q);
CSUB(aux2,p,q);
CMULT(aux,aux1,sinp);
CMULT(fact,aux2,cosp);
CSUB(*j1,aux,fact);
```

```
CMULT(aux,aux1,cosp);
CMULT(fact,aux2,sinp);
CADD(*y1,aux,fact);
CTREAL(*y1,*y1,-1.);
CMULT(aux,ci,q);
CADD(aux,p,aux);
CMULT(*h21,aux,zfact);
if(phase)
    {
    z->x = -(z->x);
    CMULT(p,*j0,ci);
    CTREAL(p,p,2.);
    CADD( *y0,*y0,p);
    CMULT(p,*y0,ci);
    CSUB(*h20,*j0,p);
    CTREAL(*j1,*j1,-1.);
    CMULT(p,*j1,ci);
    CTREAL(p,p,2.);
    CSUB(*y1,p,*y1);
    CMULT(p,*y1,ci);
    CSUB(*h21,*j1,p);
    }
wronskian:
/*wronskian*/
if( cabs(*z)<tolz) return 0;
CDIV(aux,c1,*z);
CTREAL(aux,aux,2./3.14159265358979);
CMULT(p,*j1,*y0);
CMULT(q,*j0,*y1);
CADD(q,q,aux);
CDIV(wronsk,p,q);
CSUB(wronsk,wronsk,c1);/* should be zero*/
if(cabs(wronsk)>tolw) *ivchk=10;
return *ivchk;
}


ibess(z,i,n) struct complex *z,*i;int n;
{
struct complex ci,j,zz,dummy,mult;
double theta,argmt();   int ck;
CMPLX(ci,0.,1.);
theta=argmt(z->y,z->x);
CMULT(zz,(*z),ci);
bessel(n,&zz,&j,&dummy,&dummy,&dummy,&dummy,&dummy,&ck);
if(ck)fprintf(stderr," ibess j= %le %le
ck=%d\n",j.x,j.y,ck);
if(ck || abs(j.x)==abs(errorcode))
    {
```

```
    i->x=i->y=errorcode;
    return 1;
    }
CSET(i,j);
if(theta <= pi*.5 ||theta> pi)
    {
    CTREAL(dummy,ci, -pi*.5*n);
    cexp(&dummy,&mult);
    CMULT(*i,*i,mult);
    return 0;
    }
/*else*/
CTREAL(dummy,ci, pi*1.5*n);
cexp(&dummy,&mult);
CMULT(*i,*i,mult);
return 0;

}

kbess(z,k,n) struct complex *z,*k;int n;
{
struct complex ci,j,y,h1,h2,zz,mult,dummy;
double theta,argmt();   int ck;
CMPLX(ci,0.,1.);
/*printf("entered kbess %d\n",n);*/
theta=argmt(z->y,z->x);
if(theta <= pi*.5 ||theta> pi)
    {
    CMULT(zz,(*z),ci);
    /*printf(" calling bessel\n");*/
    bessel(n,&zz,&j,&y,&h2,&dummy,&dummy,&dummy,&ck);
    /*printf(" leaving bessel y=%le %le\n",y.x,y.y);*/
    if(ck || abs(y.x)==abs(errorcode))
        {
        k->x=k->y=errorcode;
        return 1;
        }
    CMULT(dummy,ci,y);
    CADD(h1,j,dummy);
    CTREAL(dummy,ci, pi*.5*n);
    cexp(&dummy,&mult);
    CMULT(dummy,h1,mult);
    CMULT(*k,dummy,ci);
    CTREAL(*k,*k, pi*.5);
    /*printf("leaving kbess\n");*/
    return 0;
    }
/*else*/
CMULT(zz,(*z),ci);
```

```
CTREAL(zz,zz,-1.);
bessel(n,&zz,&j,&y,&h2,&dummy,&dummy,&dummy,&ck);
if( ck || abs(h2.x)==abs(errorcode))
    {
    k->x=k->y=errorcode;
    return 1;
    }
CMULT(*k,h2,ci);
CTREAL(dummy,ci, -pi*.5*n);
cexp(&dummy,&mult);
CMULT(dummy,h2,mult);
CMULT(*k,dummy,ci);
CTREAL(*k,*k,-pi*.5);
return 0;
}

double jint(n,z) double z;int n;
{
struct complex x,dummy,ans;
int ck;
x.x=z;x.y=0.;
bessel(n,&x,&ans,&dummy,&dummy,&dummy,&dummy,&dummy,&ck);
return ans.x;
}

kelvin(n,x,be,ke) double x; struct complex *be,*ke;int n;
{
struct complex mult,h2,dummy,ans,ci,y,coeff,h1;
int ck;
/*CMPLX(mult,0., .75*pi);
cexp(&mult,&coeff);
printf(" exp 3/4pii=");printc(&coeff);printf("\n");
*/
CMPLX(coeff,-.707106781,.707106781);
CMPLX(ci,0.,1.);
CTREAL(ans ,coeff,x);
bessel(n,&ans,be,&y,&h2,&dummy,&dummy,&dummy,&ck);
if( ck || abs(y.x)==abs(errorcode))
    {
    be->x=be->y=ke->x=ke->y=errorcode;
    return 1;
    }
CMULT(dummy,ci,y);
CADD(h1,(*be),dummy);
CMULT(dummy,ci,h1);
CTREAL((*ke),dummy,pi*.5);
return 0;
}
```

```
/*
Bessel functions: rational approximations
from C Mathematical Function Handbook by Louis Baker
Copyright 1991 by Louis Baker. All rights reserved.

limit   error magnitudes:  |x|<=3     |x|>3
j0                           5e-8       1.6e-8
y0                         1.4e-8     1.6e-8
j1                         1.3e-8     1.1e-8
y1                         1.1e-7     1.1e-8

limit   error magnitudes:  |x|<=3.75  |x|>3.75
i0                           1.6e-7    1.9e-7
i1                         8.e-9     2.2e-7

limit   error magnitudes:   |x|<=2     |x|>2
k0                         1.e-8     1.9e-7
k1                           8.e-9     2.2e-7
be,ke kelvin functions and derivatives, 0th order.
limit   error magnitudes:  |x|<=8.     |x|>8
ber                        1.e-9      3.e-7
bei                        1.e-9      3.e-7
ker                        1.e-8      1.e-7
kei                        3.e-9      1.e-7
ber'                       2.1e-8     3.e-7
bei'                       7.e-8      3.e-7
ker'                       8.e-8      2.e-7
kei'                       7.e-8      2.e-7

*/

#include "cmlib.h"
#include "protom.h"

double j0(x) double x;
{
double t,cos(),sqrt(),f,y,bj;
if(x<3.)
   {
   y=(x*.33333333);y=y*y;
   bj= (((((.00021*y-.0039444)*y+.0444479)*y-.3163866)*y
        +1.2656208)*y-2.2499997)*y+1.;
   return(bj);
   }
y=3./x;
if(x<1.e6)
   {
   f=(((((.00014476*y-.00072805)*y+.00137237)*y-.00009512)*y
     -.00552740)*y-.00000077)*y+.79788456;
```

```
    t=(((((.00013558*y-.00029333)*y-.00054125)*y +
        .00262573 )*y
      -.00003954)*y-.04166397)*y-.78539816+x;
    bj=f*cos(t)/sqrt(x);
    return(bj);
    }
    return(0.);
    }

double y0(x) double x;
{
double f,t,y,log(),sin(),sqrt(),j0(),by;
if(x<3. && x>=0.)
    {
    y=(x*.333333333);y=y*y;
    by=(((((-.00024846*y+.00427916)*y-
.04261214)*y+.25300117)*y
      -.74350384)*y+.60559366)*y+.36746691
      +j0(x)*log(x*.5)*.636619772;
    return(by);
    }
if(x>=3.)
    {
    y=3./x;
    if(x> 1.e6)return(0.);
    f=(((((.00014476*y-.00072805)*y+.00137237)* y
       -.00009512)*y
       -.00552740)*y-.00000077)*y+.79788456;
    t=(((((.00013558*y-.00029333)*y
       -.00054125)*y+.00262573)*y
       -.00003954)*y-.04166397)*y-.78539816+x;
    return(f*sin(t)/sqrt(x));
    }
return(-1.);
}

double j1(x)double x;
{
double y,t,f,sqrt(),cos(),bj;
if(x<=3. && x>0.)
    {
    y=(x*.333333333);y=y*y;
    bj= ( (((((.00001109*y-.00031761)*y+.00443319)*y
       -.03954289)*y
       +.21093573)*y .56249985)*y+.5)*x;
    return(bj);
    }
if(x>3.)
    {
```

```
   if(x>1.e6)return(0.);
   y=3./x;
   f=(((((-.00020033*y+.00113653)*y
      -.00249511)*y+.00017105)*y
      +.01659667)*y+.00000156)*y+.79788456;
   t=(((((-.00029166*y+.00079824)*y+.00074348)*y
      -.00637879)*y
      +.0000565)*y+.12499612)*y-2.35619449+x;
   return(f*cos(t)/sqrt(x));
   }
return(0.);
}

double y1(x) double x;
{
double y,j1(),log(),sin(),t,f,by;
if(x<3. && x>0.)
   {
   y=(x*.33333333);y=y*y;
   by=((((((.0027873*y-.0400976)*y+.3123951)*y-1.3164827)*y
     +2.1682709)*y+.2212091)*y-.6366198)/x
      +j1(x)*log(x*.5)*.636619772;
   return(by);
   }
y=3./x;
if(x>1.e6)return(0.);
   f=(((((-.00020033*y+.00113653)*y-
.00249511)*y+.00017105)*y
     +.01659667)*y+.00000156)*y+.79788456;
   t=(((((-.00029166*y+.00079824)*y+.00074348)*y-
.00637879)*y
     +.0000565)*y+.12499612)*y-2.35619449+x;
   return(f*sin(t)/sqrt(x));
}



double i0(x) double x;
{
double t,exp(),sqrt(),y;
if(x<3.75)
   {
   t=(x/3.75);t=t*t;
   y=((((((.0045813*t+.0360768)*t+.2659732)*t+1.2067492)
     *t+3.0899424)*t+3.5156229)*t+1.);
   return(y);
   }
t=3.75/x;
   y=((((((((.00392377*t-.01647633)*t+.02635537)*t
```

```
    -.02057706)*t+.00916281)*t-.00157565)*t+.00225319)*t
    +.01328692)*t+.39894228)*exp(x)/sqrt(x);
    return(y);
}

double i1(x)double x;
{
double t,y,exp(),sqrt();
if(x<3.75)
   {
   t=x/3.75;t=t*t;
   y=((((((.00032411*t+.00301532)*t+.02658733)*t
      +.15084934)*t+.51498869)*t+.87890594)*t+.5)*x;
   return(y);
   }
t=3.75/x;
   y=((((((((-.00420059*t+.01787654)*t-.02895312)*t+
      .02282967)*t-.01031555)*t+.00163801)*t-.00362018)*t
     -.03988024)*t+.39894228)*exp(x)/sqrt(x);
     return(y);
}

double k0(x)double x;
{
double t,log(),i0(),y;
if(x<2.)
   {
   t=(.5*x);t=t*t;
   y=((((((.0000074*t+.0001075)*t+.00262698)*t+
     .0348859)*t+.23069756)*t+.4227842)*t-.57721566)
     -log(.5*x)*i0(x);
     return(y);
     }
 t=2./x;
   y=((((((.00053208*t-.0025154)*t+.00587872)*t
     -.01062446)*t+.02189568)*t-.07832358)*t+1.25331414)
     *exp(-x)/sqrt(x);
     return(y);
}
double k1(x) double x;
{
   double y,t,exp(),log(),sqrt();
if(x< 2.)
   {t=(.5*x);t=t*t;
   y=((((((-.00004686*t-.00110404)*t-.01919402)*t
     -.18156897)*t-.67278579)*t+.15443144)*t+1.)/x
     +log(.5*x)*i1(x);
     return(y);
   }
```

```
t=2./x;
   y=((((((-.00068245*t+.00325614)*t-.0078353)*t
     +.01504268)*t-.03655620)*t+.23498619)*t+1.25331414)
      *exp(-x)/sqrt(x);
      return(y);
}


/* programs for computations of kelvin functions and their
   derivatives
*/

void ke(x,ker,kei,kerp,keip)double x,*ker,*kei,*kerp,*keip;
{
void be();
double y,z,al,sqrt(),log(),ber,bei,berp,beip;
struct complex CC,cex,cdum,f,phi,theta;
if(x<=8.)
   {y=x*x/64.;
   z=y*y;
   be(x,&ber,&bei,&berp,&beip);
   al=-log(.5*x);
   *ker=al* ber+.7853981634* bei
     +(((((((-.00002458*z+.00309699)*z-
.19636347)*z+5.65539121)*z
     -60.60977451)*z+171.36272133)*z-59.05819744)*z
     -.57721566);
   *kei=al* bei-.7853981634* ber
     +(((((((.00029532*z-.02695875)*z+1.17509064)*z
     -21.30060904)*z
     +124.2356965)*z-142.91827687)*z+6.76454936)*y);
   *kerp=al* berp- ber/x+beip*.7853981634
     +x*((((((-.00001075*z+.00116137)*z
     -.06136358)*z+1.4138478)*z
     -11.36433272)*z+21.42034017)*z-3.69113734)*y;
   *keip=al* beip- bei/x-.7853981634* berp
     +x*((((((.00011997*z-.00926707)*z+.33049424)*z
     -4.65950823)*z
     +19.41182758)*z-13.39858846)*z+.21139217);
   return;
   }
/*else*/

   CMPLX(CC,-.7071067812,-.7071067812);
   CTREAL(CC,CC,x);
   CTHET(-x,&y,&z);
   CMPLX(theta,y,z);
   CADD(CC,theta,CC);
   cexp(&CC,&cex);
```

```
    y=1.253314137/sqrt(x);
    CTREAL(f,cex,y);
   *ker=f.x;
   *kei=f.y;
    CPHI(-x,&y,&z);
   CMPLX(phi,y,z);/*cex now phi of AS*/
   CMULT(cdum,f,phi);
   *kerp=-cdum.x;
   *keip=-cdum.y;
return;
}

void be(X,BER,BEI,BERP,BEIP)double X, *BER, *BEI, *BERP,
*BEIP;
{
struct complex CC,cex,cdum,g,theta,phi;
double Y,Z,sqrt(),FKER,FKEI,FKERP,FKEIP;
static double PII=.3183098862;
if(X<=8.)
   {
   Y=(X/8.);Y=Y*Y;
   Z=Y*Y   ;
   *BER=((((((-.00000901*Z+.00122552)*Z-.08349609)*Z
      +2.64191397)*Z-32.36345652)*Z+113.77777774)*Z
      -64.)*Z+1.;
   *BEI=Y*((((((.00011346*Z-.01103667)*Z+.52185615)*Z
      -10.56765779)*Z+72.81777742)*Z-113.77777774)*Z+16.);
   *BERP=X*((((((-.00000394*Z+.00045957)*Z-.02609253)*Z
     +.66047849)*Z-6.06814810)*Z+14.22222222)*Z-4.)*Y;
   *BEIP=X*((((((.00004609*Z-.00379386)*Z+.14677204)*Z
     -2.31167514)*Z+11.37777772)*Z-10.66666666)*Z+.5);
   return;
    }
/*else*/

   CMPLX(CC,.7071067812,.7071067812);
   CTREAL(CC,CC,X);
   CTHET(X,&Y,&Z);
   CMPLX(theta,Y,Z);
   CADD(CC,theta,CC);
   cexp(&CC,&cex);
   Y=.3989422804/sqrt(X);
    CTREAL(g,cex,Y);
   ke(X,&FKER,&FKEI,&FKERP,&FKEIP);
   *BER=g.x-PII*FKEI;
   *BEI=g.y+PII*FKER;
   CPHI(X,&Y,&Z);
   CMPLX(phi ,Y,Z);
   CMULT(cdum,phi,g);
```

```
   *BERP= cdum.x-PII*FKEIP;
   *BEIP= cdum.y+PII*FKERP;

return;
}

CTHET(X,PARTR,PARTI)double X,*PARTI,*PARTR;
{
double Y;
   Y=8./X;
   *PARTI=((((.0000019*Y+.0000051)*Y*Y-.0000901)*Y
         -.0009765)
      *Y-.0110485)*Y-.3926991;
   *PARTR=((((.0000006*Y-.0000034)*Y-.0000252)*Y
   -.0000906)*Y*Y
   +.0110486)*Y;
return;
}
CPHI(X,PARTR,PARTI)double X,*PARTR,*PARTI;
{double Y;
   Y=8./X;
   *PARTI=(((((-.0000032*Y-.0000024)*Y
                    +.0000338)*Y+.0002452)*Y
     +.0013811)*Y-.0000001)*Y+.7071068;
   *PARTR=((((((.0000016*Y+.0000117)*Y
                    +.0000346)*Y
                    +.0000005)*Y   -.0013813)*Y
                    -.0625001)*Y+.7071068);
     return;
}
```

```
/*
Bessel function tables as a function of (integral) n

from C Mathematical Function Handbook by Louis Baker
Copyright 1991 by Louis Baker. All rights reserved.

jn
in
kn
yn
values returned in array double bessela[100];

*/

#include <stdio.h>
#include "cmlib.h"
#include "protom.h"

double bessela[100];

double jn(x,n) int n;double x;
{
int i,top,even,safety=40,k;
double mult,aux,z,y,j1(),j0(),old,older,sum,
   sqrt(),large=1.e10,ilarge;
/* will fill bessela[] with j(x) for n=0,n*/
mult=1.;
if(n<2)
   {
   if(n>0)
      {
      if(x==0.) return 0.;
      bessela[0]=j0(x);
      sum=bessela[1]=j1(x);
      return sum;
      }
   else if (!n)return bessela[0]=j0(x);
   /* else n<0*/
   if (!((-n)%2))mult=-1.;
   }
if(x==0.)return 0.;
if(n>100){
printf(" jn:n=%d exceeds size of bessela[]",n);
                     return errorcode;}
aux=2./x;
n=abs(n);
ilarge=1./large;
if( x > (double)n)
   {/*fwd*/
```

```
   bessela[0]=older=j0(x);
   bessela[1]=old=j1(x);
   for(i=1;i<n;i++)
      {
      z= i*aux*old-older;
      older=old;
      old=z;
      bessela[i+1]=z;
      }
   return z*mult;
   }
/* backward*/
even =  n+ (int)(sqrt((double)(n*safety)));
top=     (even>>1)<<1;
sum=0.;
even=0;
z=0.;
y=0.;
old=1.;
for(i=top;i>0;i--)
   {
   older=i*aux*old-z;
   if( (i-1)<=n)bessela[i-1]=older;
   z=old;
   old=older;
   if( abs(z)>large)
      { /*rescale*/
      old*=ilarge;
      z*=ilarge;
      sum*=ilarge;
      y*=ilarge;
      for(k=i-1;k<=n;k++)bessela[k]*=ilarge;
      }
   if(even)sum+=old;
/*if(even) printf(" sum,old %e %e %d\n",sum,old, i); */
   even  ^= 1;
   if(i==n)y=z;
   }
sum= 2.*sum-old;
for(i=0;i<=n;i++)bessela[i]*=(mult/sum);
return y*mult/sum;
}

double in(x,n) int n;double x;
{
int k,even,top,i,safety=40;
double aux,old,older,large=1.e10,ilarge,y,z;
if(!n){bessela[0]=aux=i0(x);return aux;}
```

```
if(n==1){bessela[1]=aux=(i1(x));bessela[0]=i0(x);return
aux;}
if(x==0.)return 0.;
n=abs(n);
if(n>100)
{printf(" kn:n=%d exceeds size of bessela[]\n",n);return er-
rorcode;}
aux=2./x;
ilarge=1./large;
/* backward*/
even =  n+ (int)(sqrt((double)(n*safety)));
top=    (even>>1)<<1;
even=0;
z=0.;
y=0.;
old=1.;
for(i=top;i>0;i--)
   {
   older=i*aux*old+z;
   z=old;
   old=older;
   bessela[i-1]=older;
   if( abs(z)>large)
      {
      old*=ilarge;
      z*=ilarge;
      y*=ilarge;
      for(k=i-1;k<=n;k++)bessela[k]*=ilarge;
      }
   if(i==n)y=z;
   }
bessela[0]=aux=i0(x);
aux/=old;
for(k=1;k<=n;k++)bessela[k]*=aux;
return y*aux;
}

double kn(x,n) double x;int n;
{
int k;
double ans,aux,old,older,k0(),k1();
if(x==0.)return errorcode;
if(n==0){bessela[0]=aux=k0(x);return aux;}
else if(n==1){bessela[1]=aux=k1(x);bessela[0]=k0(x);return
aux;}
if(n<0)n=-n;
n=abs(n);
if(n>100)
```

```
{printf(" kn:n=%d exceeds size of bessela[]\n",n);return er-
rorcode;}
aux=2./x;
bessela[0]=older=k0(x);
bessela[1]=old=k1(x);
for(k=1;k<n;k++)
   {
   ans=older+k*aux*old;
   older=old;
   old=ans;
   bessela[k+1]=ans;
   }
return ans;
}

double yn(x,n) double x;int n;
{
int k;
double mult,ans,aux,old,older,y0(),y1();
if(x==0.)return errorcode;
if(n==0){bessela[0]=aux=y0(x);return aux;}
else if(n==1){bessela[0]=y0(x);bessela[1]=aux=y1(x);return
aux;}
mult=1.;
if(n<0 &&  (-n)%2 )mult=-1.;
n=abs(n);
if(n>100){
printf(" yn:n=%d exceeds size of bessela[]\n",n)
;return errorcode;}
aux=2./x;
bessela[0]=older=y0(x);
bessela[1]=old=y1(x);
for(k=1;k<n;k++)
   {
   ans=k*aux*old-older;
   older=old;
   old=ans;
   bessela[k+1]=ans;
   }
for(k=0;k<=n;k++)bessela[k]*=mult;
return ans*mult;
}
```

```
/*
Zeros of bessel functions
from C Mathematical Function Handbook by Louis Baker
Copyright 1991 by Louis Baker. All rights reserved.

zerobes(a,n,z,d) double a,z[];int d,n;
   where a is order, z[] are first n zeros,
   d= 1 for J 2 for Y 3 for J' 4 for Y'
*/

#include <stdio.h>
#include "cmlib.h"
#include "protom.h"


#define pio2 pi*.5

double fi(y) double y;
{/* solve tan(fi)-fi=y for fi*/
double p,pp,q,r,pow(),atan();
if(y==0.)return 0.;
if(y>1.e5)return pio2;
if(y<1.)
   {
   p=pow(3.*y,.3333333333);
   pp=p*p;
   p*=(1.+pp*(-210.+pp*(27.-2.*pp)))/1575.;
   }
else
   {
   p=1./(y+pio2); pp=p*p;
   p=pio2-
p*(1.+pp*(2310.+pp*(3003.+pp*(4818.+pp*(8591.+pp*16328)))))
/3465.;
   }
q=y+p;
pp=q*q;
r=(p-atan(q))/pp;
return p-(1.+pp)*r*(1.+r/q);
}


double ybessl,sum1,sum2;

double jass(z,nu) double z,nu;
{
double term2,term,x,y,q,arg,c,s;
double zz,f1,f2,f1o,f2o,nuph,numh,npho,mu;
int k,twok,n,itmax=30;
```

```
/* INCREASING NU ONLY MAKES IT WORSE*/
/*if( abs(nu)<1.) return jass(z,nu+1.)*2.*(nu+1.)/z-
jass(z,nu+2.);*/

z=abs(z);

y= sqrt(2./(pi*z));
sum1=0.;
sum2=0.;
zz=4.*z*z;
term2=.5/z;
term=1.;
nuph=nu+.5;numh=nu-.5;npho=nu+1.5;
f1=1.e10;f2=1.e10;
mu=4.* nu*nu;
/*
for(k=0;k<itmax;k++)
    {
    f1o=f1;
    twok=k<<1;
    q=(double)(twok);
    if(term!=0.)
        {
        f1=term *gamma(nuph+q)/gamma(nuph-q);
        if( abs(f1/f1o)>1.)
            {
            term=0.;
            f1=0.;
            }
        else term*= -1./(zz*((twok+2)*(twok+1)) );
        sum1+=f1;
        }
    f2o=f2;
    if(term2!=0.)
        {
        f2=term2 *gamma(npho+q)/gamma(numh-q);
        if(abs(f2/f2o)>1.)
            {term2=0.;
            f2=0.;
            }
         else term2*= -1./(zz*((twok+3)*(twok+2)) );
        sum2+=f2;
        }
    if( (abs(term)<1.e-7 || abs(term/sum1)<1.e-6)&&
     ( abs(term2)<1.e-7 || abs(term2/sum2)<1.e-6)   )break;
    }
arg= z-pi*(nu*.5+.25);
return y*(cos(arg)*sum1-sin(arg)*sum2);
*/
```

```
/*HANKEL EXPANSION:*/
zz=1./(64.*z*z);
term=(mu-1.)*(mu-9.)*zz;
sum1=1.-term*.5+term*(mu-25.)*(mu-49.)*zz/24.;
term2=(mu-1.)*.125/z;
sum2=term2*(1.-(mu-9.)*(mu-25.)*zz/6. );
arg= z-pi*(nu*.5+.25);
c=cos(arg);s=sin(arg);
ybessl=y*(s*sum1+c*sum2);
return y*(c*sum1-s*sum2);
}

besspq(a,x,pa,qa,pa1,qa1) double a,x, *pa,*qa,*pa1,*qa1;
{
double jv,yv,s,c,chi,garb,ck;
struct complex z,jc,yc,h2,jp,yp,hp;
int n,ivk;
n=a;             z.x=x;z.y=0.;
if(x>10.)
   {
   jass(x,a); *pa=sum1;*qa=sum2;
   jass(x,a+1.); *pa1=sum1;*qa1=sum2;
   }
else
   {
   if( (a- (double)n)==0.)
      {
      bessel( n, &z,&jc,&yc,&h2,&jp,&yp,&hp,&ivk);
      jv=jc.x;yv=yc.x;
      chi=x-pi*(.25+.5*a);
      s=sin(chi);c=cos(chi);
      garb=sqrt((pi*x)*.5);
      *pa= garb*(c*jv+s*yv);
      *qa= garb*(c*yv-s*jv);
      ck= (*pa*c-*qa*s);
      n++;
      bessel( n, &z,&jc,&yc,&h2,&jp,&yp,&hp,&ivk);
      jv=jc.x;yv=yc.x;
      chi=x-pi*(.75+.5*a);
      s=sin(chi);c=cos(chi);
      *pa1= garb*(c*jv+s*yv);
      *qa1= garb*(c*yv-s*jv);
      }
   else
      {/* order not integer, not in asymptotic regime for
jas*/
      jv=jbes(x,a);yv=ybes(x,a);
      chi=x-pi*(.25+.5*a);
      s=sin(chi);c=cos(chi);
```

```
        garb=sqrt((pi*x)*.5);
        *pa= garb*(c*jv+s*yv);
        *qa= garb*(c*yv-s*jv);
        ck= (*pa*c-*qa*s);
        jv=jbes(x,a+1.);yv=ybes(x,a+1.);
        chi=x-pi*(.75+.5*a);
        s=sin(chi);c=cos(chi);
        *pa1= garb*(c*jv+s*yv);
        *qa1= garb*(c*yv-s*jv);
        }
    }
return 0;
}

zerobes(a,n,z,d) double a,z[];int d,n;
{
double e=1.e-4;/* desired accuracy. should be consistent
with
accuracy of jas p,q values*/
double ck,ckd;
double
aa,a1,a2,b,bb,c,chi,co,mu,mu2,mu3,mu4,p,pa,pa1,pp1,p0,p1,q1,
psi,q,qa,x,qq1,si,t,tt,u,v,w,xx,x4,y,sqrt(),cos(),pow()
,r0,qa1;
int j,s;
aa=a*a; mu=4.*aa;mu2=mu*mu;mu3=mu*mu2;mu4=mu2*mu2;
if(d<3)
    {
    p=7.*mu-31.;p0=mu-1.;
    if(1.+p == p) p1=q1=0.;
    else
        {
        p1=4.*(253.*mu2-3722.*mu+17869.)*p0/(p*15.);
        q1=1.6*(83.*mu2-982.*mu+3779.)/p;
        }
    }
else
    {
    p=7.*mu2+82.*mu-9.; p0=mu+3.;
    if(1.+p == p) p1=q1=0.;
    else
        {
        p1=(4048.*mu4+131264.*mu3-221984.*mu2-
417600.*mu+1012176.)/(60.*p);
        q1=1.6*(83.*mu3+2075.*mu2-3039.*mu+3537.)/p;
        }
    }
t= (d==1 || d==4)? .25 : .75;
tt=4.*t;
```

```
if(d<3)
   {pp1=5./48.;qq1=-5./36.;}
else
   {pp1=-7./48.;qq1=35/288.;}
y=.375*pi;bb= (a>=3.)? pow(a,-.6666666): 1.;
a1=3*a-8.;psi=pi*(.5*a+.25);
for(s=1;s<=n;s++)
   {
   if( s==1 && a==0. && d==3)
      {x=0.;j=0;}
   else
      {
      if( s>=a1 )
         {
         b=(s+.5*a-t)*pi;c=.0125625/(b*b);
         x=b-.125*(p0-p1*c)/(b*(1.-q1*c));
         }
      else
         {
         if(s==1)
            {
            switch (d)
               {
               case 1 : x=-2.33811;break;
               case 2 : x=-1.17371;break;
               case 3:  x=-1.01879;break;
               default: x=-2.29444;break;
               }
            }
         else
            {
            x=y*(4.*(s)-tt);v=1./(x*x);
            x= -pow(x,.6666666)*(1.+v*(pp1+qq1*v));
            }
      u=x*bb;
      v= fi(.666666*pow((-u),1.5));
      w=1./cos(v);
      xx=1.-w*w;
      c=sqrt(u/xx);
      x=w*(a+c/(48.*a*u)) *((d<3)? -5./u-c*(-10./xx+6.):
      ( 7./u+c*(-14./xx+18.)));
      }
      j=0;
      do
         {
         xx=x*x; x4=xx*xx; a2=aa-xx;
      besspq(a,x,&pa,&qa,&pa1,&qa1);
         chi=x-psi;
         si=sin(chi);co=cos(chi);
```

```
         switch (d)
            {
            case 1: r0= (pa*co-qa*si)
                        /(pa1*si+qa1*co);break;
            case 2: r0= (pa*si+qa*co)/(qa1*si-pa1*co);break;
            case 3:
               r0=a/x-(pa1*si+qa1*co)/(pa*co-qa*si);break;
            default:
               r0=a/x-(qa1*si-pa1*co)/(pa*si+qa*co);break;
            }
         j++;
         if(d<3)
            {
            u=r0;w=6.*x*(2.*a+1.);
            p=(1.-4.*a2)/w;
            q=(4*(xx-mu)-2.-12.*a)/w;
            }
         else
            {
            u=-xx*r0/a2;
            v=2.*x*a2/(3.*(aa+xx));
            w=64.*a2*a2*a2;
            q=2.*v*(1.+mu2+32.*mu*xx+48.*x4)/w;
            p=v*(1.+(-mu2+40.*mu*xx+48.*x4)/w);
            }
         w=u*(1.+p*r0)/(1.+r0*q);x+=w;
         } while( abs(w/x)>e && j<5);
      }/*else of a=0,d==3,s==1 */
   z[s-1]=x;
   }
return 0;
}
```

```
/*
test driver for bessel functions
from C Mathematical Function Handbook by Louis Baker
Copyright 1991 by Louis Baker. All rights reserved.
*/

#include <stdio.h>
#include "cmlib.h"
#include "protom.h"

extern double c1a,c2a;
extern double sphb[200];
extern int itkt;

FILE *intk,*inti,*intj,*intkt,*intit,*inty,*intjt,
*ints,*inta,*aff;

main()
{int i,m,n,rrr;double x,y,t,q,p,nu,xx,rr,r;
int check;
struct complex z,j,yy,h2,jp,yp,h2p;

intk=fopen("intk.out","w");fprintf(intk," 2\n");
ints=fopen("ints.out","w");  fprintf(ints," 3\n");
intit=fopen("intit.out","w");  fprintf(intit," 2\n");
inti=fopen("inti.out","w");  fprintf(inti," 2\n");
intkt=fopen("intkt.out","w");fprintf(intkt," 2\n");
intjt=fopen("intjt.out","w");fprintf(intjt," 2\n");
intj=fopen("intj.out","w");fprintf(intj," 2\n");
inty=fopen("inty.out","w");fprintf(inty," 2\n");
inta=fopen("inta.out","w");fprintf(inta," 2\n");
aff=fopen("af.out","w");fprintf(aff," 5\n");
for(n=0;n<10;n++)
   {
   x=(n+1)*.1;
   p=ybes(x,1.);q=y1(x);
printf(" Ybes x %e y=%e %e\n",x,p,q);
   }
for(n=0;n<10;n++)
   {
   x=(n+1)*.1;
   p=ibes(x,1.);
printf(" Ibes x %e i=%e \n",x,p);
   }
for(n=0;n<10;n++)
   {
   x=(n+1);
   p=ibes(x,1.);
printf(" Ibes x %e i=%e \n",x,p);
```

```
    }
for(n=0;n<10;n++)
    {
    x=(n+1)*.1;
    p=kbes(x,.5);
    t=ibes(x,.5);
printf(" i=%e",t);
    q=ybes(x,.5);
printf(" x %e k,y,i=%e %e %e\n",x,p,q,t);
    }
for(n=0;n<10;n++)
    {
    x=(n+1);
    p=kbes(x,.33333);
printf("  k(%e,1/3)=%e \n",x,p);
    }
for(n=0;n<10;n++)
    {
    x=(n+5);
    p=jbes(x,1.);
    q=j1(x);
printf(" x %e j1=%e %e \n",x,p,q);
    }
/* tables of bessel functions*/
for(n=0;n<10;n++)
    {
    x=.1*(n+1);
    p=jt(x);
    nu=jbes(x,.333333);
printf(" x %e jt=%e j=%e\n",x,p,nu);
    }

for(n=0;n<10;n++)
    {
    x=(n+1);
    p=jbes(x,0.);
    nu=jbes(x,1.);
    t=jbes(x,3.);
    q=jbes(x,4.);
    printf(" x %e j0=%e j1=%e \n  j3=%e j4=%e\n",x,p,nu,t,q);
    }
printf(" jas,j(2.,1/3)=%e
%e\n",jas(2.,.333333),jbes(2.,.333333333));
printf(" jas,j(3.,1/3)=%e
%e\n",jas(3.,.333333),jbes(3.,.333333333));
printf(" jas,j(4.,1/3)=%e
%e\n",jas(4.,.333333),jbes(4.,.333333333));
printf(" jas,j(5.,1/3)=%e
%e\n",jas(5.,.333333),jbes(5.,.333333333));
```

```
printf(" jas,j(10.,1/3)=%e
%e\n",jas(10.,.333333),jbes(10.,.333333333));
printf(" jas,j(15.,1/3)=%e
%e\n",jas(15.,.333333),jbes(15.,.333333333));
printf(" jas,j(20.,1/3)=%e
%e\n",jas(20.,.333333),jbes(20.,.333333333));
printf(" jas,j(2.,0.)=%e %e\n",jas(2.,0.),jbes(2.,0.));
printf(" jas,j(3.,0)=%e %e\n",jas(3.,0.),jbes(3.,.0));
printf(" jas,j(4.,0)=%e %e\n",jas(4.,0.),jbes(4.,.0));
printf(" jas,j(5.,0)=%e %e\n",jas(5.,0.),jbes(5.,.0));
printf(" jas,j(10.,0)=%e %e\n",jas(10.,0.),jbes(10.,.0));
printf(" jas,j(15.,0)=%e %e\n",jas(15.,0.),jbes(15.,.0));
printf(" jas,j(20.,0)=%e %e\n",jas(20.,0.),jbes(20.,.0));
/* functions based upn complex bessel functions*/
while(1)
   {
   printf(" enter n z-com-
plex\n");scanf("%d%le%le",&n,&q,&r);
   if(q==0. && r==0. && n==0)break;
   z.x=q;z.y=r;
   bessel(n,&z,&j,&yy,&h2,&jp,&yp,&h2p,&check);
   printf(" J,Y=");printc(&j);printc(&yy);printf("\n");
   printf(" J',Y'=");printc(&jp);printc(&yp);printf("\n");
   printf(" H2,H2'=");printc(&h2);printc(&h2p);printf("\n");
   ibess(&z,&j,n); printf("
Ibess=");printc(&j);printf("\n");
   kbess(&z,&j,n); printf("
Kbess=");printc(&j);printf("\n");
   if( r==0.)
      {printf(" jn=%le %le\n", jint(n,q),jn(q,n));
      kelvin(n,(double)q,&j,&yy);
      printf(" kelvin be=");printc(&j);
      printf(" kelvin ke=");printc(&yy);
      printf("\n");
      }
   }

printf(
"\n\n Chapter 10: Spherical Bessel functions \n\n");


/* spherical bessel functions:*/
printf(" Spherical bessel functions:\n");
while(1){
printf(" spherical i:enter n, x\n");
scanf("%d%lc",&m,&x);
if(x<0.)break;
printf(" %e\n",sinb(x,m));
for(i=0;i<=abs(m);i++)
```

```
    printf(" i[%d]=%e\n",i,sphb[i]);
if(x>0.)
    {
    if(m>0)printf(" ck: i[0]=%le\n", sinh(x)/x);
    if(m>1)printf(" ck: i[1]=%le\n",
                    (cosh(x)-sinh(x)/x)/x);
    if(m>2)printf(" ck: i[2]=%le\n",
      (-3.*cosh(x)/x+sinh(x)*(1.+3./(x*x)))/x);
    if(m<=-1)printf(" ck: i(-1) pro I[-1/2]=%le\n",
       cosh(x)/x);
    if(m<=-2)printf(" ck: i(-2) pro I[-3/2]=%le\n",
       (cosh(x)*(-1./x)+sinh(x))/x);
    if(m<=-3)printf(" ck: i(-3) pro I[-5/2]=%le\n",
       (cosh(x)*(1.+3./(x*x))-3./(x)*sinh(x))/x);
    }
}
while(1){
printf(" k:enter n, x\n");
scanf("%d%le",&m,&x);
if(x<0.)break;
printf(" %e\n",skn(x,m));
for(i=0;i<=m;i++)
    printf(" %d %e\n",i,sphb[i]);
}
while(1){
printf(" j:enter n, x\n");
scanf("%d%le",&m,&x);
if(x<0.)break;
printf(" %e\n",sjn(x,m));
for(i=0;i<=m;i++)
    printf(" %d %e\n",i,sphb[i]);
}
while(1){
printf(" y:enter n, x\n");
scanf("%d%le",&m,&x);
if(x<0.)break;
printf(" %e\n",syn(x,m));
for(i=0;i<=m;i++)
    printf(" %d %e\n",i,sphb[i]);
}

printf("\n\n Chapter 10: Airy Functions & Integrals\n\n");

for(n=0;n<10;n++)
    {
    x=.1*(n+1);
    p=ai(x);
    nu=bi(x);t=ai(-x);q=bi(-x);
printf(" x %e Ai,Bi=%e %e %e %e\n",x,p,nu,t,q);
```

```
    }
for(n=0;n<10;n++)
    {
    x=(n+1);
    p=ai(x);
    nu=bi(x);t=ai(-x);q=bi(-x);
printf(" x %e Ai,Bi=%e %e %e %e\n",x,p,nu,t,q);
    }
for(n=0;n<10;n++)
    {
    x=(n+1);
    p=dai(x);nu=dbi(x);
    t=dai(-x);q=dbi(-x);
printf(" x %e Ai',Bi'=%e %e %e %e\n",x,p,nu,t,q);
    }

for(n=0;n<10;n++)
    {
    x=.1*(n+1);
    p=ai(x);
    nu=bi(x);t= c1a*smallf(x)-c2a*smallg(x);
    q=sqrt(3.)*(c1a*smallf(x)+c2a*smallg(x));
    printf(
" x=%e Ai=%e Ai(via f,g)=%e \n   Bi=%e via(f,g)=%e\n"
    ,x,p,t,nu,q);
    }
for(n=0;n<100;n++)
    {
    x=.1*(n+1)-5.;
    p=ai(x);
    nu=bi(x);
    fprintf(aff," %le %le %le\n",x,p,nu);
    }
for(n=0;n<10;n++)
    {
    x=(n+1);
    p=IAi(x);nu=IAi(-x);t=IBi(x);q=IBi(-x);
    printf(" x %f Airy integrals=%e %e %e %e\n" ,x,p,nu,t,q);
    }
for(n=0;n<50;n++)
    {
    x=(n+1)*.2;
    p=IAi(x);nu=IAi(-x);t=IBi(x);q=IBi(-x);
    fprintf(inta," %f %e %e %e %e\n",x,p,nu,t,q);
    }

printf("\n\n Chapter 11: Integrals\n\n");

    infinite_loop
```

```
        {
        printf(
" enter x=0, r for bickley x==0 analytic \n");
        scanf("%le%le",&xx,&rr);
        if(xx<0.)break;
        printf(" x, r %le %le\n",xx,rr);
        printf("Ki=%le\n",bickley(xx,rr));
        if(xx==0.)
           {rrr=rr;
           m=rrr%2;
           if(m) {rr=(rr-1.)*.5;
                 q=
pi*.5*gamma(rr+.5)/(gamma(.5)*gamma(rr+1.));}
           else {rr*=.5;q=gamma(rr)*gamma(1.5)/gamma(rr+.5);}
           printf(" analytic %le\n",q);
           }
        }

infinite_loop
        {
        printf(" enter x, r,n[int] for Jrn")
                    ;scanf("%le%le%d",&xx,&rr,&m);
        if(xx==0. && rr==0. && m==0)break;
        printf(" x, r %le %le n=%d\n",xx,rr,m);
        printf(" rth integral:Jn=%le\n",Jrn(xx,rr,m));
        }

/* integrals of bessel functions:*/
printf(" integrals of bessel functions\n");
for(i=1;i<20;i++)
   {x=i*.5;
   y=0.;if(x>=5.)y=ii0tas(x);
   t=ii0m1t(x);
                    printf(" I0/t %e %e %e %e %e %d\n",
                    x,t,t*exp(-x),y,y*exp(-x),itkt);
   }
for(i=1;i<40;i++)
   {x=i*.25;
   t=ii0m1t(x);
   fprintf(intit," %le %le\n",x,t);
   }
for(i=1;i<10;i++)
   {x=i*.5;t=iy0t(x);printf("int Y0/t %e %e \n",x,t);}
for(i=1;i<50;i++)
   {x=i*.1;t=iy0t(x);
   fprintf(inty,"%e %e \n",x,t);
   }
for(i=0;i<10;i++)
   {x=i*.5;t=ki(x);printf(" int K0 %e %e \n",x,t);
```

```
    }
for(i=0;i<50;i++)
    {x=i*.1;t=ki(x);printf(" int K0 %e %e \n",x,t);
    fprintf(intk,"%e %e \n",x,t);
    }

for(i=1;i<20;i++)
    {x=i*.5;t=ik0t(x);
    y=0.;if(x>=4.)y=ik0tas(x);
    printf("int K0/t %e %e %e %e %e
%d\n",x,t,t*x*exp(x),y,y*x*exp(x),itkt);
    fprintf(intkt," %le %le\n",x,t);
    }

    for(i=1;i<10;i++)
    {x=i*.5;t=ij0t(x);printf("int J0/t %e %e \n",x,t);
    }
    for(i=1;i<50;i++)
    {x=i*.5;t=ij0t(x);
    fprintf(intjt," %le %le\n",x,t);
    }

for(i=1;i<25;i++)
    {x=i*.5;t=ji(x);nu=jin(x,1);
                    printf(" int J0 %le %le %le\n",x,t,nu);
    fprintf(intj," %le %le\n",x,t);
    }




infinite_loop
    {printf(" enter x for integral i0i y0i\n");
    scanf("%le",&t);if(t==0.)break;
    printf(" integrals I0 %le Y0 %le\n",i0i(t),y0i(t));
    }

for(i=0;i<50;i++)
    {t=(i+1)*.2;
    fprintf(inti,"%le %le %le\n",t,i0i(t),y0i(t));
    }


printf(
"\n\n Chapter 12: Struve and Anger-Weber functions & In-
tograls\n\n");

infinite_loop
      {printf(" enter x, nu\n");scanf("%le%le",&x,&nu);
```

```
        if(x==0. && nu==0.)break;
        printf(
" H= %le L=%le\n", StruveH(nu,x),StruveL(nu,x));
        }

for(i=0; i<50;i++)
    {t=i*.1;
    rr=i0i(t)-ModStruveI(t);
    if(t>5.)rr-= 2./pi*log(t);
    printf(
"x=%le int H %le H/t*2/pi= %le, \n  int L %le f2=%le\n"
        ,t,StruveI(t),StruveIot(t)*2./pi,ModStruveI(t),rr);
    fprintf(ints,"%le %le %le\n",t,StruveI(t),StruveIot(t));
    }


printf(" anger weber\n");
aw(.5,.5,&p,&t);
printf(" nu=x=.5, %e %e\n",p,t);
printf(" anger weber\n");
aw(.5,10.,&p,&t);
printf(" nu=.5 x=10, %e %e\n",p,t);

t=0.;
for(n=0;n<10;n++)
    {
    x=.2*(n+1);aw(t,x,&p,&nu);
    q=-StruveH(0.,x);
    printf(" x %e nu=%e J=%le j0=%le \n   E=%le %le\n"
        ,x,t,p,j0(x),nu,q);
    }
t=1.;
for(n=0;n<10;n++)
    {
    x=.2*(n+1);aw(t,x,&p,&nu);
    q= 2./(pi)-StruveH(1.,x);
    printf(" x %e nu=%e J=%le j1=%le \n   E=%le %le\n"
        ,x,t,p,j1(x),nu,q);
    }
for(n=0;n<10;n++)
    { /* ck asymptotics*/
    x=(n+1);aw(t,x,&p,&nu);
    q= 2./(pi)-StruveH(1.,x);
    printf(" x %e nu=%e J=%le j1=%le \n E=%le %le\n"
        ,x,t,p,j1(x),nu,q);
    }
infinite_loop
    {
    printf(
```

```
" enter int m, complex z for integral Anger Weber\n");
   scanf("%d%le%le",&n,&q,&p);
   if(q==0. && p==0. && n==0.)break;
   yy.x=q;yy.y=p;
   iaw(n, &yy,&z);
   printf(" answer= %le %le\n", z.x,z.y);
   }

return 0;
}
```

```
/*
test driver Bessel zero

from C Mathematical Function Handbook by Louis Baker
Copyright 1991 by Louis Baker. All rights reserved.
*/

#include <stdio.h>
#include "cmlib.h"
#include "protom.h"

main()
{
double order,z[20];
int i;
order=0.;
zerobes(order,10,z,1);
for(i=0;i<10;i++)printf(" %d zero for J %f =
%e\n",i+1,order,z[i]);
zerobes(order,10,z,2);
for(i=0;i<10;i++)printf(" %d zero for Y %f =
%e\n",i+1,order,z[i]);
zerobes(order,10,z,3);
for(i=0;i<10;i++)printf(" %d zero for J' %f =
%e\n",i+1,order,z[i]);
zerobes(order,10,z,4);
for(i=0;i<10;i++)printf(" %d zero for Y' %f =
%e\n",i+1,order,z[i]);
order=0.5;
zerobes(order,10,z,1);
for(i=0;i<10;i++)printf(" %d zero for J %f =
%e\n",i+1,order,z[i]);
order=1.;
zerobes(order,10,z,1);
for(i=0;i<10;i++)printf(" %d zero for J %f =
%e\n",i+1,order,z[i]);
return 0;
}
```

```
Output of Bessel function test driver
 Ybes x 1.000000e-01 y=-6.458951e+00 -6.458951e+00
 Ybes x 2.000000e-01 y=-3.323825e+00 -3.323825e+00
 Ybes x 3.000000e-01 y=-2.293105e+00 -2.293105e+00
 Ybes x 4.000000e-01 y=-1.780872e+00 -1.780872e+00
 Ybes x 5.000000e-01 y=-1.471472e+00 -1.471472e+00
 Ybes x 6.000000e-01 y=-1.260391e+00 -1.260391e+00
 Ybes x 7.000000e-01 y=-1.103250e+00 -1.103250e+00
 Ybes x 8.000000e-01 y=-9.781442e-01 -9.781441e-01
 Ybes x 9.000000e-01 y=-8.731266e-01 -8.731266e-01
 Ybes x 1.000000e+00 y=-7.812128e-01 -7.812128e-01
 Ibes x 1.000000e-01 i=5.006253e-02
 Ibes x 2.000000e-01 i=1.005008e-01
 Ibes x 3.000000e-01 i=1.516938e-01
 Ibes x 4.000000e-01 i=2.040268e-01
 Ibes x 5.000000e-01 i=2.578943e-01
 Ibes x 6.000000e-01 i=3.137040e-01
 Ibes x 7.000000e-01 i=3.718797e-01
 Ibes x 8.000000e-01 i=4.328648e-01
 Ibes x 9.000000e-01 i=4.971264e-01
 Ibes x 1.000000e+00 i=5.651591e-01
 Ibes x 1.000000e+00 i=5.651591e-01
 Ibes x 2.000000e+00 i=1.590637e+00
 Ibes x 3.000000e+00 i=3.953370e+00
 Ibes x 4.000000e+00 i=9.759465e+00
 Ibes x 5.000000e+00 i=2.433564e+01
 Ibes x 6.000000e+00 i=6.135377e+01
 Ibes x 7.000000e+00 i=1.560536e+02
 Ibes x 8.000000e+00 i=3.998934e+02
 Ibes x 9.000000e+00 i=1.030946e+03
 Ibes x 1.000000e+01 i=2.671039e+03
 i=2.527340e-01 x 1.000000e-01 k,y,i=3.586167e+00
-2.510528e+00 2.527340e-01
 i=3.592084e-01 x 2.000000e-01 k,y,i=2.294489e+00
-1.748561e+00 3.592084e-01
 i=4.436042e-01 x 3.000000e-01 k,y,i=1.695161e+00
-1.391669e+00 4.436042e-01
 i=5.181912e-01 x 4.000000e-01 k,y,i=1.328349e+00
-1.161980e+00 5.181912e-01
 i=5.879930e-01 x 5.000000e-01 k,y,i=1.075048e+00
-9.902461e-01 5.879930e-01
 i=6.557942e-01 x 6.000000e-01 k,y,i=8.879890e-01
-8.501491e-01 6.557942e-01
 i=7.234267e-01 x 7.000000e-01 k,y,i=7.430832e-01
-7.293953e-01 7.234267e-01
 i=7.922456e-01 x 8.000000e-01 k,y,i=6.296212e-01
-6.215057e-01 7.922456e-01
 i=8.633459e-01 x 9.000000e-01 k,y,i=5.371228e-01
-5.228015e-01 8.633459e-01
```

```
 i=9.376748e-01 x 1.000000e+00 k,y,i=4.610684e-01
-4.310990e-01 9.376748e-01
  k(1.000000e+00,1/3)=4.384301e-01
  k(2.000000e+00,1/3)=1.165444e-01
  k(3.000000e+00,1/3)=3.530490e-02
  k(4.000000e+00,1/3)=1.129832e-02
  k(5.000000e+00,1/3)=3.726599e-03
  k(6.000000e+00,1/3)=1.254692e-03
  k(7.000000e+00,1/3)=4.279600e-04
  k(8.000000e+00,1/3)=1.474329e-04
  k(9.000000e+00,1/3)=5.118021e-05
  k(1.000000e+01,1/3)=1.787452e-05
 x 5.000000e+00 j1=-3.275794e-01 -3.275791e-01
 x 6.000000e+00 j1=-2.766853e-01 -2.766839e-01
 x 7.000000e+00 j1=-4.687109e-03 -4.682827e-03
 x 8.000000e+00 j1=2.346345e-01 2.346363e-01
 x 9.000000e+00 j1=2.453119e-01 2.453118e-01
 x 1.000000e+01 j1=4.347336e-02 4.347274e-02
 x 1.100000e+01 j1=-1.767850e-01 -1.767853e-01
 x 1.200000e+01 j1=-2.234471e-01 -2.234471e-01
 x 1.300000e+01 j1=-7.031819e-02 -7.031805e-02
 x 1.400000e+01 j1=1.333751e-01 1.333752e-01
 x 1.000000e-01 jt=4.117817e-01 j=4.117824e-01
 x 2.000000e-01 jt=5.158970e-01 j=5.158972e-01
 x 3.000000e-01 jt=5.850153e-01 j=5.850153e-01
 x 4.000000e-01 jt=6.354123e-01 j=6.354117e-01
 x 5.000000e-01 jt=6.728340e-01 j=6.728313e-01
 x 6.000000e-01 jt=7.000275e-01 j=7.000276e-01
 x 7.000000e-01 jt=7.185629e-01 j=7.185631e-01
 x 8.000000e-01 jt=7.294376e-01 j=7.294381e-01
 x 9.000000e-01 jt=7.333589e-01 j=7.333602e-01
 x 1.000000e+00 jt=7.308736e-01 j=7.308768e-01
 x 1.000000e+00 j0=7.651977e-01 j1=4.400506e-01
  j3=1.956335e-02 j4=2.476639e-03
 x 2.000000e+00 j0=2.238907e-01 j1=5.767248e-01
  j3=1.289432e-01 j4=3.399572e-02
 x 3.000000e+00 j0=-2.600520e-01 j1=3.390589e-01
  j3=3.090627e-01 j4=1.320342e-01
 x 4.000000e+00 j0=-3.971499e-01 j1=-6.604346e-02
  j3=4.301715e-01 j4=2.811291e-01
 x 5.000000e+00 j0= 1.775970e 01 j1= 3.275794e 01
  j3=3.648312e-01 j4=3.912324e-01
 x 6.000000e+00 j0=1.506538e-01 j1=-2.766853e-01
  j3=1.147823e-01 j4=3.579780e-01
 x 7.000000e+00 j0=3.000807e-01 j1=-4.687109e-03
  j3=-1.675303e-01 j4=1.578330e-01
 x 8.000000e+00 j0=1.716497e-01 j1=2.346345e-01
  j3=-2.911226e-01 j4=-1.054098e-01
 x 9.000000e+00 j0=-9.033458e-02 j1=2.453119e-01
```

```
  j3=-1.809363e-01 j4=-2.655085e-01
 x 1.000000e+01 j0=-2.459360e-01 j1=4.347336e-02
  j3=5.837584e-02 j4=-2.196097e-01
 jas,j(2.,1/3)=4.430760e-01 4.429401e-01
 jas,j(3.,1/3)=-4.510974e-02 -4.496347e-02
 jas,j(4.,1/3)=-3.554584e-01 -3.554270e-01
 jas,j(5.,1/3)=-3.064191e-01 -3.064201e-01
 jas,j(10.,1/3)=-1.861455e-01 -1.861454e-01
 jas,j(15.,1/3)=8.973988e-02 8.973998e-02
 jas,j(20.,1/3)=1.760606e-01 1.760606e-01
 jas,j(2.,0.)=2.228668e-01 2.238907e-01
 jas,j(3.,0)=-2.603778e-01 -2.600520e-01
 jas,j(4.,0)=-3.971814e-01 -3.971499e-01
 jas,j(5.,0)=-1.775833e-01 -1.775970e-01
 jas,j(10.,0)=-2.459360e-01 -2.459360e-01
 jas,j(15.,0)=-1.422453e-02 -1.422453e-02
 jas,j(20.,0)=1.670247e-01 1.670247e-01
 enter n z-complex
0 1 0
 J,Y= 7.651977e-01 + 0.000000e+00 i
 8.825696e-02 + 0.000000e+00 i
 J',Y'= -4.400506e-01 + 0.000000e+00 i
 7.812128e-01 + 0.000000e+00 i
 H2,H2'= 7.651977e-01  -8.825696e-02 i
 -4.400506e-01  -7.812128e-01 i
 Ibess= 1.266066e+00 + 0.000000e+00 i
 Kbess= 4.210244e-01 + 1.307951e-13 i
 jn=7.651977e-01 7.651977e-01
 kelvin be= 9.843818e-01 + 2.495660e-01 i  kelvin ke=
2.867062e-01  -4.949946e-01 i
 enter n z-complex
0 0 1
 J,Y= 1.266066e+00 + 0.000000e+00 i
 -2.680325e-01 + 1.266066e+00 i
 J',Y'= 0.000000e+00  -5.651591e-01 i
 5.651591e-01  -3.831860e-01 i
 H2,H2'= 2.532132e+00 + 2.680325e-01 i
 -3.831860e-01  -1.130318e+00 i
 Ibess= 7.651977e-01 + 0.000000e+00 i
 Kbess= -1.386337e-01  -1.201970e+00 i
 enter n z-complex
1 1 0
 J,Y= 4.400506e-01 + 0.000000e+00 i
 -7.812128e-01 + 0.000000e+00 i
 J',Y'= 3.251471e-01 + 0.000000e+00
i  8.694698e-01 + 0.000000e+00 i
 H2,H2'= 4.400506e-01 + 7.812128e-01
i  3.251471e-01  -8.694698e-01 i
 Ibess= 5.651591e-01  -5.651591e-01 i
```

```
 Kbess= 6.019072e-01  -5.863305e-14 i
 jn=4.400506e-01 4.400506e-01
 kelvin be= -3.958683e-01 + 3.075566e-01 i  kelvin ke=
-7.403223e-01  -2.419960e-01 i
 enter n z-complex
0 1 1
 J,Y= 9.376085e-01  -4.965299e-01 i
 4.454745e-01 + 7.101586e-01 i
 J',Y'= -6.141603e-01  -3.650280e-01 i
 6.576945e-01  -6.298010e-01 i
 H2,H2'= 1.647767e+00  -9.420044e-01 i
 -1.243961e+00  -1.022723e+00 i
 Ibess= 9.376085e-01 + 4.965299e-01 i
 Kbess= 8.019773e-02  -3.572775e-01 i
 enter n z-complex
0 0 0


 Chapter 10: Spherical Bessel functions

 Spherical bessel functions:
 spherical i:enter n, x
2 2
 3.518561e-01
 i[0]=1.813430e+00
 i[1]=9.743827e-01
 i[2]=3.518561e-01
 ck: i[0]=1.813430e+00
 ck: i[1]=9.743827e-01
 spherical i:enter n, x
-2 2
 8.728813e-01
 i[0]=1.813430e+00
 i[1]=9.743827e-01
 i[2]=3.518561e-01
 ck: i(-1) pro I[-1/2]=1.881098e+00
 ck: i(-2) pro I[-3/2]=8.728813e-01
 spherical i:enter n, x
-1 -1
 k:enter n, x
2 2
 3.454493e-01
 0 1.062921e-01
 1 1.594381e-01
 2 3.454493e-01
 k:enter n, x
-2 2
 1.594381e-01
 k:enter n, x
```

```
-1 -1
 j:enter n, x
2 2
 1.984479e-01
 0 4.546487e-01
 1 4.353978e-01
 2 1.984479e-01
 j:enter n, x
-2 2
 -3.506120e-01
 j:enter n, x
-1 -1
 y:enter n, x
2 2
 -7.339914e-01
 0 2.080734e-01
 1 -3.506120e-01
 2 -7.339914e-01
 y:enter n, x
-2 2
 4.353978e-01
 y:enter n, x
-1 -1


 Chapter 10: Airy Functions & Integrals

 x 1.000000e-01 Ai,Bi=3.292032e-01 6.598619e-01
3.808488e-01 5.699992e-01
 x 2.000000e-01 Ai,Bi=3.037031e-01 7.054642e-01
4.062842e-01 5.245090e-01
 x 3.000000e-01 Ai,Bi=2.788066e-01 7.524858e-01
4.309017e-01 4.779757e-01
 x 4.000000e-01 Ai,Bi=2.547424e-01 8.017732e-01
4.542249e-01 4.300225e-01
 x 5.000000e-01 Ai,Bi=2.316936e-01 8.542771e-01
4.757283e-01 3.803529e-01
 x 6.000000e-01 Ai,Bi=2.098001e-01 9.110635e-01
4.948500e-01 3.287924e-01
 x 7.000000e-01 Ai,Bi=1.891626e-01 9.733285e-01
5.110018e-01 2.752698e-01
 x 8.000000e-01 Ai,Bi=1.698463e-01 1.042422e+00
5.235748e-01 2.198266e-01
 x 9.000000e-01 Ai,Bi=1.518867e-01 1.119873e+00
5.319621e-01 1.626356e-01
 x 1.000000e+00 Ai,Bi=1.352924e-01 1.207424e+00
5.355609e-01 1.039973e-01
 x 1.000000e+00 Ai,Bi=1.352924e-01 1.207424e+00
5.355609e-01 1.039973e-01
```

```
 x 2.000000e+00 Ai,Bi=3.492385e-02 3.298091e+00
2.274082e-01 -4.123022e-01
 x 3.000000e+00 Ai,Bi=6.589935e-03 1.403729e+01
-3.788137e-01 -1.982907e-01
 x 4.000000e+00 Ai,Bi=9.462765e-04 8.384667e+01
-7.026726e-02 3.922335e-01
 x 5.000000e+00 Ai,Bi=1.119941e-04 6.577874e+02
3.507618e-01 -1.383656e-01
 x 6.000000e+00 Ai,Bi=9.944367e-06 6.533836e+03
-3.292727e-01 -1.467730e-01
 x 7.000000e+00 Ai,Bi=7.490534e-07 8.030801e+04
1.843215e-01 2.938421e-01
 x 8.000000e+00 Ai,Bi=4.691535e-08 1.199390e+06
-5.270962e-02 -3.313097e-01
 x 9.000000e+00 Ai,Bi=2.470920e-09 2.147042e+07
-2.213936e-02 3.249867e-01
 x 1.000000e+01 Ai,Bi=1.104673e-10 4.556032e+08
4.024690e-02 -3.147075e-01
 x 1.000000e+00 Ai',Bi'=-1.591476e-01 9.324366e-01
-1.016123e-02 5.923770e-01
 x 2.000000e+00 Ai',Bi'=-5.309062e-02 4.100678e+00
6.182579e-01 2.787971e-01
 x 3.000000e+00 Ai',Bi'=-1.191376e-02 2.292215e+01
3.145864e-01 -6.756122e-01
 x 4.000000e+00 Ai',Bi'=-1.962527e-03 1.619259e+02
-7.906258e-01 -1.166765e-01
 x 5.000000e+00 Ai',Bi'=-0.000000e+00 1.435851e+03
3.271824e-01 7.784163e-01
 x 6.000000e+00 Ai',Bi'=-2.435696e-05 1.600365e+04
3.595008e-01 -8.064975e-01
 x 7.000000e+00 Ai',Bi'=-1.981725e-06 2.124672e+05
-7.774038e-01 4.876473e-01
 x 8.000000e+00 Ai',Bi'=-1.326929e-07 3.392303e+06
9.370607e-01 -1.490800e-01
 x 9.000000e+00 Ai',Bi'=-7.412614e-09 6.441012e+07
-9.749420e-01 -6.641770e-02
 x 1.000000e+01 Ai',Bi'=-3.493232e-10 1.440725e+09
9.951791e-01 1.272707e-01
 x=1.000000e-01 Ai=3.292032e-01 Ai(via f,g)=3.292031e-01
   Bi=6.598619e-01 via(f,g)=6.598617e-01
 x=2.000000e-01 Ai=3.037031e-01 Ai(via f,g)=3.037030e-01
   Bi=7.054642e-01 via(f,g)=7.054640e-01
 x=3.000000e-01 Ai=2.788066e-01 Ai(via f,g)=2.788065e-01
   Bi=7.524858e-01 via(f,g)=7.524856e-01
 x=4.000000e-01 Ai=2.547424e-01 Ai(via f,g)=2.547423e-01
   Bi=8.017732e-01 via(f,g)=8.017730e-01
 x=5.000000e-01 Ai=2.316936e-01 Ai(via f,g)=2.316936e-01
   Bi=8.542771e-01 via(f,g)=8.542769e-01
 x=6.000000e-01 Ai=2.098001e-01 Ai(via f,g)=2.098001e-01
```

```
   Bi=9.110635e-01 via(f,g)=9.110633e-01
 x=7.000000e-01 Ai=1.891626e-01 Ai(via f,g)=1.891624e-01
   Bi=9.733285e-01 via(f,g)=9.733287e-01
 x=8.000000e-01 Ai=1.698463e-01 Ai(via f,g)=1.698463e-01
   Bi=1.042422e+00 via(f,g)=1.042422e+00
 x=9.000000e-01 Ai=1.518867e-01 Ai(via f,g)=1.518868e-01
   Bi=1.119873e+00 via(f,g)=1.119873e+00
 x=1.000000e+00 Ai=1.352924e-01 Ai(via f,g)=1.352922e-01
   Bi=1.207424e+00 via(f,g)=1.207423e+00
 x 1.000000 Airy integrals=2.363173e-01 4.656740e-01
8.727691e-01 3.730050e-01
 x 2.000000 Airy integrals=3.125328e-01 9.017728e-01
2.873408e+00 1.935474e-01
 x 3.000000 Airy integrals=3.299204e-01 8.014628e-01
1.006200e+01 -1.954425e-01
 x 4.000000 Airy integrals=3.328927e-01 4.780075e-01
4.821948e+01 -5.076007e-02
 x 5.000000 Airy integrals=3.332875e-01 7.178822e-01
3.214783e+02 1.587309e-01
 x 6.000000 Airy integrals=3.333269e-01 7.326752e-01
2.838370e+03 -1.303810e-01
 x 7.000000 Airy integrals=3.333796e-01 5.534517e-01
3.180644e+04 6.491667e-02
 x 8.000000 Airy integrals=3.333333e-01 7.839826e-01
4.400653e+05 -1.475649e-02
 x 9.000000 Airy integrals=3.333333e-01 5.588196e-01
7.377921e+06 -1.033005e-02
 x 10.000000 Airy integrals=3.333333e-01 7.656984e-01
1.478098e+08 1.504037e-02


 Chapter 11: Integrals

 enter x=0, r for bickley x==0 analytic
0 1
 x, r 0.000000e+00 1.000000e+00
Ki=1.570796e+00
 analytic 1.570796e+00
 enter x=0, r for bickley x==0 analytic
0 2
 x, r 0.000000e+00 2.000000e+00
Ki=1.000000e+00
 analytic 1.000000e+00
 enter x=0, r for bickley x==0 analytic
0 3
 x, r 0.000000e+00 3.000000e+00
Ki=7.853981e-01
 analytic 7.853982e-01
 enter x=0, r for bickley x==0 analytic
```

```
0 .5
 x, r 0.000000e+00 5.000000e-01
 warning: bickley may not have achieved desired accuracy
Ki=2.621132e+00
 analytic 2.622059e+00
 enter x=0, r for bickley x==0 analytic
1 1
 x, r 1.000000e+00 1.000000e+00
Ki=3.282865e-01
 enter x=0, r for bickley x==0 analytic
0   -1 -1
 enter x, r,n[int] for Jrn1 1 0
 x, r 1.000000e+00 1.000000e+00 n=0
 rth integral:Jn=9.197304e-01
 enter x, r,n[int] for Jrn1 1 1
 x, r 1.000000e+00 1.000000e+00 n=1
 rth integral:Jn=2.348023e-01
 enter x, r,n[int] for Jrn0 0 0
 integrals of bessel functions
 I0/t 5.000000e-01 3.149527e-02 1.910285e-02 0.000000e+00
0.000000e+00 4
 I0/t 1.000000e+00 1.289794e-01 4.744889e-02 0.000000e+00
0.000000e+00 5
 I0/t 1.500000e+00 3.018715e-01 6.735663e-02 0.000000e+00
0.000000e+00 6
 I0/t 2.000000e+00 5.673537e-01 7.678298e-02 0.000000e+00
0.000000e+00 6
 I0/t 2.500000e+00 9.528591e-01 7.821544e-02 0.000000e+00
0.000000e+00 7
 I0/t 3.000000e+00 1.500125e+00 7.468681e-02 0.000000e+00
0.000000e+00 8
 I0/t 3.500000e+00 2.271508e+00 6.859360e-02 0.000000e+00
0.000000e+00 8
 I0/t 4.000000e+00 3.359670e+00 6.153450e-02 0.000000e+00
0.000000e+00 9
 I0/t 4.500000e+00 4.902333e+00 5.446000e-02 0.000000e+00
0.000000e+00 9
 I0/t 5.000000e+00 7.104776e+00 4.787161e-02 7.104925e+00
4.787261e-02 10
 I0/t 5.500000e+00 1.027436e+01 4.198898e-02 1.027436e+01
4.198898e-02 10
 I0/t 6.000000e+00 1.487192e+01 3.686381e-02 1.487192e+01
3.686381e-02 10
 I0/t 6.500000e+00 2.159491e+01 3.246663e-02 2.159491e+01
3.246663e-02 10
 I0/t 7.000000e+00 3.149947e+01 2.872380e-02 3.149947e+01
2.872380e-02 10
 I0/t 7.500000e+00 4.619036e+01 2.554717e-02 4.619036e+01
2.554717e-02 10
```

```
 I0/t 8.000000e+00 6.811823e+01 2.285112e-02 6.811823e+01
2.285112e-02 10
 I0/t 8.500000e+00 1.010384e+02 2.055811e-02 1.010384e+02
2.055811e-02 10
 I0/t 9.000000e+00 1.507223e+02 1.860061e-02 1.507223e+02
1.860061e-02 10
 I0/t 9.500000e+00 2.260650e+02 1.692138e-02 2.260650e+02
1.692138e-02 10
int Y0/t 5.000000e-01 2.696885e-01
int Y0/t 1.000000e+00 3.952729e-01
int Y0/t 1.500000e+00 2.976970e-01
int Y0/t 2.000000e+00 1.665013e-01
int Y0/t 2.500000e+00 5.158229e-02
int Y0/t 3.000000e+00 -2.987272e-02
int Y0/t 3.500000e+00 -7.441025e-02
int Y0/t 4.000000e+00 -8.613706e-02
int Y0/t 4.500000e+00 -7.340123e-02
 int K0 0.000000e+00 0.000000e+00
 int K0 5.000000e-01 9.271025e-01
 int K0 1.000000e+00 1.242510e+00
 int K0 1.500000e+00 1.394582e+00
 int K0 2.000000e+00 1.473657e+00
 int K0 2.500000e+00 1.516366e+00
 int K0 3.000000e+00 1.539944e+00
 int K0 3.500000e+00 1.553160e+00
 int K0 4.000000e+00 1.560648e+00
 int K0 4.500000e+00 1.564927e+00
 int K0 0.000000e+00 0.000000e+00
 int K0 1.000000e-01 3.421644e-01
 int K0 2.000000e-01 5.471164e-01
 int K0 3.000000e-01 7.019641e-01
 int K0 4.000000e-01 8.255929e-01
 int K0 5.000000e-01 9.271025e-01
 int K0 6.000000e-01 1.011906e+00
 int K0 7.000000e-01 1.083598e+00
 int K0 8.000000e-01 1.144734e+00
 int K0 9.000000e-01 1.197217e+00
 int K0 1.000000e+00 1.242510e+00
 int K0 1.100000e+00 1.281764e+00
 int K0 1.200000e+00 1.315907e+00
 int K0 1.300000e+00 1.345694e+00
 int K0 1.400000e+00 1.371746e+00
 int K0 1.500000e+00 1.394582e+00
 int K0 1.600000e+00 1.414640e+00
 int K0 1.700000e+00 1.432286e+00
 int K0 1.800000e+00 1.447836e+00
 int K0 1.900000e+00 1.461555e+00
 int K0 2.000000e+00 1.473657e+00
 int K0 2.100000e+00 1.484380e+00
```

```
int K0 2.200000e+00 1.493873e+00
int K0 2.300000e+00 1.502284e+00
int K0 2.400000e+00 1.509744e+00
int K0 2.500000e+00 1.516366e+00
int K0 2.600000e+00 1.522247e+00
int K0 2.700000e+00 1.527474e+00
int K0 2.800000e+00 1.532123e+00
int K0 2.900000e+00 1.536261e+00
int K0 3.000000e+00 1.539944e+00
int K0 3.100000e+00 1.543226e+00
int K0 3.200000e+00 1.546150e+00
int K0 3.300000e+00 1.548758e+00
int K0 3.400000e+00 1.551084e+00
int K0 3.500000e+00 1.553160e+00
int K0 3.600000e+00 1.555013e+00
int K0 3.700000e+00 1.556668e+00
int K0 3.800000e+00 1.558146e+00
int K0 3.900000e+00 1.559467e+00
int K0 4.000000e+00 1.560648e+00
int K0 4.100000e+00 1.561704e+00
int K0 4.200000e+00 1.562649e+00
int K0 4.300000e+00 1.563494e+00
int K0 4.400000e+00 1.564250e+00
int K0 4.500000e+00 1.564927e+00
int K0 4.600000e+00 1.565533e+00
int K0 4.700000e+00 1.566075e+00
int K0 4.800000e+00 1.566561e+00
int K0 4.900000e+00 1.566997e+00
int K0/t 5.000000e-01 6.657510e-01 5.488189e-01
0.000000e+00 0.000000e+00 5
int K0/t 1.000000e+00 2.085183e-01 5.668115e-01
0.000000e+00 0.000000e+00 6
int K0/t 1.500000e+00 8.237150e-02 5.537452e-01
0.000000e+00 0.000000e+00 7
int K0/t 2.000000e+00 3.617749e-02 5.346350e-01
0.000000e+00 0.000000e+00 8
int K0/t 2.500000e+00 1.690871e-02 5.149758e-01
0.000000e+00 0.000000e+00 8
int K0/t 3.000000e+00 8.236313e-03 4.962923e-01
0.000000e+00 0.000000e+00 9
int K0/t 3.500000e+00 4.132592e-03 4.789843e-01
0.000000e+00 0.000000e+00 10
int K0/t 4.000000e+00 2.120423e-03 4.630846e-01
2.120418e-03 4.630835e-01 10
int K0/t 4.500000e+00 1.107205e-03 4.485032e-01
1.107210e-03 4.485054e-01 11
int K0/t 5.000000e+00 5.863563e-04 4.351150e-01
5.863612e-04 4.351186e-01 12
int K0/t 5.500000e+00 3.141558e-04 4.227927e-01
```

```
3.141564e-04 4.227935e-01 12
int K0/t 6.000000e+00 1.699666e-04 4.114165e-01
1.699659e-04 4.114149e-01 13
int K0/t 6.500000e+00 9.272327e-05 4.008817e-01
9.272255e-05 4.008786e-01 14
int K0/t 7.000000e+00 5.094819e-05 3.911004e-01
5.094710e-05 3.910919e-01 14
int K0/t 7.500000e+00 2.816903e-05 3.819810e-01
2.816852e-05 3.819741e-01 15
int K0/t 8.000000e+00 1.566025e-05 3.734603e-01
1.566002e-05 3.734549e-01 16
int K0/t 8.500000e+00 8.749377e-06 3.655099e-01
8.748504e-06 3.654734e-01 16
int K0/t 9.000000e+00 4.909004e-06 3.580026e-01
4.908647e-06 3.579766e-01 17
int K0/t 9.500000e+00 2.765079e-06 3.509366e-01
2.764933e-06 3.509182e-01 18
int J0/t 5.000000e-01 3.100699e-02
int J0/t 1.000000e+00 1.211652e-01
int J0/t 1.500000e+00 2.622772e-01
int J0/t 2.000000e+00 4.419194e-01
int J0/t 2.500000e+00 6.450916e-01
int J0/t 3.000000e+00 8.561467e-01
int J0/t 3.500000e+00 1.060700e+00
int J0/t 4.000000e+00 1.247237e+00
int J0/t 4.500000e+00 1.408187e+00
 int J0 5.000000e-01 4.896805e-01 6.153019e-02
 int J0 1.000000e+00 9.197304e-01 2.348023e-01
 int J0 1.500000e+00 1.241450e+00 4.881723e-01
 int J0 2.000000e+00 1.425770e+00 7.761092e-01
 int J0 2.500000e+00 1.467981e+00 1.048384e+00
 int J0 3.000000e+00 1.387567e+00 1.260052e+00
 int J0 3.500000e+00 1.223306e+00 1.380128e+00
 int J0 4.000000e+00 1.024734e+00 1.397150e+00
 int J0 4.500000e+00 8.418625e-01 1.320543e+00
 int J0 5.000000e+00 7.153119e-01 1.177597e+00
 int J0 5.500000e+00 6.689145e-01 1.006844e+00
 int J0 6.000000e+00 7.062212e-01 8.493547e-01
 int J0 6.500000e+00 8.114767e-01 7.399054e-01
 int J0 7.000000e+00 9.546403e-01 6.999207e-01
 int J0 7.500000e+00 1.099171e+00 7.336603e-01
 int J0 8.000000e+00 1.210747e+00 8.283492e-01
 int J0 8.500000e+00 1.264948e+00 9.580608e-01
 int J0 9.000000e+00 1.252266e+00 1.090334e+00
 int J0 9.500000e+00 1.179442e+00 1.193929e+00
 int J0 1.000000e+01 1.067011e+00 1.245936e+00
 int J0 1.050000e+01 9.438016e-01 1.236648e+00
 int J0 1.100000e+01 8.397926e-01 1.171190e+00
 int J0 1.150000e+01 7.790062e-01 1.067654e+00
```

```
 int J0 1.200000e+01 7.741205e-01 9.523107e-01
 enter x for integral i0i y0i
1
 integrals I0 1.086521e+00 Y0 -6.370694e-01
 enter x for integral i0i y0i
10
 integrals I0 3.021987e+03 Y0 2.412904e-01
 enter x for integral i0i y0i
.1
 integrals I0 1.000834e-01 Y0 -2.174306e-01
 enter x for integral i0i y0i
0

 Chapter 12: Struve and Anger-Weber functions & Integrals

 enter x, nu
1 0
 H= 5.686566e-01 L=7.102431e-01
 enter x, nu
10 0
 H= 1.187437e-01 L=2.815652e+03
 enter x, nu
.1 0
 H= 6.359126e-02 L=6.373274e-02
 enter x, nu
1 1
 H= 1.984574e-01 L=2.267644e-01
 enter x, nu
0 0
x=0.000000e+00 int H 0.000000e+00 H/t*2/pi= 1.000000e+00,
  int L 0.000000e+00 f2=0.000000e+00
x=1.000000e-01 int H 3.181331e-03 H/t*2/pi= 9.594865e-01,
  int L 3.184868e-03 f2=9.689850e-02
x=2.000000e-01 int H 1.270413e-02 H/t*2/pi= 9.190630e-01,
  int L 1.276072e-02 f2=1.879069e-01
x=3.000000e-01 int H 2.850499e-02 H/t*2/pi= 8.788190e-01,
  int L 2.879147e-02 f2=2.734661e-01
x=4.000000e-01 int H 5.047880e-02 H/t*2/pi= 8.388431e-01,
  int L 5.138423e-02 f2=3.539812e-01
x=5.000000e-01 int H 7.847957e-02 H/t*2/pi= 7.992227e-01,
  int L 8.069011e-02 f2=4.298247e-01
x=6.000000e-01 int H 1.123216e-01 H/t*2/pi= 7.600436e-01,
  int L 1.169055e-01 f2=5.013393e-01
x=7.000000e-01 int H 1.517810e-01 H/t*2/pi= 7.213892e-01,
  int L 1.602736e-01 f2=5.688401e-01
x=8.000000e-01 int H 1.965974e-01 H/t*2/pi= 6.833407e-01,
  int L 2.110865e-01 f2=6.326173e-01
x=9.000000e-01 int H 2.464761e-01 H/t*2/pi= 6.459762e-01,
  int L 2.696871e-01 f2=6.929382e-01
```

```
x=1.000000e+00 int H 3.010904e-01 H/t*2/pi= 6.093708e-01,
  int L 3.364726e-01 f2=7.500486e-01
x=1.100000e+00 int H 3.600841e-01 H/t*2/pi= 5.735958e-01,
  int L 4.118970e-01 f2=8.041753e-01
x=1.200000e+00 int H 4.230744e-01 H/t*2/pi= 5.387187e-01,
  int L 4.964751e-01 f2=8.555272e-01
x=1.300000e+00 int H 4.896550e-01 H/t*2/pi= 5.048028e-01,
  int L 5.907867e-01 f2=9.042970e-01
x=1.400000e+00 int H 5.593992e-01 H/t*2/pi= 4.719071e-01,
  int L 6.954811e-01 f2=9.506624e-01
x=1.500000e+00 int H 6.318631e-01 H/t*2/pi= 4.400856e-01,
  int L 8.112825e-01 f2=9.947874e-01
x=1.600000e+00 int H 7.065895e-01 H/t*2/pi= 4.093877e-01,
  int L 9.389960e-01 f2=1.036823e+00
x=1.700000e+00 int H 7.831112e-01 H/t*2/pi= 3.798573e-01,
  int L 1.079514e+00 f2=1.076910e+00
x=1.800000e+00 int H 8.609543e-01 H/t*2/pi= 3.515335e-01,
  int L 1.233823e+00 f2=1.115177e+00
x=1.900000e+00 int H 9.396428e-01 H/t*2/pi= 3.244496e-01,
  int L 1.403013e+00 f2=1.151743e+00
x=2.000000e+00 int H 1.018701e+00 H/t*2/pi= 2.986339e-01,
  int L 1.588285e+00 f2=1.186719e+00
x=2.100000e+00 int H 1.097659e+00 H/t*2/pi= 2.741086e-01,
  int L 1.790962e+00 f2=1.220207e+00
x=2.200000e+00 int H 1.176053e+00 H/t*2/pi= 2.508907e-01,
  int L 2.012499e+00 f2=1.252302e+00
x=2.300000e+00 int H 1.253434e+00 H/t*2/pi= 2.289917e-01,
  int L 2.254495e+00 f2=1.283091e+00
x=2.400000e+00 int H 1.329364e+00 H/t*2/pi= 2.084172e-01,
  int L 2.518708e+00 f2=1.312655e+00
x=2.500000e+00 int H 1.403427e+00 H/t*2/pi= 1.891678e-01,
  int L 2.807067e+00 f2=1.341070e+00
x=2.600000e+00 int H 1.475227e+00 H/t*2/pi= 1.712382e-01,
  int L 3.121689e+00 f2=1.368406e+00
x=2.700000e+00 int H 1.544392e+00 H/t*2/pi= 1.546184e-01,
  int L 3.464899e+00 f2=1.394727e+00
x=2.800000e+00 int H 1.610577e+00 H/t*2/pi= 1.392929e-01,
  int L 3.839245e+00 f2=1.420094e+00
x=2.900000e+00 int H 1.673465e+00 H/t*2/pi= 1.252416e-01,
  int L 4.247522e+00 f2=1.444562e+00
x=3.000000e+00 int H 1.732773e+00 H/t*2/pi= 1.124393e-01,
  int L 4.692798e+00 f2=1.468184e+00
x=3.100000e+00 int H 1.788248e+00 H/t*2/pi= 1.008567e-01,
  int L 5.178432e+00 f2=1.491008e+00
x=3.200000e+00 int H 1.839675e+00 H/t*2/pi= 9.046014e-02,
  int L 5.708112e+00 f2=1.513078e+00
x=3.300000e+00 int H 1.886873e+00 H/t*2/pi= 8.121196e-02,
  int L 6.285879e+00 f2=1.534438e+00
x=3.400000e+00 int H 1.929699e+00 H/t*2/pi= 7.307088e-02,
```

```
  int L 6.916164e+00 f2=1.555127e+00
x=3.500000e+00 int H 1.968046e+00 H/t*2/pi= 6.599227e-02,
  int L 7.603826e+00 f2=1.575180e+00
x=3.600000e+00 int H 2.001847e+00 H/t*2/pi= 5.992848e-02,
  int L 8.354192e+00 f2=1.594633e+00
x=3.700000e+00 int H 2.031071e+00 H/t*2/pi= 5.482913e-02,
  int L 9.173103e+00 f2=1.613518e+00
x=3.800000e+00 int H 2.055726e+00 H/t*2/pi= 5.064151e-02,
  int L 1.006696e+01 f2=1.631864e+00
x=3.900000e+00 int H 2.075858e+00 H/t*2/pi= 4.731088e-02,
  int L 1.104280e+01 f2=1.649701e+00
x=4.000000e+00 int H 2.091545e+00 H/t*2/pi= 4.478088e-02,
  int L 1.210832e+01 f2=1.667054e+00
x=4.100000e+00 int H 2.102905e+00 H/t*2/pi= 4.299383e-02,
  int L 1.327196e+01 f2=1.683951e+00
x=4.200000e+00 int H 2.110085e+00 H/t*2/pi= 4.189113e-02,
  int L 1.454300e+01 f2=1.700413e+00
x=4.300000e+00 int H 2.113265e+00 H/t*2/pi= 4.141360e-02,
  int L 1.593159e+01 f2=1.716465e+00
x=4.400000e+00 int H 2.112655e+00 H/t*2/pi= 4.150181e-02,
  int L 1.744890e+01 f2=1.732128e+00
x=4.500000e+00 int H 2.108492e+00 H/t*2/pi= 4.209647e-02,
  int L 1.910714e+01 f2=1.747426e+00
x=4.600000e+00 int H 2.101037e+00 H/t*2/pi= 4.313874e-02,
  int L 2.091976e+01 f2=1.762377e+00
x=4.700000e+00 int H 2.090574e+00 H/t*2/pi= 4.457053e-02,
  int L 2.290146e+01 f2=1.777003e+00
x=4.800000e+00 int H 2.077406e+00 H/t*2/pi= 4.633486e-02,
  int L 2.506843e+01 f2=1.791323e+00
x=4.900000e+00 int H 2.061852e+00 H/t*2/pi= 4.837613e-02,
  int L 2.743838e+01 f2=1.805361e+00
 anger weber
 nu=x=.5, 8.010519e-01 3.886429e-01
 anger weber
 nu=.5 x=10, -1.308975e-01 -2.212582e-01
 x 2.000000e-01 nu=0.000000e+00 J=9.900250e-01 j0=9.900250e-
01
   E=-1.267590e-01 -1.267590e-01
 x 4.000000e-01 nu=0.000000e+00 J=9.603982e-01 j0=9.603982e-
01
   E=-2.501497e-01 -2.501497e-01
 x 6.000000e-01 nu=0.000000e+00 J=9.120049e-01 j0=9.120049e-
01
   E=-3.669113e-01 -3.669114e-01
 x 8.000000e-01 nu=0.000000e+00 J=8.462874e-01 j0=8.462874e-
01
   E=-4.739943e-01 -4.739943e-01
 x 1.000000e+00 nu=0.000000e+00 J=7.651977e-01 j0=7.651977e-
01
```

```
   E=-5.686565e-01 -5.686566e-01
 x 1.200000e+00 nu=0.000000e+00 J=6.711327e-01 j0=6.711327e-
01
   E=-6.485498e-01 -6.485499e-01
 x 1.400000e+00 nu=0.000000e+00 J=5.668551e-01 j0=5.668551e-
01
   E=-7.117923e-01 -7.117924e-01
 x 1.600000e+00 nu=0.000000e+00 J=4.554022e-01 j0=4.554022e-
01
   E=-7.570252e-01 -7.570254e-01
 x 1.800000e+00 nu=0.000000e+00 J=3.399864e-01 j0=3.399864e-
01
   E=-7.834520e-01 -7.834523e-01
 x 2.000000e+00 nu=0.000000e+00 J=2.238908e-01 j0=2.238908e-
01
   E=-7.908585e-01 -7.908588e-01
 x 2.000000e-01 nu=1.000000e+00 J=9.950083e-02 j1=9.950083e-
02
   E=6.281540e-01 6.281541e-01
 x 4.000000e-01 nu=1.000000e+00 J=1.960266e-01 j1=1.960266e-
01
   E=6.030271e-01 6.030272e-01
 x 6.000000e-01 nu=1.000000e+00 J=2.867010e-01 j1=2.867010e-
01
   E=5.620400e-01 5.620401e-01
 x 8.000000e-01 nu=1.000000e+00 J=3.688420e-01 j1=3.688420e-
01
   E=5.064972e-01 5.064973e-01
 x 1.000000e+00 nu=1.000000e+00 J=4.400506e-01 j1=4.400506e-
01
   E=4.381623e-01 4.381624e-01
 x 1.200000e+00 nu=1.000000e+00 J=4.982891e-01 j1=4.982891e-
01
   E=3.591978e-01 3.591979e-01
 x 1.400000e+00 nu=1.000000e+00 J=5.419477e-01 j1=5.419477e-
01
   E=2.720916e-01 2.720917e-01
 x 1.600000e+00 nu=1.000000e+00 J=5.698959e-01 j1=5.698959e-
01
   E=1.795724e-01 1.795725e-01
 x 1.800000e+00 nu=1.000000e+00 J=5.815169e-01 j1=5.815170e-
01
   E=8.451751e-02 8.451755e-02
 x 2.000000e+00 nu=1.000000e+00 J=5.767248e-01 j1=5.767248e-
01
   E=-1.014409e-02 -1.014406e-02
 x 1.000000e+00 nu=1.000000e+00 J=4.400506e-01 j1=4.400506e-
01
 E=4.381623e-01 4.381624e-01
```

```
 x 2.000000e+00 nu=1.000000e+00 J=5.767248e-01 j1=5.767248e-
01
 E=-1.014409e-02 -1.014406e-02
 x 3.000000e+00 nu=1.000000e+00 J=3.390589e-01 j1=3.390590e-
01
 E=-3.834899e-01 -3.834900e-01
 x 4.000000e+00 nu=1.000000e+00 J=-6.604337e-02
j1=-6.604332e-02
 E=-4.331067e-01 -4.331071e-01
 x 5.000000e+00 nu=1.000000e+00 J=-3.275791e-01
j1=-3.275791e-01
 E=-1.711912e-01 -1.711923e-01
 x 6.000000e+00 nu=1.000000e+00 J=-2.766836e-01 j1=
-2.766839e-01
 E=1.584468e-01 1.584444e-01
 x 7.000000e+00 nu=1.000000e+00 J=-4.687109e-03 j1=
-4.682827e-03
 E=2.896732e-01 2.903140e-01
 x 8.000000e+00 nu=1.000000e+00 J=2.346345e-01 j1=2.346363e-
01
 E=1.481146e-01 1.485036e-01
 x 9.000000e+00 nu=1.000000e+00 J=2.453119e-01 j1=2.453118e-
01
 E=-1.121729e-01 -1.119228e-01
 x 1.000000e+01 nu=1.000000e+00 J=4.347336e-02 j1=4.347274e-
02
 E=-2.553813e-01 -2.552129e-01
 enter int m, complex z for integral Anger Weber
0 0 .5
 answer= 1.505452e-01 4.598652e-01
 enter int m, complex z for integral Anger Weber
0 0 6
 answer= 1.177203e+00 3.870830e-01
 enter int m, complex z for integral Anger Weber
0 -.5 5
 answer= 1.473493e+00 6.066011e-01
 enter int m, complex z for integral Anger Weber
0 1 0
 answer= 5.933585e-01 0.000000e+00
 enter int m, complex z for integral Anger Weber
1 1 0
 answer= -0.000000e+00 3.289242e-01
 enter int m, complex z for integral Anger Weber
0 1 1
 answer= 7.191210e-01 2.845165e-01
 enter int m, complex z for integral Anger Weber
0 0 0
```

```
Output of test driver for zerobess()
1 zero for J 0.000000 = 2.404826e+00
 2 zero for J 0.000000 = 5.520078e+00
 3 zero for J 0.000000 = 8.653728e+00
 4 zero for J 0.000000 = 1.179153e+01
 5 zero for J 0.000000 = 1.493092e+01
 6 zero for J 0.000000 = 1.807106e+01
 7 zero for J 0.000000 = 2.121164e+01
 8 zero for J 0.000000 = 2.435247e+01
 9 zero for J 0.000000 = 2.749348e+01
 10 zero for J 0.000000 = 3.063461e+01
 1 zero for Y 0.000000 = 8.935770e-01
 2 zero for Y 0.000000 = 3.957678e+00
 3 zero for Y 0.000000 = 7.086051e+00
 4 zero for Y 0.000000 = 1.022234e+01
 5 zero for Y 0.000000 = 1.336110e+01
 6 zero for Y 0.000000 = 1.650092e+01
 7 zero for Y 0.000000 = 1.964131e+01
 8 zero for Y 0.000000 = 2.278203e+01
 9 zero for Y 0.000000 = 2.592296e+01
 10 zero for Y 0.000000 = 2.906403e+01
 1 zero for J' 0.000000 = 0.000000e+00
 2 zero for J' 0.000000 = 3.831706e+00
 3 zero for J' 0.000000 = 7.015587e+00
 4 zero for J' 0.000000 = 1.017347e+01
 5 zero for J' 0.000000 = 1.332369e+01
 6 zero for J' 0.000000 = 1.647063e+01
 7 zero for J' 0.000000 = 1.961586e+01
 8 zero for J' 0.000000 = 2.276008e+01
 9 zero for J' 0.000000 = 2.590367e+01
 10 zero for J' 0.000000 = 2.904683e+01
 1 zero for Y' 0.000000 = 2.197141e+00
 2 zero for Y' 0.000000 = 5.429681e+00
 3 zero for Y' 0.000000 = 8.596006e+00
 4 zero for Y' 0.000000 = 1.174916e+01
 5 zero for Y' 0.000000 = 1.489744e+01
 6 zero for Y' 0.000000 = 1.804340e+01
 7 zero for Y' 0.000000 = 2.118807e+01
 8 zero for Y' 0.000000 = 2.433194e+01
 9 zero for Y' 0.000000 = 2.747529e+01
 10 zero for Y' 0.000000 = 3.061829e+01
 1 zero for J 0.500000 = 3.141593e+00
 2 zero for J 0.500000 = 6.283185e+00
 3 zero for J 0.500000 = 9.424778e+00
 4 zero for J 0.500000 = 1.256637e+01
 5 zero for J 0.500000 = 1.570796e+01
 6 zero for J 0.500000 = 1.884956e+01
 7 zero for J 0.500000 = 2.199115e+01
 8 zero for J 0.500000 = 2.513274e+01
```

```
9 zero for J 0.500000 = 2.827433e+01
10 zero for J 0.500000 = 3.141593e+01
1 zero for J 1.000000 = 3.831706e+00
2 zero for J 1.000000 = 7.015587e+00
3 zero for J 1.000000 = 1.017347e+01
4 zero for J 1.000000 = 1.332369e+01
5 zero for J 1.000000 = 1.647063e+01
6 zero for J 1.000000 = 1.961586e+01
7 zero for J 1.000000 = 2.276008e+01
8 zero for J 1.000000 = 2.590367e+01
9 zero for J 1.000000 = 2.904683e+01
10 zero for J 1.000000 = 3.218968e+01
```

Chapter 10

Bessel Functions of Fractional Order

Introduction

There are two categories of special interest here: spherical Bessel functions and Airy functions.

Spherical Bessel Functions

Spherical Bessel functions are Bessel functions of half-integral order, i.e., 1/2, 3/2, etc. The notation j_n for $J_{n+1/2}$, and similarly for the other Bessel functions, is often used. These arise in solving the Helmholtz equation $(\nabla^2 + k^2)\varphi = 0$ in spherical coordinates, and are well known to students of quantum mechanics, who have probably seen scattering problems treated with a "partial wave" expansion. (The Helmholtz equation is merely the wave equation $(\nabla^2 - \frac{1}{v^2}\frac{\partial^2}{\partial t^2})\varphi = 0$ where v is the wave velocity, and the wave amplitude function is assumed to have a time dependence $e^{i\omega t}$. Then $k = \frac{\omega}{v}$ is the wavenumber. The Helmholtz equation holds for any Fourier component of the wave amplitude, and so may be used with Fourier analysis to analyze general time dependences.) These functions are called spherical Bessel functions for this reason. Such functions can be expressed in terms of the elementary transcendental functions sin(), sinh(), etc.

Airy Functions

The Airy functions may be defined by:

$$Ai(z) = \frac{1}{2\pi}\int_{-\infty}^{\infty} e^{-i(t^3/3 + zt)}\,dt = \frac{1}{\pi}\int_{0}^{\infty} \cos(t^3/3 + zt)\,dt$$

$$\text{and } Bi(z) = \frac{1}{\pi}\int_{0}^{\infty} e^{(-t^3/3 + zt)} + \sin(t^3/3 + zt)\,dt\,.$$

These are sometimes called the Miller-type or Keller-type Airy functions. The Airy functions may be defined for complex arguments (see Chapter 13) using path integrals, and V. A. Fock developed and used such representations in his treatment of scattering and diffraction, with notation $w_1 = \sqrt{\pi}[\, Bi(t) + iAi(t)\,]$ and $w_2 = \sqrt{\pi}[\, Bi(t) - i\,Ai(t)\,]$. Various integrals involving these functions are of interest in scattering problems, and are given in FOCK.CPP discussed in Chapter 29. J. Keller in his celebrated Geometrical Theory of Diffraction (GTD) used the Miller form.

Bessel functions of order 1/3 and 2/3 are related to the Airy functions discussed previously. The Airy functions will also be discussed in Chapter 13. Different authors use different versions, however, so be careful! Generally, the notations $Ai(z)$ and $Bi(z)$ are reserved for the type of Airy function discussed here. We include a plot of the Airy functions, Fig. 10-1, generated with the code of this chapter and the plotting package GraphiC, because it is impossible to understand their applications without such a picture.

Applications

Asymptotics

Airy functions occur in asymptotic expressions for Bessel functions of large order. See, for example, 9.3.4-9.3.6 for such approximations for $Y_\nu(\nu z)$ and $J_\nu(\nu z)$, among others, and more complicated but more accurate uniform asymptotic expansions for the same $Y_\nu(\nu z)$ and $J_\nu(\nu z)$. These are of use in a number of physical problems. Landau and Lifshitz discuss them in the context of Bremsstrahulung (they call it "Radiation in the case of Coulomb interaction") as well as synchrotron radiation (which they call "Magnetic Bremsstrahulung"). The Airy functions also occur in asymptotic expressions for the Parabolic Cylinder functions (see 19.20.3-4 in Abramowitz and Stegun).

Caustics

Imagine the effect of a superposition of many rays of light from a source of uniform intensity. This gives rise to an integral of the form $\int e^{id(t)}\,dt$ where t is the position on the source and $d(t)$ is the distance from that point to the observation point. The exponential factor accounts for the phase difference between different points of the source. (Of course, $d(t)$ must be suitably non-dimensional in the above expression.) Now expand $d(t)$ in a Taylor series, retaining termus up to t^3. The constant term may be taken out of the integral and does not affect the results. Airy considered the behavior near a *caustic,* where the second derivative term vanishes, i. e., a point of inflection in the distance function. Caustics can arise, for example,

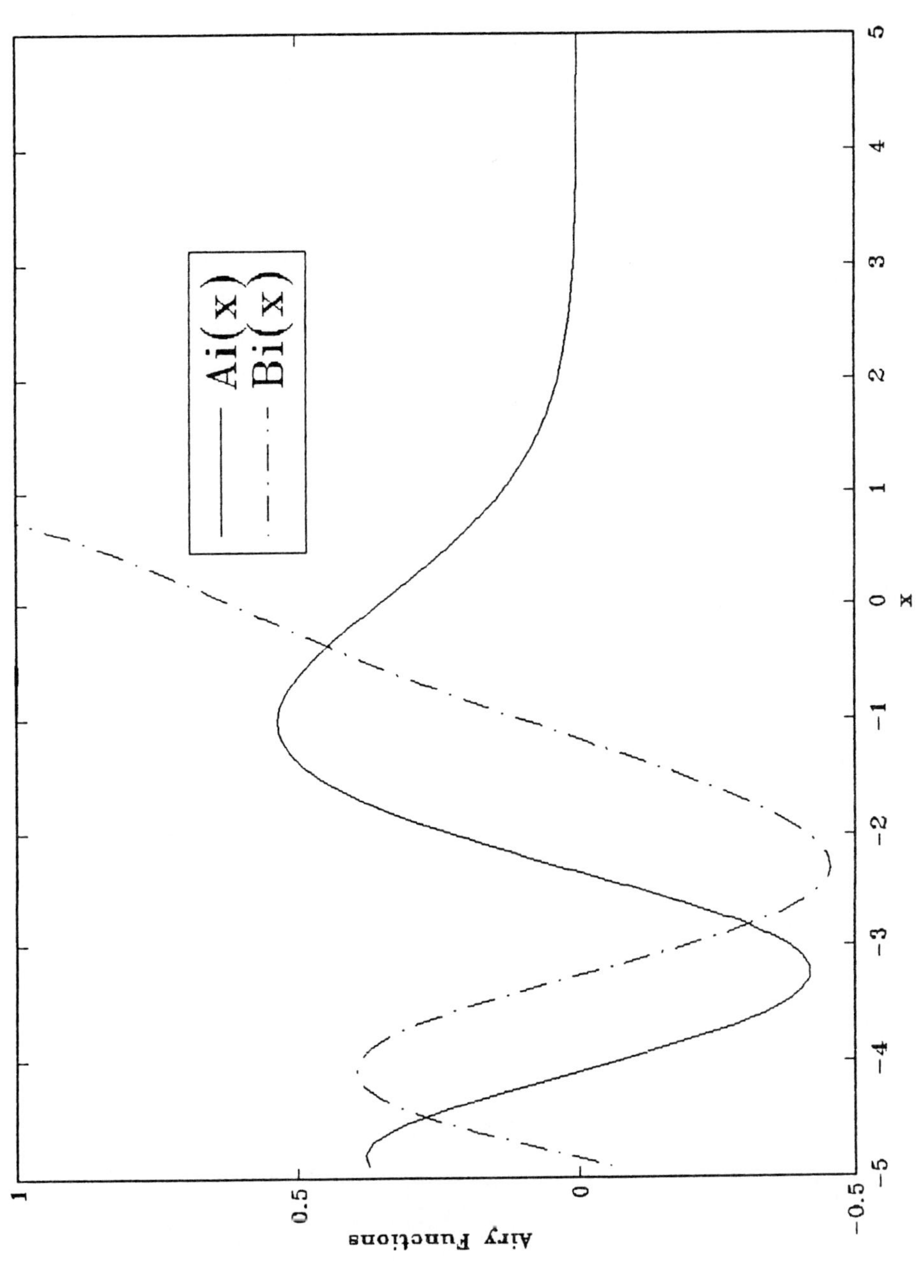

Fig. 10-1: Airy Functions.

in reflection from a concave surface such as the inside of a coffee cup. Then we have an integral of the form $\int e^{i(xt+at^3)}\,dt$. Consideration of such integrals give rise to Airy functions. (Airy apparently did not notice the connection to Bessel functions, but Stokes did.) Note that the approximations made apply only in the vicinity of the caustic. Therefore, the Airy function solution will not represent the actual amplitude except near the caustic.

Schroedinger's Equation, Turning Points and the WKB Method

A related situation arises in using the WKB approximation in treating wave equations such as Schroedinger's. This equation may be written in time-independent form (for the determination of the eigenvalue E, which characterizes the energy of the state): $\frac{h^2}{8\pi^2 m}\nabla^2\psi + (E-V)\psi = 0$. Here V is the potential energy and is typically a function of position in problems of interest. Now consider applying the WKB approximation (named after Wentzel, Kramers, and Brillouin, who developed it for application to quantum mechanics. Also called the WKBJ approximation to honor Jeffreys' contribution as well.) Consider an expansion of the form $y(x) = \exp(\frac{1}{\delta}\sum_{n=0}^{\infty}\delta^n S_n(x))$ applied to the second-order equation (presumed to be a form of the wave or Helmholtz equation) $y'' = Q(x)\,y$. Plugging in, we find for the first term of the expansion $S_0(x) = \int \sqrt{Q(t)}\,dt$. If we stop here, we have the so-called geometrical-optics approximation, which solves the eikonal equation, $S_0'^2 = Q(x)$. This approximation in a wave equation is equivalent to assuming the field does not diffract, i. e., moves in straight lines. Solving the next level of approximation, $S_1(x) = -\frac{1}{4}\ln Q(x)$. This is called the physical-optics approximation, and solves the so-called transport equation. The physical optics approximation is often used for computing scattering cross sections to a first approximation.

The validity of the WKB expansion requires that δ be a small parameter. Physically, the WKB approximation assumes that the wavelength is small compared to scales of interest. The eikonal or geometrical optics approximation is equivalent to assuming a wavelength of zero. For Schroedinger's equation, the wavelength is given by deBroglie's relation h/p where p is the momentum, $p = \sqrt{E/(2m)}$, where E is the particle's energy. The WKB approximation breaks down when the function $Q(x)$

vanishes. Such points are called turning points, because they are points at which, according to classical physics, the particle hits a potential barrier which reflects it. It is possible to "patch" asymptotic expansions together at such points (Jeffreys was very instrumental in this development). For a full discussion, see Bender and Orszag, whose treatment we have followed. Other similar treatments of the caustic problem are given in Landau and Lifshitz as well as Hochstadt's book, and in Airy's original treatment. As might be expected from the discussion on caustics above, near a turning point we expand $Q(x)$ in a Taylor series, getting to lowest order and equation of the form: $y'' = xy$ which causes Airy functions to show up in such matching formulae.

We provide a figure (10-1) showing the behavior of the Airy functions, because it is important to the physical role of these functions. The functions are oscillatory for negative argument. The function $Ai(z)$ decays exponentially for positive z while $Bi(z)$ grows exponentially. This behavior is characteristic of the difference between the illuminated and shadow regions near caustics and in scattering problems. The oscillations manifest themselves physically as interference fringes. It is well to bear in mind that the approximate expansions used near caustics and turning points typically do not hold at any great distance away from such points. Therefore, approximate solutions involving Airy functions typically are not valid more than a few wavelengths from the origin, i. e., are valid for small $|z|$ only. Beyond this, the assumptions used to obtain the equation $y'' - zy = 0$ break down.

Methods

The recurrence relations are used to find the spherical Bessel functions. Series and asymptotic formulae are used for the Airy functions Ai and Bi, their derivatives, and integrals, for real arguments. General real orders and arguments are treated by other routines using series and asymptotic formulae. The programs of Chapter 13 are general, i. e., suitable for complex orders and arguments.

For an alternative method, based upon continued fractions, see the article by Press and Teukolsky and the references cited therein.

The IAi Function

The test case involving the integral of the Airy function $Ai(x)$ illustrates some important behavior. The asymptotic formula does not give exact agreement with the comparison value, as should be expected, since there is a limit on the accuracy which can be obtained by an asymptotic formula.

Increasing the crossover value between the use of "exact" series and asymptotic formulae produces even poorer results for these same values of x, at least on a 80386/80387 machine! Examination of the computation shows that the "exact" solution computes two series and the result for $IAi(x)$ is the difference between these two series. As x increases, these two series get larger and closer to one another. Consequently, there is a great loss of significance for large x in the "exact" computation. Be forewarned.

References

G. B. Airy, *Trans. Cambridge Phil. Soc.*, **6**, 1838.

C. M. Bender and S. A. Orszag, *Advanced Mathematical Methods for Scientists and Engineers* (N. Y.: McGraw-Hill, 1978).

H. Hochstadt, *The Functions of Mathematical Physics* (N. Y.: Dover, 1986).

L. D. Landau and E. M. Lifshitz, *The Classical Theory of Fields*, 4th English ed. (Oxford: Pergamon Press, 1975).

W. H. Press and S. A. Teukolsky, *Computers in Physics*, p. 244, Mar./Apr. 1991.

```
/*
spherical bessel functions and allied routines
C Mathematical Function Handbook
Copyright L. Baker 1991. All rights reserved.
sjn(x,n)   returns jn(x) and sets sphb[] array i=0,...n
syn(x,n)   ditto yn(x)
skn(x,n)   ditto kn(x)
sinb(x,n)  all n. (named so as not to conflict with
sine[x]=sin(x) )
sj0,sj1,sy0,sy1,si0,si1,sim1,sim2,sk0,sk1- spherical bessel
functions
 for n=0,1 (for i, -1 and -2 as well) for j,y,i,k.

for negative n, note: k[x,n]= k[x,-n-1]. e.g. k[x,-1]=k[x,0]
   also y(x,n)= -1^(n+1) j(x,-n-1)
   e. g.  y(x,0) = -j(x,-1)
   Thus j[x,-1] = y[x,0] and y[x,-1]= j[x,0]
*/
#include <stdio.h>
#include "cmlib.h"
#include "protom.h"
#include "complex.h"
#define max(a,b)  ((a)<(b)?(b):(a))
#define min(a,b)  ((a)>(b)?(b):(a))

double sj0(x) double x;
{double sin();
if(x==0.)return 1.;
return sin(x)/x;
}
double sy0(x) double x;
{double cos();
if(x==0.)return errorcode;
return -cos(x)/x;
}
double sj1(x) double x;
{double sin(),cos();
if(x==0.)return 0.;
return (sin(x)/x-cos(x))/x;
}
double sy1(x) double x;
{double cos(),sin();
if(x==0.)return errorcode;
return -(cos(x)/x+sin(x))/x;
}

static double y,z,sr;
double si0(x) double x;
{double sinh(),sqrt();
```

```
if(x==0.)return 1.;
z=sinh(x)/x;
return z;
}

double sim1(x) double x;
{double cosh(),sqrt();
if(x==0.)return errorcode;
z=cosh(x)/x;
return z;
}
double sim2(x) double x;
{double cosh(),sqrt();
if(x==0.)return errorcode;
z=(sinh(x)-cosh(x)/x)/x;
return z;
}
double si1(x) double x;
{double sinh(),cosh(),sqrt();
if(x==0.)return 0.;
y=(cosh(x)-sinh(x)/x)/x;
return y;
}
double sk0(x) double x;
{double exp(),sqrt(),q;
if(x==0.)return errorcode;
q=pi/(2.*x);
z=q*exp(-x);
return z;
}
double sk1(x) double x;
{double exp(),sqrt(),q;
if(x==0.)return errorcode;
q=pi/(2.*x);
y=q*exp(-x)*(1.+1./x);
return y;
}

double sphb[100];

double sjn(x,n)double x;int n;
{/* as with J, use fwd for x>n else backward*/
int i,m;double old,older,new,sqrt(),s0,s1,mult,syn();
if(n<0)
    {m=-n-1;/* j(x,-1)= -y(x,0)*/
    return (sphb[0]=(m%2?1.:-1.)*syn(x,m));
    }

sphb[0]=s0=sj0(x);
```

```
if(!n)return s0;
sphb[1]=s1=sj1(x);
if(n==1)return s1;
if( x>(double)n )
   {
   old=s1;older=s0;sphb[0]=s0;sphb[1]=s1;mult=3.;
   for(i=1;i<n;i++)
      {
      new= old*(mult)/x-older;
      sphb[i+1]=new;mult+=2.;
      older=old;old=new;
      }
   return new;
   }
/* backward*/
if(x==0.)return 0.;
m= min((100-3),n+max(10,sqrt(n*2.)));
/*printf(" m=%d %e\n",m,x);*/
sphb[m+1]=0.;sphb[m]=1.;
for(i=m;i>0;i--)
   sphb[i-1]=((i<<1)+1.)*sphb[i]/x-sphb[i+1];
if(sphb[0]!=0.)new=sj0(x)/sphb[0];
else new=sj1(x)/sphb[1];
/* use when table needed of all n=0 to n */
for(i=0;i<=n;i++)sphb[i]*=new;
return sphb[n];
}

double syn(x,n)double x;int n;
{/*  use fwd */
int i,m;double old,older,new,sqrt(),s0,s1,term,sjn();
if(n<0)
   {m=-n-1;
   return (m%2?1.:-1.)*sjn(x,m);
   }
sphb[0]=s0=sy0(x);
if(!n)return s0;
sphb[1]=s1=sy1(x);
if(n==1)return s1;
   old=s1;older=s0;sphb[0]=s0;sphb[1]=s1;term=3.;
   for(i=1;i<n;i++)
      {
/*       new= old*((i<<1)+1.)/x-older;*/
      new= old*(term)/x-older;
      sphb[i+1]=new;term+=2.;
      older=old;old=new;
      }
   return new;
}
```

```
double sinb(x,n)double x;int n;
{/*  use backward */
int i,m,neg,nn;double old,older,new,sqrt(),s0,s1,mult;
sphb[0]=s0=si0(x);
if(!n)return s0;
sphb[1]=s1=si1(x);
if(n==1)return s1;
if(n>0 && x==0.)
    {
    for(i=0;i<=min(n,99);i++)sphb[i]=0.;
    return 0.;
    }

if(n==-1)return sim1(x);
if(n==-2)return sim2(x);
nn=abs(n);
if(n<0)neg=1;
else neg=0;
/* backward*/
m= min((100-3),nn+max(10*(neg+1),sqrt(nn*2.)));
/*printf(" m=%d %e\n",m,x);*/
sphb[m+1]=0.;sphb[m]=1.;
if(neg)
    {
    s1=sim1(x);
    /*if(x<nn)*/
        {/* forward*/
        sphb[0]=s0;sphb[1]=s1;new=1./x;mult=-1.;
        for(i=2;i<=nn;i++)
            {sphb[i]=sphb[i-2]+mult*new*sphb[i-1];mult-=2.;}
        return sphb[nn];
        }
    /*mult= 1.-(m<<1);
    for(i=m;i>0;i--)
        {sphb[i-1]=sphb[i+1]-(mult)*sphb[i]/x;
        mult+=2.;
        } backward recursion not good negative n*/
    }
else
    {/* n>0 backward recursion*/
    mult= (m<<1)+1.;
    for(i=m;i>0;i--)
        {sphb[i-1]=sphb[i+1]-(mult)*sphb[i]/x; mult-=2.;
        }
    }
/*printf(
" sphb[0]=%le %le %le\n",sphb[0],sphb[1],sphb[2]);*/
if(sphb[0]!=0.)new=s0/sphb[0];
```

```
else new=s1/sphb[1];
/* use when table needed of all n=0 to n */
/*printf(
" ck s1=%le new %le,sphb[1] %le rest %le\n"
,s1,new,sphb[1],new*sphb[1]);*/
for(i=0;i<=nn;i++)sphb[i]*=new;
for(i=1; i<=n;i+=2)sphb[i]=-sphb[i];
return sphb[nn];
}

double skn(x,ni)double x;int ni;
{/*  use fwd */
int i,m,n;double old,older,new,sqrt(),s0,s1,mult;
n=ni;
if(n<0) n= -ni-1;
sphb[0]=s0=sk0(x);
if(!n)return s0;
sphb[1]=s1=sk1(x);
if(n==1)return s1;
   mult=3.;
   old=s1;older=s0;sphb[0]=s0;sphb[1]=s1;
   for(i=1;i<n;i++)
      {
      new=older +old*mult/x;
      mult+=(2.);
      sphb[i+1]=new;
      older=old;old=new;
      }
   return new;
}
```

```
/*
Airy,Bessel functions and integrals thereof
from C Mathematical Function Handbook by Louis Baker
Copyright 1991 by Louis Baker. All rights reserved.
jt   J(x) for order  1/3
jmt   J(x) for order -1/3
it   I(x) for order  1/3
imt   I(x) for order -1/3
jbes   J(x,nu)
jas   J asymptotic large x
ybes   Y(x,nu)
kbes   K(x,nu)
ibes  I(x,nu)
Ai
Bi
dai
dbi
IAi
IBi
*/
#include <stdio.h>
#include "cmlib.h"
#include "protom.h"
#include "complex.h"

double jt(z) double z;
{
double pow(),sqrt(),x,y,zz,nu,sum,term;
int k,n,itmax=30;
y= pow(z*.5,.33333333);
sum=0.;
zz=z*z*3.;
term=1.;
for(k=0;k<itmax;k++)
   {
   sum+=term;
   term*= -.25*zz/(double)((k+1)*(3*k+4));
   if( abs(term)<1.e-6 || abs(term/sum)<1.e-5)break;
   }
return sum*y/.892979;

}
double jmt(z) double z;
{
double pow(),sqrt(),x,y,zz,nu,sum,term;
int k,n,itmax=30;
y= pow(z*.5,-.33333333);
sum=0.;
zz=z*z*3.;
```

```
term=1.;
for(k=0;k<itmax;k++)
   {
   sum+=term;
   term*= -.25*zz/(double)((k+1)*(3*k+2));
   if( abs(term)<1.e-6 || abs(term/sum)<1.e-5)break;
   }
return sum*y/1.354118;
}

double it(z) double z;
{
double pow(),sqrt(),x,y,zz,nu,sum,term;
int k,n,itmax=30;
y= pow(z*.5,.33333333);
x=z*sqrt(3.);
sum=0.;
zz=x*x*.25;
term=1.;
for(k=0;k<itmax;k++)
   {
   sum+=term;
   term*= zz/(double)((k+1)*(3*k+4));
   if( abs(term)<5.e-7 || abs(term/sum)<1.e-6)break;
   }
return sum*y/.892979;

}
double imt(z) double z;
{
double pow(),sqrt(),x,y,zz,nu,sum,term;
int k,n,itmax=30;
y= pow(z*.5,-.33333333);
x=z*sqrt(3.);
sum=0.;
zz=x*x;
term=1.;
for(k=0;k<itmax;k++)
   {
   sum+=term;
   term*= .25*zz/(double)((k+1)*(3*k+2));
   if( abs(term)<5.e-7 || abs(term/sum)<1.e-7)break;
   }
return sum*y/1.354118;
}

static double asympt=6.;

double jbes(z,nu) double z,nu;
```

```
{
double pow(),sqrt(),jas(),gamma(),x,y,zz,sum,term,denom;
int k,n,itmax=50;
if( abs(z)>= asympt)return jas(z,nu);
if( abs(nu)<1. && z!=0.) return jbes(z,nu+1.)*2.*(nu+1.) /z-
jbes(z,nu+2.);
x=z*.5;
y=1.;
if(nu!=0.)y= pow(x,nu);
sum=0.;
zz=x*x;
term=1.;
for(k=0;k<itmax;k++)
   {denom=gamma(nu+1.+k);
   if( abs(denom)<1.e-6)
      {
      fprintf(stderr,
                     " warn denom=%e nu %e k %d in jbes()\n",
         denom,nu,k);
      break;
      }
   sum+=term/denom;
   term*= -zz/( ((double) (k+1)) );
   if( abs(term)<5.e-7 || abs(term)<1.e-7*abs(sum))break;
   }
return sum*y;
}

double ybessel;

double jas(z,nu) double z,nu;
{
double cos(),sin(),sum,sum2,term2,term,x,y,q,arg,c,s;
double
pow(),sqrt(),gamma(),zz,f1,f2,f1o,f2o,nuph,numh,npho,mu;
int k,twok,n,itmax=30;
/* INCREASING NU ONLY MAKES IT WORSE*/
/*if( abs(nu)<1.) return jas(z,nu+1.)*2.*(nu+1.)/z-
jas(z,nu+2.);*/
y= sqrt(2./(pi*z));
sum=0.;
sum2=0.;
zz=4.*z*z;
term2=.5/z;
term=1.;
nuph=nu+.5;numh=nu-.5;npho=nu+1.5;
f1=1.e10;f2=1.e10;
mu=4.* nu*nu;
/*
```

```
for(k=0;k<itmax;k++)
    {
    f1o=f1;
    twok=k<<1;
    q=(double)(twok);
    if(term!=0.)
        {
        f1=term *gamma(nuph+q)/gamma(nuph-q);
        if( abs(f1/f1o)>1.)
            {
            term=0.;
            f1=0.;
            }
        else term*= -1./(zz*((twok+2)*(twok+1)) );
        sum+=f1;
        }
    f2o=f2;
    if(term2!=0.)
        {
        f2=term2 *gamma(npho+q)/gamma(numh-q);
        if(abs(f2/f2o)>1.)
            {term2=0.;
            f2=0.;
            }
         else term2*= -1./(zz*((twok+3)*(twok+2)) );
        sum2+=f2;
        }
    if( (abs(term)<1.e-7 || abs(term/sum)<1.e-6)&&
     ( abs(term2)<1.e-7 || abs(term2/sum2)<1.e-6)  )break;
    }
arg= z-pi*(nu*.5+.25);
return y*(cos(arg)*sum-sin(arg)*sum2);
*/
/*HANKEL EXPANSION:*/
zz=1./(64.*z*z);
term=(mu-1.)*(mu-9.)*zz;
sum=1.-term*.5+term*(mu-25.)*(mu-49.)*zz/24.;
term2=(mu-1.)*.125/z;
sum2=term2*(1.-(mu-9.)*(mu-25.)*zz/6. );
arg= z-pi*(nu*.5+.25);
c=cos(arg);s=sin(arg);
ybessel=y*(s*sum+c*sum2);
return y*(c*sum-s*sum2);
}

double ybes(z,nu) double z,nu;
{
int n,iv;
struct complex zz,jj,yy,dummy;
```

```
double x;
n=nu;
if( ( nu-((double)(n))) ==0.)
   {/* call bessel return y*/
   zz.x=z;zz.y=0.;
   bessel(n,&zz,&jj,&yy,&dummy,&dummy,&dummy,&dummy,&iv);
   return yy.x;
   }
if( abs(z)>asympt)
   {
   x=jbes(z,nu);
   return ybessel;
   }
x=(jbes(z,nu)*cos(pi*nu)-jbes(z,-nu))/sin(pi*nu);
/*printf(" y returning %e\n",x);*/
return  x;
}

double kbes(z,nuu) double z,nuu;
{
int n;
struct complex zz,ans;
double tol=1.e-6,x,y,sum,term,factor,pow,old,mu,nu;
/* not valid z<0*/
nu=abs(nuu);
if(z<0.)return errorcode;
n=nu;
if( (nu-((double)(n)))==0.)
   {/* call kbess return k*/
   zz.x=z;zz.y=0.;
   kbess(&zz,&ans,n);
   return ans.x;
   }
/* for z<0 fix */
if( (z)>=asympt)
   {
   x= 1./(8.*z);
   mu=nu*nu*4.;
   sum=1.+(mu-1.)*x*((mu-9.)*x*.5*(1.+(mu-
25.)*x*.33333)+1.);
   return exp(-z)*sqrt(pi/(2.*z))*sum;
   }
/* below not used in asymptotic regime where sign of nu ir-
relevant*/
return pi*.5*( ibes(z,-nu)-ibes(z,nu))/sin(nu*pi);
}

/* NOT STATIC- MAKE c1,c2 PUBLIC and usable
c1a = Ai(0)
```

```
c2a= -Ai'(0)
*/
double c1a=.355028053887817,c2a=.258819403792807;

double smallf(z) double z;
{
double x,y,zz,nu,sum,term;
int k,n,itmax=50;
sum=0.;
zz=z*z*z;
term=1.;
for(k=0;k<itmax;k++)
    {
    sum+=term;
    y= zz/((double)((3*k+2)*(3*k+3)));
    term*=y;
    if( abs(term)<5.e-7 || abs(term/sum)<5.e-7)break;
    }
return sum;

}
double smallg(z) double z;
{
double pow(),sqrt(),x,y,zz,nu,sum,term;
int k,n,itmax=50;
sum=0.;
zz=z*z*z;
term=1.;
for(k=0;k<itmax;k++)
    {
    sum+=term;
    term*= zz/((double)((3*k+3)*(3*k+4)));
    if( abs(term)<5.e-7 || abs(term/sum)<5.e-7)break;
    }
return z*sum;

}

double ai(z) double(z);
{
int i,itmax=40;
double
x,zeta,zi,pow(),sqrt(),arg,exp(),c,d,term,term2,old,old2,
   tol=1.e-6,factor,sum,sin(),cos(),sum2;
if(z==0.) return c1a;
x=abs(z);
if(x>=asympt)
    {
    zeta= x*sqrt(x)*.6666666;
```

```
   zi=1./zeta;
   if(z>0.)
      {
      sum=0.;
      c=term=1.;
      old=1.;
      for(i=0;i<itmax;i++)
         {
         sum+=term;
         if(!i)factor=15.;
         else factor*= (6*i-5)*(6*i-3)*(6*i-1)/(2*i-1);
         c*=factor/(216.*(i+1));
         term*=-zi*c;
         if( abs(c)<tol || abs(c)<tol*abs(sum)) break;
         if( abs(term)>abs(old))break;
         old=term;
         }
      return .5/sqrt(pi*sqrt(x))*exp(-zeta)*sum;
/*printf(" asymp Ai %e\n", .5/sqrt(pi*sqrt(x))*exp(-
zeta)*sum);*/
      }
else
   {
   arg=zeta+pi*.25;
   sum=sum2=0.;
   d=c=term=1.;term2=-1.;
   old=old2=1.;
   for(i=0;i<itmax;i++)
      {
      if(i%2)sum2+=term2;
      else sum+=term;
      if(!i)factor=15.;
      else factor*= (6*i-5)*(6*i-3)*(6*i-1)/(2*i-1);
      c*=factor/(216.*(i+1));
      term*=-zi*c;
      term2*=-zi*c;
      if( abs(c)<tol || abs(c)<tol*abs(sum)) break;
      if( abs(term)>abs(old))break;
      old=term;
      }
   return (sin(arg)*sum-cos(arg)*sum2)/sqrt(pi*sqrt(x));
/*printf(" Ai-=%e\n",(sin(arg)*sum-
cos(arg)*sum2)/sqrt(pi*sqrt(x)));*/
   }
   }
if(z>0.)
   {
   x=sqrt(z);
   arg=.666666*x*z;
```

```
   return    .33333333*x*( imt(arg)-it(arg) );
/*return c1a*smallf(z)-c2a*smallg(z);*/
   }
x=sqrt(x);
arg=.666666*x*abs(z);
return .33333333*x*( jt(arg)+jmt(arg));
}


double bi(z) double(z);
{
int i,itmax=40;
double
x,zeta,zi,pow(),sqrt(),arg,exp(),c,d,term,term2,old,old2,
   zz,tol=1.e-6,factor,sum,sin(),cos(),sum2;
if(z==0.) return c1a*sqrt(3.);
x=abs(z);
if(x>=asympt)
   {
   zeta= x*sqrt(x)*.6666666;
   zi=1./zeta;
   if(z>0.)
      {
      sum=0.;
      c=term=1.;
      old=1.;
      for(i=0;i<itmax;i++)
         {
         sum+=term;
         if(!i)factor=15.;
         else factor*= (6*i-5)*(6*i-3)*(6*i-1)/(2*i-1);
         c*= factor/(216.*(i+1));
         term*=zi*c;
         if( abs(c)<tol || abs(c)<tol*abs(sum)) break;
         if( abs(term)>abs(old))break;
         old=term;
         }
      return 1./sqrt(pi*sqrt(x))*exp(zeta)*sum;
/*printf(" Bi=%e\n", 1./sqrt(pi*sqrt(x))*exp(zeta)*sum);*/
      }
else
   {
   arg=zeta+pi*.25;
   sum=sum2=0.;
   d=c=term=1.;term2=-1.;
   old=old2=1.;
   for(i=0;i<itmax;i++)
      {
      if(i%2)sum2+=term2;
```

```
        else sum+=term;
        if(!i)factor=15.;
        else factor*= (6*i-5)*(6*i-3)*(6*i-1)/(2*i-1);
        c*=factor/(216.*(i+1));
        term*=-zi*c;
        term2*=-zi*c;
        if( abs(c)<tol || abs(c)<tol*abs(sum)) break;
        if( abs(term)>abs(old))break;
        old=term;
        }
    return (cos(arg)*sum+sin(arg)*sum2)/sqrt(pi*sqrt(x));
/*printf(" Bi-=%e\n",
(cos(arg)*sum+sin(arg)*sum2)/sqrt(pi*sqrt(x)));*/
    }
    }
zz=sqrt(x);
arg=.666666*x*zz;
if(z>=0.)
return    zz*( imt(arg)+it(arg) )/sqrt(3.);
/*
return sqrt(3.)*(c1a*smallf(z)+c2a*smallg(z));*/
return zz/sqrt(3.)*(jmt(arg)-jt(arg));
}

double ibes(z,nu) double z,nu;
{
double
pow(),exp(),sqrt(),gamma(),x,y,zz,sum,term,mu,ser,asym;
int k,n,itmax=500;
x=z*.5;
y=1.;
if(nu!=0.)y= pow(x,nu);
if(z<asympt)
    {
    sum=0.;
    zz=x*x;
    term=1.;
    for(k=0;k<itmax;k++)
        {
        asym=gamma(nu+1.+k);
        if(asym==0.)fprintf(stderr," pblm in ibes() gamma=%e
nu=%e\n",asym,nu);
        sum+=term/asym;
        term*= zz/( ((double) (k+1)) );
        if( abs(term)<5.e-8 || abs(term)<1.e-
8*abs(sum))return sum*y;
        }
fprintf(stderr,
" i bessel: precision not achieved, sum=%e\n",sum);
```

```
    return sum*y;
    }
/*else*/
mu=4.*nu*nu;
term=.125/z;/* for z>0 only:*/
return exp(z)/sqrt(2.*pi*z)*
        (1.+(mu-1.)*term*
        ((.5-(mu-25.)*term*.1666666)*term*(mu-9.)-1.));
}

double dai(x) double x;
{
int k,itmax=40;
double
zeta,zi,pow(),sqrt(),arg,exp(),c,d,term,term2,old,old2,
    tol=1.e-6,factor,sum,sin(),cos(),sum2;
double z,zz;
if(x==0.)return -c2a;
z=abs(x);
if(z>=asympt)
    {
    zeta= z*sqrt(z)*.6666666;
    zi=1./zeta;
    if(x>0.)
        {
        sum=0.;
        c=term=1.;
        old=1.;
        for(k=0;k<itmax;k++)
            {
            sum+=term;
            if(!k)factor=15.;
            else factor*= (6*k-5)*(6*k-3)*(6*k-1)/(2*k-1);
            c*=factor/(216.*(k+1));
            d=-(6*k+1.)/(6*k-1.)*c;
            term*=-zi*d;
            if( abs(c)<tol || abs(c)<tol*abs(sum)) break;
            if( abs(term)>abs(old))break;
            old=term;
            }
        return -.5*sqrt(sqrt(z)/pi)*exp(-zeta)*sum;
/*printf(" DAi=%e\n", -.5*sqrt(sqrt(z)/pi)*exp(-
zeta)*sum);*/
        }
else
    {
    arg=zeta+pi*.25;
    sum=sum2=0.;
    d=c=term=1.;
```

```
   term2=-1.;
   old=old2=1.;
   for(k=0;k<itmax;k++)
      {
      if(k%2)sum2+=term2;
      else sum+=term;
      if(!k)factor=15.;
      else factor*= (6*k-5)*(6*k-3)*(6*k-1)/(2*k-1);
      c*=factor/(216.*(k+1));
      d=-(6*k+1.)/(6*k-1.)*c;
      term*=-zi*d;
      term2*=-zi*d;
      if( abs(c)<tol || abs(c)<tol*abs(sum)) break;
      if( abs(term)>abs(old))break;
      old=term;
      }
   return -(cos(arg)*sum+sin(arg)*sum2)*sqrt(sqrt(z)/pi);
/*printf(" Dai-=%e\n", -
(cos(arg)*sum+sin(arg)*sum2)*sqrt(sqrt(z)/pi));*/
   }
   }
if(x<0.)
   {
   z=-x;
   zz=.666666*z*sqrt(z);
   return z*.333333*( jbes(zz,.666666)-jbes(zz,-.666666));
   }
zz=.666666*x*sqrt(x);
return -x*.333333*( ibes(zz,-.666666)-ibes(zz,.666666));
}

double dbi(x) double x;
{
double
zeta,zi,pow(),sqrt(),arg,exp(),c,d,term,term2,old,old2,
   tol=1.e-6,factor,sum,sin(),cos(),sum2;
int k,itmax=40;
double z,zz;
if(x==0.)return c2a*sqrt(2.);
z=abs(x);
if(z>=asympt)
   {
   zeta= z*sqrt(z)*.6666666;
   zi=1./zeta;
   if(x>0.)
      {
      sum=0.;
      c=term=1.;
      old=1.;
```

```
        for(k=0;k<itmax;k++)
            {
            sum+=term;
            if(!k)factor=15.;
            else factor*= (6*k-5)*(6*k-3)*(6*k-1)/(2*k-1);
            c*=factor/(216.*(k+1));
            d=-(6*k+1.)/(6*k-1.)*c;
            term*= zi*d;
            if( abs(c)<tol || abs(c)<tol*abs(sum)) break;
            if( abs(term)>abs(old))break;
            old=term;
            }
        return sqrt(sqrt(z)/pi)*exp(zeta)*sum;
/*printf(" DBi=%e\n",sqrt(sqrt(z)/pi)*exp(zeta)*sum);*/
        }
else
    {
    arg=zeta+pi*.25;
    sum=sum2=0.;
    d=c=term=1.;term2=-1.;
    old=old2=1.;
    for(k=0;k<itmax;k++)
        {
        if(k%2)sum2+=term2;
        else sum+=term;
        if(!k)factor=15.;
        else factor*= (6*k-5)*(6*k-3)*(6*k-1)/(2*k-1);
        c*=factor/(216.*(k+1));
        d=-(6*k+1.)/(6*k-1.)*c;
        term*=-zi*d;
        term2*=-zi*d;
        if( abs(c)<tol || abs(c)<tol*abs(sum)) break;
        if( abs(term)>abs(old))break;
        old=term;
        }
    return (sin(arg)*sum-cos(arg)*sum2)*sqrt(sqrt(z)/pi);
/*printf("DBi-=%e\n", (sin(arg)*sum-
cos(arg)*sum2)*sqrt(sqrt(z)/pi));*/
    }
    }
if(x<0.)
    {
    z=-x;
    zz=.666666*z*sqrt(z);
    return z*.57735027*(jbes(zz,-.666666)+jbes(zz,.666666));
    }
zz=.666666*x*sqrt(x);
return x*.57735027*(ibes(zz,-.666666)+ibes(zz,.666666));
}
```

```
double bigf(z) double z;
{
double pow(),sqrt(),x,y,zz,nu,sum,term,tk;
int k,n,itmax=5000;
sum=0.;
zz=z*z*z;
term=1.;
for(k=0;k<itmax;k++)
   {
   sum+=term;       tk=3.*k;
/*   term*=
zz*((double)(3*k+1))/((double)((3*k+2)*(3*k+3)*(3*k+4)));*/
   term*= zz*(tk+1.)/((tk+2.)*(tk+3.)*(tk+4.));
   if( abs(term)<1.e-8 || abs(term/sum)<1.e-8) goto done;
   }
fprintf(stderr," bigf did not achieve desired precision\n");
done: return z*sum;
}
double bigg(z) double z;
{
double pow(),sqrt(),x,y,zz,nu,sum,term,tk;
int k,n,itmax=5000;
sum=0.;
zz=z*z*z;
term=.5;
for(k=0;k<itmax;k++)
   {
   sum+=term;tk=3.*k;
/*   term*=
zz*((double)(3*k+2))/((double)((3*k+3)*(3*k+4)*(3*k+5)));
*/
   term*= zz*((tk+2.))/(((tk+3.)*(tk+4.)*(tk+5.)));

   if( abs(term)<1.e-8 || abs(term/sum)<1.e-8)goto done;
   }
fprintf(stderr," bigg did not achieve desired precision\n");
done: return z*z*sum;
}

#define IAap  7.5
#define IAan 10.5
#define IBap 10.5
#define IBan 10.5

double IAi(z) double z;
{
double bigf(),bigg(),sqrt(),exp(),sin(),cos(),pow,x32,x34;
if( z==0.)return 0.;
if( z>0.)
```

```
    {
    if(z> IAap )
        {
        x32= z*sqrt(z);
        return 1./3.-.5/(sqrt(pi*x32))*exp(-.6666666*x32);
        }
    return c1a*bigf(z)-c2a*bigg(z);
    }
/*z<0.*/
if(z> - ( IAan ) )
    return -c1a*bigf(z)+c2a*bigg(z);
x32= -z*sqrt(-z);
return 2./3.-cos(.666666*x32+.25*pi)/sqrt(pi*x32);
}

double IBi(z) double z;
{
double sqrt(),exp(),sin(),cos(),pow,x32,x34;
if( z==0.)return 0.;
if( z>0.)
    {
    if(z>  IBap )
        {
        x32= z*sqrt(z);
        return exp(.6666666*x32)/(sqrt(pi*x32));
        }
    return sqrt(3.)*(c1a*bigf(z)+c2a*bigg(z));
    }
/*z<0.*/
if(z> - ( IBan ) )
    return -sqrt(3.)*(c1a*bigf(z)+c2a*bigg(z));
x32= -z*sqrt(-z);
return sin(.66666666*x32+.25*pi)/sqrt(pi*x32);
}

#define tolaw 1.e-8

aw(nu,z,jj,e) double z,nu,*jj,*e;
{
double x,zz,sum,term,term2,factor,
    arg,c,s,hnu,sum2,old,old2;
int k,l,n,itmax=500;

if(z>asympt)
    {
    x=1./z*z;
    factor=nu*nu;
    sum=1.;
    sum2=1.;
```

```
   old=old2=1.;
   term=term2=1.;
   for(k=1;k<itmax;k+=2)
      {
      term*=-x*((k*k) -factor);
      if( abs(term)>abs(old))term=0.;
      old=term;
      sum+=term;
      l=k+1;
      term2*=-x*((l*l) -factor);
      if(abs(term2)>abs(old2))term2=0.;
      sum2+=term2;
      old2=term2;
      if( (abs(term)< tolaw || abs(term)< tolaw*abs(sum))
      &&(abs(term2)< tolaw || abs(term2)<
tolaw*abs(sum2)))break;
      }
   sum2*=nu/z;
   *jj= jbes(z,nu)+ sin(nu*pi)/(pi*z)*(sum-sum2);
   zz=cos(nu*pi);
   *e=-ybessel-((1.+zz)*sum+(1.-zz)*sum2 )/(pi*z);
/* printf(" asympt %e %e\n",*jj,*e);*/
    return 0;
   }
x=z*.5;
hnu=.5*nu;
sum=sum2=0.;
zz=x*x;
factor=1.;
for(k=0;k<itmax;k++)
   {term=factor/(gamma(1.+k-hnu)*gamma(hnu+1.+k));
   sum+=term;
   term2=factor/(gamma(1.5+k-hnu)*gamma(hnu+1.5+k));
   sum2+=term2;
   factor*= -zz;
   if( abs(term2)<tolaw*abs(sum2))goto d1;
   }
fprintf(stderr," tolerance not met aw series %le
%le\n",term2,sum2);
d1:sum2*=x;
arg= pi*hnu;
c=cos(arg);s=sin(arg);
*jj= c*sum+s*sum2;
*e= s*sum-c*sum2;
return 0;
}
```

Chapter 11

Integrals of Bessel Functions

Introduction

Programs for computation of the integrals of Bessel functions are given here. These make use of a gamut of methods, including results expressed in terms of the Struve and modified Struve functions of the next chapter, series, asymptotics, and rational approximation. Note that the integrals of the Airy functions are contained in file **abb.c** which is discussed in the previous chapter. The Bickley functions and repeated integrals of J, which are merely mentioned in Abramowitz and Stegun, are provided with computational methods here.

Applications

The integrals of Bessel functions often appear as the result of Laplace transforms. A common example is the solution of a ladder network. Details may be found in papers by Carson and the book by Gardner and Barnes.

Methods

Many of the functions are evaluated directly from expressions involving the Struve functions, or series of Bessel functions.

Bickley Functions

The Bickley function is defined as a repeated integral of the modified Bessel function: $Ki_1(z) = \int_z^\infty K_0(x)\,dx$,

$Ki_n(z) = \int_z^\infty Ki_{n-1}\,dx = \int_z^\infty \ldots \int_z^\infty K_0(x)\,dx$,. It may be written as an integral:

$Ki_n(z) = \int_z^\infty \frac{exp[-z\cosh t\ ]}{\cosh^n t}\,dt$. In this latter representation, the parameter n need not be an integer. It was found most efficient to use the adaptive quadrature method of C Tools, after transforming this integral to a finite interval by the variable substitution $t = exp(-x)$. The convergence gets better as the parameter n increases. The adaptive quadrature routine **adsimp()** from *C Tools* is used to compute this integral.

Adaptive Quadrature

The quadrature routine has an error tolerance and a maximum depth of recursion (subdivision of intervals) specified. Global integer variables are used to specify the maximum level of subdivision (maxlev) as well as returning the maximum level actually used (levmax). If levmax equals maxlev upon the end of integral computation, it is possible that the required accuracy has not been obtained. The Bickley function computation routine will then print a warning to **stderr**. Note that merely changing the error tolerance will not in general increase the accuracy of the solution if **adsimp()** it is already bumping its head against maxlev.

Repeated integrals of J_n

These are similar to the Bickley functions except that they are between the limits of 0 and *z*, and have integrands of J_n instead of K_0. These are computed using Abramowitz and Stegun 11.2.4, an infinite sum which converges rapidly. The routines of Chapter 9, which compute a table of values for a single call, are used for efficiency. The upper limit on order in this table is chosen from tests and is suitable for all reasonable cases, but extreme cases might require higher upper limits on the order of Bessel functions included in the sum.

Other integrals

For rapid computation, some of the rational approximations given in Abramowitz and Stegun are reproduced here as C functions. Series and asymptotic expansions are also provided if greater precision is required. The comments in the previous chapter concerning asymptotic expansions remain relevant.

References

J. R. Carson, *J. Am. Inst. Elec. Eng.,* **38**, pp. 345-427, 1919.

J R. Carson, *Bell System Tech. J.,* pp. 44-55, Nov., 1922.

M. F. Gardner and J. L. Barnes, *Transients in Linear Systems (vol. 1)* (New York: J. Wiley, 1942).

N. W. McLaclan, *Bessel Functions for Engineers* (Oxford: Clarendon Press, 1955).

Figures of Integrals of Bessel Functions

Plots are shown for integrals of Bessel functions in Figures 11-1 to 11-9. They were produced using *GraphiC* from files generated by the test driver. Only functions not plotted in Abramowitz and Stegun are displayed.

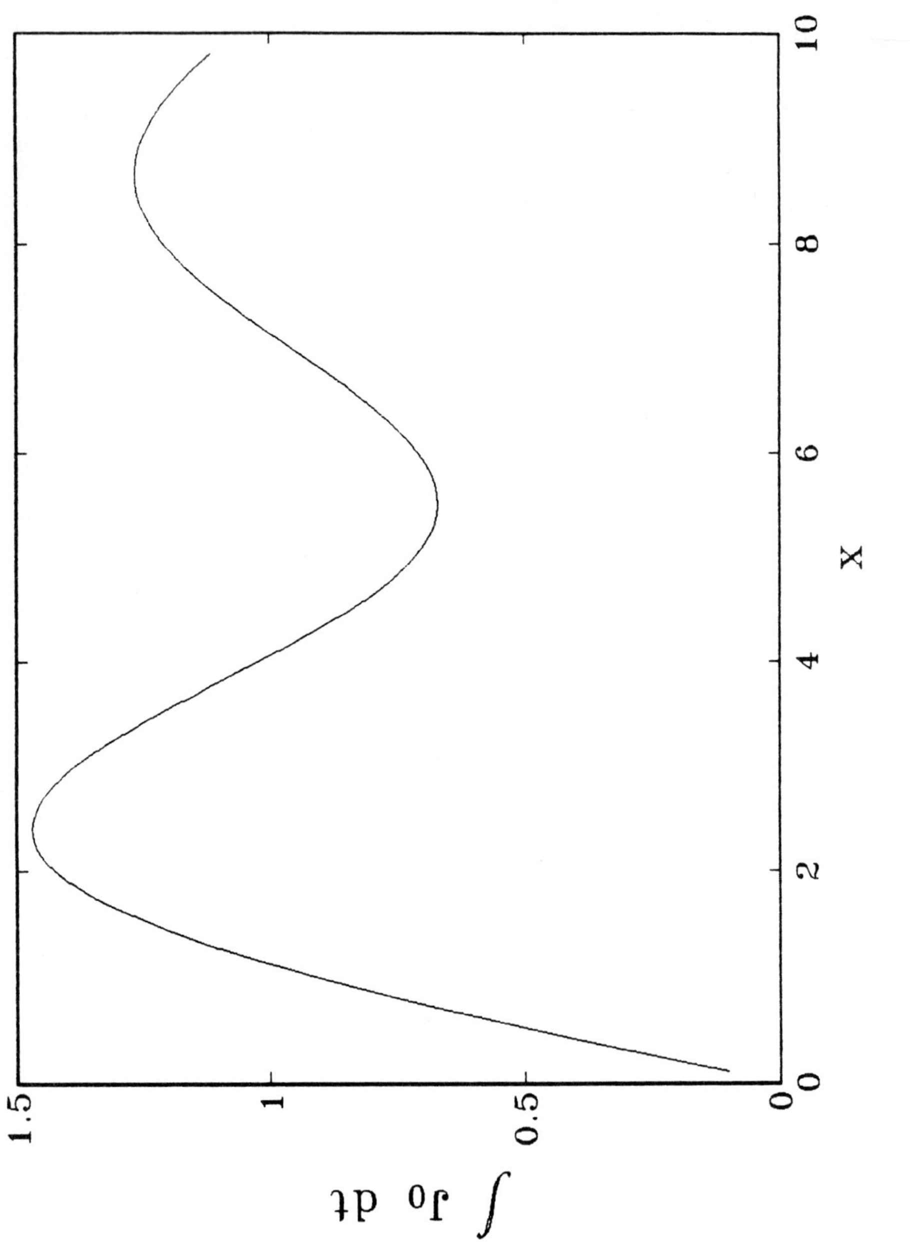

Fig. 11-1: Integral of J_0.

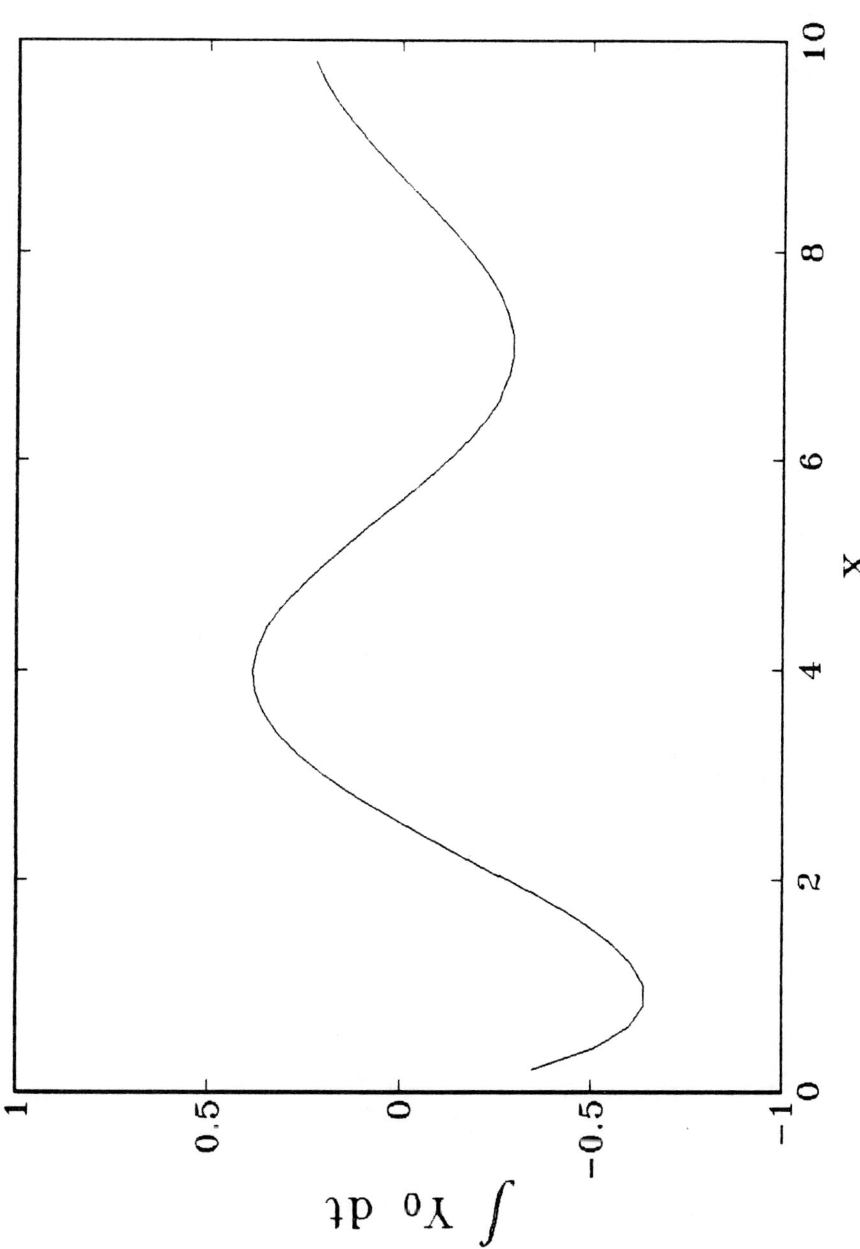

Fig. 11-2: Integral of Y_0.

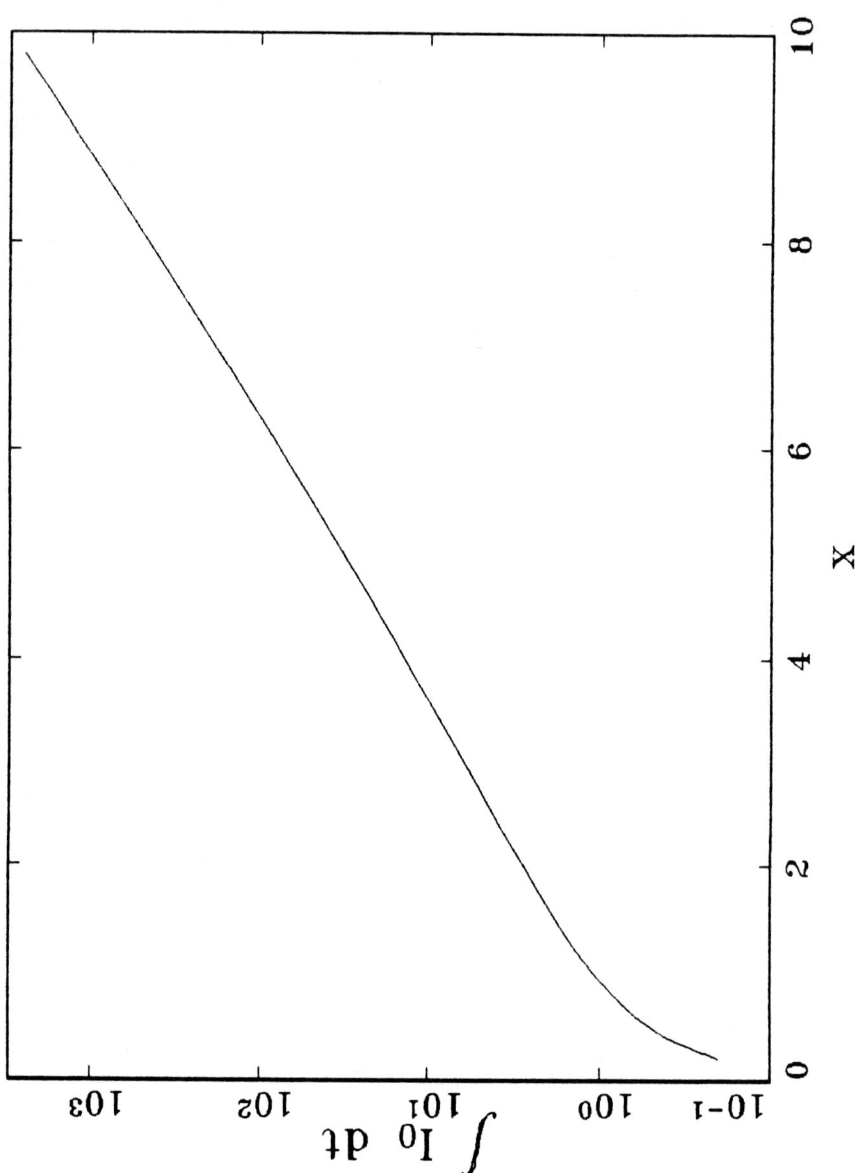

Fig. 11-3: Integral of I_0.

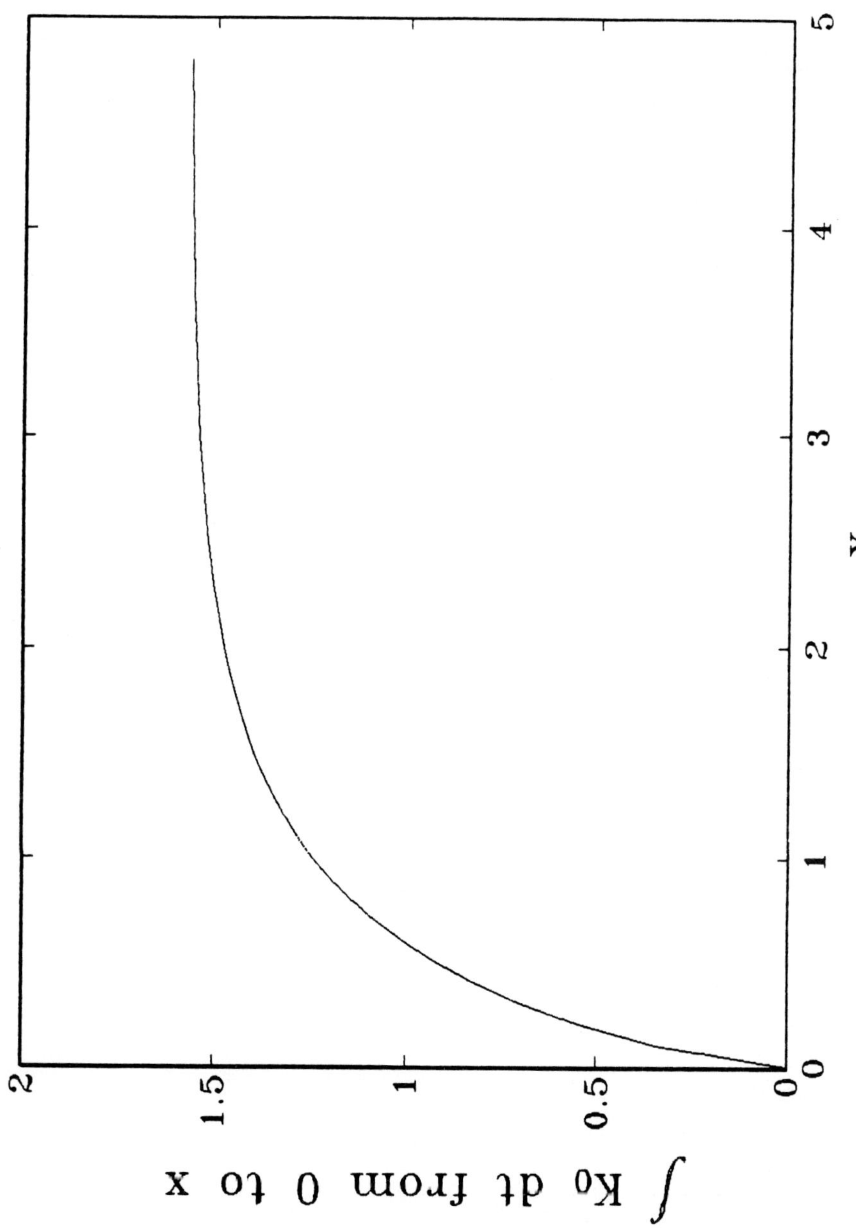

Fig. 11-4: Integral of K_0.

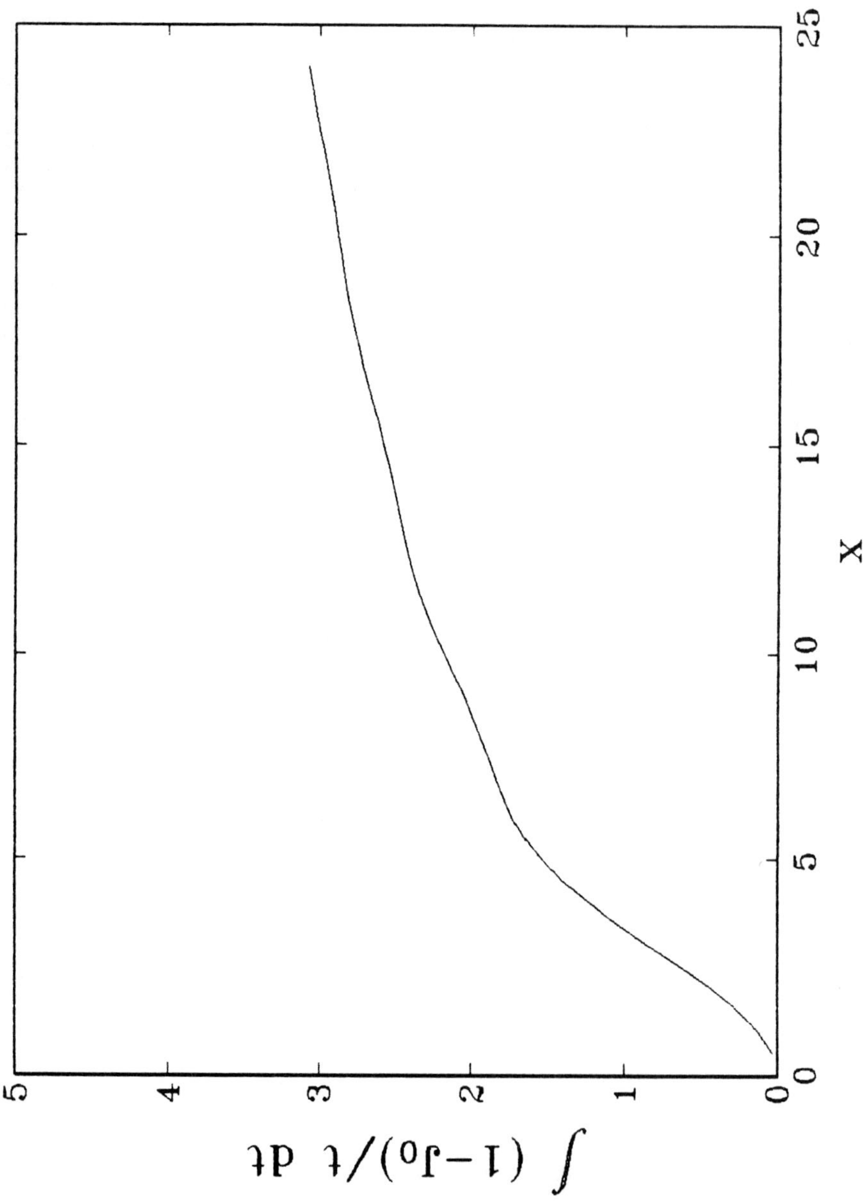

Fig. 11-5: Integral of *(1—J0)/t*.

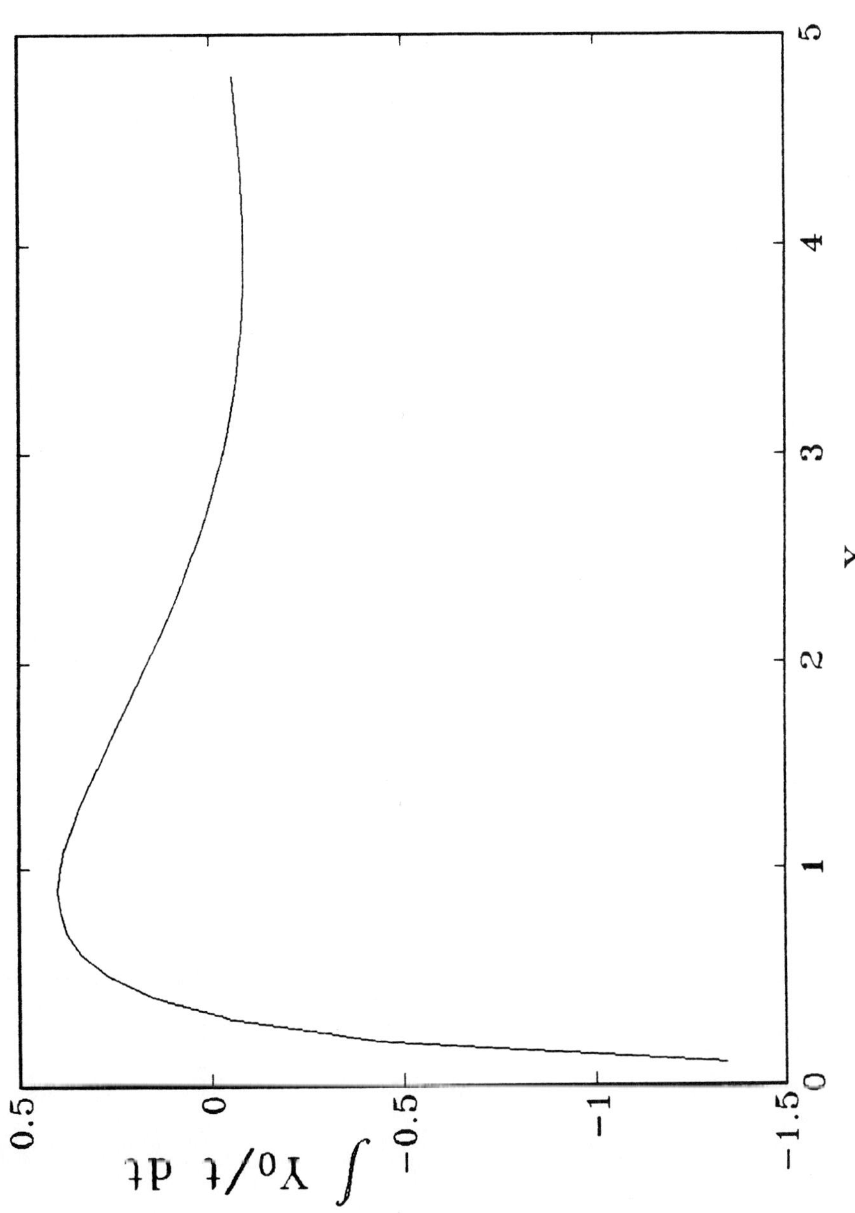

Fig. 11-6: Integral of Y_0/t.

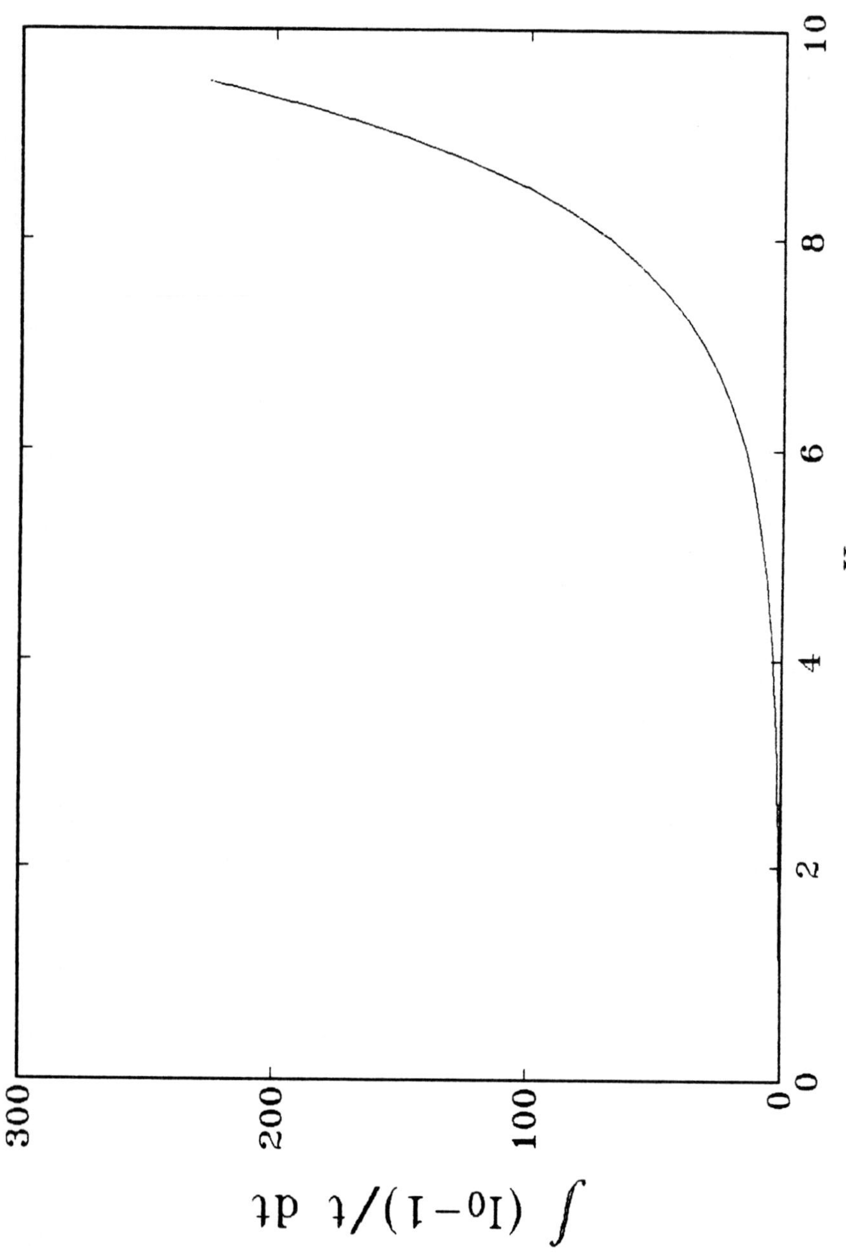

Fig. 11-7: Integral of $(I_0-1)/t$.

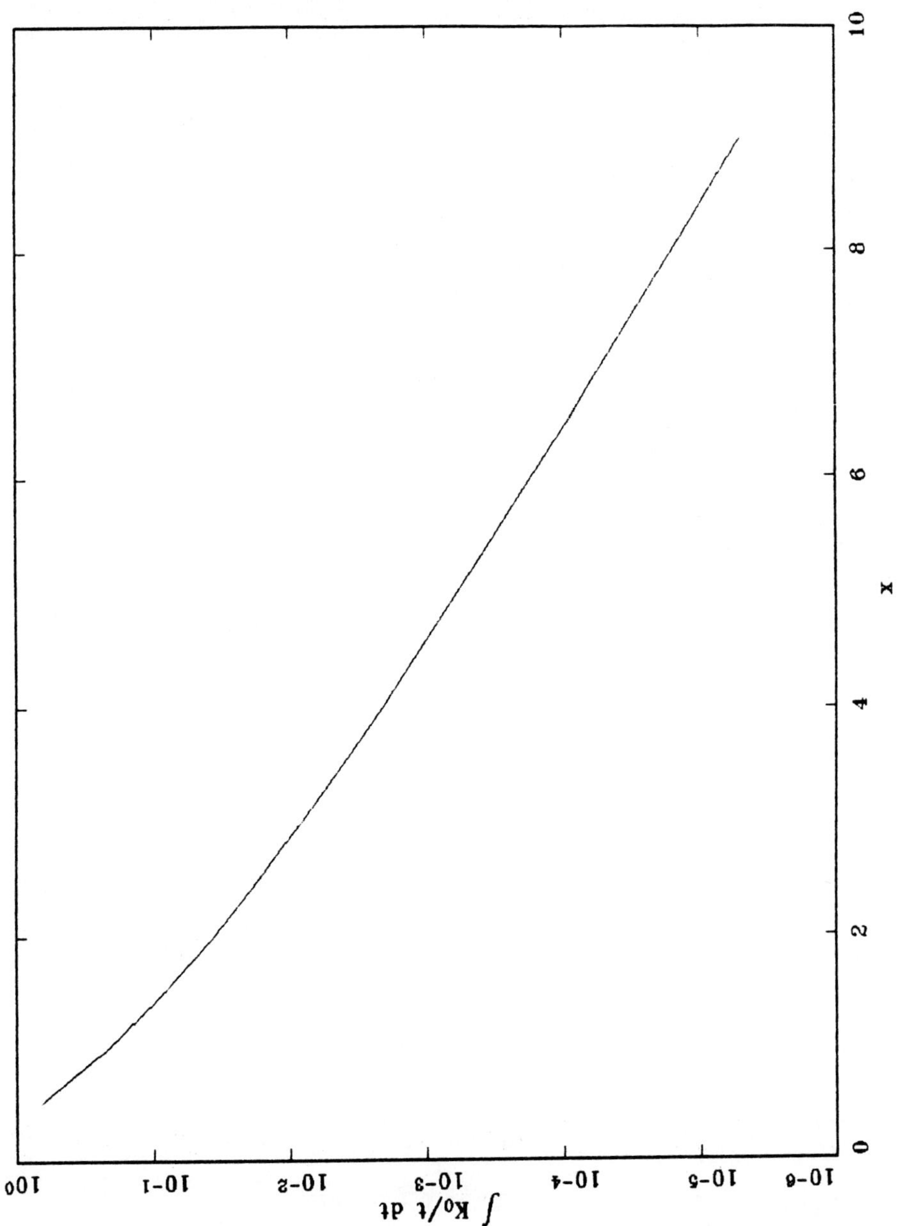

Fig. 11-8: Integral of K_0/t.

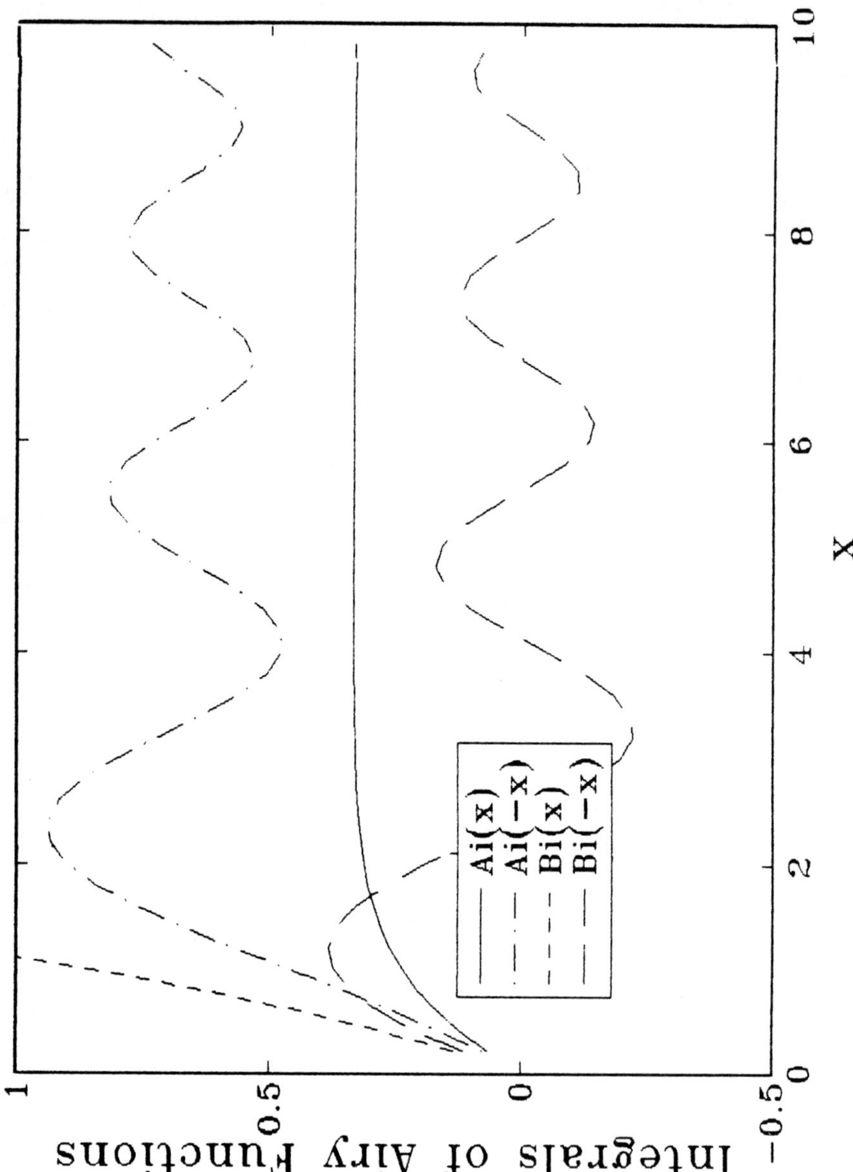

Fig. 11-9: Integrals of Airy functions.

```
/*
Integrals of Bessel functions
from C Mathematical Function Handbook by Louis Baker
Copyright 1991 by Louis Baker. All rights reserved.

ji   integral of J0
jii   1. - integral of J0
jin   integral of Jn
jiotn   integral of Jn/t dt
ki   integral of K0 from 0 to x
kii   pi/2 - integral of K0 above = integral of K0 from x
to infinity
ij0t   integral (1-J0_/t dt
ii0m1t   integral (I0 - 1)/t
iy0t   integral Y0/t dt
ik0t   integral K0/t dt
y0i   integral of y0   uses Struve functions
i0i   integral of i0   "     "        "

*/

#include "cmlib.h"
#include "protom.h"

#define gamma   Egamma
#define eps   3.e-7
#define epsk   1.e-8

/*static int itkt;*/
extern int itkt;

double ji(x) double x;
{
double y,p,q,r,ans;
y=j0(x);
p=j1(x);
q=h0(x);
r=h1(x);
return x*(y+.5*pi*(q*p-r*y));
/*return x*(y+.5*pi*(h0(x)*j1(x)-h1(x)*y));*/
}

double jii(x) double x;
{
double ji(),z;
return 1.-ji(x);
}

double jin(x,n) int n;double x;
```

```
{/* integral from 0 to x of j[n](x)*/
int k,m;
double sum,jn(),ji();
sum=0.;
m=n>>1;
if( n%2)
   {/* n odd*/
   if(n==1) return 1.-j0(x);
   for(k=1;k<=m;k++)
      sum+=jn(x,k<<1);
   return 1.-j0(x)-2.*sum;
   }
for(k=0;k<m;k++)
   {
   sum+= jn(x, (k<<1)+1 );
   }
return ji(x)-sum*2.;
}

double jiotn(x,n) int n;double x;
{
int k,m,halfn;
double sum,jn(),y,z,ji(),j1();
if(n<1)return errorcode;
sum=0.;
halfn=n>>1;
if( n%2)
   {/* n odd*/
   if(x==0.)return 0.;
   if(n==1) return ji(x)-j1(x);
   for(k=1;k<=halfn;k++)
      sum+=jn(x,k<<1)*k;
   return (ji(x)-j1(x)-4./x*sum)/(2*halfn+1);
   }
for(k=1;k<=halfn;k++)
   {
   m=(k<<1)-1;
   sum+= m*jn(x, m );
   }
return (1.-sum*2./x)/(2*halfn);
}

double ki(x) double x;
{/* integral from 0 to x of K0*/
double y,exp(),sqrt(),l0(),k0(),l1(),k1(),p,q,r,ans;
if(x==0.)return 0.;
if(x>7.)
   {
    y=7./x;
```

```
     return pi*.5-exp(-x)/sqrt(x)*
     ((((((.00033934*y-.00163271)*y+.00417454)*y
     -.00933994)*y+.02576746)*y-.11190289)*y+1.25331414);
    }
/* x<7*/
/* a triple sum! A&S p 480*/
/* or use  11.1.8 with K0,K1,L0,L1 L the Modifed Struve
functions*/
y=k0(x);
p=k1(x);
q=l0(x);
r=l1(x);
ans= x*(y+pi*.5*(y*r+q*p ));
return ans;
}


double kii(x) double x;
{
double ki(),z;
return pi*.5-ki(x);
}



double ii0m1t(x) double x;
{
int k;double sum,term,factor,y,fk,ii0tas();
if(x>5.)return ii0tas(x);
sum=0.;
term=1.;factor=1.;
y=x*x;
for(k=1;k<50;k++)
    {
    fk=k;
    factor*= y*.25/(fk*fk);
    term=factor/k;
    sum+=term;
    if(abs(term)<eps || abs(sum)*eps>abs(term))break;
    }
itkt=k;
return sum*.5;
}

double ij0t(x) double x;
{       int k;
double log(),y,z,sum,term,fk,factor,digamma();
y=.5*x;
sum=0.;y*=y;factor=1.;fk=1.;
```

```
for(k=1;k<50;k++)
   {
   factor*=-y/(fk*fk);
   term=factor/fk;
   sum+=term;
   if( abs(sum)*eps>abs(term))break;
   fk+=1.;
   }
itkt=k;
return -.5*sum;
}

double iy0t(x) double x;
{       int k;
double log(),y,z,sum,term,fk,factor,digamma();
y=.5*x;
z=log(y);
sum=0.;y*=y;factor=1.;fk=1.;
for(k=1;k<50;k++)
   {
   factor*=-y/(fk*fk);
   term=factor/fk*(digamma(1.+fk)+.5/fk-z);
   sum+=term;
   if( abs(sum)*eps>abs(term))break;
   fk+=1.;
   }
itkt=k;
return -z*z/pi-2./pi*gamma*z+(pi*pi/6.-gamma*gamma+sum)/pi;
}

double ik0t(x) double x;
{       int k;
double log(),y,z,sum,term,fk,factor,digam-
ma(),ik0tas(),digam();
/*if(x>5.)return ik0tas(x);*/
y=.5*x;
z=log(y);
sum=0.;y*=y;factor=1.;fk=1.;
for(k=1;k<50;k++)
   {
   factor*=y/(fk*fk);
   term=factor/fk*(digamma(1.+fk)+.5/fk-z);
   sum+=term;
   if(abs(sum)*epsk>abs(term))break;
   fk+=1.;
   }
itkt=k;
return z*z*.5+gamma*z+pi*pi/24.+gamma*gamma*.5-.5*sum;
}
```

```
double ii0tas(x) double x;
{
double sqrt(),exp(),y,sum;int i;
double b[11]={
.3989314,.1332055,-.0493843,1.4780044,
-8.6556013,28.1221478,-48.0524115,
40.3947340,-11.9094395,-3.5195009,2.1945464};
if(x<5.)return errorcode;sum=b[10];y=5./x;
for(i=9;i>=0;i--) sum=(b[i]+sum*y);
return  sum/(sqrt(x)*x*exp(-x));
}

double ik0tas(x) double x;
{
double sqrt(),exp(),y,sum;int i;
double b[7]={1.2533141,-.5091339,.3219184,
-.2621446,.2060126,-.1110396,.02724};
if(x<4.)return errorcode;
sum=b[6];y=4./x;
for(i=5;i>=0;i--) sum=(b[i]+sum*y);
return  sum/(sqrt(x)*x*exp(x));
}


double y0i(x) double x;
{double h0(),h1(),y0(),y1(),y;
y=y0(x);
return x*(y+pi*.5*(h0(x)*y1(x)-h1(x)*y));
}

double i0i(x) double x;
{double i,ii,s0,s1;struct complex ans,arg;
/*i=i0(x);
return x*(i+pi*.5*(l1(x)*i-l0(x)*i1(x)));*/
/*i=in(x,0);
return x*(i+pi*.5*(l1(x)*i-l0(x)*in(x,1)));*/
CMPLX(arg,x,0.);
ibess(&arg,&ans,0);
i=ans.x;
ibess(&arg,&ans,1);
ii=ans.x;
s0=StruveL(0.,x);
s1=StruveL(1.,x);
/*printf(" i0 %le i1 %le L0 %le L1 %le\n",i,ii,s0,s1);*/
return x*(i+pi*.5*(s1*i-s0*ii));
}
```

```
/*
Bessel function integrals

from C Mathematical Function Handbook by Louis Baker
Copyright 1991 by Louis Baker. All rights reserved.

bii   integrand for adaptive quadrature for bickley func-
tions
bickley   repeated integral of K0
Jrn   repeated integral of Jn

*/
#include <stdio.h>
#include "cmlib.h"
#include "protom.h"
#define max(a,b) ((a)>(b)?(a):(b))

static double z,r;
extern int level,maxlev,feval,levmax;

double bii(double x)
{double y,ans,num,denom;
if( x==0.) {if(z==0.)
       {if(r==1.)return 2.;
       if(r>1.)return 0.;
       /*r<1.*/
       return pow(2.,r);
       }
   return 0.;}
y= .5*(x+1./x);
num= (z==0.)? 1.: exp(-z*y);
denom= (r==0.)? 1.:pow(y,r);
ans= num/(x* denom );
return ans;
}

/*CAVEAT: should not be used for r <1. Strictly speaking,
r should be an integer>= 1*/

double bickley(double x, double rr)
{
double a,b,adsimp(),ans,dx,cutoff;int i,lim, lm;
r=rr;z=x; maxlev= 9/*6*/;cutoff=.00015625*.5;
lim=3;if(rr<2.)lim=8/max(rr,.01);ans=0.;
a=0.;dx=cutoff/lim;b=dx;lm=0;
for(i=0;i<lim;i++,a+=dx,b+=dx)
    {
    ans+= adsimp(a,b,1.e-7,bii);
    lm=max(lm,levmax);
```

```
    }
lim=3;dx= (1.-cutoff)/lim;a=cutoff;b=a+dx;
for(i=0;i<lim;i++,a+=dx,b+=dx)
    {
    ans+= adsimp(a,b,1.e-7,bii);
    lm=max(lm,levmax);
    }
    if( lm>=maxlev)
        fprintf(stderr,
            " warning: bickley may not have achieved desired
accuracy\n");

return ans;
}


#define tol 1.e-7

extern double bessela[100];

#define FILL 25

double Jrn(double x, double r, int n)
{int method,k,intnr,id,lim=99;double sum,term,factor,jj,rv;
/*printf(" entered Jrn\n");printf(" x=%le r=%le
n=%d\n",x,r,n);*/
method=r; if(abs(r-method)<tol && r<=0.)return errorcode;
method=1;sum=n+r;intnr=(int)sum;
if( (sum-(double)intnr) ==0. && intnr>=0)
    {method=0;
    sum=jn(x,FILL); /*set up bessela array*/
    /*for(k=0;k<100;k++)
        {printf(" J[%d]=%le\n",k,bessela[k]);}*/
    }
/*printf(" method=%d\n",method);*/

for(factor=1.,sum=0.,k=0;k<lim;k++)
    {
    if(method)jj=jbes(x,r+(double)(n+(k<<1)));
    else { id=intnr+(k<<1);if(id> FILL-1 )break;
    jj=bessela[id];}
    term=gamma((double)k+r)*factor*jj;
    sum+=term;
    if(abs(term)<abs(sum)*tol)break;
    factor/= (k+1.);
    }
rv=pow(2.,r)/gamma(r)*sum;
return rv;
}
```

Chapter 12

Struve and Anger-Weber Functions

Introduction

Struve Functions

The Struve function **H** was defined as the solution of an inhomogeneous version of Bessel's equation, with the modified Struve function **L** the analogous solution of the modifed Bessel equation. It is perhaps more naturally defined in terms of the integral:

$\boldsymbol{H}_\nu(z) = \dfrac{2(\frac{z}{2})^\nu}{\sqrt{\pi}\Gamma(\nu + \frac{1}{2})} \int_0^\pi sin(\,z\cos\theta)\sin^{2\nu}\theta\, d\theta$, with the modified Struve function defined by $\boldsymbol{L}_\nu(z) = \dfrac{2(\frac{z}{2})^\nu}{\sqrt{\pi}\Gamma(\nu + \frac{1}{2})} \int_0^\pi sinh(\,z\cos\theta)\sin^{2\nu}\theta\, d\theta$. The Struve functions are of interest in relation to the integrals of Bessel functions.

Anger-Weber Functions

Consider the integral $\boldsymbol{J}_\nu(z) + i\,\boldsymbol{E}_\nu(z) = \dfrac{1}{\pi}\int_0^\pi e^{\nu\theta - z\sin\theta} d\theta$. Note that this integral may easily be split into its real and imaginary parts for real z. The real part is called Anger's function, and the imaginary part is called Weber's function. Note that for integer ν, the Anger function becomes identical with the Bessel function J_ν, but for non-integral n the two are different. The Lommel-Weber function is defined $\Omega_\nu = -\boldsymbol{E}_\nu$. It is natural to call the integral the Anger-Weber function. This complex function, and its integral, arise in the study of loop antennas, and in the synthesis of circular aperture antennas. See Collin and Zucker, for example, for King's article on the loop antenna as well as that by Schell and Ishimaru on antenna pattern synthesis. The integral $W_n(S) = \frac{1}{2}\int_0^{-2iS} [\Omega_n(x) + i\,J_n(x)]\,dx$ arises in these works. The definition used here and the computational formulae are from Blackburn and Wilton, and is motivated by calculations in the Laplace transform domain with variable S. Their computational formulae are based upon the work of Baum et al. The work of King cited uses the Fourier domain, with frequency ω. The formula as given here has positive imaginary arguments corresponding to King's real arguments.

For n zero or a positive integer, Watson gives a formula relating $\mathbf{E_n}$ and

$$\mathbf{H_n}:\ E_n = \frac{1}{\pi}\sum_{m=0}^{<\frac{n}{2}} \frac{\Gamma(m+.5)\,(\frac{z}{2})^{n-2m-1}}{\Gamma(n+.5-m)} - H_n$$

(their sum is a polynomial in z). This is used as a check on the values of $\mathrm{E_n}$.

Note that the parabolic cylinder function D_n is often called Weber's function. Therefore, be sure the Weber's function of interest is the correct one!

Methods

Series and asymptotic expansions are used. There is a cancellation and loss of accuracy for the integral of the Anger-Weber function for large ν. This forces us to use the asymptotic formula for smaller values of the argument that we would rather. For $|z|$ on the order of 20, the accuracy may only be 10% or so for the integral of the Anger-Weber function!

References

R. F. Blackburn and D. R. Wilton, *Evaluation of the Integral of the Anger-Weber Function with a Complex Argument*, Phillips Laboratory, Kirtland AFB Math Note 57, Jan. 1978. (Available from DTIC, the Defense Technical Information Center.)

C. A. Baum, H. Chang, J. P. Martinez, *Analytical Approximations and Numerical Techniques for the Integral of the Anger-Weber Function* , Phillips Laboratory, Kirtland AFB Math Note 25, Aug. 1972. (Available from DTIC, the Defense Technical Information Center.)

R. E. Collin & F. J. Zucker, *Antenna Theory, Part 1* (N. Y.: McGraw-Hill, 1969).

R. P. W. King and G. S. Smith, *Antennas in Matter* (Cambridge: MIT Press, 1981).

Figures

Fig. 12-1 shows the integrals of the Struve functions $\mathbf{H}_0(t)$ and $\mathbf{H}_0(t)/t$. Fig. 12-2, taken from Mathematics Note 25, shows the integral of the Anger-Weber function for $n = 4$.

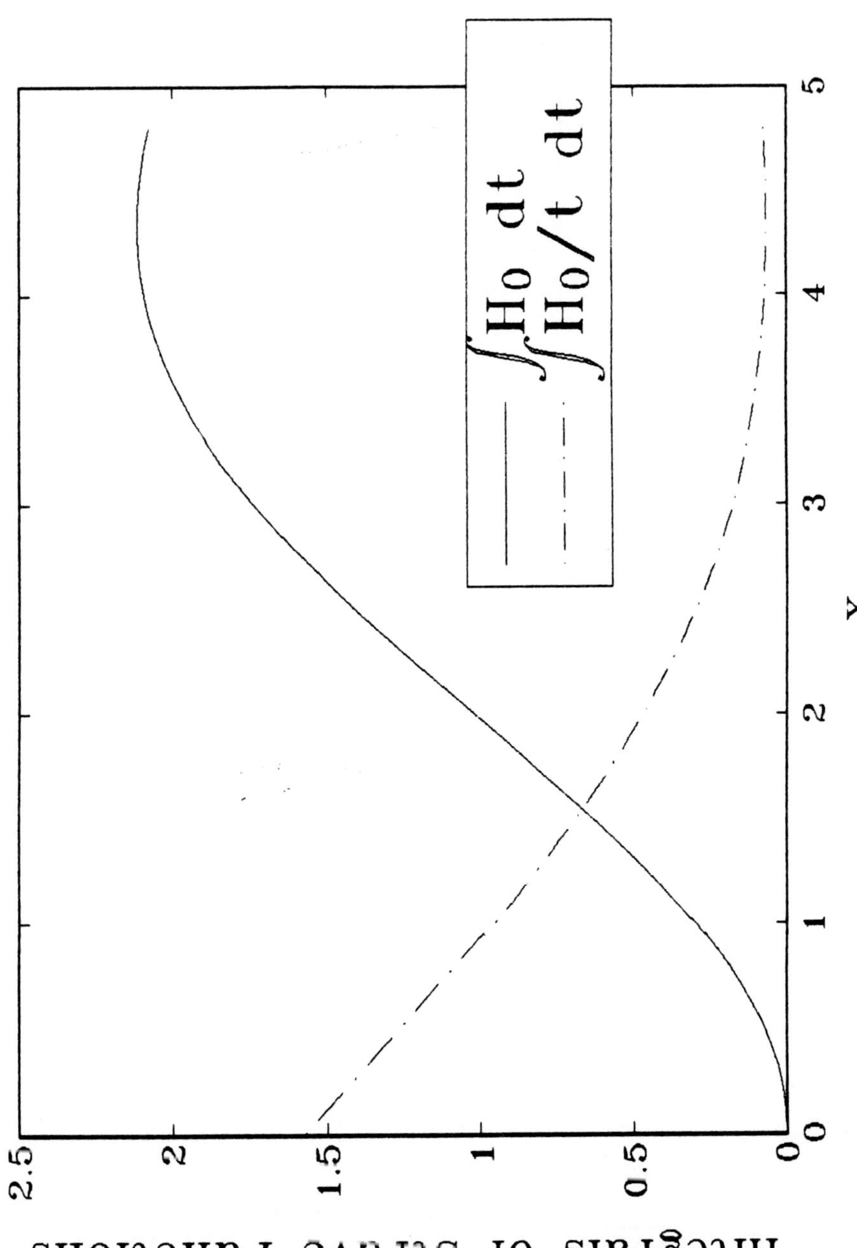

Fig. 12-1: Integrals of the Struve function H_0.

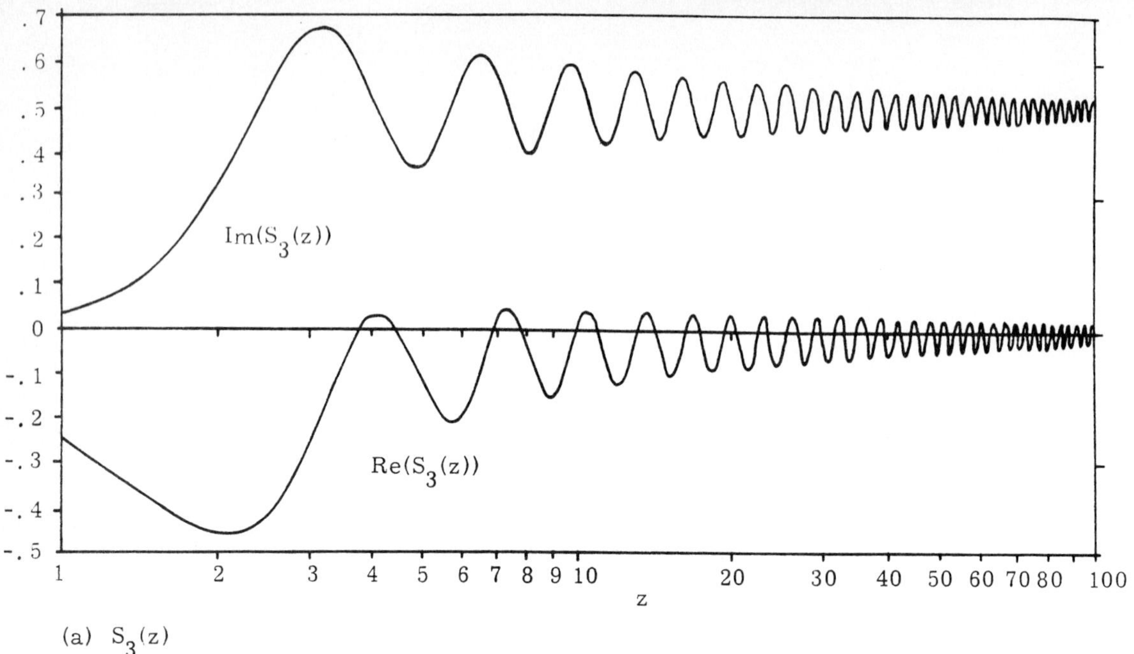

(a) $S_3(z)$

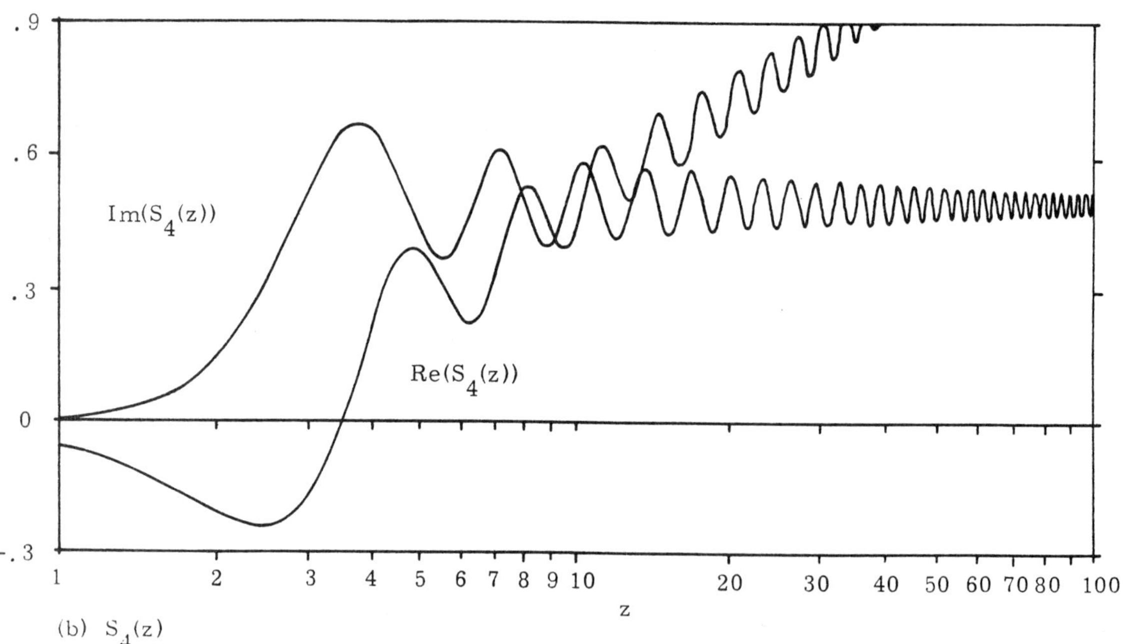

(b) $S_4(z)$

Fig. 12-2: Integral of Anger-Weber function for $n = 4$.The dependent variable z here is to be taken as imaginary.

```
/*
Struve functions general order
from C Mathematical Function Handbook by Louis Baker
Copyright 1991 by Louis Baker. All rights reserved.

StruveL L
StruveH H
struve   service routine not intended to be called by user
*/

#include <stdio.h>
#include "cmlib.h"
#include "protom.h"

#define tol 1.e-8
#define tolas 1.e-7
#define xcrit 20.

/* prototype for struve: omit or comment out if not using
ANSI compiler*/
double struve( double nu, double x, int l);


double struve(nu,x,l) double nu,x; int l;
   {double y,z,sum,factor,term,oldterm,mult,add;int k;
   if(x<0.)return errorcode;
   if(x>xcrit && abs(nu-((int)nu))<tol)
      {/* attempt to  use asymptotic formula*/
      y=2./x;
      z=y*y;
      mult=1.;
      if(l){z=-z;mult=-1.; add= in((int)(abs(nu)),z);}
      /* for integer nu, I of order -nu = I of order nu*/
      else add=yn(z, (int)nu);
      for(k=1,sum=term=oldterm=1.;k<1000;k++)
         {
         term *= z*(k-.5)*(.5+nu-k);
         /*printf(" %d oldsum oldterm,term %le %le
%le\n",k,sum,oldterm,term);*/
         if( (abs(oldterm)<abs(term) ||
abs(term)<tol*abs(sum))
            && k>nu-.5)break;
         sum+=term;
         oldterm=term;
         }
      if( abs(term)>tolas*abs(sum))
         {
         fprintf(stderr,
```

```
        " struve: asympt. inaccurate using series term=%le
sum=%le\n"
           ,term,sum);
        goto series;
        }
      return pow(y,1.-
nu)*mult/(sqrt(pi)*gamma(.5+nu))*sum+add;
      }
   series:
   y=x*.5;
   z=y*y;
   if(!l)z=-z;
   for (k=1,sum=term=1.;k<1000;k++)
      {term *=z/((.5+k)*(.5+k+nu));
      sum+=term;
      if(abs(term)<tol*abs(sum))goto fini;
      }
   fprintf(stderr," struve-series-tolerance not met\n");
   fini:return pow( y,
nu+1.)*2./(sqrt(pi)*gamma(nu+1.5))*sum;
   }



double StruveH(nu,x) double nu,x;
   {return struve(nu, x,0);}
double StruveL(nu,x) double nu,x;
   {return struve(nu, x,1);}
```

```
/*
Struve functions lowest order
from C Mathematical Function Handbook by Louis Baker
Copyright 1991 by Louis Baker. All rights reserved.

h0
h1
l0
l1
h0a,l0a,l1a,h1a asymptotic
*/

#include <stdio.h>
#include "cmlib.h"
#include "protom.h"

double h0a(x) double x;
{
int i,itmax=30,k;
double sq,sum,rx,term,oldterm;
sum=0.;
rx=1./x;
term=1.;
sq=rx*rx;
for(i=0;i<itmax;i++)
   {
   sum+=term;
   oldterm=term;
   k= (i<<1) +1;
   k *=k;
   term*= -sq*(k);
   if (abs(term)>abs(oldterm) || abs(term)<1.e-6) break;
   }
return 2./pi*rx*sum+y0(x);
}

double h1a(x) double x;
{
int i,itmax=30,k;
double sq,sum,rx,term,oldterm;
sum=0.;
rx=1./x;
term=1.;
sq=rx*rx;
for(i=0;i<itmax;i++)
   {
   sum+=term;
   oldterm=term;
   if(!i) k=-1;
```

```
   else
      {
      k= (i<<1)-1;
      k *=(k+2);
      }
   term*= -sq*(k);
   if (abs(term)>abs(oldterm) || abs(term)<1.e-6) break;
   }
return 2./pi*sum+y1(x);
}

double l0a(x) double x;
{
int i,itmax=30,k;
double sq,sum,rx,term,oldterm,i0();
sum=0.;
rx=1./x;
term=-1.;
sq=rx*rx;
for(i=0;i<itmax;i++)
   {
   sum+=term;
   oldterm=term;
   k= (i<<1)+1;
   k *=k;
   term*= -sq*(k);
   if (abs(term)>abs(oldterm) || abs(term)<1.e-6) break;
   }
return 2./pi*rx*sum+i0(x);
}

double l1a(x) double x;
{
int i,itmax=30,k;
double sq,sum,rx,term,oldterm,i1();
sum=0.;
rx=1./x;
term=-1.;
sq=rx*rx;
for(i=0;i<itmax;i++)
   {
   sum+=term;
   oldterm=term;
   if(!i) k=-1;
   else
      {
      k= (i<<1)-1;
      k *=(k+2);
      }
```

```
    term*= -sq*(k);
    if (abs(term)>abs(oldterm) || abs(term)<1.e-6) break;
    }
return 2./pi*sum+i1(x);
}

double l0(x)
double x;
{
double term,count,sq,sum,xa=10.,l0a(),tol=1.e-6;
int i,top=20;
if(x==0.)return 0.;
if(x>xa) return l0a(x);
sq=x*x;
for(i=0,sum=0.,count=3.,term=x;i<top;i++)
    {
    sum +=term;
    if( sum)
        {
        if( (i>3) & (abs(term/sum)<tol) )return 2./pi*sum;
        }
    term *=   sq/(count*count);
    count += 2.;
    }
return 2./pi*sum;
}

double l1(x)
double x;
{
double term,count,sq,sum,xa=10.,l1a(),tol=1.e-6;
int i,top=20;
if(x==0.)return 0.;
if(x>xa) return l1a(x);
sq=x*x;
for(i=0,sum=0.,count=3.,term=sq/3.;i<top;i++)
    {
    sum +=term;
    if (sum)
        {
        if((i>3) & (abs(term/sum)<tol) )return 2./pi*sum;
        }
    term *=   sq/(count*(count+2.));
    count += 2.;
    }
return 2./pi*sum;
}
double h0(x)
double x;
```

```
{
double term,count,sq,sum,h0a(),xa=10.,tol=1.e-6;
int i,top=30;
if(x==0.)return 0.;
if(x>xa) return h0a(x);
sq=x*x;
for(i=0,sum=0.,count=3.,term=x;i<top;i++)
   {
   sum +=term;
   if( sum)
      {
      if( (i>3) & (abs(term/sum)<tol) )return 2./pi*sum;
      }
   term *=   -sq/(count*count);
   count += 2.;
   }
return 2./pi*sum;
}

double h1(x)
double x;
{
double term,count,sq,sum,xa=10.,h1a(),tol=1.e-6;
int i,top=20;
if(x==0.)return 0.;
if(x>xa) return h1a(x);
sq=x*x;
for(i=0,sum=0.,count=3.,term=sq/3.;i<top;i++)
   {
   sum +=term;
   if (sum)
      {
      if((i>3) & (abs(term/sum)<tol) )return 2./pi*sum;
      }
   term *=   -sq/(count*(count+2.));
   count += 2.;
   }
return 2./pi*sum;
}
```

```
/*
integrals of struve H0, H0/t, L0
from C Mathematical Function Handbook by Louis Baker
Copyright 1991 by Louis Baker. All rights reserved.

double ModStruveI(x) double x;  integral of L from 0 to x
double StruveI(x) double x;     integral of H from 0 to x
double StruveIot(x) double x;   integral of H/t from 0 to x

*/

#include <stdio.h>
#include "cmlib.h"
#include "protom.h"

#define tol 1.e-8

double ModStruveI(x) double x;
{/* integral from 0 to x of L0(x)*/
double z,term,factor,sum;int i;
if(x==0.)return 0.;
z=x*x;sum=z*.5;term=z*z/36.;
for(i=5;i<10000;i+=2)
   {
   sum+=term;
   if( abs(term)<tol*abs(sum))goto fini;
   factor=i;
   term*= z*(factor-1.)/(factor*factor*(factor+1.));
   }
fprintf(stderr,
" ModStruveI could not meet error tolerance\n");
fini:return 2./pi*sum;
}

double StruveI(x) double x;
{/* integral from 0 to x of H0(x)*/
double z,term,factor,sum;int i;
if(x==0.)return 0.;
z=x*x;sum=z*.5;term=-z*z/36.;
for(i=5;i<10000;i+=2)
   {
   sum+=term;
   if( abs(term)<tol*abs(sum))goto fini;
   factor=i;
   term*= -z*(factor-1.)/(factor*factor*(factor+1.));
   }
fprintf(stderr,
" StruveI could not meet error tolerance\n");
fini:return 2./pi*sum;
```

```
}

double StruveIot(x) double x;
{/* integral from x to infinity of H0(x)/x*/
double z,term,factor,sum;int i;
if(x==0.)return pi/2.;
z=x*x;sum=x;term=-z*x/27.;
for(i=5;i<10000;i+=2)
   {
   sum+=term;
   if( abs(term)<tol*abs(sum))goto fini;
   factor=i;
   term*= -z*(factor-2.)/(factor*factor*(factor));
   }
fprintf(stderr," StruveI/t could not meet error
tolerance\n");
fini:return pi/2.*(1.-4./(pi*pi)*sum);
}
```

```
/*
integral of Anger-Weber function
from C Mathematical Function Handbook by Louis Baker
Copyright 1991 by Louis Baker. All rights reserved.

based upon algorithm (but not code) of
by R. F Blackburn and D. R. Wilton
Math Note 57 AFWL Kirtland AFB, NM
*/

#include <stdio.h>
#include "cmlib.h"
#include "protom.h"


#define imax 500
#define tol 1.e-10
#define asympl 15.

/* caveat: making topgam too large will cause overflows!*/
#define topgam 160
static double gammi[topgam],gammh[topgam],gammnh[topgam];


/* call with x==0 to initialize*/
static int cginit=0;

gaminit()
   { double sp,z; int i;
   sp=sqrt(pi);
   /* gammh[z]= gamma(z+.5)*/
   gammh[0]=sp;z=.5;
   for(i=1;i<topgam;i++)
      {
      gammh[i]=gammh[i-1]*z;
      z+=1.;
      }
   /* gammn[z]= gamma(-z)*/
   gammnh[1]= -2.*sp;z=-.5;
   for(i=2;i<topgam;i++)
      {
      z-=1.;
      gammnh[i]=gammnh[i-1]/z;
      }
   /* gammi[z]= gamma(z)*/
   gammi[0]=errorcode;
   gammi[1]=1. ;z=1.;
   for(i=2;i<topgam;i++)
      {
```

```
        gammi[i]=gammi[i-1]*z;
        z+=1.;
        }
    }

double gamtab(double x)
    {
    int i,type; double z,sp;
    if(!cginit) gaminit();
    if(x==0.)
        {
        return errorcode;
        }
    else
        {
        i=(int)(2.*x);
        if( abs(2.*x-(double)i) > tol)
            {fprintf(stderr,
             " arg to gamtab %le not half integer\n",x);
            return gamma(x);
            }
        if(i%2)
            {/* half-integral or error*/
            type=1;
            }
        else type=0;
        }
    switch (type)
        {
        case 0: /* integer*/
            i=(int)x;
            if(i>=topgam)
                {
                fprintf(stderr,
                " out of gamtab range %le\n",x);
                return gamma(x);
                }
            return gammi[i ];
        case 1: /* half-integer*/
            i= (int)(x-.5);
            if(i>=topgam || -i<=-topgam)
                {
                fprintf(stderr,
                " out of gamtab range %le\n",x);
                return gamma(x);
                }
            if(x>0.)return gammh[i];
            return gammnh[-i];
        }
```

```
    }


iaw(m,s,ans) int m; struct complex *s,*ans;
{int i,j;
struct complex sum,x,term;
double gamma(),factor,agam;
if (cabs( *s) > asympl && ( s->y!=0. || s->x >=0.) ) goto
asympt;
CMPLX(sum,0.,0.);factor=-1.;
CLET(x,*s);
gamtab(0.);
/*infinite_loop
    {
    printf(" enter x for gamtab (0 to end)\n");
    scanf("%le",&factor);
    if(factor==0.)break;
    printf(" gamtab(%le)=%le\n",factor,gamtab(factor));
    }
*/
for (i=0;i<imax;i++)
    {
    agam=.5*(i-m)+1.;j=agam;
    /*printf(" agam=%e %d\n",agam,i);*/

    if( !(j<=0 && ((double)j)==agam) )
        {
        agam=gamtab((agam));
        factor= 1./((i+1)*gamtab(1.+.5*(i+m))*agam);
        if(i%2)factor=-factor;
        CTREAL(term,x,factor);
/*printf(" i=%d agam %le factor %le |term|%le |sum| %le\n"
    ,i,agam,factor,cabs(term),cabs(sum));*/
        CADD(sum,sum,term);
        if( cabs(term)<cabs(sum)*tol)break;
        }
    CMULT(term,x,*s);
    CLET(x,term);
    }
switch (m%4)
    {
    case 0 : ans->x=sum.x;ans->y=sum.y;return 0;
    case 1 : ans->x=-sum.y;ans->y=sum.x;return 0;
    case 2 : ans->x=-sum.x;ans->y=-sum.y;return 0;
    default: ans->x=sum.y;ans->y=-sum.x;return 0;
    }

asympt:
CMPLX(x,0.,.5*(m+1.)*pi); CTREAL(sum,*s,-2.);CADD(x,x,sum);
```

```
cexp(&x,&sum); CLET(x,*s);
CTREAL(x,x,pi);
ctreal(&x,.5,&term);
CDIV( x,sum,term);CTREAL( x,x, -.5);
CMPLX(sum, 0,.5);CADD(sum,sum,x);
CMPLX( x, s->y  , -(s->x)); clog( &x, &term);
term.x -= digamma( .5*(1.+m));
CTREAL(term,term, (m%2? 0.:2. )/pi*.5);
CADD(*ans,sum,term);
return 0;


}
```

Chapter 13

Confluent Hypergeometric Functions and Relatives

Introduction

It strikes me as somewhat bass-ackwards to discuss the Confluent Hypergeometric function before discussing the Hypergeometric function, but if we wish to preserve the ordering of Abramowitz and Stegun, we must.

The Hypergeometric function, as usually defined, has singularities at 0, 1, and infinity. It may be generalized somewhat with relatively little difficulty to an equation with singularities at 0, *a*, and infinity (see Chapter 15). The Confluent Hypergeometric functions are the solutions of this equation as $c \to \infty$. The two solutions are generally called M and U. M is the solution regular for small z, and has the expansion $M(a, b, z) = \sum_{n=1}^{\infty} \frac{(a)_n}{(b)_n n!} z^n$.

Here $()_n$ is Pochhammer's symbol, which has been used in chapter 8 and will be discussed in Chapter 15. This compares to the Hypergeometric function's expansion. Note that *M* is often denoted as ${}_1F_1(a;b;z)$. In general ${}_mF_n$ will denote a generalized Hypergeometric function with m parameters appearing in Pochhammer symbols in the numerator in the series expansion, and n in the denominator. Chapter 29 will provide C++ functions for these generalized Hypergeometric functions.

These functions M(a,b,z) and U(a,b,z) solve the equation $z \frac{d^2w}{dz^2} + (b - z) \frac{dw}{dz} - aw = 0$. Whittaker and Watson (reference in Chapter 9) discuss a modified form of the equation $\frac{d^2w}{dz^2} + [-\frac{1}{4} + \frac{\kappa}{z} + \frac{(\frac{1}{4} - \mu^2)}{z^2}] w = 0$, with solutions

$$M_{\kappa,\mu}(z) = \exp(-\frac{1}{2}z)\, z^{\frac{1}{2}\mu} M(\frac{1}{2}+\mu-\kappa\,,\, 1+2\mu\,,\, z)$$ and

$$W_{\kappa,\mu}(z) = \exp(-\frac{1}{2}z)\, z^{\frac{1}{2}\mu} U(\frac{1}{2}+\mu-\kappa\,,\, 1+2\mu\,,\, z)\,.$$

There are a number of functions related closely to the Confluent Hypergeometric function. Among these are the parabolic cylinder function and the Coulomb wave functions. In addition, the Bessel functions are related to either *M* or *U*. Finally, a number of exotic functions are listed in Chapter 13 of Abramowitz and Stegun, including the Toronto, Cunningham, and Bateman functions as well as the Poisson-Charlier polynomials.

Formula 13.1.3 and the discussion following it note that
$$U(a,b,z) = \frac{\pi}{\sin\pi z}\left[\frac{M(a,b,z)}{\Gamma(1+a-b)\Gamma(b)} - z^{1-b}\frac{M(1+a-b,2-b,z)}{\Gamma(a)\Gamma(2-b)}\right]$$

with the principal branch given by $-\pi < arg\; z < \pi$. Thus, we can express U in terms of M for non-integral *b*. If *b* is negative or zero, U will be undefined, while for positive integral *b* we use 13.1.6
$$U(a,n+1,z) = \frac{(-1)^{n+1}}{n!\Gamma(a-n)}\,[\,M(a,n+1,z)\ln z\; +$$

$$+\sum_{r=0}^{\infty}\frac{(a)_r z^r}{(n+1)_r r!}[\psi(a+r)-\psi(1+r)-\psi(1+n+r)]$$

$$+\frac{(n-1)!}{\Gamma(a)}z^{-n}M(a-n,1-n,z)_n]$$ where the last function is to be interpreted as the sum to n terms, taking the value of 0 when $n = 0$. This is still not useful if a = n, for which we use a Kummer transform, Abramowitz and Stegun 13.1.29. Note also that, using 13.6.27, we see that $U(0,b,z) = 1$ because the Laguerre polynomial $L_0^{(\alpha)}(z) = 1$.

When *a* in *M(a,b,z)* is a negative integer, the series terminates (the pochhammer symbols become zero in the numerator) and *M* is a polynomial in *z*. If *b* is a negative integer, *M* is undefined for the same reason, unless *a* is also a negative integer and $b < a$ ($|b| > |a|$), so that the series can terminate before a zero denominator is encountered. If *b* is a negative integer and *a* is not a larger negative integer, $\frac{M(a,b,z)}{\Gamma(b)}$ is defined. The program provided will return this value in such a case as a complex number, with the function returning — 1 to signal this anomolous condition (it returns 0 under normal circumstances). (A similar situation arises for the Hypergeometric function. See Chapter 15.)

Airy Functions

We can use Abramowitz and Stegun's 10.4.6 $Bi(z) = e^{i\pi/6} Ai(z e^{2\pi i/3}) + e^{-i\pi/6} Ai(z e^{-2\pi i/3})$

and 13.6.26 $Ai(z) = U(5/6, 5/3, 4/3\, z^{2/3})\, z/\pi^{1/2} \dfrac{2^{-2/3}}{3^{5/6}} e^{-2/3\, z^{3/2}}$

to express the Airy functions in terms of the Confluent Hypergeometric function U. This works everywhere except for Ai(z) for real z<0. This is related to Stoke's phenomenon on the negative real axis. If in the computation of z^{1-b}, we add 2 π to the logarithm, i. e., if we move the branch cut from the negative real axis to the positive real axis, it gets the correct answer! Note that, for z<0, the argument of U is on the negative imaginary axis, not the branch cut of U. That is, this is not the problem. Comparisons with *Mathematica's*® results for U show that we should not modify our means of computing U along the negative imaginary axis.

To permit computing *Ai(z)*, we provide a modified version of cpow(), called **Cpow()**, which allows the increased generality of adding a multiple of 2pi to the logarithm before taking the exponential. This function may be useful in other contexts, such as computing multiple roots. Note that you should not have to use a non-zero value of this multiplier, argpow, for computing *U*. Note also that, if your complier cannot be made case-sensitive, and complains of multiple functions named **CPOW**, simply change its name. It is only referenced once. You will have to have a context-sensitive editor, of course, but these are the norm.

Applications

The Confluent Hypergeometric functions are most often used as solutions to a variety of differential equations. They are used here to provide methods for complex arguments and parameters for some more common functions, such as the Bessel functions, discussed previously. We also present a file of more exotic functions, such as Cunningham's, Bateman's, and Poisson-Charlier polynomials.

One example of the Confluent Hypergeometric function appearing in a solution of interest is in meteorologist J. Charney's model for baroclinic instability. This is an instability in which a horizontal temperature gradient supplies the potential energy for the motion.

Methods

Series and asymptotic expansions are used. U is related to M by the formula 13.1.3 for non-integral n $U(a,b,z) = \frac{\pi}{\sin\pi b}\left[\frac{M(a,b,z)}{\Gamma(1+a-b)\Gamma(b)} - \frac{M(1+a-b,2-b,z)}{\Gamma(2-b)\Gamma(a)}\right]$ and by 13.1.4 for integral $\mathrm{m}U(a,n+1,z) = \frac{(-1)^{n+1}}{n!\,\Gamma(a-n)}[M(a,n+1,z)\ln z + SUM + TERM]$.

with $SUM = \sum_{r=0}^{\infty}\frac{(a)_r z^r}{(n+1)_r r!}(\psi(a+r)) - \psi(1+r) - \psi(1+n+r))$ and $TERM = \frac{(n-1)!}{\Gamma(n)} z^{-a} M(a-m,1-n,z)_n$. Here M_n denotes the summation is to include only up to the n-th term. Note that our M function supports this by allowing the user to specify n, with n = 0 taken to specify that TERM is zero. If a negative n is specified through the dummy argument **top**, the number of terms summed is determined by convergence only. The evaluations of the Bessel and other functions follow the definitions in Tables 13.6 and 13.7 of Abramowitz and Stegun. Use of the series is forced if the dummy argument **top** is not negative. If b is a negative integer, the series will be summed if a is a larger negative integer or if **top** is not negative. Otherwise, $\frac{M(a, b, z)}{\Gamma(b)}$ will be computed and returned.

Temme's procedure for evaluating the function $U(a,b,z)$ for real $z > 0$ uses a variety of procedures in different regimes, including recurrence relations, asymptotic formulae, and the relationship with the modified Bessel function K. In our implementation, this last procedure is not used, as better results seemed to be obtained without it. The code which selects this option has been defeated by including a term of the form: && 0, which will of course always evaluate to false. The user may easily omit this. Temme evaluated the Bessel functions with a function he had previously developed (and referenced in Chapter 9).

References

H. Bucholz, *The Confluent Hypergeometric Function* (Berlin: Springer Verlag, 1969).

J. G. Charney, *J. Meteorology*, **4**, 135, 1963.

N. M. Temme, *Numerische Mathematic*, **41**, 63-82, 1983.

```
/*
confluent hypergeometric function complex arguments
from C Mathematical Function Handbook by Louis Baker
Copyright 1991 by Louis Baker. All rights reserved.

c1f1 confluent hypergeometric function of the first kind: M
cu      "            "            "       "  "  second kind: U

c1f1(a,c,x,top, ans).
   For top=-1, infinite series is used.
   in some applications, finite value of integer top needed
   If a is negative integer, polynomial.
   If c is negative integer, undefined unless
      a is a negative integer and |a|<|c|, i. e. a>c
   in this case, return 1F1/Gamma(c). function return -1

Cpow   x^n for complex x, n differs from cpow in that
   while both use x^n= exp( n log x), for cpow
   log x has branch cut on neg. x axis, Cpow is adjustable.
   It adds two*pi*argrot, argot a global integer variable.

   For argrot=1, argument of log x ranges from 0 to 2pi,
   rather than from -pi to pi.
   Cpow can therefore be used to find multiple roots by
   giving it argrot= 0,1,...
   For its use with cu, see text.

CAVEAT: YOU SHOULD SET argrot=0 BEFORE CALLING cu EXCEPT IN
VERY SPECIAL CIRCUMSTANCES (see text).
*/

#include <stdio.h>
#include "cmlib.h"
#include "protom.h"


/* to= i*fm*/
#define CTI(to,fm) {(to).x=-(fm).y;(to).y=(fm).x;}
#define cdigam cdigamma

#define tol 1.e-6
#define eps 1.e-7
#define topkt 1000

int argrot=0;/*default initialization. */

/* base ^ expon with ability to adjust log. principal value
range*/
```

```
Cpow(struct complex *base,struct complex *expon,struct
complex *ans)
{struct complex l,d;
clog(base,&l); l.y+=(2.*pi)*argrot;
CMULT(d,l,*expon);cexp(&d,ans);
return 0;
}

c1f1(a,c,x,top,ans)struct complex  *a,*c,*x,*ans;int top;
{/* complex confluent hypergeometric function 1F1(a,b;c;x)*/
double oldterm,newterm,gamma(),digamma();int m,i;struct com-
plex s,z;
int aa,bb,cc,aint,cint,l,mpl,topin;
struct complex term,sum,ratio,factor,p,q,r,t,term1,term2,cl;
double count;
struct complex savec,delta;
topin=top;
CLET(savec,*c);

if(top<0)top=topkt;
if(!top)
   {CMPLX((*ans),0.,0.);return 0;}
CLET(p,*a);CLET(r,*c);

if(cabs(*x)<eps){
   /*printf("small x=%le\n",cabs(*x));*/
   CMPLX((*ans),1.,0.);return 0;}
/* Kummer transformation- good idea?*/
/* suppress except for real arguments?*/
if(x->x <0.   /* &&  x->y ==0.*/ )
   {
   /*printf(" M:Kummer xfm\n");*/
   CTREAL(z,*x,-1.);  CSUB(p,*c,*a);
   c1f1(&p,c,&z,-1,&q);
   cexp(x,&p);
   CMULT((*ans),p,q);
   return 0;
   }

/* is a a negative integer or zero?*/
aint=0;
if( abs(a->y)<eps)
   {oldterm= a->x;aint=oldterm;
   if( aint <=0) aint= (abs(aint-oldterm))<eps ;
   else aint=0;
   }
/* is c a negative integer or zero?*/
cint=0;
if( abs(c->y)<eps)
```

```
   {oldterm= c->x;cint=oldterm;
   if( cint <=0) cint= (abs(cint-oldterm))<eps ;
   else cint=0;
   }
/*printf(" aint, cint top=%d %d %d\n",aint,cint,top);*/

if(cint && topin== -1 )
   {
   /*fprintf(stderr," warn: log case 1f1\n");*/
   if( !aint || cint>= aint)
      {
      CMPLX(s,1.,0.);CSUB(term,s,*c);CADD(sum,term,*a);
      c1f1(&sum,&term,x,top,&s);cpow(x,&term,&sum);
      CMULT(p,s,sum);CTREAL(p,p,1./gamma( 1.+term.x));
      cpochhammer(a,(int)(term.x),&s);
      CMULT(*ans,s,p);
      return -1;
      }
   }

if(cabs(*x)<=20.  || aint )
      {/*series*/
/*printf(" M:series\n");*/

      for(i=0,term.x=sum.x=1.,term.y=sum.y=0.;i<top;i++)
         {
         count=(double)(i+1);
         if(cabs(r)==0.)
            {
            fprintf(stderr," r=0 i=%d top=%d\n",i,top);
            /* once r== 0, will always be*/
            CSET(ans,sum); return 1;
            }
         CDIV(ratio,p,r);
         ratio.x/=count;ratio.y/=count;
         CMULT(s,*x,ratio);
         CMULT(ratio,term,s);CLET(term,ratio);
         CADD(sum,sum,term);
         /*CDIV(ratio,term,sum);*/
         if( cabs(term)< tol*cabs(sum))
            {
      /*printc(c);printf(
                  " = c  series normal before cset\n");*/
            CSET(ans,sum);
            CSUB(delta,savec,*c);
            return 0;
            }
         p.x+=1.;r.x+=1.;
         }
```

```
if(top==topkt)
fprintf(stderr," 1f1:requested accuracy not met\n");
/*otherwise, top was positive on entry for specified term
count*/
/*printc(ans);printf("=M series\n");*/
      CSET(ans,sum);return 0;
      }
/*printf("M:asymptotic\n");*/
/* asymptotic expansion*/
CMPLX(p,1.,0.);CDIV(z,p,*x);
CSUB(p,*c,*a);CMPLX(r,1.,0.);CSUB(r,r,*a);
oldterm=1.e30;
for(i=0,term.x=sum.x=1.,term.y=sum.y=0.;i<top;i++)
      {
      count=(double)(i+1);
      CMULT(ratio,p,r);
      ratio.x/=count;ratio.y/=count;
      CMULT(s,z,ratio);
      CMULT(ratio,term,s);CLET(term,ratio);
      CADD(sum,sum,term);
      /*CDIV(ratio,term,sum);*/
      if( cabs(term)< tol*cabs(sum))break;
      newterm=cabs(term);
      if(oldterm>newterm)oldterm=newterm;
      else break;
      p.x+=1.;r.x+=1.;
      }
CSUB(q,*a,*c);cpow(x,&q,&p);CMULT(q,p,sum);
cexp(x,&p);CMULT(sum,p,q);
cgamma(a,&p,&q);CDIV(term1,sum,p);
CTREAL(z,z,-1.);
CLET(p,*a);CMPLX(r,1.,0.);CSUB(r,r,*c);CADD(r,r,*a);
oldterm=1.e30;
for(i=0,term.x=sum.x=1.,term.y=sum.y=0.;i<top;i++)
      {
      count=(double)(i+1);
      CMULT(ratio,p,r);
      ratio.x/=count;ratio.y/=count;
      CMULT(s,z,ratio);
      CMULT(ratio,term,s);CLET(term,ratio);
      /*term *=(x*(a+i)/((c+i)*count));*/
      CADD(sum,sum,term);
      /*CDIV(ratio,term,sum);*/
      newterm=cabs(term);
      if(oldterm>newterm)oldterm=newterm;
      else break;
      if( cabs(term)< tol*cabs(sum))break;
      p.x+=1.;r.x+=1.;
      }
```

```
cpow(x,a,&p);CDIV(q,sum,p);CLET(r,*a);
CTREAL(r,r,-pi);CTI(s,r);
cexp(&s,&p);CMULT(sum,p,q);
CSUB(r,*c,*a);cgamma(&r,&p,&q);CDIV(term2,sum,p);
CADD(term2,term2,term1);
cgamma(c,&r,&s);CMULT((*ans),term2,r);
return 0;
}


cu(a,c,x,ans)struct complex  *a,*c,*x,*ans;
{double oldterm,newterm,digamma(),gamma();
struct complex z,s,term1,term2,term,sum; int m,i,top=100;
int aa,bb,cc,aint,l,mpl;
struct complex ratio,factor,p,q,r,t,cl;
double count;
if(cabs(*a)<eps)
   {CMPLX((*ans),1.,0.); return 0;}
if(cabs(*x)>8.)
   {/* asymptotic expansion*/
   /*printf(" asymptotic case\n");*/
   CMPLX(p,-1.,0.);CDIV(z,p,(*x));
   CLET(p,*a);CMPLX(r,1.,0.);CADD(r,r,*a);CSUB(r,r,*c);
   oldterm=1.e30;
   for(i=0,term.x=sum.x=1.,term.y=sum.y=0.;i<top;i++)
         {
         count=(double)(i+1);
         CMULT(ratio,p,r);
         ratio.x/=count;ratio.y/=count;
         CMULT(s,z,ratio);
         CMULT(ratio,term,s);CLET(term,ratio);
         /*term *=(x*(a+i)/((c+i)*count));*/
         CADD(sum,sum,term);
         /*CDIV(ratio,term,sum);*/
         if( cabs(term)< tol*cabs(sum))break;
         newterm=cabs(term);
         if(oldterm>newterm)oldterm=newterm;
         else break;
         p.x+=1.;r.x+=1.;
         }
      cpow(x,a,&p);CDIV((*ans),sum,p);return 0;
   }
m=c->x;
if( abs(c->y)<eps && abs(c->x-m)<eps)
   {/* c (b in A&S) is an integer*/
   /*printf(" integer case\n");*/

   if(m<1)
```

```
    {/*m =1-n  n=1-m>0  */
    /*printf(" integer case m \n");*/
    CLET(p,*a);p.x+=1.-m; CMPLX(q,2.-m,0.);
    cu(&p,&q,x,&s);
    /*printc(&s);printf("= U(recursive)\n");*/
    CMPLX(p,1.-m,0.);cpow(x,&p,&r);CMULT((*ans),r,s);
    return 0;
    }
/* m=n+1 m at least 1*/
CMPLX(term1,1.,0.);
CADD(term1,term1,*a);
CSUB(term1,term1,*c);
if( cabs(term1) < eps)
    {/* log. solution has pblm a=n for c=n+1.
    use Kummer  13.1.29 */
    CMPLX(term2,2.,0.);CSUB(term2,term2,*c);
    cu(&term1,&term2,x,&p);
    CMPLX(term2,1.,0.);CSUB(term2,term2,*c);
    cpow(x,&term2,&term1);/* x^(1-b)*/
    CMULT( *ans, term1,p);
    return 0;
    }
CMPLX(term1,0.,0.);
if(m>1)
    {
    /*printf(" integer case m1 \n");*/
    CMPLX(q,2.-m,0.);CLET(p,*a);p.x-=(m-1);
    c1f1(&p,&q, x,(m-2),&term1);/* was m-1*/
    /*printc(&term1);printf("= M m=%d\n",m);*/
    CTREAL(r,term1,gamma((double)(m-1)) );
    cgamma(a,&p,&q);CDIV(s,r,p);
    CMPLX(r,(m-1),0.);
    cpow(x,&r,&t);CDIV(term1,s,t);
    }
clog(x,&s);
c1f1(a,c,x,-1,&t);
/*printc(&t);printf("= M\n");*/
CMULT(term2,s,t);
CLET(p,*a);CLET(r,*c);
CMPLX(sum,-digamma(1.),0.);
cdigam(a,&s);cdigam(c,&t);CADD(sum,sum,s);CSUB(sum,sum,t)
for(i=0,term.x=1.,term.y=0.;i<top;i++)
        {
        count=(double)(i+1);
        CDIV(ratio,p,r);
        ratio.x/=count;ratio.y/=count;
        CMULT(s,*x,ratio);
        CMULT(ratio,term,s);CLET(term,ratio);
        CMPLX(factor,-digamma(count+m)
```

```
-digamma(count+1.),0.);
        CLET(t,*a);t.x+=count;
        cdigam(&t ,&s);CADD(factor,factor,s);
        CMULT(t,ratio,factor);
        /*term *=(x*(a+i)/((c+i)*count));*/
        CADD(sum,sum,t);
        /*CDIV(ratio,term,sum);*/
        if( cabs(t)< tol*cabs(sum))break;
        p.x+=1.;r.x+=1.;
        }
   CADD(term2,term2,sum);
   CTREAL(term2,term2, ((m%2)?-1.:1.)/gamma((double)m) );
   CLET(p,*a);p.x-=(m-1);
   cgamma(&p,&q,&r);CDIV(s,term2,q);CADD((*ans),term1,s);
   return 0;
   }
/* x not large, b not integer*/
   {
   /*printf(" x not large, b no integer: use M\n");*/
   c1f1(a,c,x,-1,&s);
   cgamma(c,&t,&p);CDIV(q,s,t);
   CMPLX(p,1.,0.);CADD(p,p,*a);
   CSUB(p,p,*c);cgamma(&p,&s,&t);CDIV(term1,q,s);
   CMPLX(q,2.,0.);CSUB(q,q,*c);
   c1f1(&p,&q ,x,-1,&s);
   CMPLX(q,2.,0.);CSUB(q,q,*c);
   cgamma(a,&t,&p);CDIV(term2,s,t);
   cgamma(&q,&t,&s);CDIV(s,term2,t);
   CMPLX(p,1.,0.);CSUB(p,p,*c);
   /*CPOW(X,&p,&q);For Airy for Real arguments*/
   Cpow(x,&p,&q);
   CMULT(term2,s,q);
   CSUB(term1,term1,term2);CTREAL(term1,term1,pi);
   CTREAL(q,*c,pi);csin(&q,&s);
   CDIV((*ans),term1,s);
   return 0;
   }
}
```

```
/* functions defined in terms of Confluent Hypergeometric
Function

from C Mathematical Function Handbook by Louis Baker
Copyright 1991 by Louis Baker. All rights reserved.

Jbessel  I Associated Bessel function for complex order,ar-
gument
Ibessel  I Associated Bessel function for complex order,ar-
gument
Kbessel  K Associated Bessel function for complex order,ar-
gument
Airy   Ai CAVEAT: SEE TEXT!!!!!!!!!!!!!!!!!!!!!!
BiAiry   Bi
The following functions are included, but have not been
benchmarked
against any standard:

bateman
Charlier
cunningham
Toronto

*/

#include <stdio.h>
#include "cmlib.h"
#include "protom.h"

/* multiply by i */
#define CTI(to,fm) {(to).x=-(fm).y;(to).y=(fm).x;}

extern int argrot;
/* some cpow() below could be ctreal()*/

Jbessel(order,arg, ans) struct complex *order,*arg,*ans;
   {struct complex a,b,c,d,iarg;int top=-1;
   CLET(a,*order);CTI(iarg,*arg);
   a.x += .5;/* a= order+.5*/
   CTREAL(b,a,2.);CLET(c,iarg);CTREAL(c,c,2.);
   c1f1(&a,&b,&c,top,ans);
   /*printc(ans);printf(" =M\n");*/
   CTREAL(b,iarg,-1.);
   cexp(&b,&a);
   CMULT(b,*ans,a);
   CTREAL(a,*arg,.5);
   cpow(&a,order,&c);CMULT(a,b,c);
   CLET(c,*order);c.x+=1.;
   cgamma(&c,&b,&d);
```

```
    CDIV((*ans),a,b);
    return 0;
    }

Ibessel(order,arg, ans) struct complex *order,*arg,*ans;
    {struct complex a,b,c,d;int top=-1;
    CLET(a,*order);
    a.x += .5;/* a= order+.5*/
    CTREAL(b,a,2.);CLET(c,(*arg));CTREAL(c,c,2.);
    c1f1(&a,&b,&c,top,ans);
    /*printc(ans);printf(" =M\n");*/
    CTREAL(b,*arg,-1.);
    cexp(&b,&a);
    CMULT(b,*ans,a);
    CTREAL(a,*arg,.5);
    cpow(&a,order,&c);CMULT(a,b,c);
    CLET(c,*order);c.x+=1.;
    cgamma(&c,&b,&d);
    CDIV((*ans),a,b);
    return 0;
    }

Kbessel(order,arg, ans) struct complex *order,*arg,*ans;
    {struct complex a,b,c;
    CLET(a,*order);
    a.x += .5;/* a= order+.5*/
    CTREAL(b,a,2.);CLET(c,(*arg));CTREAL(c,c,2.);
    cu(&a,&b,&c,ans);
    cexp(arg,&a);
    CDIV(b,(*ans),a);/*b=U exp(-x)*/
    CTREAL(a,*arg,2.);
    cpow(&a,order,&c);CMULT(a,b,c);/* a= Uexp()(2x)^n*/
    CTREAL((*ans),a,sqrt(pi));
    return 0;
    }

Airy(z,ans) struct complex *z,*ans;
    {struct complex a,b,c,d,z3h;double factor;double
pow(),sqrt();
    int oldarg;
    oldarg=argrot;
    CMPLX(a,5./6.,0.);
    CMPLX(b,5./3.,0.);
    CMPLX(c,1.5,0.);
    factor= pow(3.,-5./6.)*pow(2.,2./3.)/sqrt(pi);

    cpow(z,&c,&d);CTREAL(z3h,d,4./3.);/*z3h= 4/3 z^(3/2)*/
    if(z->y==0.)
       {if( z->x <0.) {z3h.x=0.;argrot=1;}
```

```
        else z3h.y=0.;
        }
    /*printc(&z3h);printf(" U arg=4/3z^3/2 \n");*/
    cu(&a,&b,&z3h,&c);
    /*printc(&c);printf(" U, argrot=%d\n",argrot);*/
    CMULT(a,c,(*z));
    CTREAL(a,a,factor);
    CTREAL(z3h,z3h,-.5);
    cexp(&z3h,&b);
    argrot=oldarg;
    CMULT(*ans,b,a);return 0;
    }

BiAiry(z,ans) struct complex *z,*ans;
    {struct complex a,b,c,d,x,c1,c2,a1,a2,one;int oldrot;
    CMPLX(a,0., pi/6.);
    CMPLX(b,0., 2.*pi/3.);
    CMPLX(one,1.,0.);
    cexp(&a,&c1);
    CDIV(c2,one,c1);
    cexp(&b,&a1);
    CDIV(a2,one,a1);
    CMULT(x,a1,*z);    CLET(a1,x);
    CMULT(x,a2,*z);    CLET(a2,x);
    oldrot=argrot;argrot=0;
    Airy(&a1,&a);
    Airy(&a2,&b);
    CMULT(c,a,c1);CMULT(d,b,c2);CADD( *ans, c,d);
    argrot=oldrot;
    return 0;
    }


bateman(nu,x,ans) struct complex *nu,*x,*ans;
    {
    struct complex a,b,c,d;
    CLET(a,*nu);CTREAL(a,a,-.5);
    CMPLX(b,0.,0.);
    CTREAL(c,*x,2.);
    cu(&a,&b,&c,&d);
    cexp(x,&a);CDIV(b,d,a);
    CTREAL(a,*nu,.5);a.x+=1.;
    cgamma(&a,&c,&d);CDIV((*ans),b ,d);return 0;
    }

cunningham(n,m,x,ans)struct complex *n,*m,*x,*ans;
    {
    struct complex a,b,c,d,diff;
    CTREAL(b,*m,.5);CSUB(diff,b,*n);/* diff= m/2-n */
```

```
    CLET(c,*m); c.x+=1.;
    cu(&diff,&c,x,&d);
    CMPLX(a,1.,0.);CSUB(a,a,diff);/* a=1-diff= 1+n-m/2*/
    cgamma(&a,&b,&c);CDIV(c,d,b);
    CTI(b,diff);CTREAL(b,b,pi);CSUB(d,*x,b);CTREAL(d,d,-1.);
    cexp(&d,&b);CMULT((*ans),b,c);
    return 0;
    }
/* note that n is integer-Pochhammer symbol does not make
sense otherwise*/
charlier(n,nu,x,ans) struct complex *nu,*x,*ans;int n;
    {
    struct complex a,b,c,d,e,f;int top=40;
    double gam;
    CMPLX(a,(double)(-n),0.);CADD(b,*nu,a);b.x+=1.;
    c1f1(&a,&b,x,-1,&d);
    cpochhammer(&b,n,&a);CMULT(f,a,d);
    gam=1./sqrt(gamma((double)(n+1)));
    CMPLX(b,-n*.5,0.);
    cpow(x,&b,&a); CTREAL(a,a,gam);
    CMULT((*ans),a,f);
    return 0;
    }

toronto(m,n,r,ans) struct complex *m,*n,*r,*ans;
    {struct complex mm,nn,rsq,a,b,c,d;int tol=50;
    CMULT(rsq,*r,*r);
    CLET(mm,*m);mm.x+=1.;CTREAL(mm,mm,.5);/* mm= .5(m+1) */
    CLET(nn,*n);nn.x+=1.;
    c1f1(&mm,&nn,&rsq,tol,&a);
    CTREAL(c,rsq,-1.);
    cexp(&c,&d);CMULT(c,a,d);/* c=Mexp(-r^2) */
    cgamma(&mm,&a,&b);CMULT(b,a,c);
    cgamma(&nn,&a,&c);CDIV(c,b,a);/*divide by n!=Gamma(n+1)*/
    CTREAL(a, *n,2.);CADD(a,a,*m); a.x-=1.;
    cpow( r,&a,&b); CMULT( (*ans),b,c);
    return 0;
    }

Laguerre( a, n, x,ans) struct complex *a,*x,*ans;int n;
    {
    struct complex p,q,r,s;
    CMPLX(q,n+1.,0.);
    cgamma(&q,&r,&p);/* r=Gamma(n+1)*/
    CMPLX(p,-n,0.);
    CLET(q,*a);q.x+=1.;/* q= a+1*/
    c1f1(&p,&q,x,-1,&s);
    CDIV( p,s,r);
    cpochhammer(&q,n,&s);
```

```
CMULT((*ans),s,p);
return 0;
}
```

```
Whittaker confluent hypergeometric functions

/* confluent hypergeometric function complex arguments

from C Mathematical Function Handbook by Louis Baker
Copyright 1991
by Louis Baker. All rights reserved.

Mwhit   : Whittaker confluent hypergeometric function of
the first
kind Wwhit   :     "            "            "          "
"  "  second
kind

*/ #include "cmlib.h" #include "protom.h"

Mwhit(k,mu,x,ans) struct complex *k,*mu,*x,*ans; {struct
complex a,b,c,d; CMPLX(a,.5,0.);CADD(a,a,*mu);CSUB(a,a,*k);
CMPLX(b,1.,0.);CTREAL(c,*mu,2.);CADD(b,b,c);
c1f1(&a,&b,x,-1,&d);
if(d.x==errorcode) {ans->x=ans->y=errorcode; return 1;}
CMPLX(c,.5,0.);CADD(c,c,*mu);cpow(x,&c,&a);CMULT(c,d,a);
CTREAL(a,*x,-.5);cexp(&a,&b);CMULT((*ans) ,b,c);return 0; }

Wwhit(k,mu,x,ans) struct complex *k,*mu,*x,*ans; {struct
complex a,b,c,d; CMPLX(a,.5,0.);CADD(a,a,*mu);CSUB(a,a,*k);
CMPLX(b,1.,0.);CTREAL(c,*mu,2.);CADD(b,b,c);
cu(&a,&b,x,&d);
if(d.x==errorcode) {ans->x=ans->y=errorcode; return 1;}
CMPLX(c,.5,0.);CADD(c,c,*mu);cpow(x,&c,&a);CMULT(c,d,a);
CTREAL(a,*x,-.5);cexp(&a,&b);CMULT((*ans) ,b,c);return 0; }
```

```
/*
Test Driver Confluent Hypergeometric Function
from C Mathematical Function Handbook by Louis Baker
Copyright 1991 by Louis Baker. All rights reserved.
*/

#include <stdio.h>
#include "cmlib.h"
#include "protom.h"

extern int argrot;

#define cdigam cdigamma
extern double digammin;

main()
{struct complex aa,bb,z,ans,w,f,g,h;double a,b,c,
digamma(),d,e,ff;
int n,k;
argrot=0;
while(1)
   {printf(" enter x+iy for log\n");scanf("%le%le",&a,&b);
   if(a==0.&&b==0.)break;
   CMPLX(z,a,b);clog(&z,&ans);printc(&ans);printf(
                    " log\n");
   }
while(1)
   {printf(
" enter complex arg a,b z for confl. hypergom. 1f1 M\n");

scanf("%le%le%le%le%le%le",&a,&b,&c,&d,&e,&ff);CMPLX(aa,a,b);

   if( a==0.&&b==0.)break;
   CMPLX(bb,c,d);CMPLX(z,e,ff);
   c1f1(&aa,&bb,&z,-1,&ans);
printc(&ans);printf("=answer\n");
   }
while(1)
   {printf(" enter complex arg a,b z for confl. hypergom.
U\n");

scanf("%le%le%le%le%le%le",&a,&b,&c,&d,&e,&ff);CMPLX(aa,a,b);

   if( a==0.&&b==0.)break;
   printf(" enter argrot\n");scanf("%d",&argrot);
   CMPLX(bb,c,d);CMPLX(z,e,ff);
   cu(&aa,&bb,&z,&ans);
printc(&ans);printf("=answer\n");
   }
```

```
    while(1)
        {
         printf(" enter digammin, x for digamma\n");
        scanf("%le%le",&digammin,&a);
        if(a==0.)break;
        printf(" psi(%le)=%le,floor=%le\n"
                     ,a,digamma(a),digammin);
        }
    while(1)
        {
         printf(" enter digammin, y for digamma(1+iy)\n");
        scanf("%le%le",&digammin,&a);
        if(a==0.)break;
        CMPLX(w,1.,a);cdigam(&w,&f);
        printc(&f);
        }
    while(1)
        {
         printf(" K:enter order,arg\n");
        scanf("%le%le%le%le",&a,&b,&c,&d);
        if(a==0.&&b==0. && c==0. &&d==0.)break;
        CMPLX(w,a,b);
        CMPLX(g,c,d);
        Kbessel(&w,&g,&f);
        printc(&f);
        }
    while(1)
        {
         printf(" J:enter order,arg\n");
        scanf("%le%le%le%le",&a,&b,&c,&d);
        if(a==0.&&b==0. && c==0. &&d==0.)break;
        CMPLX(w,a,b);
        CMPLX(g,c,d);
        Jbessel(&w,&g,&f);
        printc(&f);
        }
    while(1)
        {
        printf(
" I:enter order,arg\n");scanf("%le%le%le%le",&a,&b,&c,&d);
        if(a==0.&&b==0. && c==0. &&d==0.)break;
        CMPLX(w,a,b);
        CMPLX(g,c,d);
        Ibessel(&w,&g,&f);
        printc(&f);
        }
    while(1)
        {
        printf(" Airy:arg\n");
```

```
      /*scanf("%le%le%d",&a,&b,&argrot);*/
      scanf("%le%le",&a,&b);
      if(a==0.&&b==0.)break;argrot=0;
      /*printf(" argrot=%d \n",argrot);*/
      CMPLX(w,a,b);
      Airy(&w,&f);
      printc(&f);
      }
   while(1)
      {
      printf(" Bi(Airy):arg\n");
      scanf("%le%le",&a,&b);
      if(a==0.&&b==0.)break;
      CMPLX(w,a,b);argrot=0;
      BiAiry(&w,&f);
      printc(&f);
      }
   while(1)
      {
      printf(" gamma:arg\n");scanf("%le%le",&a,&b);
      if(a==0.&&b==0.)break;
      CMPLX(w,a,b);
      cgamma(&w,&f,&g);
      printc(&f);printc(&g);
      }
   while(1)
      {
       printf(" Erfc via Whittaker:arg\n");
      scanf("%le%le",&a,&b);
      if(a==0.&&b==0.)break;
      CMPLX(w,a,b);
      CMULT(h,w,w);CMPLX(aa,-.25,0.);CMPLX(bb,.25,0.);
      Wwhit(&aa,&bb,&h,&f);
      CTREAL(h,h,-.5);cexp(&h,&aa);CMULT(g,aa,f);
      /* Caveat: Whittaker & Watson p. 341
      definition of Erfc different from A&S 7.1.2
      */
      CTREAL(g,g,1./sqrt(pi));
      ctreal(&w,-.5,&f);CMULT(aa ,f,g);
      printc(&aa);
      }
   while(1)
      {
      printf(" Poisson-Charlier:
n,nu,x\n");scanf("%d%le%le",&n,&b,&a);
      /* A&C call x, nu what Erdelyi calls a, x respective-
ly*/
      if(a==0.&&b==0. && !n)break;
      CMPLX(w,a,0.); CMPLX(f,b,0.);
```

```
        charlier(n,&f,&w,&g);
        printc(&g);printf("=from chf\n");
        ff=pow(a,(double)(-n*.5))*sqrt(gamma(1.+n));
        c=laguerre((b-n), n ,a);
        printf(" from Laguerre %le,coef %le ans: %le\n"
        ,c,ff,c*ff);
        /* check lag via recur*/
        c=1.;d=1.+b-n-a;  if(n==1)ff=d;if(!n)ff=c;
        for(k=1;k<n;k++)
            {
            ff= ((2*k+b-n+1.-a)*d-(k+b-n)*c)/(k+1.);
            c=d;d=ff;
            }
        printf(" Lag. by recursion=%le\n",ff);
        CMPLX(bb,b-n,0.);
        Laguerre(&bb,n,&w,&g);
        printc(&g);printf("=Lag. by 1F1\n");
        }
return 0;
}
```

```
/*
Confluent Hypergeometric function U
for real positive argument and real parameters

from C Mathematical Function Handbook by Louis Baker
Copyright 1991 by Louis Baker. All rights reserved.

Based on N M Temm, Numer. Math. 41,63-82 (1983)

uabx(a,b,x,eps,uprime) returns U and uprime =U'
chu(a,b,x,kmax,eps,u,uprime) where u is an array from 0 to
kmax
 giving Gamma(a+k)/Gamma(a) U(a+k,b,x) 0<=k<=kmax and
 uprime= Gamma(a+kmax)/Gamma(a)U'(a+kmax,b,x)
*/
#include <alloc.h>
#include <stdio.h>
#include "cmlib.h"
#include "protom.h"

#define entier(x) ((x>0.)?(int)x:((int)x)-1)

brec(a,b,k,f,g,x)double a,b,*f,*g,x;int k;
{
int i,km;
double h;km=k-1;
for(i=0;i<km;i++)
   {
   h=*f-*g;
   *g=((i+b)* *g-a* *f)/x;
   *f=h;
   }
return 0;
}

chu(a,b,x,kmax,eps,u,uprime)
double a,b,x,eps,u[],*uprime; int kmax;
{/* gamma(a+k)/gamma(k)*u(a+k,b,x) for k=0,1,kmax and
u'(a+k,b,x)*/
int i,j,kk,l,m,p,q,r,s,n,nu,k0,k1,largex; double
ar,br,cr,m0,m1;
double pr,qr,rr,sr,vr,bb[9],bb1[9],bx[9],fi[10],
sqrt(),sin(),log(),exp();
double c,d,e,f,g,h,w,a1,b1,*v,pow(),delta,t0,t1,
gamma(),lou, u0,u1,u2,u3,x2,y,z,t,mr,er,p2,p1,p0;
if(a<0. || x<0. || kmax<0 || eps<0.)
                     {*u=*uprime=errorcode;return 0;}
if(a==0.)
   {
```

```
        u[0]=1;
        *uprime=0.;
        for( i=1;i<=kmax;i++)u[i]=0.;
        return;
        }
    if(b<0.)
        {
        v=(double *) malloc( sizeof(double) * (kmax+1));
        c=a-b+1.;
        d=pow(x,-b);
        chu(c,1.-b,x,kmax,eps,v,&w);
        for(j=0;j<=kmax;j++)
            {
            e=(a+j)/d;
            v[j]=-e*v[j];
            d=e/(c+j);
            }
        *uprime=v[kmax];
        u[kmax]=-x*(*uprime*e*w)/(a+kmax);
        c+=x;
        for(j=kmax-1;j>=0;j--)
            {
            u[j]=(-x*v[j+1]+(c+j)*u[j+1])/(a+j);
            }
        return;
        }
    if(b>1.)
        {
        n=entier(b);
        b1=b-n;
        a1=a+kmax;
        c=b-a-1.;
        e=c-x;
        m=entier(e);
        if( ((double)m)==e)m--;
        p=    c>=0. && (c==((double)((int)c)));
        q= kmax<=c;
        r=kmax<=m;s=m>=0;
        if(!kmax){r=s=1;}
        if(r){m=kmax; kk= (p?c:n)-m;}
        if(!r)
            {
            if(p&&q)
                {
                g=1;
                i=kmax-1;
                for(j=0;j<=i;j++)
                    g*=(j+a);
                f=g*pow(x,-a1);
```

```
        g=-a1*f/x;
        brec(a1,a1+1,c-kmax,&f,&g,x);
        }
    else
        {
        chu(a,b1,x,kmax,eps,u,&u3);
        f=u[kmax];
        g=u3;
        brec(a1,b1,n,&f,&g,x);
        if( !p&&s)
            {
            for(j=kmax;j>0;j--)
                u3-=u[j];
                vr=u[0];
                w=u3;
                d=b1;
            }
        n=m+1;
        u[kmax]=f;
        *uprime=g;
        if(!s)n=0;
        }/* else  (if p&&q)*/
    for(j=kmax-1;j>=n;j--)
        {
        h=(-x*g+(j-e)*f)/(a+j);
        g-=f;
        f=u[j]=h;
        }
    }/* !r  */
    if(s)
        {
        if(p)
            {
            vr=pow(x,-a);
            w=-a*vr/x;
            d=a+1.;
            }
        else if(r)
            {
            chu(a,b1,x,0,eps,u,&w);
            vr=u[0];
            d=b1;
            }
        brec(a,d,kk,&vr,&w,x);
        e=b-n-x;
        for(j=0;j<=m;j++)
            {
            if(!j)
                {
```

```
                f=u[0]=vr;
                g=w;
                }
            else
                {
                h=-w;
                g=w=-((a+j-1)*vr-(j+e)*w)/x;
                vr=u[j]=h;
                }
            brec(a+j,b+j-m,m-j,&(u[j]),&g,x);
            if(m==kmax)*uprime=g;
            }
        }/* if s */
    }/*b>1*/
else if(x<=1.4 && 0 )
/* defeat with && 0  CAN GIVE poor acc. due to bessel */
    {
    /*printf(" x case\n");*/
    n=9;
    vr=12.56637;
    rr=(x-vr*(b+1.))*.5;
    lou=rr*rr+4.*n*x;
    if(lou<0.){fprintf(stderr," U:lou=%e\n",lou);lou=0.;}
    d=(vr*n+rr-sqrt(lou))/(2.*n);
    if(d<4.7124){d=4.7124;vr=w=1;}
    else {vr=abs(sin(d));w=pow(vr,-1.-b);}
    w*=exp(.5*x*(1./vr+1./d));
    delta= eps*exp(-.5*x+(n-1.-b)*log(d))/w;
    z=.5/delta;
    vr=.5-b;
    i=n-1;
    for(j=1;j<=i;j++) z*=(j+vr);
    i=0;
    t=sqrt(x)*pow(z,.5/n);
    e=log(delta)+n-n*log(x);
    label: rr=n+b+t;
    sr=1.+b+t;
    pr=log(rr);
    qr=log(sr);
    f=(log(t+.5)-2.*n*log(t)+(rr-.5)*pr-(sr-.5)*qr-e)
        /(1./(t+.5)-2.*n/t+.5*(n-1)/(rr*sr)+pr-qr);
    if(f<0.)
        {
        t-=f;
        t=sqrt(t*t+2.*x);
        i++;
        if(i<10)goto label;
        }
    else
```

```
        {k0=1+ entier(t*t/x-a);}
    /*printf("k0=%d t=%e\n",k0,t);*/
    nu= kmax>=k0 ? 1+kmax : k0 ;
    rr=a+nu;
    w=sqrt(x/rr);
    vr=2.*rr*w;
    t0=kbes( vr,-b);
    t1=kbes( vr,1.-b);
    /*printf(
" K(vr) for orders -b,1-b,b=%e %e %e %e\n",t0,t1,vr,b);*/
    vr=pow(w,-b);
    bb[0]=bb1[0]=bx[0]=1.;
    u1=fi[0]=vr*t0;
    u0=fi[1]=vr*w*t1;
    x2=x*x;
    bx[1]=-x/12.;
    bx[2]=x2/288;
    bx[3]=-x*(5.*x2-72.)/51840.;
    bx[4]=x2*(5*x2-288.)/2488320.;
    bx[5]=-x*(x2*(7.*x2-1008.)+6912.)/209018880.;
    bx[6]=x2*(x2*(35.*x2-10080.)+279936.)/75246796800.;
    bx[7]=-x*(x2*(x2*(x2*5.-2520.)+176256.)-
                    746496.)/902961561600.;
    bx[8]=x2*(x2*(x2*(x2*5.-4032.)+566784.)-
                    9953280.)/86684309913600.;
    bb[1]=.5;
    bb[2]=(3.*b-1.)/24.;
    bb[3]=b*(b-1.)/48.;
    bb[4]=(b*(b*(b*15.-30.)+5.)+2.)/5760.;
    bb[5]=b*(b*(b*(b*3.-10.)+5.)+2.)/11520.;
    bb[6]=(b*(b*(b*(b*(b*63.-315.)+315.)+91.)-42.)-
                    16.)/2903040.;
    bb[7]=b*(b*(b*(b*(b*(b*9.-63.)+105.)+7.)-42.)-
                    16.)/5806080.;
    bb[8]=(b*(b*(b*(b*(b*(b*(b*135.-1260.)+3150.)-840.)-
                    2345.)-540.)
        +404.)+144.)/1393459200.;
    for(i=1;i<n;i++)
        {
        t0=bb[i];
        t1=bb1[i]=(b-i)*t0;
        for(j=1;j<i;j++)
            {
            t0+=bb[i-j]*bx[j];
            t1+=bb1[i-j]*bx[j];
            }
        t0=bx[i]+b*t0;
        t1+=bx[i];
        fi[i+1]=(x*fi[i-1]+(i-b)*fi[i])/rr;
```

```
            u0+=t0*fi[i+1];
            u1+=t1*fi[i];
            /*printf(" i=%d u0 u1 %e %e\n",i,u0,u1);*/
            }
        w=2.*exp(.5*x)/gamma(1.+a);
        u2=w*u0;
        u3=-w*u1;
        vr=a+1.-b+x;
        k1=nu-1;
        for(j=k1;j>0;j--)
            {
            u1=(-x*u3+(vr+j)*u2)/(a+j);
            u3-=u2;
            u2=u1;
            if(j<=kmax) u[j]=a*u2;
            if(j==kmax)*uprime=a*u3;
            }
        u[0]=-x*u3+vr*u2;
        if(!kmax) *uprime=a*(u3-u2);
        /*printf(" answer=%e\n" ,u[0]);*/
        return;
        }

else/* x>1.4 */
        {
        n=a;
        if( (a-(double)n)==0.)
            {
            n--;
            a-=n;
            kmax+=n;
            }
        largex= x>6.5 && a!=b;
        if(largex) mr=1.;
        else
            {
            mr=0.;
            if(a==b)
                {
                m0=a;
                m1=1.;
                }
            else/* gets wrong answers for a!=b, 1.4<x<6.5 must be
here!*/
            /* for a approx=b, should bet m0 approx a, m1 approx
1*/
                {
                m0=0.;
                m1=vr=1.;
```

```
        for(r=1;vr>eps*m1;r++)
            {
/* Temme vr*=vr/r I believe is typo */
            vr*=x/r;
            m0+=vr;
            vr*=(a+r)/(b+r);
            m1+=vr;
/*printf(" r=%d vr=%e m0 m1 %e %e\n",r,vr,m0,m1);*/
            }
        vr=exp(-x)*gamma(a+1.)/gamma(b+1.);
        m0=vr*(b+a*m0);m1*=vr;
/*        printf(" m0=%e(a=%e)m1=%e(1) %e\n",m0,a,m1,vr);*/
        }
      }/* else*/
   c=a-b;
   cr=2.+c;
   br=x+a+cr;
   p0=0.;
   vr=p1=er=1.;r=0;
   for(ar=a+r;r<=kmax;)
      {
      p2=(br*p1-ar*p0)/cr;
      er*=ar/cr;
      r++;
      if(largex) mr*=(1.+c/r);
      vr=er/p2;
      br+=2.;
      cr+=1.;
      p0=p1;
      p1=p2;
      }
   w=p0*p1/er;

   for(ar=a+r;vr*(w/p0+mr*(2.+a/r))>=eps;ar+=1.)
      {
      p2=(br*p1-ar*p0)/cr;
      er*=ar/cr;
      r++;
      if(largex) mr*=(1.+c/r);
      vr=er/p2;
      br+=2.;
      cr+=1.;
      p0=p1;
      p1=p2;
      }
   c+=1.;
   vr=x+c;
   u2=1.;
   w=0.;
```

```
    u3=-2.*r/(x+sqrt(x*(x+4.*r)));

    for(r--;r>0;r--)
        {
        if(largex)
            {
            w+=mr*u2;
            mr*=(r+1)/(c+r);
            }

        u1=(-x*u3+(vr+r)*u2)/(a+r);
        u3-=u2;
        u2=u1;
        if(r>=n && r<=kmax) u[r-n]=u2;
        if(r==kmax)*uprime=u3;
        }
    u1=-x*u3+vr*u2;
    u3-=u2;
    vr=a;
    kk=n-1;
    if(kmax==0) *uprime=u3;
    kmax-=n;

    w= largex ? pow(x, -a)/(a*(w+c*u2)+u1):
             pow(x,-b)/(u1*m1-u3*m0);
    for(r=0;r<=kk;r++)vr/=(a+r);
    if(n)kk=0;
    else
        {
        kk=1;
        u[0]=w*u1;
        }
    w*=vr;
    *uprime *=w;
    for(r=kk;r<=kmax;r++) u[r] *=w;
    }
return;
}

double uabx(a,b,x,eps,uprime) double a,b,x,eps,*uprime;
{
double a1,c,p,q,r,u[1]; int j,n;
n= (a<0.)? (int)a -1 :0;
q=a1=a-n;
u[0]=1.;
if(n<0 && a==b)
    {
    if(a1>0.)chu(a1,a1,x,0,eps,u,&q);
    p=u[0];
```

```
    r=p-q;
    for(j=1;j<=(-n);j++)
        {
        r*=x;q=(a1-j)*p;
        p=r-q;
        }
    }
else
    {
    /*if(n<0)printf(" a1=%e\n",a1);*/
    if(a1>0.)chu(a1,b,x,0,eps,u,&q);
    /*if(n<0)printf(" q=%e n=%d\n",q,n);*/
    c=1.+a1-b+x;
    a1-=1.;
    p=u[0];
    if(n<0)    for(j=1;j<=(-n);j++)
        {
        /*printf(" j=%d\n",j);*/
        r=(c-j)*p-x*q;
        q=(a1-j)*(q-p);
        p=r;
        }
    }
*uprime=q;
return p;
}
```

```
/*
test driver U.c
from C Mathematical Function Handbook by Louis Baker
Copyright 1991 by Louis Baker. All rights reserved.
*/

#include <stdio.h>
#include "cmlib.h"
#include "protom.h"
main()
{float e,a,b,x;int i;
double exp(),aa,bb,xx,z,er,eps=1.e-6,u,up,uabx(),sqrt();
/* Ei test*/
for (i=1;i<=10;i++)
   { xx= i;aa= exp(-xx)*uabx(1.,1.,xx,eps,&up);
/*uabx(1.,1.,-xx,eps,&up); xx<0 not allowed
   aa*=-exp(xx);                          */
   bb=aa*xx*exp(xx);
   printf(" x=%e E1=%e scaled=%e\n",xx,aa,bb);
   }
for (i=1;i<=10;i++)
   { xx= i;aa= exp(-
xx*xx)*uabx(.5,.5,xx*xx,eps,&up)/sqrt(pi);
   bb=aa*xx*exp(xx*xx);
   printf(" x=%e erfc=%e scaled=%e\n",xx,aa,bb);
   }
while(1)
{
printf("enter a,b,x,eps");scanf("%f%f%f%f",&a,&b,&x,&e);
aa=a;bb=b;xx=x;                           eps=e;
printf(" %e\n",uabx(aa,bb,xx,eps,&up));
}
}
```

Test Output: Confluent Hypergeometric funct.

```
 enter x+iy for log
 0 0
 enter complex arg a,b z for confl. hypergom. 1f1 M
-1 0 .5 0 10 0
 -1.900000e+01 + 0.000000e+00 i =answer
 enter complex arg a,b z for confl. hypergom. 1f1 M
0 0 0 0 0 0
 enter complex arg a,b z for confl. hypergom. U
1 0 2 0 3 0
 enter argrot
0
 3.333333e-01 + 0.000000e+00 i =answer
 enter complex arg a,b z for confl. hypergom. U
1 0 1 0 1 0
 enter argrot
0
 5.963474e-01 + 0.000000e+00 i =answer
 enter complex arg a,b z for confl. hypergom. U
0 0 0 0 0 0
 enter digammin, x for digamma
0 0
 enter digammin, y for digamma(1+iy)
0 0
 K:enter order,arg
1 0 1 0
 6.019072e-01  -1.639156e-17 i  K:enter order,arg
0 0 1 0
 4.210245e-01 + 0.000000e+00 i  K:enter order,arg
2 0 1 0
 1.624839e+00 + 0.000000e+00 i  K:enter order,arg
 K:enter order,arg
0 0  .7071 -.7071
 2.867128e-01 + 4.949981e-01 i  K:enter order,arg
0 0 .7071 -.7071
 2.867128e-01 + 4.949981e-01 i  K:enter order,arg
0 0 .7071 .7071
 2.867128e-01  -4.949981e-01 i  K:enter order,arg
0 0 0 0
 J:enter order,arg
3 0 3 0
 3.090627e-01  -3.033851e-08 i  J:enter order,arg
0 0 .7071 -.7071
 9.843825e-01 + 2.495613e-01 i  J:enter order,arg
0 0 0 0
 I:enter order,arg
0 0 .4 0
 1.040402e+00 + 0.000000e+00 i  I:enter order,arg
1 0 .4 0
```

```
 2.040268e-01 + 0.000000e+00 i  I:enter order,arg
0 0 0 0
 Airy:arg
1 0
 1.352924e-01 + 0.000000e+00 i  Airy:arg
-1 0
 5.355609e-01  -1.724609e-08 i  Airy:arg
0 0
 Bi(Airy):arg
1 0
 1.207424e+00 + 1.110223e-16 i  Bi(Airy):arg
-1 0
 1.039973e-01  -5.551115e-17 i  Bi(Airy):arg
0 0
 gamma:arg
0 0
 Erfc via Whittaker:arg
1 0
 1.572992e-01 + 0.000000e+00 i  Erfc via Whittaker:arg
2 0
 4.677602e-03 + 0.000000e+00 i  Erfc via Whittaker:arg
0 0
 Poisson-Charlier: n,nu,x
2 .6 .3
 -1.202082e+00 + 0.000000e+00 i =from chf
 from Laguerre -2.550000e-01,coef 4.714045e+00 ans:
-1.202082e+00
 Lag. by recursion=-2.550000e-01
 -2.550000e-01 + 0.000000e+00 i =Lag. by 1F1
 Poisson-Charlier: n,nu,x
0 0 0
```

Test Output: U

```
 x=1.000000e+00 E1=2.193839e-01 scaled=5.963474e-01
 x=2.000000e+00 E1=4.890051e-02 scaled=7.226572e-01
 x=3.000000e+00 E1=1.304838e-02 scaled=7.862512e-01
 x=4.000000e+00 E1=3.779352e-03 scaled=8.253826e-01
 x=5.000000e+00 E1=1.148296e-03 scaled=8.521109e-01
 x=6.000000e+00 E1=3.600825e-04 scaled=8.716058e-01
 x=7.000000e+00 E1=1.154817e-04 scaled=8.864877e-01
 x=8.000000e+00 E1=3.766562e-05 scaled=8.982371e-01
 x=9.000000e+00 E1=1.244735e-05 scaled=9.077576e-01
 x=1.000000e+01 E1=4.156969e-06 scaled=9.156333e-01
 x=1.000000e+00 erfc=1.572992e-01 scaled=4.275836e-01
 x=2.000000e+00 erfc=4.677735e-03 scaled=5.107914e-01
 x=3.000000e+00 erfc=2.209050e-05 scaled=5.370035e-01
 x=4.000000e+00 erfc=1.541726e-08 scaled=5.479978e-01
 x=5.000000e+00 erfc=1.537460e-12 scaled=5.535232e-01
 x=6.000000e+00 erfc=2.151974e-17 scaled=5.566594e-01
 x=7.000000e+00 erfc=4.183826e-23 scaled=5.586004e-01
 x=8.000000e+00 erfc=1.122430e-29 scaled=5.598813e-01
 x=9.000000e+00 erfc=4.137032e-37 scaled=5.607695e-01
 x=1.000000e+01 erfc=2.088488e-45 scaled=5.614099e-01
enter a,b,x,eps1 2 3 1.e-5
 3.333333e-01
enter a,b,x,eps1 1 1 1.e-5
 5.963474e-01
```

Chapter 14

Coulomb Wave Functions

Introduction

The Coulomb Wave functions are the solutions to the equation, which is the equation for the radial wave function when Schroedinger's equation is separated in spherical polar coordinates. There are a number of cases of interest. Repulsive and attractive forces need to be considered. For repulsive forces, there are no bound states, and hence the particle energy is positive. The equation, $\frac{d^2w}{d\rho^2} + [1 - \frac{2\eta}{\rho} - \frac{L(L+1)}{\rho^2}]w = 0$, given in Abramowitz and Stegun, corresponds to the Schroedinger equation for positive energy (unbound) states and with positive η corresponding to repulsive forces and negative η corresponding to attractive forces. The angular momentum term, containing L, corresponds the the centrifugal force, so it behaves as a repulsive ficticious force for nonzero L. For attractive forces, bound states, i. e., eigenstates, are possible; for these, the total energy is negative. The usual Coulomb Wave functions can accommodate either attractive or repulsive forces, but assume positive energy (unbound) states. The Coulomb Wave functions are therefore of interest in scattering problems, both nuclear and molecular, in which a collision occurs between two particles, one approaching from a large distance and hence unbound.

The solutions can be written in terms of the Parabolic Cylinder function (Chapter 19) as well as the Confluent Hypergeometric function (Chapter 13). Davydov gives the solution which, in the notation used here, is $exp(\pm i\rho)\,\rho^{l+1} M(L+1 \pm i\eta, 2L+2, \mp 2i\rho)$ for attractive forces. Note that the first parameter is complex and the argument is imaginary. This solution will work for positive energy states; for repulsive forces the solution is $exp(\pm i\rho)\,\rho^{l+1} M(L+1 \pm i\eta, 2L+2, \pm 2i\rho)$. Note the subtle difference between these two solutions. For attractive forces with negative energies, i. e., bound states, we are interested in the equation of the normalized form $\frac{d^2w}{d\rho^2} + [-1 + \frac{2\eta}{\rho} - \frac{L(L+1)}{\rho^2}]w = 0$, where h is now positive for cases of interest. Bound states that vanish for large ρ now will exist for a discrete spectrum, i. e., only for particular values of η with our normalization convention. Of course, in the physical problem we fix the force (by fixing the charge on the particles of interest) and find the energy eigenvalues: $\frac{d^2w}{d\rho^2}+[-\alpha^2+\frac{2Z}{\rho}-\frac{L(L+1)}{\rho^2}]\,w=0$, where $\alpha^2=-2E>0$, E being the magnitude of the energy of the bound state and the particles having charges of 1 and Z. The solution is then capable of being expressed as in terms of generalized Laguerre polynomials, multiplied by exp($-\alpha\rho$). In terms of the Confluent Hypergeometric function, the solution is of the form $\exp(-Z\rho/n)\,(2Z\rho/n)^L M(-n+L+1, 2L+2, 2Z\rho\, n)$. Here n is the principal quantum number, an eigenvalue of the solution. The generalized Laguerre polynomials are in turn related to the Confluent Hypergeometric function $L_n^c(z)=\Gamma(n+1)\,M(-n,1,z)$. If $c=\pm\frac{1}{2}$, the associate (called generalized by Davydov) Laguerre polynomials become Hermite polynomials. Depending upon which text you pick, you may find solutions expressed in any of these forms. Pauling and Wilson give the solution as proportional to $R(r)=\exp(-\rho/2)\,\rho^L L_{n+L}^{2L+2}(\rho)$ where $\rho=\frac{2Zr}{na}$ where a is the Bohr radius, r the radial coordinate, and the other parameters are as before.

Here, we are interested in positive energy, unbound states, which are of interest in scattering problems. These are the regular solution F_L and the irregular solution G_L. G_L becomes infinite at the origin. Plots of the functions for $\eta=1$ are shown. Asymptotically, for large ρ, the functions oscillate like trigonometric functions. (Note that, in the discrete case, the eigenfunctions have a finite number of zero crossings equal to the principal quantum number n.)

Schroedinger's equation in a Coulomb field is also separable in parabolic coordinates. See Schiff's book for a discussion. Morse and Feshbach note this and discuss the relationship to Parabolic Cylinder functions (see also 19.25.1-3 in Abramowitz and Stegun. For $\eta = 0$, the equation reduces to a form of Bessel's, with solutions proportional to spherical Bessel functions. For example, for $\eta = L = 0$, $F=\sin\rho$ and $G=\cos\rho$. This case is of little interest, as there will be no scattering from a particle with zero ($\eta = 0$) charge.

Methods

The methods used might be called a "brute force" application of the series given in Abramowitz and Stegun. The adaptive quadrature program **adsimp()** from *C Tools* is used with the integral representation of 14.3.3 of Abramowitz and Stegun for the irregular Coulomb Wave function *G*. See the paper below by Boersma for an alternate method, and the paper by Cody and Hillstrom for approximations to the phase shift. (These papers appeared after the publication of Abramowitz and Stegun.) The article by Press and Teukolsky, cited in Chapter 10, uses a method applied by Steed et al. to the Coulomb Wave functions. See that paper for the relevant references.

References

J. Boersma, *Math. Comp.*, **23**, 51, 1969.

W. J. Cody and K. E. Hillstrom, *Math. Comp.*, **24**, 671, 1970.

A. S. Davydov, *Quantum Mechanics* (D. ter Haar, translator), (Oxford: University Press and Reading, MA: Addison-Wesley, 1965).

P. Morse & H. Feshbach, *Methods of Theoretical Physics* (N. Y.: McGraw-Hill, 1953).

L. Pauling and E. B. Wilson, Jr., *Introduction to Quantum Mechanics* (N. Y.: McGraw-Hill, 1935). (Reprinted by Dover Publ.)

L. I Schiff, *Quantum Mechanics* (N. Y.: McGraw-Hill, 1968).

Figure

The Coulomb Wave functions F and G for L = 0 are shown in Fig. 14-1.

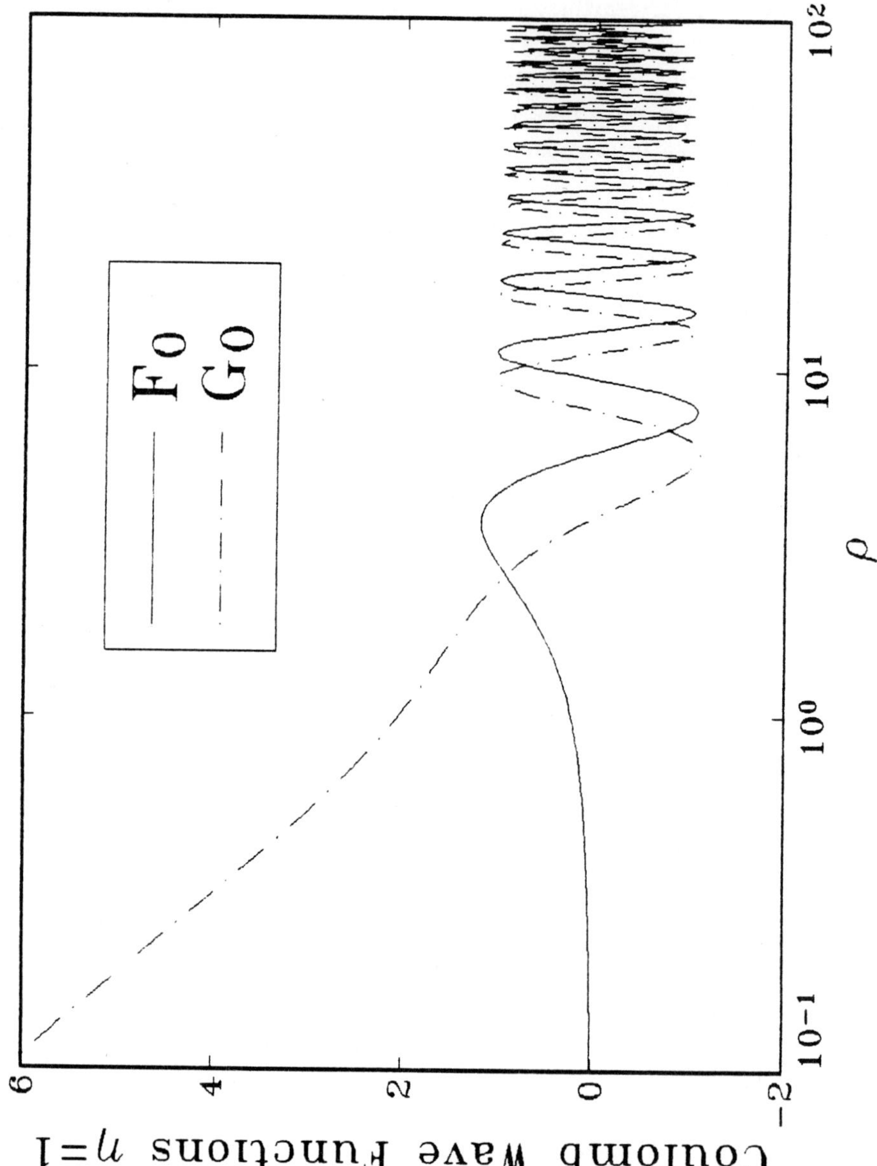

Fig. 14-1. Coulomb Wave Functions for L=0.

```
/*
Coulomb Wave functions
from C Mathematical Function Handbook by Louis Baker
Copyright 1991 by Louis Baker. All rights reserved.
*/

#include <stdio.h>
#include "cmlib.h"
#include "protom.h"

#define min(a,b) ((a)<(b)?(a):(b))
#define tol 1.e-6
#define MAXIT 500

static double g0;

double coulombf(eta,rho,l) int l;double eta,rho;
{
/* flp is derivative */
int i,small;
double exp(),pow(),log(),term,sum,sqrt(),c,cf,c0,
power,a,aold,aolder,gl,fl;
double theta,psi,d,qp,sump,flp,termp,rhol;
double sa,saold,saolder,pl,rl,terms;
if(rho>35.)
   {cwfa(l,eta,rho,&fl,&gl,&flp,&qp);
   if(!l)g0=gl;
   return fl;
   }
term=2.*pi*eta;
if( eta==0.)
   {
   /*if(!l)return sin(rho);*/
   return (rho)*sjn(rho, l);
   }
if(eta<1.e-10)c0=1.;
else c0=sqrt(term/(exp(term)-1.));
c=c0;
for(i=1;i<=l;i++)
     c*=sqrt( eta*eta+i*i)/(i*(2*i+1));
printf(" c0=%e\n",c0);
power=rho; aolder=1.;aold=eta/(1.+l);sum=aolder+aold*power;
sump= (l+1.+ aold*(l+2.)*power);
saolder=1.;saold=0.;
/*d= 1./(c*(2*l+1.));*/
pl= c*c/(c0*c0)*eta*(2*(2*l+1));
i=2;
if(!l)
   {sa= (2.*eta*saold-saolder-pl*(2*i-1)*aold)/
```

```
((i-l-1)*(i+l));
   psi=1.+ saold*rho+sa*rho*rho;
   saolder=saold;saold=sa;
   }
for(small=0,i=3;i<MAXIT;i++)
   {
   power*=rho;
   a= (2.*eta*aold-aolder)/((double)((l+l+i)*(i-1)));
   if(!l)
      {
      sa= (2.*eta*saold-saolder-pl*(2*i-1)*a)/((i-l-
1)*(i+l));
      terms=sa*power*rho;
      psi+=terms;
      }
   term=power*a;
   sum+=term;
   termp=term*(i+l);
   sump+=termp;
   /*printf(" sum, term, %le %le %d\n",sum,term,i);*/
   if( abs(sum)*tol>abs(term)&&abs(sump)*tol>abs(term))
      {if(!small)small=1;
      if(small)break;/* two in a row*/
      }
   else small=0;
   aolder=aold;aold=a;
   saolder=saold;saold=sa;
   }
if(l)    rhol=pow(rho,(double)(l));
else    rhol=1.;
fl= c*sum*rho*rhol;
flp= c*sump*rhol;
if(rho>34.5)
   {
   cwfa(l,eta,rho,&saold,&gl,&saolder,&qp);
   theta= ((rho-34.5)/(35.-34.5));
/*printf(" theta=%e %e %e\n",theta,fl,saold);*/
   fl= fl*(1.-theta)+saold*(theta);
   flp=flp*(1.-theta)+saolder*(theta);
   if(!l)g0=gl;
   }
printf(" flp=%e\n",flp);
return fl;
}

static double etaparm,rhoparm;
static int lparm;

double gl(q) double q;
```

```
{double x,y,z,pow(),exp(),tanh(),atan(),sin(),tan(),
t,cos(),jacob,ans;
if(q<.5*pi)t=tan(q);
else t=1.e12;
x=tanh(t);y=1.-x*x;z=1.;
if(lparm>0){z=1.+t*t;if(lparm>1)z=pow(z,(double)lparm);}
jacob=cos(q);
jacob=1./(jacob*jacob+1.e-8);
if(lparm>0)y=pow(y,1.+lparm);
ans= (z*exp(-rhoparm*t+2.*etaparm*q)
   -y*sin(rhoparm*x-2.*etaparm*t))*jacob;
return ans;
}

double coulombg(eta,rho,l) int l;double eta,rho;
{
int i; double term,coef,c0,c,exp(),pow(),gamma(),
adsimp(),as,sqrt(),btm,top,delta;
etaparm=eta;rhoparm=rho,lparm=l;
/*if(!l && eta<1.)
   {coef=coulombf(eta,rho,l);return g0;
   }
*/
term=2.*pi*eta;
if(eta<1.e-10)c0=1.;
else c0=sqrt(term/(exp(term)-1.));
c=c0;
for(i=1;i<=l;i++)
      c*=sqrt( eta*eta+i*i)/(i*(2*i+1));
coef=exp(-pi*eta)*pow(rho,1.+l)/(gamma(2*l+2.)*c);
as=0.;
btm=0.;top=.025;delta=.05;
for( i=0;btm<.5*pi;i++)
   {as+=adsimp(btm ,top ,tol,gl);btm=top;
   top= min(.5*pi,top+delta);}
/*as=adsimp(0.,.02,tol,gl)+adsimp(.02,.1,tol,gl)+ad-
simp(.1,.25*pi,tol,gl)
+adsimp(.25*pi,.5*pi,tol,gl);*/
return as*coef;
}

cwfa(l,eta,rho,fl,gl,flp,glp) int l; double
eta,rho,*fl,*gl,*flp,*glp;
{
struct complex carg,cans,cdummy;
double
c,theta,sigma,f,g,fs,gs,fold,gold,d,ct,st,log(),argmt(),
   fsold,gsold,a,b,fsum,gsum,fssum,gssum,cos(),sin();
int k;
```

```
fold=1.;gold=fsold=0.;gsold=1.-eta/rho;
fsum=fold;gsum=gold;gssum=gsold;fssum=fsold;
d=eta*eta+l*(l+1);
for( k=1;k<100;k++)
   {
   c=1./((2*k+2)*rho);
   a=(2*k+1)*eta*c;
   b=(d-k*(k+1))*c;
   f=a*fold-b*gold;
   g=a*gold+b*fold;
   fs=a*fsold-b*gsold-f/rho;
   gs=a*gsold+b*fsold-g/rho;
   if(k>1)
      {
      if( abs(fsum)*tol>abs(f)  || abs(f)>abs(fold))break;
      if( abs(gsum)*tol>abs(g)  || abs(g)>abs(gold))break;
      }
   fsum+=f;gsum+=g;fssum+=fs;gssum+=gsum;
   gold=g;fold=f;fsold=fs;gsold=gs;
   }
carg.x=1.+l;carg.y=eta;cgamma(&carg,&cans,&cdummy);
sigma=argmt(cans.y,cans.x);
theta= rho-eta*log(2.*rho)-.5*pi*l+sigma;
ct=cos(theta);st=sin(theta);
*fl=gsum*ct+fsum*st;
*gl=fsum*ct-gsum*st;
*flp=gssum*ct+fssum*st;
*glp=fssum*ct-gssum*st;
return 0;
}
```

```
/*
test driver Coulomb Wave functions
from C Mathematical Function Handbook by Louis Baker
Copyright 1991 by Louis Baker. All rights reserved.
*/

#include <stdio.h>
#include "cmlib.h"
#include "protom.h"

FILE *outc;

main()
{
int l;float e,r;double eta,rho,f,g,fl,gl,fls,gls;

outc=fopen("cwf.plt","w");
fprintf(outc," 3\n");
printf(" enter eta\n");scanf("%le",&eta);
for(l=0;l<50;l++)
   {
   rho= .1*l;
   g=coulombg(eta,rho,0);
   f=coulombf(eta,rho,0);
   fprintf(outc,"%le %le %le\n",rho,f,g);
   }

while(1)
   {
   printf(" enter l=0 eta rho ");
   scanf("%d%f%f",&l,&e,&r);eta=e;rho=r;
   if(l<0)break;
   printf(" result %e %e\n",coulombf(eta,rho,l),
   /*,coulombg(eta,rho,l)*/
   coulombg(eta,rho,l));
   cwfa(l,eta,rho,&fl,&gl,&fls,&gls);
   printf(" asmpt %e %e %e %e\n",fl,gl,fls,gls);
   }
}
```

```
Test Output: Coulomb Wave functions
 enter eta
.5
 enter l=0 eta rho 0 .5 1
 result 5.166014e-01 1.197487e+00
 asmpt 1.459404e-01 1.435525e+00 -4.856363e-03
-1.682163e-01
 enter l=0 eta rho 0 5 1
 result 2.041301e-05 8.085524e+03
 asmpt 5.893231e+00 -4.571086e+00 1.916634e+01 2.505245e+00
 enter l=0 eta rho 0 .5 5
 result -4.904552e-01 -9.349270e-01
 asmpt -3.756309e-01 -9.940918e-01 -5.732032e-01
1.847418e-01
```

Chapter 15

The Hypergeometric Function

Introduction

The definition of the Hypergeometric function $_2F_1$ is given implicitly in Chapter 13, $_2F_1\,(a, b; c; z) = \sum_{n=1}^{\infty} \frac{(a)_n (b)_n}{(c)_n\, n!} z^n$. There are two Pochhammer symbols in the numerator and one in the denominator, as the notation tells us. It solves the equation $z\,(1-z)\frac{d^2w}{dz^2} + [c-(a+b+1)\,z\,]\frac{dw}{dz} - abw = 0$. Note the notation in which semicolons rather than commas are used to separate parameters in the numerator from those in the denominator, as well as from the independent variable.

The Hypergeometric function is closely related to the Legendre functions P and Q of Chapter 8, and we provide here functions for the evaluation of these functions for complex arguments and parameters. Note that the definition of P in terms of $_2F_1$ involves a denominator of $\Gamma\,(1-\mu\,)$, which will be undefined (infinite) for μ a positive integer. However, so will $_2F_1$, and we use 15.2.1 of Abramowitz and Stegun,

$$\lim_{c\to -m} \frac{1}{\Gamma(c)}\ F(a,b;c;z) = (a)_{m+1}\,(b)_{m+1}\,z^{m+1}F(a+m+1,b+m+1;m+2;z)$$

to obtain the finite result.

Differential equations can be classified by their singularities, and these can to some degree be moved by proper transformation of the independent variable. The Hypergeometric equation has regular singular points at 0, 1, and ∞, and is a special case of the Riemann differential equation

$$\frac{d^2w}{dz^2} + [\frac{1-a-a'}{z-a} + \frac{1-b-b'}{z-b} + \frac{1-c-c'}{z-c}]\frac{dw}{dz} +$$

$$[\frac{aa'(a-b)(a-c)}{z-a} + \frac{bb'(b-a)(b-c)}{z-b} + \frac{cc'(c-a)(c-b)}{z-c}]$$

$\frac{w}{(z-a)(z-b)(z-c)} = 0$ (called the Papperitz equation in Morse and Feshbach) which has such points at a, b, and c. Regular singular points have solutions which have a pole at such points, i. e., behave like $\frac{1}{(z-a)^b}$ for a pole at a for some b and independent variable z. Irregular singular points have an essential singularity at such points. An example of such a function is $e^{1/z}$ near $z = 0$.

The ability to move singularities by transformations allows standard forms to be defined for differential equations that have a limited number of singularities (three in the case of second-order differential equations). See Moon and Spencer for an exhaustive (and exhausting) discussion.

Applications

The Hypergeometric function appears to be used primarily to represent other functions.

Methods

The linear transformation in section 15.3 of Abramowitz and Stegun are used to make the series convergent over the complex plane. Due to the many special cases, the work is split over a number of C functions.

In the test examples, a number of cases are chosen, including the example used in the *Mathematica*® advertisement.

References

N. N. Lebedev, *Special Functions and Their Applications* (N. Y.: Dover, 1972).

O. I. Marichev, *Handbook of Integral Transforms of Higher Transcendental Functions* (Chichester: Ellis Horwood, 1983).

P. Moon and D. E. Spencer, *Field Theory Handbook*, 2nd ed. (N. Y. : Springer, 1971 hardcover, 1988 paperback).

P. M. Morse and H. Feshbach, *Methods of Theoretical Physics (N.* Y.: McGraw-Hill, 1953).

E. T. Whittaker and G. N. Watson, *A Course of Modern Analysis, 4th ed.* (Cambridge: University Press, 1952).

```
/*
hypergeometric function complex arguments

from C Mathematical Function Handbook by Louis Baker
Copyright 1991 by Louis Baker. All rights reserved.
*/

#include <stdio.h>
#include "cmlib.h"
#include "protom.h"

#define CTI(to,fm) {(to).x=-(fm).y;(to).y=(fm).x;}
#define eps 5.e-8
#define tol 1.e-7
#define DEBUG 0
#undef DEBUG

#define cdigam cdigamma

cpochhammer(x,n,ans) struct complex *x,*ans;int n;
{/* cannot use gamma(x+n)/gamma(x) as x may be 0 or neg. in-
teger*/
struct complex product,factor,temp;int i;
if(!n){CMPLX(*ans,1.,0.);return 0;}
CLET(product,*x);
if(n==1){CSET(ans,product);return 0;}
for(i=1;i<n;i++)
   {
   CLET(factor,*x);factor.x+=(double)i;
   CMULT(temp,factor,product);
   CLET(product,temp);
   }
CSET(ans,product);return 0;
}

/*#define tol 1.e-6*/

cf21(a,b,c,x,ans)struct complex  *a,*b,*c,*x,*ans;
{/* complex hypergeometric function 2F1(a,b;c;x)*/
double gamma(),digamma();int m,i;struct complex s,z;
int aa,bb,cc,aint,bint,cint,top,l,mpl;
struct complex term,sum,ratio,factor,p,q,r,t,term1,term2,cl;
double count;
top=40;
#ifdef DEBUG
printf(" entered f21\n");
printc(a);printc(b);printc(c);printc(x);
printf(" arg f21\n");
#endif
```

```
if(cabs(*x)<1.e-8 || cabs(*a)<1.e-8 || cabs(*b)<1.e-8)
    {CMPLX(*ans,1.,0.);return 0 ;}
if(abs(a->y)<1.e-8)
   {aa=a->x;if((a->x-aa)==0.)aint=1;else aint=0;}else
{aint=0;}
if(abs(b->y)<1.e-8)
   {bb=b->x;if((b->x-bb)==0.)bint=1;else bint=0;}else
{bint=0;}
if(abs(c->y)<1.e-8)
   {cc=c->x;if((c->x-cc)==0.)cint=1;else cint=0;}else
{cint=0;}
/*degenerate cases */
/* c,a or b negative integers- finite series n=0 to m, m=-a
or b A&S 15.4.2*/
if(cint && cc<=0)
   {
   if (aint && aa<=0  && aa>cc)
      {
#ifdef DEBUG
      printf(" 2f1 degenerate series case\n");
#endif
      top=-aa;goto series2;}
   if (bint && bb<=0 && bb>cc )
      {
#ifdef DEBUG
      printf(" 2f1 degenerate series case\n");
#endif
      top=-bb;goto series2;}
   }
/* if c is 0 or neg. integer, returns F/Gamma(c) A&S
15.1.2*/
if(cint && cc<=0)
   {m=-cc;/*m>=0*/ count=1./ gamma(2.+m);/*count=m+1 !*/
   m++;
   cpochhammer(a,m,&p);cpochhammer(b,m,&q);CMULT(r,p,q);
   CTREAL(r,r,count);CMPLX(s,(double)m,0.);cpow(x,&s,&t);
   CMULT(s,r,t);
   CMPLX(term,(double)m,0.);CADD(term,term,*a);
   CMPLX(sum,(double)m,0.);CADD(sum,sum,*b);
   CMPLX(ratio,(double)m+1.,0.);
   cf21(&term,&sum,&ratio,x,&factor);
   CMULT((*ans),factor,s);
   return 2;
   }
/* a or b negative integers, c not- polynomial finite
series A&S 15.4.1*/
if((aint && aa<0 )||(bint && bb<0)) goto series;
```

```
/* c-a integer? */
CSUB(p,*c,*a);
if(abs(p.y)<1.e-7 && abs(p.x-((int)p.x))<1.e-7)
   {/*c-a integer*/
#ifdef DEBUG
printf(" c-a integer\n");
#endif
   if(p.x==0.){/*c-a=0,f=1/(1-z)^(-b)*/
         CMPLX(q,1.,0.);CSUB(q,q,*x);CSUB(p,p,*b);
/*p was 0 now -b*/
         cpow(&q,&p,ans);return 0;}
   if(p.x<0.)/* c-a negative integer- get polynomial/(1-
z)^power A&S 15.3.3*/
      {CMPLX(q,1.,0.);CSUB(q,q,*x);CSUB(r,p,*b);/*r= c-a-b*/
      cpow(&q,&p,&term1);CSUB(s,*c,*b);
      cf21(&p,&s,c,x,&term2);CMULT((*ans),term1,term2);
      return 0;}
   /*c-a positive integer: on to appropriate form*/
   }
#ifdef DEBUG
printc(c);printf(" c after int c-a \n");
#endif

/*x==1., Real(c-a-b)>0, c!= 0,-1,-2,...*/
#ifdef DEBUG
if(abs(x->y)<1.e-8 ) printf(" real argument\n");
if(abs(x->x-1.)<1.e-8)printf(" Re(z)==1\n");
if( (c->x)>(a->x+b->x))printf(" Re(c)Re(a+b) \n");
#endif

if((abs(x->y)<1.e-8) && (abs(x->x-1.)<1.e-8)
&&( (c->x)>(a->x+b->x)))
   {if(!cint || c->x>0.)/* do if not real, or not int, or
positive*/
      {/*A&S 15.1.20*/
#ifdef DEBUG
printf(" 2f1 x==1\n");
#endif
      cgamma(c,&p,&ratio);
      CSUB(q,*c,*a);cgamma(&q,&r,&ratio);
      CDIV(ratio,p,r);/*ratio= gamma(c)/gamma(c-a)*/
      CSUB(q,*c,*b);cgamma(&q,&r,&s);
      CSUB(p,*c,*a);CSUB(p,p,*b);cgamma(&p,&s,&q);
      CDIV(p,s,r);CMULT((*ans),p,ratio);/* ans GcGc-a-b/Gc-
a/Gc-b*/
      return 0;
      }
   }
/* Erdelyi(4) 15.3.9 as check on other stuff*/
```

```
/*
#ifdef DEBUG
printc(c);printf(" c before(4) \n");
#endif

CMPLX(r,1.,0.);CDIV(z,r,*x);CSUB(r,r,z);
if(cabs(r)<1. && cabs(*x)>1.)
   {printf(" Erdeyli (4) as check?\n");
   CMPLX(p,1.,0.);CADD(p,p,*a);CADD(p,p,*b); CSUB(p,p,*c);
   CMPLX(q,1.,0.);CADD(q,q,*c); CSUB(q,q,*a); CSUB(q,q,*b);
   if(!((q.x-(int)q.x)==0. && q.x<0.)&&
      !((p.x-(int)p.x)==0. && p.x<0.))
      {
#ifdef DEBUG
printf(" (4) OK\n");
#endif
      CMPLX(s,1.,0.);CADD(s,s,*a); CSUB(s,s,*c);
      cf21(a,&s,&p,&r,&t);
#ifdef DEBUG
printc(&t);printf(" first call returned\n");
#endif

      cpow(x,a,&s);CDIV(term1,t,s);
      cgamma(c,&r,&s);
      CSUB(t,*c,*a);CSUB(t,t,*b);cgamma(&t,&s,&p);
      CMULT(q,t,s);CMULT(t,term1,q);
      CSUB(p,*c,*a);cgamma(&p,&r,&s);
      CSUB(p,*c,*b);cgam-
ma(&p,&q,&s);CMULT(p,r,q);CDIV(term1,t,p);
#ifdef DEBUG
printc(&term1);printf(" first term\n");
#endif
      CMPLX(q,1.,0.);CADD(q,q,*c); CSUB(q,q,*a);
CSUB(q,q,*b);
      CMPLX(r,1.,0.);CDIV(z,r,*x);CSUB(r,r,z);
      CSUB(s,*c,*a);
      CMPLX(t,1.,0.);CSUB(t,t,*a);
      cf21(&s,&t,&q,&r,&p);
#ifdef DEBUG
printc(&p);printf(" 2nd call\n");
#endif

CMPLX(q,1.,0.);CSUB(q,q,*x);CSUB(r,*c,*a);CSUB(r,r,*b);
      cpow(&q,&r,&s);CMULT(t,s,p);
      CSUB(q,*a,*c);cpow(x,&q,&s);CMULT(term2,s,t);
      cgamma(c,&r,&s);
      CADD(t,*b,*a);CSUB(t,t,*c);cgamma(&t,&s,&p);
      CMULT(q,t,s);CMULT(t,term2,q);
```

```
       cgamma(a,&r,&s);
       cgamma(b,&q,&s);CMULT(p,r,q);CDIV(term2,t,p);
#ifdef DEBUG
printc(&term2);printf(" 2nd term\n");
#endif
       CADD((*ans),term1,term2);
       return 0;
       }
    }
*/

CLET(q,*x);q.x-=1.;
if(cabs(q)<1. && x->x >.5){ f211(a,b,c,x,ans);return 0;}
else if(cabs(*x)<1.)/*series solution A&S 15.1.1*/
   {
   series:
   if(!(cint && cc<=0))/* c not 0 or negative integer*/
       {
       series2:
#ifdef DEBUG
printf(" 2f1 series\n");
#endif
       CLET(p,*a);CLET(q,*b);CLET(r,*c);
#ifdef DEBUG
printc(c);printc(&r);printf(" initial c term\n");
#endif
       for(i=0,term.x=sum.x=1.,term.y=sum.y=0.;i<top;i++)
          {
          count=(double)(i+1);
#ifdef DEBUG
printc(&p);printc(&q);printc(&r);
#endif
          CMULT(s,p,q);CDIV(ratio,s,r);
#ifdef DEBUG
printc(&ratio);printf(" p,q,r,ratio\n");
#endif
          ratio.x/=count;ratio.y/=count;
          CMULT(s,*x,ratio);
#ifdef DEBUG
printc(&s);
#endif
          CMULT(ratio,term,s);CLET(term,ratio);
#ifdef DEBUG
printc(&ratio);printf(" s, term\n");
#endif
          /*term *=(x*(a+i)*(b+i)/((c+i)*count));*/
          CADD(sum,sum,term);
          /*CDIV(ratio,term,sum);*/
#ifdef DEBUG
```

```
printc(&term);printc(&sum);
printf(" term,sum 2f1 series\n");
#endif
        if( cabs(term)<
tol*cabs(sum)){CSET(ans,sum);return 0;}
        p.x+=1.;q.x+=1.;r.x+=1.;
        }
     printf(" 2f1 tolerance not met series \n");
     CSET(ans,sum);return 0 ;
     }
   /* if c negative integer but a or b=n<m use A&S 15.1.2
   F is proportional to Gamma(c) which is infinite.*/
   CMPLX(*ans,errorcode,0.);
   return 0 ;/* c negative integer, no fixing*/
   }
else if(cabs(*x)>1.) {f21big(a,b,c,x,ans);return 0;}
if((cabs(*x)-1.)<1.e-7)/* on unit circle*/
   {if( a->x+b->x-c->x>= 1.){printf(" 2f1 divergent on unit
circle\n");
      CMPLX(*ans,errorcode,0.);return 0 ;}
   /*divergent Erdelyi p.57 2.1.1 Vol.1*/
#ifdef DEBUG
   printf(" f21: |x|=1, conditionally convergent, attempt-
ing series\n");
#endif
   goto series;/*conditional convergence, try series*/
   }
/* never should get here? */
CMPLX(*ans,errorcode,errorcode);return 0;
}
```

```
/* hypergeometric function complex arguments

from C Mathematical Function Handbook by Louis Baker
Copyright 1991 by Louis Baker. All rights reserved.
*/

#include <stdio.h>
#include "cmlib.h"
#include "protom.h"

#define cdigam cdigamma
#define tol 1.e-10
#define eps 5.e-8
#define DEBUG 1
#undef DEBUG

f21big(ain,bin,c,x,ans)struct complex *ain,*bin,*c,*x,*ans;
{double gamma(),digamma();
struct complex *a,*b;
int top=1000,i,l,m,mpl;
struct complex term,sum,ratio,fac-
tor,p,q,r,t,z,term1,term2,cl,s;
double count,rr;
#ifdef DEBUG
printf(" entered f21\n");
#endif
a=ain;b=bin;
CMPLX(p,1.,0.);CDIV(z,p ,(*x));/* z=1/x*/
CSUB(p,*b,*a);m=p.x;
if(abs(p.y)<1.e-7 && abs(p.x-m)<1.e-2)
   {/* near pole neg. integer 1-b+a or 1-a+b */
   if(m<0){m=-m;b=ain;a=bin;}
   CSUB(q,*c,*a); mpl=q.x;   l=mpl-m-1;
   if(abs(q.y)<1.e-7 && abs(q.x-mpl)<1.e-7 && q.x>0 && l>=0)
      {/* |z|>1, c-a,b-a integers b=a+m,c=a+m+l+1 m,l
      nonegative
       use Erdelyi 2.10(9) pp,109-110 NOT in A&S */
      CMPLX(term2,0.,0.);/* zero out for m==0 case*/
#ifdef DEBUG
printf(" b-a integer, c-a also Erdelyi(9) m=%d l=%d\n",m,l);
#endif
      if(m)
         {
         CLET(p,*a);CMPLX(q,(double)(m),0.);
         CMPLX(r,m+l+1,0.);
         CMPLX(term,gamma((double)m)/
         gamma((double)(m+l+1)),0.);
         CLET(sum,term);
```

```
        CMPLX(t,0.,0.);CSUB(t,t,z);/*t=(-1/z)*/
        for(i=1;i<m;i++)
            {
            count=(double)(i);
            CMULT(s,p,q);CDIV(ratio,s,r);
            ratio.x/=count;ratio.y/=count;
            CMULT(s,z,ratio);
            CMULT(ratio,term,s);CLET(term,ratio);
            CADD(sum,sum,term);
            /*if( cabs(ratio)< tol*cabs(term))break;*/
            p.x+=1.;q.x+=1.;r.x+=1.;
            }
        cpow(&t,a,&r);
        CMULT(term2,r,sum);/*term2=1st finite sum*/
        }
#ifdef DEBUG
printc(&term2);printf(" m sum\n");
#endif
        /*infinite sum*/
        cpochhammer(a,m+l+1,&term);
        CTREAL(q,term,1./(gamma(2.+l+m)*gamma(2.+l)));
        CMPLX(p,(double)(l+1),0.);
        cpow(&z,&p,&t);/* t= z^-(l+1)  */
        CMULT(term,q,z);
        CLET(sum,term);
        CMPLX(q,1.,0.);
        CMPLX(r,(double)(m+l+2),0.);
        CLET(p,*a);p.x+=(m+l+1);
        /* sum= n=l+1 term by here*/
        for(i=l+2;i<top;i++)
            {
            count=(double)(i);/*count=n*/
            CMULT(s,p,q);CDIV(ratio,s,r);
            ratio.x/=count;ratio.y/=count;
            CMULT(s,z,ratio);
            CMULT(ratio,term,s);CLET(term,ratio);
            CADD(sum,sum,term);
            if( cabs(term)< tol*cabs(sum))break;
            p.x+=1.;q.x+=1.;r.x+=1.;
            }
        CMPLX(s,0.,0.);CSUB(s,s,z);
        CLET(r,*a);r.x+=(double)m;
        cpow(&s,&r,&t);
        CMULT(term1,t,sum);
        CTREAL( term1,term1,((m+l+1)%2?-1.:1.));
#ifdef DEBUG
printc(&term1);printf(" infinite sum\n");
#endif
        CADD(term1,term1,term2);/*term1 first two terms*/
```

```
        /* last finite sum*/
        CMPLX(s,0.,0.);CSUB(s,s,*x);
         clog(&s,&cl);/*s= log(-x) */
         CMPLX(sum, digamma(1.+m)+digamma(1.)-
        digamma(1.+l),0.);
        CMPLX(q,(double)m,0.);CADD(q,q,*a);cdigam(&q,&p);
        CSUB(sum,sum,p);CADD(sum,sum,cl);/* sum=h'[0]*/
#ifdef DEBUG
printc(&sum);printf(" [log+] in n==0 term of lsum\n");
#endif
        cpochhammer(a,m,&t);
#ifdef DEBUG
printc(&t);printf(" pochhammer (a)m\n");
#endif
        CMPLX(s,(double)(-(m+l)),0.);
        cpochhammer(&s,m,&q);
#ifdef DEBUG
printc(&q);printf(" pochhammer -(m+l)m m=%d l=%d\n",m,l);
#endif
        CMULT(term,q,t);
        CTREAL(term,term,1./gamma((double)(m+1)));
#ifdef DEBUG
printf("  %e gamma in denom\n",gamma((double)(m+1)));
#endif
        CMULT(sum,term,sum);/*sum=(n=0
term)=term*[h'+log]*/
#ifdef DEBUG
printc(&sum);printf("  n==0 term of lsum\n");
#endif
        CLET(p,*a);p.x+=(double)m;
        CMPLX(q,(double)(-(l)) ,0.);
        CMPLX(r,(double)(m+1),0.);
        for(i=0;i<l;i++)/* n=i+1, sum to n=l */
           {
           count=(double)(i+1);
           CMULT(s,p,q);CDIV(ratio,s,r);
           ratio.x/=count;ratio.y/=count;
           CMULT(s,z,ratio);
           CMULT(ratio,term,s);CLET(term,ratio);
           CMPLX(factor,
             digamma(count+1.)+digamma(count+m+1.)
            -digamma(1.+l-count),0.);
           CLET(s,*b);s.x+=(count);/* b+n=a+m+n */
           cdigam(&s,&t);
           CSUB(factor,factor,t);
           CADD(factor,factor,cl);
           CMULT(t,factor,term);
           CADD(sum,sum,t);
           p.x+=1.;q.x+=1.;r.x+=1.;
```

```
            }
#ifdef DEBUG
printc(&sum);printf("  n==0 term of lsum\n");
#endif
        CMPLX(p,0.,0.);CSUB(p,p,z);
        cpow(&p,b,&r);CMULT(p,sum,r);
#ifdef DEBUG
printc(&p);printf(" scaled by (-x)^-b\n");
#endif
        CTREAL(p,p,1./gamma((double)(m+l+1)));
#ifdef DEBUG
printc(&p);printf(" l sum\n");
#endif
        CADD(term1,term1,p);/* all terms*/
        cgamma(c,&t,&r);CMULT(r,term1,t);/*c=a+m+l+1*/
        cgamma(b,&t,&q);CDIV((*ans),r,t);/*b=a+m*/
        return;
        /* end (9)*/
        }
    /* b-a,integer c-a not 0 or pos. integer:
      Erdelyl 2.10(7) A&S 15.3.13(m=0) and 14*/
#ifdef DEBUG
printf(" Edelyi (7) b-a integer, c-a not 0 or pos in-
teger,m=%d\n",m);
#endif
      CMPLX(term1,0.,0.);/* for m==0*/
      if(m)
        {
        CSUB(q,*c,*a);cgamma(&q,&p,&s);
        CMPLX(t,gamma((double)m),0.);
        CDIV(sum,t,p);/* sum=  n==0 term */
        CMPLX(term,1.,0.);CLET(q,*a);
        for(i=1;i<m;i++)/*i=n*/
           {
           count=(double)(i);/*n=count*/
           CMPLX(p,gamma((double)(m-i)),0.);
           CLET(r,*c);CSUB(r,r,*a);r.x-=count;
           cgamma(&r,&s,&t);/*s=Gc-a-n*/
           CDIV(factor,p,s);/*factor= Gm-n/Gc-a-n*/
           CTREAL(term,term,1./count);
           CMULT(s,z,term);CMULT(t,s,q);
           CLET(term,t);/*term=(a)n z^n/n!*/
           CMULT(ratio,factor,term);
           CADD(sum,sum,ratio);
           q.x+=1.;
           }
        CMPLX(p,0.,0.);CSUB(p,p,*x);cpow(&p,a,&r);
        CDIV(term1,sum,r);/*term1=first term*/
        }
```

```
#ifdef DEBUG
printc(&term1);printf("=finite term\n");
#endif
        /* infinite sum in 15.3.14*/
        CMPLX(s,0.,0.);CSUB(s,s,*x);
        clog(&s,&cl);
#ifdef DEBUG
printc(&z);printf("z=1/x\n");
#endif
        cpochhammer(a,m,&s);/* s= (a)m*/
#ifdef DEBUG
printc(&cl);printc(&s);printf(" log(-x)  poch (a)m\n");
#endif
        CMPLX(p,1.,0.);CADD(p,p,*a);CSUB(p,p,*c);/*p=1+a-
c*/
        cpochhammer(&p,m,&t);
#ifdef DEBUG
printc(&t);printf(" poch 1+a-c)m\n");
#endif
        CMULT(term,t,s);CTREAL(term,term,1./gamma(1.+m));
#ifdef DEBUG
printc(&term);printf(" initial term value\n");
#endif
        CMPLX(factor,digamma(1.+m)+digamma(1.),0.);
        CADD(factor,factor,cl);
        cdigam(b,&s);CSUB(factor,factor,s);
        CSUB(s,*c,*b);
        cdigam(&s,&t);CSUB(factor,factor,t);
/*CMPLX(factor,1.,0.); old error-test to see effect*/
#ifdef DEBUG
printc(&factor);
printf(" factor inn==0 term in infinite sum\n");
#endif
        CMULT(sum,term,factor);/*sum = n==0 term*/
        CMPLX(q,1.+m,0.);CSUB(q,q,*c);CADD(q,q,*a);
        /*CMPLX(r,(double)(m+1),0.);*/rr=(double)(m+1);
        CLET(p,*b);
#ifdef DEBUG
printc(&q);printc(&p);printf("=initial q,p\n");
#endif
        for(i=0;i<top;i++)
           {/*n=i+1=count*/
           count=(double)(i+1);
           CMULT(s,p,q);CTREAL(ratio,s,1./(rr*count));
           /*ratio.x/=count;ratio.y/=count;*/
           CMULT(s,z,ratio);
#ifdef DEBUG
printc(&s);printf(" ratio new term/old\n");
#endif
```

```
            CMULT(ratio,term,s);CLET(term,ratio);
            CMPLX(factor,
            digamma(count+1.)+digamma(count+m+1),0.);
            CLET(s,*b);s.x+=(count);/*s=b+n=a+m+n*/
            if(abs(s.y)<eps){CMPLX(t,digamma(s.x),0.);}
            else cdigam(&s,&t);
            CSUB(factor,factor,t);
            CSUB(s,*c,*b);s.x-=count;/*s=c-b-n=c-a-m-n*/
            if(abs(s.y)<eps){CMPLX(t,digamma(s.x),0.);}
            else cdigam(&s,&t);
            CSUB(factor,factor,t);
            CADD(factor,factor,cl);/*factor=h+log*/
            CMULT(t,factor,term);
            CADD(sum,sum,t);
#ifdef DEBUG
printc(&sum);printc(&t);printc(&factor);printc(&term);
printf(" sum,factor,term,i %d\n",i);
#endif
            if( cabs(t)< tol*cabs(sum))break;
            p.x+=1.;q.x+=1.;rr+=1.;
            }
        CTREAL(s,(*x),-1.);
        cpow(&s,b,&r);CDIV(p,sum,r);
        CSUB(q,*c,*a);
        cgamma(&q,&t,&s);CDIV(r,p,t);
        CADD(term1,term1,r);
#ifdef DEBUG
printc(&r);printc(&term1);printf(" inf sum tot\n");
#endif
        cgamma(c,&s,&t);CMULT(r,term1,s);
        cgamma(b,&s,&t);CDIV((*ans),r,s);
        return;
}
/* Erdelyi 2.10(2) A&S15.3.7  B1 & B2 */
#ifdef DEBUG
printf(" Erdelyi(2)\n");
#endif
cgamma(c,&term2,&ratio);
CSUB(q,*c,*a);cgamma(&q,&r,&ratio);
CDIV(ratio,term2,r);/*ratio= gamma(c)/gamma(c-a)*/
CSUB(q,*b,*a);cgamma(&q,&r,&s);
cgamma(b,&s,&q);
CDIV(p,r,s);CMULT(s,p,ratio);/* s=GcGb-a/Gc-a/Gb =B1*/
CMPLX(p,0.,0.);CSUB(p,p,*x);cpow(&p,a,&r);CDIV(t,s,r);
/*t=(-x)^-aB1*/
CMPLX(p,1.,0.);CDIV(z,p,(*x));/* z=1/x*/
CMPLX(r,1.,0.);CADD(r,r,*a);CSUB(r,r,*b);/*r=1+a-b*/
CMPLX(q,1.,0.);CADD(q,q,*a);CSUB(q,q,*c);/*q=1+a-c*/
cf21(a,&q,&r,&z,&s);CMULT(term1,s,t);
```

```
/*term2= Gc at this point*/
cgamma(a,&r,&ratio);
CDIV(ratio,term2,r);/*ratio= Gc/Ga */
CSUB(q,*a,*b);cgamma(&q,&r,&s);
CSUB(p,*c,*b);cgamma(&p,&s,&q);
CDIV(p,r,s);CMULT(s,p,ratio);/* s=B2= GcGa-b/Ga/Gc-b*/
CMPLX(p,0.,0.);CSUB(p,p,*x);cpow(&p,b,&r);CDIV(t,s,r);
/*t=B2*(-x)^-b*/
CMPLX(q,1.,0.);CADD(q,q,*b);CSUB(q,q,*c);
CMPLX(r,1.,0.);CADD(r,r,*b);CSUB(r,r,*a);
cf21(b,&q,&r,&z,&s);CMULT(term2,s,t);
CADD((*ans),term1,term2);
return;
}
```

```
/* hypergeometric function

from C Mathematical Function Handbook by Louis Baker
Copyright 1991 by Louis Baker. All rights reserved.
*/

#include <stdio.h>
#include "cmlib.h"
#include "protom.h"
#define cdigam cdigamma
#define tol 1.e-7
#define DEBUG 1
#undef DEBUG
/* handles cases associated with series in (1-x) rather
than x or 1/x*/
f211(a,b,c,x,ans) struct complex *a,*b,*c,*x,*ans;
   {double gamma(),digamma();
   int top=200,l,mpl,m,i;
   struct complex term,sum,ratio,factor,p,q,r,s,t,
     term1,term2,cl,z;
   double count;

   CADD(q,*a,*b);CSUB(p,*c,q);m=p.x;/*p=c-(a+b)*/
   if(abs(p.y)<1.e-7 && abs(p.x-m)<1.e-2)
      {/* Erdelyi 2.10(12)A&S 15.3.10-11 near pole */
#ifdef DEBUG
printf(" 2f1 Erdelyi(12) case A&S 10 or 11\n");
#endif
      if(m>=0)
      {
      CMPLX(z,1.,0.);CSUB(z,z,*x);/*z=1-x*/
      cgamma(c,&term1,&term2);/*term1=Gc*/
      CMPLX(term2,0.,0.);/* zero out for m==0 case*/
      if(m)
         {
         CLET(p,*a);CLET(q,*b);CMPLX(r,1.-m,0.);
         for(i=1,term.x=sum.x=1.,term.y=sum.y=0.;i<m;i++)
            {
            count=(double)(i);/*i=n*/
            CMULT(s,p,q);CDIV(ratio,s,r);
            ratio.x/=count;ratio.y/=count;
            CMULT(s,z,ratio);
            CMULT(ratio,term,s);CLET(term,ratio);
            CADD(sum,sum,term);
            if( cabs(term)< tol*cabs(sum))break;
            p.x+=1.;q.x+=1.;r.x+=1.;
            }
         CMPLX(p,gamma((double)m),0.);
         CMPLX(q,(double)m,0.);
```

```
    CADD(r,q,*a);CADD(s,q,*b);
    cgamma(&r,&t,&q);cgamma(&s,&q,&term2);
    CDIV(term2,p,t);/* Gm/Gm+a */
    CDIV(p,term2,q);/* p= Gm/Gm+a/Gm+b*/
    CMULT(term2,p,sum);/*term2= Sum*G/GG*/
    }
    /* infinite sum first find h[0]*/
    clog(&z,&cl);
    CMPLX(sum, digamma(1.+m)+digamma(1.),0.);
    CSUB(sum,sum,cl);
    CMPLX(q,(double)m,0.);CADD(q,q,*a);cdigam(&q,&p);
    CSUB(sum,sum,p);
    CMPLX(q,(double)m,0.);CADD(q,q,*b);cdigam(&q,&p);
    CSUB(sum,sum,p);/*sum=h[0]*/
    CLET(p,*a);CLET(q,*b);CMPLX(r,(double)(m+1),0.);
    p.x+=(double)m;
    q.x+=(double)m;
    CMPLX(term,1./gamma((double)(m+1)),0.);
    CMULT(sum,term,sum);/* sum now n=0 term in sum*/
    for(i=0;i<top;i++)
       {
       count=(double)(i+1);
       CMULT(s,p,q);CDIV(ratio,s,r);
       ratio.x/=count;ratio.y/=count;
       CMULT(s,z,ratio);
       CMULT(ratio,term,s);CLET(term,ratio);
       CMPLX(factor,
         digamma(count+1.)+digamma(count+m+1),0.);
       CLET(s,*a);s.x+=(m+count);
       cdigam(&s,&t);
       CSUB(factor,factor,t);
       CLET(s,*b);s.x+=(m+count);
       cdigam(&s,&t);
       CSUB(factor,factor,t);
       CSUB(factor,factor,cl);/*factor=h*/
       CMULT(t,factor,term);
       CADD(sum,sum,t);
       if( cabs(t)< tol*cabs(sum))break;
       p.x+=1.;q.x+=1.;r.x+=1.;
       }
    CMPLX(q,(double)m,0.);
    cpow(&z,&q,&r);CMULT(p,sum,r);
    CTREAL(p,p,((m%2)?-1.:1));
    cgamma(a,&t,&q);CDIV(r,p,t);
    cgamma(b,&t,&q);CDIV(q,r,t);
    CADD(p,q,term2);CMULT((*ans),p,term1);
    return;
}
/* m negative integer  Erdelyi(14) A&S 12*/
```

```
m=-m;
CMPLX(z,1.,0.);CSUB(z,z,*x);/*z=1-x*/
cgamma(c,&term1,&term2);/*term1=Gc*/
CMPLX(term2,0.,0.);/* zero out for m==0 case*/
if(m)
    {
    CLET(p,*a);p.x-=m;CLET(q,*b);q.x-=m;
    CMPLX(r,1.-m,0.);
    for(i=1,term.x=sum.x=1.,term.y=sum.y=0.;i<m;i++)
        {
        count=(double)(i);
        CMULT(s,p,q);CDIV(ratio,s,r);
        ratio.x/=count;ratio.y/=count;
        CMULT(s,z,ratio);
        CMULT(ratio,term,s);CLET(term,ratio);
        CADD(sum,sum,term);
        if( cabs(term)< tol*cabs(sum))break;
        p.x+=1.;q.x+=1.;r.x+=1.;
        }
    CMPLX(q,(double)(-m),0.);
    cpow(&z,&q,&p);
    CTREAL(p,p,gamma((double)m));
    cgamma(a,&t,&q);cgamma(b,&q,&term2);
    CDIV(term2,p,t);/* term2= (1-x)^-m Gm/Ga */
    CDIV(p,term2,q)
    CMULT(term2,p,sum);/*term2= finite term Sum*G/GG*/
    }
    /* infinite sum first find h[0]*/
    clog(&z,&cl);
    CMPLX(sum, digamma(1.+m)+digamma(1.),0.);
    CSUB(sum,sum,cl);
    CMPLX(q,(double)m,0.);CADD(q,q,*a);cdigam(&q,&p);
    CSUB(sum,sum,p);
    CMPLX(q,(double)m,0.);CADD(q,q,*b);cdigam(&q,&p);
    CADD(sum,sum,p);/*sum=h[0]*/
    CLET(p,*a);CLET(q,*b);CMPLX(r,(double)(m+1),0.);
    CMPLX(term,1./gamma((double)(m+1)),0.);
    CMULT(sum,term,sum);/* sum now n=0 term in sum*/
    for(i=0;i<top;i++)
        {
        count=(double)(i+1);
        CMULT(s,p,q);CDIV(ratio,s,r);
        ratio.x/=count;ratio.y/=count;
        CMULT(s,z,ratio);
        CMULT(ratio,term,s);CLET(term,ratio);
        CMPLX(factor,
          digamma(count+1.)+digamma(count+m+1),0.);
        CLET(s,*a);s.x+=(count);
        cdigam(&s,&t);
```

```
                CSUB(factor,factor,t);
                CLET(s,*b);s.x+=(count);
                cdigam(&s,&t);
                CADD(factor,factor,t);
                CSUB(factor,factor,cl);/*factor=h*/
                CMULT(t,factor,term);
                CADD(sum,sum,t);
                if( cabs(t)< tol*cabs(sum))break;
                p.x+=1.;q.x+=1.;r.x+=1.;
                }
            CTREAL(sum,sum,((m%2)?-1.:1));
            CLET(p,*a);p.x-=m;
            cgamma(&p,&t,&q);CDIV(r,sum,t);
            CLET(p,*b);p.x-=m;
            cgamma(&p,&t,&q);CDIV(q,r,t);
            CADD(p,q,term2);CMULT((*ans),p,term1);
            return;
        }
    /* c not a+b +/- positive integer*/
    /* A&S 15.3.6  z=1.-x  A1 A2 coef. Erdelyi 2.10(1)*/
#ifdef DEBUG
printf(" 2f1 Erdelyi (1) A&S 6\n");
#endif
    cgamma(c,&term2,&ratio);
    CSUB(q,*c,*a);cgamma(&q,&r,&ratio);
    CDIV(ratio,term2,r);/*ratio= gamma(c)/gamma(c-a)*/
    CSUB(q,*c,*b);cgamma(&q,&r,&s);
    CSUB(p,*c,*a);CSUB(p,p,*b);cgamma(&p,&s,&q);
    CDIV(p,s,r);CMULT((*ans),p,ratio);
/* ans= GcGc-a-b/Gc-a/Gc-b*/
    CMPLX(z,1.,0.);CSUB(z,z,*x);CMPLX(q,1.,0.);
CADD(q,q,*a);CADD(q,q,*b);
    CSUB(q,q,*c);
    cf21(a,b,&q,&z,&t);CMULT(term1,*ans,t);/*first term*/
    cgamma(a,&r,&s);cgama(b,&p,&s);
    CDIV(s,term2,r);CDIV(r,s,p);
    CADD(p,*a,*b);CSUB(p,p,*c);cgamma(&p,&s,&q);
    CMULT((*ans),s,r);
    /*ans= GcGa+b-c/GaGb*/
    CSUB(p,*c,*a);CSUB(q,*c,*b);CMPLX(r,1.,0.);CADD(r,r,*c);
    CSUB(r,r,*a); CSUB(r,r,*b);
    cf21(&p,&q,&r,&z,&term2);CMULT(p,term2,(*ans));/*p=A*f*/
    CSUB(q,*c,*a); CSUB(q,q,*b);
    cpow(&z,&q,&r);CMULT((*ans),r,p);CADD(*ans,*ans,term1);
    return;
    }
```

```
/*
Legendre function P for complex parameters
from C Mathematical Function Handbook by Louis Baker
Copyright 1991 by Louis Baker. All rights reserved.
*/

#include <stdio.h>
#include "cmlib.h"
#include "protom.h"
#include "complex.h"
#define eps 1.e-8
/* to= i from */
#define CTI(to,from) {to.x=-from.y;to.y=from.x;}

cp(z,mu,nu,ans) struct complex *z,*mu,*nu,*ans;
{
/* need cf21 such that if c neg. integer, returns
F/Gamma(c)*/
double sqrt(),gamma(),x,y;
struct complex a,b,c,d,e,f,one,term1,term2,ccos,csin,p,q;
int j,k;
x=z->x;y=z->y;one.x=1.;one.y=0.;
if(abs(y)<eps && abs(x)<=1.)
   {/* on cut  use Bateman 3.4(10) if mu not an integer*/
/*printf(" on cut\n");*/
   if( abs(abs(x)-1.)<eps)
         {/* |x|=1 */
         /*printf(" |x|=1  %le\n",x);*/
         if(cabs(*mu)>eps)/* mu nonzero*/
            {
            /* x=-1 return zero*/
            if( abs(x+1.)<eps)
                     {CMPLX(*ans,0.,0.);return 0;}
            /* if mu is an integer return zero*/
            if(abs(mu->y )<eps && abs(mu->x-(int)
                           (mu->x))<eps)
                     {CMPLX(*ans,0.,0.);}
            else{CMPLX((*ans),errorcode,0.);}
            return 0;
            }
         /*   mu==0   */
         if(x==1.){CMPLX((*ans),1.,0.);}
         if(x==-1.)
            {if(cabs(*mu)<eps)
               {CMPLX((*ans),
                 (((int)nu->x)%2?-1.:1.),0.);}
            else{CMPLX((*ans),errorcode,0.);}
            }
         return 0;
```

```
        }
/*printf(" on cut but not at end of cut %le\n",x);*/
   CLET(b,one);CADD(b,b,*nu);
   CMPLX(a,0.,0.);CSUB(a,a,*nu);
   CMPLX(f,1.,0.);CSUB(e,f,(*z));CTREAL(f,e,.5);
/*f=.5(1-Z)*/
   CMPLX(c,1,0.);CSUB(c,c,*mu);
   /*printf(" cf call\n");printc(&a);
   printc(&b);printc(&c); printc(&f);*/
   k=cf21(&a,&b,&c,&f,&e);/*printc(&e);
   printf(" =2F1 return code %d\n",k);*/
   if(cabs(*mu)>eps)
      {
      CMPLX(a,(1.+x)/(1.-
x),0.);CTREAL(b,*mu,.5);cpow(&a,&b,&c);
      CMULT(f,c,e);
      }
   else {CLET(f,e);}/* mu=0 */
   /* if mu is a positive integer, use F/Gamma(c) from f21*/
   if(abs(mu->y)<eps && abs(mu->x - ((int)mu->x))<eps && mu-
>x>0.)
      { CSET(ans,f);}
   /* otherwise, divide by GAMMA(1-MU)*/
   else   {CSUB(a,one,*mu);cgam-
ma(&a,&b,&c);CDIV((*ans),f,b);}
   return 0;
   }
/*printf(" off cut\n");*/
CLET(b,one);CADD(b,b,*nu);
CMPLX(a,0.,0.);CSUB(a,a,*nu);
CMPLX(f,1.,0.);CSUB(e,f,(*z));CTREAL(f,e,.5);/*f=.5(1-Z)*/
CMPLX(c,1,0.);CSUB(c,c,*mu);
/*printf(" cf call\n");
printc(&a);printc(&b);printc(&c);printc(&f);*/
cf21(&a,&b,&c,&f,&e);
/*printc(&e);printf(" =2F1 return code=%d\n",k);*/
CLET(b,one);CLET(c,one); CADD(b,b,*z); CSUB(c,c,*z);
CDIV(a,b,c);
CTREAL(b,*mu,.5);cpow(&a,&b,&c);CMULT(f,e,c);
if(abs(mu->y)<eps && abs(mu->x - ((int)mu->x))<eps
   && mu->x>0.)
   {CSET(ans,f);}
   /* mu pos integer do not divide by Gamma */
   else {
   CSUB(a,one,*mu);cgamma(&a,&b,&c);CMULT((*ans),f,b);
   }
return 0;
}
```

```
/*
Legendre Q for complex arguments
from C Mathematical Function Handbook by Louis Baker
Copyright 1991 by Louis Baker. All rights reserved.
*/

#include <stdio.h>
#include "cmlib.h"
#include "protom.h"

/* to= i from */
#define CTI(to,from) {to.x=-from.y;to.y=from.x;}

cq(z,mu,nu,ans) struct complex *z,*mu,*nu,*ans;
{
double sqrt(),gamma(),x,y;
struct complex a,b,c,d,e,f,one,term1,term2,ccos,csin,p,q;
int j,k;
x=z->x;y=z->y;one.x=1.;one.y=0.;
if(abs(y)<1.e-8 && abs(x)<1.)
   {/* on cut  use Bateman 3.4(10) if mu not an integer*/
   /*printf(" on cut\n");*/
   if(!(abs(mu->y)<1.e-8 && abs(mu->x-((int)mu->x))<1.e-7))
   {
   /*printf(" munnot integer in effect A&S 8.1.6\n");*/
   CLET(d,one);CSUB(d,d,*z);CTREAL(d,d,.5);
   CMPLX(a,0.,0.);CSUB(a,a,*nu);
   CLET(b,one);CADD(b,b,*nu);
   CLET(c,one);CADD(c,c,*mu);
   cf21(&a,&b,&c,&d,&term1);
   CTREAL(d,*mu,.5);
   CMPLX(e, (1.-x)/(1.+x) ,0.);
   cpow(&e,&d,&f);CMULT(term2,term1,f);
   CTREAL(f,term2,.5);
   CLET(d,one);CADD(d,d,*nu); CADD(d,d,*mu);
   cgamma(&d,&e,&term1);CMULT(term1,e,f);
   CMPLX(d,0.,0.);CSUB(d,d,*mu);cgamma(&d,&e,&f);
   CMULT(f,term1,e);
   CLET(d,one); CADD(d,d,*nu);CSUB(d,d,*mu);
   cgamma(&d,&e,&term1);CDIV(term1,f,e);
 /*printc(&term1);printf(" first term in sum\n");*/
   CLET(c,one);CSUB(c,c,*mu);
   cf21(&a,&b,&c,&d,&term2);
   CTREAL(d,*mu,.5);
   CMPLX(e, (1.+x)/(1.-x) ,0.);
   cpow(&e,&d,&f);CMULT(e,term2,f);
   CTREAL(e,e,.5);cgamma(mu,&a,&b);CMULT(f,a,e);
   CTREAL(a,*mu,pi);
   ctrig(&a,&b,&c);CMULT(term2,b,f);/* 2nd arg cos*/
```

```
   CADD( *ans,term1,term2);
/*printc(&term2);printf(" 2nd term in sum\n");*/
   return;
   }
/*printf(" integer mu on cut Erdelyi 3.4(12)\n");*/
   CLET(a,*nu);CADD(a,a,*mu);CTREAL(a,a,-.5);
   CLET(b,one);CADD(b,b,*nu);CSUB(b,b,*mu);CTREAL(b,b,.5);
   CLET(c,one);CTREAL(c,c,.5);
/*c=1/2 b= (1+n-m)/2 a=-(n+m)/2*/
   CMULT(d,*z,*z);
   cf21(&a,&b,&c,&d,&term1);
/*printc(&term1);printf(" second f21\n");*/
   b.x+=.5;cgamma(&b,&e,&f);CDIV(f,term1,e);CTREAL(f,f,.5);
/*printc(&f);
printf(" second term before tan/G((1-nu-mu)/2)\n");*/
   CADD(e,*mu,*nu);CTREAL(e,e,-.5);CTREAL(q,e,-pi);
   j=(int)e.x;
   ctrig(&q,&ccos,&csin);
   a.x+=.5;CLET(term2,f);
   CADD(p,*mu,*nu);k=(int)p.x;
   /* tan inf. if mu+nu odd integer*/
   if(!( abs(p.y)<1.e-8 && abs(p.x-(k))<1.e-8 && k%2))
      {
      cgamma(&a,&q,&term1);CDIV(term1,f,q);
      CMULT(f,term1,csin);CDIV(term2,f,ccos);
      }
   else
      {k>>=1;
      CTREAL(term2,term2,((k%2)?-1.:1.)*gamma(1.+k));
      }
/*printc(&term2);printf(" second term \n");*/

   CMPLX(c,1.5,0.);
   cf21(&a,&b,&c,&d,&term1);
   CMULT(f,*z,term1);
   CADD(a,a,*nu);cgamma(&a,&q,&c);CDIV(term1,f,q);
/*printc(&term1);printf(" first term before cot/G\n");*/
   if(!( abs(e.y)<1.e-8 && abs(e.x-(j))<1.e-8 && e.x <=1.e-
8))
      {/*printc(&e);
      printf(" cut,NOT: mu+nu 0 or even integer\n");*/
      cgamma(&e,&p,&q);CDIV(q,f,p);
      CMULT(p,q,ccos);CDIV(term1,p,csin);
      }
   else
      {/*ratio of cot(pi*e/2)/Gamma(-e/2)*/
      /*printf(" mu+nu even integer %d\n",j);*/
      j=(-j);
      CTREAL(term1,term1,( (j)%2?-1.:1.)*
```

```
        gamma((double)j+1.));
        }
/*printc(&term1);printf(" first term \n");*/
   CSUB(term1,term1,term2);
   CTREAL((*ans),term1,sqrt(pi));
   if(cabs(*mu)>1.e-8)
        {
        CMPLX(c,2.,0.);cpow(&c,mu,&a);CMULT(term1,a,*ans);
        CSUB(d,one,d);CTREAL(a,*mu,-.5);cpow(&d,&a,&c);
        CMULT((*ans),term1,c);
        }
   return;
   }
/*printf(" off cut\n");*/
CLET(b,one);CADD(b,b,*mu); CADD(b,b,*nu); CTREAL(b,b,.5);
CMPLX(a,.5,0.);CADD(a,a,b);
CMPLX(f,1.,0.);CDIV(e,f,(*z));CMULT(f,e,e);/*f=1/z^2*/
CMPLX(c,1.5,0.);CADD(c,c,*nu);
/*printf(" cf
call\n");printc(&a);printc(&b);printc(&c);printc(&f);*/
cf21(&a,&b,&c,&f,&e);/*printc(&e);printf(" answer\n");*/
CTREAL(e,e,sqrt(pi));
CMPLX(a,-
1.,0.);CSUB(a,a,*mu);CSUB(a,a,*nu);cpow(z,&a,&b);CMULT(f,e,b)
;
CTREAL(b,*mu,.5);CMULT(a,*z,*z);CSUB(a,a,one);cpow(&a,&b,&c);
CMULT(e,f,c);
CTI(a,(*mu));CTREAL(a,a,pi);cexp(&a,&b);CMULT(f,e,b);
CMPLX(a,-1.,0.);CSUB(a,a,*nu);CMPLX(b,2.,0.);cpow(&b,&a,&c);
CMULT(e,f,c);
CLET(a,one);CADD(a,a,*mu);CADD(a,a,*nu);
cgamma(&a,&c,&f);CMULT(f,e,c);
CMPLX(b,1.5,0.);CADD(b,b,*nu);
cgamma(&b,&d,&e);CDIV((*ans),f,d);return;
}
```

```
/*
test driver 2F1
from C Mathematical Function Handbook by Louis Baker
Copyright 1991 by Louis Baker. All rights reserved.
*/

#include <stdio.h>
#include "cmlib.h"
#include "protom.h"
#define cdigam cdigamma

main()
{struct complex a,b,c,d,e;float
f,g,h,i,j,k,l,m,n,o,p;double z,digamma();
printf(" test driver for Gauss hypergeometric & related
functions\n");
while(1)
   {printf(" enter real x for digamma\n");scanf("%e",&p);
   if(p==0.)break; z=p;  CMPLX(a,z,0.);cdigam(&a,&b);
   printf(" digamma=%le digam=%le\n",digamma(z),digam(z));
   printc(&b);printf("=cdigam\n");
   }

while(1)
{printf(" enter as complex numb a,b,c,x\n");
scanf("%e%e%e%e%e%e%e%e",&f,&g,&h,&i,&j,&k,&l,&m);
if(f==0. && g==0. && l==0. &&m==0. &&j==0. &&k==0. &&h==0.
&&i==0.)break;
CMPLX(a,f,g);CMPLX(b,h,i);CMPLX(c,j,k); CMPLX(d,l,m);
cf21(&a,&b,&c,&d,&e);printf("answer= %e %e ",e.x,e.y);
}

while(1)
{printf(" Legendre P:enter as complex numb mu,nu,x\n");
scanf("%e%e%e%e%e%e",&f,&g,&h,&i,&j,&k);
if(f==0. && g==0. &&j==0. &&k==0. &&h==0. &&i==0.)break;
CMPLX(a,f,g);CMPLX(b,h,i);CMPLX(c,j,k);
cp(&c,&a,&b,&e);
printc(&e);printf("=answer\n");
}
while(1)
{printf(" Legendre Q:enter as complex numb mu,nu,x\n");
scanf("%e%e%e%e%e%e",&f,&g,&h,&i,&j,&k);
if(f==0. && g==0. &&j==0. &&k==0. &&h==0. &&i==0.)break;
CMPLX(a,f,g);CMPLX(b,h,i);CMPLX(c,j,k);
cq(&c,&a,&b,&e);
printc(&e);printf("=answer\n");
}
}
```

```
 Output: Gauss Hypergeometric functions
 enter real x for digamma
0
 enter as complex numb a,b,c,x
7 0 5 0 4.1 0 3 -1
answer= -4.037611e-03 -2.956632e-03  enter as complex numb
a,b,c,x
0 0 0 0 0 0 0 0
 Legendre P:enter as complex numb mu,nu,x
1 0 1 0 .5 0
 -8.660254e-01 + 0.000000e+00 i =answer
 Legendre P:enter as complex numb mu,nu,x
0 0 0 0 0 0
 Legendre Q:enter as complex numb mu,nu,x
1 0 1 0 .5 0
 -1.053063e+00  -6.493721e-33 i =answer
 Legendre Q:enter as complex numb mu,nu,x
0 0 0 0 0 0
```

```
/*
real hypergeometric function and relatives.
 simple,naive,
from C Mathematical Function Handbook by Louis Baker
Copyright 1991 by Louis Baker. All rights reserved.

f21 2F1 (Gauss Hypergeometric)
f12 1F2
f01 0F1

Note: confluent is 1F1
*/
#include "cmlib.h"
#include "protom.h"

double f21(a,b,c,x)
double a,b,c,x;
{/*hypergeometric function 2F1(a,b;c;x)*/
double sum,term,count,tol=1.e-12;
int top=40,i;
if(x==0.)return 1.;
for(i=0,term=sum=1.;i<top;i++)
   {
   count=(double)(i+1);
   term *=(x*(a+i)*(b+i)/((c+i)*count));
/*   printf(" term=%f sum=%f %d\n",term,sum,i);
*/
   if( abs(term)< tol*abs(sum) )return sum;
   sum+=term;
   }
return(sum);
}

double f12(a,b,c,x)
double a,b,c,x;
{/*hypergeometric function 1F2(a;b,c;x)*/
double sum,term,count,tol=1.e-6;
int top=40,i;
if(x==0.)return 1.;
for(i=0,term=sum=1.;i<top;i++)
   {
   count=(double)(i+1);
   term *=(x*(a+i)/((c+i)*(b+i)*count));
/*   printf(" term=%f sum=%f %d\n",term,sum,i);
*/
   if( abs(term/sum)< tol)return sum;
   sum+=term;
   }
return(sum);
```

```
}
double F01(c,x)
double c,x;
{/*hypergeometric function 0F1(;c;x)*/
double sum,term,count,tol=1.e-6;
int top=40,i;
if(x==0.)return 1.;
for(i=0,term=sum=1.;i<top;i++)
   {
   count=(double)(i+1);
   term *=(x/((c+i)*count));
/*   printf(" term=%f sum=%f %d\n",term,sum,i);
*/
   if( abs(term/sum)< tol)return sum;
   sum+=term;
   }
return(sum);
}
```

Chapter 16

The Elliptic Functions

Introduction

Abramowitz and Stegun devote three full chapters to the Elliptic functions. Rather than introduce them piecemeal and repeat information, the definitions and inter-relationships will be discussed here, just as we concentrated the discussion of the Bessel functions in a single chapter. In discussing the Theta functions, Abramowitz and Stegun refer to a "bewildering" variety of notations. It is generally true that Elliptic functions are written in a variety of ways as dependent upon a variety of parameters, so always be careful to be sure as to what the arguments, etc., really are.

Note that Chapter 29 will present C++ programs for the general case of complex modulus. This case is typically of little practical interest, however. In association with these three chapters, we provide C code for dealing with complex arguments but real moduli.

Note also that there are a number of ways of writing these functions and the parameter on which they depend. Be sure that a result in a book, say, *jn*(*x*,.5) means m=.5 and not k=.5, for example.

Historically, elliptic integrals were the first functions in this class to be studied. It was shown by Legendre that integrals involving the square root of a cubic polynomial could be reduced to combinations of three basic integrals, the elliptic integrals of the first $F(\varphi,k)=\int_0^{\varphi}\frac{dt}{\sqrt{1-k^2\sin^2 t}}$, second $E(\varphi,k)=\int_0^{\varphi}dt\sqrt{1-k^2\sin^2 t}$, and third kind $\Pi(\varphi,k,n)=\int_0^{\varphi}\frac{dt}{(1-n\sin^2 t)\sqrt{1-k^2\sin^2 t}}$. The parameter m is called the modulus, where $k^2=m$, while in turn $k=\sin\alpha$. The integrals are often written as a function of any of these three parameters, e. g., $F(\phi,k)$ or $F(\phi\backslash a)$ or

$F(\phi \mid m)$. Often, the variable u is used instead of ϕ, meaning the corresponding value of F for the given m. This argument is often used with the Jacobian Elliptic functions as well as $E(u|m)$. Be careful which version of the parameter is being specified, as this notation is not universal. When the range of integration is from 0 to $\pi/2$, these are called complete elliptic integrals. The complete elliptic integrals of the first and second kinds are written $K(m)$ and $E(m)$, respectively. It is common to encounter m' and k' where $m + m' = 1$ and $m' = k'^2$. With this notation, $K' = K(m')$, etc.

Consider the formula $x = \int_0^{sin(x)} \frac{dt}{\sqrt{1-t^2}}$. This may be used as the definition of the sine function. We can then define the Jacobian Elliptic functions analgously, as inverses of the elliptic integral of the first kind. For the definition of the Jacobian Elliptic function $sn(u,m)$, $sn\, u = \sin \varphi$ where $u = F(\varphi,m)$. Then $cn\, u = \cos \varphi$ and $dn\, u = sn\, u / cn\, u$. Additionally, we define $am\ u$ by $am\, u = \varphi = arcsin(\, sn\, u)$ and $dn\, u = \Delta(\varphi) = \sqrt{1 - m \sin^2 \varphi}$. There are a total of twelve Jacobian Elliptic functions, involving the distinct combinations of $s\ n\ d\ c$ taken two at a time; for example, $cd\, u = cn\, u / dn\, u$. Note that they are in a sense inverses of the elliptic integrals.

We can define the Weierstrass function $\wp(x)$ by $x = \int_\infty^{\wp(x)} \frac{dt}{\sqrt{4t^3 - g2\,t - g3}}$.

It will then be seen to be similar in character to a Jacobian Elliptic function, i.e., the inverse of an elliptic integral. Historically, Jacobi used a different route, generalizing $\frac{1}{\sin^2 x} = \sum_{n=-\infty}^{\infty} \frac{1}{(x - n\pi)^2}$ to

$$\wp(x) = \frac{1}{x^2} + \sum_{n,m}^{\infty}{}' \left[\frac{1}{(x - 2m\omega - 2n\omega')^2} - \frac{1}{(2m\omega + 2n\omega')^2} \right].$$

Here the summation is over all integral n and m except for the case $n=m=0$. Related to this function are the zeta and sigma functions, with the definitions $\zeta'(z) = -\wp(z)$ and $\frac{\sigma'(z)}{\sigma(z)} = \zeta(z)$.

The Jacobian elliptic function and the Weierstrass function are doubly periodic. That is, there are two different complex numbers a and b which are not integral multiples of one another such that $F(x)=F(x+a)=F(x+b)$, where F is sn or cn or ... (There are degenerate cases in which this is not true,

i. e., one of the periods is zero. Such cases are not of much interest, however.)

We can define the elliptic logarithm, given by $\int_{\infty}^{x} \frac{dt}{\sqrt{t^3 - a t^2 - bt}}$, and its inverse, the elliptic exponential. See Chapter 29 for C++ implementations.

Also related are the Jacobi theta functions. There are four of them, defined by:

$$\theta_1 (z,q) = 2q^{1/4} \sum_{n=0}^{\infty} (-1)^n q^{n(n+1)} \sin(2n+1) z,$$

$$\theta_2 (z,q) = 2q^{1/4} \sum_{n=0}^{\infty} q^{n(n+1)} \cos(2n+1) z \quad , \quad \theta_3 (z,q) = 1 + 2 \sum_{n=0}^{\infty} q^{n^2} \cos 2n\ z,$$

$\theta_4 (z,q) = 1 + 2 \sum_{n=0}^{\infty} (-1)^n q^{n^2} \cos 2n\ z$. The variable q is called the nome.

The Jacobi Zeta function (a capital zeta instead of the many zeta functions which use a lower-case zeta) is $Z(\varphi|m) = E(\varphi|m) - \frac{E(m)}{K(m)} F(\varphi|m)$.

Heumann's Lamba function is $\Lambda_0 = \frac{F(\varphi|1-m)}{K(1-m)} + \frac{2}{\pi} Z(\varphi|1-m)$. There are also the Neville theta functions, defined by $\theta_s (u) = \frac{\theta_1 (v)}{\theta_1{}' (0)}$,

$\theta_c (u) = \frac{\theta_1 (v + \frac{\pi}{2})}{\theta_1 (\frac{\pi}{2})}$, $\theta_d (u) = \frac{\theta_4 (v + \frac{\pi}{2})}{\theta_4 (\frac{\pi}{2})}$, $\theta_n (u) = \frac{\theta_4 (v)}{\theta_4 (0)}$. Here $v = \frac{\pi u}{2K}$, where K is the complete elliptic integral for m. Once again, as noted in Abramowitz and Stegun, a variety of notations and arguments exist for theta functions. Note also that $\theta_1{}' (0) = \pi \theta_2 (0) \theta_3 (0) \theta_4 (0)$, which enables us to avoid having to evaluate derivatives of theta functions in determining the Neville theta functions.

The Jacobian Elliptic functions may be defined as the ratio of theta functions.

Finally, there are the elliptic modular functions, which are defined by the ratios of theta functions: $f(\tau) = \frac{\theta_2^4 (0|\tau)}{\theta_3^4 (0|\tau)}$, $g(\tau) = \frac{\theta_4^4 (0|\tau)}{\theta_3^4 (0|\tau)}$,

$h(\tau) = -\frac{f(\tau)}{g(\tau)}$. Here $\tau = -\frac{i}{\pi}\log q = i\frac{K'}{K}$. These functions may be written as rational functions of q. They may be used to relate the modulus m, or equivalently, *k*, to the ratio of the periods of the elliptic function in question, i. e., determining *q* from *k* and vice versa.

Applications

The elliptic integrals occur in a variety of physical problems, most notably in the motion of a pendulum with a swing of finite amplitude. The Jacobian Elliptic functions, because of their doubly periodic nature, show up in conformal mappings and similar applications in which the domain is rectangular. They show up, for example, in determining the impedance of microstrip transmission lines; see Love and Carlisle. (Such solutions can also be written in terms of the theta functions; see Gupta et al.) Another use for the Jacobian Elliptic functions is in the design of elliptic filters. Developed by W. Cauer, these are electrical filters (ladder networks of inductors and capacitors) which are designed to pass or reject various frequencies. Any filter design is a compromise between flatness of response in the passband and maximal rejection of the stopband. Elliptic filters have ripples of constant amplitude in the passband (they are sometimes called "equiripple" filters) and are often used. See Zverev's book for details.

Methods

There is an iteration, called the arithmetic-geometric mean (AGM), which converges very rapidly and is useful for computing many of the Elliptic functions. It will be used here, in the following two chapters and in Chapter 29. It involves starting with two values a_0 and b_0, and iterating forming $a_{n+1} = (a_n + b_n)/2$, $b_{n+1} = (a_n b_n)^{1/2}$, and $c_{n+1} = a_n - b_n$ and iterating until c is smaller than a desired error tolerance. Depending upon the starting values chosen, various elliptic integrals and other functions may be calculated, either from the final value of $a_n = b_n$ in some cases or some function of the sequence of values in others.

Interestingly, the AGM has been applied to computing π to 200 million digits by Kanada.

The Neville theta functions may be computed from the Jacobian elliptic functions. The Weierstrass functions, after suitable manipulation to determine the appropriate modulus, can also be computed from the Jacobian elliptic functions. There are efficient expansions for determining m from q and *q* from *m*, at least when m is not very close to one. However, brute force is used here for the theta functions and their logarithmic derivatives.

For additional methods, see Chapter 29, which uses the AGM for the Neville and Jacobi theta functions.

Programs given in Math. Notes 14 and 70 have been adapted for computing elliptic integrals. They have been enhanced and corrected (see code).

For alternative programs, see the papers cited by Bulirsch and the article by Press and Teukolsky.

Smirnov's *Course of Higher Mathematics*, Vol. III, Part Two, provides good coverage of elliptic functions, including the reduction of the integrals to standard forms, elliptic coordinates, the Lamé equation, use in conformal transformations, and others.

References

T. Brown, Math. Note 14, *TEF: A Subroutine for the Calculation of the Incomplete Elliptic Integrals of the First and Second Kind*, Phillips Lab., Kirtland AFB (available from Defense Technical Information Center, DTIC), August 1970.

R. Bulirsch, *Numerische Mathematik*, **7**, 78, 1965.

R. Bulirsch, *Numerische Mathematik*, **7**, 353, 1965.

R. Bulirsch, *Numerische Mathematik*, **13**, 266, 1969.

R. Bulirsch, *Numerische Mathematik*, **13**, 305, 1969.

G. W. Carlisle, *Impedance and Fields of Two Parallel Plates of Unequal Breadths*, Sensor and Simulation Note 90, Phillips Lab., Kirtland AFB (available from Defense Technical Information Center, DTIC), July 1969.

D. V. Giri, T. Brown, J. P. Martinez, *Numerical Evaluation of Jacobian Elliptic Functions, Elliptic Integrals of All Three Kinds and the Jacobi Zeta Function*, Math. Note 70, Phillips Lab., Kirtland AFB (available from Defense Technical Information Center, DTIC), April 1, 1981.

K. C. Gupta, R. Garg, I. J. Bahl, *Microstrip Lines and Slotlines* (Boston: ARTECH, 1979).

Y. Kanada, *Supercomputing 88, Vol. II* (Washington: IEEE Press, 1988), p. 117.

A. F. H. Love, *Proc. London Math. Soc.*, **22**, 337, 1923.

W. H. Press and S. A. Teukolsky, *Computers in Physics*, p. 92, Jan/Feb. 1990.

V. I. Smirnov, *A Course of Higher Mathematics* Vol. III, Part Two (Oxford: Pergamon Press, 1964).

A. Zverev, *Handbook of Filter Synthesis* (N. Y.: J. Wiley, 1967).

Figure

Fig. 16-1 shows the Jacobian Elliptic functions for typical moduli.

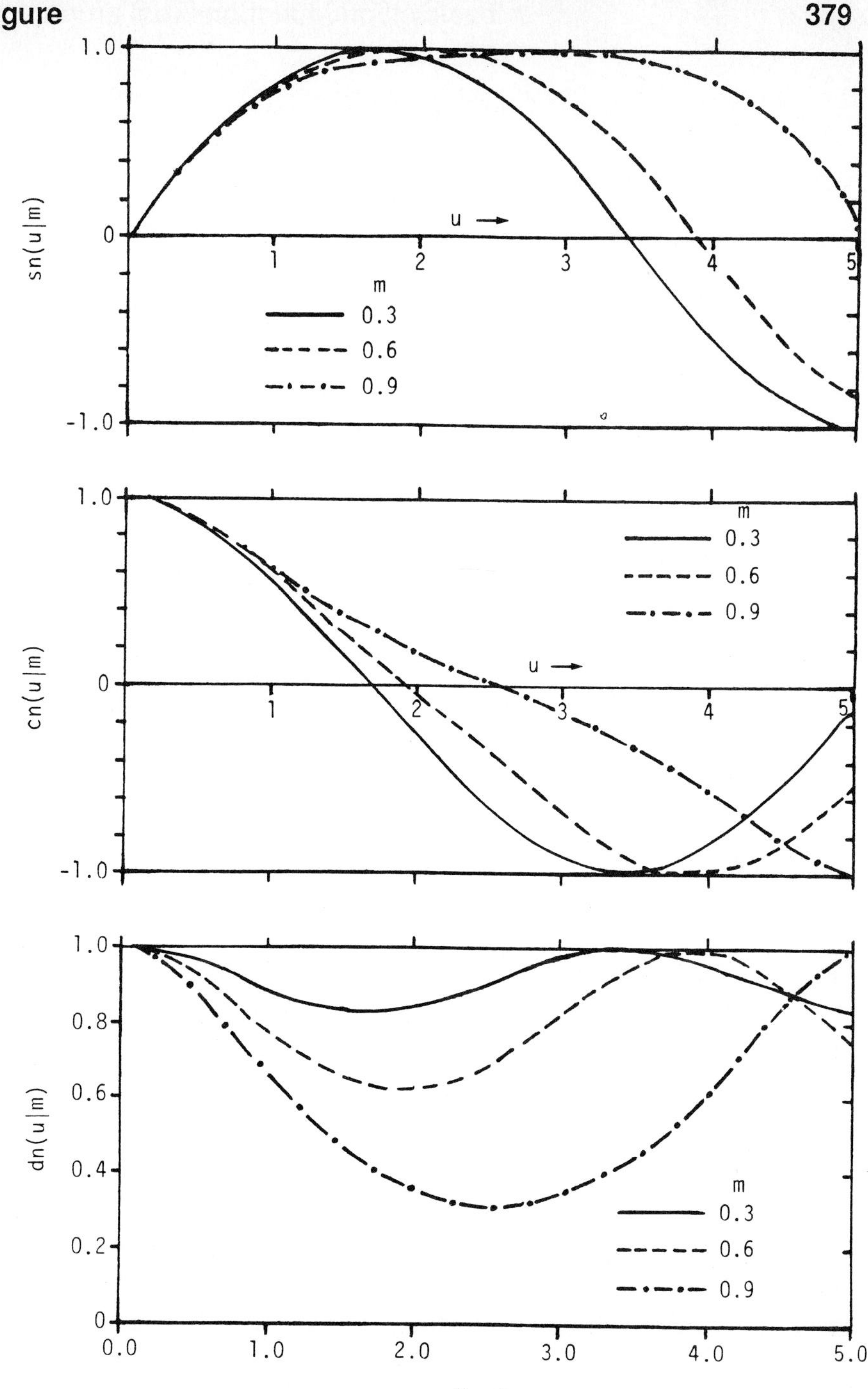

Fig. 16-1: Jacobian Elliptic functions *sn*, *cn*, *dn* for three moduli.

```
/*
basic elliptic functions real arguments
   copyright 1991 Louis Baker. All rights reserved.

   tek()   returns complete elliptic integrals 1st,2nd kind
      id=0 for 2nd argument m else =1 for m1 supplied
      0<=m<=1

   tef()   incomplete elliptic integrals of 1st,2nd kind
      as functions of phi,m. see e3m.c for third kind
      any real m

   jzeta   Jacobian Capital Zeta function

   am()    amplitude

   jef()   Jacobian elliptic function sn,cn,dn all real m
      returns in global double amplitude am

   heuman   Heuman's Lambda function

   theta   Jacobian theta functions i=1,4 real u,m

   neville   Neville theta functions

tek,tef,jef jzeta based upon routines in AFWL math notes.
Modified to handle  m<0 and m>1, m==0,1 as special cases,
calculate Capital Theta, return amplitude from jef
*/


#include "cmlib.h"
#include "protom.h"
static teff(double phi,double m,double sig,double *f,double
*e);

double kimag,eimag;

tek(id,m,k,e)
double m,*k,*e;int id;
{/* complete elliptic integrals of 1st,2nd kinds*/
int i,n;
double sqrt(),log(),
   rpk,rkn,rkp[60],tol=1.e-6,pk2,pkp,gol,
gk,fk,fe,ge,c,d,h,t1,t2,aux;
kimag=eimag=0.;
if(id) rpk=sqrt(m);
if(!id)aux=m;else aux=1.-m;
if(aux>1. )
```

```
    {
    aux=1./aux;
    h=sqrt(aux);d=(1.-aux);
    tek(0,aux, &fk,&fe);
    tek(0,d, &gk,&ge);
    *k=h*fk;kimag=h*gk;
    *e=(fe-fk*d)/h;eimag=(ge-aux*gk)/h;
    return 0;
    }
if(m==1.)
    {*k=1.e60; *e=1.;return 0;}
*k=pi*.5;
*e=*k;
if(aux<0.)
    {
    aux= -aux/(1.-aux);
    h=sqrt(1.-aux);
    tek(0,aux,k,e);
    (*k) *=h; (*e)/=h;
    return 0;
    }
if(m==0.)return 0;
if(m> .999)
    rpk=sqrt(1.-m);
else
    {
    rkn=sqrt(m);
    for(i=0;i<60;i++)
        {
        rkp[i]=aux= sqrt(1.-rkn*rkn);
        rkn= (1.-aux)/(1.+aux);
        if(i && rkn<tol)break;
        }
    n=i;
    for(i=n;i>=0;i--)
        {
        rkn=rkp[i];
        aux=1.+rkn;
        *k *= 2./aux;
        *e= aux* *e -*k *rkn;
        }
    return 0;
    }
/* m>.999 */
pk2=rpk*rpk;
pkp=pk2;
gol= log(4./rpk);
gk=gol-1.;
fk=.25;
```

```
fe=.25;
*k=gol+fk*gk*pkp;
*e=1.+.5*(gol-.5)*pkp;
ge=gk;
for(i=2;i<2000;i++)
   {
   aux=i+1;
   d=i;
   pkp=pkp*pk2;
   c=d/aux;
   *k *= d*d/(aux*aux);
   *e *=c;
   h=1./(d*aux);
   gk -= 1./(d*d);
   ge-=h;
   t1= *k *gk*pkp;
   *k += t1;
   t2= fe*ge*pkp;
   *e += t2;
   if(t1<tol && t2<tol)return 0;
   fe *=c;
   ge -=h;
   }
return 0;
}

tef(phi,m,sig,f,e) double phi,m,sig,*f,*e;
{ double sin(),log(),tan(),sqrt(),sin(),asin(),am();
double  u,ff,ec,w,plus,plus1,t,u1,a,p,r,bd,ek,ee;
struct complex carg,cans;
if(m==0.)
   {*e=*f=phi;return 0;}
if(m==1.)
   {
   *e=sin(phi);*f= log(tan(pi*.25+.5*phi));
   return 0;
   }
if(m>1.)
   {/* A&S 17.4.15-16*/
   plus= sqrt(m);plus1=1./m;
   ff=plus*sin(phi);
   if(ff>1. || ff<-1.)
      {/* imaginary angle theta- need complex functions*/
      *f=*e=errorcode;return 1;
      }
   t= asin(ff);
   u=sig;
   tef(t,plus1,u,&ff,&ec);
   *f= ff/plus; /* *f= u */
```

```
    w=*f*plus; p=am(w,plus1);/*am plus1 or m???*/
    tef(p,plus1,sig,&ff,&ec);
    *e= plus*ec-(m-1.)* *f;
    return 0;
    }
else if(m<0.)
    {
    /* A&S 17.4.17 F, homebrew E note A&S use -m for m */
    plus=1./(1.-m);plus1=-m*plus;
    tek(0,plus1,&ek,&ee);
    tef(.5*pi-phi,plus1,sig,&ff,&ec);
    r=sqrt(plus);bd=1./r;
    *f= r*( ek-ff);
    w= *f *bd;
    u=sqrt(plus1);u1=sqrt(1.-plus1);
    r=sin(phi);a= u*r;ek=sqrt(u1*u1+ a*a);
    a= r/ek;
    bd=asin(a);
    tef(bd,plus1,sig,&ff,&ec);p=u*a;
    *e= (ec-plus1*a*cos(bd)/sqrt(1.-p*p))/u1;
    return 0;
    }
teff(phi,m,sig,f,e);
return 0;
}

static teff(phi,m,sig,f,e) double phi,m,sig,*f,*e;
{/* CAVEAT- USER SHOULD CALL TEF, NOT TEFF*/
double sqrt(),tan(),atan(),sin(),cos(),asin(),log(),tol=1.e-
8;
double phii,ek,ee,plus,plus1,w,signem,ph,rk,ss,sk,alphar;
double
d,g,ps,u1,u,h,a,ap,cnk,be,reler,oreler,p,or,pr,bf,s,c;
double sumem,bd,r,t,p2,t1,t2,pk,ce,ff,am(),b,lou;
double aa[50],bb[50],cc[50],psav[50];
int i,j,n,nk,stop,ios,ins,i4,nq,m2p,it,k;
if(phi<0.)
    {
    w=-1.;
    ph=-phi;
    }
else
    {
    w=1.;
    ph-phi;
    }
rk=sqrt(m);
n=ph/(2.*pi);
a=ph- n*2.*pi;
```

```
b=a/pi *2.;
k=b;
nq=k+1;
switch (nq)
   {
   case 1: nk= (n<<2);
      signem=1.;
      ap=a;
      break;
   case 2:
      nk= (n<<2)+2;
      signem=-1.;
      ap=pi-a;
      break;
   case 3:
      nk=(n<<2)+2;
      signem=1.;
      ap=a-pi;
      break;
   default:
      nk= (n<<2)+4;
      signem=-1;
      ap= 2.*pi-a;
      break;
   }
cnk=nk;
phii=ap;
tek(0,m,&ek,&ee);
plus=cnk*ek;
plus1=cnk*ee;
it=0;
if(abs(phii-.5*pi)<tol)it=1;
if(abs(rk-1.)<tol)
   {
   it++;
   if(it==2)
      {
      *f=w*1.e70; *e= w*(plus1+signem);return 0;
      }
   *f=w*(plus+signem*log(tan(phii*.5+.785398163397448)));
   *e=w*(plus1+signem*sin(phii));
   return 0;
   }
if(abs(rk)<tol)
   {
   *f= w*(plus+signem*phii);
   *e=w*(plus1+signem*phii);
   return 0;
   }
```

```
it++;
if(it==2)
    {
    tek(0,m,&ek,&ee);
    *f=w*(plus+signem*ek);
    *f=w*(plus1+signem*ee);
    return 0;
    }
if(abs(phii)<1.e-30)
    {
    *f=w*plus;
    *e=w*plus1;
    return 0;
    }
if(m<=.75)
{
tek(0,m,&ek,&ee);
s=sin(phii);
c=cos(phii);
sk=m;
ce=2.*phii/pi;
t2=ce*ek;
t1=ce*ee;
a=.5;
t=.5*a*sk;
r=t;
ss=s*s;
ps=1.;
h=.5;
ff=.5;
pk=sk;
u1=10.;
for(i=2;i<20000;i++)
    {
    j=i<<1;
    d= j-1;
    g=j-3;
    ee=1./j;
    ps *=ss;
    a=ee*(d*a+ps);
    ff*=d*ee;
    h*=g*ee;
    pk*=sk;
    u=ff*a*pk;
    if( u1*u1/(u1-u) < sig)break;
    u1=u;
    t+=u;
    r+=h*a*pk;
    }
```

```
(*f)=w*((t2-s*c*t)*signem+plus);
(*e)=w*((t1+s*c*r)*signem+plus1);
return 0;
}
   /* else m>=.75   */
   alphar=asin(rk);
   aa[0]=1.;
   bb[0]=cos(alphar);stop=49;
   for(i=1;i<50;i++)
      {j=i-1;
      aa[i]=.5*(aa[j]+bb[j]);
      bb[i]=sqrt(aa[j]*bb[j]);
      cc[i]=.5*(aa[j]-bb[j]);
      if(abs(cc[i])<sig){stop=i;break;}
      }
   p=phii;
   p2=1.;
   nq=0;
   ios=1;
   m2p=0;
   i4=0;
   oreler=1.e20;
   or=oreler;
   for(i=0;i<=stop;i++)
      {
      psav[i]=p;
      p2 *=2.;
      bd= tan(p)*bb[i]/aa[i];
      bf=atan(bd);
      label1:
         ins= (bf<0.) ? -1 : 1 ;
      if( ios*ins < 0)
         {
         nq++;
         nq%=4;
          }
      switch (nq)
         {
         case 0:
            if(i4)
               {
               i4=0;
               m2p++;
               }
            be=bf+(2*m2p)*pi;
            break;
         case 1:
         case 2:
            be=bf+(2*m2p)*pi+pi;
```

```
                break;
            case 3:
                be=bf+(2*m2p)*pi+2.*pi;
                i4=1;
            }
        ios=ins;
        pr=p/be;
        reler= abs(or-pr)/(pr+or);
        if( oreler<reler )
                {
                ios=-ios;
                goto label1;
                }
        p +=be;
        or=pr;
        oreler=reler;
        }
    lou=(p/(p2*aa[stop]));
    *f= w*(plus+signem*lou);
    tek(0,m,&ek,&ee);
/*printf(" debug K,E=%le %le lou=%le\n",ek,ee,lou);*/
    sumem=0.;
    for(i=1;i<=stop;i++)
        sumem += cc[i]*sin(psav[i]);
/* not F(phi) but transformed phi needed here? */
    *e=w*(plus1+signem*(ee/ek* (lou) + sumem));
/*   INCORRECT CODE FROM MN70:
    *e=w*(plus1+signem*(ee/ek* *f + sumem));*/
/*printf(" E debug: plus1=%le sumem=%le F=%le, sigmen=%le\n"
,plus1,sumem,*f,signem);*/
    return 0;
}

double jzeta(phi,m) double phi,m;
{/*jacobian zeta function*/
double k,e,f,ee,sig=1.e-5;
tek(0,m,&k,&e);
tef(phi,m,sig,&f,&ee);
if(ee==errorcode || f==errorcode)return errorcode;
return ee-f*e/k;
}

double am(u,m) double u,m;
{/* returns phi= am u inverse function of u=F(phi,m=sin^2
alpha) */
/* asin() returns within range -pi/2 to pi/2  am(u+2K)=
pi+am(u) */
double sn,cn,dn,asin(),mult,e,k,offset;
offset=0.;mult=1.;
```

```
if(u<0.){u=-u;mult=-1.;}
tek(0,m,&k,&e);e=((int)(u/(2.*k)));
u-=e;offset=pi*e;
jef(u,m,&sn,&cn,&dn);
return  mult*(asin(sn)+offset);
}


double jtheta,amplitude;

jef(u,m,sn,cn,dn) double u,m,*sn,*cn,*dn;
{
int i,n;
double a[200],c[200],phi[200],v,am,am1,b,argu,t,
   asin(),sin(),cos(),sqrt(),pow(),tol=1.e-7;

/* Jacobian theta function valid for all real m<=1 */
double exp(),log(),twon,term,k,sum,lou,sqrtm1,mu,mu1;

if(m<0.)
   {/* A&S 16.10.1-4*/
   t=-m;mu= t/(1.+t);mu1=1./(1.+t);k=sqrt(mu1);v=u/k;
   jef(v,mu,&term,&sum,&lou);
   *dn= 1./lou;
   *sn= k* term* *dn;
   *cn= sum* *dn;
   return 0;
   }
if(m>1.)
   { /* A&S 16.11.1-4*/
   mu=1./m; k=sqrt(mu);v=u/k;
   jef(v,mu,&term,&sum,&lou);
   *sn=k*term;
   *cn=lou;
   *dn=sum;
   return 0;
   }
v=u;am=m;
if(m==0.)
   {
   *sn=sin(u);
   *cn=cos(u);
   *dn=1.;
   return 0;
   }
else if(m==1.)
   {
   *sn=tanh(u);
   *cn=1./sinh(u);
```

```
    *dn=*cn;
    return 0;
    }
am1=1.-am;
a[0]=1.;
sqrtm1=sqrt(am1);
b=sqrtm1;
/*c[0]=sqrt(m);not used anywhere*/
for(i=1;i<200;i++)
    {
    a[i]=.5*(a[i-1]+b);
    c[i]=.5*(a[i-1]-b);
    if(abs(c[i])<tol)break;
    b=sqrt(b*a[i-1]);
    }
n=i;
twon=pow(2., (double)(n));
phi[n]=a[n]*v* twon;

sum=0.;
term= .5/twon;
for(i=n;i>0;i--)
    {
    argu=c[i]*sin(phi[i])/a[i];
    t=asin(argu);
    phi[i-1]=.5*(t+phi[i]);
    sum-= term*log(cos(2.*phi[i-1]-phi[i]));
    term*=2.;
    }
argu=phi[0]; amplitude=argu;
*sn=sin(argu);
*cn=cos(argu);
lou= cos(phi[1]-argu);
*dn= *cn/lou;
tek(0,m,&k,&term);
jtheta=sum+.5*log(2.*sqrtm1/pi*k * lou/cos(argu));
jtheta=exp(jtheta);
return 0;
}

double heuman(phi,m) double phi,m;
{
double k,e,ff,ee;
tek(0,m,&k,&e);
tef(phi,1.-m,1.e-3,&ff,&ee);
return 2./pi*(k*ee-(k-e)*ff);
}

theta(v,m,t1,t2,t3,t4)
```

```
double v,m,*t1,*t2,*t3,*t4;
{
double sn,cn,dn,bigk,k,kp,e,u,srk,srkp;
tek(0,m,&bigk,&e);
u=2.*bigk*v/pi;
jef(u,m,&sn,&cn,&dn);
k=sqrt(m);kp=sqrt(1.-m);srk=sqrt(k);srkp=sqrt(kp);
*t1= sn*srk*jtheta;
*t2=cn*srk/srkp*jtheta;
*t3=dn/srkp*jtheta;
*t4=jtheta;
return 0;
}

neville(u,m,ts,tc,td,tn) double u,m,*ts,*tc,*tn,*td;
{
double v,e,bigk,t1,t2,t3,t4,t10,t20,t30,t40;
tek(0,m,&bigk,&e);
v=u*pi/(2.*bigk);
theta(v,m,&t1,&t2,&t3,&t4);
theta(0.,m,&t10,&t20,&t30,&t40);
*ts=t1*bigk*2./(pi*t20*t30*t40);
*tc=t2/t20;
*td=t3/t30;
*tn=t4/t40;
return 0;
}
```

```
/*
Elliptic Integral of Third Kind

from C Mathematical Function Handbook by Louis Baker
Copyright 1991 by Louis Baker. All rights reserved.
*/

#include <stdio.h>
#include "cmlib.h"
#include "protom.h"

double e3(n,phi,m,sig) double n,phi,m,sig;
{
int choice;
double eps=1.e-6,sin(),cos(),pye,ms,cs,new,p1,y,dp,x,
dnr,ddr,t1,t2,t3,   atan(),tan(),log(),sqrt(),
fp,ep,sinp,secp,tanp,snp,snm,sqn,sqm,tpd,tpn,
ca,tp,rhs,py,dpn,dpd,s2p,sgn;
choice=0;
if(n==0.)
   {if(m==0.)return phi;tef(phi,m,sig,&fp,&ep);return fp;
   }
if(n>0. && n<m)choice=1;
if(n>1.)choice=2;
if(n>m && n<1.)choice=3;
if(n<0.)choice=4;
if( abs(n)<=eps && m>eps)choice=5;
if( abs(n)<=eps && m<=eps)choice=6;
if(m<eps && abs(n)>eps)choice=7;
if(m==1. && n!=1.)choice=8;
ms=sqrt(m);
if( abs(n-ms)<=eps || abs(n+ms)<=eps)choice=9;
cs=sqrt(1.-m);
if( abs(n-1.-cs)<eps || abs(n-1.+cs)<eps)choice=11;
if(abs(n-m)<=eps)choice=13;

switch (choice)
{
case 1:
   e3n1m(n,phi,m,sig,&pye);
   return pye;
case 2:
   new=m/n;
   p1=sqrt((m-1.)*(1.-new));
   tef(phi,m,sig,&fp,&ep);
   y=sin(phi);
   dp=sqrt(1.-m*y*y);
   x=p1*tan(phi);
   dnr=dp+x;
```

```
   ddr=dp-x;
   t3=.5/p1*log(dnr/ddr);
   e3nlm(new,phi,m,sig,&pye);
   pye= -pye+fp+t3;
   return pye;
case 3:
   e3mln(n,phi,m,sig,&pye);
   return pye;
case 4:
   new=(m-n)/(1.-n);
   p1=sqrt(-n*new);
   e3mln(new,phi,m,sig,&pye);
   t1=sqrt((1.-new)*(1.-m/new))*pye;
   tef(phi,m,sig,&fp,&ep);
   t2=m/p1*fp;
   x=sin(phi);
   dp=sqrt(1.-m*x*x);
   t3=atan(.5*p1*sin(2.*phi)/dp);
   pye=(t1+t2+t3)/sqrt((1.-n)*(1.-m/n));
   return pye;
case 5:
   tef(phi,m,sig,&pye,&ep);
   return pye;
case 6:   return phi;
case 7:
   if(n==1.)
      return tan(phi);
   if(n<1.)
      p1=sqrt(1.-n);
   else
      p1=sqrt(n-1.);
   return atan(p1*tan(phi))/p1;
case 8:
   secp=1./cos(phi);
   sinp=sin(phi);
   tanp=sinp*secp;
   t1= log(tanp+secp);
   sqn=sqrt(n);
   x=sqn*sinp;
   snp=1.+x;
   snm=1.-x;
   t2=.5*sqn*log(snp/snm);
   return (t1-t2)/(1.-n);
case 9:
   tp=tan(phi);
   x=sin(phi);
   dp=sqrt(1.-m*x*x);
   sqm=sqrt(m);
   if(abs(n-ms)<=eps) sgn=-1.;
```

```
    else sgn=1.;
    y=1.+sgn*sqm;
    rhs=atan(y*tp/dp);
    py=rhs/y;
    tef(phi,m,sig,&fp,&ep);
    return .5*(py+fp);
 case 11:
    tp=tan(phi);
    x=sin(phi);
    ca=sqrt(1.-m);
    dp=sqrt(1.-m*x*x);
    y=tp*dp;
    tpn=1.+y;
    tpd=1.-y;
    if(abs(n-1.+cs)<=eps)sgn=-1.;
    else sgn=1.;
    y=ca*tp;
    dpn=dp+y;
    dpd=dp-y;
    tef(phi,m,sig,&fp,&ep);
    t1= sgn*.5*log(tpn/tpd);
    t2=.5*log(dpn/dpd);
    t3=-sgn*(1.-sgn*ca)*fp;
    return (t1+t2+t3)/(2.*ca);
 case 13:
    tef(phi,m,sig,&fp,&ep);
    p1=1./(1.-m);
    t2=m*p1;
    s2p=sin(2.*phi);
    y=sin(phi);
    dp=sqrt(1.-m*y*y);
    t1=p1*ep;
    t2 *=s2p/(2.*dp);
    return t1-t2;
/*if( abs(n-1.)<eps && m>eps)
    {
    }*/
default:
tef(phi,m,sig,&fp,&ep);
tp=tan(phi);
y=sin(phi);
p1=1./(1.-m);
dp=sqrt(1.-m*y*y);
pye=fp-p1*ep+p1*tp*dp;
return pye;
}
}

e3nlm(n,phi,m,sig,pye) double n,phi,m,sig,*pye;
```

```
{
int i;
double
x,k,e,b,fe,ee,asin(),sqrt(),exp(),tan(),sin(),tol=1.e-7,

xq,q,q2,m1,y,z,d1,v,ris,term,sum1,sum2,cotb,k1,e1,fp,ep,arg;
x=n/m;
e=asin(sqrt(x));
tef(e,m,sig,&fe,&ee);
tek(0,m,&k,&e);
b=pi*.5*fe/k;
cotb=1./tan(b);
m1=1.-m;
tek(0,m1,&k1,&e1);
tef(phi,m,sig,&fp,&ep);
arg=-pi*k1/k;
q=exp(arg);
v=pi*.5*fp/k;
xq=1.;
d1=sqrt(n/((1.-n)*(m-n)));
sum1=sum2=0.;
for(i=1;i<200;i++)
    {
    ris=i;
    xq*=q;
    if(xq<1.e-15)break;
    term=2.*xq*sin(2.*ris*v)*sin(2.*ris*b)/(ris*(1.-xq*xq));
    sum1+=term;
    if(i>1 && (abs(term)<tol)||( abs(term)/sum1 <sig)) break;
    }
y=sin(2.*b);
z=cos(2.*b);
xq=1.;
q2=q*q;
for(i=0;i<200;i++)
    {
    xq*=q2;
    if(xq<1.e-14)break;
    term=4.*xq*y/(1.+xq*(xq-2.*z));
    sum2+=term;
    if(i && (abs(term)<tol)||( abs(term)/sum2 <sig)) break;
    }
*pye=d1*(v*(cotb+sum2)-sum1);
return 0;
}

e3mln(n,phi,m,sig,pye) double n,phi,m,sig,*pye;
{
int i,iq;
```

```
double
cosh(),sinh(),pow(),exp(),asin(),sqrt(),tanh(),atan(),
e,m1,fe1,e1,fp,ep,km1,em1,b,q,xx,term,
   ris,s2sv,sb,sb2,km,em,qs,arg,
   sum1,sum2,sum3,sgn,q2,q2s,d2,v,
tol=1.e-7,qs2,mu,lm,thb,tv;
e=asin(sqrt((1.-n)/(1.-m)));
m1=1.-m;
tef(e,m1,sig,&fe1,&e1);
tek(0,m,&km,&em);
tef(phi,m,sig,&fp,&ep);
tek(0,m1,&km1,&em1);
b=.5*pi*fe1/km;
arg=-pi*km1/km;
q=exp(arg);
xx=fp/km;
if(xx>.99999)xx=.99999;
v=.5*pi*xx;
d2=sqrt(n/((1.-n)*(n-m)));
q2=q*q;
q2s=1.;
sum1=sum2=sum3=0.;
sgn=-1.;
for(i=1;i<200;i++)
   {
   ris=i;
   sgn=-sgn;
   q2s*=q2;
   s2sv=sin(2.*ris*v);
   sb2=2.*ris*b;
   if(abs(sb2)>10.)
      {
      sb=1.e10;
      if(sb2<-10.) sb=0.;
      }
   else sb=sinh(sb2);
   term=2.*sgn*q2s*s2sv*sb/(ris*(1.-q2s));
   sum1+=term;
   if(i>1 && (abs(term)<tol)||( abs(term)/sum1 <sig)) break;
   }
qs2=q;
for(i=1;i<200;i++)
   {
   ris=i;
   sb2=2.*ris*b;
   term=ris*qs2*sinh(sb2);
   sum2+=term;
   iq=(i<<1)+1;
   qs2*= pow(q,(double)iq);
```

```
    if(qs2<1.e-8)break;
    if(i>1 && (abs(term)<tol)||( abs(term)/sum2 <sig)) break;
    }
qs=q;
for(i=1;i<200;i++)
    {
    ris=i;
    sb2=2.*ris*b;
    term=2.*cosh(sb2)*qs;
    sum3+=term;
    iq=(i<<1)+1;
    qs2*= pow(q,(double)iq);
    if(qs2<1.e-8)break;
    if(i>1 && (abs(term)<tol)||( abs(term)/sum3 <sig)) break;
    }
thb=tanh(b);/* b as in my FTN or of sb2 math notes?*/
tv=tan(v);
lm=atan(thb*tv)+sum1;
mu=sum2/(1.+sum3);
*pye=d2*(lm-4.*mu*v);
return 0;
}
```

```
/*
Jacobian elliptic function complex argument
   and Weierstrass P, sigma, zeta functions

from C Mathematical Function Handbook by Louis Baker
Copyright 1991 by Louis Baker. All rights reserved.

cjef   complex jacobian elliptic functions sn,cn,dn
weier   Weierstrass function P,derivative P',
eta=zeta(ometa),etc.
sigma   call weier and then use parameters to obtain
Weierstrass sigma

ctld-logarithmic derivative of the theta functions, and
zeta, the Weierstrass zeta function, should be used with
caution.

Note zeta has a singularity at the origin

*/
#include <stdio.h>
#include "cmlib.h"
#include "protom.h"

cjef(u,m,sn,cn,dn) double m; struct complex *u,*sn,*cn,*dn;
{double w,s,c,d,s1,c1,d1;struct complex z;
jef(u->x,m,&s,&c,&d);
jef(u->y,1.-m,&s1,&c1,&d1);
w=1./( c1*c1+m*s*s*s1*s1);
CMPLX(z,w*(s*d1),w*(c*d*s1*c1));CSET(sn,z);
CMPLX(z,w*(c*c1),-w*(s*d*s1*d1));CSET(cn,z);
CMPLX(z,w*(d*c1*d1),-w*(s*m*s1*c));CSET(dn,z);
return 0;
}

static double ratiov;

double ratmp(m) double m;
{double x,y,z,p;
x=m-2.;y=2.*m-1.;z=m+1.;p=m*(m-1.)+1.;
if(p==0. || y==0.)
   {fprintf(stderr,
   " zero denom. in ratmp m=%le x=%le y=%le\n",m,x,y);
   return errorcode;}
return .25*x*x*y*y*z*z/(p*p*p)-ratiov;
}

double ratmm(m) double m;
{double x,y,p;
```

```
/* return negative infinity for m=.5*/
if(m>=.5)return -1.e37;/* avoid overflw if single prec*/
x=32.*m*(m-1.)-1.;y=2.*m-1.;p=16.*m*(m-1.)+1.;
/*printf(" ratmm x y %le %le\n",x,y);*/
if(x==0. || y==0.)
   {fprintf(stderr,
   " zero denom. in ratmm m=%le x=%le y=%le\n",m,x,y);
   return errorcode;}
return (p*p*p)/(x*x*y*y)-ratiov;
}

#define maxit 30
#define tol 1.e-5

double solvem(ratio,mu,ml,ratv) double ratio,mu,ml,
(*ratv)();
{
 int i;
 double x,mbtm,mtop,value, topv,btmv,reltol=1.e-
4,abstol=1.e-8,brent();
/* does it change sign from ml to mu? if not can't use
brent*/
mbtm=ml;mtop=mu;     ratiov=ratio;
topv=ratv(mu);btmv=ratv(ml);
if(topv*btmv<0.)  return brent(mbtm,mtop,rel-
tol,abstol,ratv);
/* cant use brent  use bisection????????*/
fprintf(stderr,
" solvem using bisection, not brent %le %le\n",topv,btmv);
 for(i=0;i<maxit;i++)
   {
   x=.5*(mbtm+mtop);
   value=ratv(x);
/*printf(" value=%le for x=%le\n",value,x);*/
   if(value==0.)return x;
   else if(value>0.) mbtm=x;
   else mtop=x;
   if( abs(value)<tol)break;
   }
value=.5*(mbtm+mtop);
/*printf(" solvem rv=%le %le %le %d\n",value,
mbtm,mtop,i);*/
return value;

}

#define critm .066987398
/*critm=.5-sqrt(3)/4 */
```

```
double getm(g2,g3,d) int d; double g2,g3;
{double ml,mu,x,pow(),rat,rv;
if(d)
   {/* disc >0*/
   rat=g3*g3*27./(g2*g2*g2);
   ml=0.;mu=.5;
   return solvem(rat,mu,ml,ratmp);
   }
else
   {/* disc <0 */
   rat=(g2*g2*g2)/(27.*g3*g3);
   if (rat>=0.)
      {mu= critm ;
      ml=0.;
      }
   else
      {
      ml= critm ;
      mu=.5;
      }
/*printf(" getm: ml, mu %le %le\n",ml,mu);*/
   rv=solvem(rat,mu,ml,ratmm);
/*printf(" solvem returned %le\n",rv);*/
   return rv;
   }
return 0.;
}

weir(z,g2,g3,p,pp,mp,kp,ep,omegap,eta,ehp)
double g2,g3,*mp,*kp,*ep,*omegap,*ehp,*eta; struct complex
*z,*p,*pp;
{
int dpos;
struct complex ci,x,q,qp,aux,sn,cn,dn,aux2;
double pow(),discr,d1,d2,sqrt(),k,e,m,omega,
om2,e1,e2,e3,h2,c,ee,getm();

CMPLX(ci,0.,1.);
if(g3<0.) {
CMULT(x,ci,*z);weir(&x,g2,g3,&q,&qp,mp,kp,ep,omegap,eta,ehp);

   CMPLX(aux,0.,0.);CSUB(*p,aux,q);CSUB(*pp,aux,qp);
   return 1;
   }
d1= 27.*g3*g3;d2=(g2*g2*g2);
discr=d2-d1;
/*printf(" discr=%le\n",discr);*/
if( discr==0.) /* DEGENERATE CASE not doubly-periodic */
   { /* g3>=0*/
```

```
    if( g3==0. /* && g2==0. */)
       {
       CMPLX(aux,1.,0.);CDIV(q,aux,*z);CDIV((*p),aux,*z);
       CDIV((*pp),*p,*z);CTREAL(*pp,*pp,-2.);return 0;
       }
    c=sqrt(abs(g2/12.));
    CMPLX(aux,c,0.); if(g2<0.){CMULT(q,ci,aux);CLET(aux,q);}
    /*p= -c+3c/ {sin [sqrt(3c)z]}^2*/
    ee=sqrt(3.*c);
    CTREAL( aux, *z,ee);csin(&aux,&aux2);
    CMULT(aux,aux2,aux2);
CMPLX(aux2,3.*c,0.);CDIV(q,aux2,aux);
    CLET(*p,q);p->x -=c;
    ccot(&aux,&qp);CTREAL(qp,qp,-2.*ee);CMULT(*pp,qp,q);
    return 1;
    }
else if(discr>0.)
    {
    /*find 0<m<.5*/
    if(g3==0.)m=.5;
    else m=getm(g2,g3,1);
    tek(0,m,&k,&ee);
    omega= sqrt(sqrt(4./3.*(m*(m-1.)+1.)/g2))*k;
    e= k*k/(3.*omega*omega);
    e1=e*(2.-m);e3=-e*(1.+m);e=sqrt(abs(e1-e3));
/*printf(" omega=%e,e1=%e,e3=%e, sqrt(dif)
%e\n",omega,e1,e3,e);*/
    *omegap=omega; *ehp=e;
    *eta= k/(3.*omega)*(3.*ee+(m-2.)*k);
    if((e1-e3)>0.){CMPLX(aux,e,0.);}
    else   {CMPLX(aux,0.,e);}
    CMULT(x,*z,aux);
    cjef(&x,m,&sn,&cn,&dn);
    CMULT(aux2,sn,sn);
    CMPLX(q,(e1-e3),0.);
    CDIV(qp,q,aux2);
    qp.x+=e3;CSET(p,qp);
    CMULT(q,aux2,sn);
    CDIV(qp,cn,q);
    CMULT(q,qp,dn);
    CTREAL(q,q,-2.*(e1-e3));
    CMULT(*pp ,q,aux);
    }
else    /* discr<0.*/
    {
    /* find m*/
    /*   printf(" discr\n");*/
    if(g2==0.) m= critm ;
    else m=getm(g2,g3,0);
```

```
/*printf(" after getm m=%le g2,3 %le %le\n",m,g2,g3);*/
   tek(0,m,&k,&ee);
   om2= k*pow( 8.*(2.*m-1.)*(32.*m*(m-1.)-
1.)/(27.*g3),1./6.) ;
   if(om2==0.)
      {fprintf(stderr," om2==0. in weir\n");
      p->x=errorcode;p->y=errorcode;
      pp->x=errorcode;pp->y=errorcode;
      return 1;
      }
   e=k*k/(3.*om2*om2);
   e2=2.*(1.-2.*m)*e;
   h2= .75*e2/(.5-m);
   e=sqrt(abs(h2));
/*printf(" omega2=%e,e2=%e,h2=%e, sqrt(dif)
%e\n",om2,e2,h2,e);*/
   *omegap=om2;*ehp=h2;
   *eta=k/(3.*om2)*(6.*ee+(4.*m-5.)*k);
   if(h2>0.){CMPLX(aux,e,0.);}
   else{CMPLX(aux,0.,e)};
   CMULT(x,*z,aux);
   CTREAL(x,x,2.);
   cjef(&x,m,&sn,&cn,&dn);
   CLET(q,cn);q.x+=1.;
   CMPLX(aux2,1.,0.);CSUB(aux2,aux2,cn);
   if(cabs(aux2)==0.)
      {fprintf(stderr," cn= %e %e divide
error\n",cn.x,cn.y);
      p->x=errorcode;p->y=errorcode;
      pp->x=errorcode;pp->y=errorcode;
      return 1;
      }
   CDIV(qp,q,aux2);
   CTREAL(qp,qp,h2);qp.x+=e2;CSET(p,qp);
   CMULT(qp,aux2,aux2);
   if(cabs(qp)==0.)
      {fprintf(stderr," qp==0. in weir\n");
      p->x=errorcode;p->y=errorcode;
      pp->x=errorcode;pp->y=errorcode;
      return 1;
      }
   CMULT(q,sn,dn);CDIV(aux2,q,qp);
   CMULT(q,aux2,aux);
   CTREAL(q,q,-4.*h2);CSET(pp,q);
   }
*mp=m;*ep=e;*kp=k;
return 0;
}
```

```
ctld(v,q,t1,t2,t3,t4) struct complex *v,*q,*t1,*t2,*t3,*t4;
{/* log derv. theta functions*/
double si;
struct complex
sin,cos,denom,qn,q2n,one,ti,fact1,fact2,q2,x,e2ui,e2uii;
struct complex q2e2,q2e2i,qe2,qe2i;
struct complex term1,term2,term3,term4,sum1,sum2,sum3,sum4;
int n,itmax=1000;
CMPLX(one,1.,0.); CMPLX(ti,0.,2.);
ctrig(v,&cos,&sin);
CDIV((*t1),cos,sin);CDIV((*t2),sin,cos);CTREAL(*t2,*t2,-1.);
CMPLX(*t4,0.,0.); CSET(t3,*t4);
/*printf(" cot %e %e\n",t1->x,t1->y);*/
CLET(qn,*q);CMULT(q2,qn,qn);CLET(q2n,q2);
CMPLX(sum1,0.,0.);
CLET(sum2,sum1);CLET(sum3,sum1);CLET(sum4,sum1);si=-1.;
CMULT(x,ti,*v);cexp(&x,&e2ui);CDIV(e2uii,one,e2ui);
CSUB(x,e2uii,e2ui); /*if( cabs(x)<1.e-10) return;*/
CMULT(q2e2,q2n,e2ui);CMULT(q2e2i,q2n,e2uii);
CMULT(qe2,qn,e2ui);CMULT(qe2i,qn,e2uii);
if(cabs(qn)>=1.)printf(" warn ctld q= %e %e
|q|1\n",qn.x,qn.y);
for(n=1;n<itmax;n++)
   {
   CSUB(denom,one,q2n);
   CSUB(x,q2e2,q2e2i);CDIV(term1,x,denom);
   CLET(term2,term1);
   CTREAL(term2,term2,si);
   CSUB(x,qe2,qe2i);CDIV(term4,x,denom);
   CLET(term3,term4);
   CTREAL(term3,term3,si);
   CADD(sum1,sum1,term1);
/*printf(" sum1, term1 %e %e %e %e
%d\n",sum1.x,sum1.y,term1.x,term1.y,n);*/
   CADD(sum2,sum2,term2);
   CADD(sum3,sum3,term3);
   CADD(sum3,sum4,term4);
   if(cabs(sin)>1.e-3){
   if( cabs(term4)<tol*cabs(sum2) &&
cabs(term1)<tol*cabs(sum1))break;}
   if( cabs(sum1)<tol && n>10)break;
   /* for u=0,pi/2 type cases*/
   CMULT(sin,q2e2,q2);CMULT(q2e2,sin,e2ui);
   CMULT(sin,q2e2i,q2);CMULT(q2e2i,sin,e2uii);
   CMULT(sin,qe2,qn);CMULT(qe2,sin,e2ui);
   CMULT(sin,qe2i,qn);CMULT(qe2i,sin,e2uii);
   si=-si;
   /* avoid an overflow*/
   if( cabs(term4)>1.e10 || cabs(term1)>1.e10)break;
```

```
   }
CMULT(sin,sum1,ti);
/*printf(" sum1 %e %e,term1 %e %e
%d\n",sum1.x,sum1.y,term1.x,term1.y,n);*/
CMULT(cos,sum2,ti);
CMULT(*t3,sum3,ti);
CMULT(*t4,sum4,ti);
CADD(*t1,*t1,sin);CADD(*t2,*t2,cos);
return 0;
}

sigma(z,ans,k,omega,eta,m,g2,g3) struct complex *z,*ans;
double k,omega,eta,m,g2,g3;
{struct complex v,dum1,dum2,q,t1,t2,t3,t4;double
kp,ep,exp(),delta;
CLET(v,*z);CTREAL(v,v,pi*.5/omega);
/*printf(" omega= %e m= %e eta=%e k=%e\n",omega,m,eta,k);*/
CMULT(dum1,*z,*z);CTREAL(dum1,dum1,eta/(2.*omega));
cexp(&dum1,&dum2);
/*printf(" before tek\n");*/
tek(0,1.-m,&kp,&ep);
/*printf(" after tek\n");*/
delta= g2*g2*g2-27.*g3*g3;
if(delta>0.)
   {CMPLX(q,exp(-pi*kp/k) ,0.);}
else
   {CMPLX(q,0.,exp(-pi*.5*kp/k));}
/*printf(" before ctheta v= %e %e q=%e
%e\n",v.x,v.y,q.x,q.y);*/
ctheta(&v,&q,&t1,&t2,&t3,&t4);
/*printf(" after ctheta\n");*/
CMULT(v,t1,dum2);/*v= exp()*t1(v)*/
CMPLX(dum1,0.,0.);
/*printf(" before theta(0)\n");*/
ctheta(&dum1,&q,&t1,&t2,&t3,&t4);
/*printf(" after theta(0)\n");*/
CDIV(dum1,v,t2);CDIV(dum2,dum1,t3);CDIV((*ans) ,dum2,t4);
CTREAL (*ans,*ans,2.*omega/pi);
return 0;
}

zetaw(z,ans,k,omega,eta,m,g2,g3)
struct complex *z,*ans;double k,omega,eta,m,g2,g3;
{struct complex v,dum1,dum2,q,t1,t2,t3,t4;
double kp,ep,exp(),pow(),delta,mp,op,et,ehp,g2n,g3n;int n;
/* convergence trouble in cthld if |Im(z)| big */

/* try to use period relations to reduce Im z */
if(abs(z->y)>2.)
```

```
    {
    tek(0,1.-m,&kp,&ep);op=omega*kp/k;
    delta= g2*g2*g2-27.*g3*g3;
    if( delta>0.)   n=(int)((z->y)/(2.*op));
    else
        {/*op=omega2',want complex omega*/
        n=(int)(z->y/(op));
        }
/*printf(" reducing? op=%e n %d\n",op,n);*/
    if(n)
        {
        CLET(v,*z);
        if(delta>=0.)
            {v.y-=n*2.*op;
            CMPLX(dum2,0.,(eta*op-.5*pi)/omega);}
        else
            {v.y-=n*op;v.x-=n*omega;
            CMPLX(dum2,0.,(eta*op-pi)/omega);}
        zetaw(&v,&dum1,k,omega,eta,m,g2,g3);
        CTREAL(dum2,dum2, 2.*n);
        CADD(*ans,dum1,dum2);
        return 0;
        }
    }
if(abs(z->y)>.5 && omega>1.1)
/* if omega not big no use only reduce once*/
    {/* for big |Im(z)| use */
    g2n=g2/pow(omega,4.);g3n=g3/pow(omega,6.);
/*printf(" reducing omega=%e,g2n g3n %e
%e\n",omega,g2n,g3n);*/
    CLET(v,*z);CTREAL(v,v,1./omega);
    weir(&v,g2n,g3n,&t1,&t2,&mp,&kp,&ep,&op,&et,&ehp);
    zetaw(&v,&t3,kp,op,et,mp,g2n,g3n);
/*printf(" redu return\n");*/
    CTREAL(t3,t3,1./omega);
    CSET(ans,t3);
    return 0;
    }

CLET(v,*z);CTREAL(v,v,pi*.5/omega);
tek(0,1.-m,&kp,&ep);
delta= g2*g2*g2-27.*g3*g3;
printf(" g2, g3 delta %e %e %e\n",g2,g3,delta);
if(delta>0.)
    {CMPLX(q,exp(-pi*kp/k) ,0.);}
else
    {CMPLX(q,0.,exp(-pi*.5*kp/k));}
CSET(ans,*z);CTREAL(*ans,*ans,eta/omega);
ctld(&v,&q,&t1,&t2,&t3,&t4);
```

```
CTREAL(t1,t1,pi/(2.*omega));
CADD(*ans,*ans,t1);
return 0;
}
```

```
/*
Complex Elliptic Theta functions
   Copyright 1989,1991 Louis Baker. All rights reserved.
ctheta   theta functions complex v,q. v is (pi/2) times
   the value 2v used in Jahne & Emde's tables.
q   nome q given m for 0<= m,q <= 1
mq   m given q for 0<= m,q <= 1
emf   elliptic modular function m given q for complex q
emft     "         "        "       m given t complex t, q=
exp( i pi t)
amc   amplitude given complex m,u (see te.c for real values,
   set either by am() or in global double amplitude set by
jef)

*/
#include "cmlib.h"
#include "protom.h"

#define max(a,b) ((a)>(b)?(a):(b))
#define min(a,b) ((a)<(b)?(a):(b))
#define itmax 5000
#define tol 1.e-7

/* v is complex. q is complex, |q|<1, q= exp( -piK'/K)
v=pi*u/(2K)
where u is the argument of big-theta, sn, etc.*/

ctheta(v,q,ct1,ct2,ct3,ct4)struct complex
*v,*q,*ct4,*ct3,*ct1,*ct2;
{/* t1,t2 converge more slowly that t3,t4 for larger |q|-
it may be desirable to split the evaluation into separate
functions
in some applications if only t3 or t4 desired*/
struct complex sum,p2,d1,d2,one,term,logq,d3,d4,sum3;
struct complex sum1,sum2,qn1,s1,c1,ci,expiz;
double magv,si,old,older,oldest,worst;int vnonz;long int i;
old=older=oldest=10.; CMPLX(ci,0.,1.);
CMPLX(sum,1.,0.);CMPLX(d1,0.,2.);CMULT(p2,d1,(*v));
CMPLX(one,1.,0.);CLET(sum3,sum);
magv = cabs((*v));vnonz= magv>1.e-15;
if( vnonz)ctrig(v,&c1,&s1);
else {CMPLX(c1,1.,0.);CMPLX(s1,0.,0.);}
CLET(sum1,s1);CLET(sum2,c1);
CTREAL(sum1,sum1,2.);CTREAL(sum2,sum2,2.);CTREAL(c1,p2,.5);
if(vnonz)cexp(&c1,&expiz);
else{CLET(expiz,one);};
if(cabs((*q))>=1.)
    {
    ct1->x=ct2->x=ct3->x=ct4->x=errorcode;
```

```
   ct1->y=ct2->y=ct3->y=ct4->y=errorcode;return 1;
   }
si=-1.;clog(q,&logq);
for(i=11;i<itmax;i++)
   {
   CTREAL(d1,logq,(double)i*i);cexp(&d1,&d2);
   CTREAL(d1,logq,(double)i*(i+1));cexp(&d1,&qn1);
   if(vnonz)
      {
      CTREAL(d1,p2,(double)i);cexp(&d1,&d3);
      if(cabs(d3)>1.e-20){CDIV(d4,one,d3);}
      else {CMPLX(d4,1.e20,0.);}
      CADD(d4,d4,d3);
      }
   else     {CMPLX(d3,1.,0.);CMPLX(d4,2.,0.);}
   CMULT(term,d2,d4);
/*printf(" cabs term %e %e\n",term.x,term.y);*/
   oldest=cabs(term);
   CADD(sum3,sum3,term);
   CTREAL(term,term,si);
   CADD(sum,sum,term);
   CMULT(d1,d3,expiz);
/*printf(" cabs d1 %e %e\n",d1.x,d1.y);*/
   if(cabs(d1)>1.e-20){CDIV(d4,one,d1);}
   else {CMPLX(d4,1.e20,0.);}
   CADD(c1,d1,d4);
   CMULT(term,qn1,c1);
   CADD(sum2,sum2,term);
/*printf(" cabs term %e %e\n",term.x,term.y);*/
   older=cabs(term);
   CSUB(term,d1,d4);CMULT(s1,term,ci);CTREAL(s1,s1,-1.);
   CMULT(term,qn1,s1);
   CTREAL(term,term,si);
   CADD(sum1,sum1,term);
/*printf(" cabs term %e %e\n",term.x,term.y);*/
   old=cabs(term);
/*   worst= max(old,max(older,oldest));*/
/*printf(" cabs term %e %e %e %e %e %e\n",
   sum1.x,sum1.y,sum2.x,sum2.y,sum.x,sum.y);*/
   if( cabs(sum1)*tol>old && cabs(sum2)*tol>older
   && cabs(sum)*tol>oldest )break;
/*   oldest=older;
   older=old;*/
   si=-si;
   }
CSET(ct4,sum); CSET(ct3,sum3);
CTREAL(logq,logq,.25);cexp(&logq,&term);
CMULT( *ct1,term,sum1);CMULT(*ct2,term,sum2);
return 0;
```

```
}
/* given complex theta4, sn,cn,dn, theta1=
sn*theta4(v)*theta2/theta3,
 2= cn*theta4(v)*theta2/theta4, 3=
dn*theat4(v)*theta3/theta4*/

double q(m) double m;
{double k,alpha,cos(),c,asin(),src,eps,e4,q,a;
int flip;
/*k=sqrt(m); alpha= asin(k);     c=cos(alpha);*/
if(m==1.)return 1.;
/* better convergence for eps near 1/2 to switch k,k' and
use
log q * log q' = pi^2*/
flip=0;
if(m> .5 )
   {flip=1;
   c=sqrt(m);
   }
else c= sqrt(1.-m);/* suffices for 0<=m<=1*/
src=sqrt(c);
eps=.5*(1.-src)/(1.+src);
e4= eps*eps; e4*=e4;
a=15.*e4;/* ratio of coeff. is abt 15 at final retained
term,
asymptotes to 16. e4 is <= 1/16 . approx sum geometric
series
for omitted terms as 1/(1-a)*/
q=eps*
 (1.+e4*(2.+e4*(15.+e4*(150.+e4*(1701.+e4*(20910.

+e4*(268616.+e4*(3567400.+e4*(48555069.+e4*(673458874./(1.-
a)))))))))));
if(flip)
   {q= exp(pi*pi/log(q)); }
return q;
}

#define itlimit 50
#define tol 3.e-8
int itermq;

double mq(q) double q;
{double eps,ep-
sold,q8,q4,q2,nmult,num,denom,dmult,nterm,dterm,k;
q2=q*q;q4=q2*q2;q8=q4*q4;itermq=0;
nterm=q*q4*q4;num= q;nmult=q8*q8;
denom=1.;dterm=2.*q4;dmult=q4*q8;
epsold=0.;
```

```
while(itermq<itlimit)
   {num+=nterm;
   denom+=dterm;
   eps=num/denom;
   /*printf(" eps,epsold %le %le %le\n",
    eps, epsold,eps-epsold);*/
   if( abs(eps-epsold)<tol && eps<=.5)break;
   epsold=eps;
   nterm*=nmult;
   nmult*=q8;
   dterm*=dmult;
   dmult*=q8;
   itermq++;
   }
eps=min(.5,eps);
eps*=2.;
k = (1.-eps)/(1.+eps);
k*=k;/* epsold= (1+eps*(eps-2.))/(1+eps*(eps+2.));
printf(" k, alternate %le %le\n",k,epsold);*/
return 1.-(k*k);
}

emf(q,m) struct complex *q,*m;
{struct complex zero,rat,rat2,t1,t2,t3,t4;
CMPLX(zero,0.,0.);
ctheta(&zero,q,&t1,&t2,&t3,&t4);
CDIV(rat,t2,t3);CMULT(rat2,rat,rat);
CMULT((*m),rat2,rat2);
return 0;
}

emft(t,m)struct complex *t,*m;
{struct complex q,cip,arg;
CMPLX(cip,0.,pi);CMULT(arg,cip,(*t));cexp(&arg,&q);
emf(&q,m);
return 0;
}

amc(x,m,ans) double m;struct complex *x,*ans;
{
struct complex ci,z2,arg,sum,z,cn,dn;
cjef(x,m,&z,&cn,&dn);
CMULT(z2,z,z);
CMPLX(ci,0.,1.);CMPLX(arg,1.,0.);CSUB(arg,arg,z2);
clog(&arg,&sum);CTREAL(sum,sum,.5);cexp(&sum,&arg);
CMULT(sum,z,ci);CADD(sum,sum,arg);clog(&sum,&arg);
CMULT(sum,arg,ci);CTREAL((*ans),sum,-1.);
return 0;
}
```

```
/* for Am(z) use asin( sn(z)); if complex,
   asin = -i log(iz+sqrt(1-z^2)) */
```

```
 Output: Test Driver for Elliptic functions
E(u) enter mag u, theta(deg), m(==0. to quit)
1.5 20 .6
 for m=6.000000e-01 theta(rad)=3.490659e-01,|u|=1.500000e+00
 1.104633e+00 + 2.300319e-01 i  E(u) enter mag u,
theta(deg), m(==0. to quit)
.5 220 .9
 for m=9.000000e-01 theta(rad)=3.839724e+00,
|u|=5.000000e-01
 -3.983972e-01  -2.880332e-01 i  E(u) enter mag u,
theta(deg), m(==0. to quit)
1 100 .3
 for m=3.000000e-01 theta(rad)=1.745329e+00,|u|=1.000000e+00
 -2.507125e-01 + 1.089930e+00 i  E(u) enter mag u,
theta(deg), m(==0. to quit)
0 0 0
 K,E(m) enter m(==0. to quit)
.25
 K,E= 1.685750e+00 1.467462e+00
 K,E(m) enter m(==0. to quit)
.75
 K,E= 2.156516e+00 1.211056e+00
 K,E(m) enter m(==0. to quit)
0
 for tef(incomplete): enter m (-1 to quit) .25
enter phi.52359878
 at phi=5.235988e-01,m=2.500000e-01,F=5.294290e-01
E=5.178819e-01 Z=5.700875e-02
 for tef(incomplete): enter m (-1 to quit) .75
enter phi.78539816
 at phi=7.853982e-01,m=7.500000e-01,F=8.512266e-01
E=7.282241e-01 Z=2.501923e-01
 for tef(incomplete): enter m (-1 to quit) -1
 tef: enter m -1. to quit -1
 complete integrals
 5.000000e-02 1.591003e+00 1.550973e+00
 1.000000e-01 1.612441e+00 1.530758e+00
 1.500000e-01 1.635257e+00 1.510122e+00
 2.000000e-01 1.659624e+00 1.489035e+00
 2.500000e-01 1.685750e+00 1.467462e+00
 3.000000e-01 1.713889e+00 1.445363e+00
 3.500000e-01 1.744351e+00 1.422691e+00
 4.000000e-01 1.777519e+00 1.399392e+00
 4.500000e-01 1.813884e+00 1.375402e+00
 5.000000e-01 1.854075e+00 1.350644e+00
 5.500000e-01 1.898925e+00 1.325024e+00
 6.000000e-01 1.949568e+00 1.298428e+00
 6.500000e-01 2.007598e+00 1.270707e+00
 7.000000e-01 2.075363e+00 1.241671e+00
```

```
 7.500000e-01 2.156516e+00 1.211056e+00
 8.000000e-01 2.257205e+00 1.178490e+00
 incomplete, 30deg
 alpha=0.261799 0.0669873  5.251436e-01 5.220747e-01
 alpha=0.523599 0.25  5.294679e-01 5.178778e-01
 alpha=0.785398 0.5  5.357661e-01 5.120406e-01
 alpha=1.047198 0.75  5.424824e-01 5.060853e-01
 jzeta
 5.700875e-02
 jacobian elliptic
 .2|.81 sn=1.976208e-01 cn=9.802785e-01 dn=9.840560e-01
8.032024e-01
 .2|.19 sn=1.984231e-01 cn=9.801165e-01 dn=9.962527e-01
jtheta=9.755420e-01
 .75342|.7 sn=6.513735e-01 cn=7.587572e-01 dn=8.384502e-01
9.376462e-01
 .6|.36 sn=5.546958e-01 cn=8.320532e-01 dn=9.429913e-01
9.735688e-01
 heuman=4.677347e-01
 neville s,c,d,n 5.367643e-01 8.657458e-01 9.826509e-01
1.018642e+00
 e3: enter n phi m  all 0 to end.
0 .52359878 .25
 0 0.523599 0.250000 5.294369e-01
 e3: enter n phi m  all 0 to end.
.6 .52359878 .25
 0.6 0.523599 0.250000 5.600123e-01
 e3: enter n phi m  all 0 to end.
.1 .52359878 .25
 0.1 0.523599 0.250000 5.341253e-01
 e3: enter n phi m  all 0 to end.
.1 .52360 .75
 0.1 0.523600 0.750000 5.471092e-01
 e3: enter n phi m  all 0 to end.
.1 1.57079 .75
 0.1 1.570790 0.750000 2.293381e+00
 e3: enter n phi m  all 0 to end.
0 0 0
 Weierstrass:enter z=x+iy,g2,g3 quit z==0.1 .03 -10 2
 P and P': 7.658833e+01  -5.050379e+01 i   -1.127488e+03 +
1.348203e+03 i
 m= 4.086745e-01 K=1.783584e+00 E=1.271800e+00 omega(2)
1.402409e+00 e or h2 1.617475e+00
 sigma= 1.000001e-01 3.000051e-02
 g2, g3 delta -1.000000e+01 2.000000e+00 -1.108000e+03
zetaw 9.233817e+00 -2.734598e+00
 Weierstrass:enter z=x+iy,g2,g3 quit z==0.07 .1 10 2
 zero denom. in ratmp m=5.000000e-01 x=-1.500000e+00
y=0.000000e+00
```

```
 zero denom. in ratmp m=5.000000e-01 x=-1.500000e+00
y=0.000000e+00
 P and P': -2.297450e+01  -6.305323e+01 i   1.062359e+03 +
2.842641e+02 i
 m= 4.029158e-01 K=1.779547e+00 E=1.772736e+00 omega(2)
1.003842e+00 e or h2 1.772736e+00
 sigma= 6.999990e-02 1.000011e-01
 g2, g3 delta 1.000000e+01 2.000000e+00 8.920000e+02
zetaw 4.695312e+00 -6.715526e+00
 Weierstrass:enter z=x+iy,g2,g3 quit z==01.75 3.6 7 6
 P and P': -9.608987e-01  -3.830738e-01 i   -5.573073e-01 +
1.200471e+00 i
 m= 1.014366e-02 K=1.574803e+00 E=1.581444e+00 omega(2)
9.958003e-01 e or h2 2.500966e+00
 sigma= 9.885612e+00 -7.671989e+01
 g2, g3 delta 7.000000e+00 6.000000e+00 -6.290000e+02
zetaw 7.535906e-01 -2.929088e+00
 Weierstrass:enter z=x+iy,g2,g3 quit z==015 73 8 4
 zero denom. in ratmp m=5.000000e-01 x=-1.500000e+00
y=0.000000e+00
 zero denom. in ratmp m=5.000000e-01 x=-1.500000e+00
y=0.000000e+00
 P and P': -5.774259e-01 + 6.779957e-02 i   2.986033e-01  -
4.560798e-01 i
 m= 1.458979e-01 K=1.633329e+00 E=1.618034e+00 omega(2)
1.009453e+00 e or h2 1.618034e+00
 sigma= 0.000000e+00 0.000000e+00
 g2, g3 delta 8.000000e+00 4.000000e+00 8.000000e+01
zetaw 1.205592e+01 -1.739054e+01
 Weierstrass:enter z=x+iy,g2,g3 quit z==0.8 .4 7 6
 P and P': 8.532482e-01  -6.435885e-01 i   -6.912597e-03 +
3.705272e+00 i
 m= 1.014366e-02 K=1.574803e+00 E=1.581444e+00 omega(2)
9.958003e-01 e or h2 2.500966e+00
 sigma= 8.146576e-01 3.881948e-01
 g2, g3 delta 7.000000e+00 6.000000e+00 -6.290000e+02
zetaw 1.013647e+00 -6.096445e-01
 Weierstrass:enter z=x+iy,g2,g3 quit z==0.4 1.3 8 4
 zero denom. in ratmp m=5.000000e-01 x=-1.500000e+00
y=0.000000e+00
 zero denom. in ratmp m=5.000000e-01 x=-1.500000e+00
y=0.000000e+00
 P and P': -8.714132e-01  -1.127497e-01 i   6.819606e-01  -
8.774822e-02 i
 m= 1.458979e-01 K=1.633329e+00 E=1.618034e+00 omega(2)
1.009453e+00 e or h2 1.618034e+00
 sigma= 2.780800e-01 1.272785e+00
 g2, g3 delta 8.000000e+00 4.000000e+00 8.000000e+01
zetaw 3.578191e-01 -5.313742e-01
```

```
 Weierstrass:enter z=x+iy,g2,g3 quit z==00 0 0
0
 m given q
 q=5.000000e-02 m=5.518703e-01 or 5.518703e-01 0.000000e+00
 q=1.000000e-01 m=8.024033e-01 or 8.024033e-01 0.000000e+00
 q=1.500000e-01 m=9.157098e-01 or 9.157098e-01 0.000000e+00
 q=2.000000e-01 m=9.658522e-01 or 9.658522e-01 0.000000e+00
 q=2.500000e-01 m=9.871356e-01 or 9.871356e-01 0.000000e+00
 q=3.000000e-01 m=9.956044e-01 or 9.956044e-01 0.000000e+00
 q=3.500000e-01 m=9.986789e-01 or 9.986789e-01 0.000000e+00
 q=4.000000e-01 m=9.996641e-01 or 9.996641e-01 0.000000e+00
 q=4.500000e-01 m=9.999314e-01 or 9.999314e-01 0.000000e+00
 q=5.000000e-01 m=9.999895e-01 or 9.999895e-01 0.000000e+00
 q=5.500000e-01 m=9.999989e-01 or 9.999989e-01 0.000000e+00
 q=6.000000e-01 m=9.999999e-01 or 9.999999e-01 0.000000e+00
 q=6.500000e-01 m=1.000000e+00 or 1.000000e+00 0.000000e+00
 q=7.000000e-01 m=1.000000e+00 or 1.000000e+00 0.000000e+00
 q=7.500000e-01 m=1.000000e+00 or 1.000000e+00 0.000000e+00
 q=8.000000e-01 m=1.000000e+00 or 1.000000e+00 0.000000e+00
 q=8.500000e-01 m=1.000000e+00 or 1.000000e+00 0.000000e+00
 q=9.000000e-01 m=1.000000e+00 or 1.000000e+00 0.000000e+00
 q=9.500000e-01 m=1.000000e+00 or 1.000000e+00 0.000000e+00
 q=1.000000e+00 m=1.000000e+00 or 1.000000e+00 0.000000e+00
 q=1.000000e-02 m=1.478744e-01 1.478744e-01
 q=2.000000e-02 m=2.739749e-01 2.739749e-01
 q=3.000000e-02 m=3.815732e-01 3.815732e-01
 q=4.000000e-02 m=4.734281e-01 4.734281e-01
 q=5.000000e-02 m=5.518703e-01 5.518703e-01
 q=6.000000e-02 m=6.188731e-01 6.188731e-01
 q=7.000000e-02 m=6.761095e-01 6.761095e-01
 q=8.000000e-02 m=7.250005e-01 7.250005e-01
 q=9.000000e-02 m=7.667551e-01 7.667551e-01
 q=1.000000e-01 m=8.024033e-01 8.024033e-01
 q=1.100000e-01 m=8.328239e-01 8.328239e-01
 q=1.200000e-01 m=8.587676e-01 8.587676e-01
 q=1.300000e-01 m=8.808764e-01 8.808764e-01
 q=1.400000e-01 m=8.997001e-01 8.997001e-01
 q=1.500000e-01 m=9.157098e-01 9.157098e-01
 q=1.600000e-01 m=9.293096e-01 9.293096e-01
 q=1.700000e-01 m=9.408462e-01 9.408462e-01
 q=1.800000e-01 m=9.506176e-01 9.506176e-01
 q=1.900000e-01 m=9.588796e-01 9.588796e-01
 q=2.000000e-01 m=9.658522e-01 9.658522e-01
 q for .9997 4.038202e-01
 theta:enter v,q both complex.5 0 .5 0
 ans=4.115265e-01 5.421011e-20 1.484397e+00 -5.421011e-20
4.027686e-01 2.917423e-18 1.484216e+00 1.458812e-18
 theta:enter v,q both complex0 0 0 0
```

```
 quartic 1.000000e+00 0.000000e+00 0.000000e+00 -
1.000000e+00 0.000000e+00 1.000000e+00 -1.000000e+00
0.000000e+00
 enter real m, complex z for cef.25 1 1
 e 1.743938e+00 -2.366206e-01 f 9.252520e-01 1.105634e+00
 enter real m, complex z for cef0 0 0
 enter complex z, real g2 g3 for invw test
1 1 -10 2
 answer 6.301454e-01 2.392589e-01
```

Chapter 17

The Elliptic Integrals

Introduction

Here, results are presented for real and complex arguments for the incomplete elliptic integrals of the first and second kinds, as well as more specialized routines for the complete and incomplete integrals for real arguments. See Chapter 29 for general complex parameters and Chapter 16 for a discussion of Elliptic functions.

Numerous books discuss the reduction of integrals involving rational functions of x and $\sqrt{ax^3 + bx^2 + cx + d}$. See, for example, Hancock and Korn and Korn. Byrd and Friedman have rather exhaustive tables of such integrals.

Caveat

The elliptic integrals are the inverse functions of the doubly periodic elliptic functions, and are therefore multiple valued. This affects the AGM computations (see Chapter 16) in the need for taking arc-tangents or arc-sines, which are multiple-valued. The net result is that it is very easy to get wrong answers! Version 1.2 of *Mathematica*®, for example, will return EllipticF[1.8,.9] as 1.90046 (version 2.0beta1 for SPARC returns the correct value 3.25572). Most frustrating was the incomplete elliptic integral of the second kind, *E*. For negative *m*, the integrand is well-behaved and easily calculated with adaptive quadrature. We do not use Abramowitz and Stegun 17.4.18 for *E*. The AGM as supplied in Chapter 29 will correctly evaluate E in this case, as does the expression used, which is based upon results in Korn and Korn (from Erdelyi; see previous chapter for reference). It is $E(\tilde{\varphi}, \tilde{m}) = [\, E(\varphi, m) - m \frac{\sin\varphi \cos\varphi}{\Delta}] \frac{1}{k'}$ where $m = -\tilde{m} / (1 - \tilde{m})$, $\sin\varphi = \frac{\sin\tilde{\varphi}}{\sqrt{k'^2 + k^2 \sin^2 \tilde{\varphi}}}$ and $\Delta = \sqrt{1 - k^2 \sin^2 \varphi}$. Care should be exercised as it has been impossible to check these routines as thoroughly as desired for unusal cases, due in part to the untrustworthiness of the version of *Mathematica*® presently available. Cross-checks between the programs presented here and in Chapter 29, comparison with published tables and direct integration have been used to verify correctness.

References

P. F. Byrd and M. D. Friedman, *Handbook of Elliptic Integrals for Engineers and Scientists* 2nd ed. (N. Y.: Springer Verlag, 1971).

H. Hancock, *Theory of Elliptic Functions (N. Y.: Dover, 1958).*

G. Korn & T. Korn, *Mathematical Handbook for Engineers and Scientists*, 2nd ed. (N. Y.: McGraw-Hill, 1968).

Figures

Fig. 17-1 plots the complete Elliptic integrals of the first and second kind. Fig. 17-2 plots the related Jacobi Zeta function. Fig. 17-3 plots the Elliptic Integral of the third kind.

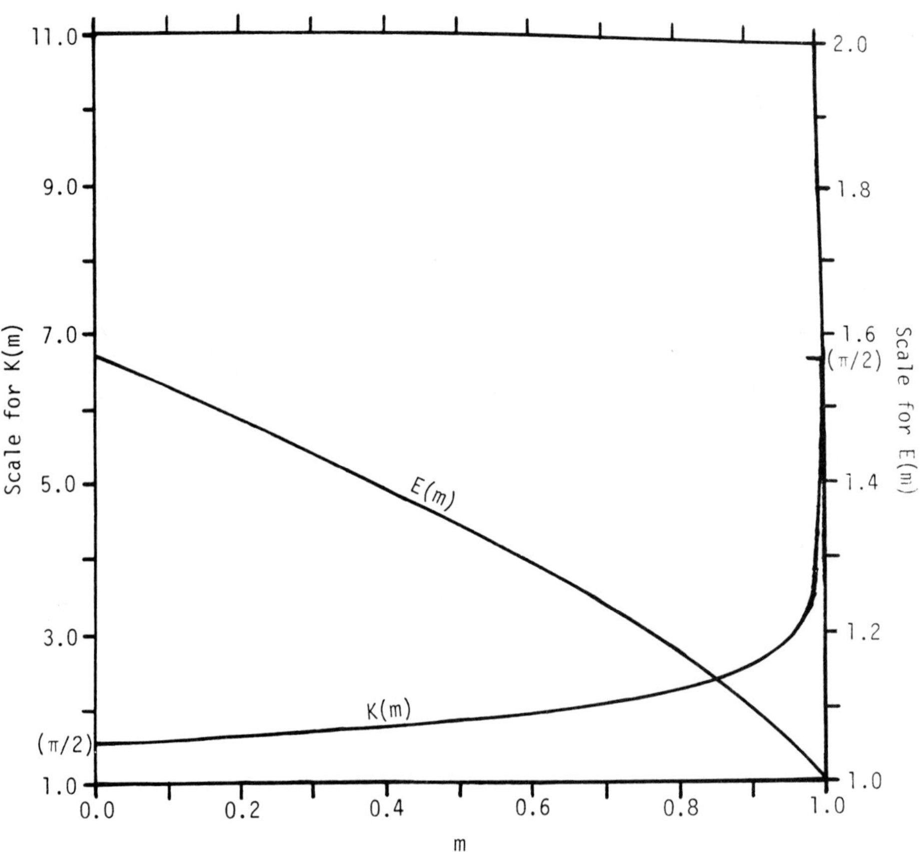

Fig. 17-1: Complete Elliptic Integrals of the first and second kind.

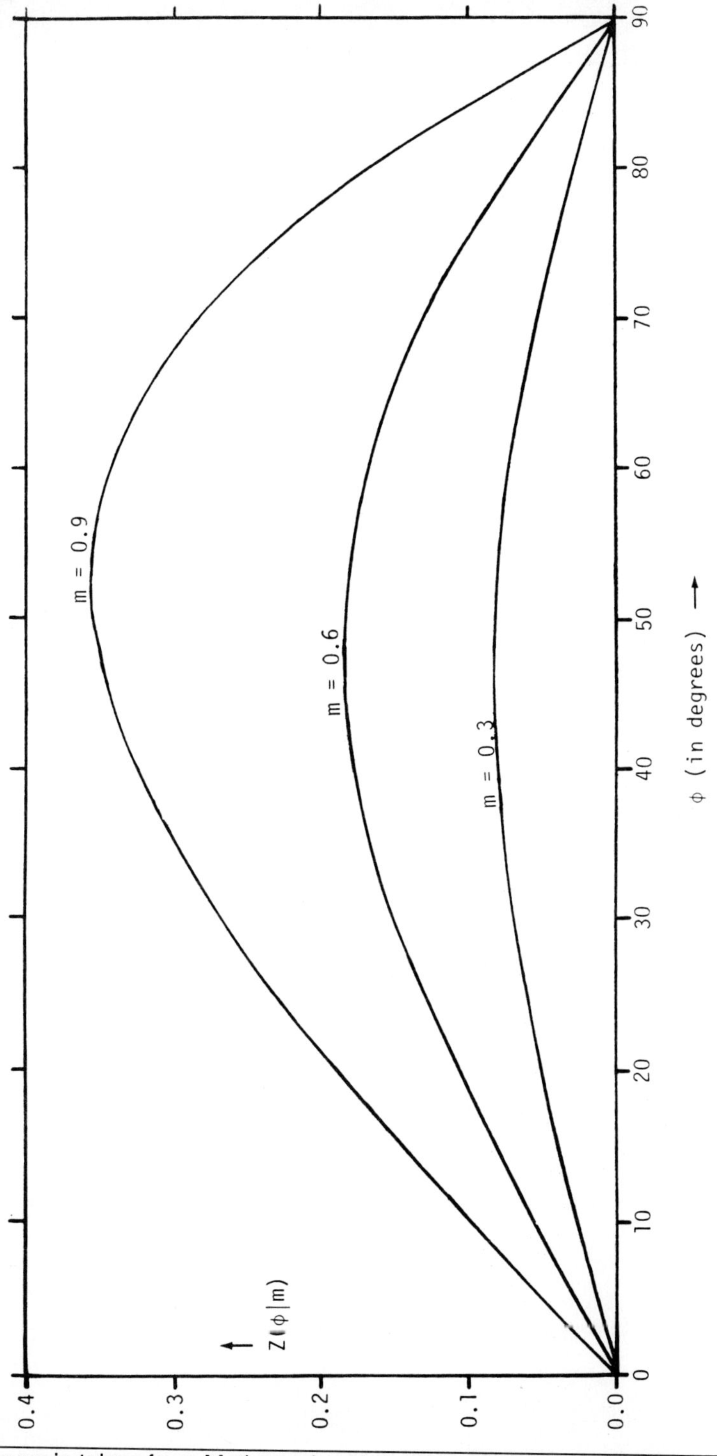

Fig. 17-2: Jacobian Zeta function.

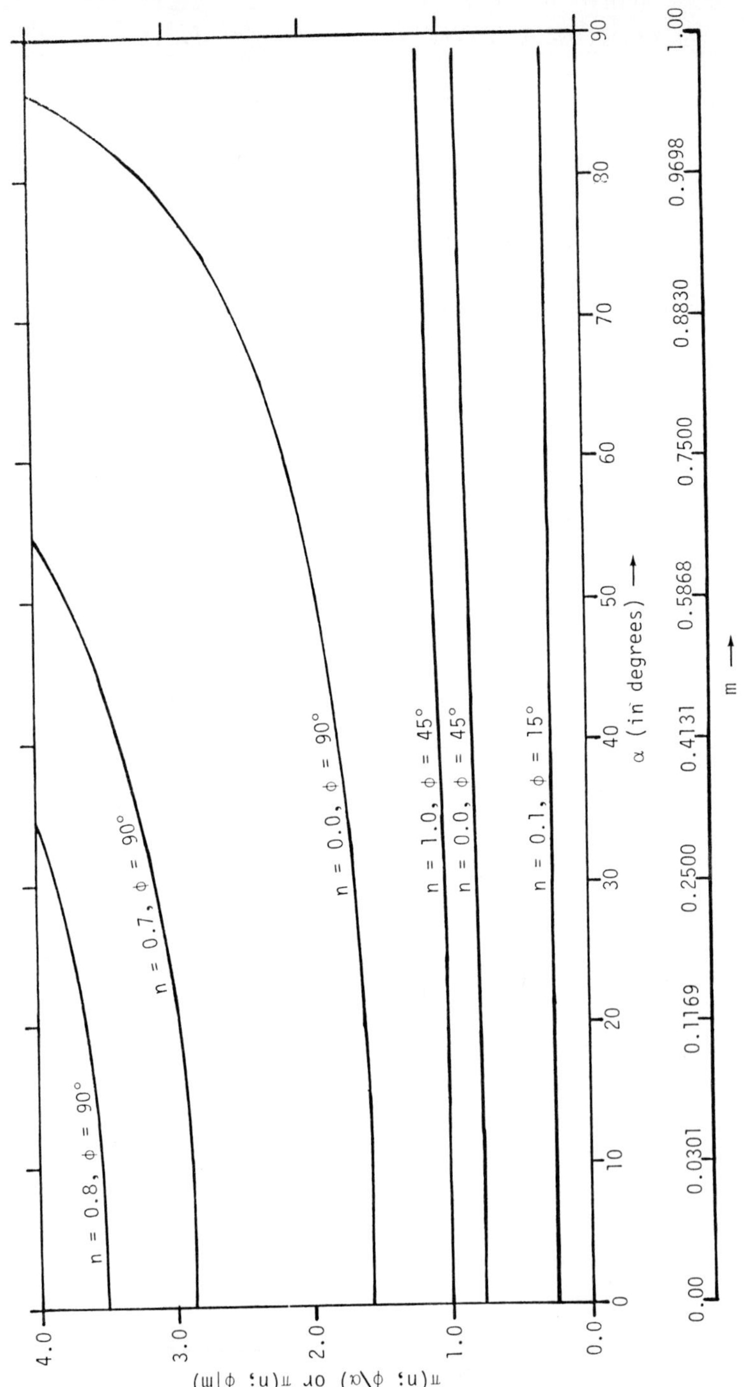

Fig. 17-3: Incomplete Elliptic Integral of the third kind.

```
/*
Complex Elliptic Integrals of 1st,2nd kind

from C Mathematical Function Handbook by Louis Baker
Copyright 1991 by Louis Baker. All rights reserved.
*/
#include <stdio.h>
#include "cmlib.h"
#include "protom.h"

cef(m,z,e,f,sig) struct complex *e,*z,*f;double m,sig;
{
double m1,k,alpha,
phi,psi,lambda,sinh(),sin(),cos(),cot,sinhp,cscp,
tan(),atan(),asin(),b1,b2,b3,mu,b,c,r1,r2,rp,sqrt(),cotl,b4,b
5;
struct complex du1,du2;
m1=1.-m;
phi=z->x;psi=z->y;
cot= 1./tan(phi);cot*=cot;
cscp= 1./sin(phi);cscp*=cscp;sinhp=sinh(psi);sinhp*=sinhp;
b= -(cot+m*cscp*sinhp-m1);
c= -m1*cot;
lambda=b*b-4.*c ;
if(lambda<0.){fprintf(stderr," cef root would be com-
plex\n");
                    e->x=e->y=f->x=f->y=errorcode;return 1;}
r1=-b*.5;r2=.5*sqrt(lambda);
cotl=r1+r2; if(cotl<0.)cotl=r1-r2;
if(cotl<0.){fprintf(stderr," cef can't find positive
root\n");
                    e->x=e->y=f->x=f->y=errorcode;return 2;}
lambda= atan( 1./sqrt(cotl));
if(m==0.) {mu=pi*.5;if(abs(cotl-cot)<1.e-6)mu=0.;}
else { b4= (cotl/cot)-1.;
                    if(b4<0.){
                    fprintf(stderr,
                    " warn mu imaginary %e %e %e %e\n",b4,cotl,cot,lam
                    mu=0.;}
                    else mu=atan(sqrt(abs(b4/m)));}
/*k=sqrt(m); alpha=asin(k);*/
b= sin(lambda);
c=sin(mu);r1=cos(mu);
b4=1.-m*b*b; b5= 1.-m1*b*b;
b1= m*b*cos(lambda)*c*c*sqrt(abs(b4));
b2=c*r1*b4*sqrt(abs(b5));
b3=r1*r1+m*b*b*c*c;
tef(lambda,m,sig,&b,&c);
/*printf("tef real: f e  %e %e\n",b,c);*/
```

```
tef(mu,m1,sig,&r1,&r2);
/*printf(" b1 b2 b3 %e %e %e\n",b1,b2,b3);*/
f->x =b; f->y=r1;
e->x=c;
e->y=r2-r1;
if(b4>=0.)e->x+=(b1/b3);
else e->y+=(b1/b3);
if(b5>=0.)e->x+=(b2/b3);
else e->y+=(b2/b3);
return 0;
}

czeta(m,z,ans,sig) double m,sig;struct complex *z,*ans;
{struct complex e,f,phi,term,ee,ff;double tanh(),am(),u;
if(m==0.){ans->x=0.;ans->y=0.;return 0;}
phi.x=pi*.5;phi.y=0.;
cef(m,&phi,&e,&f,sig);
cef(m,z,&ee,&ff,sig);
CDIV(phi,e,f);CMULT(term,phi,ff);
CSUB((*ans),ee,term);
return 0;
}
```

```
/*  ce
E for complex argument 0 <= m <= 1

from C Mathematical Function Handbook by Louis Baker
Copyright 1991 by Louis Baker. All rights reserved.

*/
#include <stdio.h>
#include "cmlib.h"
#include "protom.h"
#define zerotol 1.e-8
#define eps 1.e-6

ce(u,m,ce) double m; struct complex *u,*ce;
{
double wr,wi,s,t,c,d,m1,s1,c1,d1,ep,em,uphi,vphi,fm,fm1,em1;
struct complex z,cs,cc,cd,cim;int ic;
ep=zerotol; em=-ep;CMPLX(cim,0.,-1.);
wr=u->x;wi=u->y;s=abs(wr);t=abs(wi);
if(s<ep && t < ep)
   {ce->x=0.;ce->y=0.;return 0;}
if(wr>ep && wi>ep)ic=1;/* quadrant*/
if(wr<em && wi>ep)ic=2;
if(wr<em && wi<em)ic=3;
if(wr>ep && wi<em)ic=4;
if(t<=ep && wr>=ep)ic=5;/* 5,6 pure real arg*/
if(t<=ep && wr<=em)ic=6;
if(s<=ep && wi>=ep)ic=7;/*pure imaginary arg*/
if(s<=ep && wi<=em)ic=8;
m1=1.-m;
/*printf(" debug ic=%d\n",ic);*/
if(ic<5)
   {
   CMPLX(z,s,t);
   cjef(&z,m,&cs,&cc,&cd);
/*   printc(&cs);printf("= sn(u+iv)\n");*/
   jef(s,m,&s,&c,&d);
   jef(t,m1,&s1,&c1,&d1);
   uphi= asin(s);
   vphi=asin(s1);
   tef(uphi,m,eps,&fm,&em);
   tef(vphi,m1,eps,&fm1,&em1);
   d= s1/c1;
   CMPLX(*ce,em,(t+d1*d-em1));
   CTREAL(cs,cs,m*s*d);
/*   printc(&cs);printf("= sn(u+iv)scaled\n");*/
   CMULT(cd,cim,cs);
/*   printc(&cd);printf("= cd\n");*/
   CADD(*ce,*ce,cd);
```

```
/*   printc(ce);printf("= ce\n");*/
   s=ce->x;t=ce->y;
   switch (ic)
      {
      case 2: s=-s;break;
      case 4: t=-t;break;
      case 3:   s=-s;t=-t;break;
      default: break;
      }
   CMPLX((*ce),s,t);
   /*printc(ce);printf("= ce\n");*/
   return 0;
   }

if(ic<7)
   {
   jef(s,m,&s1,&c,&d);
   uphi=asin(s1);
   tef(uphi,m,eps,&fm,&em);
   if(ic==6) em=-em;
   CMPLX(*ce,em,0.);
   return 0;
   }
jef(t,m1,&s,&c,&d);
uphi=asin(s);
tef(uphi,m1,eps,&fm,&em);
em= (t+d*s/c-em);
if(ic==8) em=-em;
CMPLX(*ce,0.,em);
return 0;
}
```

Chapter 18

The Weierstrass Elliptic Function and Relatives

Introduction

Here, results are presented for Weierstrass' $\wp$ (and its derivative), as well as the related zeta and sigma functions. Following Abramowitz and Stegun and *Mathematica*®, the parameters g_2 and g_3 are assumed real. There seems to be little or no interest in more general circumstances, although these could be calculated using the functions of Chapter 29 in conjunction with the root finders of Chapter 3. We also provide a program which will find the inverse of the Weierstrass $\wp$ function. See Chapter 16 for the definitions of these functions.

Suppose you are given the period ratio (called a in the examples at the end of Chapter 18 of Abramowitz and Stegun). How do you then go on to determine the other parameters and values? The elliptic modular functions, discussed in Chapter 16, may be used to find the value of modulus m corresponding to the period ratio of interest, determining the nome q. One can then compute the associated values of g_2 or g_3, given the sign of the determinant, and compute $\wp$.

Note that zeta is a popular letter to denote functions. Be sure you want this zeta, and not Jacobi's zeta, or Riemann's zeta, etc.

The Lamé equation can be expressed in a number of forms, some involving the Weierstrass function or Jacobian Elliptic functions. Its solution is not generally simply expressible as one, however. The solutions, called Lamé functions, are sufficiently difficult to deal with that they are not generally used. The Lamé equation can be used to express Laplace's equation in a class of coordinate systems called biquartic. In elliptic coordinates, one special case of these, we can solve the Laplace equation $\nabla^2 \psi = 0$, by separating variables, i. e., looking for a solution of the form $\psi = U(u)V(v)W(w)$. Each of the functions U, V, W, satisfy an equation of the form

$\frac{d^2U}{du^2} + [A + B\wp(u)]\,U = 0$. The equation $\frac{d^2y}{du^2} + [A + 2\wp(u)]\,y = 0$, with the condition that $\wp(a) = A$, has the solutions $y_1 = e^{-u\zeta(a)}\frac{\sigma(u+a)}{\sigma(u)}$ and $y_2 = e^{u\zeta(a)}\frac{\sigma(u-a)}{\sigma(u)}$. See Akhiezer for a discussion. Whittaker and Watson have an extensive discussion of the Lamé equation, and Moon and Spencer discuss the Lamé equation and its relatives, the Wangerin and Heine equations. Note that the Lamé equation, among its many forms, can be written without explicitly occuring Elliptic functions. It then has four singular points. See Smirnov (referenced in Chapter 16) and Whittaker and Watson's *Course in Modern Analysis* (referenced in Chapter 9) for more details. In standard form $\frac{d^2y}{du^2} + [\,a + b\wp(u)]\,y = 0$, a must be of the form $a = -n\,(\,n + 1\,)$, $n = 0, 1, 2, ...$ for the general solution to be a single-valued function of u. For a given n, we then have an eigenvalue problem for b for a well-behaved solution to Laplace's equation. The corresponding eigen-solutions will, in general, be polynomials in $\wp(u)$, of the nth degree, possibly multiplied by a factor $\sqrt{\wp(u) - e_i}$ where e_i is one of the roots of the cubic $4t^3 - g_2 t - g_3$. There will generally be $2n + 1$ choices of b for a given a, and $2n + 1$ solutions to Laplace's equation. Nobody said life was simple. I have not encountered a numerical application of these functions, i. e., someone actually calculating quantitative answers to a problem in ellipsoidal (or any other) coordinates using the Weierstrass $\wp$ or any of its relatives.

Given the cubic expression in the radical, we can form the discriminant $g_2^3 - 27g_3^2$. As this expression is real, it must be either positive, negative, or zero. If zero, we have a degenerate case which is not truly doubly periodic. The other two cases, which have either three real roots or one real and two conjugate roots, give rise to different procedures for determining $\wp$. The case g=0, g=1 is called the Lemniscatic case, because it arises in integrals related to determining the arc length of the lemniscate, while g=0, g=1 is called the the equiharmonic case.

For general, complex values of g_2 or g_3 one can find the roots of the cubic and then one has a problem involving an elliptic integral of the first kind with complex parameters. The routines of Chapter 29 can then be used to evaluate this elliptic integral for determining the value of $\wp^{-1}$ or evaluating the appropriate Jacobian Elliptic function to determine the inverse of this integral, i. e., $\wp$. Similarly, the elliptic logarithm and its inverse, the elliptic exponential, can be evaluated as elliptic integrals or their inverses. (See Chapter 29 for details and definitions.)

See the papers by Eckhart for routines for the computation of the lemniscatic and equiharmonic cases.

Methods

The methods follow the procedures in Chapter 18 of Abramowitz and Stegun. An implementation of the root finder of R. P. Brent is supplied to determine the modulus m. This root finder is the method of choice when the root is bracketed, i. e., known to be in an interval in which the function changes sign.

The test examples are mostly taken from the Abramowitz and Stegun examples for $\wp$, σ, and inverse $\wp$. Note that in Example 14, Abramowitz and Stegun give the inverse $\wp$ as $z = .772247 - .239258\,i$, whereas the code computes $.630148 - .2392589\,i$. The latter is also correct, using the double periodicity of $\wp$ and the period $\omega_2 = 1.4023948$.

References

N. I. Akhiezer, *Elements of the Theory of Elliptic Functions* (Providence, R. I.: American Math. Soc., 1990).

R. P. Brent, *Computer Journal*, **14**, 422, 1971. Also *Algorithms for Minimization without Derivatives* (Englewood Cliffs, N. J.: Prentice Hall, 1973).

U. Eckhart, *Mathematics of Computation*, **30**, 818, 1976.

U. Eckhart, *Computing*, **18**, 341, 1977.

```
/*
Inverse of Weierstrass Elliptic P

from C Mathematical Function Handbook by Louis Baker
Copyright 1991 by Louis Baker. All rights reserved.
*/

#include <stdio.h>
#include "cmlib.h"
#include "protom.h"

#define sig 1.e-6

invp(g2,g3,z,ans)struct complex *z,*ans;double g2,g3;
{double
delta,r,q,ss,sqrt(),pp,ppp,lambda,m,acos(),asin(),phi,rt1,rt2
,rt3;
int roottp;
struct complex s,s1,s2,r1,r2,r3,factor,num,denom,acoss;
roottp=cubic(0.,-g2*.25,-g3*.25,&rt1,&rt2,&rt3);
if (roottp)
    {
    /*CMPLX(r1,rt1,0.);
    CMPLX(r2,rt2,rt3);
    CMPLX(r3,rt2,-rt3);*/
    /*printf(" delta");*/
    ss= rt1;
    pp= 3.*ss*ss-g2*.25;
    if(pp<0.){fprintf(stderr," pblm p'real
root=%e\n",ss);return 0;}
    ppp=6.*ss;
    pp=sqrt(pp);
    m= .5-.125*ppp/pp;
    lambda=sqrt(pp);
    /*printf(" lambda=%e m=%e\n",lambda,m);*/
    CLET(num,*z);num.x-=(ss+pp);
    CLET(denom,*z);denom.x+= pp-ss;
    /*printf(" denom=%e %e\n",denom.x,denom.y);*/
    CDIV(s,num,denom);
    /*printf(" calling cacos,x=%e %e\n",s.x,s.y);*/
    cacos(&s,&acoss);
    /*printf(" acoss=%e %e\n",acoss.x,acoss.y);*/
    cef( m,&acoss,&factor,&s,sig);
    CTREAL(*ans,s,.5/lambda);
    return 0;
    }
/* 3 real roots- sort them*/
if(rt1<rt2){q=rt1;rt1=rt2;rt2=q;}
if(rt1<rt3){q=rt1;rt1=rt3;rt3=q;}
```

```
if(rt2<rt3){q=rt2;rt2=rt3;rt3=q;}
if( rt1<rt2 || rt1<rt3 ||rt2<rt3){printf(" bad sort %e %e
%e\n",rt1,rt2,rt3);
   return 1;}
lambda= rt1-rt3;
if(lambda<0.){fprintf(stderr," invw: bad roots %e %e
%e\n",rt1,rt2,rt3);return 1;}
/*printf(" all real roots\n");*/
lambda=.5*sqrt(lambda);
m= (rt2-rt3)/(rt1-rt3);
/*printf(" m= %e lambda=%e\n",m,lambda);*/
CLET(num,*z);num.x-=rt1;
CLET(denom,*z);denom.x-= rt3;
CDIV(s,num,denom);
if(cabs(s)>1.e-10)
   {clog(&s,&factor);CTREAL(factor,factor,.5);cexp(&fac-
tor,&s);}
/*printf(" s= %e %e\n",s.x,s.y);*/
cacos(&s,&acoss);
/*printf(" acoss= %e %e\n",acoss.x,acoss.y);*/
cef(m, &acoss,&factor,&s,sig);
/*printf(" cef returned\n");*/
CTREAL(*ans,s,.5/lambda);
return 0;
}
```

```
/*
brent root finder
        for real roots of a real function
        root must be bracketed beforehand a<root<b
        function f must change sign: f(a)f(b)<0

from C Mathematical Function Handbook by Louis Baker
Copyright 1991 by Louis Baker. All rights reserved.
*/

#include <stdio.h>
#include "cmlib.h"

#define min(a,b) (((a)<(b))? (a): (b))
#define max(a,b) (((a)>=(b))? (a): (b))

double brent(a,b,eta,t,f)
double a,b,eta,t, (*f) ();
{
double c,d,e,fa,fb,fc,tol,pwr2(),m,p,q,r,s;
fa=(*f)(a);fb=(*f)(b);
init:
   c=a;fc=fa;d=e=b-a;
ext:
   if (abs(fc)<abs(fb) )
      {
      a=b;
      b=c;
      c=a;
      fa=fb;
      fb=fc;
      fc=fa;
      }
tol=2.*eta*abs(b)+t;
m=.5*(c-b);
if(abs(m)>tol &&fb!=0.)
    {
         if(abs(e)<tol || abs(fa)<abs(fb) )
              {
         d=e=m;
              }
         else
            {
                 s=fb/fa;
                 if(a==c)
         {/*linear interp*/
                   p=(2.*m*s);
                   q=1.-s;
                   }
```

```
            else
         {/*inver. quadr. interp*/
                    q=fa/fc;
                    r=fb/fc;
                    p=s*(2.*m*q*(q-r)-(b-a)*(r-1.))    ;
         q=(q-1.)*(r-1.)*(s-1.);
                    }
            if(p>0.) q*=-1.;
            else     p*=-1.;
            s=e;
       e=d;
       if(2.*p< 3.*m*q-abs(tol*q) && p<abs(.5*s*q))
                      d=p/q;
            else
          {d=e=m;}

      }/* else abs()<tol...*/
        a=b;
        fa=fb;
        b+=(  abs(d)>tol ? d :(m>0.?tol:-tol)  );
    fb=(*f)(b);
    if((fb>0.)==(fc>0.)) goto init;
goto ext;
           }
 return(b);
 }
```

Chapter 19

The Parabolic Cylinder Functions

Introduction

The Parabolic Cylinder functions are the solutions $U(a,x)$ and $V(a,x)$ of $\frac{d^2w}{dx^2} - [\frac{1}{4}x^2 + a]\, w = 0$ and are related to the Confluent Hypergeometric functions. Whittaker defines the function $D_{-a-1/2}(x) = U(a,x)$, with the other solution given by $V(a,x) = \frac{1}{\pi}\Gamma(a + \frac{1}{2})\,[\sin \pi a\, D_{-a-1/2}(x) + D_{-a-1/2}(-x)]$. There is also the modified parabolic cylinder equation, $\frac{d^2w}{dx^2} + [\frac{1}{4}x^2 - a]\, w = 0$ with solutions $W(a,x)$ and $W(a, -x)$.

The Schroedinger equation for a harmonic oscillator potential in one dimension has the form of the parabolic cylinder equation. Parabolic cylinder coordinates have been used, for example in problems involving diffraction from a straight edge.

Methods

The methods of Chapter 19 of Abramowitz and Stegun, including the asymptotic expressions involving the Airy functions, are used.

Figures

Fig. 19-1 shows the Parabolic Cylinder functions U and V for a=1, while Fig. 19-2 shows $W(1,x)$ and $W(1, -x)$.

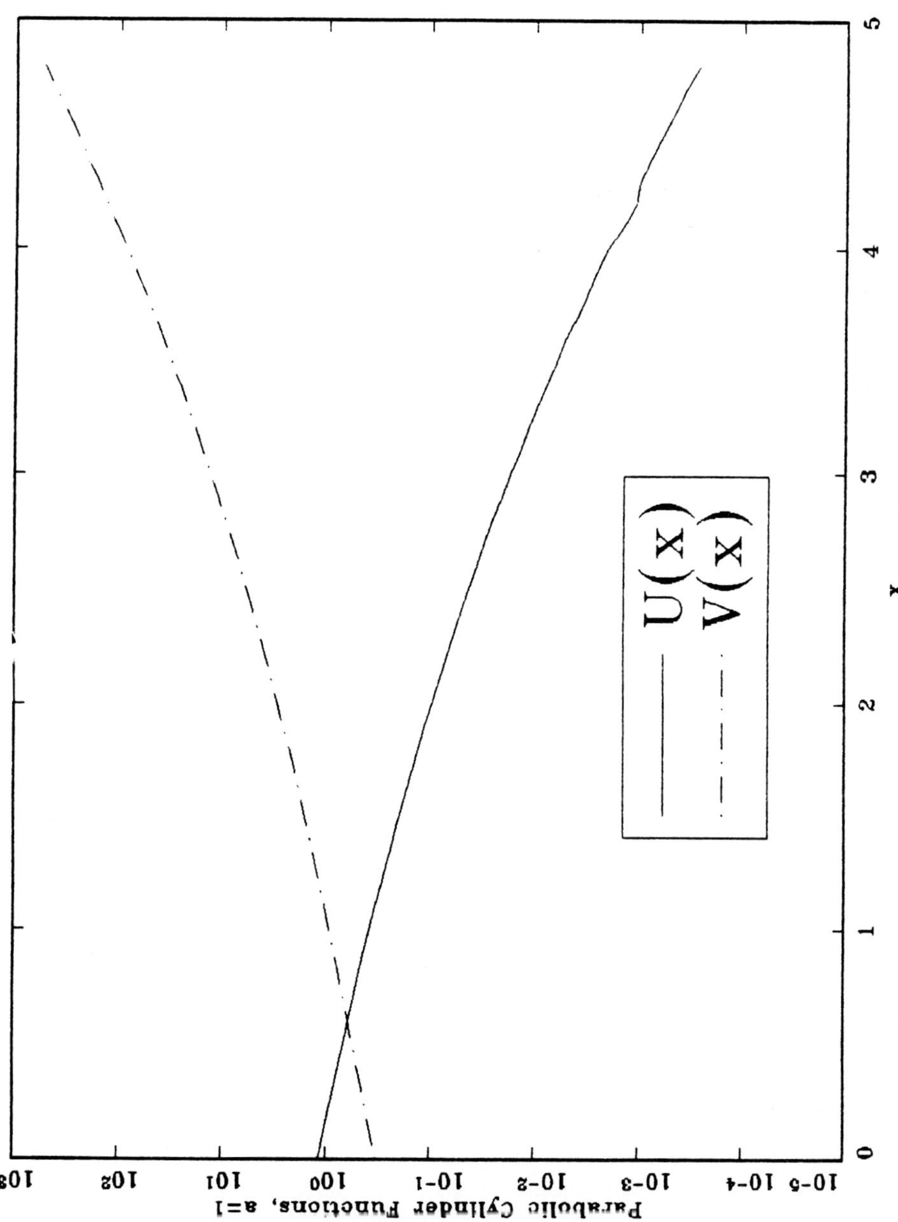

Fig. 13-1: Parabolic Cylinder functions $U(1,x)$ and $V(1,x)$.

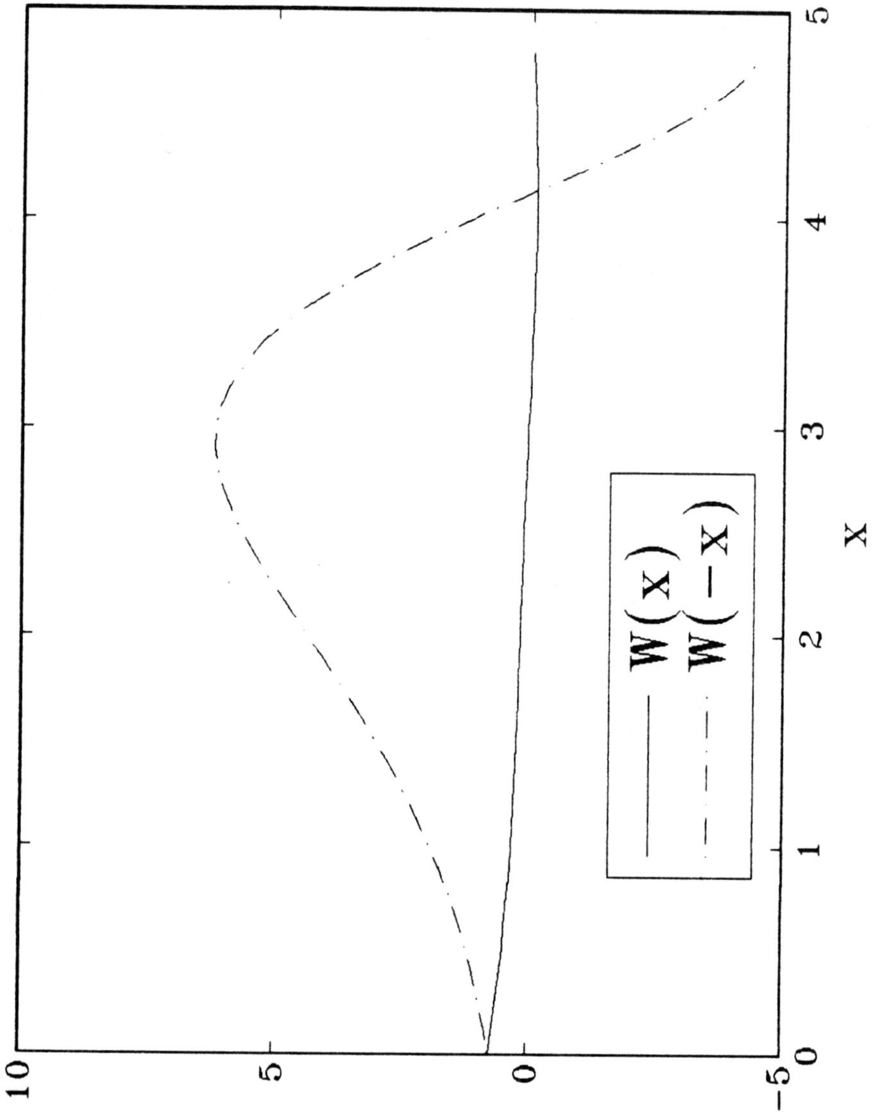

Fig. 19-2: Parabolic Cylinder functions $W(1,x)$ and $W(1,-x)$.

```
/*
Parabolic cylinder functions
and related confluent hypergeometric functions

from C Mathematical Function Handbook by Louis Baker
Copyright 1991 by Louis Baker. All rights reserved.

upcf   U
vpcf   V
wpcf   W: Associated pcf (for x, -x independent solutions)

uses confluent hypergeometric function

*/

#include <stdio.h>
#include "cmlib.h"
#include "protom.h"



double wpcf(a,xx) double a,xx;
{
int i,twoi,itmax=100;
struct complex ag,loggam,gam;
double g1,g3,y1,y3,term1,term3,x,tol=1.e-7,wa(),sqrt();
double z,oold,oolder,eold,eolder,new,f1,f3,sign,wairy();
x=abs(xx);
if(a>4.) return wairy(a,xx);
if( x>8. && x> abs(a)*4.) return wa(a,xx);

if(xx>=0.)
   {
   sign=-1.;
   }
else
   {
   sign=1.;
   }
ag.x=.25;ag.y=.5*a;
cgamma(&ag,&gam,&loggam);
g1= cabs(gam);
ag.x=.75;ag.y=.5*a;
cgamma(&ag,&gam,&loggam);
g3= cabs(gam);
z=x*x;
oolder=eolder=1.;
eold=oold=a;
f1=.5*z;
```

```
f3=.1666666*z;
y1=1.+a*f1;
y3=1.+a*f3;
for (i=2;i<itmax;i++)
    {
    twoi=i<<1;
    new= a*eold-.25*(twoi-2)*(twoi-3)*eolder;
    f1*= z/((twoi)*(twoi-1));
    term1=f1*new;
    y1+=term1;
    eolder=eold;
    eold=new;
    new= a*oold-.25*(twoi-2)*(twoi-1)*oolder;
    f3*= z/((twoi+1)*(twoi));
    term3=f3*new;
    y3+= term3;
    oolder=oold;
    oold=new;
    if( abs(term1)<tol && abs(term3)<tol)break;
    }
y3*=x;
f1=sqrt(g1/g3);
f3=sign*sqrt(2.*g3/g1);
return  sqrt(sqrt(2.))*.5*(f1*y1+f3*y3);
}

double wa(a,xx) double a,xx;
{
int i,itmax=6;
struct complex ag,loggam,ans,ans1;
double arg,sqrt(),log(),cos(),sin(),x,y,phi,s1,s2,k,exp(),
term1,term2,factor,tol=1.e-6,old1,old2;
printf(" entered wa\n");
if(a<=0.) return errorcode;
ag.x=.5; ag.y=a;
x=abs(xx);
y=exp(pi*a);
k= sqrt(1.+y*y)-y;
cgamma(&ag,&ans,&loggam);
phi=loggam.y;
arg= .25*x*x-a*log(x)+.25*pi+.5*phi;
y=.5/(x*x);
factor=y;
s1=1.;
s2=0.;
old1=old2=1.e10;
for(i=1;i<itmax;i++)
    {
    ag.x=.5+((double) (i<<1));ag.y=a;
```

```
    cgamma(&ag,&ans1,&loggam);
    CDIV(loggam,ans1,ans);
    switch (i%4)
       {
       case 1:
          term1=loggam.y;
          term2=-loggam.x;
          break;
       case 2:
          term1=-loggam.x;
          term2=-loggam.y;
          break;
       case 3:
          term1=-loggam.y;
          term2=loggam.x;
       default:
          term1=loggam.x;
          term2=loggam.y;
       }
    term1*=factor;
    term2*=factor;
    if(abs(term1)>abs(old1) || abs(term2)>abs(old2)) break;
    s1+=term1;
    s2+=term2;
    if( abs(term1)<tol && abs(term2)<tol)break;
    if( abs(term1)<tol*abs(s1) &&
abs(term2)<tol*abs(s2))break;
    factor*=y/(i+1);
    old1=term1;
    old2=term2;
    }
if(xx>=0.)
    {return sqrt(2.*k/(x))*(s1*cos(arg)-s2*sin(arg));}
/*else*/
    return sqrt(2./(k*x))*(s1*sin(arg)+s2*cos(arg));
}

#define acosh arccosh

double wairy(a,xx) double a,xx;
{
double sqrt(),pow(),acos(),acosh(),
bi(),ai(),xi,t,tau,th,x,exp(),airy,ex,c;
/* a>>0 */
xi= abs(xx/(2.*sqrt(a)) ) ;
if(xi<1.)
    {
    th= .25*(acos(xi)-xi*sqrt(1.-xi*xi));
    t=-pow(1.5*th,.6666666);
```

```
   }
else
   {
   th= .25*(xi*sqrt(xi*xi-1.)-acosh(xi));
   t=pow(1.5*th,.6666666);
   }
t*=pow(4.*a,.666666);
if(t!=0.)c=sqrt(pi*sqrt(t/((4.*a)*(xi*xi-1.))));
else c=sqrt(pi/sqrt(4.*a));
ex=exp(-.5*pi*a);
if(xx>0.)
   return c*ex*bi(-t);
return 2.*c/ex*ai(-t);

}

double upcf(nu,x)double nu,x;
{
double u(),m(),mult=4.,sqrt(),gamma();
double a,b,c,d;

if( x> 4. && x> abs(nu)*mult)
   {
   a=.5/(x*x);
   d= exp(-.25*x*x)/pow(x,nu+.5)*
      (1.+(nu+.5)*(nu+1.5)*a*((nu+2.5)*(nu+3.5)*a*.5-1.));
   printf(" asymptotic u=%e\n",d);
   }

if(x>0.)
return exp(-.25*x*x)/pow(2.,
.25+.5*nu)*u(.25+.5*nu,.5,x*x*.5);
/*else*/
a= sqrt(pi)*exp(-.25*x*x)/pow(2.,.25+nu*.5);
b=gamma(.75+.5*nu);
c=gamma(.25+.5*nu);
d= a*
   (m(.5*nu+.25,.5,.5*x*x)/b
   -x*sqrt(2.)*m(.5*nu+.75,1.5,.5*x*x)/c);
return d;
}

double vpcf(nu,x)double nu,x;
{
double a,b,c,d,mult=4.;
if( x> 4. && x> abs(nu)*mult)
   {
   a=.5/(x*x);
   d= exp(.25*x*x)*pow(x,nu-.5)*sqrt(2./pi)*
```

```
    (1.+(nu-.5)*(nu-1.5)*a*((nu-2.5)*(nu-3.5)*a*.5+1.));
printf(" asymptotic v=%e\n",d);
   }
a= gamma(nu+.5)/pi;
b=sin(pi*nu);
c=upcf(nu,x);
d=upcf(nu,-x);
return a*(b*c+d);
}

/* whittaker functions M and W */

double mwhit(k,mu,z) double k,mu,z;
{
double m();
return m(.5+mu-k,1.+2.*mu,z)*exp(-z*.5)*pow(z,.5+mu);
}

double wwhit(k,m,z) double k,m,z;
{
double u();
return u(.5+m-k,1.+2.*m,z)*exp(-z*.5)*pow(z,.5+m);
}

/* simple versions of confluent hypergeometric functions M
and U
for real arguments*/

double m(a,b,x)
double a,b,x;
{
double sum,term,newterm,count,tol=1.e-
6,pow(),exp(),gamma(),oldterm;
int top=40,i,k,itmax=40;

if(x==0.)return 1.;
if((b-(double)((int)b))==0.  && b<0. &&
   (a-(double)((int)a))==0. && b<a)return(errorcode);
if(x> 10.)
   {
   sum=1.;term=1.;oldterm=1.e30;
   for (i=0;i<itmax;i++)
      {
      k=i+1;
      term*=(b-a+i)*(k-a)/(x*(k));
      newterm=abs(term);
      if(newterm>oldterm)break;
      oldterm=newterm;
      sum+=term;
```

```
      if((abs(term)<tol||abs(term)<tol*abs(sum)))break;
      }
   return exp(x)*pow(x,a-b)*gamma(b)/gamma(a)*sum;
   }
for(i=0,term=sum=1.;i<top;i++)
   {
   count=(double)(i+1);
   term *=(x*(a+i)/((b+i)*count));
   if( abs(term)< tol*abs(sum))return sum;
   sum+=term;
   }
return(sum);
}

double u(a,b,x)
double a,b,x;
{
double pow(),sin(),fac(),m(),eps=1.e-4,gamma(),tol=1.e-
6,exp(),cos();
double sum,term,count,ret,factor;
int i,top=40;

/* wont work for integer b*/
 if(abs(x)<5.)
   {
   help:
/*printf(" after help x, a b %f %f %f\n",x,a,b);*/
if((b-(double)((int)b))==0. ) {b+=eps;/* avoid
sin(pi*b)=0*/}
   if(x>0.)
   return pi/(sin(pi*b))*(m(a,b,x)/(gamma(1.+a-b)*gamma(b))
   -m(a+1.-b,2.-b,x)/(gamma(a)*fac(1.-b))* pow(abs(x),
     1.- b));
   sum=-(x);
   /* factor= exp i pi (1-b) */
   factor= cos( pi*(1.-b));/*neglect imaginary part sin(),
if any for now*/
   return pi/(sin(pi*b))*exp(-sum)*(m(b-
a,b,sum)/(gamma(1.+a-b)*gamma(b))
   -m(1.-a,2.-b,x)*factor/(gamma(a)*gamma(2.-b))*pow(sum,1.-
b));
   }
/*else*/
/*printf(" asympt u a=%f b=%f x=%f\n",a,b,x);*/
for (i=0,term=1.,sum=1.;i<top;i++)
   {
   count=(double)(i+1);
   factor=(a+i)*(a-b+count)/(-x*count);
   if(abs(factor)>1.)
```

```
   /* asympt. series invalid once terms increase*/
      {
   /*   printf(
" term=%d sum=%f term=%f,factor=%f\n",i,sum,term,factor);*/
      if (abs(term/sum)<1.e-3)return sum/pow(x,a);
/*      printf(" getting help,would be %f\n",
sum/pow(x,a));*/
      goto help;
      }
   term*=factor;
   sum +=term;/*sum must be nonzero here */
   if(abs(term/sum)<tol)return (sum/pow(x,a));
   }
/*printf(" asympt non converge %f %f %f\n",
factor,term,sum);*/
return sum/pow(x,a);/*keep desmet happy*/
}
```

```
/*
test driver parabolic cylinder function
and relatives
from C Mathematical Function Handbook by Louis Baker
Copyright 1991 by Louis Baker. All rights reserved.
*/

#include <stdio.h>
#include "cmlib.h"
#include "protom.h"

FILE *outp;

main()
{
double a,x,w,u,v,z;int i;
outp=fopen("pcf.out","w");fprintf(outp,"5\n");
printf(" enter a\n");scanf("%le",&a);
for(i=0; i<50;i++)
    {x=i/10.;
    u=upcf(a,x);v=vpcf(a,x);
    w=wpcf(a,x);
    z=wpcf(a,-x);
    fprintf(outp,"%le %le %le %le %le\n",x,u,v,w,z);
    }
infinite_loop
    {printf(" enter a, x. x1000 to quit\n");
    scanf("%le%le",&a,&x);
    if(x>1000.)break;
    u=upcf(a,x);v=vpcf(a,x);
    printf(" U= %le, V %le\n",u,v);
    w=wpcf(a,x);
    z=wpcf(a,-x);
    printf(" W(%le,%le)=%le and for -x:%le\n",a,x,w,z);
    }
return 0;
}
```

Test Output for Parabolic Cylinder Functions

```
 enter a
-2
 enter a, x. x1000 to quit
-2 0
 U= -6.081402e-01, V -4.574753e-01
 W(-2.000000e+00,0.000000e+00)=6.002746e-01
and for -x:6.002746e-01
 enter a, x. x1000 to quit
2 0
 U= 8.108537e-01, V 3.431063e-01
 W(2.000000e+00,0.000000e+00)=6.002746e-01
and for -x:6.002746e-01
 enter a, x. x1000 to quit
-2 1
 U= 5.156671e-01, V -5.417693e-01
 W(-2.000000e+00,1.000000e+00)=-4.870414e-01
and for -x:6.597537e-01
 enter a, x. x1000 to quit
2 1
 U= 1.832067e-01, V 1.439015e+00
 W(2.000000e+00,1.000000e+00)=1.615054e-01
and for -x:2.415599e+00
 enter a, x. x1000 to quit
2000
```

Chapter 20

The Mathieu Functions

Introduction

These functions are solutions to Mathieu's equation. They arise principally from two circumstances. In one, an oscillator is periodically driven. This is the well-known "parametric amplifier." In such problems, the limits of stability (eigenvalues) of the system are typically of interest, rather than the solutions themselves. Behavior such as sub-harmonic resonance is typical. (A child "pumping" a swing by pulling themselves up and down, and/or swinging their legs to move their center of gravity up and down, is often cited as an example of these systems. Note that the child varies his parameters at twice the frequency of the swing, moving the center of gravity up twice for each full swing. However, no experiment is ideal, and there are torque effects as well which make the demonstration less than ideal.) These may be found using the functions given here. In the other principal route to Mathieu's equation, Laplace's equation is solved in elliptic cylinder coordinates.

Mathieu's equation may be written as $\frac{d^2y}{dx^2} + (a - q\cos 2x)y = 0$, which clearly shows the periodic forcing term. By the substitution t = cos x we can get a purely algebraic equation $(1 - t^2)\frac{d^2y}{dt^2} - t\frac{dy}{dt} + (a + 2q - 4qt^2)y = 0$. The theory of equations with periodic coefficients, as in the first form given here for Mathieu's equation, is called Floquet theory. Given a value of q, there are characteristic values for a which will give periodic solutions. There can be solutions of period π or 2π. The eigenvalues are different for even and odd periodic solutions. The odd and even periodic solutions are denoted *se* or *ce*, respectively. Generally, these are the solutions of interest. The modified equation in which cosh replaces cos in the first form above, is of interest as radial solutions of the wave equation in elliptic coordinates. Elliptic coordinates are a two-dimensional system of confocal ellipses and hyperbolas (see Fig.

20-1). These coordinates, ρ, u, v, may be defined by $x = \rho \cosh u \cos v, y = \rho \sinh u \sin v$, z = z. It's solutions are denoted by Se and Ce, for solutions of the first kind, and are related by relations such as $Se(x) = se(ix)$, to solutions of the corresponding unmodified equation. The solutions of the second kind are denoted by Mc and Ms, and are again closely related in form but involve Bessel function products in the sum.

Hill's equation is a generalization involving a number of forcing functions at differing periods.

Method

The functions of CALGO 352 are used. A continued fraction method is used for determining the eigenvalues (characteristic values). The solutions are expanding in series of sines or cosines (sinh or cosh for the modified functions), with the coefficients coming from the same continued fraction method. Math. Note 31 was used to check the results. It contains a discussion of the problem for complex parameters.

References

D. S. Clemm, CALGO Algorithm 352, *Characteristic Values and Associated Solutions of Mathieu's Differential Equation.*

R. J. Lytle, D. L. Lager, *Solutions of the Scalar Helmholtz Equation in the Elliptic Cylinder Coordinate System*, Mathematics Note 31, Phillips Lab, Kirtland AFB (available through the Defense Technical Information Center, DTIC), Oct. 15, 1973.

W. Magnus and S. Winkler, *Hill's Equation*, (N. Y.: Dover, 1979).

Figures

Fig. 20-1 Shows Elliptic Cylinder or Ellipsoidal coordinates. Fig. 20-2 shows plots of Mathieu functions, and Fig. 20-3 shows plots of the Radial Mathieu functions.

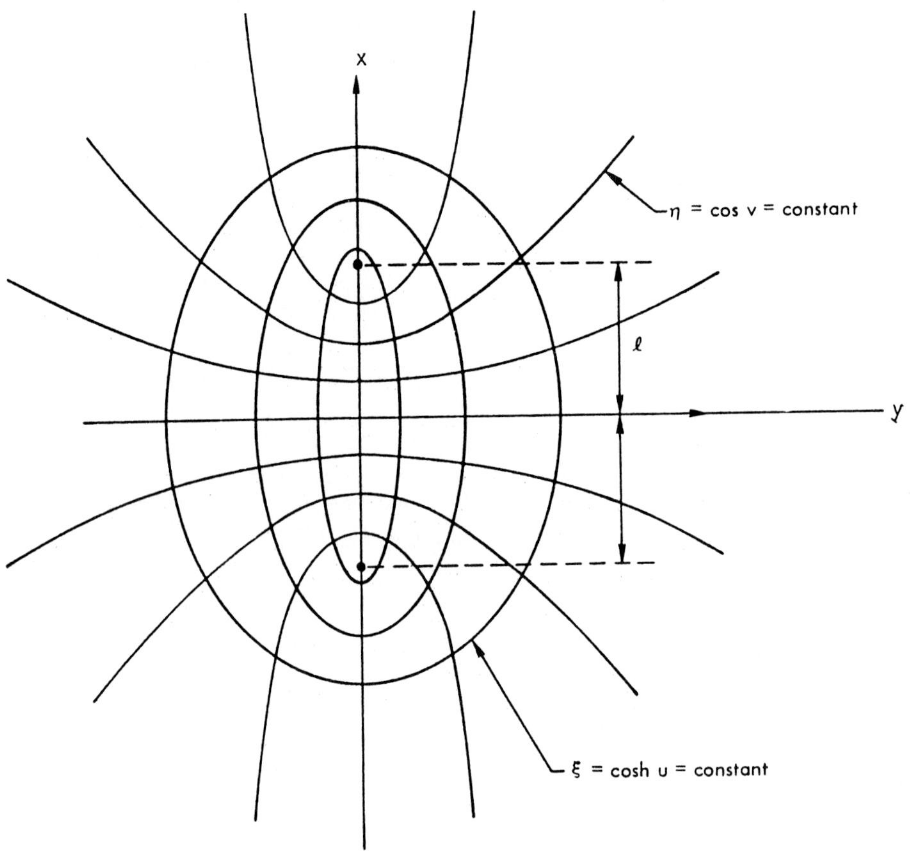

Fig. 20-1: Ellipsoidal coordinates

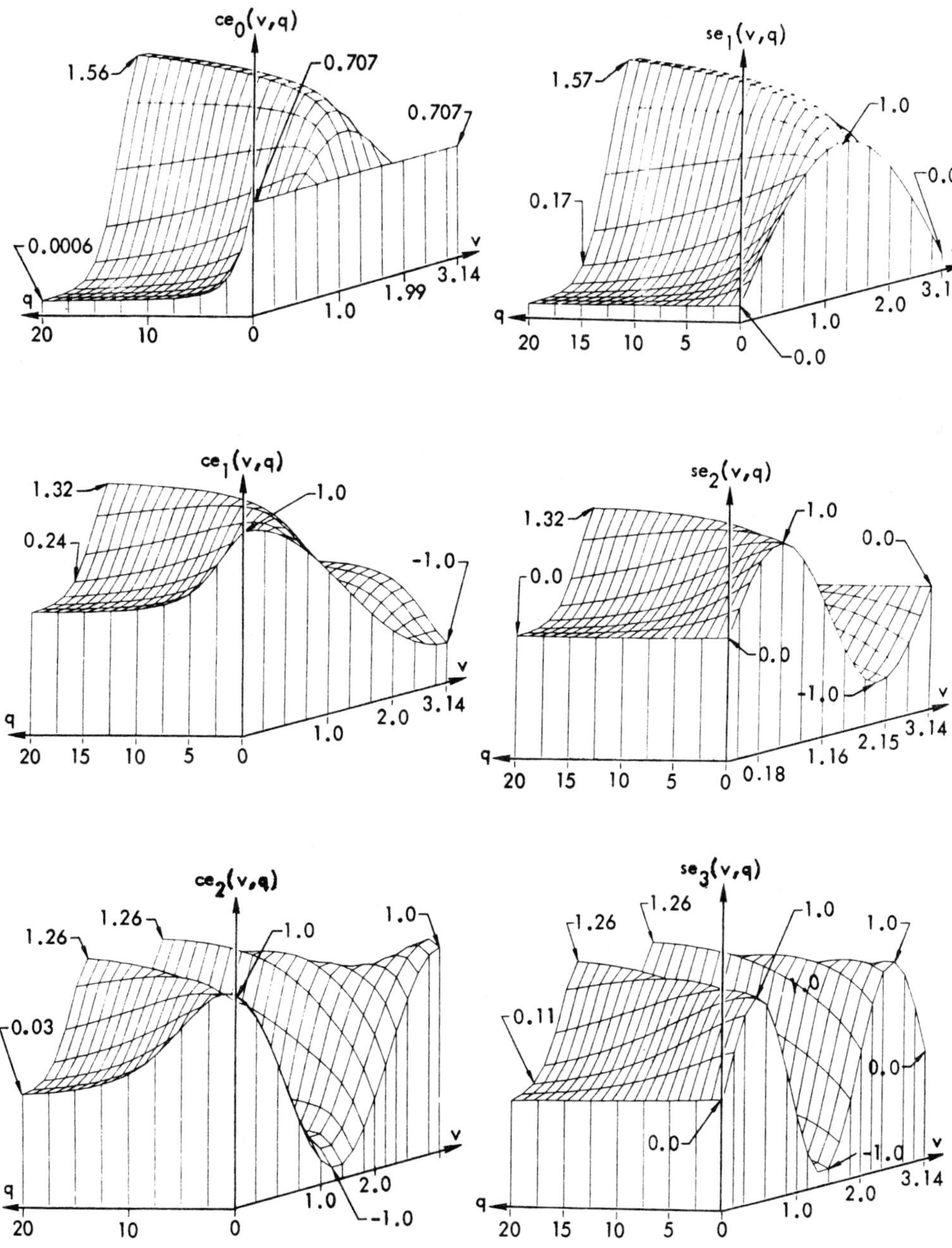

Fig. 20-2: Mathieu functions

This figure is taken from Mathematics Note 31 by Lytle and Lager. It is the property of the U. S. Government and not subject to copyright.

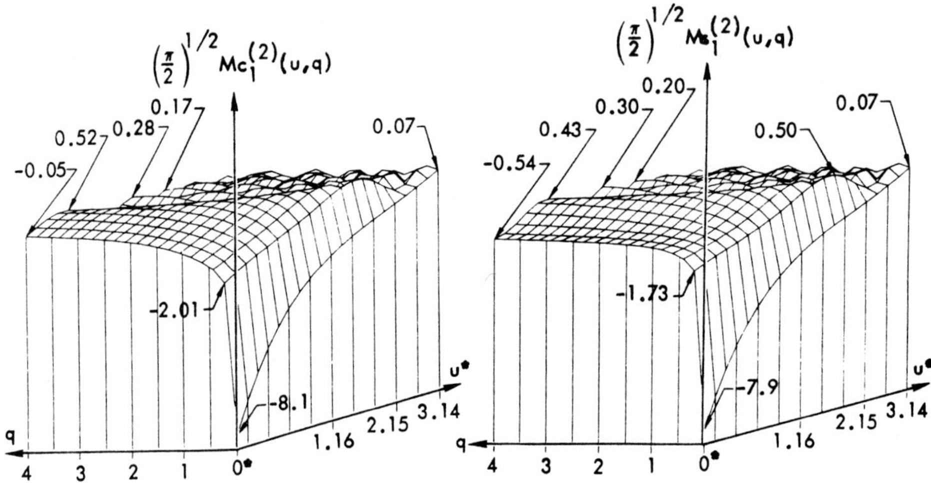

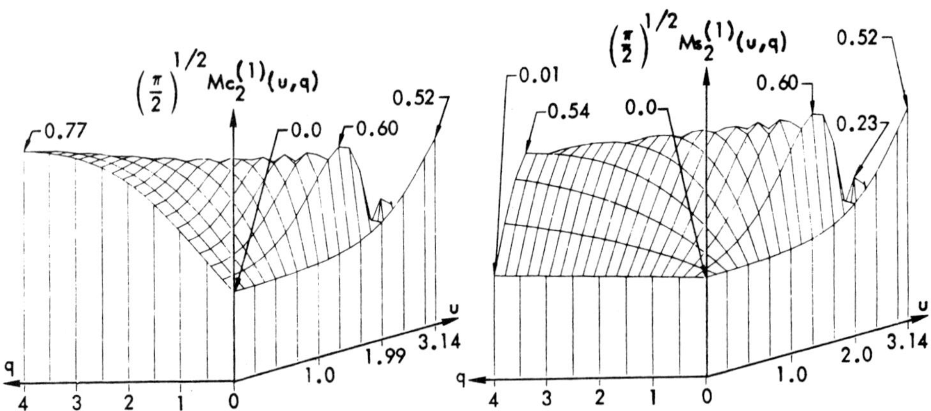

*Note that the lower bound of u is 0.01 (not 0.00) because the $Mc_1^{(2)}$ and $Ms_1^{(2)}$ functions go to $-\infty$ at $u = 0$, $q = 0$.

Fig. 20-3: Radial (associated) Mathieu functions.

```
/*
Mathieu functions

from C Mathematical Function Handbook by Louis Baker
Copyright 1991 by Louis Baker. All rights reserved.

based upon FORTRAN code of CALGO 352 of D. S. Clemm
*/

#include <stdio.h>
#include <alloc.h>
#include "cmlib.h"
#include "protom.h"

#define min(a,b) ((a)<(b)?(a):(b))
#define max(a,b) ((a)>(b)?(a):(b))
#define INDEX(i,j) [(j)+(i)*(coln)]

static double qmath,tol,qinv;
static double a,a0,a1;
static int type;

static double gmath[2][200],dg[2][200];
static int mf,m0,m1,m2s;
#define fl 1.e30

/* the following prototypes are not intended to be
global, as they have fairly common names.
comment the prototypes out if your C compiler is not
ANSI compatible
*/
static int coef( void);

int tmofa(alfa,tm,dtm) double alfa,*tm,*dtm;
{int k,kk,kt,l;
/* NOT modified to do c.f. the Lenz/Thompson/Barnett
method*/
double aa,dtype,
q1,q2,t,tt,sqrt(),a[3],b[3],aux;

kt=0;aa=alfa;dtype=type;
for(l=0;l<2;l++) {for(k=0;k<200;k++)
        {gmath[l][k]=dg[l][k]=0.;}
     }
if( (type%2))m0=3;
else m0=type+2;
k=.5*sqrt(max(0.,3.*qmath+aa));
m2s=min(2*k+m0+4,398+m0%2);
a[0]=1.;a[1]= (aa-(m2s+2.)*(m2s+2.))*qinv;
```

```
b[0]= (aa-m2s*m2s)*qinv;
b[1]=a[1]*b[0]-1.;
q1=a[1]/b[1];
kt=1;
for(k=0;k<200;k++)
   {
   mf=m2s+4+2*k;
   t=(aa-mf*mf)*qinv;
   a[2]=t*a[1]-a[0];
   b[2]=t*b[1]-b[0];
   q2=a[2]/b[2];
   if(abs(q1-q2)<tol){kt=0;break;}
   q1=q2;
   a[0]=a[1];b[0]=b[1];
   a[1]=a[2];b[1]=b[2];
   /* no need to renormalize???*/
   }
t=1./t;
tt=-t*t*qinv;
l=mf-m2s;
for(k=2;k<=l;k+=2)
   {
   t=1./(qinv*(aa-(mf-k)*(mf-k))-t);
   tt=t*t*(tt-qinv);
   }
kk= m2s>>1;
if(kt==1)q2=t;
gmath[1][kk]=.5*(q2+t);
dg[1][kk]=tt;
gmath[0][1]=1.;
for(k=m0;k<=m2s;k+=2)
   {
   kk=k>>1;
   if(k<5)
      {
      if(k<3)
         {
         gmath[0][1]=aa*qinv;
         dg[0][1]=qinv;
         }
      else if(k==3)
         {
         gmath[0][1]=(aa-1.)*qinv+dtype-2.;
         dg[0][1]=qinv;
         }
      else
         {
         aux=gmath[0][1];
         gmath[0][2]=(aa-4.)*qinv+(dtype-2.)/aux;
```

```
            dg[0][2]=qinv+(2.-dtype)*dg[0][1]/(aux*aux);
            if(type==2)gmath[0][1]=0.;
            }
         }
      else
         {
         aux=gmath[0][kk-1];
         gmath[0][kk]=(aa-(k-2)*(k-2))*qinv-1./aux;
         dg[0][kk]=qinv+ dg[0][kk-1]/(aux*aux);
         }
      if(abs(gmath[0][kk])<1.)goto stage2;
      }
/* backtrack*/
*tm= gmath[1][kk]-gmath[0][kk];
*dtm=dg[1][kk]-dg[0][kk];
m1=m2s;
kt=m2s-m0;
for(l=2;l<=kt;l+=2)
   {
   k=m2s-l;
   kk=k>>1;
   gmath[1][kk]=1./(qinv*(aa-k*k)-gmath[1][kk+1]);
   aux= gmath[1][kk];
   dg[1][kk]=-aux*aux*(qinv-dg[1][kk+1]);
   if(k<=2)
      {
      gmath[1][1]*=2.;
      dg[1][1]*=2.;
      }
   t= gmath[1][kk]-gmath[0][kk];
   if(abs(t)<abs(*tm))
      {*tm=t;*dtm= dg[1][kk]-dg[0][kk];m1=k;}
   }
stage2:
m1=k; k=m2s;kk=k>>1;
redo:
   if(k==m1)
   {
   if(k<=2)
      {gmath[1][1]*=2.;dg[1][1]*=2.;}
   *tm=gmath[1][kk]-gmath[0][kk];
   *dtm=dg[1][kk]-dg[0][kk];
   return 0;
   }
k-=2;
kk--;
t= (aa-k*k)*qinv-gmath[1][kk+1];
if(abs(t)>=1.)
   {again:
```

```
   gmath[1][kk]=1./t;
   dg[1][kk]=( dg[1][kk+1]-qinv)/(t*t);
   goto redo;
   }
if(k==m1)
   {
   if(t==0.)return 1;
   goto again;
   }
q1= dg[1][kk+1]-qinv;
while(1)
{
gmath[1][kk]=f1;
gmath[0][kk]=t;
k-=2;
kk--;
q2= t*(aa-k*k)*qinv-1.;
if(k==m1)
   {
   if(q2==0.)return 1;
   gmath[1][kk]=t/q2;
   dg[1][kk]= (q1-qinv*t*t)/(q2*q2);
   goto redo;
   }
if(abs(q2)-abs(t)<0.)
   {q1=q1/(t*t)-qinv;
   t=q2/t;
   continue;
   }
else/* was goto 280*/
   {
   gmath[1][kk]=t/q2;
   dg[1][kk]= (q1-qinv*t*t)/(q2*q2);
   goto redo;
   }
}/*stage3 loop*/
}

static int l,s,p,klast,kmax,mm,ml,n;
static double a,dmax,dlast,total,t,ab[200],u1,u2,x;

static int coef()
{int k,ka,kb,kk,m;
double log(),v2=1.e-15;
m=tmofa(a,&t,&t);/*set mf,etc and g*/
if(m){fprintf(stderr,
     " failure in tmfoa from coef\n");return m;}
for(k=0;k<200;k++)ab[k]=0.;
ka=m1-m0+2;
```

```
for(k=2;k<=ka;k+=2)
    {
    kk=(m1-k)>>1;
    if(k<=2)ab[kk]=1.;
    else ab[kk]=ab[kk+1]/gmath[0][kk+1];
    }
ka=0;
for (k=m1;k<=m2s;k+=2)
    {
    kk=k>>1;
    ml=k;
    if( gmath[1][kk]!=fl)ab[kk]=ab[kk-1]*gmath[1][kk];
    else
        {
        t=ab[kk-2];
        if(k==4 && m1==2)t+=t;
        ab[kk]=t/( (a-(k-2)*(k-2))*qinv*gmath[0][kk]-1.);
        }
    if( abs(ab[kk])>=1.e-12)ka=0;
    if(ka==5)goto norm;
    ka++;
    }
t=log(abs(ab[kk])/v2)/ log(1./abs(gmath[1][kk]));
ka=2*t;
ml=ka+2+m2s;
if(ml>399)
    {
    fprintf(stderr," ml ka m2s %d %d %d %e\n",ml,ka,m2s,t);
    return -1;
    }
kb=ka+2+mf;
t=1./(qinv*(a-kb*kb));
kk=mf-m2s;
for(k=2;k<=kk;k+=2) t=1./(qinv*(a-(kb-k)*(kb-k))-t);
kk=(ml>>1);
gmath[1][kk]=t;
for(k=2;k<=ka;k+=2)
    {kk=(ml-k)>>1;
    gmath[1][kk]=1./( qinv*(a-(ml-k)*(ml-k))
     -gmath[1][kk+1]);
    }
ka=m2s+2;
for(k=ka;k<=ml;k+=2)
    {
    kk=k>>1;
    ab[kk]=ab[kk-1]*gmath[1][kk];
    }
norm: t=ab[0];
mm= type%2; ka=mm+2;
```

```
for(k=ka;k<=ml;k+=2)
   {kk=k>>1;
   if( abs(t)<abs(ab[kk]))
      {
      t=ab[kk];mm=k;
      }
   }
for(k=0;k<=kk;k++) ab[k]/=t;
return 0;
}

/* fj returns J(n)  for z= u1; fy returns J or Y  z=u2,
depending on sol
dy,dj return the corresponding derivatives*/
double ju1[200],jyu2[200],dju1[200],djyu2[200];


double fj(n) int n;
{return ju1[n];
}

double fy(n) int n;
{return jyu2[n];
}

double dy(n) int n;
{return djyu2[n];
}

double dj(n) int n;
{return dju1[n];
}



double ds(kk)int kk;
{
double dsv;
int k,n1,n2;
k=kk;
n1=k-s;n2=k+s+p;
dsv= ab[k]*( fj(n1)*fy(n2)-fj(n2)*fy(n1));

/*printf(" ds %d %d %d %le %le %le %le %le\n"
   ,k,n1,n2,ab[k],fj(n1),fy(n2),fj(n2),fy(n1));
*/
if( (k+n)%2)dsv=-dsv;return dsv;
}
```

```
double dc(kk)int kk;
{
double dsv;
int k,n1,n2;
k=kk;
n1=k-s;n2=k+s+p;
dsv= ab[k]*( fj(n1)*fy(n2)+fj(n2)*fy(n1));
/*printf(" dc %d %d %d %le %le %le %le %le\n"
   ,k,n1,n2,ab[k],fj(n1),fy(n2),fj(n2),fy(n1));
*/
if((s+p)==0.)dsv*=.5;
if( (k+n)%2)dsv=-dsv;return dsv;
}


double dds(kk)int kk;
{
double dsv;
int k,n1,n2;
k=kk;
n1=k-s;n2=k+s+p;
dsv= ab[k]*(u2*fj(n1)*dy(n2)-fj(n2)*dy(n1))-
u1*(fy(n2)*dj(n1)-fy(n1)*dj(n2));
if( (k+n)%2)dsv=-dsv;return dsv;
}
double ddc(kk)int kk;
{
double dsv;
int k,n1,n2;
k=kk;
n1=k-s;n2=k+s+p;
dsv= ab[k]*(u2*fj(n1)*dy(n2)+fj(n2)*dy(n1))-
u1*(fy(n2)*dj(n1)+fy(n1)*dj(n2));
if((s+p)==0.)dsv*=.5;
if( (k+n)%2)dsv=-dsv;return dsv;
}

double ps(k)
{double sin();
return ab[k]*sin( x*(p+(k<<1)));
}

double pc(k)
{double cos();
return ab[k]*cos( x*(p+(k<<1)));
}

double dps(k)
{double cos();
```

```
t=p+(k<<1);
return ab[k]*t*cos( x*t);
}
double dpc(k)
{double sin();
t=p+(k<<1);
return -ab[k]*t*sin( x*t);
}


#define normlim  1.e-14

sum(func) double (*func)();
{       int k;
k=0; total= func(0); dmax=total;t=abs(total); kmax=0;
if(t<normlim)/* for x= pi/2 when f should be zero*/
   {
   kmax=klast=0;
   dmax=total=0.;
   t=1.; /* prevent division by zero*/
   return 1;
   }
/*printf(" in sum l=%d\n",l);*/
for(klast=1;klast<=l;klast++)
   {
   dlast= func(klast);
   /*printf(" func(%d=klast)=%le\n",klast,dlast);*/
   total+=dlast;
   if(t<abs(dlast))
      {
      dmax=dlast;
      t=abs(dmax);
      kmax=klast;
      }
   if(klast>s)
      {/* stop if "many" (3) small terms*/
      if( abs(dlast)/t> 1.e-12)k=0;
      k++;
      if(k>=3)break;
      }
   }
return 0;
}

bessinit(sol,n)
{struct complex z,j,y,h,jprime,yprime,hprime;int i,iv;
z.x=u1;z.y=0.;
/*printf(" bessinit u1=%le u2=%le n=%d\n",u1,u2,n);*/
for(i=0;i<=n;i++)
```

```
    {
    bessel(i,&z,&j,&y,&h,&jprime,&yprime,&hprime,&iv);
    if(iv)fprintf(stderr," bessint: pblm %d\n",iv);
    ju1[i]= j.x;
    dju1[i]=jprime.x;
    /*printf(" j,dj[%d]=%le %le\n",i,ju1[i],dju1[i]);*/
    }
z.x=u2;z.y=0.;
for(i=0;i<=n;i++)
    {
    bessel(i,&z,&j,&y,&h,&jprime,&yprime,&hprime,&iv);
    jyu2[i]= (sol==1)? j.x: y.x;
    djyu2[i]= (sol==1)? jprime.x: yprime.x;
    /*printf(" jy,djy[%d]=%le %le\n",i,jyu2[i],djyu2[i]);*/
    }
return 0;
}

int math(xx,qq,r,cv,sol,fnc,norm,f,k) double xx,qq,cv,f[];
int sol,fnc,norm,k[],r;
/* sol= 1 radial,first kind 2 second 3 periodic
at point x, order r, qq, cv=characteristic value a[r](q) or
b[r](q)
fnc= 1 b  2 a 3 deriv b 4 deriv a
norm= 1 neutral 2 Ince 3 Stratton
f[3] solution value, largest mag series term last term in
summation
k[2] 1 indices of terms in 2nd,3rd element of f */
{
int i,ll,m;
double sqrt(),aux;
if( sol<1 ||sol>3 ||fnc<1 ||fnc>4)goto bomb;
a=cv;qmath=qq; if(qmath!=0.)qinv=1./qmath;
tol=1.e-8;type=  ((fnc%2)<<1) + r%2;
m=coef();
if(m){fprintf(stderr," mathieu:coef failed\n");goto bomb; }
n=r>>1;
p=r%2;
s=mm>>1;
l=ml>>1;
x=xx;
t=1.;
if(sol==3) /* periodic case*/
    {
    switch(fnc)
        {
        case 1: sum(ps);break;
        case 2: sum(pc);break;
        case 3: sum(dps);break;
```

```
        default: sum(dpc);
        }
    if(norm==2)
        {
        t= ab[0]; t*=t;
        if(!type)t+=t;
        for(i=0;i<l;i++) {aux=ab[i+1];t+=aux*aux;}
        t=sqrt(t);
        i=m0>>1;
        if(ab[i-1]<0.)t=-t;
        }
    else if(norm>2)
        {
        if(type<=1)
            {
            t=ab[0];
            for (i=0;i<l;i++)
                {
                t+=ab[i+1];
                }
            }
        else
            {
            t=ab[0]*p;
            for(i=0;i<l;i++)
                {
                t+=ab[i+1]*(2*i+p);
                }
            }
        }
    }
else /* radial case*/
    {
    u1= sqrt(qmath)*exp(-x);
    u2=qmath/u1;
    ll=l+s+p;
    bessinit(sol,ll);
    switch (fnc)
        {
        case 1: sum(ds);break;
        case 2: sum(dc);break;
        case 3: sum(dds);break;
        default: sum(ddc);break;
        }
    }
/*printf(" t, total %le %le\n",t,total);*/
f[0]=total/t;f[1]=dmax/t;f[2]=dlast/t;
k[0]=kmax;k[1]=klast;
return m;
```

```
bomb:
f[0]=f[1]=f[2]=0.; k[0]=k[1]=0;
return ierrorcode;
}


/* parameter n not used- is this so in original code?*/
int bounds(k,approx,tola,cv,coln) int coln,k;double ap-
prox,tola,*cv;
{int m,ka,km;
double dtm,d0,d1,tm;
ka=0;km=k-1;
if(k!=1 && approx<= cv INDEX(0,km-1))
   a0= 1.+cv INDEX(0,km-1);
else
   a0=approx;
while(1)
{/* label 30*/
m=tmofa(a0,&tm,&dtm);
if(m>0)return m;
d0=-tm/dtm;
if(d0==0.)
   { cv INDEX(0,km)=a0; cv INDEX(1,km)=0.; return -1;}
if(d0>0.)
   {/* a0=lower, search for upper*/
   while(1)
      {
      a1=a0+d0+.1;
      m=tmofa(a1,&tm,&dtm);
      if(m>0)return m;
      d1=-tm/dtm;
      if(d1==0.)
         {cv INDEX(0,km)=a1;cv INDEX(1,km)=0.;return -1;}
      else if(d1>0.)
         {
         a0=a1;d0=d1;ka++;
         if(ka>=4)return 2;
         }   /* inifinite loop if d1<0. a1 doesn't change*/
      else goto 1200;
      }
   }
/* a1 upper search for lower*/
while(1)
   {
   a1=a0;d1=d0;
   a0= max(a1+d1-.1,-2.*qmath);
   if(k==1 || a0>cv INDEX(0,km-1))
      {
      m=tmofa(a0,&tm,&dtm);
```

```
        if(m>0)return m;
        d0=-tm/dtm;
        if(d0==0.){ cv INDEX(0,km)=a0; cv INDEX(1,km)=0.;
return -1;}
        else if(d0>0.)goto 1200;
        ka++;
        if(ka>=4)return 2;
        }
    else break;
    }
ka++;
if(ka>=4)return 2;
a0=a1+max(tola,abs(d1));
/* goto 30*/}
1200:a=.5*(a0+d0+a1+d1);
if(a<=a0 || a>=a1)a=.5*(a0+a1);
return m;
}

int mfitr8(tola,cv,dcv) double *dcv,*cv,tola;
{int m,n,last;
double a2,d,tm,dtm;
n=0;last=0;
while(1)
    {
    n++;
    m=tmofa(a,&tm,&dtm);
    if(m>0){*cv=*dcv=0.;return m;}
    d=-tm/dtm;
    if(n>=40 || a-a0 <=tola ||a1-a<=tola
 ||abs(d)<tola)last=1;
    if(d==0.){*cv=a;*dcv=0.;return m;}
    else if(d<0.)a1=a;
    else a0=a;
    a2=a+d;
    if(last)
        {
        if(a2>a0 && a2<a1)
            {
            m=tmofa(a2,&tm,&dtm);
            if(m>0){*cv=*dcv=0.;return m;}
            *dcv=d=-tm/dtm;
            *cv=a2;
            return m;
            }
        else
            {
            *cv=a;*dcv=d; return m;
            }
```

```
        }
    if(a2>a0 && a2<a1) a=a2;
    else a=.5*(a0+a1);
    }
}

/* matheign: compute the eigenvalues
and place in the array eigenv

q= parameter
r= count of desired eigenvalues
odd= 1(true) if odd else 0 for even eigenfunctions

returns the count of eigenvalues actually found
*/
int matheign(q,r,odd,eigenv) int r,odd;double q,eigenv[];
{
int i,j,coln; double *cv;
if(odd)n=r;
else n=r+1;
coln=n;
cv=(double *)malloc( sizeof(double)*coln*6);
j=mfcval(n,r,q,cv,coln);
for(i=0;i<j;i++) eigenv[i]=cv INDEX(0,i) ;
free(cv);
return j;
}


/* return value of mathieu functions
x= argument q=parameter
eigenv= array, previously computed. size r;

sol= 1 radial, first kind
     2 radial, second kind
     3 periodic

fnc= 1 odd solution
     2 even
     3 derivative of odd
     4 derivative of even

norm=1 neutral
     2 Ince
     3 Stratton
*/

double mathieu(x,q,r,eigenv,sol,fnc,norm)
int sol,fnc,norm,r;double x,q,eigenv[];
```

```
{
double fval,f[3];
int k[2],l;
l=math(x,q,r,eigenv[r],sol,fnc,norm,f,k); fval=f[0];
return fval;
}

int mfcval(n,r,qq,cv,coln) double *cv,qq; int n,r,coln;
{int j,k,kk,km,l,m;
double a,dtm,t,tm,tola,sqrt();
tol=1.e-3;
if(n>r) l=2;
else   l=1;
qmath=qq;if(qmath!=0.)qinv=1./qmath;
for(k=1;k<=n;k++)
   {
   j=k;km=k-1;
   if (qmath==0.)
      {
      m=k-l+1;
      cv INDEX(0,km)= cv INDEX(2,km)=cv INDEX(4,km)=m*m;
      cv INDEX(1,km)= cv INDEX(3,km)=cv INDEX(5,km)=0.;
      }
   else if(qmath<0.)
      { return 0;}
   else
      {
      kk=min(k,4);
      type= ((l%2)<<1)+ (k-l+1)%2 ;
      switch (kk)
         {
         case 1:
            {
            if(qmath<1.)
               {
               if(l==1)
                  a=1.-qmath-.125*qmath*qmath;
               else
                  {
                  a=qmath*qmath;
                  a*=(.0546875*a-.5);
                  }
               break;
               }
            else
               {
               if(qmath<2.)
                  {
                  if(l==1)
```

```
                    a=1.033-1.0746*qmath
                    -.0688*qmath*qmath;
                 else
                    a=.23-.459*qmath-.191*qmath*qmath;
                 break;
                 }
              a=-.25-2.*qmath+2.*sqrt(qmath);break;
              }
           }
        case 2:
           {t=l;
           if(qmath*t<6.)
              {
              if(l==1)
                 a=4.01521-qmath*(.046+qmath*.0667867);
              else
                 a=1.+1.05007*qmath-
                   .180143*qmath*qmath;
              break;
              }
           t=k-1;
           a= cv INDEX(0,km-1)-t+4.*sqrt(qmath);break;
           }
        case 3:
           if(qmath<8.)
              {
              if(l==1)
                 a=8.93867+.178156*qmath
                   -qmath*qmath*.0252132;
              else
                 a=3.70017+.953485*qmath-
.0475065*qmath*qmath;
              break;
              }
           t=k-1;
           a= cv INDEX(0,km-1)-t+4.*sqrt(qmath);break;

        case 4:
           a= cv INDEX(0,km-1)-cv INDEX(0,km-2);
           a=3.*a+cv INDEX(0,km-3);
           break;
        default:
           return (0)/* trouble*/;
        }
     }
   if(qmath<1.)
     {if(k==1)tola= max(min(tol,abs(a)),1.e-7);
     else tola=tol*abs(a);
     }
```

```
   else
      {
      tola=tol*max(qmath,abs(a));
      tola= max(min(.4*sqrt(qmath),min(tola,abs(a))),
               1.e-7);
      }
   m=bounds(k,a,tola,cv,coln);
   if(m>0)return --j;
   else if(!m)/* m==0*/
      {
      m=mfitr8(tola,&(cv INDEX(0,km)),&(cv INDEX(1,km)));
      if(m>0)return --j;
      }
   t= cv INDEX(0,km)-tola;
   m=tmofa(t,&tm,&dtm);
   if(m>0){cv INDEX(2,km)=cv INDEX(3,km)=0.;continue;}
   else
      {
      cv INDEX(2,km)=t;
      cv INDEX(3,km)=-tm/dtm;
      }
   t= cv INDEX(0,km)+tola;
   m=tmofa(t,&tm,&dtm);
   if(m>0){cv INDEX(4,km)=cv INDEX(5,km)=0.;continue;}
   else
      {
      cv INDEX(4,km)=t;
      cv INDEX(5,km)=-tm/dtm;
      }
   }/* loop over values*/
return j;
}
```

```
/*
Mathieu functions test driver

from C Mathematical Function Handbook by Louis Baker
Copyright 1991 by Louis Baker. All rights reserved.
*/

#include <stdio.h>
#include "cmlib.h"
#include "protom.h"

#define INDEX(i,j) [(j)+(i)*(coln)]

double cv[120];/* 6 x 20*/

main()
{
int l,n,r,coln,i,j,sol,fnc,norm,k[2],odd;
double q,x,f[3],cvv,fval[3],y;
coln=20;n=5;r=5/*5 odd or 4 even*/;q=5.;
printf(" enter q value\n");scanf("%le",&q);
printf(" q=%le\n",q);
printf(" enter fnc value 1=odd 2=even 3 deriv,odd 4
deriv,even\n");
scanf("%d",&fnc);
printf(" enter r\n");
scanf("%d",&r);
printf(" fnc=%d r=%d\n",fnc,r,n);

/* direct user interface*/
if(fnc%2){/*odd*/n=r;}
else n=r+1;
j=mfcval(n,r,q,cv,coln);
printf(" j=%d\n",j);
for(i=0;i<j;i++)printf("r=n %e\n",cv INDEX(0,i) );

/* a more user friendly interface function: */
odd= fnc%2;
matheign(q,r,odd,cv);
for(i=0;i<j;i++)printf("r=n %e\n",cv INDEX(0,i) );

/* for each order */
for(i=0;i<j;i++)
   {r=i;
   printf(" r=%d\n",i);
   cvv=cv INDEX(0,i);/*q unchanged*/
   sol=3;x= .0*pi;
   printf(" x     norm:neutral  Ince   Stratton\n");
   for(norm=1;norm<4;norm++)
```

```
      {
      l=math(x,q,r,cvv,sol,fnc,norm,f,k);
fval[norm-1]=f[0];
      }
   printf(" x=%f %le %e %e %d\n",
    x,fval[0],fval[1],fval[2],l);
   norm=2;
   y=mathieu(x,q,r,cv,sol,fnc,norm);
   printf(" Ince=%le\n",y);
   x=.5*pi;
   for(norm=1;norm<4;norm++)
      {
      l=math(x,q,r,cvv,sol,fnc,norm,f,k);
fval[norm-1]=f[0];
      }
   printf(" x=%f %le %e %e
%d\n",x,fval[0],fval[1],fval[2],l);
   }
printf(" radial mathieu functions\n");
for(i=0;i<j;i++)
   {r=i;
   cvv=cv INDEX(0,i);/*q unchanged*/
   fnc=2;sol=1;x= .50*pi;
  /* sol for radial first kind norm irrel*/
   norm=1;
      {
      l=math(x,q,r,cvv,sol,fnc,norm,f,k);
       fval[norm-1]=f[0];
      }
   printf(" x=%f %le %d\n",x,fval[0],l);
   }
}
```

Test Output: Mathieu functions

```
enter q value
5
 q=5.000000e+00
 enter fnc value 1=odd 2=even 3 deriv,odd 4 deriv,even
2
 enter r
20
 fnc=2 r=20
 j=21
r=n -5.800046e+00
r=n 1.858188e+00
r=n 7.449110e+00
r=n 1.154883e+01
r=n 1.709658e+01
r=n 2.554997e+01
r=n 3.636090e+01
r=n 4.926145e+01
r=n 6.419884e+01
r=n 8.115645e+01
r=n 1.001264e+02
r=n 1.211042e+02
r=n 1.440874e+02
r=n 1.690744e+02
r=n 1.960641e+02
r=n 2.250558e+02
r=n 2.560490e+02
r=n 2.890434e+02
r=n 3.240387e+02
r=n 3.610347e+02
r=n 4.000313e+02
r=n -5.800046e+00
r=n 1.858188e+00
r=n 7.449110e+00
r=n 1.154883e+01
r=n 1.709658e+01
r=n 2.554997e+01
r=n 3.636090e+01
r=n 4.926145e+01
r=n 6.419884e+01
r=n 8.115645e+01
r=n 1.001264e+02
r=n 1.211042e+02
r=n 1.440874e+02
r=n 1.690744e+02
r=n 1.960641e+02
r=n 2.250558e+02
r=n 2.560490e+02
r=n 2.890434e+02
```

```
r=n 3.240387e+02
r=n 3.610347e+02
r=n 4.000313e+02
 r=0
 x     norm:neutral  Ince  Stratton
 x=0.000000 -7.145368e-02 4.480970e-02 1.000000e+00 0
 Ince=4.480970e-02
 x=1.570796 -2.128536e+00 1.334838e+00 2.978904e+01 0
 r=1
 x     norm:neutral  Ince  Stratton
 x=0.000000 3.364641e-01 2.565416e-01 1.000000e+00 0
 Ince=2.565416e-01
 x=1.570796 0.000000e+00 0.000000e+00 0.000000e+00 0
 r=2
 x     norm:neutral  Ince  Stratton
 x=0.000000 1.124922e+00 7.352943e-01 1.000000e+00 0
 Ince=7.352943e-01
 x=1.570796 -1.108390e+00 -7.244882e-01 -9.853036e-01 0
 r=3
 x     norm:neutral  Ince  Stratton
 x=0.000000 1.558878e+00 1.111248e+00 1.000000e+00 0
 Ince=1.111248e+00
 x=1.570796 0.000000e+00 0.000000e+00 0.000000e+00 0
 r=4
 x     norm:neutral  Ince  Stratton
 x=0.000000 1.390582e+00 1.193331e+00 1.000000e+00 0
 Ince=1.193331e+00
 x=1.570796 9.554846e-01 8.199511e-01 6.871114e-01 0
 r=5
 x     norm:neutral  Ince  Stratton
 x=0.000000 1.212432e+00 1.124807e+00 1.000000e+00 0
 Ince=1.124807e+00
 x=1.570796 0.000000e+00 0.000000e+00 0.000000e+00 0
 r=6
 x     norm:neutral  Ince  Stratton
 x=0.000000 1.132931e+00 1.079697e+00 1.000000e+00 0
 Ince=1.079697e+00
 x=1.570796 -9.785704e-01 -9.325896e-01 -8.637512e-01 0
 r=7
 x     norm:neutral  Ince  Stratton
 x=0.000000 1.092713e+00 1.055880e+00 1.000000e+00 0
 Ince=1.055880e+00
 x=1.570796 0.000000e+00 0.000000e+00 0.000000e+00 0
 r=8
 x     norm:neutral  Ince  Stratton
 x=0.000000 1.068912e+00 1.041698e+00 1.000000e+00 0
 Ince=1.041698e+00
 x=1.570796 9.868651e-01 9.617409e-01 9.232430e-01 0
 r=9
```

```
x      norm:neutral   Ince   Stratton
x=0.000000 1.053425e+00 1.032426e+00 1.000000e+00 0
Ince=1.032426e+00
x=1.570796 0.000000e+00 0.000000e+00 0.000000e+00 0
r=10
x      norm:neutral   Ince   Stratton
x=0.000000 1.042724e+00 1.025994e+00 1.000000e+00 0
Ince=1.025994e+00
x=1.570796 -9.912509e-01 -9.753469e-01 -9.506356e-01 0
r=11
x      norm:neutral   Ince   Stratton
x=0.000000 1.034985e+00 1.021325e+00 1.000000e+00 0
Ince=1.021325e+00
x=1.570796 0.000000e+00 0.000000e+00 0.000000e+00 0
r=12
x      norm:neutral   Ince   Stratton
x=0.000000 1.029195e+00 1.017822e+00 1.000000e+00 0
Ince=1.017822e+00
x=1.570796 9.937933e-01 9.828108e-01 9.656022e-01 0
r=13
x      norm:neutral   Ince   Stratton
x=0.000000 1.024744e+00 1.015121e+00 1.000000e+00 0
Ince=1.015121e+00
x=1.570796 0.000000e+00 0.000000e+00 0.000000e+00 0
r=14
x      norm:neutral   Ince   Stratton
x=0.000000 1.021249e+00 1.012998e+00 1.000000e+00 0
Ince=1.012998e+00
x=1.570796 -9.953810e-01 -9.873389e-01 -9.746705e-01 0
r=15
x      norm:neutral   Ince   Stratton
x=0.000000 1.018448e+00 1.011293e+00 1.000000e+00 0
Ince=1.011293e+00
x=1.570796 0.000000e+00 0.000000e+00 0.000000e+00 0
r=16
x      norm:neutral   Ince   Stratton
x=0.000000 1.016172e+00 1.009906e+00 1.000000e+00 0
Ince=1.009906e+00
x=1.570796 9.964344e-01 9.902901e-01 9.805767e-01 0
r=17
x      norm:neutral   Ince   Stratton
x=0.000000 1.014294e+00 1.008760e+00 1.000000e+00 0
Ince=1.008760e+00
x=1.570796 0.000000e+00 0.000000e+00 0.000000e+00 0
r=18
x      norm:neutral   Ince   Stratton
x=0.000000 0.000000e+00 0.000000e+00 0.000000e+00 0
Ince=0.000000e+00
x=1.570796 0.000000e+00 0.000000e+00 0.000000e+00 0
```

```
r=19
x     norm:neutral  Ince  Stratton
x=0.000000 0.000000e+00 0.000000e+00 0.000000e+00 0
Ince=0.000000e+00
x=1.570796 0.000000e+00 0.000000e+00 0.000000e+00 0
r=20
x     norm:neutral  Ince  Stratton
x=0.000000 0.000000e+00 0.000000e+00 0.000000e+00 0
Ince=0.000000e+00
x=1.570796 0.000000e+00 0.000000e+00 0.000000e+00 0
radial mathieu functions
x=1.570796 -7.459304e-01 0
x=1.570796 -8.123138e-01 0
x=1.570796 1.421395e+00 0
x=1.570796 5.609594e-01 0
x=1.570796 0.000000e+00 0
x=1.570796 0.000000e+00 0
x=1.570796 0.000000e+00 0
x=1.570796 0.000000e+00 0
x=1.570796 0.000000e+00 0
x=1.570796 0.000000e+00 0
x=1.570796 0.000000e+00 0
x=1.570796 0.000000e+00 0
x=1.570796 -1.000000e+00 0
x=1.570796 1.000000e+00 0
x=1.570796 0.000000e+00 0
x=1.570796 0.000000e+00 0
x=1.570796 0.000000e+00 0
x=1.570796 0.000000e+00 0
x=1.570796 0.000000e+00 0
x=1.570796 0.000000e+00 0
x=1.570796 0.000000e+00 0

C:\CMATHLIB\CMATH\S91 mathieu
 enter q value
5
 q=5.000000e+00
 enter fnc value 1=odd 2=even 3 deriv,odd 4 deriv,even
1
 enter r
20
 fnc=1 r=20
 j=20
r=n -5.790081e+00
r=n 2.099460e+00
r=n 9.236328e+00
r=n 1.664822e+01
r=n 2.551082e+01
r=n 3.635887e+01
```

```
r=n 4.926138e+01
r=n 6.419884e+01
r=n 8.115645e+01
r=n 1.001264e+02
r=n 1.211042e+02
r=n 1.440874e+02
r=n 1.690744e+02
r=n 1.960641e+02
r=n 2.250558e+02
r=n 2.560490e+02
r=n 2.890434e+02
r=n 3.240387e+02
r=n 3.610347e+02
r=n 4.000313e+02
r=n -5.790081e+00
r=n 2.099460e+00
r=n 9.236328e+00
r=n 1.664822e+01
r=n 2.551082e+01
r=n 3.635887e+01
r=n 4.926138e+01
r=n 6.419884e+01
r=n 8.115645e+01
r=n 1.001264e+02
r=n 1.211042e+02
r=n 1.440874e+02
r=n 1.690744e+02
r=n 1.960641e+02
r=n 2.250558e+02
r=n 2.560490e+02
r=n 2.890434e+02
r=n 3.240387e+02
r=n 3.610347e+02
r=n 4.000313e+02
 r=0
 x     norm:neutral  Ince  Stratton
 x=0.000000 0.000000e+00 0.000000e+00 -0.000000e+00 0
 Ince=0.000000e+00
 x=1.570796 0.000000e+00 0.000000e+00 -0.000000e+00 0
 r=1
 x     norm:neutral  Ince  Stratton
 x=0.000000 0.000000e+00 0.000000e+00 0.000000e+00 0
 Ince=0.000000e+00
 x=1.570796 2.080092e+00 1.556723e+00 3.353511e+00 0
 r=2
 x     norm:neutral  Ince  Stratton
 x=0.000000 0.000000e+00 0.000000e+00 -0.000000e+00 0
 Ince=0.000000e+00
 x=1.570796 0.000000e+00 0.000000e+00 -0.000000e+00 0
```

```
r=3
x      norm:neutral  Ince   Stratton
x=0.000000 0.000000e+00 0.000000e+00 0.000000e+00 0
Ince=0.000000e+00
x=1.570796 1.907908e-01 1.672275e-01 2.498752e-01 0
r=4
x      norm:neutral  Ince   Stratton
x=0.000000 0.000000e+00 0.000000e+00 0.000000e+00 0
Ince=0.000000e+00
x=1.570796 0.000000e+00 0.000000e+00 0.000000e+00 0
r=5
x      norm:neutral  Ince   Stratton
x=0.000000 0.000000e+00 0.000000e+00 0.000000e+00 0
Ince=0.000000e+00
x=1.570796 9.107599e-01 8.910574e-01 7.081400e-01 0
r=6
x      norm:neutral  Ince   Stratton
x=0.000000 0.000000e+00 0.000000e+00 0.000000e+00 0
Ince=0.000000e+00
x=1.570796 0.000000e+00 0.000000e+00 0.000000e+00 0
r=7
x      norm:neutral  Ince   Stratton
x=0.000000 0.000000e+00 0.000000e+00 0.000000e+00 0
Ince=0.000000e+00
x=1.570796 9.156271e-01 9.117296e-01 8.036136e-01 0
r=8
x      norm:neutral  Ince   Stratton
x=0.000000 0.000000e+00 0.000000e+00 0.000000e+00 0
Ince=0.000000e+00
x=1.570796 0.000000e+00 0.000000e+00 0.000000e+00 0
r=9
x      norm:neutral  Ince   Stratton
x=0.000000 0.000000e+00 0.000000e+00 0.000000e+00 0
Ince=0.000000e+00
x=1.570796 9.483635e-01 9.469221e-01 8.876124e-01 0
r=10
x      norm:neutral  Ince   Stratton
x=0.000000 0.000000e+00 0.000000e+00 0.000000e+00 0
Ince=0.000000e+00
x=1.570796 0.000000e+00 0.000000e+00 0.000000e+00 0
r=11
x      norm:neutral  Ince   Stratton
x=0.000000 0.000000e+00 0.000000e+00 0.000000e+00 0
Ince=0.000000e+00
x=1.570796 9.644117e-01 9.637485e-01 9.253451e-01 0
r=12
x      norm:neutral  Ince   Stratton
x=0.000000 0.000000e+00 0.000000e+00 0.000000e+00 0
Ince=0.000000e+00
```

```
x=1.570796 0.000000e+00 0.000000e+00 0.000000e+00 0
r=13
x     norm:neutral  Ince  Stratton
x=0.000000 0.000000e+00 0.000000e+00 0.000000e+00 0
Ince=0.000000e+00
x=1.570796 9.740074e-01 9.736588e-01 9.463366e-01 0
r=14
x     norm:neutral  Ince  Stratton
x=0.000000 0.000000e+00 0.000000e+00 0.000000e+00 0
Ince=0.000000e+00
x=1.570796 0.000000e+00 0.000000e+00 0.000000e+00 0
r=15
x     norm:neutral  Ince  Stratton
x=0.000000 0.000000e+00 0.000000e+00 0.000000e+00 0
Ince=0.000000e+00
x=1.570796 9.801803e-01 9.799794e-01 9.594390e-01 0
r=16
x     norm:neutral  Ince  Stratton
x=0.000000 0.000000e+00 0.000000e+00 0.000000e+00 0
Ince=0.000000e+00
x=1.570796 0.000000e+00 0.000000e+00 0.000000e+00 0
r=17
x     norm:neutral  Ince  Stratton
x=0.000000 0.000000e+00 0.000000e+00 0.000000e+00 0
Ince=0.000000e+00
x=1.570796 9.843855e-01 9.842615e-01 9.682194e-01 0
r=18
x     norm:neutral  Ince  Stratton
x=0.000000 0.000000e+00 0.000000e+00 0.000000e+00 0
Ince=0.000000e+00
x=1.570796 0.000000e+00 0.000000e+00 0.000000e+00 0
r=19
x     norm:neutral  Ince  Stratton
x=0.000000 0.000000e+00 0.000000e+00 0.000000e+00 0
Ince=0.000000e+00
x=1.570796 9.873793e-01 9.872985e-01 9.744071e-01 0
radial mathieu functions
x=1.570796 -7.454145e-01 0
x=1.570796 -8.040226e-01 0
x=1.570796 1.428913e+00 0
x=1.570796 1.110052e+00 0
x=1.570796 -9.159019e-01 0
x=1.570796 -1.040612e+00 0
x=1.570796 9.647921e-01 0
x=1.570796 1.019700e+00 0
x=1.570796 -9.798531e-01 0
x=1.570796 -1.011954e+00 0
x=1.570796 9.868271e-01 0
x=1.570796 1.008077e+00 0
```

```
x=1.570796 -9.906872e-01 0
x=1.570796 -1.005840e+00 0
x=1.570796 9.930585e-01 0
x=1.570796 1.004426e+00 0
x=1.570796 -9.946228e-01 0
x=1.570796 -1.003472e+00 0
x=1.570796 9.957102e-01 0
x=1.570796 1.002799e+00 0
```

Chapter 21

The Spheroidal Wave Functions

Introduction

The Spheroidal Wave functions are solutions to Laplace's equation when separated in prolate or oblate spheroidal coordinates. The angular functions are related to Legendre functions, and the radial functions are related to Bessel functions.

We provide here the $d_{\rho l n}$ coefficients mentioned in Abramowitz and Stegun as well as the other functions given there. We also provide the normalization factor N_{nm} and the coefficient ρ_{nm}, following Flammer, as well as results therein for negative m.

Spheroidal Wave Functions

The Spheroidal Wave functions solve the Helmholtz wave equation in spheroidal coordinates with solutions of the form , $R_{mn}^{(i)}(c,\xi)\, S_{mn}^{(i)}(c,\eta) e^{\pm i m \varphi}$, where R is the radial solution, S the angular solution, and the superscript i is either 1 or 2 to denote solutions of the first and second kinds, respectively. Prolate spheroidal coordinates are the (two-dimensional) elliptic coordinates of the previous chapter, rotated about the major axis of the ellipse. Oblate coordinates result from rotation about the minor axis of the ellipse. The coordinates are confocal ellipses and hyperbolas (see Figs. 21-1 and 21-2). The prolate wave functions satisfy the equation $\frac{d}{dx}[(1-x^2)\frac{dy}{dx}] + (\lambda_{mn} - c^2x^2 - \frac{m^2}{1-x^2})\, y = 0$, where x is either ξ or η. The oblate satisfy the same equation with the substitutions $c \to \pm ic, \xi \to \mp i\xi$. Thus, the oblate radial functions are written $R_{mn}^{(1)}(-ic, i\xi)$, for example. The radial and angular eigen-solutions satisfy the same equations. (Different authors exchange which variable is which. Page and Adams use the opposite convention of that of Abramowitz and Stegun.) The eigenvalue λ_{mn} is chosen so that the solutions are finite at ± 1. For prolate spheroidal coordinates, the coordinates are related to the cartesian coordinates by $x = l\sqrt{(1-\eta^2)(\xi^2-1)}\cos\varphi$, $y = l\sqrt{(1-\eta^2)(\xi^2-1)}\sin\varphi$, $z = l\eta\xi$. For oblate spheroidal coordinates, they are related to the cartesian coordinates by $x = l\sqrt{(1-\eta^2)(\xi^2+1)}\cos\varphi$, $y = l\sqrt{(1-\eta^2)(\xi^2+1)}\sin\varphi$, $z = l\eta\xi$. Note that authors differ as to which axis is used for rotation (as Abramowitz and Stegun), and other details. The variables range $-1 \le \eta \le 1$ and, for prolate coordinates, $1 \le \xi \le \infty$ while for oblate coordinates $0 \le \xi \le \infty$. Note also that, in analogy to the Hankel functions, one can define

$R^{(3)} = R^{(1)} + i\,R^{(2)}$ and $R^{(4)} = R^{(1)} - i\,R^{(2)}$. Note that the ellipses have different eccentricities, and approach spheres for large ξ. The behavior of the solutions for prolate and oblate coordinates are rather different. The wave functions are developed as series in Legendre functions for the angular functions and spherical Bessel functions for the radial functions. $S^{(1)}_{mn}$ is written as a sum over even or odd $P_n^m(\eta)$, while $S^{(2)}_{mn}$ is the analogous sum over $Q_n^m(\eta)$. Simlarly, the $R^{(p)}_{mn}(c,\xi)$ can be written as a series in spherical Bessel functions (with a multiplicative factor $\left(\frac{\xi^2-1}{\xi^2}\right)^{m/2}$ and a normalizing factor), using $J_{n+1/2} = j_n$ for p = 1 and $Y_{n+1/2} = y_n$ for p = 2. Notice that one can use expansions in these functions instead of spheroidal wave functions if it is not required to expand in eigenvalues. This is often done. See, for example, the discussion of the electromagnetic oscillations of a perfectly conducting prolate spheroid in Page and Adams. See also *Electromagnetic and Acoustic Scattering by Simple Shapes*, referenced in Chapter 29. See Interaction Note 235 by Lytle and Deadrick for the eigenvalues of spheroids (called "natural frequencies" by them, and "free oscillations" in Page and Adams). These are determined, for example, by the condition $R^{(4)}_{1n}(c,\xi_0) = 0$ for TE modes and prolate spheroids, and by the condition $\left(\frac{\partial}{\partial\xi}[\sqrt{\xi^2-1}\,R^{(4)}_{1n}(c,\xi)]\right)_{\xi=\xi_0} = 0$ for TM modes. Similar conditions can be for the oblate spheroids. Formally, at least, the treatment is much simpler using the Spheroidal Wave functions. Prolate spheroids are suited to modeling scatterers such as wires, while oblate spheroids are suited to modeling disks. See the paper by Fletcher and Harrison for the application of the oblate spheroidal wave functions to diffraction at an aperture in a screen. After all, a hole in an infinitesimally thin sheet is a disk.

Prolate spheroidal wave functions have been used as windowing functions for spectrum estimation. See the article by Thomson. The S_{0n} appear here because they are eigenfunctions of the Dirichlet kernel: $\mu_n(c)\, S_{0n}(c,z) = \int_{-1}^{1} \frac{\mathrm{sinc}(z-t)}{\pi(z-t)} S_{0n}(c,z)\, dt$. They form a complete, orthogonal set of functions on this interval, as well as $(-\infty,\infty)$. Slepian has a series of articles in the *Bell System Technical J.* on the subject. See also the book by Papoulis.

Generalized Spheroidal Wave Functions

Slepian defines so-called generalized spheroidal wave functions, for application to laser resonator eigenmode calculations. These satisfy the equation $(1-x^2)\frac{d^2y}{dx^2} - 2x\frac{dy}{dx} + (\chi - c^2x^2 + \frac{1/4 - N^2}{x^2})\, y = 0$. This generalizes the equation for order zero (m = 0). Note that this equation is not a generalization of the general spheroidal wave function. It may be treated by methods very similar to those of this chapter.

Caveat

Table 21.5 of Abramowitz and Stegun lists Prolate Joining factors of the first kind $\kappa^{(1)}_{mn}$. Results of the programs presented agree with those in this table for m,n sets 00,11,12,13,22. For 02, they are one-half of the values given in this table. For 01, they are different as well. The first value listed in that table for 01, .9422, appears to be the value for the first d_{mn} coefficient. Because of the agreement with the other listed values, it is believed that the tabulated values which disagree with the computed values are wrong.

Method

All the code of this section is original, and was checked against the results in Lytle and Deadrick. The methods are rather similar to those of the preceding chapter, with a continued fraction method used to determine the eigenvalues and expansion coefficients. We use the normalization of Flammer, i. e., that of Abramowitz and Stegun. Note that the the index of the d_r^{mn} and $d_{\rho|r}^{mn}$ coefficients in their arrays is somewhat tricky, especially for negative values of r for the former and for all of the latter. If you intend to use these coefficients directly, be sure you understand the code thoroughly.

References

C. Flammer, *Spheroidal Wave Functions* (Stanford, C. A.: University Press, 1957).

H. J. Fletcher, *Evaluation of the Oblate Spheroidal Wave Functions*, Math. Note 60, Phillips Lab., Kirtland AFB (available through DTIC—see previous chapter), Dec. 9, 1978.

H. J. Fletcher & A. Harrison, *Diffraction Through a Circular Aperture in a Screen Separating Two Different Media,* Interaction Note 352, Phillips Lab., Kirtland AFB (available through DTIC—see previous chapter), Dec. 1978.

R. J. Lytle, F. J. Deadrick, *Prolate and Oblate Spheroidal Wave Functions of Complex Argument*, Math. Note 32, Phillips Lab., Kirtland AFB (available through DTIC—see previous chapter), Oct. 24, 1973.

R. J. Lytle, F. J. Deadrick, *Determining the Natural Frequencies of Spheroids via the Boundary-Value Problem Formulation*, Interaction Note 235, Phillips Lab., Kirtland AFB (available through DTIC—see previous chapter), April 24, 1975.

L. Page and N. I. Adams, Jr., *Electrodynamics* (N. Y.: Dover, 1940).

A. Papoulis, *Signal Analysis* (N. Y.: McGraw-Hill, 1977).

D. Slepian, H. J. Landau, H. O. Pollack, *Bell System Technical J.*, **40,** 43, 1961.

D. Slepian, *Bell System Technical J.*, **43,** 3009, 1964.

D. J. Thomson, *Proc. IEEE*, **70**, p. 1055, 1982.

Figures

Figs. 21-1 and 21-2 show the spheroidal coordinate systems. Figs. 21-3 through 21-7 show plots of various Spheriodal functions.

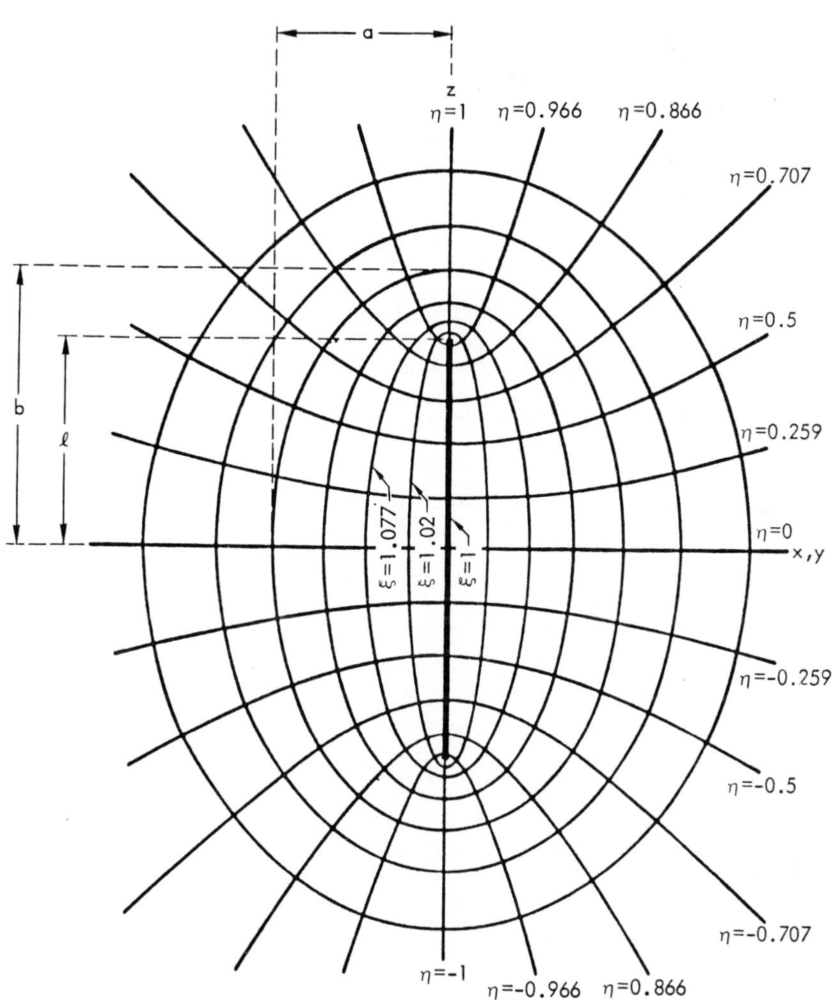

Fig. 12-1: Prolate Spheroidal coordinates.

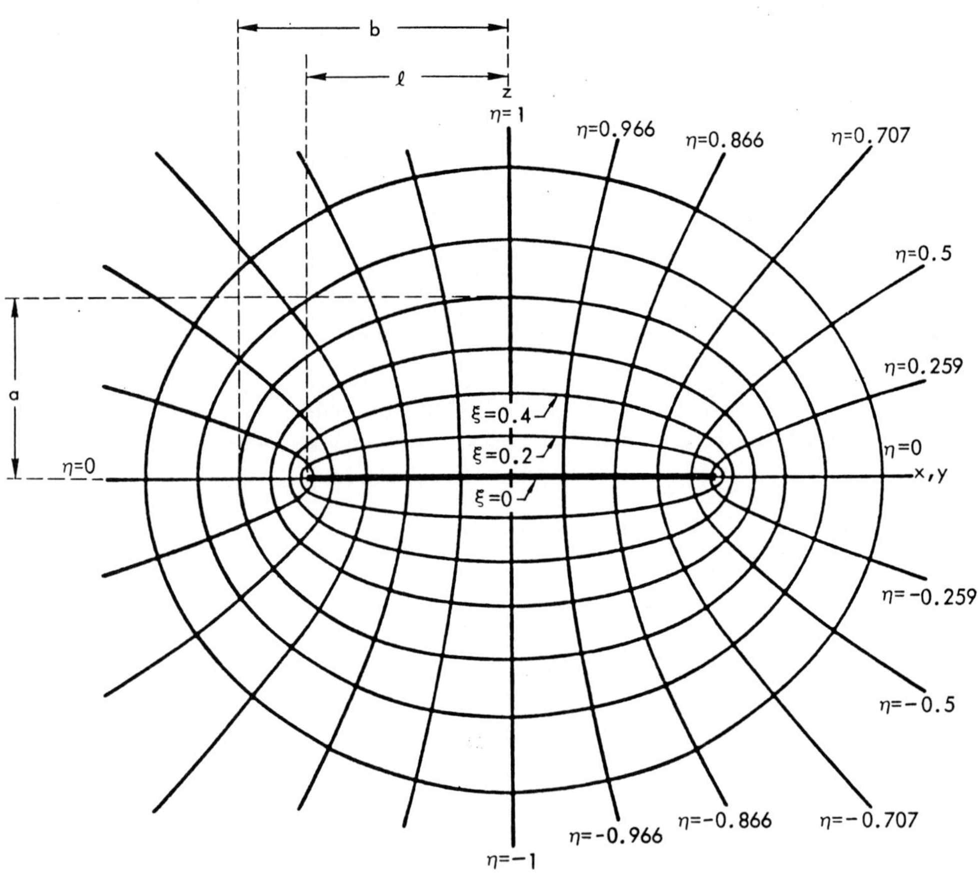

Fig. 12-2: Oblate Spheroidal coordinates.

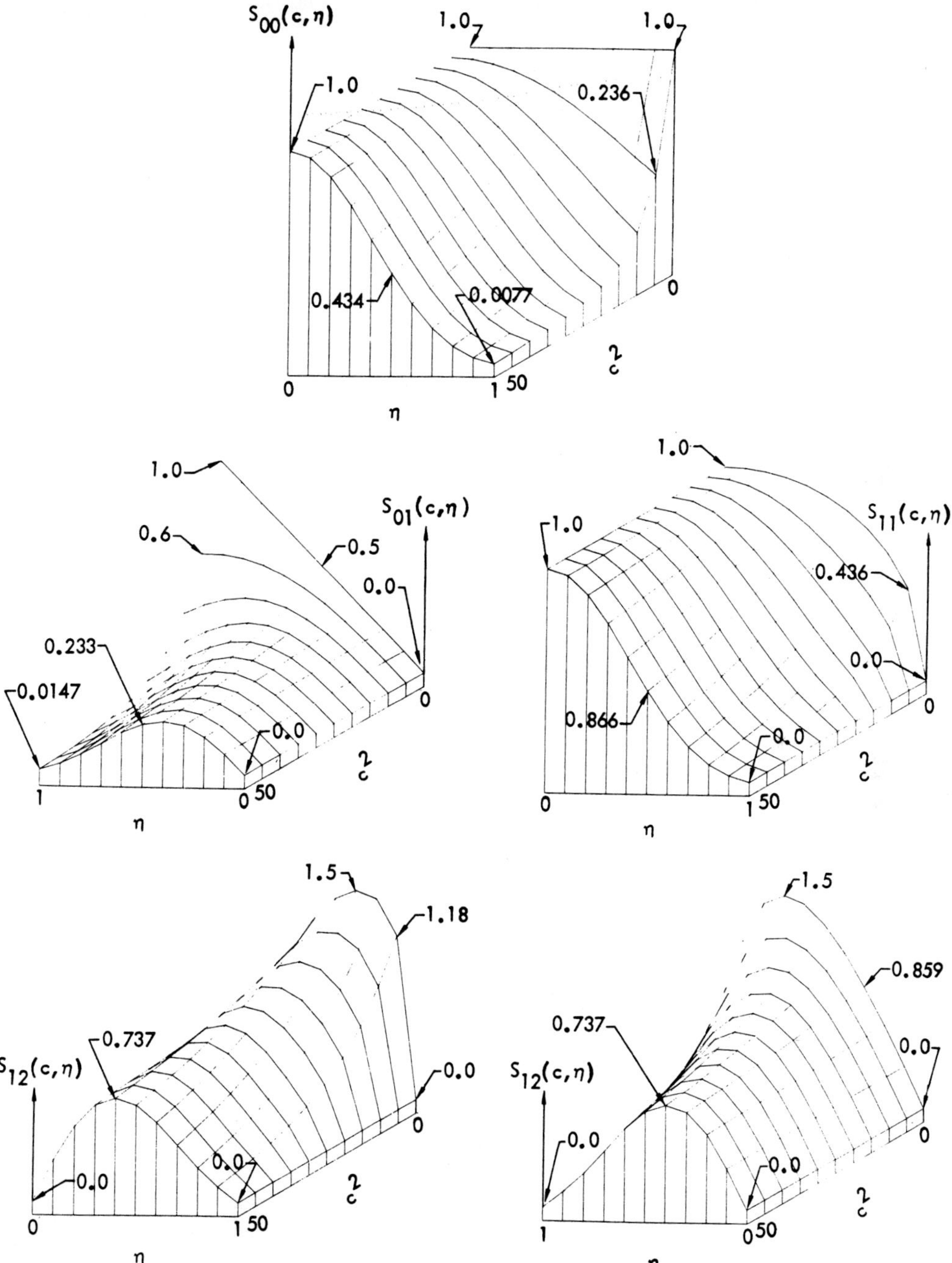

Fig. 21-3: Prolate spheroidal angular wave functions.

This figure is taken from Mathematics Note 32 by Lytle and Deadrick. It is the property of the U. S. Government and not subject to copyright.

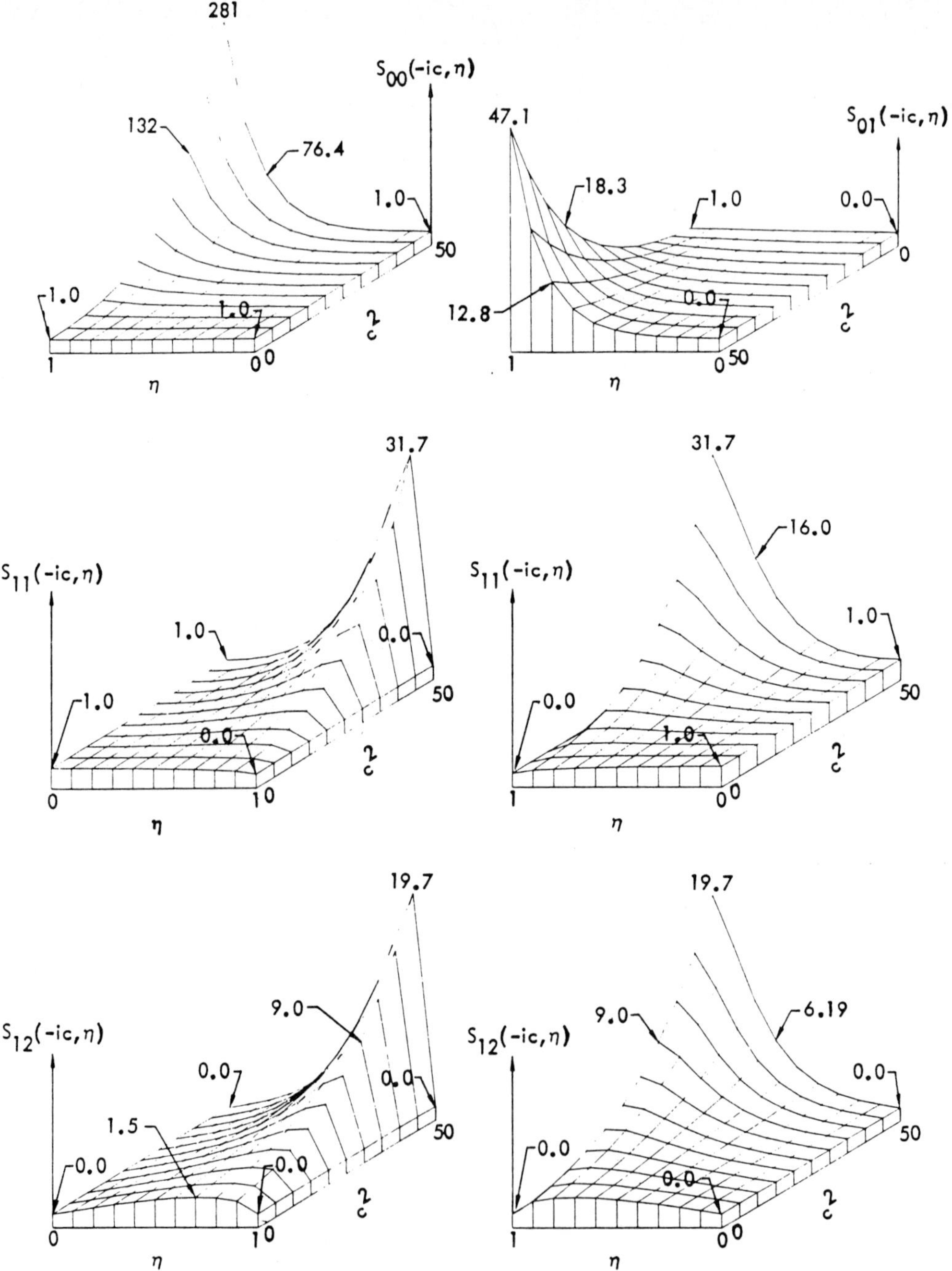

Fig. 21-4: Oblate spheroidal angular wave functions.

This figure is taken from Mathematics Note 32 by Lytle and Deadrick. It is the property of the U. S. Government and not subject to copyright.

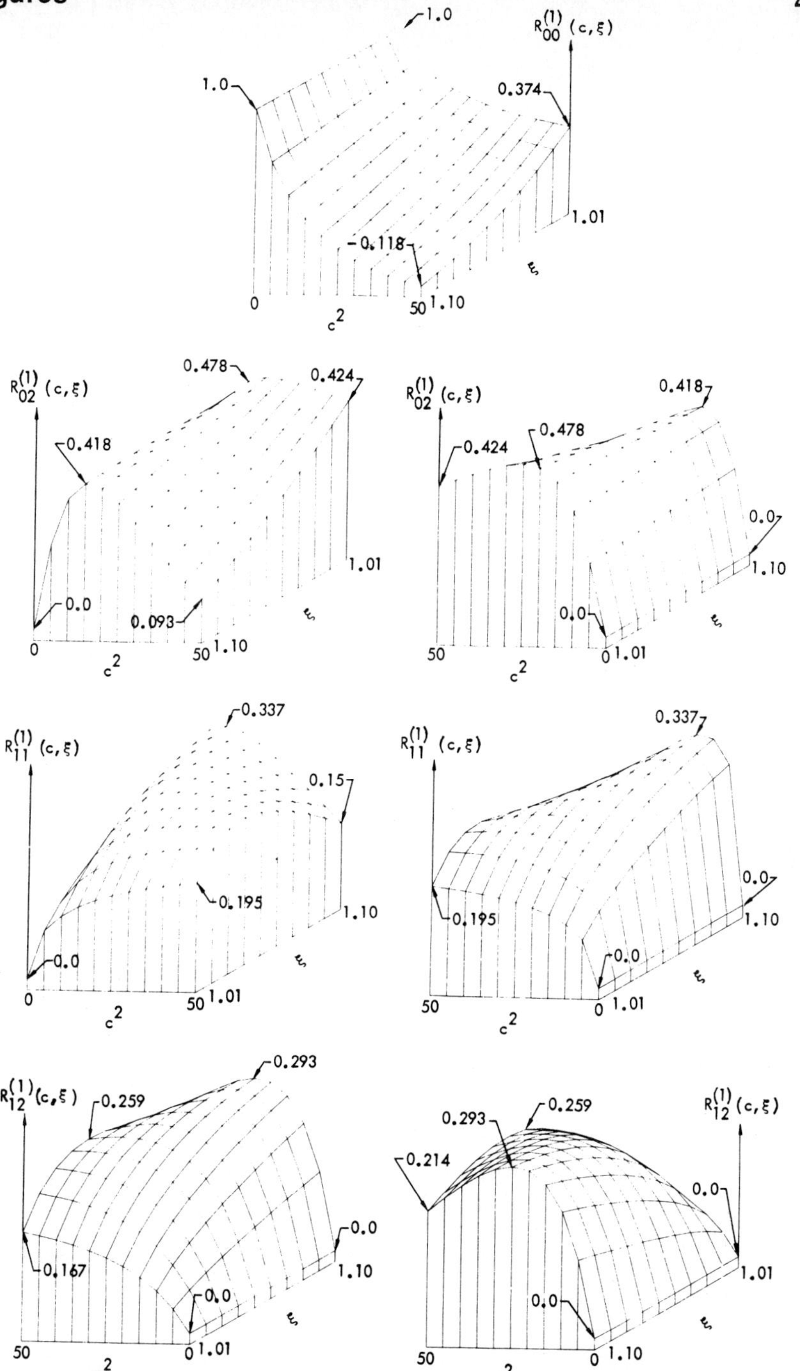

Fig. 21-5: Prolate spheroidal radial wave functions.

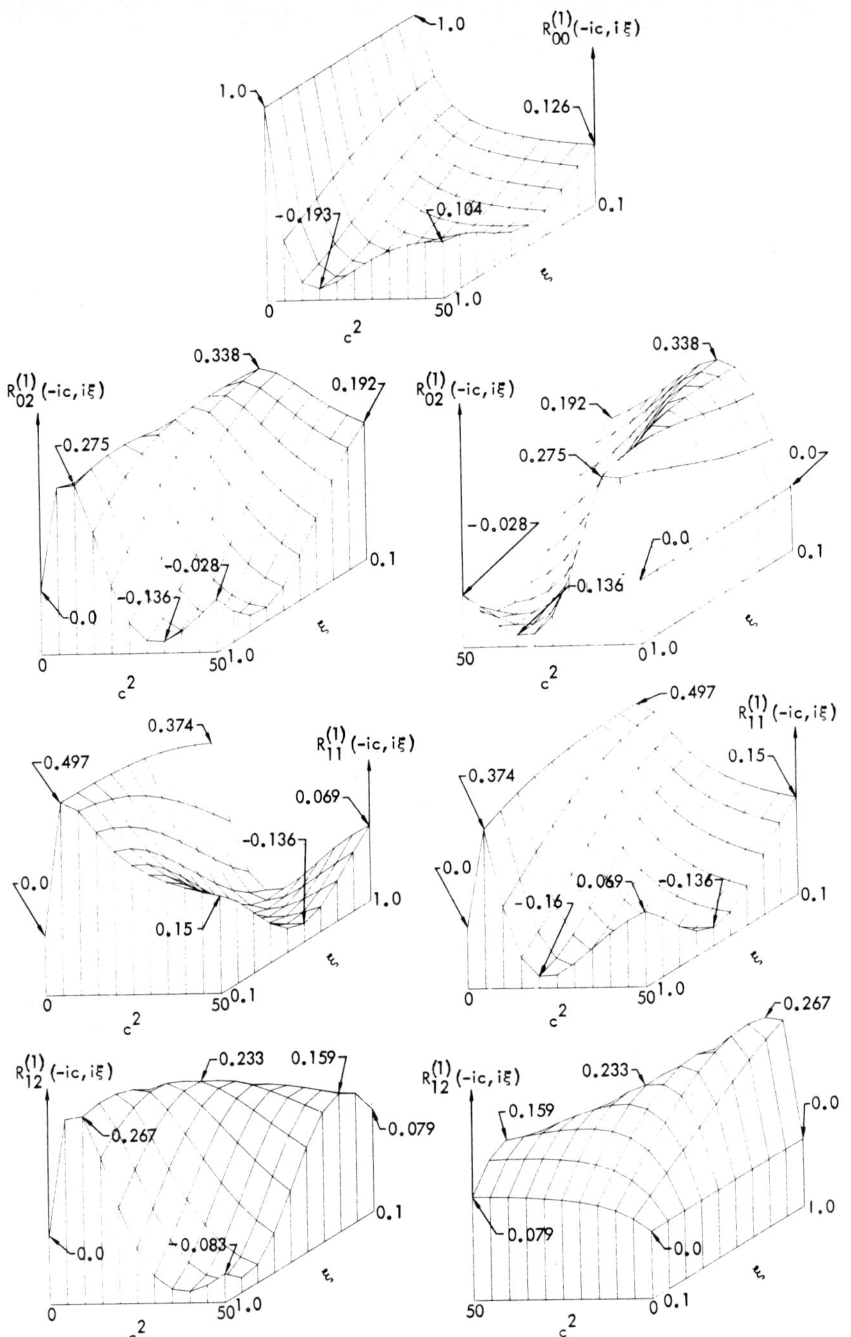

Fig. 21-6: Prolate and oblate spheroidal radial wave functions.

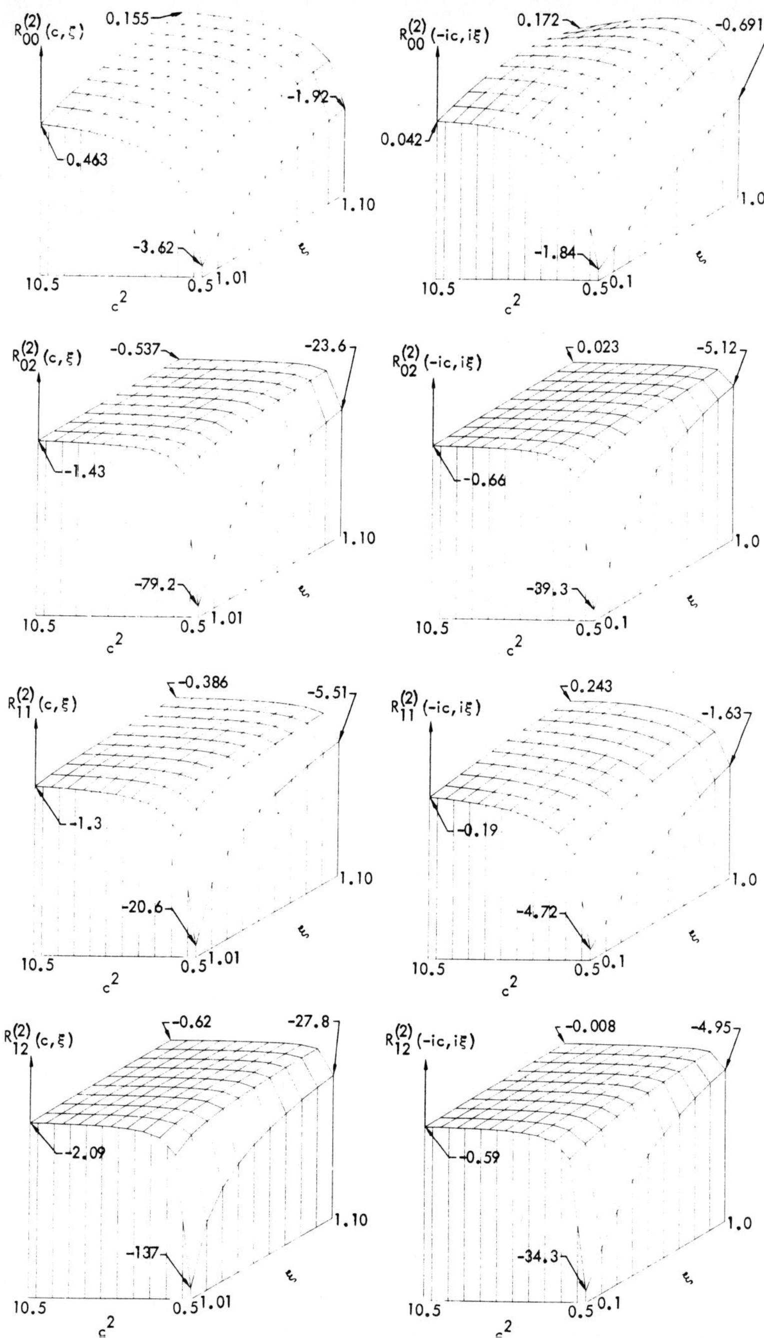

Fig. 21-7: Prolate and oblate spheroidal radial wave functions.

```
/*
Spheroidal Wave Functions

from C Mathematical Function Handbook by Louis Baker
Copyright 1991 by Louis Baker. All rights reserved.
*/

#include <stdio.h>
#include "cmlib.h"
#include "protom.h"

#define sign(a,b)    ( (b>0.)? a: -a)
#define min(a,b)  ((a)<(b)?(a):(b))
#define max(a,b)  ((a)<(b)?(b):(a))

static double ratios[100];

extern double leg[100],sphb[100];
/* spherical bessel function i for negative indices n=1
means -1, etc.*/
/* sinb will also work!*/

double simb(x,n)double x;int n;
{/*  use backward in order, forward in -order: -1,-2,-
3,etc. function grows*/
int i;double sqrt(),sm1,sm2,mult,sinh(),cosh(),s,c;
s=sinh(x);c=cosh(x);
sphb[0]=s/x;
sphb[1]=sm1=c/x;
if(n==1)return sm1;
sphb[2]=sm2= (s-c/x)/x;
if(n==2)return sm2;
/* forward recursion*/
mult=-3.;
for(i=3;i<=n;i++)
{sphb[i]= sphb[i-2]+sphb[i-1]*mult/x;mult-=2.;}
return sphb[n];
}

/* caveat c is c^2, which is >0 prolate <0 oblate */
/* renamed to avoid name conflict*/
double dssph(c,s) double c,s;
{return s*(s+1.)+c*(2.*s*s*(2.*s+3.)-1.)/((2*s-
1.)*(2.*s+1.)*(2.*s+3.));}
double fs(c,s) double c,s;
{return s*(s+1.)+c*(2.*s*s+2.*s-3.)/((2*s-1.)*(2.*s+3.));}
double es(c,s) double c,s;
{double sqrt();
```

```
return
c*(s+1.)*(s+2.)/((2.*s+3.)*sqrt((2.*s+1.)*(2.*s+5.)));}
double gs(c,s) double c,s;
{double sqrt();
return
c/(2.*s+3.)*sqrt(s*(s+1.)*(s+2.)*(s+3.)/((2.*s+1.)*(2.*s+5.))
);}
/* based upon Eispack, ste finds eigenvalues of symm.
tridi. matrix*/
int ste(d,e,n) double d[],e[];int n;
{int i,l,m,iterkt;double b,c,f,g,p,r,s,eps,sqrt();
eps=1.e-12;
for(l=0;l<n;l++)
   {
   iterkt=0;/*search for small subdiagonal element*/
   iterate:
   for(m=l;m<n;m++)
      {
      if((m==n-
1)||abs(e[m])<eps*(abs(d[m])+abs(d[m+1])))break;
      }
   p=d[l];
   if(m!=l)
      {
      if(iterkt>=30){return -n-l;/*error*/}
      iterkt++;
      /*shift*/
      g=(d[l+1]-p)*.5/e[l];
      r=sqrt(g*g+1.);
      g=d[m]-p+e[l]/(g+sign(r,g));
      s=c=1.;p=0.;
      for(i=m-1;i>=l;i--)
         {
         f=s*e[i];b=c*e[i];
         if(abs(f)>=abs(g))
            {
            c=g/f;
            r=sqrt(c*c+1.);
            e[i+1]=f*r;
            s=1./r;
            c*=s;
            }
         else
            {
            s=f/g;
            r=sqrt(s*s+1.);
            e[i+1]=g*r;
            c=1./r;
            s*=c;
```

```
            }
         g=d[i+1]-p;
         r=(d[i]-g)*s+2.*c*b;
         p=s*r;
         d[i+1]=g+p;
         g=c*r-b;
         }
      d[l]-=p;
      e[l]=g;
      e[m]=0.;
      goto iterate;
      }
   else
      {
      if(!l){d[0]=p;}
      else
         {for(i=l;i>=1;i--)
            {
            if(p>=d[i-1]){d[i]=p;break;}
            d[i]=d[i-1];
            }
         }
      }
   }
return 0;
}

double diag[100],sdiag[100];
double ab[100],bl[100];
/* solve, figi set up eigenvalue problem for spheroidal
wave functions*/
int solve(c,prolate,odd,order, nmax)double c;int pro-
late,odd,nmax,order;
{
double cc, (*dia)(),(*subd)();
/* odd=0 even 1 odd*/
int i,offset,j;double s;
if(nmax>100)
   {fprintf(stderr," nmax too big\n");return -1;}
if(((double)nmax)*((double)nmax)< 2.*c)
   {fprintf(stderr," nmax too small for accuracy\n");}
offset=0;
if(!prolate)cc=-c;
else   cc=c;
if(order<2)
   {
   if(order && !odd)offset=2;
   if(order){dia=fs;subd=gs;}
   else {dia=dssph;subd=es;}
```

```
    for(i=0;i<nmax;i++)
        {
        j=2*i+odd+offset;s=j;
        diag[i]= dia(cc,s);
        sdiag[i]=subd(cc,s);
        }
    }
else
    {
    for(i=0;i<nmax;i++)
        {
        j=2*i+odd;
        bl[i]= cc*j*(j-1)/((2*(order+j)-3)*(2*(order+j)-1));
        ab[i]= cc*(2*order+j+2)*(2*order+j+1)
            /((2*(order+j)+3)*(2*(order+j)+5));
        diag[i]=(j+order)*(j+order+1)
        +cc*(2*(order+j)*(order+j+1)-2*order*order-1.)
        /((2.*(order+j)-1.)*(2.*(order+j)+3));
        }
    i=figi(ab,bl,nmax);
    if(i)fprintf(stderr," figi pblm %d\n",i);
    }
i=ste(diag,sdiag,nmax);
if(i)fprintf(stderr," ste pblme index %d",-(i+nmax));
return i;
}

int figi(above,below,nmax)int nmax;double above[],below[];
{
int i,j;   double p,sqrt();
/* note that first nonzero below diagonal element is
below[1],not below[0]
 and that there are nmax-1 super/subdiagonal elements each,
not nmax*/
for(i=0;i<nmax-1;i++)
    {j=i+1;
    p=above[i]*below[j];
    if(p<0.)
        {fprintf(stderr, " swf:figi: i %d %e %e\n"
                ,i,above[i],below[j]);
        return -nmax-i;}
    else if(p==0.)
        {if( above[i]!=0. || below[j]!=0.)
            {
        fprintf(stderr,
         " swf|figi: i %d %e %e\n",i,above[i],below[j]);
            return -3*nmax-i;}
        }
    sdiag[i]=sqrt(p);
```

```
    }
return 0;
}

static int nmmodd,firstrho;
double lmn,csquare;
double nsph[100],dsph[100],dsphn[200];

double nmn(m,n,limit) int m,n,limit;
{int odd,k;double r,sum,factor,gamma(),d,twom;
odd=(n-m)%2;r=odd;/*r= 0 or 1.*/
twom=(m<<1);
factor=gamma(twom+r+1.)/gamma(twom+2.*(r+1.));
for(sum=0.,k=0;k<limit;k++,r+=2.)
   {d=dsph[k];
   sum+=d*d*factor;
   fac-
tor*=(twom+r+1.)*(twom+r+2.)/((twom+2.*r+3.)*(twom+2.*r+5.));

/*printf(" nmm sum factor now %e %e\n",sum,factor);*/
   }
return 2.*sum;
}

double rho(m,n,limit) int m,n,limit;
{int odd,k;double c,r,sum,fac-
tor,gamma(),d,twom,pow(),sqrt();
odd=(n-m)%2;r=odd;/*r= 0 or 1.*/
twom=(m<<1);
c=sqrt(abs(csquare));
factor=gamma( twom+r+1.)/gamma((r+1.));
for(sum=0.,k=0;k<limit;k++,r+=2.)
   {d=dsph[k];
   sum+=d*factor;
   factor*=(twom+r+1.)*(twom+r+2.)/((r+1.)*(r+2.));
/*printf(" rho sum factor now %e %e\n",sum,factor);*/
   }
return ((m-n)%2?-1.:1.)* pow(c,m)/sum;
}


double gamsph(m,r) int m,r;
{
double f,g;
f=m+r;g=2.*f;
return f*(f+1.)+.5*csquare*(1.-(4*m*m-1.)/((g-1.)*(g+3.)));
}

double betsph(m,r) int m,r;
```

```
{
double f,g,h;
g=2*(m+r); h=2*m+r;
f=g-1.;f*=f;
return r*(r-1)*(h)*(h-1.)*csquare*csquare/
((g-3.)*(g+1.)*f);
}

double asph(m,r) int m,r;
{double twom,g,h;
twom=2.*m;g=twom+r;h=twom+2.*r;
return csquare*g*(g-1.)/((h-1.)*(h+1.));
}
double csph(m,r) int m,r;
{double twom,h;
twom=2.*m;h=twom+2.*r;
return csquare*(r+1.)*(r+2.)/((h+3.)*(h+1.));
}
double bsph(m,r) int m,r;
{double twom,h,f;
twom=2.*m;h=twom+2.*r;f=m+r;
return f*(f+1.)-lmn+csquare*(2.*f*(f+1.)-twom*m-1.)
   /((h-1.)*(h+3.));
}

int tridi(bl,diag,ab,c,n) int n; double
bl[],diag[],ab[],c[];
{  int i;double pivot;
if(n==1)
   {c[0]/=diag[0];return 0;}
for(i=1;i<n;i++)
   {
   pivot=diag[i-1];
   if(pivot==0.){fprintf(stderr,
               " tridi:bad pivot\n");return -1;}
   pivot= bl[i]/pivot;
   diag[i]-=pivot*ab[i-1];c[i]-=pivot*c[i-1];
   }
c[n-1]/=diag[n-1];
for(i=n-2;i>=0;i--)
   c[i]= (c[i]-ab[i]*c[i+1])/diag[i];
return 0;
}

/*double nfwd(m,r) int r,m;
{
if(r<2){return -1;}
if(r==2) return gamsph(m,0)-lmn;
if(r==3) return gamsph(m,1)-lmn;
```

```
return gamsph(m,r)-lmn-betsph(m,r)/nfwd(m,r-2);
}                    */

#define tol 1.e-10

int setd(mm,n)int mm,n;
{/* starting from n<(1/2)<100 set the d coefficients by
backward recursion*/
int i,j,k,r,s,t,l,m; double
sum,alpha,gamma(),temp,scale,pow(),legendrea();
double p,pold,polder,q,qold,qolder,a,b,ratio,newrat;
l=32;
k=l;
m=abs(mm);/* d's are same for pos, neg m except for a scal-
ing done in angular()*/
if(n<m){fprintf(stderr," swf:setd: n=%d\n",n,m);
   return -1;}
nmmodd=(n-m)%2 ;/*? 1: 0; don't need the ?1:0  test*/
nsph[0]=1.;
if(k+1>=100){fprintf(stderr,
          " swf:setd:l too big in setd\n"); return -1;}
/* fill d array with N */
nsph[k+1]=dsph[k+1]=0.;
/* down to i=2 r=2i+nmmodd=4 or 5 */
for(i=k;i>=1;i--)
   {r=(i<<1)+nmmodd;nsph[i]= betsph(m,r)/
                 (gamsph(m,r)-lmn-nsph[i+1]);
   }
sum=nsph[1];
nsph[1]=gamsph(m, nmmodd)-lmn;
/* special treatment not needed? */
if( abs(sum-nsph[1])> 1.e-4)
   {fprintf(stderr,
    " swf:setd:trouble nsph[1]=%e %e\n",sum,nsph[1]);
   return -1;}
/* temporary norm of d s.t. d[0]=1*/
dsph[0]=1.;
j=(m<<1);
for(i=1;i<=k;i++)
   {
   r=nmmodd+(i<<1); s=j+r;t=j+(r<<1);
   dsph[i]=-dsph[i-1]*nsph[i]*((double)(t-
1)*(t+1))/(csquare*(s)*(s-1));
   if(abs(dsph[i])<tol){k=i;break;}
   }
sum=0.;
/* flammer normalization corrected sign of N*/
if(!nmmodd)
   {
```

```
    alpha= gamma(2.*m+1.)/gamma((double)m+1.);
    for (i=0;i<k;i++)
       {
       r=i<<1;
       temp=alpha;
       sum+=temp;
       if(abs(temp)<tol*abs(sum)){k=i;break;}
       scale=-
.25*(double)((r+2+j)*(r+1+j))/((double)((i+1)*(i+1+m)));
       alpha=temp*scale*dsph[i+1]/dsph[i];
       }
    alpha= gamma((double)n+m+1)*(((n-m)>>1)%2?-1:1)
    /(sum*pow(2.,(double)n-m)*
     gamma(.5*(n-m)+1.)*gamma(.5*(n+m)+1.));
    }
else
    {
    alpha=.5*gamma(2.*m+3.)/gamma(m+2.);
    for (i=0;i<k;i++)
       {
       r=1+(i<<1);
       temp=alpha;
       sum+=temp;
       if(abs(temp)<tol*abs(sum)){k=i;break;}
       scale=-.25*(r+2+j)*(r+3+j)/((i+1)*(i+2+m));
       alpha=temp*scale*dsph[i+1]/dsph[i];
       }
    alpha= gamma((double)n+m+2)*(((n-m-1)>>1)%2?-1:1)
    /(sum*pow(2.,(double)n-m)*
     gamma(.5*(n-m-1)+1.)*gamma(.5*(n+m+1)+1.));
    }
for(i=0;i<=k;i++) dsph[i]*=(alpha);
/* set drm for r=-2m or -2m+1*/
if(!m){dsphn[0]=dsph[0];}
else
    {/* setup tridiag  bl  diag ab   = sdiag*/
    i=0;bl[0]=0.;
    r=nmmodd-2;/*r= -2 or -1*/
    diag[0]=bsph(m,r); ab[0]=csph(m,r-2);
    dsphn[0]=-dsph[0]*asph(m,r+2);
/*printf(" r= i=%d %d %e %e %e %e\n",r,i,
dsphn[i],diag[i],ab[i],bl[i]);*/
    i=1;/* r initially -4 or -3 in for loop*/
    for(r=nmmodd-4;r>=nmmodd-j;r-=2,i++)
       {
       dsphn[i]=0.;
       diag[i]=bsph(m,r);
       ab[i]=csph(m,r-2);
       bl[i]=asph(m,r+2);
```

```
/*printf(" r= i=%d %d %e %e %e
%e\n",r,i,dsphn[i],diag[i],ab[i],bl[i]);*/
      }
/*printf(" calling tridi with i=%d\n",i);*/
   tridi(bl,diag,ab,dsphn,i);
/*for(l=0;l<i;l++)printf(" dsphn[%d]=%e\n",l,dsphn[l]);*/
   }
/* set d rho|r. first value */
if(nmmodd)
   sum=1./((1.-j)*(3.-j));
else
   sum=1./((1.-j)*(1.+j));
pold=0.;polder=1.;qolder=0.;qold=1.;ratio=0.;
for(i=m+1;i<100;i++)
   {
   r=nmmodd-(i<<1);
   if(i==(m+1))a=1.;
   else a= -csph(m,r)*asph(m,r+2);
   b=bsph(m,r);
   p=a*polder+b*pold;
   q=a*qolder+b*qold;
   newrat=p/q;
   if(abs(ratio-newrat)< 1.e-6)break;
   ratio=newrat;
   polder=pold;pold=p;qolder=qold;qold=q;
   }
r=m;if(!m)r=1;
dsphn[r]=-dsphn[r-1]*csquare*sum*newrat;
s= m? 0:1;
firstrho=r;
/*printf(" FIRST d-rho: dsphn[%d]=%e \n",r,dsphn[r]);*/
for(i=m+2;i<100;i++)
   {
        pold=0.;polder=1.;qolder=0.;qold=1.;ratio=0.;
   for(l=i-1;l<25;l++)
      {
      r=-((l<<1)+2-nmmodd);
      if(l==i-1)a=asph(m,r+2);
      else a= -csph(m,r)*asph(m,r+2);
      b=bsph(m,r);
      p=a*polder+b*pold;
      q=a*qolder+b*qold;
      newrat=p/q;
      if(abs(ratio-newrat)< 1.e-6)break;
      ratio=newrat;
      polder=pold;pold=p;qolder=qold;qold=q;
      }
   dsphn[i-1+s]=-dsphn[i-2+s]*newrat;
   if(abs(dsphn[i-1])<1.e-10)break;
```

```
    }
return k;
}

static int nlimit;

double angular(mm,n,kind,eta,imag)double eta;int
kind,mm,n,imag;
{int i,r,btm,nn,m;
double sum,qlm(),qli(),qbig,qbigger,q;
/*first set up d array*/
/*if(abs(eta)<=1.)*/
{
m=abs(mm);
nlimit=setd(m,n);
btm= (n-m)%2;
sum=0.;
if(kind==1)
    {
    if(imag){for(i=0;i<(nlimit<<1)+m;i++)
            leg[i]=legendrea(m,i+m,eta,0);
        }
    else legptable(eta,(nlimit<<1)+m,m);
    for(i=0,r=btm;i<nlimit;i++)
        {sum+=dsph[i]*leg[r];r+=2;}
    if(m!=mm)
        {/*negative m*/
        sum*=(m%2?-1.:1.)*gamma(n-m+1.)/gamma(n+m+1.);
        }
    return sum;
    }
/* kind==2*/
if(abs(eta)==1. && !imag)return errorcode;
if(!imag)leg2(eta,m,nlimit,6,leg);
else {/*printf(
"Oblate Radial case: imag. eta for leg2 %e\n" ,eta);*/
    /* need Q(ix) here */
    if(m || eta!=0.)qleg(m,(nlimit<<1)+m,eta,0,ratios,leg);
    else for(i=0;i<=(nlimit<<1)+m;i++)leg[i]=qli(i,eta);
      }
for(i=0,r=m+btm;i<nlimit;i++)/* r>=0 Q terms*/
    {
    sum+=dsph[i]*leg[r];r+=2;
/*printf(" q sum now %e latest factors %e
%e\n",sum,dsph[i],leg[r-2]);*/
    }
if(m)/* skip if m==0*/
    {
    if(m==1)
```

```
        {
        if(btm){q=leg[0];qbig=leg[1];qbigger=leg[2];}
        else/*m=1, (n-m)even, dsphn[0]*Q-1,m */
            {
            qbig=leg[0];qbigger=leg[1];
            q=(eta*qbig-(1-m)*qbigger)/m;/* n=-1*/
            }
        }
    else/* for m>1, dsphn[0] multiples Qn,m n>=0 */
        {
        r=btm-(m%2);/*r=-1 or 0*/
        if(!r)r=-2;/* r = -1 or -2 highest neg. index*/
        nn=m+r;/* nn for Qnn,m of highest neg. dsphn[0] term*/
        q=leg[nn];qbig=leg[nn+1];qbigger=0.;
/*printf(" q,qbig,qbigger %e %e %e %d %d
nn=%d\n",q,qbig,qbigger,r,btm,nn);*/
        }
    for(i=0;i<firstrho;i++)
        {sum+=dsphn[i]*q;
        nn--;
        if(!(m+1+nn))break;
        qbigger=qbig;
        qbig=q;
        q=(eta*(2*nn+3)*qbig-qbigger*(2+nn-m))/(m+nn+1);
        nn--;
        if(!(m+1+nn))break;
        qbigger=qbig;
        qbig=q;
        q=(eta*(2*nn+3)*qbig-qbigger*(2+nn-m))/(m+nn+1);
        }
    }
/*if(imag)printf(" before p terms %d %d
sum=%e\n",nlimit,m,sum);*/
/* need P(ix) for oblate radial case*/
if(imag){for(i=0;i<(nlimit<<1)+m;i++)
leg[i]=legendrea(m,i+m,eta,0);}
else legptable(eta,(nlimit<<1)+m,m);
r=(1-btm);
/*if(imag)printf(" legp/legendrea returned r=%d
firstrho=%d\n",r,firstrho);*/
for(i=firstrho;i<nlimit;i++)
    { sum+=q=dsphn[i]*leg[r];r+=2;
/*printf(" P sum now %e term=%e P=%e dsphn=%e i=%d
r=%d\n",sum,q,leg[r-2],dsphn[i],i,r-2);*/
    }
return sum;
}
}
```

```
double radswf(m,n,kind,eta)double eta;int kind,m,n;
{int i,r,btm,twom,k,limit;
double sum,qlm(),etasq,coef,c,factor,fsave,pow(),gamma(),z;
/*first set up d array*/
if( (abs(eta)>1.&&csquare>0.) ||(csquare<0.))
{
/*printf(
" eta %e csquare %e m n kind %d %d %d radial\n"
,eta,csquare,m,n,kind);*/
twom=m<<1;
nlimit=setd(m,n);
btm= (n-m)%2;
sum=0.;
if(!m) factor=1.;
else
   {if(btm)factor=gamma(twom+2.);
    else factor=gamma(twom+1.);}
r=btm;fsave=factor;
for(k=0;k<(nlimit);k++)
   {sum+= dsph[k]*factor;
   r+=2.;        factor*=(twom+r)*(twom+r-1.)/(r*(r-1.));
   }
etasq=eta*eta;
if(csquare>=0.){ coef=1.;c=sqrt(csquare);}/*prolate*/
else {coef=-1.;c=sqrt(-csquare);}/*oblate*/
coef=(etasq-coef)/etasq;
coef= pow(coef,.5*m)/sum;
sum=0.;
limit=(nlimit<<1)+m;
z=c*eta;
if(kind==1)
   {
   if(csquare>0.)sjn(z,limit);
   else {sinb(z,limit);
        for(k=1;k<=limit;k+=2)sphb[k]=-sphb[k];}
        }
else
   {
   printf(" CAVEAT:poor convergence 2nd kind RADIAL
SPHER.WAVE FUNCT\n");
   if(csquare>0.)syn(z,limit);
   else {sinb(z,limit);return errorcode;}
   /* oblate radial,second kind not supported through
radial()*/
   }
factor=fsave;
for(i=0,r=btm;i<nlimit;i++)
   {sum+=factor*dsph[i]*sphb[r+m];r+=2;
```

```
/*printf(" r=%d m=%d %d bes=%e sum %e
\n",r,m,r+m,sphb[r+m],sum);*/
     factor*=-(twom+r)*(twom+r-1.)/(r*(r-1.));}
return sum*coef;
}
/* eta<1.*/
return errorcode;
}

double radial(m,n,kind,xi) int m,n,kind; double xi;
{double coef,angular(),sphjoin(),z;    int limit,imag;
limit=setd(m,n);
coef=sphjoin(m,n,kind,limit);
if(csquare<0.)imag=1;
else imag=0.;
if(coef==0.){fprintf(stderr,
          " warn sphjoin=0. in radial\n");
   return errorcode;}
z=angular(m,n,kind,xi,imag)/coef;
/*printf("radial =%e kappa=%e\n",z,coef);*/
return z;
}

double sphjoin(m,n,kind,limit) int m,n,kind,limit;
{
double sign,sqrt(),c,coef,pow(),r,gamma(),sum,fac-
tor,twom;int k,btm,oblate,ms;
/*printf(" in sphjoin %d %d %d %d\n",m,n,kind,limit);*/
/* including sign of factors of -i^ -m,-m+1 (1 even/odd) 1-
m,2-m oblate
but NOT factor of i if imaginary*/
btm=(n-m)%2;twom=m<<1;
sum=0.;
if(!m) factor=1.;
else
   {if(btm)factor=gamma(twom+2.);
    else factor=gamma(twom+1.);}
r=btm;
for(k=0;k<(limit);k++)
   {sum+= dsph[k]*factor;
   r+=2.;        factor*=(twom+r)*(twom+r-1.)/(r*(r-1.));
   }
if(csquare<0.){c=sqrt(-csquare);oblate=1;ms=m%4;}
else {c=sqrt(csquare);oblate=0;}
if(kind==1)
   {
   coef=1.;
   if(btm)
      {
```

```
        if(oblate) coef= (ms==1 || ms==2)?-1.:1.;
        return coef*sum*gamma(2.+n+m)*(twom+3.)

/(pow(2.,(double)(n+m))*dsph[0]*pow(c,1.+m)*gamma(1.+m)
        *gamma(1.+.5*(n+m+1))*gamma(1.+.5*(n-m-1)));}
    {
    if(oblate) coef= (ms)>1?-1.:1.;
    return coef*sum*gamma(1.+n+m)*(twom+1.)

/(pow(2.,(double)(n+m))*dsph[0]*pow(c,(double)m)*gamma(1.+m)
    *gamma(.5*(n+m)+1.)*gamma(.5*(n-m)+1.));}
    }
/* kind==2*/
    coef= firstrho-1 >=0 ? dsphn[firstrho-1] : dsphn[0];
    sign=1.;
/*printf(" coef=%e sum=%e\n",coef,sum);*/
    if(btm)/*odd*/
        {if(oblate)sign=((ms)<2?-1.:1.);
        factor= -sum*pow(2.,(double)n-m)*gamma(twom+1.)
        *gamma(.5*(n-m-1)+1.)*gamma(.5*(n+m+1)+1.)*coef
        /((twom-3.)*(twom-
1.)*gamma(m+1.)*gamma(2.+n+m)*pow(c,m-2.));
        return factor*sign;}
        {if(oblate)sign=(ms==3||!ms?-1.:1.);
        return sum*pow(2.,(double)n-m)*gamma(twom+1.)
        *gamma(.5*(n-m)+1.)*gamma(.5*(n+m)+1.)*coef*sign
        /((twom-1.)*gamma(m+1.)*gamma(1.+n+m)*pow(c,m-1.));}

}
```

```
/*
legptable Pn,m for n=m to ntop.
used with sjn by spheroidal wave functions.
from C Mathematical Function Handbook by Louis Baker
Copyright 1991 by Louis Baker. All rights reserved.
*/

#include "cmlib.h"
#include "protom.h"

double leg[100];

legptable(x,ntop,m)int ntop,m;double x;
{/* table of P(x)nm, n=m to ntop*/
int i,twom;
double sqrt(),y,new,term;
y=(1.-x*x);
if(x<-1.||x>1.)y=sqrt(-y);
else y=sqrt(y);
twom=m<<1;
if(!m)new=1.;/* P 0,0*/
else new=-y;/*P 1,1*/
/* first find Pm,m*/
term=3.;
for(i=2;i<=m;i++){new*= -y*term;term+=2.;}
/* new = P m,m old= p m-1,m-1*/
leg[0]=new;
leg[1]=(twom+1)*x*new;/*Pm+1,m */
for(i=2;i<=ntop;i++)
   { leg[i]=((((m+i)<<1)-1.)*x*leg[i-1]-(i-1+twom)*leg[i-
2])/(i);}
return 0;
}
```

```
/*
test driver Spheroidal Wave Functions
 and friends
from C Mathematical Function Handbook by Louis Baker
Copyright 1991 by Louis Baker. All rights reserved.
*/

#include <stdio.h>
#include "cmlib.h"
#include "protom.h"

extern double
diag[100],dsph[100],dsphn[100],sphb[100],leg[100]
   ,lmn,csquare;

main()
{int i,m,ntop;float xx;double x,cos(),sphjoin(),c,an-
gular(),zz,yy;
double radial(),rad(),sinh(),cosh(),simb();
 int prolate,odd,nmax,ans,p,o,nn,z;float cc;
 while(1)
{printf(" enter c,prolate, odd, order,nmax\n");
scanf("%e%d%d%d%d",&cc,&p,&odd,&z,&nmax);c=cc;
if(c<0.)break; prolate=p;
solve(c,p,odd,z,nmax);
for(ans=0;ans<nmax;ans++)printf(" eigenv=%e\n",diag[ans]);
printf(" enter i for ith eigenvalue\n");
scanf("%d", &o);lmn=diag[o];
nn=odd;
while(nn<z)nn+=2;
nn+=(o<<1);
printf("  nn=%d\n",nn);
/*printf(" enter n\n");scanf("%d",&nn);printf("
n=%d\n",nn);*/
printf(" lambda=%e n=%d\n",lmn,nn);if(nn==100)break;
p=z;csquare=c;if(!prolate)csquare=-csquare;ans=setd(p,nn);
for(p=0;p<ans;p++)printf(" d=%e %e\n",dsph[p],dsphn[p]);
printf(" join factor first kind:%e N=%e rho=%e\n",
   sphjoin(z,nn,1,ans),nmn(z,nn,ans),rho(z,nn,ans));
printf(" Angular:\n");
for(p=0;p<10;p++){x=p/10.;if(prolate)x=cos(p*pi/18.);
   printf(" %f %d %e\n",x,p,angular(z,nn,1,x,0));}
printf(" Radial, 1st kind:\n");
for(p=0;p<10;p++){x=p/5.;if(prolate)x=1.005+.005*p;
   printf(" %f %d %e\n",x,p,radial(z,nn,1,x));}
printf(" Radial, 2nd kind:\n");
for(p=0;p<10;p++){x=p/5.;if(prolate)x=1.005+.005*p;
   printf(" %f %d %e\n",x,p,radial(z,nn,2,x));}
}
```

```
/* spherical bessel check*/
for(m=1;m<=10;m++){
x= .5*m;
zz= cosh(x)*(3./(x*x*x)+1./x)-3./(x*x)*sinh(x);
yy= cosh(x)/x;
c= sinh(x)/x-cosh(x)/(x*x);
printf(" x=%e returned:%e  -1:%e -2:%e -
3:%e\n",x,simb(x,5),yy,c,zz);
for(i=0;i<=5;i++)
   printf(" %d %e\n",i,sphb[i]);
}
while(1){
printf(" i:enter n, x\n");
scanf("%d%e",&m,&xx);x=xx;
if(xx<0.||m<0)break;
printf(" %e\n",sinb(x,m));
for(i=0;i<=m;i++)
   printf(" %d %e\n",i,sphb[i]);
}
while(1){
printf(" k:enter n, x\n");
scanf("%d%e",&m,&xx);x=xx;
if(xx<0.||m<0)break;
printf(" %e\n",skn(x,m));
for(i=0;i<=m;i++)
   printf(" %d %e\n",i,sphb[i]);
}
while(1){
printf(" j:enter n, x\n");
scanf("%d%e",&m,&xx);x=xx;
if(xx<0.||m<0)break;
printf(" %e\n",sjn(x,m));
for(i=0;i<=m;i++)
   printf(" %d %e\n",i,sphb[i]);
}
while(1){
printf(" y:enter n, x\n");
scanf("%d%e",&m,&xx);x=xx;
if(xx<0.||m<0)break;
printf(" %e\n",syn(x,m));
for(i=0;i<=m;i++)
   printf(" %d %e\n",i,sphb[i]);
}
while(1){
printf(" P;enter ntop,m x\n");
scanf("%d%d%e",&ntop,&m,&xx);x=xx;
if(xx<0.||m<0)break;
legptable(x,ntop,m);
for(i=0;i<ntop;i++)
```

```
    printf(" P(%d,%d)%e\n",m+i-1,m,leg[i]);
}
return 0;
}
```

```
Test Output: Spheroidal Wave functions
 enter c,prolate, odd, order,nmax
25 1 0 0 20
 eigenv=4.195129e+00
 eigenv=2.017691e+01
 eigenv=3.389710e+01
 eigenv=5.508096e+01
 eigenv=8.482593e+01
 eigenv=1.227104e+02
 eigenv=1.686473e+02
 eigenv=2.226090e+02
 eigenv=2.845840e+02
 eigenv=3.545667e+02
 eigenv=4.325542e+02
 eigenv=5.185450e+02
 eigenv=6.125379e+02
 eigenv=7.145324e+02
 eigenv=8.245280e+02
 eigenv=9.425244e+02
 eigenv=1.068521e+03
 eigenv=1.202519e+03
 eigenv=1.344517e+03
 eigenv=1.494762e+03
 enter i for ith eigenvalue
0
  nn=0
 lambda=4.195129e+00 n=0
 d=5.603176e-01 5.603176e-01
 d=-6.956126e-01 -1.320314e+00
 d=2.154763e-01 6.763189e-01
 d=-3.272121e-02 -1.420245e-01
 d=2.935928e-03 1.630445e-02
 d=-1.731790e-04 -1.173674e-03
 d=7.208307e-06 5.772965e-05
 d=-2.227028e-07 -2.059049e-06
 d=5.304469e-09 5.562550e-08
 join factor first kind:8.964522e-02 N=7.593153e-01
rho=1.990850e+01
 Angular:
 1.000000 0 5.022979e-02
 0.984808 1 5.844048e-02
 0.939693 2 8.608309e-02
 0.866025 3 1.418569e-01
 0.766044 4 2.380257e-01
 0.642788 5 3.839276e-01
 0.500000 6 5.742243e-01
 0.342020 7 7.775588e-01
 0.173648 8 9.383359e-01
 0.000000 9 1.000000e+00
```

```
 Radial, 1st kind:
 1.005000 0 5.315016e-01
 1.010000 1 5.033380e-01
 1.015000 2 4.758236e-01
 1.020000 3 4.489548e-01
 1.025000 4 4.227279e-01
 1.030000 5 3.971391e-01
 1.035000 6 3.721844e-01
 1.040000 7 3.478595e-01
 1.045000 8 3.241603e-01
 1.050000 9 3.010821e-01
 Radial, 2nd kind:
 1.005000 0 -2.911724e-01
 1.010000 1 -1.516538e-01
 1.015000 2 -6.304382e-02
 1.020000 3 8.849687e-04
 1.025000 4 5.053710e-02
 1.030000 5 9.068807e-02
 1.035000 6 1.239639e-01
 1.040000 7 1.519817e-01
 1.045000 8 1.758187e-01
 1.050000 9 1.962350e-01
 enter c,prolate, odd, order,nmax
25 0 0 0 20
 eigenv=-1.607904e+01
 eigenv=-2.448599e+00
 eigenv=8.630396e+00
 eigenv=2.991688e+01
 eigenv=5.973618e+01
 eigenv=9.765266e+01
 eigenv=1.436069e+02
 eigenv=1.975791e+02
 eigenv=2.595609e+02
 eigenv=3.295483e+02
 eigenv=4.075393e+02
 eigenv=4.935326e+02
 eigenv=5.875275e+02
 eigenv=6.895235e+02
 eigenv=7.995203e+02
 eigenv=9.175177e+02
 eigenv=1.043516e+03
 eigenv=1.177514e+03
 eigenv=1.319513e+03
 eigenv=1.469758e+03
 enter i for ith eigenvalue
0
  nn=0
 lambda=-1.607904e+01 n=0
 d=7.888440e+00 7.888440e+00
```

```
 d=1.833047e+01 5.623847e+03
 d=6.972705e+00 3.994399e+03
 d=1.174403e+00 9.664167e+02
 d=1.121396e-01 1.200675e+02
 d=6.894334e-03 9.088450e+00
 d=2.955547e-04 4.628189e-01
 d=9.334829e-06 1.693152e-02
 d=2.261770e-07 4.663396e-04
 d=4.336188e-09 1.001663e-05
 join factor first kind:4.371632e+00 N=2.165409e+02
rho=2.899782e-02
 Angular:
 0.000000 0 1.000000e+00
 0.100000 1 1.081675e+00
 0.200000 2 1.342473e+00
 0.300000 3 1.832972e+00
 0.400000 4 2.649029e+00
 0.500000 5 3.951714e+00
 0.600000 6 6.001025e+00
 0.700000 7 9.210683e+00
 0.800000 8 1.423594e+01
 0.900000 9 2.211365e+01
 Radial, 1st kind:
 0.000000 0 2.287475e-01
 0.200000 1 1.597143e-01
 0.400000 2 1.348714e-03
 0.600000 3 -1.367605e-01
 0.800000 4 -1.654779e-01
 1.000000 5 -7.936226e-02
 1.200000 6 4.473455e-02
 1.400000 7 1.025353e-01
 1.600000 8 -2.709500e-02
 1.800000 9 -8.485211e-01
 Radial, 2nd kind:
 0.000000 0 -1.154846e-03
 0.200000 1 1.538005e-01
 0.400000 2 2.057829e-01
 0.600000 3 1.263601e-01
 0.800000 4 -1.959127e-02
 1.000000 5 -1.257049e-01
 1.200000 6 -1.218818e-01
 1.400000 7 -8.136757e-04
 1.600000 8 3.374430e-01
 1.800000 9 1.918045e+00
 enter c,prolate, odd, order,nmax
25 1 0 0 20
 eigenv=4.195129e+00
 eigenv=2.017691e+01
 eigenv=3.389710e+01
```

```
 eigenv=5.508096e+01
 eigenv=8.482593e+01
 eigenv=1.227104e+02
 eigenv=1.686473e+02
 eigenv=2.226090e+02
 eigenv=2.845840e+02
 eigenv=3.545667e+02
 eigenv=4.325542e+02
 eigenv=5.185450e+02
 eigenv=6.125379e+02
 eigenv=7.145324e+02
 eigenv=8.245280e+02
 eigenv=9.425244e+02
 eigenv=1.068521e+03
 eigenv=1.202519e+03
 eigenv=1.344517e+03
 eigenv=1.494762e+03
 enter i for ith eigenvalue
3
  nn=6
 lambda=5.508096e+01 n=6
 d=2.435288e-03 2.435288e-03
 d=3.415319e-02 1.666377e-03
 d=2.495722e-01 6.008399e-04
 d=1.010976e+00 3.056314e-04
 d=-2.513478e-01 -1.775589e-04
 d=2.609302e-02 2.665926e-05
 d=-1.574801e-03 -2.060777e-06
 d=6.346476e-05 1.003854e-07
 d=-1.847228e-06 -3.411752e-09
 d=4.087498e-08 8.612673e-11
 d=-7.131478e-10 -1.685676e-12
 join factor first kind:1.373514e+02 N=1.452608e-02
rho=9.342571e-01
 Angular:
 1.000000 0 1.070369e+00
 0.984808 1 8.372139e-01
 0.939693 2 2.752036e-01
 0.866025 3 -2.639455e-01
 0.766044 4 -4.183833e-01
 0.642788 5 -1.205252e-01
 0.500000 6 2.660405e-01
 0.342020 7 2.772922e-01
 0.173648 8 -8.425988e-02
 0.000000 9 -3.125000e-01
 Radial, 1st kind:
 1.005000 0 8.388055e-03
 1.010000 1 9.001430e-03
 1.015000 2 9.633146e-03
```

```
1.020000 3 1.028329e-02
1.025000 4 1.095195e-02
1.030000 5 1.163919e-02
1.035000 6 1.234507e-02
1.040000 7 1.306965e-02
1.045000 8 1.381296e-02
1.050000 9 1.457505e-02
Radial, 2nd kind:
1.005000 0 -2.158118e+01
1.010000 1 -1.519958e+01
1.015000 2 -1.175009e+01
1.020000 3 -9.553909e+00
1.025000 4 -8.003258e+00
1.030000 5 -6.836967e+00
1.035000 6 -5.920328e+00
1.040000 7 -5.175425e+00
1.045000 8 -4.553438e+00
1.050000 9 -4.021893e+00
enter c,prolate, odd, order,nmax
```

Chapter 22

Orthogonal Polynomials

Introduction

In this chapter, functions are provided for evaluating a number of polynomials for real arguments. Some, like the Legendre functions, are treated elsewhere. The methods used here could obviously be generalized to handle complex arguments. This would in fact be quite simple using the methods of C++ given in Chapter 29.

Contents

We provide functions for the Laguerre, Tchebychev (first and second kinds), Gegenbauer ultraspherical, Jacobi, Hermite, and Legendre.

Applications

The orthogonal polynomials are generally used for fitting functions over specified intervals. The Gegenbauer ultraspherical polynomials are generalizations of the Legendre functions to more than three dimensions. See in particular Hochstadt's book, referenced in Chapter 8, on this subject. See, for example, Lebedev's book, also referenced in Chapter 8, on the applications of orthogonal polynomials.

Method

The recurrences in section 22.18 of Abramowitz and Stegun are used.

```
/*
orthogonal polynomials

from C Mathematical Function Handbook by Louis Baker
Copyright 1991 by Louis Baker. All rights reserved.

backp   service routine-not intended for direct user call
Pjacobi      Jacobi polynomials
laguerre   Laguerre
Cgegenbauer   Gegenbauer
Tcheby      Chebyshev, 1st kind
Ucheby      Chebyshev, 2nd kind
Plegendre   Legendre
Hermite      Hermite
*/

#include <stdio.h>
#include "cmlib.h"
#include "protom.h"

static double  apass,bpass;
static int odd;

double backp(n,cc,typep,x)double x; int n,cc,typep;
{
int m;   double a,f,b,c;
switch(cc)
   {
   case 1:f=x;break;
   case 2:f=x*x;break;
   case 3: f=1.-x;break;
   default:printf(" base case=%d\n",cc);return errorcode;
   }
for(a=1.,m=n;m>0;m--)
   {
   switch(cc)
      {
      case 1: /* Gen Laguerre*/
         b=n-m+1.;
         c=m*(apass+m);
         break;
      case 2:/* all else*/
         switch(typep)
            {
            case 1:/* gegenbauer*/
               b=2.*(n-m+1.)*(apass+n+m+odd-1.);
               c= m*(((m+odd)<<1)-1);
               break;
            case 2:/* Chebyshev T*/
```

```
                b=2.*(n-m+1.)*(n+m+odd-1);
                c= m*(((m+odd)<<1)-1);
                break;
             case 3:/* Chebyshev U (shifted)*/
                b=2.*(n-m+1.)*(n+m+odd);
                c= m*(((m+odd)<<1)-1);
                break;
             case 4: /* legendre*/
                b=(n-m+1)*(((n+m)<<1)+odd-1);
                c= m*(((m+odd)<<1)-1);
                break;
             case 5: /* Hermite*/
                b=2.*(n-m+1);
                c= m*(((m+odd)<<1)-1);
                break;
             }
          break;
       case 3:/*Jacobi P*/
          b=(n-m+1.)*(apass+bpass+n+m);
          c=2.*m*(apass+m);
          break;
       }
    a=1.-b/c*f*a;
    }
return a;
}

double Pjacobi(alpha,beta,n,x) int n; double alpha,beta,x;
{double gamma(),d;
apass=alpha;bpass=beta;
d= gamma(alpha+n+1.)/(gamma(alpha+1.)*gamma((double)n+1.));
return d*backp(n,3,0,x);
}

double laguerre(alpha,n,x) int n; double alpha,x;
{double gamma(),d;
apass=alpha;
d= gamma(alpha+n+1.)/(gamma(alpha+1.)*gamma((double)n+1.));
return d*backp(n,1,0,x);
}

double Cgegenbauer(alpha,n,x) int n; double alpha,x;
{double gamma(),d;
int m;m=n/2;odd=n%2;
apass=alpha;
d=((m%2)?-1.:1.)*pochhammer(alpha,m+odd)/gamma(m+1.);
if(odd)d*=2.*x;
return d*backp(m,2,1,x);
}
```

```
double Tcheby(n,x) int n; double x;
{double gamma(),d;
int m;m=n/2;odd=n%2;
d=((m%2)?-1.:1.);
if(odd)d*=(n)*x;
return d*backp(m,2,2,x);
}

double Ucheby(n,x) int n; double x;
{double gamma(),d;
int m;m=n/2;odd=n%2;
d=((m%2)?-1.:1.);
if(odd)d*=2.*(m+1)*x;
return d*backp(m,2,3,x);
}

double Plegendre(n,x) int n; double x;
{double pow(),gamma(),d;
int m;m=n/2;odd=n%2;
d=((m%2)?-1.:1.)*gamma((double)n+1.)
  /(pow(4.,(double)m)*gamma((double)m+1.)*
   gamma((double)(m+odd+1)));
if(odd)d*=(m+1.)*x;
return d*backp(m,2,4,x);
}

double Hermite(n,x) int n; double x;
{double pow(),gamma(),d;
int m;m=n/2;odd=n%2;
d=((m%2)?-1.:1.)*gamma(n+1.)
  /(gamma((double)m+1.));
if(odd)d*=2.*x;
return d*backp(m,2,5,x);
}
```

```
/*

test driver orthogonal polynomials
from C Mathematical Function Handbook by Louis Baker
Copyright 1991 by Louis Baker. All rights reserved.
*/

#include <stdio.h>
#include "cmlib.h"
#include "protom.h"

main()
{
double a,b,x;float aa,bb,xx;int n;
while(1)
    {
    printf(" Jacobi enter a,b n x\n");
    scanf("%e%e%d%e",&aa,&bb,&n,&xx);
    a=aa;b=bb;x=xx;
    if(n<0||x<0.||a<0.||b<0.)break;
    printf(" %e\n",Pjacobi(a,b,n,x));
    }
while(1)
    {
    printf(" C gegenbauer enter a n x\n");
    scanf("%e%d%e",&aa,&n,&xx);
    a=aa;x=xx;
    if(n<0||x<0.||a<0.)break;
    printf(" %e\n",Cgegenbauer(a,n,x));
    }
while(1)
    {
    printf(" gen. Laguerre enter a n x\n");
    scanf("%e%d%e",&aa,&n,&xx);
    a=aa;x=xx;
    if(n<0||x<0.||a<0.)break;
    printf(" %e\n",laguerre(a,n,x));
    }
while(1)
    {
    printf(" P legendre enter n x\n");
    scanf("%d%e",&n,&xx);
    x=xx;
    if(n<0||x<0.)break;
    printf(" %e\n",Plegendre(n,x));
    }
while(1)
    {
    printf(" Tcheby enter n x\n");
```

```
   scanf("%d%e",&n,&xx);
   x=xx;
   if(n<0||x<0.)break;
   printf(" %e\n",Tcheby(n,x));
   }
while(1)
   {
   printf(" U Tcheby enter n x\n");
   scanf("%d%e",&n,&xx);
   x=xx;
   if(n<0||x<0.)break;
   printf(" %e\n",Ucheby(n,x));
   }
while(1)
   {
   printf(" Hermite enter n x\n");
   scanf("%d%e",&n,&xx);
   x=xx;
   if(n<0||x<0.)break;
   printf(" %e\n",Hermite(n,x));
   }

}
```

```
Test Output for Orthogonal Polynomials
 Jacobi enter a,b n x
.5 .5 2 .6
 2.750001e-01
 Jacobi enter a,b n x
-1 -1 -1 -1
 C gegenbauer enter a n x
2 3 1
 2.000000e+01
 C gegenbauer enter a n x
-1 -1 -1
 gen. Laguerre enter a n x
0 11 1
 4.801342e-01
 gen. Laguerre enter a n x
0 6 5
 -2.090278e+00
 gen. Laguerre enter a n x
-1 -1 -1
 P legendre enter n x
2 .5
 -1.250000e-01
 P legendre enter n x
-1 -1
 Tcheby enter n x
6 0
 -1.000000e+00
 Tcheby enter n x
6 1
 1.000000e+00
 Tcheby enter n x
-1 -1
 U Tcheby enter n x
6 1
 7.000000e+00
 U Tcheby enter n x
-1 -1
 Hermite enter n x
11 3
 -1.042502e+07
 Hermite enter n x
-1 -1
```

Chapter 23

Bernoulli & Euler Numbers and Polynomials, Riemann Zeta Function

Introduction

In this chapter, we present functions that return the Bernoulli and Euler numbers, as well as evaluating the associated polynomials. We also provide functions for the Riemann zeta function for real arguments, and for associated functions such as the Debye function of Chapter 27, whose evaluation requires the use of Bernoulli numbers. We also provide routines for related sums. See Chapter 29 for C++ programs which can treat the Riemann zeta functions for complex arguments, and generalizations such as the Hurwitz zeta and Lerch Phi Transcendent.

Riemann Zeta Function

The Riemann Zeta function is defined by: $\zeta(s) = \sum_{n=1}^{\infty} \frac{1}{n^s}$. It clearly has a pole at $s = 1$, because the harmonic series $1 + \frac{1}{2} + \frac{1}{3} + \frac{1}{4} + \ldots$ is well known to diverge. Although the sum will not converge for $Re(s) < 1$, the zeta function can be analytically continued over the rest of the complex plane.

Generalized functions such as the Hurwitz zeta function $\zeta(s,a) = \sum_{n=0}^{\infty} \frac{1}{(n+a)^s}$ and the Lerch Phi Transcendent $\Phi(s,a,z) = \sum_{n=0}^{\infty} \frac{z^n}{(n+a)^s}$. See Chapter 29 for methods for these functions. There are also the sums

$$\eta(s) = \sum_{n=1}^{\infty} (-1)^{n-1} \frac{1}{n^s} = (1 - 2^{1-s})\, \zeta(s),$$

$\lambda(s) = \sum_{n=0}^{\infty} \frac{1}{(2n+1)^s} = (1 - 2^{-s})\,\zeta(s)$, $\beta(s) = \sum_{n=0}^{\infty} (-1)^n \frac{1}{(2n+1)^s}$. These sums are meaningful for integral s. They are related to Riemann Zeta function as shown above, as well as being expressible in terms of Bernoulli and Euler polynomials. The value *beta*(2) = .9159655941... is called Catalan's constant.

Bernoulli Polynomials and Numbers

The Bernoulli polynomials $B_n(t)$ are defined by the generating function $\frac{te^{xt}}{e^t - 1} = \sum_{n=0}^{\infty} B_n(t) \frac{t^n}{n!}$. The Bernoulli numbers are the constant terms in the polynomials, i. e., $B_n(0)$. The first few nonzero values are $B_0 = 1$, $B_1 = -1/2$, $B_2 = 1/6$, $B_3 = -1/30$. Note that, except for n = 1, the numbers are zero for odd n. Also note the alternating signs. Some authors, particularly older books, often define the Bernoulli numbers so that they are always positive! The Bernoulli numbers appear in computation of the Riemann zeta function.

Euler Polynomials and Numbers

The Euler polynomials $E_n(t)$ are defined by the generating function $\frac{2e^{xt}}{e^t + 1} = \sum_{n=0}^{\infty} B_n(t) \frac{t^n}{n!}$, obviously quite similar to the one above for Bernoulli polynomials.

Methods

For the zeta function, results in Tuma are used for real arguments. For complex arguments, the formula in Hutchinson is used. See references by Edwards and by Titchmarsh for theory, and by Cody et al. for rational approximations.

References

W. J. Cody, K. E. Hillstrom, H. C. Thacher, Jr., *Math. Comp.*, **25**, p. 537, 1971.

H. M. Edwards, *Riemann's Zeta Function* (N. Y.: Academic Press, 1974).

J. T. Hutchinson, *Trans. American Math. Soc.*, **27**, 49, 1925.

E. C Titchmarsh, *The Theory of Functions (Oxford: University Press, 1939).*

J. J. Tuma, *Handbook of Numerical Calculations in Engineering (N. Y.: McGraw-Hill, 1989).*

```
/*
Riemann Zeta (real arg.)
 and related functions
from C Mathematical Function Handbook by Louis Baker
Copyright 1991 by Louis Baker. All rights reserved.

zeta      Riemann Zeta
bernoulli(n)   Bernoulli numbers
bernpoly(n,x)   Bernoulli polynomial
euler      Euler numbers
debye      integral
dilog
clausen   clausen integral (Ch. 27)
*/

#include "cmlib.h"
#include "complex.h"
#include "protom.h"
#include <stdio.h>
#define itmax 1000
extern int itkt;

/* ibkeven is the integer power such that x^i is more cheap-
ly calculated using pow() than x*x*... i times*/
int ibkeven=11,dbkeven=3,lbkeven=4;
/*default guess 387/386 TURBOC*/

double zeta(r) double r;
{
double pow(),bernoul-
li(),term,sum,g,sin(),gamma(),values[11]=
   {1.6449340668,1.20205690316,1.0823232337,1.0369277551,

1.017343061984,1.0083492773819,1.00407735619,1.0020083928,
   1.000994575127,1.000494188604,1.000246086553};
int i,j,k,ir,intlim,rint,m;
if(r==1.)return errorcode;
if(r==0.)return -.5;
ir=(int)r;
rint= (r==(double)ir);
if(rint &&ir>1)
   {
   if(ir<13) return values[ir-2];
   /* if even,could either continue on to sum, or
   zeta(2m)= -1^(m+1) (2pi)^2m D[2m]/(2*(2m)!)*/
   }
if(rint &&ir<0)
   {
   if( !((-ir)%2 ))return 0.;/*even*/
```

```
   ir= (1-ir);
   return -bernoulli(ir)/(ir);
   }
if(r<0.)
   {
   return zeta(1.-r)*pow(2.*pi,r-
1.)*2.*sin(pi*.5*r)*gamma(1.-r);
   }
if(r>1.)
   {
   intlim= pow( 32767.,1./r);/* max int we can safely raise
to power*/
   sum=0;
   rint= rint && (ir<intlim);
   for(i=1;i<itmax;i++)
      {
      if(rint &&(i<intlim))
         { m=k=(i<<1)-1 ;
         for(j=2;j<=ir;j++)m*=k;
         term=m;
         }
      else if(i<32767)term= pow( (double)((i<<1)-1),-r);
      /* if rint, ir<5 use long int possible*/
      else term= pow( 2.*((double)i)-1.,-r);
      sum+=term;
      }
   g=pow(2.,r);
   return sum*g/(g-1.);
   }
/* 0<r<1*/
g=-1.;sum=1.;
for(i=2;i< 20000;i++)
   {
   term= pow((double)i,-r);
   sum+=g*term;
   g=-g;
   if(abs(term)<1.e-5 || abs(term)<1.e-5*abs(sum))break;
   }
return sum/(1.-pow(2.,1.-r));
}

double bernoulli(n) int n;/* n even 0<=n*/
{
double r,sum,term,x,b0=1.,b1=-.5,b2=.166666666,g;
int i;
if(n==0)return b0;
if(n==2)return b2;
if(n==1)return b1;
if(n%2==1)return 0.;
```

```
r=(double) n;
if(n>3)
    {
    sum=0;
    for(i=1;i<itmax;i++)
        {
        term= pow( (double)(i) ,-r);
        sum+=term;
        if(abs(term)<5.e-7 || abs(term/sum)<5.e-7)break;
        }
    g=pow(2.*pi,r);
    x=1.;
    if((n>>1)%2 ==0)x=-1.;
    return 2.*sum*gamma(r+1.)/g*x;
    }
return 0.;
}

double bernpoly(n,x) double x;int n;
{int i; double sum,fact;
fact=1.;
sum= bernoulli(0);
for(i=1;i<=n;i++)
    {
    fact*=((double) (n+1-i))/((double)(i));
/*printf(" i %d sum %d fact %e\n",i,sum,fact);*/
    sum=sum*x+ fact*bernoulli(i);
    }
return sum;
}

double eulerpoly(n,x) int n; double x;
{int m;double y,z;
m=n+1;y=x*.5;
return 2./m*(bernpoly(m,x)-bernpoly(m,y)*pow(2.,(double)m));
}


double euler(n) int n;
{
double e[7]={1.,-1.,5.,-61.,1385.,-50521.,2702765.};
double r,g,sum,term,x;
int i;
itkt=0;
if(!n)return c[0];
if(n%2==1 ) return 0./*no such*/;
if( n<=12)
    {i=n>>1;return e[i];}
r=(double) (n);
```

```
if(n>3)
   {
   sum=0;
   x=1.;
   for(i=1;i<itmax;i++)
      {
      term= x*pow( (double)((i<<1)-1) ,-(r+1.));
      sum+=term;
      x=-x;
      itkt=i;
      if(abs(term)<1.e-10 || abs(term/sum)<1.e-8)break;
      }
   g=pow(2./pi,r+1.);
   x=-1.;
   if((n>>1)%2 ==0)x=1.;
   /*printf(" euler itkt=%d %e %e\n",itkt,term,sum);*/
   return x*sum*g*2.*gamma(r+1.);
   }
return 0.;
}

double debye(x,n) int n; double x;
{
int k,l;
double nn,np,nm,sum,term,interm,fk,factor,tt;
/*printf(" enter debye x=%le n=%d\n",x,n);*/
nn=n;np=nn+1.;
sum=0.;
factor=x*x;
term=factor;
if(x<.15 )
   {
   for(k=1;k<itmax;k++)
      {
      tt=term*bernoulli(2*k)/(2*k+n);
      sum+=tt;
      if(abs(tt)<1.e-5 || abs(tt/sum)<1.e-5)break;
      term*=factor/(2*(k+1)*(2*k+3));
      }
   return pow(x,nn)*(1./n-.5*x/np+sum);
   }

fk= exp(-x);
factor=fk;
for(k=1;k<itmax;k++)
   {
   term=0.;nm=nn;
   interm= pow(x, (double)n)/k;
   for(l=0;l<=n;l++)
```

```
        {
        term+=interm;
        interm*=(nm/(k*x));
        nm--;
        }
    term*= factor;
    factor*=fk;
    sum+=term;
    if(abs(term)<1.e-5 || abs(term/sum)<1.e-5)break;
    }
return zeta( np) *gamma(np)-sum;
}

double dilog(x) double x;
{
double log(),t;
if(x!=0.)t=log(x);
else t= -1.e60;
/* x=0 -> t= -infinity. do not use errorcode here, as user
might change it from -1.e60 */

if(x>1.)
    {
    return -t*t*.5-debye(t,1);
    }
return debye(-t,1);
}


double clausen(theta) double theta;
{
int k;
double sum,term,sq,ans1,ans2,tt,t;
/*printf(" entered clausen theta= %le %le\n",theta,
theta*180./pi);*/
if(theta==0.)return 0.;
if(theta<0. || theta>pi)return errorcode;
if(theta<=.5* pi )
    {
    sum=0.;
    sq=theta*theta;
    term=.25*theta*sq;
    for(k=1;k<itmax;k++)
        {
        tt=term*bernoulli(2*k)/((double)(k*((k<<1)+1)));
        sum+=tt;
/*printf(" debug sum term %e %e\n",sum,term);*/
        term*= -sq/((double)(2*(k+1)*(2*k+1)) );
        if((abs(tt)<5.e-7 || abs(tt)<1.e-6*abs(sum))  )break;
```

```
        itkt=k;
        }
    ans1=theta-theta*log(theta)+sum; return ans1;
    }
/* theta >= pi/2*/
/*printf(" debug  pi/2\n");*/

t= pi -theta;
sum=0.;
sq=t*t;
term=.25*t*sq;
for(k=1;k<itmax;k++)
    {
    tt=term*bernoulli(2*k)*(pow(2.,2.*k)-
1.)/((double)(k*(2*k+1)));
    sum+=tt;
/*printf(" debug sum term %e %e\n",sum,tt);*/
    term*= -sq/(2.*(k+1)*(2*k+1) );
    if(abs(tt)<5.e-7 || abs(tt)<1.e-6*abs(sum))break;
    itkt=k;
    }
ans2=t*log(2.)-sum;
/*
sum=0.;
for(k=1;k<itmax;k++)
    {
    term= sin(k*theta)/((double)(k*k));
    sum+=term;
    printf(" debug sin sum term %e %e\n",sum,term);
    if((abs(term)<5.e-7 || abs(term)<1.e-6*abs(sum))&&
k>40)break;
    itkt=k;
    }
ans1=sum;*/
/*printf(" clausen sin sum=%le %le\n",ans1,ans2);*/
return ans2;
/*return ans1;*/
/* leads to infinite loop theta>pi/2
t=theta*.5;
return 2.*(clausen(t*.5)-clausen(pi-t));
*/
}


double zeta1(z) double z;
{double bigphi();/* for faster see ebz.c*/
return bigphi(1.,z,1.);
}
```

```
double zeta2(z,a)double z,a;
{/* "Hurwitz" zeta function*/
int i,top,topl=12,inta;/*topl chosen for efficiency*/
double zeta(),sum,pow(),term,tol=1.e-6,denom;
if(a==0.)return errorcode;
if(z==0.)return .5-a;
if (((z-(double)((int)z))==0.) && z<0.)
   {/* z negative integer*/
   return -bernpoly((int)(1.-z),a)/(z+1.);
   }
inta=((a-(double)((int)a))==0.);
if(  inta && a>0.)
   {/* a is a positive  integer*/
   if(a==1.)return zeta(z);
   top= (int)a;
   if(top<topl)
      {
      sum=0.;
      for(i=1;i<top;i++)
         {
         term=pow(((double)i) ,-z);
         sum+=term;
         if( abs(term)<tol*abs(sum))break;
         }
/*       printf(" answer shortcut %e\n",zeta(z)-sum);*/
      return zeta(z)-sum;
      }
   }
sum=0.;
for(i=0;i<itmax;i++)
   {
   denom=a+((double)i);
   if(denom!=0.)term=pow( denom,-z);
   sum+=term;
   if( abs(term)<tol*abs(sum))break;
   }
return sum;
}


double bigphi(z,s,v) double z,s,v;
{
double sum,term,pow(),denom,power,tol=1.e-6;
int i;
sum=0.;
power=1.;
for(i=0;i<itmax;i++)
   {
```

```
   denom=v+((double)i);
   term=pow(denom ,-s)*power;
   sum+=term;
   if( abs(term)<tol*abs(sum))break;
   power*=z;
   }
return sum;
}

double betacat(s) double s;
{double pow();/* Catalan beta= sum k=0 to inf. (-1)^k
(2k+1)^-s*/
if(s==1.) return pi*.25;
if(s==2.) return .915965594177219;
if(s==3.)return pi*pi*pi*.03125;
return bigphi(-1.,s,.5)*pow(2.,-s);}

double lambda(s) double s;
{double pow(),zeta();/* sum k=0 to infinity (2k+1)^-s */
return (1.-pow(2.,-s))*zeta(s);
}

double eta(s) double s;
{double pow(),zeta();/* sum from k=1 to infinity -1^k k^-n
*/
return zeta(s)*(1.-pow(2.,1.-s));
}

double ifermi(mu,s)double mu,s;
{/* integral from 0 to infinity of k^s/(exp(k-mu)+1) dk */
double exp(),gamma(),e;e=exp(mu);
return e*gamma(1.+s)*bigphi(-e,1.+s,1.);
}
```

```
/*
test driver Riemann zeta(real)
     , Bernoulli/Euler, relatives.

from C Mathematical Function Handbook by Louis Baker
Copyright 1991 by Louis Baker. All rights reserved.
*/

#include <stdio.h>
#include "cmlib.h"
#include "protom.h"

main()
{
int i; double a,b,c,d;
infinite_loop
   {printf(" enter z for Riemann zeta =1 to end\n");
   scanf("%le",&a);
   if(a==1.)break;
   printf(" zeta=%le also %le\n",zeta(a), zeta2(a,1.));
   printf(" Catalan beta=%le lambda=%le eta=%le\n"
      ,betacat(a),lambda(a),eta(a));
   }
infinite_loop
   {printf(" enter n for Bernoulli, Euler (-1 to end)\n");
   scanf("%d",&i);
   if(i==-1)break;
   printf(" Bernoulli= %le Euler=%le\n",bernoul-
li(i),euler(i));
   printf(" now enter x for poly\n");scanf("%le",&a);
   printf(" Bernoulli, Euler poly values %le %le\n"
      ,bernpoly(i,a),eulerpoly(i,a));
   }
infinite_loop
   {printf(" enter z,mu for fermi integral -1 -1to end\n");
   scanf("%le%le",&a,&b);
   if(a==-1. && b==-1.)break;
   printf(" ifermi=%le\n",ifermi(b,a));
   }

}
```

Test Output: Riemann Zeta, Bernoulli, Euler Num.

```
 enter z for Riemann zeta =1 to end
7
 zeta=1.008349e+00 also 1.008349e+00
 Catalan beta=9.995545e-01 lambda=1.000472e+00
eta=9.925938e-01
 enter z for Riemann zeta =1 to end
6
 zeta=1.017343e+00 also 1.017343e+00
 Catalan beta=9.986851e-01 lambda=1.001447e+00
eta=9.855511e-01
 enter z for Riemann zeta =1 to end
1
 enter n for Bernoulli, Euler (-1 to end)
10
 Bernoulli= 7.575757e-02 Euler=-5.052100e+04
 now enter x for poly
11
 Bernoulli, Euler poly values 1.574305e+10 1.471234e+10
 enter n for Bernoulli, Euler (-1 to end)
11
 Bernoulli= 0.000000e+00 Euler=0.000000e+00
 now enter x for poly
1 0
 Bernoulli, Euler poly values 0.000000e+00 1.727500e+02
 enter n for Bernoulli, Euler (-1 to end)
12
 Bernoulli= -2.531136e-01 Euler=2.702765e+06
 now enter x for poly
1
 Bernoulli, Euler poly values -2.530297e-01 -1.767907e-04
 enter n for Bernoulli, Euler (-1 to end)
-1
 enter z,mu for fermi integral -1 -1to end
.5 -.5
 ifermi=4.497932e-01
 enter z,mu for fermi integral -1 -1to end
-1 -1
```

Chapter 24

Combinatorics. Stirling Numbers.

Introduction

This chapter discusses a number of functions of interest to combinatorics and number theory. In the former category are the Stirling numbers of the first and second kinds and the binomial coefficients. In the latter category are number theoretic functions such as those of Mobius, Euler's totient function, etc., as well as the table of primes and factorizations. The partition functions represent an intermediate class of functions of interest to both, the formulae being obtained from analytic number theoretic arguments.

The Stirling and Fibonacci numbers are computed by programs in this chapter, and the binomial coefficients by a function given in Chapter 26. The number theoretic functions require the use of arbitrary precision integer arithmetic if reasonable capability in handling interesting numbers is to be provided. Such a package would require a book in itself for a proper treatment. Packages with such functionality are discussed in Chapter 28.

Note that some authors, such as Graham et al., define Stirling numbers of the first kind such that they are positive. We provide routines for both conventions.

Methods

Recurrences are used for the Stirling numbers. The closed form for Fibonacci numbers are used. The binomial coefficients are first tested for special cases, with the gamma function used for large values. (Recurrence relations are a poor choice for computing the binomial coefficients.)

References

R. L. Graham, D. Knuth, O. Patashnik, *Concrete Mathematics* (Reading, M. A.: Addison Wesley, 1989).

```
/*
Stirling numbers first and second kind

from C Mathematical Function Handbook by Louis Baker
Copyright 1991 by Louis Baker. All rights reserved.
*/
#include "cmlib.h"
#include "protom.h"

double stirl2(int n, int m)
{
if (m<0 || n<0 || m>n ) return errorcode;
if(m==n)return 1;
if( !m) return 0;
if(m==1)return 1;
if(m==2) return pow(2., (double)(n-1)) -1;
return m* stirl2(n-1,m)+ stirl2(n-1,m-1);
}

double stirl1(int n, int m)
{
if (m<0 || n<0 || m>n ) return errorcode;
if(m==n)return 1;
if( !m) return 0.;
if(m==1)return  gamma( (double)(n));
return (n-1)* stirl1(n-1,m)+ stirl1(n-1,m-1);
}

double stirlingf(int n, int m)
{
return stirl1(n,m)*((n-m)%2?-1:1);
}
```

```
/*
Fibonacci numbers
from C Mathematical Function Handbook by Louis Baker
Copyright 1991 by Louis Baker. All rights reserved.
*/
double fib(n) int n;
{
double a=1.6180339887498948204,b=-.6180339887498948204;
/*a= .5*(1+sqrt(5)), b=.5(1-sqrt(5))*/
double p,pow();
p=n;
return( pow(a,p)-pow(b,p))*.447213595;/*1/sqrt(5)*/
}
```

```
/*
binomial coefficients
from C Mathematical Function Handbook by Louis Baker
Copyright 1991 by Louis Baker. All rights reserved.
*/

#include <stdio.h>
#include "cmlib.h"
#include "protom.h"

double binom(double n, double m)
{
double k;
if(m>n) return 0l;
/* ?  if m=3,n=2: 2!/3!-1! -1!=Gamma(0)=infinity=> 0 ans*/
if(m==0. || m==n)return 1l;
if(m==1.)return n;
if(n-m== 1.)return n;
k=n+1.;
return gamma(k)/(gamma(k-m)*gamma(m+1.));
/* slow for large n:*/
k=n-1.;
return binom(k,m)+binom(k,m-1.);
}
```

```
/*
test driver for stirling numbers
from C Mathematical Function Handbook by Louis Baker
Copyright 1991 by Louis Baker. All rights reserved.
*/

#include <stdio.h>
#include "cmlib.h"
#include "protom.h"

#include <stdio.h>

/* test driver stirling, fibonacci, binomial coef.

from C Mathematical Function Handbook by Louis Baker
Copyright 1991 by Louis Baker. All rights reserved.
*/

#include <stdio.h>
#include "cmlib.h"
#include "protom.h"

main()
{int n=1,k=1;
for(;;)
   {
   printf(" enter n,k ");
   scanf("%d%d",&n,&k);
   printf(" echo n, k %d %d\n",n,k);
   if(n<=0  || k<=0 )break;
   printf(" first %le %le second %le\n"
      ,stirl1(n,k),stirlingf(n,k),stirl2(n,k));
   }
for(;;)
   {
   printf(" enter n for FIBONACCI ");
   scanf("%d",&n);if(n<=0)break;
   printf(" %le\n",fib(n));
   }
for(;;)
   {
   printf(" enter n,m for binomial coeff");
   scanf("%d%d",&n,&k);if(n<=0)break;
   printf(" %le\n",binom((double)n,(double)k));
   }
}
```

```
Test Output: Stirling, Fibonacci, Binomial coef.
 enter n,k 10 4
 echo n, k 10 4
 first 7.236800e+05 7.236800e+05 second 3.410500e+04
 enter n,k 10 5
 echo n, k 10 5
 first 2.693250e+05 -2.693250e+05 second 4.252500e+04
 enter n,k 0 0
 echo n, k 0 0
 enter n for FIBONACCI 1
 1.000000e+00
 enter n for FIBONACCI 2
 1.000000e+00
 enter n for FIBONACCI 3
 2.000000e+00
 enter n for FIBONACCI 4
 3.000000e+00
 enter n for FIBONACCI 5
 5.000000e+00
 enter n for FIBONACCI 6
 8.000000e+00
 enter n for FIBONACCI 7
 1.300000e+01
 enter n for FIBONACCI 0
 enter n,m for binomial coeff19 5
 1.162800e+04
 enter n,m for binomial coeff0 0
```

Chapter 25

Numerical Analysis

Discussion

Abramowitz and Stegun present here basic formulae relevent to numerical analysis, specifically, interpolation, integration, and finite-difference methods. Much of this is outdated. Adaptive quadrature is very commonly used now. It places the points of function evalution where they are most effective. See *C Tools*. Of course, Gaussian quadrature and its relatives (e. g., Lobatto quadrature) have many applications. See *More C Tools* for a discussion of these methods and their uses in a variety of applications. Finite-element and multi-grid methods are often used in preference to finite-difference formulations.

Multi-grid methods, of course, use a series of finite-difference grids which share points but vary in coarseness. They therefore make use of the typical stencils found in Chapter 25 of Abramowitz and Stegun. Multi-grid methods are discussed in *More C Tools*.

Iterative methods have been popular lately, in part because of their ability to vectorize and parallelize, as well as their ability to handle sparse systems well. So-called "semi-iterative" methods, which converge to the exact answer in a finite number of iterations, in principle, i. e., with exact arithmetic, are among the most popular. These include the conjugate gradient method, discussed in *More C Tools*, which is applicable to positive-definite systems, and more general methods, such as ORTHOMIN or GMRES or the Biconjugate-Gradient Method. For all of these methods, good preconditioning is required to achieve economy of computation. Preconditioning is a subject of very active research at present. It would be unfair to list references here, as they would be quickly out-of-date; it would be best to consult recent issues of *SIAM J. Num. Analysis* or similar journals. Dagonet software offers a package of C routines for solving sparse linear systems.

Finally, splines of various kinds are now regularly used for interpolation, again providing more flexibility in locating points. An introduction to B-splines is in *C Tools*. They are discussed there from the point of view of interpolating splines, i. e., splines that pass through their specified control points. Many splines used in graphics, such as Bezier splines, do not pass through their control points. There are many variants of B-Splines, NURBS (non-uniform rational B-splines) being an example. In these applications, the spline curve does not pass through the control points. See, e. g., Foley, van Dam, Feiner, and Hughes for a general discussion of splines as applied to graphics.

Reference

J. D. Foley, A. van Dam, S. K. Feiner, J. F. Hughes, *Computer Graphics*, 2nd. ed. (Reading, M. A.: Addison-Wesley, 1990).

Chapter 26

Statistical Functions, Probability Distributions, and Random Variables

Introduction

This chapter contains a number of packages. There is a "calculator" with the statistical functions of Chapter 26 of Abramowitz and Stegun, including such functions as the *F* distribution and its inverse, based upon one in *More C Tools*. There are packages for producing random numbers and random variables from a wide variety of distributions, and there are functions for calculating various probability distributions.

The calculator package is enhanced with the bivariate normal distribution and the sign test from **stath.c** in *More C Tools*. The calculator package is self-contained. It goes well beyond Abramowitz and Stegun in functionality.

The random variables packages are based upon **random.c** in *More C Tools*. Additional distributions have been added, in files **dist.c** and **rrice.c.** The distribution functions, as well as the ability to generate random variables from these distributions, are supplied.

Methods

See *More C Tools* for references, a complete discussion of methods, and test cases for the two packages taken from that book. The random distribution functions are based largely upon Hastings and Peacock (with a number of corrections).

References

N. A. J. Hastings and J. B. Peacock, *Statistical Distributions* (London: Butterworths, 1975).

S. Kokoska and C. Nevison, *Statistical Tables and Formulae,* (N. Y.: Springer, 1989).

```
/*
package of routines to generate and apply
random numbers
from More C Tools for Scientists and Engineers by L. Baker
Copyright 1991 by Louis Baker. All rights reserved.
*/
/* You may change stmt below, replacing randm() with u16()
or u32() */
/* randm() was called random() but this conflicted with sys-
tem routine
  you may use that routine, but note that it had arguments.
check
your system for details as to required arguments and
type of return value.

Stdlib.h, in Turbo C, defines random as an inline function
returning
type int and taking as input a seed int.  It calls rand(),
which
uses type long return value and has no argument. see for
rand() set
by call to srand.
*/

#include "cmlib.h"
#include "protom.h"

#define urand()  randm()

long int seed;
int naflag,nflag;
long int s1,seed2;
int s16,s26,s36;

double erlang(k,mean) int k; double mean;
{
double exp(),expon(),emult,sum;
int i;
emult= mean/k;
sum=0.;
for (i=0;i<k;i++) sum+=exp(expon(emult));
return(sum);
}

double expon(mean) double mean;
{/* assumes rand has been seeded with proper iy*/
double log(),urand();
return(-mean*log(urand()) );
}
```

```
double cauchy()
{
return  tan((pi-randm())*.5);
}

double logistic(a,k) double a,k;
{
/* logistic distribution F= 1/{1+exp-(x-a)/k }
   mean a, variance b^2= (k*pi)^2/3  */
double x;
x=randm();
return a+k*log(x/(1.-x));
}

int randi(nvalue,probd) int nvalue;float probd[];
/* random integer betwen 1-nvalue in accord with probd dis-
trib.*/
{
int i,n1;
double u;
u=randm();/* u(0,1) uniform random */
n1=nvalue-1;
for (i=0;i<n1;i++) if(u<probd[i])return(i);
return(nvalue);
}

double uniform(a,b) double a,b;
{
double urand();
return(a+(b-a)*urand());
}

double normal(mean,sd,s1,s2) double mean,sd,*s1,*s2;
{
double log(),urand(),sqrt(),r1,r2,v1,v2,s,ss;
int iter;
iter=0;
while(1)
   {
   r1=urand();r2=urand();
   v1=2.*r1-1.;v2=2.*r2-1.;
   s=v1*v1+v2*v2;
   if (s<1.)
      {
      ss=sqrt(-2.*log(s)/s)*sd;
      *s1=v1*ss+mean;
      *s2=v2*ss+mean;
      return(*s1);
```

```
        };
/*    iter++;
   if(iter>10)
      {
      printf(" trouble in normal %f %f %f\n",r1,r2,s);
      break;
      }
*/
   };/*end while*/
   return(0.);/* Keep DeSmet happy*/
}

double snorm1,snorm2;

double norm(mean,sd) double mean,sd;
{
/* nflag must be initialized to 1 before first call*/
nflag^=1;
if(nflag)return snorm2;
return normal(mean,sd,&snorm1,&snorm2);
}


double u32()
{/*32 bit*/
long int z,k;
k= s1/ 53668;
s1= 40014*(s1-k*53668)-k*12211;
if(s1<0) s1+=2147483563;
k= seed2/52774;
seed2=40692*(seed2-k*52774)-k*3791;
if(seed2<0)seed2+=2147483399;
z=s1-seed2;
if(z<1)z+=2147483562;
return z*4.656613e-10;
}


double u16()
{/*16 bit*/
int z,k;
k= s16/ 206;
s16= 157*(s16-k*206)-k*21;
if(s16<0) s16+=32363;
k= s26/217;
s26=146*(s26-k*217)-k*45;
if(s26<0)s26+=31727;
k= s36/222;
s36=142*(s36-k*222)-k*133;
```

```
if(s36<0)s36+=31657;
z=s16-s26;
if(z>706)z-=32362;
z+=s36;
if(z<1)z+=32362;
return z*3.0899e-5;
}

double randm()
{
long int a=16807,m=2147483647,q=127773,r=2836;
long int lo,hi,test;
hi= seed / q;
lo= seed % q;
test= a*lo-r*hi;
seed=(test>0)?test: test+m;
return (double) seed/m;
}

double ex()
{
static double ln2=.6931471805599453,a=5.7133631526454228,
b=3.4142135623730950, c=-1.6734053240284925,
p=.9802581434685472,q=5.6005707569738080,
r=3.3468106480569850, h=.0026106723602095,
d=.08576764376269050;
double g,aux,u,up,y,aux2,aux1,H=2.28421e-4;
/*H=h*d/p;*/
u=randm();
g=c;
dbl: u=u+u;
if(u<1.)
   {
   g+=ln2;
   goto dbl;
   }
u--;
if(u<p) return (g+q/(r-u));
while(1)
   {
   u=randm();
   aux=b-u;
   y= a/aux;
   up=randm();
   aux1=(up*H+d)*aux*aux;       aux2=exp(-(y+c));
   if( aux1 <= aux2 )return (g+y);
   }
return(0.);/*for DeSmet*/
}
```

```
double ca()
{
static double a=.6380631366077803,b=.5959486060529070,
q=.9339962925760365 6,w=.2488703380083841,c=.6366197723675813,

d=.5972997593539963,h=.0214949094570452,p=4.9125013953033204;

double u,t,s,up,x;
u=randm();
t=u-.5;
s=w-t*t;
if(s>0.0)return t*(c/s+d);
while(1)
    {
    u=randm();
    t=u-.5;
    s=.25-t*t;
    up=randm();
    x=t*(a/s+b);
    if( s*s*((1+x*x)*(h*up+p)-q)+s<=.5)return x;
    }
return(0.);
}
static double y;

double na()
{
int b;
double t,up,u,e,s,ca,x,r;
static double a=.6380631366077803,g=.5959486060529070,
q=.93399629257603656,w=.2488703380083841,c=.6366197723675813,

d=.5972997593539963,h=.0214949094570452,p=4.9125013953033204;

/* initialize naflag=1*/
naflag ^= 1;
if(naflag) return y;
u=randm();
b=(u<.5)? 0:1;
e=ex();
r=e+e;
/* ca= cauchy dist*/
u= (b)? u+u-1. : u+u;
t=u-.5;
s=w-t*t;
if(s>0.0) ca=t*(c/s+d);
else while(1)
    {
```

```
    u=randm();
    t=u-.5;
    s=.25-t*t;
    up=randm();
    ca=t*(a/s+g);
    if( s*s*((1+ca*ca)*(h*up+p)-q)+s<=.5)break;
    }
x=sqrt(r/(1.+ca*ca));
y=ca*x;
if(!b) return x;
else return -x;
return 0.;
}
```

```
/*
Random Distributions
Copyright 1991 by Louis Baker. All rights reserved.

a) cumm. prob distributions-
   binomial, negative binomial, Poisson, hypergeometric
b) random numbers for distrib.:
      binomial,neg. binomial,chisq,geometric,hyper-
geometric,Poisson
      lognormal, weibull,extreme, Pareto

Based largely on Hastings and Peacock, with errors in rng
for
 neg. binomial and hypergeometric fixed and chi-sq and
 error hypergeom dist fixed.

*/
#include "cmlib.h"
#include "protom.h"
#include <stdio.h>

#define urand() u16()

/* cummulative binomial, neg. binomial, poisson, hyper-
geometric dist*/

double binomial_dist(int x,int n, double p)
{
/* also related to incomplete Beta function */
 int i;
 double sum,ratio,q,pow(),term;
 if(p<=0. || p>=1. || x>n || x<0 || n<0 )
    return errorcode;
 q=1.-p;
 if(q!=0.)ratio=p/q;
 else ratio=1.;/* q=0 => p=1 */
 term= sum= pow(q,(double)n);
for(i=1;i<=x;i++){term *= (ratio*(n-i+1))/(double)i;
                 sum += term;}
return sum;
}

double neg_binomial_dist(int x,int y, double p)
{
 int i;
 double sum,ratio,q,pow(),term,gamma();
 if(p<=0. || p>=1. || y<0 ||x<1) return errorcode;
 q=1.-p;ratio=q;
 term= sum=1.;
```

```
for(i=1;i<=y;i++){term *= (ratio*(x+i-1))/(double)i;
                sum += term;}
return pow(p,(double)x)*sum;
}

double poisson_dist(int x,double lambda)
{
double sum,exp(),term;
int i;
sum=term=1.;
for(i=1;i<=x;i++){term*= lambda/i ;sum+=term;}
return exp(-lambda)*sum;
}

double hypergeometric_dist(int N, int m, int k, int x)
{double binomial_coef(),sum,term; int r;
double z;
/* N balls in urn, k white; draw m;
cumm prob, i.e. prob that up to x white are drawn H*P has
error
in prob dist. function!*/
if(x<0||N<1||k>N||x>m || m>N ) return errorcode;
if(x>k)x=k;/* cummulative prob. includes x>N*/
if(x>m)x=m;
/*printf(" N %d m%d k%d x%d\n",N,m,k,x);*/
/* prob no success f(0)=*/
sum=term= binomial_coef(N-k,m)/binomial_coef(N,m);
if(sum==0.)
   {
   /*fprintf(stderr,
   " hypergeom dist warn:prob of drawing no white balls is
zero\n");*/
   for(sum=0.,r=0;r<=x;r++)
      {
      sum+= binomial_coef(k,r)*binomial_coef(N-k,m-r);
      }
   return sum/binomial_coef(N,m);
   }
for(r=0;r<x;r++)
   {
   /*printf(" prob of %d white balls=%le\n",r,term);*/
   z=((double)((r+1)*(N-m-k+r+1)));
   if(z<=0.)
      {/* term does not contribute: m so large, must draw
      more than r white balls. Eg if N=4, k=3, m=2 must
draw at least 1 wht
      So   f(0)=0, do not get here.
      */
      fprintf(stderr,
```

```
      " error in hypergeometric distribution N M k x %d %d
%d %d\n"
      ,N,m,k,x);
      exit(1);
      }
   term*=(m-r)*(k-r)/z;
   sum+=term;
   }
return sum;
}

double erlang_dist(double b,int c,double x)
{double sum,term,factor,exp(); int i;
sum=term=1.;factor=x/b;
for(i=1;i<c;i++)
   {term*= factor/i;
   sum+=term;
   }
return 1.-exp(-factor)*sum;
}


extern double random(),u16(),u32();
extern long int seed,s1,s2; extern int s26,s16,s36;

double randn;

#define smallp  .1
#define nlimbi  0

int binomial(int n, double p)
{
int i,kount;double g,log(),sum,a,q;
q=1.-p;
if(p<=0. || p>=1.) return errorcode;
if(p<smallp && n>nlimbi)
   {
   q= 1./log(1.-p);kount=0;sum=0.;
   while(sum<n)
      {
      a=urand();
      if(a<=0.)
         {/* it is possible that urand=0.but unlikely*/
         continue;}
      g= log(a)*q;sum+=g;kount++;
      }
   }
 else
   for(i=kount=0;i<n;i++)if(urand()<p)kount++;
```

```
return kount;
}

int neg_binomial(int x, double p)
{/* p success prob.  return number of failures before x suc-
cesses */
int i,kountl,kountm;double g,log(),sum,a,q;
if(p<=0. || p>=1.) return errorcode;
if(p<smallp && x<nlimbi)
    {
    q= 1./log(1.-p);sum=0.;
    for(i=1;i<=x;i++)
        {
        a=urand(); randn=a;
        if(a<=0.)
            {/* it is possible that urand=0.but unlikely*/
            fprintf(stderr," warn bad urand %le\n",a);
            continue;}
        g= log(a);sum+=g;
        }
    return (int)(sum*q-x +.5);/* round to nearest int*/
    }
else
    {
    kountl=kountm=0;
    while(1)
        {
        a=urand();
randn=a;
/*printf(" random =%le\n",randn);*/
        if(a<=p)kountl++;/* a<p= failure p=1 all failures*/
        else   kountm++;/*a>=p a sucess */
/*      if(kountm>=x)return kountl;*//* x sucesses-return
failure kt*/
        if(kountl>=x)return kountm;  /* x failures-return suc-
cess????*/
        }
    }
return  ierrorcode;
}

extern nflag;

double chisq(int v)
{
int limit,i;
double add,norm(),urand(),prod=1.,log();
/* call nflag only once for maximum efficiency if will be
```

```
many calls to chisq or to norm().  That is, pull stmt from
below! */

/* method adding normal^2  works well but is expensive*/
/*
add=0.;
for(i=1;i<=v;i++){prod=norm(0.,1.);randn=prod;add+=prod*prod;
}
return add;
*/

/*nflag=1;*/
if( v%2)
   {
   limit=(v-1)>>1;/* -1 not really needed, as shift will do
it*/
   add= norm(0.,1.);add*=add;
   }
else
   {
   limit= v>>1;
   add=0.;
   }
for(prod=1.,i=1;i<=limit;i++)
   prod*= urand();
if(prod<=0.) return errorcode;
return add-2.*log(prod);/* H&P give .5 not 2.*/

}

double extreme (double a, double b)
{
double log(),urand(),y,z;
y=0;while(y==0.)y=urand();/*nonzero y*/
z=-log(y);/* as 0<y<=1, log(y) <0 . z>0 */
return a+b*log(z);
}

int geometric(double p)
{double log();return  (int)(log(urand())/log(1.-
p)+.99999999);}

int hypergeometric(int N, int X, int smalln)
{/* N balls, X white draw smalln without reeplacement
 return count of white balls drawn */
int i,n,kount=0;double p,d,a;
p=((double)X)/((double)N);/* prob. of drawing a white ball*/
n=N;/* number of balls to draw from*/
for (i=1;i<=smalln;i++)
```

```
    {
    a=urand();
    d=(a>=p)?1:0;/* what did we draw? 1=black, 0=white*/
    if(!d)kount++;/* equiv, if a<p*/
/*   p= (n*p-d)*(N-i); WRONG?????*/
    p=( p*n-1.+d)/((double)(n-1));/*new prob. of white ball
draw*/
    n--;/*=(1-d);not unchanged. is this function of d,ie n-
=d or n-= 1-d?*/
    }
return kount;
}

double lognormal(double median, double sigma)/* sigma=shape
parameter*/
{
double exp(),norm();
/* see comments on nflag in chisq() */
/*nflag=1;*/
return median*exp(sigma*norm(0.,1.));
}

double pareto( double c)
{double urand(),pow();
return pow( urand(), -1./c);
}


int poisson(double lambda)
{
int x;
/*        */
double f,urand(),exp(),a,sum;
sum=f= exp(-lambda);a=urand();
for(x=0; x<1000;x++)
    {
    if( a<sum)return x;
    f*= lambda/(x+1);
    sum += sum+f;
    }
return x;
}

double weibull(double b, double c)
{
double urand(),pow(),log(),d;
d=0.;
while(d<=0.)d= urand();
return b*pow(-log(d), 1./c);
```

```
}

double binomial_coef(int n, int m)
{ double M,N,a,b,c;
if(m==n)return 1.;
if(!m)return 1.;
if(m>n)return 0.;/*term does not contribute. */
M=m+1;N=n+1;
/*printf(" M,N in b_coef: %le %le\n",M,N);*/
a=gamma(N);b=gamma(M);c=gamma( abs(N-M)+1.);
/*printf(" a,b,c %le %le %le\n",a,b,c);*/
return a/(b*c);
/*return gamma(N)/(gamma(M)*gamma(abs(N-M)));*/
}
```

```
/*
test driver for random number
generators and distributions
from C Mathematical Function Handbook by Louis Baker
Copyright 1991 by Louis Baker. All rights reserved.
*/

#include <stdio.h>
#include "cmlib.h"
#include "protom.h"

#define urand()  randm()

extern long int seed;
extern int naflag,nflag;
extern long int s1,seed2;
extern int s16,s26,s36;
/* TEST CODE BELOW
*/
main(argc,argv) int argc; char **argv;
{
int i,k,l,N,X;
double urand(),nor-
mal(),sd,y,x,xs,ys,rk,meant,m2,mu3,mu4,skew,kurt;
double a,b,sum,sq,mean,var,me,ve,p,q,lambda;
double sum1,sum2,sum3,sum4;
double u;
long int outseed;
seed=1;
naflag=1;
nflag=1;
s1=12345;seed2=67890;
s16=12;s26=23;s36=34;
for(i=0;i<=10000;i++)
    {outseed=seed;
    u=randm();
    }
printf(" u=%f seed = %ld \n",u,outseed);
printf(" results of u16:\n");
for(i=0;i<=1000;i++)
    {u=u16();
    if(i%100 ==0)printf(" u=%f \n",u);
    }
printf(" results of u32:\n");
for(i=0;i<=1000;i++)
    {u=u32();
    if(i%100 ==0)printf(" u=%f \n",u);
    }
/* now test distributions */
```

```
mean=0.;sd=1.;
while(1)
{printf(" enter count");scanf("%d",&k);
if(k<=0)break;
printf(" kount=%d\n",k);
sum1=sum2=sum3=sum4=0.;
for (i=0;i<k;i++)
   {
   u=normal(mean,sd,&x,&y);
/*   printf(" return normal %f %f\n",x,y);*/
   sum1=sum1+x+y;
   xs=x*x;ys=y*y;
   sum2=sum2+xs+ys;
   sum3=sum3+xs*x+ys*y;
   sum4=sum4+xs*xs+ys*ys;
   }
printf(" tabulating\n");
rk=.5/k;
meant=sum1*rk;
m2=meant*meant;
var=sum2*rk-m2;
mu3=(sum3-3.*sum1*sum2*rk)*rk+2.*meant*m2;
mu4=sum4*rk-3.*m2*m2+6.*m2*sum2*rk-4.*sum3*sum1*rk*rk;
skew=mu3/(var*sqrt(var));
kurt=(mu4/(var*var)-3.)*.5;
/* mean should equal 0. approximately.
   var    "     "   1.     "         (variance=sd*sd)
  skewness          0.
kurtosis            0.                as defined here,
which is
CRC Basic Stat. tables definition.  Others define kurtosis
without
the fact of .5 and/or without the -3.
*/

printf("
mean=%f,var=%f,skew=%f,kurt=%f\n",meant,var,skew,kurt);
}/* end while*/
mean=0.;sd=1.;
printf(" now fast normal dist mean=0 var=1\n");
while(1)
{printf(" enter count");scanf("%d",&k);
if(k<=0)break;
printf(" kount=%d\n",k);
sum1=sum2=sum3=sum4=0.;
for (i=0;i<k;i++)
   {
   x=na();y=na();
   sum1=sum1+x+y;
```

```
    xs=x*x;ys=y*y;
    sum2=sum2+xs+ys;
    sum3=sum3+xs*x+ys*y;
    sum4=sum4+xs*xs+ys*ys;
    }
printf(" tabulating\n");
rk=.5/k;
meant=sum1*rk;
m2=meant*meant;
var=sum2*rk-m2;
mu3=(sum3-3.*sum1*sum2*rk)*rk+2.*meant*m2;
mu4=sum4*rk-3.*m2*m2+6.*m2*sum2*rk-4.*sum3*sum1*rk*rk;
skew=mu3/(var*sqrt(var));
kurt=(mu4/(var*var)-3.)*.5;
/* mean should equal 0. approximately.
   var     "       "  1.      "          (variance=sd*sd)
  skewness            0.
kurtosis              0.                  as defined here,
which is
CRC Basic Stat. tables definition.  Others define kurtosis
without
the fact of .5 and/or without the -3.
*/
printf("
mean=%f,var=%f,skew=%f,kurt=%f\n",meant,var,skew,kurt);
}/* end while*/
printf(" now exponential dist\n");
mean=0.;sd=1.;
while(1)
{printf(" enter count");scanf("%d",&k);
if(k<=0)break;
printf(" kount=%d\n",k);
sum1=sum2=sum3=sum4=0.;
for (i=0;i<k;i++)
    {
    x=ex();y=ex();
/*   printf(" return normal %f %f\n",x,y);*/
    sum1=sum1+x+y;
    xs=x*x;ys=y*y;
    sum2=sum2+xs+ys;
    sum3=sum3+xs*x+ys*y;
    sum4=sum4+xs*xs+ys*ys;
    }
printf(" tabulating\n");
rk=.5/k;
meant=sum1*rk;
m2=meant*meant;
var=sum2*rk-m2;
mu3=(sum3-3.*sum1*sum2*rk)*rk+2.*meant*m2;
```

```
mu4=sum4*rk-3.*m2*m2+6.*m2*sum2*rk-4.*sum3*sum1*rk*rk;
skew=mu3/(var*sqrt(var));
kurt=(mu4/(var*var));
/* mean should equal 0. approximately.
   var    "      "  1.     "          (variance=sd*sd)
  skewness          0.
kurtosis            0.                 as defined here,
which is
CRC Basic Stat. tables definition.  Others define kurtosis
without
the fact of .5 and/or without the -3.
*/

printf("
mean=%f,var=%f,skew=%f,kurt=%f\n",meant,var,skew,kurt);
}/* end while*/
mean=0.;sd=1.;
printf(" now cauchy\n");
while(1)
{printf(" enter count");scanf("%d",&k);
if(k<=0)break;
printf(" kount=%d\n",k);
sum1=sum2=sum3=sum4=0.;
for (i=0;i<k;i++)
    {
    x=ca();y=ca();
/*   printf(" return normal %f %f\n",x,y);*/
    sum1=sum1+x+y;
    xs=x*x;ys=y*y;
    sum2=sum2+xs+ys;
    sum3=sum3+xs*x+ys*y;
    sum4=sum4+xs*xs+ys*ys;
    }
printf(" tabulating\n");
rk=.5/k;
meant=sum1*rk;
m2=meant*meant;
var=sum2*rk-m2;
mu3=(sum3-3.*sum1*sum2*rk)*rk+2.*meant*m2;
mu4=sum4*rk-3.*m2*m2+6.*m2*sum2*rk-4.*sum3*sum1*rk*rk;
skew=mu3/(var*sqrt(var));
kurt=(mu4/(var*var));
/* mean should equal 0. approximately.
   var    "      "  1.     "          (variance=sd*sd)
  skewness          0.
kurtosis            0.                 as defined here,
which is
CRC Basic Stat. tables definition.  Others define kurtosis
without
```

```
the fact of .5 and/or without the -3.
*/

printf("
mean=%f,var=%f,skew=%f,kurt=%f\n",meant,var,skew,kurt);
}/* end while*/

/*sum=0.;
for(i=0;i<1000;i++){a=random();sum+=a;}
printf(" average random=%le\n",sum/1000.);
sum=0.;
for(i=0;i<1000;i++){a=u16();sum+=a;}
printf(" average u16=%le\n",sum/1000.);*/
while(1)
   {
   printf(" enter int N int k, int m int x for Hyper-
geom.cumm\n");
   scanf("%d%d%d%d",&N,&k,&l,&X);
   if(N==0)break;
   printf(" N=%d k=%d l=%d X= %d\n",N,k,l,X);
   printf(" =%le\n", hypergeometric_dist(N,l,k,X));
   }
while(1)
   {
   printf(" enter b, int m int x for Erlang.cumm\n");
   scanf("%le%d%d",&p,&k,&X);
   if(k==0)break;
   printf(" =%le\n", erlang_dist(p,k,X));
   }

/*rm=0.;
while(1)
   {printf(" enter neg binomial int x,p ,iter kt\n");
   scanf("%d%le%d",&N,&p,&k);
   if(k<=0 ||p<=0.)break;
   sum=sq=0.;
   for(i=0;i<k;i++)
      {b=neg_binomial(N,p);
      printf(" b=%le %le\n",b,randn);
      rm+=randn;
      sum+=b;sq+=b*b;
      }
   sum/=k;sq/=k;rm/=k;
   q=1.-p;    me= N*q/p;ve=me/(p);
   mean=sum/me;
   var= (sq-sum*sum)/(ve);
   printf(" norm mean,var %e %e sum=%e\n",mean,var,sum);
   }
a=0.;
```

```
while(1)
   {printf(" enter integer v chisq,iter kt\n");
   scanf("%d%d",&l,&k);
   if(k<=0 ||l<=0)break;
   sum=sq=0.;
   for(i=0;i<k;i++)
      {b=chisq(l);
      printf(" b=%e\n",b);
      sum+=b;sq+=b*b;
      }
   sum/=k;sq/=k;
   mean=sum/l;
   var= (sq-sum*sum)/(2*l);
   printf(" normalized mean,var %e %e
lambda=%e\n",mean,var,sum);
   }

while(1)
   {
   printf(" enter int X, lambda for Poisson cumm\n");
   scanf("%d%le",&X,&lambda);
   if(lambda==0.)break;
   printf(" =%le\n", poisson_dist(X,lambda));
   }
while(1)
   {
   printf(" enter int N int X, p for binomial cumm\n");
   scanf("%d%d%le",&N,&X,&lambda);
   if(lambda==0.)break;
   printf(" =%le\n", binomial_dist(X,N,lambda));
   }*/
while(1)
   {
   printf(" enter int X int Y, p for neg binomial cumm\n");
   scanf("%d%d%le",&X,&N,&lambda);
   if(lambda==0.)break;
   printf(" =%le\n", neg_binomial_dist(X,N,lambda));
   }

while(1)
   {printf(" enter lognormal mean,sigma,iter kt\n");
   scanf("%le%le%d",&p,&q,&k);
   if(k<=0 ||p<=0.)break;
   sum=sq=0.;
   for(i=0;i<k;i++)
      {b=lognormal(p,q);
      sum+=b;sq+=b*b;
      }
   sum/=k;sq/=k;
```

```
   a= exp(q*q*.5);me=p*(a);b=a*a;ve=p*p*b*(b-1.);
   mean=sum/me;
   var= (sq-sum*sum)/(ve);
   printf(" norm mean,var %e %e lambda=%e\n",mean,var,sum);
   }

while(1)
   {printf(" enter extreme a,b,kt\n");
   scanf("%le%le%d",&p,&q,&k);
   if(k<=0 ||p<=0.)break;
   sum=sq=0.;
   for(i=0;i<k;i++)
      {b=extreme(p,q);
      sum+=b;sq+=b*b;
      }
   sum/=k;sq/=k;
   me=(p)-.57721*q;ve=q*q*pi*pi/6.;
   mean=sum/me;
   var= (sq-sum*sum)/(ve);
   printf(" norm mean,var %e %e lambda=%e\n",mean,var,sum);
   }

while(1)
   {printf(" weibull b,c,kt\n");
   scanf("%le%le%d",&p,&q,&k);
   if(k<=0 ||p<=0.)break;
   sum=sq=0.;
   for(i=0;i<k;i++)
      {b=weibull(p,q);
      sum+=b;sq+=b*b;
      }
   sum/=k;sq/=k;
   me= p*gamma((q+1.)/q);ve=p*p*gamma((q+2.)/q) -me*me;
   mean=sum/me;
   var= (sq-sum*sum)/(ve);
   printf(" norm mean,var %e %e lambda=%e\n",mean,var,sum);
   }


while(1)
   {printf(" enter Pareto c,kt\n");
   scanf("%le%d",&p,&k);
   if(k<=0 ||p<=0.)break;
   sum=sq=0.;
   for(i=0;i<k;i++)
      {b=pareto(p);
      sum+=b;sq+=b*b;
      }
   sum/=k;sq/=k;
```

```
   me=(p)/(p-1.);ve=p/(p-2.)-me*me;
   mean=sum/me;
   var= (sq-sum*sum)/(ve);
   printf(" norm mean,var %e %e lambda=%e\n",mean,var,sum);
   }

/*while(1)
   {printf(" enter binomial n,p ,iter kt\n");
   scanf("%d%le%d",&N,&p,&k);
   if(k<=0 ||p<=0.)break;
   sum=sq=0.;
   for(i=0;i<k;i++)
      {b=binomial(N,p);
      sum+=b;sq+=b*b;
      }
   sum/=k;sq/=k;
   q=1.-p;   me= N*p;ve=N*p*(q);
   mean=sum/me;
   var= (sq-sum*sum)/(ve);
   printf(" norm mean,var %e %e lambda=%e\n",mean,var,sum);
   }
*/
/*while(1)
   {printf(" enter geometric p ,iter kt\n");
   scanf("%le%d",&p,&k);
   if(k<=0 ||p<=0.)break;
   sum=sq=0.;
   for(i=0;i<k;i++)
      {b=(double)geometric(p);
      sum+=b;sq+=b*b;
      }
   sum/=k;sq/=k;
   q=1.-p;   me= 1./p;ve=q/(p*p);
   mean=sum/me;
   var= (sq-sum*sum)/(ve);
   printf(" norm mean,var %e %e lambda=%e\n",mean,var,sum);
   }
*/
/*
while(1)
   {printf(" enter hypergom int N,X,n,iter kt\n");
   scanf("%d%d%d%d",&N,&X,&nn,&k);
   if(k<=0 ||N<0)break;
   sum=sq=0.;
   for(i=0;i<k;i++)
      {b=hypergeometric(N,X,nn);
      sum+=b;sq+=b*b;
      }
   sum/=k;sq/=k;
```

```
    me= (double)(nn*X)/((double)N);
    ve=me*(1.-(double)X/(double)N)*(N-nn)/(N-1.);
    mean=sum/me;
    var= (sq-sum*sum)/(ve);
    printf(" norm mean,var %e %e lambda=%e\n",mean,var,sum);
    }
*/
while(1)
    {printf(" enter lambda for Poisson random,iter kt\n");
    scanf("%le%d",&a,&k);
    if(k<=0 ||a<=0.)break;
    sum=sq=0.;
    for(i=0;i<k;i++)
        {b=poisson(a);
        sum+=b;sq+=b*b;
        }
    sum/=k;sq/=k;
    mean=sum/a;
    var= (sq)/(a+a*a);/* NOTvar abt mean, origin*/
    ve= (sq-sum*sum)/(a);/* NOTvar abt mean, origin*/
    printf(" norm mean,var %e %e lambda=%e\n",mean,var,ve);
    }
return 0;
}
```

```
Test Output: Random numbers and Distributions
 u=0.740342 seed = 1043618065
 results of u16:
 u=0.103635
 u=0.670879
 u=0.657284
 u=0.139756
 u=0.310937
 u=0.235265
 u=0.333524
 u=0.073571
 u=0.858158
 u=0.911335
 u=0.880405
 results of u32:
 u=0.943597
 u=0.477201
 u=0.284022
 u=0.557013
 u=0.089085
 u=0.818510
 u=0.155531
 u=0.667918
 u=0.283165
 u=0.884450
 u=0.996507
 enter count1000
 kount=1000
 tabulating
 mean=-0.007287,var=0.966434,skew=-0.023269,kurt=0.044017
 enter count1000
 kount=1000
 tabulating
 mean=-0.027800,var=1.015423,skew=0.076596,kurt=-0.010348
 enter count-1
 now fast normal dist mean=0 var=1
 enter count1000
 kount=1000
 tabulating
 mean=0.020240,var=1.002613,skew=-0.007044,kurt=-0.009048
 enter count1000
 kount=1000
 tabulating
 mean=-0.028241,var=1.006372,skew=0.012394,kurt=-0.067061
 enter count-1
 now exponential dist
 enter count1000
 kount=1000
 tabulating
```

```
 mean=0.986053,var=0.996615,skew=1.869641,kurt=7.487452
 enter count1000
 kount=1000
 tabulating
 mean=1.008006,var=0.984463,skew=1.986757,kurt=9.294343
 enter count-1
 now cauchy
 enter count1000
 kount=1000
 tabulating

mean=3.366806,var=9114.885355,skew=29.095584,kurt=1037.079786

 enter count1000
 kount=1000
 tabulating
 mean=-0.505607,var=261.736133,skew=-
6.590927,kurt=173.908391
 enter count-1
 enter int N int k, int m int x for Hypergeom.cumm
5 3 1 0
 N=5 k=3 l=1 X= 0
 N 5 m1 k3 x0
 M,N in b_coef: 2.000000e+00 3.000000e+00
 a,b,c 2.000000e+00 1.000000e+00 1.000000e+00
 M,N in b_coef: 2.000000e+00 6.000000e+00
 a,b,c 1.200000e+02 1.000000e+00 2.400000e+01
 =4.000000e-01
 enter int N int k, int m int x for Hypergeom.cumm
^C

C:\CMATHLIB\CMATH\S91
 u=0.740342 seed = 1043618065
 results of u16:
 u=0.103635
 u=0.670879
 u=0.657284
 u=0.139756
 u=0.310937
 u=0.235265
 u=0.333524
 u=0.073571
 u=0.858158
 u=0.911335
 u=0.880405
 results of u32:
 u=0.943597
 u=0.477201
 u=0.284022
```

```
u=0.557013
u=0.089085
u=0.818510
u=0.155531
u=0.667918
u=0.283165
u=0.884450
u=0.996507
enter count1000
kount=1000
tabulating
mean=-0.007287,var=0.966434,skew=-0.023269,kurt=0.044017
enter count1000
kount=1000
tabulating
mean=-0.027800,var=1.015423,skew=0.076596,kurt=-0.010348
enter count-1
now fast normal dist mean=0 var=1
enter count1000
kount=1000
tabulating
mean=0.020240,var=1.002613,skew=-0.007044,kurt=-0.009048
enter count1000
kount=1000
tabulating
mean=-0.028241,var=1.006372,skew=0.012394,kurt=-0.067061
enter count-1
now exponential dist
enter count1000
kount=1000
tabulating
mean=0.986053,var=0.996615,skew=1.869641,kurt=7.487452
enter count1000
kount=1000
tabulating
mean=1.008006,var=0.984463,skew=1.986757,kurt=9.294343
enter count-1
now cauchy
enter count1000
kount=1000
tabulating

mean=3.366806,var=9114.885355,skew=29.095584,kurt=1037.079786

enter count-1  1000
kount=1000
tabulating
mean=-0.505607,var=261.736133,skew=-
6.590927,kurt=173.908391
```

```
 enter count-1
 enter int N int k, int m int x for Hypergeom.cumm
5 4 2 1
 N=5 k=4 l=2 X= 1
 =4.000000e-01
 enter int N int k, int m int x for Hypergeom.cumm
8 2 2 0
 N=8 k=2 l=2 X= 0
 =5.357143e-01
 enter int N int k, int m int x for Hypergeom.cumm
-1 -1 -1 -1
 N=-1 k=-1 l=-1 X= -1
 =-1.000000e+60
 enter int N int k, int m int x for Hypergeom.cumm
0 0 0 0
 enter b, int m int x for Erlang.cumm
.5 2 1
 =5.939942e-01
 enter b, int m int x for Erlang.cumm
0 0 0
 enter int X int Y, p for neg binomial cumm
4 4 .2
 =5.628160e-02
 enter int X int Y, p for neg binomial cumm
0 0 0
 enter lognormal mean,sigma,iter kt
.5 .5 100
 norm mean,var 9.657800e-01 9.332939e-01
lambda=5.471861e-01
 enter lognormal mean,sigma,iter kt
.3 .4 1000
 norm mean,var 9.990491e-01 1.023750e+00
lambda=3.246771e-01
 enter lognormal mean,sigma,iter kt
0 0 0
 enter extreme a,b,kt
.1 .2 1000
 norm mean,var -2.524207e-01 9.891661e-01
lambda=3.897881e-03
 enter extreme a,b,kt
0 0 0
 weibull b,c,kt
.1 .2 1000
 norm mean,var 6.481180e-01 1.096799e-01 lambda=7.777416e+00
 weibull b,c,kt
.1 .2 1000
 norm mean,var 8.500665e-01 1.201716e-01 lambda=1.020080e+01
 weibull b,c,kt
0 0 0
```

```
 enter Pareto c,kt
.5 1000
 norm mean,var -6.418243e+02 -1.698234e+08
lambda=6.418243e+02
 enter Pareto c,kt
.5 1000
 norm mean,var -5.079515e+03 -1.262761e+10
lambda=5.079515e+03
 enter Pareto c,kt
0 0
 enter lambda for Poisson random,iter kt
.5 1000
 norm mean,var 7.840000e-01 5.226667e-01
lambda=4.766720e-01
 enter lambda for Poisson random,iter kt
.5 1000
 norm mean,var 7.460000e-01 4.973333e-01
lambda=4.677420e-01
 enter lambda for Poisson random,iter kt
.5 1000
 norm mean,var 7.460000e-01 4.973333e-01
lambda=4.677420e-01
 enter lambda for Poisson random,iter kt
.5 1000
 norm mean,var 7.740000e-01 5.160000e-01
lambda=4.744620e-01
 enter lambda for Poisson random,iter kt
0 0
```

```
/*
calculator version of stat.c routines
routines for statistical functions and auxilliar functions
used in their
computation

chisq() Chi-square
studt() Student's-t distribution
fdist() F distribution
Hot()   Hotelling's T-squared distribution ( generalized t
dist)
prob() probability integral
cump() cummulative probability integral (P)
icump() inverse cummulative prob. integral
erf()   error function (related simply to probability in-
tegral)
ierf()  inverse of the error function
loggam() logarithm of the absolute value of the gamma func-
tion
gamma()  gamma function
beta()    beta function
incbeta() incomplete beta function
incgam() incomplete gamma function
finv()   inverse of F distribution (F value given con-
fidence,d.f.'s)
tinv()   inverse of student's t (t value given con-
fidence,d.f.) two-sided.
chiinv()  "  of chi-sq
ks()    Kolmogorov-Smirnov distribution (1 sample)
wilcoxon() Wilcoxon cummulative count (integer)
mannw()    Mann-Whitney confidence (calls wilcoxon)
sign_crit() sign test
invnr()  auxilliary routine to use Newton-Raphson iteration
for
      use with finv,tinv.
ncf()   noncentral f distribution
ncc()     "      chi-sq
nct()     "          Student's t
incf()     "       f distribution inverse
inct()    "       t       "         "
incc()    "       chi-sq  "         "

P,Q   PROBABILITY INTEGRALS P+Q=1
L   Bivariate Normal distribution
from More C tools for scientists and engineers by L. Baker
*/
#include <alloc.h>
#include <stdio.h>
#define DOFOR(i,to) for(i=0;i<to;i++)
```

```
#define abs(x) ((x)>0.? (x):-(x))
#define max(a,b) ((a)>(b)? (a):(b))
#define min(a,b) ((a)<(b)? (a):(b))
#define pi 3.14159265358979
#define errorcode -1.
#define D sizeof(double)
/*double P(x) double x;{return cump(x);}*/
#define P(x) cump(x)

static double tolrel=1.e-7,tolabsg=1.e-5,tolabsb=1.e-5,
                    conabs=1.e-5,conrel=1.e-3;
static int iterkti,iterkt,wilcox;

#define MAXZ 50
main(argc,argv) int argc;char **argv;
{int i,j,k,m,n,df1,df2;
float zz,rr,qq;
double x,Hot(),ierf(),erf(),y,z,q,r,exp(),
loggam(),gamma(),ks(),mannw();
double prob(),chisq(),studt(),fdist(),incgam(),
incbeta(),cump(),icump();
double
finv(),tinv(),chiinv(),ncf(),ncc(),nct(),incf(),inct(),incc()
,pow();
double Q(),L(),zn(),Z[ MAXZ ]; int sign_crit();
FILE *fileid,*in;
/*in=fopen("CON:","r");
if(!in)printf(" pblm opening for input\n");*/
/*BEGIN SPECIAL PLOTTING SECTION*/
/*fileid=fopen("PLOT.GAM","w");
fprintf(fileid,"1 \n");
for(i=0;i<100;i++)
   {
   x=(i-50)*.1+.05;
   fprintf(fileid," %f %e\n",x,gamma(x));
   }
fclose(fileid);
fileid=fopen("PLOT.FEW","w");
fprintf(fileid," 6 \n");
for(i=0;i<50;i++)
   {
   x=(i)*.1+.05;
   fprintf(fileid," %f %e %e %e %e %e\n"
,x,loggam(x),erf(x),ierf(x/5.1),prob(x),cump(x),icump(x));
   }
fclose(fileid);
*/
/*
fileid=fopen("PLOT.PRB","w");
```

```
fprintf(fileid,"6 \n");
for(i=0;i<50;i++)
   {
   x=(i)*.1+.05;
   y=i*.02;
   fprintf(fileid," %f %e %e %e %e %e %e\n",
x,chisq(x,10.),studt(x,10.),fdist(x,10.,5.),fdist(x,5.,10.)
,incbeta(.5,.5,y),incgam(2.,x));
   }
fclose(fileid);
fileid=fopen("PLOT.inv","w");
fprintf(fileid,"4 \n");
for(i=0;i<50;i++)
   {
   x=(i)*.01+.05;
   fprintf(fileid," %f %e %e %e %e\n"
,x,tinv(x,10.),finv(x,5.,10.),chiinv(x,10.),finv(x,10.,20.));

   }
fclose(fileid);
*/
/*END SPECIAL PLOTTING SECTION.*/
k=1;m=1;q=1.;x=1.;/*defaults*/
iterkt=iterkti=0;
while(1)
{
printf(
" enter: 1 for F, 2 chi-sq, 3 Student's 4 Hotelling gen.
t\n");
printf(
" 5 z-p 6 p-z 7 gamma 8 erf 9 inverse erf 10 prob\n");
printf(
" 11 inc beta 12 inc gamma 13 t-inv 14 F-inv 15 chi-sq
inv\n");
printf(
" 16 noncentral F 17 chi-sq 18 t 19 inv-F 20 inv-t 21 inv-
chi\n");
printf(
" 22 Kolmogorv-Smirnov 23 Mann Whitney 24 Wilcoxon 25conv
param\n");
printf(
" 26 P,Q 27 Bivariate Normal L 28 sign test 29 Z\n");
j=scanf("%d", &i);
if(j==-1)printf(" trouble\n");
if(i==2)
   {
   printf(" enter chi-sq value ");j=scanf("%f",&zz);
   z=zz;
```

```
   printf(" enter degrees of freedom(integer)
");j=scanf("%d",&k);
   if(k>0)x=k;
   y=chisq(z,x);q=1.-y;
   printf(" z=%f df=%f chisq(z,df)=%e %e\n",z,x,y,q);
   }
else
   if(i==3)
   {
   printf(" enter student t value ");j=scanf("%f",&zz);z=zz;
   printf(" enter degrees of freedom(integer)
");j=scanf("%d",&k);
   if(k>0)x=k;
   y=studt(z,x); q=1.-y;r=q*.5;
   printf(" student's-t(z=%f,df=%f)=%e\n",z,x,y);
   printf("significance levels= %e[1-sided] %e[2-sided]\n"
,r,q);
   r=1.-r;
   printf(" cummulative t[1-sided]=%f %f[two-sided]\n",r,y);
   }
else if(i==1)
   {
   printf(" enter F value ");j=scanf("%f",&zz);x=zz;
   if(j!=-1)printf(" echo F value=%f\n",x);
   else
      printf(" input error\n");
   printf(" enter degrees of freedom(2 integers)
");j=scanf("%d %d",&k,&m);
   if(k>0)z=k;
   if(m>0)q=m;
   y=fdist(x,z,q);
   printf(" F=%f fdist(F,%d,%d)=%e\n",x,k,m,y);
   }
else if(i==4)
   {
      printf(" enter as integers degrees of freedom n and
k\n");
      scanf("%d%d",&m,&k);
      if(m>0) n=m;
      printf(" enter value for T (NOT square)\n");
      scanf("%f",&zz);
      x=zz;
      printf(" echo n %d k %d T %f\n",n,k,z);
       y=Hot(x,n,k);
      printf(" generalized t dist=%e\n",y);
   }
else if (i==5)
   {
   printf(" enter z score\n");
```

```
    scanf("%f",&zz);
    x=zz;
    y=cump(x);/*.5*(1.+erf(.7071*x));*/
    printf(" z score=%e\n",y);
    }
else if (i==6)
    {
    printf(" enter p score\n");
    scanf("%f",&zz);
    x=zz;
    y=icump(x);/*1.4142*(ierf(2.*x-1.));*/
    printf(" p score=%e\n",y);
    }
else if (i==7)
    {
    printf(" enter x\n");scanf("%f",&zz);x=zz;
    printf(" gamma(%f)=%f\n", x,gamma(x));
    }
else if (i==8)
    {
    printf(" enter x\n");scanf("%f",&zz);x=zz;
    printf(" erf(%f)=%f\n", x,erf(x) );
    }
else if (i==9)
    {
    printf(" enter x\n");scanf("%f",&zz);x=zz;
    printf(" %f=erf(%f)\n", ierf(x),x );
    }
else if (i==10)
    {
    printf(" enter x\n");scanf("%f",&zz);x=zz;
    printf(" %f=prob(%f)\n", prob(x),x );
    }
else if (i==11)
    {
    printf(" enter x,a,b\n");scanf("%f%f%f",&zz,&rr,&qq);
    x=zz;r=rr;q=qq;
    printf(" %f=inc.beta(%f|%f,%f) %d\n", in-
cbeta(r,q,x),x,r,q,iterkt );
    }
else if (i==12)
    {
    printf(" enter x,a\n");scanf("%f%f",&zz,&qq);
    x=zz;q=qq;
    printf(" %f=inc gamma(%f,%f)\n", incgam(q,x),q,x );
    }
else if (i==13)
    {
```

```
   printf(" enter 2-sided con-
fid.,nu\n");scanf("%f%f",&zz,&qq);
   x=zz;q=qq;
   if(x<=0. || x>=1.)
          printf(" confidence must be between 0 and 1\n");
   else
          {
          printf(" %f=inverse t(%f,%f)\n", tinv(x,q),x,q);
          }
   }
else if (i==14)
   {
   printf(" enter con-
fid,d.f.1,2\n");scanf("%f%f%f",&zz,&qq,&rr);
   x=zz;q=qq;r=rr;
   if(x<=0. || x>=1.)
          printf(" confidence must be between 0 and 1\n");
   else
      {
      printf(" %f=inv F(%f,%f,%f)\n", finv(x,q,r),x,q,r);
      }
   }
else if (i==15)
   {
   printf(" enter 1-sided con-
fid.,nu\n");scanf("%f%f",&zz,&qq);
   x=zz;q=qq;
   if(x<=0. || x>=1.)
          printf(" confidence must be between 0 and 1\n");
   else
          {
          printf(" %f=inverse chi-sq(%f,%f)\n",
chiinv(x,q),x,q);
          }
   }
else if (i==16)
   {
   printf(
   " enter  F, df1,df2, noncentrality.df integers\n");
   scanf("%f%d%d%f",&zz,&df1,&df2,&qq);
   x=zz;q=qq;
   if(x<=0. )
          printf(" noncentrality must be positive");
   else
          {
          printf(" noncentral F=%f\n", ncf(x,q,df1,df2) );
          }
   }
else if (i==17)
```

```
   {
   printf(" enter  chisq, df,noncentrality.df integer\n");
   scanf("%f%d%f",&zz,&df1,&qq);
   x=zz;q=qq;
   if(x<=0. )
         printf(" noncentrality must be positive");
   else
         {
         printf(" noncentral chisq=%f\n", ncc(x,q,df1) );
         }
   }
else if (i==18)
   {
   printf(" enter  t, df, noncentrality.df integer\n");
   scanf("%f%d%f",&zz,&df1,&qq);
   x=zz;q=qq;
   if(x<=0. )
         printf(" noncentrality must be positive");
   else
         {
         printf(" noncentral t=%f\n", nct(x,q,df1) );
         }
   }
else if (i==19)
   {
   printf(" enter  confidence, df1,df2, noncentrality.df in-
tegers\n");
   scanf("%f%d%d%f",&zz,&df1,&df2,&qq);
   x=zz;q=qq;
   if(q<=0. )
         printf(" noncentrality must be positive");
   else
         {
         printf(" inverse noncentral F=%f\n",
incf(x,df1,df2,q) );
         }
   }
else if (i==20)
   {
   printf(
   " enter  confidence, df, noncentrality.df integer\n");
   scanf("%f%d%f",&zz,&df1,&qq);
   x=zz;q=qq;
   if(q<=0. )
         printf(" noncentrality must be positive");
   else
         {
         printf(" inverse noncentral t=%f\n", inct(x,df1,q)
);
```

```
        }
    }
else if (i==21)
    {
    printf(
    " enter  confidence, df, noncentrality.df integer\n");
    scanf("%f%d%f",&zz,&df1,&qq);
    x=zz;q=qq;
    if(q<=0. )
         printf(" noncentrality must be positive");
    else
         {
         printf(" inverse noncentral chisq=%f\n",
incc(x,df1,q) );
         }
    }
else if(i==22)
    {
    printf(" enter d, n for kolmogorov smirnov\n");
    scanf("%e%d",&zz,&n);z=zz;
    q=ks(z,n);r= (1.-q);
    printf(" answer=%e siglevel=%e\n",q,r);
    }
else if(i==23)
    {
    printf(
    " enter n,m,u integers for Wilcoxon (Mann-Whitney) 2
sample statistic\n");
    scanf("%d%d%d",&n,&m,&k);
    i= m*n+(m*(m+1)>>1)-k;
    printf(" Wilcoxon=%d T=%d, mann-whitney= %e\n",
     wilcox,i,mannw(n,m,k));
    }
else if(i==24)
    {
    printf(
" enter n,m integers for Wilcoxon matched pair signed
rank\n");
    scanf("%d%d",&n,&m);
    j=wilcoxs(n,m);
    printf(" count=%d, prob.= %e\n",j,j/pow(2.,(double)n));
    }
else if(i==25)
    {
    printf(" previous iteration count %d\n",iterkt);
    printf(" enter tolabsg=%e,tolabsb=%e,tolrel=%e nonzero
to alter\n"
    ,tolabsg,tolabsb,tolrel);
    scanf("%e%e%e",&zz,&qq,&rr);
```

```
    if(zz!=0.) {tolabsg=zz;printf(
              " new tolabsg=%e\n",tolabsg);}
    if(qq!=0.) {tolabsb=qq;printf(
              " new tolabsb=%e\n",tolabsb);}
    if(rr!=0.) {tolrel=rr;printf(
                  " new tolrel=%e\n",tolrel);}
    printf(
      " inverse funct. last iteration count=%d\n",iterkti);
    printf("conabs=%e,conrel=%e enter nonzero to alter\n"
    ,conabs,conrel);
    scanf(" %e %e",&zz,&qq);
    if(zz!=0.) {conabs=zz;printf(" new conabs=%e\n",conabs);}
    if(qq!=0.) {conrel=qq;printf(" new conrel=%e\n",conrel);}
    }
else if (i==26)
    {
    printf(" enter  x\n");
    scanf("%f",&zz);
    x=zz;
    printf(" P(x)=%le Q(x)=%le\n", P(x),Q(x) );
    }

else if (i==27)
    {
    printf(" enter h,k,rho\n");
    scanf("%f%f%f",&zz,&qq,&rr);
    x=zz;q=qq;r=rr;
    if(r<-1. || r>1.) printf(
    " correlation must be between -1 and 1\n");
    else
       printf(" L(%le,%le,%le)=%le\n",x,q,r,L(x,q,r));
    }
else if (i==28)
    {
    printf(" enter n,alpha sign test (two-tailed) critical
value\n");
    scanf("%d%f",&n ,&zz);x=zz;
    printf(" %d\n", sign_crit(x,n) );
    }

else if (i==29)
    {
    printf(
   " enter n,x Z(n)[x]=n-th derivative of Normal prob.\n");
    scanf("%d%f",&n ,&zz);x=zz;if(n>MAXZ)n=MAXZ;
    printf(" %le\n", zn(x,n,Z ));
    /* out of memory=no room to print Z*/
    }
```

```
else
   {printf(" terminating j i %d %d\n",j,i);break;}
}
exit(0);
}
double arr(m,n)int m,n;
{/* m+n!/m!n! */
double product;
int i,nn,mm;
if(n>m){nn=n;mm=m;}
else{nn=m;mm=n;}
product=1.;
for(i=1;i<=mm;i++)
   {product*=(((double)(nn+i))/((double)i));
   }
return product;
}
int wilcoxs(ni,mi) int ni,mi;
{
int n,m,x;
if(mi<0)return 0;
if(!mi)return 1;
x=(ni*(ni+1)) >>1;
if(mi>x) return wilcoxs(ni,x);
m=mi;n=ni;
if(n<0 || m<0 )printf(" warn n %d m%d\n",n,m);
return wilcoxs(n-1,m)+wilcoxs(n-1,m-n);
}

int wilcoxon(ni,mi,ui) int ni,mi,ui;
{
int n,m,u;
if(ui>ni*ni) return -1;
if(ui>=mi*ni) return (int)(arr(mi,ni) +.5);
if(ui<0)return 0;
if(!ui)return 1;
if(!mi)return 1;
u=ui;
if(mi>0 && ni>0 && ni<mi) {m=ni;n=mi;}else{m=mi;n=ni;}
if(n<0 || m<0 )printf(" warn n %d m%d\n",n,m);
return wilcoxon(n-1,m,u-m)+wilcoxon(n,m-1,u);
}


double mannw(n,m,u) int n,m,u;
{int a;double arr(),denom;
a=wilcoxon(n,m,u);
wilcox=a;
```

```
denom=arr(m,n);
return (double)a/denom;
}

int sign_crit(double two_tail,int n)
{
/* for one-tailed use twice the one-sided value for
two_tail*/
double pow(),sum,term,stop;int i;
sum=term=1.;stop =.5*two_tail*pow(2.,(double)n);
for(i=0;i<n;i++)
   {term*= (n-i)/(i+1.);
   sum+=term;
   if(sum>=stop)return i;
   }
return -1;
}




double ks(d,n) double d;int n;
{
int ind,ndt,ndp,ndd,nddp,i,j,k,jmax,na=75;
double dk;
double nd,*q,*f,sum,ft,fu,fv,fn,ci,pow(),sqrt(),exp(),mult;

if(n>na)
   {
   d*=sqrt((double)n);
/*   fv= d+1./(sqrt((double)n)*6.);
   ft= exp(-2.*fv*fv);
   fn=1.-2.*ft;
*/
   fu=exp(-2.*d*d)*(1.-d/sqrt((double)n)*.66666666);
   sum=1.-2.*fu;
/*   printf(" fn, sum %e %e\n",fn,sum);*/
   return sum;
   }
/* na chosen to avoid overflow problems for large n*/
if(n==1)return 2.*d-1.;/* pblms d<.5???*/
nd= n*d;
fn=(double)n;
ndt= 2.*nd;
if(ndt<1)return 0.;
ind=nd;
ndp=ind+1;
ndd= min(n,ind<<1);
f=malloc( D * (n+2) );
```

```
q=malloc( D * (n+2) );
nddp=ndd+1;
ci=1.;
f[0]=1.;
for(i=0;i<n;i++)
   {
   f[i+1]=f[i]*ci;
   ci++;
   }
mult=f[n]/pow(fn,fn);
/* might be efficient to invert the f[i] here*/
for(i=0;i<=n;i++) f[i]=1./f[i];
q[0]=1.;
if(ndd)
   {
   ci=1.;
   for(i=1;i<=ndd;i++)
      {
      q[i]=pow(ci,(double)i)*f[i];
      ci++;
      }

   if(ndp>n) goto r1;
   fv= ndp-nd;
   jmax= fv+1;
   for(i=ndp;i<=ndd;i++)
      {
      sum=0.;
      ft=nd;
      k=i;
      fu=fv;
      for(j=0;j<jmax;j++)
         {sum+=pow(ft,(double)j-1)*pow(fu,(double)k)*
            (f[j]*f[k]);
         ft++;fu--;k--;
         }
      q[i]-=2.*nd*sum;
      jmax++;
      fv++;
      }
   if(ndd==n)goto r1;
   }
for(i=nddp;i<=n;i++)
   {
   sum=0.;
   ci=1.;
   ft=2.*nd;
   for(j=1;j<=ndt;j++)
      {
```

```
        ft--;
        k=i-j;
        sum+= ci*pow(ft,(double)j)*q[k]*f[j];
        ci=-ci;
        }
    q[i]=sum;
    if(sum<0. || sum*mult>1.)
        {/*trouble*//*printf(
         " trouble k-s:  sum=%e\n",i,sum);
        for(j=1;j<=i;j++)printf(
         " q[%d]=%e f=%e\n",j,q[j],f[j]);*/
        return 1.;
        }
    }
r1:
free(f);free(q);
return q[n]*mult ;
}

double gamma(x) double x;
{
double y,z,exp(),loggam();
y=exp(loggam(x));
if(x>=0.)return(y);
z=  2*(((int)(-x))%2) -1;
return(y*z);
}

double loggam(x) double x;
{
int i;
double z,tmp,ser,log(),sin(),*coeff;
static double logsr2pi=.918938533;
static double b[9]={.035868343,-.193527818,.482199394,
-.756704078, .918206857,-.897056937,.988205891,
-.577191652,1.0};

/*if( x<0.&& x> -1. )
    {
    return((loggam(1.+x)-log(-x)));
    }
else requires two levels of recursion and  log call,not sin
*/
if (x<-0.) /*was x< -1. when above implemented */
      {/*transform to x>0. will blow up if x integer, as it
should*/
      z=1.-x;/* z>2. */
      return(log(pi/abs(sin(pi*z)))-loggam(z) );
      }
```

```
else
   if (x<=1.)/* 0<=x<1 */
      {
      /*z=1.-x*/;/*  0<=z<1*/
      /*return( log(z*pi/sin(pi*z))-loggam(1.+z));*/
      /* Ab& Stegun-takes less than half the time*/
      if(x==0.)return 0.;
      tmp=b[0];
      coeff=&(b[1]);
      for(i=1;i<9;i++)tmp= tmp*x+ *(coeff++);
      return(log(tmp/x));
      }
/* use below for x>1.*/
else
   if(x<=2.)
      {
      tmp=b[0];
      coeff=&(b[1]);
      z=x-1.;
      for(i=1;i<9;i++)tmp= tmp*z+ *(coeff++);
      return(log(tmp));
      }
z=1./x;
tmp=z*z;
/*ser= (1./12.+tmp*(-1./360.+tmp*(1/1260.-tmp/1680.)
))/x;*/
ser= (.08333333333333+tmp*(tmp*(0.000793650793-
.000595238095*tmp)
   -.002777777777))*z;
return (logsr2pi-x+(x-.5)*log(x)+ser);
}
#define small 1.e-30

double incgam(a,x) double x,a;
{
int i,itmax=100;
double gln,exp(),log(),loggam(),sum,ap,del,fi,start,
tol=3.e-7,c0,d0,an,ana,anf,old,offset,mult,delta;
/* error condition return -1 on invalid arguments*/
if( x< 0. || a<0. ) return(-1.);
if(x==0.)return(0.);
gln=loggam(a);
if (x< (a+1.))
   {
   /*series*/
   offset=0.;
   mult=1.;
   ap=a;
   sum=1./a;
```

```
    del=sum;
    DOFOR(i,itmax)
        {
        ap++;
        del*=x/ap;
        sum+=del;
        if( abs(del)<abs(sum)*tol) goto fini;
        }
        printf(" trouble incomplete gamma series\n");
    }
else
    {
    offset=1.;
    mult=-1.;
    old=0.;
    start=small;
    sum=start;
    d0=0.;c0=sum;
    DOFOR(i,itmax)
        {
        fi=i;
        if(i)ana=fi;
        else ana=1.;
        d0= (x+d0*ana);
        c0=(x+ana/c0);
        if(d0==0.)d0=small;
        if(c0==0.)c0=small;
        d0=1./d0;
        delta=d0*c0;sum*=delta;
        ana=fi+1.-a;
        d0= (1.+d0*ana);
        c0=(1.+ana/c0);
        if(d0==0.)d0=small;
        if(c0==0.)c0=small;
        d0=1./d0;
        delta=d0*c0;sum*=delta;
        if( abs(delta-1.)<tol)
            {sum-=start;goto fini;}
        }
    printf(" trouble incomplete gamma cont. fract\n");
    }
/*return(-1.);*/
fini:return(offset+mult*sum*exp(-x+a*log(x)-gln));
}

double chisq(csq,nu) double csq,nu;
{
double incgam();
return (incgam(.5*nu,.5*csq));
```

```
}


double incbeta(aa,bb,x) double aa,bb,x;
{
int itmax=25,m;
/* uses Abramowitz and Stegun 26.5.8 for Ix(a,b)
26.5.9 seems less reliable */
double offset,bmult,exp(),log(),loggam(),a,b,z;
double error,fm,twicefm,dc,aplusb,am1,ap1, factor,
tol=1.e-7,h,d,c,delta;
iterkt=0;
if(x<0. || x>1.) return(errorcode);
if(aa==0. )return(1.e10);
if (x==1.||x==0.) return  x ;
bmult= exp(loggam(aa+bb)-loggam(aa)-log-
gam(bb)+aa*log(x)+bb*log(1.-x));
/*printf(" incbeta x,aa,bb=%e %e %e bt=%e\n",x,aa,bb,bt);*/
 if(x <((aa+1.)/(aa+bb+2.)) )
     {
     a=aa;
     b=bb;
     z=x;
     offset=0.;
    bmult/=aa;
    }
else
    {
    a=bb;
    b=aa;
    z=1.-x;
    bmult=-bmult/bb;
    offset=1.;
    };
aplusb=a+b;
am1=a-1.;
ap1=a+1.;
d=0.;h=small;c=h;
for(m=0;m<=itmax;m++)
    {
    fm=(double)(m);
    twicefm=(double)(m<<1);
    if(m)
       dc=fm*(b-fm)*z/((am1+twicefm)*(a+twicefm));/*d2m*/
    else
       dc=1.;
    d=1.+d*dc;
    c=1.+dc/c;
    if(d==0.)d=small;
```

```
   if(c==0.)c=small;
   d=1./d;
   delta=d*c;
   h*=delta;
   dc=-
(a+fm)*(aplusb+fm)*z/((a+twicefm)*(ap1+twicefm));/*d2m+1*/
   d=1.+d*dc;
   c=1.+dc/c;
   if(d==0.)d=small;
   if(c==0.)c=small;
   d=1./d;
   delta=d*c;
   h*=delta;
   if(abs(delta-1.)<tol)return h*bmult+offset;
   iterkt++;
    };
/*printf(" inc. beta noconv.\n");*/
return (errorcode);/*or return best guess (of-
fset+bmult*conv)*/
}

double beta(a,b) double a,b;
{
double exp(),loggam();
return  exp( loggam(a)+loggam(b)-loggam(a+b));
}

/*26.5.4 series expansion-
use only as a check on incbeta*/
/*
double IncBeta(a,b,x) double a,b,x;
{
int n,nmax=25;
double sum,term,log(),ap1,aplusb,pow,exp()
,factor,beta(),fn;
ap1=a+1.;
aplusb=a+b;
factor= exp(a*log(x)+b*log(1.-x))/(beta(a,b)*a);
sum=1.;
pow=x;
iterkt=0;
for(n=1;n<nmax;n++)
   {
   fn=(double)n;
   term= pow*beta(ap1,fn)/beta(aplusb,fn);
   sum+=term;
   if( abs(term/sum)<tolrel ||
abs(term)<tolabsb)return(sum*factor);
   pow*=x;
```

```
   iterkt++;
   }
printf("IncBeta warn\n");
return(sum*factor);
}
*/

double studt(t,nu) double t,nu;
{
double incbeta();
return(1.-incbeta(nu*.5,.5, nu/(nu+t*t)) );
}

double Hot(t,n,k) double t;int n,k;
{
double incbeta(),nu;
nu=n-1;
return(1.-incbeta(nu*.5,.5*k,nu/(nu+t*t)) );
}

double fdist(f,nu1,nu2) double f,nu1,nu2;
{
double incbeta();
return(incbeta(.5*nu2,.5*nu1,nu2/(nu2+nu1*f)) );
}


int g_df1,g_df2;
double g_noncent;

double ncf(f,noncen,df1,df2)
double f,noncen; int df1,df2;
{
/* fdist returns Q want P=1-Q for P' then take 1-P' */
int i,itmax=10;
double nu1,nu2,exp(),fdist(),tol=1.e-
3,term,sum,coef,arg1,arg2;
nu1=df1;nu2=df2;
arg1=noncen*.5;
coef=1.;
for (i=0,sum=0.;i<itmax;i++)
   {
   coef /= (double) max(i,1) ;
   term= coef*(1.- fdist(f, nu1+2.*i,nu2) );
   sum=sum+term;
   if( abs(term/sum) < tol)break;
   coef *= arg1;
   }
if(i>itmax)
```

```
    {
    printf(" no convergence in noncentral F\n");
    return(-1.);
    }
/*printf(" number of terms for noncentral F=%d\n",i+1);*/
return( 1.- exp(-arg1)*sum);
}

double nct(f,noncen,df1)
double f,noncen; int df1;
{
/* fdist returns Q want P=1-Q for P' then take 1-P' */
int i,itmax=10;
double nu1,nu2,exp(),incbeta(),tol=1.e-
3,term,sum,coef,arg1,arg2;
nu1=df1;
arg1=noncen*noncen*.5;
nu2= nu1/(nu1+f*f);
coef=1.;
for (i=0,sum=0.;i<itmax;i++)
    {
    coef /= ((double) max(i*2-1,1) )*((double) max(i*2,1));
    term= coef*(incbeta(nu1*.5,.5+i,nu2) );
    sum=sum+term;
    if( abs(term/sum) < tol)break;
    coef *= arg1;
    }
if(i>itmax)
    {
    printf(" no convergence in noncentral t\n");
    return(-1.);
    }
/*printf(" number of terms for noncentral t=%d\n",i+1);*/
return( 1.- exp(-arg1)*sum);
}

double ncc(f,noncen,df1)
double f,noncen; int df1;
{
/* fdist returns Q want P=1-Q for P' then take 1-P' */
int i,itmax=10;
double nu1,nu2,y,exp(),chisq(),tol=1.e-
3,term,sum,coef,arg1,arg2;
nu1=df1;
arg1=noncen*.5;
coef=1.;
for (i=0,sum=0.;i<itmax;i++)
    {
    coef /= (double) max(i,1) ;
```

```
   y=chisq(f, nu1+2.*i);
   term= coef*(y );
   sum=sum+term;
   if( abs(term/sum) < tol)break;
   coef *= arg1;
   }
if(i>itmax)
   {
   printf(" no convergence in noncentral chisq\n");
   return(-1.);
   }
/*printf(" number of terms for noncentral
chisq=%d\n",i+1);*/
return( exp(-arg1)*sum);
}

double finv(f,nu1,nu2) double f,nu1,nu2;
{
double
sqrt(),invnr(),fdist(),icump(),guess,exp(),a,b,h,y,l,w;
   /*guess for F dist*/
if(nu1==1. || nu2==1.)
   {
   if(f>.5)guess=.7;
   else
   guess= 1./sqrt(f);
   }
else
   {
   y=icump(1.-f);
   l=(y*y-3.)/6.;
   h=2./(1./(nu2-1.)+1./(nu1-1.));
   w= y*sqrt(h+l)/h-(l+5./6.-2./(3.*h))*
     (1./(nu1-1.)-1./(nu2-1.));
   guess=exp(w);
/*printf(" debug guess=%f\n");*/
   }
return (invnr(0,f,nu1,nu2,fdist,guess)) ;
}


double ncf3(f,nu1,nu2) double f,nu1,nu2;
{
return ncf(f,g_noncent,g_df1,g_df2);
}

double nct3(f,nu1) double f,nu1;
{
return nct(f,g_noncent,g_df1);
```

```
}
double ncc3(f,nu1) double f,nu1;
{
return ncc(f,g_noncent,g_df1);
}

double incf(f,df1,df2,noncen) double f,noncen;
int df1,df2;
{
double nu1,nu2;
double
sqrt(),invnr(),ncf(),ncf3(),icump(),guess,exp(),a,b,h,y,l,w;
nu1=df1;nu2=df2;
g_df1=df1;g_df2=df2;g_noncent=noncen;
   /*guess for F dist*/
if(nu1==1. || nu2==1.)
   {
   if(f>.5)guess=.7;
   else
   guess= 1./sqrt(f);
   }
else
   {
   y=icump(1.-f);
   l=(y*y-3.)/6.;
   h=2./(1./(nu2-1.)+1./(nu1-1.));
   w= y*sqrt(h+l)/h-(l+5./6.-2./(3.*h))*
     (1./(nu1-1.)-1./(nu2-1.));
   guess=exp(w);
/*printf(" debug guess=%f\n");*/
   }
return (invnr(0,f,nu1,nu2,ncf3,guess)) ;
}

double tinv(a,nu) double a,nu;
{
double p,t,x;
double
y,invnr(),studt(),iguess,icump(),term2,term3,term4,nui;
      /* guess for student's t*/
/*CAVEAT- INAACURATE FOR SMALL NU*/
nui=1./nu;
p=(1.-a)*.5;
t=icump(1.-p);
y=t*t;
term2=t/96.*(3.+y*(16.+5.*y));
term3=t/384.*(-15.+y*(17.+y*(19.+3.*y)));
term4=t/92160.*(-945.+y*(-1920.+y*(1482.+y*(776.+y*79.))));
```

```
iguess=
t*(1.+(.25*(1.+t*t)+(term2+(term3+term4*nui)*nui)*nui)*nui);
/*attempt itertive improvement*/
return (invnr(1,a,nu,0.0,studt,iguess)) ;
}

double chiinv(a,nu) double a,nu;
{
double p,t,x;
double y,sqrt(),invnr(),chisq(),iguess,icump();
/* approx. for large nu>30 */
x= icump(1.-a);
p=2./(9.*nu);
t= 1.-p+x*sqrt(p);
t=t*t*t;
iguess= nu*t;
return(invnr(1,a,nu,0.0,chisq,iguess));
}

double invnr(narg,x,nu1,nu2,value,iguess)
int narg;
double x,nu1,nu2,(*value)(),iguess;
{
double y,z,zold,znew,dz0=.005,dz,zp,v;
double deriv,delta,deltas,resid,rnew,rold;
double sqrt();
int maxit=40,halvetop=10,i,j;
z=iguess;
iterkti=0;
j=0;
if(narg)
   { dz0=.05;
   }
for(i=0;i<maxit;i++)
   {
   iterkti++;
   dz= dz0+.001*z;
   zp=z+dz;
/*    v= (narg)? value(z,nu1):value(z,nu1,nu2);
   y= (narg)? value(zp,nu1):value(zp,nu1,nu2);
*/
   if(narg)
      {v=value(z,nu1);
       y=value(zp,nu1);
       }
   else
      {v=value(z,nu1,nu2);
       y=value(zp,nu1,nu2);
      }
```

```
/*if(narg)printf(" debug z=%f v=%f y=%f\n",z,v,y);*/
   deriv=(y-v)/dz;
   resid= v-x;
   delta= -resid/(deriv+.0001);
   resid*=resid;/*square residual as metric*/
   if(resid<conabs|| abs(delta/resid)< conrel) return(z);
/*if(narg)
printf(" debug deriv %f resid %f
delta=%f\n",deriv,resid,delta);*/
   z+=delta;
   deltas=delta;
   z= max(z,0.001);
   z=min(z,1.e4);/*no reasonable F should exceed this*/
   for(j=0;j<halvetop;j++)
      {
/*      v= (narg)? value(z,nu1):value(z,nu1,nu2);*/
      if(narg)
         {v=value(z,nu1);}
      else
         {v=value(z,nu1,nu2);
         }
      rnew=v-x;
      rnew*=rnew;
      if(rnew<resid)break;
/*if(narg)printf(" worse z=%f rn=%f old=%f v=%f %d\n"
,z,rnew,resid,v,j);*/
         delta*=.5;
         z-=delta;
      if(halvetop-j==1){/* no soap*/
                  z-=deltas*.5;/* try other direction*/
                  }
      }
   }

   printf(
" iter=maxit trouble resid=%f z=%f narg=%d,iguess=%f x=%f\n"
   ,resid,z,narg,iguess,x);
   if(narg)printf(" nu1=%f\n",nu1);
   else
      printf(" nu1,nu2 %f %f\n",nu1,nu2);
return(z);
}


double erf(x) double x;
{
double exp(),t,z,sign=1.;
if (x<0.)sign=-1.;
x=abs(x);
```

```
t= 1./(1.+x*.3275911);
z=((((t*1.061405429-1.453152027)*t+1.421413741)*t-
.284496736)*t
   +.254829592)*t;
return (1.-exp(-x*x)*z)*sign;
}

double ierf(y) double y;
{
int i,maxi=20;
double test,sqrt(),pow(),t,z,q,log(),c,x,dx,f,df;
if(y==0.)return(0.);
if(y>=1.)return(1.e10);
if(y<0.) return(-ierf(-y));
c= 1./ sqrt(sqrt(1.-y));
c=sqrt(sqrt(c));/* for higher power version*/
/*guess*/
x=1.;
if(y<1.)x=y*.7;

for(i=0;i<=maxi;i++)
   {
   f=(((((.0000430638*x+.0002765672)*x+.0001520143)*x+
   .0092705272)*x+.0422820123)*x+.0705230784)*x+1.-c;

df=(((((6.*.0000430638*x+5.*.0002765672)*x+4.*.0001520143)*x+

   3.*.0092705272)*x+2.*.0422820123)*x+.0705230784);


/*lower power version
   f= 1.-c+(((.078108*x+.000972)*x+.230389)*x+.278393)*x;
   df= (((4.*.078108*x+3.*.000972)*x+2.*.230389)*x+.278393);
   */
   dx= -f/df;
   x=x+dx;
   test=abs(dx);
/*low power
   if( test < 1.e-6 || test< .0001*x)break;
*/
   if( test < 1.e-8 || test< .0000001*x)break;
/*printf(" iter=%d x=%f dx=%f \n",i,x,dx);*/
   }
if(i==maxi)printf(" ierf max
it=%d,x=%f,dx=%f,arg=%f\n",i,x,dx,y);
return (x);
}

double prob(x) double x;
```

```
{
double erf();
return(erf(x*.707106781));
}

double cump(x) double x;
{/* area under normal curve from -infinty to x*/
static double rt=.7071067812;
double erf();
return(.5*(1.+erf(x*rt)));
}

double icump(x) double x;
{
double ierf();
static double rti=1.414213562;
return(rti*(ierf(2.*x-1.)));
}

double inct(a,df1,noncen) double a,noncen;
int df1;
{
double nu1,nu2;
double invnr(),nct(),icump(),guess;
double nui,t,y,term2,term3,term4,p;
g_noncent=noncen;g_df1=df1;
nu1=df1;nu2=0.;
   /*guess for t dist*/
      /* guess for student's t*/
/*CAVEAT- INAACURATE FOR SMALL NU*/
nui=1./nu1;
p=(1.-a)*.5;
t=icump(1.-p);
y=t*t;
term2=t/96.*(3.+y*(16.+5.*y));
term3=t/384.*(-15.+y*(17.+y*(19.+3.*y)));
term4=t/92160.*(-945.+y*(-1920.+y*(1482.+y*(776.+y*79.))));
guess=
t*(1.+(.25*(1.+t*t)+(term2+(term3+term4*nui)*nui)*nui)*nui);
return (invnr(1,a,nu1,nu2,nct3,guess)) ;
}

double incc(a,df1,noncen) double a,noncen;
int df1;
{
double nu1,nu2;
double sqrt(),invnr(),nct(),icump(),guess,exp(),p,t,x;
nu1=df1;nu2=0.;
g_noncent=noncen;g_df1=df1;
```

```
/* approx. for large nu>30 */
x= icump(1.-a);
p=2./(9.*nu1);
t= 1.-p+x*sqrt(p);
t=t*t*t;
guess= nu1*t;
return (invnr(1,a,nu1,nu2,ncc3,guess)) ;
}

#define tol 1.e-10

double zn(x,n,z) double x,z[];int n;
{double p;int i;
z[0]=p= exp(-.5*x*x)/sqrt(2.* pi );
if(!n)return p;
z[1]=-p*x;
if(n==1)return z[1];
for(i=2;i<=n;i++)
    {z[i]=-(x*z[i-1]+z[i-2]*(i-1.));
    }
return z[n];
}



double Q(x) double x;
{return 1.-P(x);
}

double L(h,k,rho) double h,k,rho;
{/* L(h,0,rho)*/
int n;
double sum,term,factor,z0[51],z[51];
factor=rho;
term=zn(k,25,z0);
term=zn(h,25,z);
sum=0.;
for(n=0;n<25;n++)
    {
    term=factor*z0[n]*z[n];
    if(abs(term)<tol)break;
    sum+=term;
/*printf(" n=%d z0=%le z=%le term %le
sum=%le\n",n,z0[n],z[n],term,sum);*/
    if(abs(term)<abs(sum)*tol)break;
    factor *= rho/(n+1.);
    }
```

```
if(abs(term)>tol*abs(sum)){printf(" for L abs. error %le ex-
ceeds tol\n",term);}
/*return Q(h)*.5 + sum;L(h,0,rho)*/
return Q(h)*Q(k)+ sum;
}
```

Chapter 27

Miscellaneous Functions

Introduction

Included here are the functions of Chapter 27, such as the Sievert integral and Clausen's integral, and Clebsch-Gordon and related symbols. Some of these miscellaneous functions are related to those developed in previous chapters, such as Ritchie's integral and the Debye functions, and are given in the relevant preceding chapter. The polylogarithms are included as well as implementations of the dilogarithm function. The f functions, which it seems appropriate to name Abramowitz functions, are included for general n. In addition to the functions of Abramowitz and Stegun, we add a number of relatives to the Clebsh-Gordon coefficients, as well as the Lobachevski integral and the function $\mu(\alpha,\beta,x)$ and its relatives.

Debye Functions

The Debye functions are defined by the integral $\int_0^x \frac{t^n}{e^t - 1}\,dt$. They arise from quantum statistical calculations in which Bose-Einstein statistics are obeyed. They are of use, therefore, in solid-state problems involving phonons, for example.

When Fermi-Dirac statistics are obeyed, the integrals of interest are of the general form: $\int_0^x \frac{t^n}{e^{t-\mu} + 1}\,dt$. The parameter μ is the chemical potential, which is zero in the Debye function. This integral would arise in studies of electron transport properties of semiconductors, for example. This integral is generally difficult to deal with. See Cody and Thacher for the special cases $x = \infty, n = -\frac{1}{2}, \frac{1}{2}, \frac{3}{2}$.

Method

The relationship with the Bernoulli numbers is used, along with the functions of Chapter 23.

Sievert

The Sievert Integral is defined by $\int_0^{\theta} e^{-x \sec \varphi}\, d\varphi$.

Method

Formula 27.4.2, with the routines for exponential integrals, is used.

Abramowitz and Kruse-Ramsey

The functions $f_m(x) = \int_0^{\infty} t^m e^{-t^2 - x/t}\, dt$ I have chosen to call Abramowitz functions, as they were studied by Abramowitz. For $m = 1, 2, 3$, they may be evaluated using the results contained in Abramowitz and Stegun, and these functions are provided here. The functions defined by $g_1 + g_2 = f_3\,(ix)$ are from work by Kruse and Ramsey. Complex versions of the f_m are provided in Chapter 29.

Method

The formulae of 27.5 are used.

Ritchie

The Ritchie integral is $\int_0^{\infty} \frac{e^{-x^2}}{t+x}\, dt$.

Method

Relation 27.6.2, along with the functions from Chapter 7 for the exponential integral Ei(x) and Dawson's integral, is used.

Dilogarithm and Polylogarithms

Abramowitz and Stegun use Spence's Integral (for $n = 2$), $f(x) = -\int_1^{x} \frac{\ln t}{t-1}\, dt$. This is not the usual definition, however.

Polylogarithms are defined by $F_n(x) = \sum_{h=1}^{\infty} \frac{z^h}{h^n}$, which would give an integral $Li_2(x) = -\int_0^x \frac{ln(1-t)}{t} dt$. Note that $Li_2(x) = f(1-x)$.

Method

For Spence's dilogarithm, we use the formulae of Abramowitz and Stegun. For the dilogarithm, we use CALGO 490 by Ginsberg and Zaborowski's method. The dilogarithm (for the usual definition) is real for $x \le 1$ and complex for larger x. Consequently, the **Dlog()** routine supplied can be used to supply the real part of the dilogarithm for positive real x. However, for $x > 1$, the imaginary part is simply $-\pi \ln(x)$. For the polylogarithm, we provide a general routine as well as two rational fits to the dilogarithm and trilogarithm, from *Electromagnetic and Acoustic Scattering by Simple Shapes.*

Claussen

Claussen's integral $f(\theta) = -\int_0^\theta \ln(2\sin\frac{t}{2})\, dt.$

Method

The series in Abramowitz and Stegun, 27.8.2 and 27.8.3, with 27.8.4, are used.

Lobachevsky

This integral is $Lob(\theta) = -\int_0^\theta \ln(\cos t)\, dt.$ It is defined in Gradshteyn and Ryzhik.

Method

Series are used, along with transformations to reduce the maximum values of theta needed.

Clebsch-Gordon and Relatives

A variety of coefficients arise in the quantum-mechanical theory of angular momentum. The Clebsch-Gordon coefficients express the contribution to a given angular momentum state by the component states. The Clebsch-Gordon coefficient < j_1 j_2 m_1 m_2 | j_1 j_2 j_m> applies to a system with total momentum j and momentum in the z-direction m composed of two components denoted by the subscripts 1 and 2. In quantum mechanics, the angular momenta must all be integral or half-integral, the j's must be positive, $|m| \le j$ for each of the components and the entire system, and various other constraints (triangle conditions) apply if the coefficients are to be nonzero. Closely related is the Wigner 3j symbol $\begin{pmatrix} j1 & j2 & j3 \\ m1 & m2 & m3 \end{pmatrix}$. Various associated symbols exist, such as Wigner's 6-j symbol $\begin{Bmatrix} a & b & c \\ d & e & f \end{Bmatrix}$, the related Racah function $W(a\ b\ c\ d;\ e\ f)$, the 9-j symbol (for coupling three angular momenta) $\begin{Bmatrix} a & b & c \\ d & e & f \\ g & h & i \end{Bmatrix}$. Note that we provide a number of alternative methods for some of the symbols, as a check.

Method

The formulae of Racah and others are used.

ν and Relatives

Define $\mu(x,\alpha,\beta) = \int_0^{\infty} \frac{x^{\alpha+t} t^{\beta}}{\Gamma(\beta+1)\Gamma(\alpha+t+1)} dt$. Then define $\nu(x) = \mu(x,0,0)$, $\nu(x,a) = \mu(x,\alpha = a,\beta = 0)$, $\mu(x,\beta) = \mu(x,\alpha = 0,\beta)$. These are defined in *Higher Transcendental Functions.* Note that in *Integral Transforms,* also edited by Erdelyi as part of the Bateman Manuscript Project, $\mu(x,a)$ is defined without the normalizing factor of $\Gamma(1+a)$ as it would have if the definition were consistent with *Higher Transcendental Functions.* Note also that in that book the order of the α and β parameters is the opposite of that given here; it seems more natural to have alpha preceed beta. For that reason we have explicitly shown the alpha and beta parameters in the above definitions. These functions appear to be of most interest because they are involved in some inverse Laplace transforms of interest, e. g., that of $\frac{p^{-\alpha}}{\log p}$, $\alpha > 0$ is $\nu(t,\alpha-1)$, and that of $\frac{\Gamma(\alpha)}{p(\log p)^{\alpha}}$, $\mathrm{Re}\, p > 1$ is $\mu(t,\alpha-1)$, where the definition of μ in *Integral Transforms,* without the normalizing factor of $\Gamma(\beta+1)$, is used. Note that for large x, $\nu(x) \sim exp(x)$, and $\mu(x,\alpha,\beta) \sim \frac{(x-\alpha)^{\beta}\, exp(x)}{\Gamma(\beta+1)}$. This may be verified using Laplace's method of steepest descent.

Method

It was found that a straightforward integration was the best approach. Note that the integrand may be simplified, with some factors pulled out from within the integral.

References

D. M. Brink & G. R. Satchler, *Angular Momentum,* 2nd ed, corrected reprinting (Oxford: University Press, 1971).

W. J. Cody & H. C. Thatcher, Jr., *Mathematics of Computation*, **21**, 30, 1967.

E. S. Ginsberg & D. Zaborowski, CALGO 490, *The Dilogarithm Function of a Real Argument.*

I. S. Gradshteyn and I. W. Ryzhik, *Tables of Integrals, Series, and Products* (N. Y.: Academic Press, 1965).

Higher Transcendental Functions, *Bateman Manuscript Project* (ed. A. Erdelyi) (N. Y. : McGraw-Hill, 1953).

Integral Transforms, Bateman Manuscript Project (ed. A. Erdelyi), (N. Y. : McGraw-Hill, 1953).

L. Lewin, *Polylogarithms and Associated Functions* (N. Y.: North Holland, 1981).

M. Mizushima, *Theoretical Physics* (N. Y.: J. Wiley, 1972).

E. W. Ng and C. J. Devine, *Mathematics of Computation*, **24**, 405, 1970.

G. Racah, *Phys. Rev.*, **62**, 438, 1942.

Figures

Figs. 27-1 through 27-8 plot the miscellaneous functions.

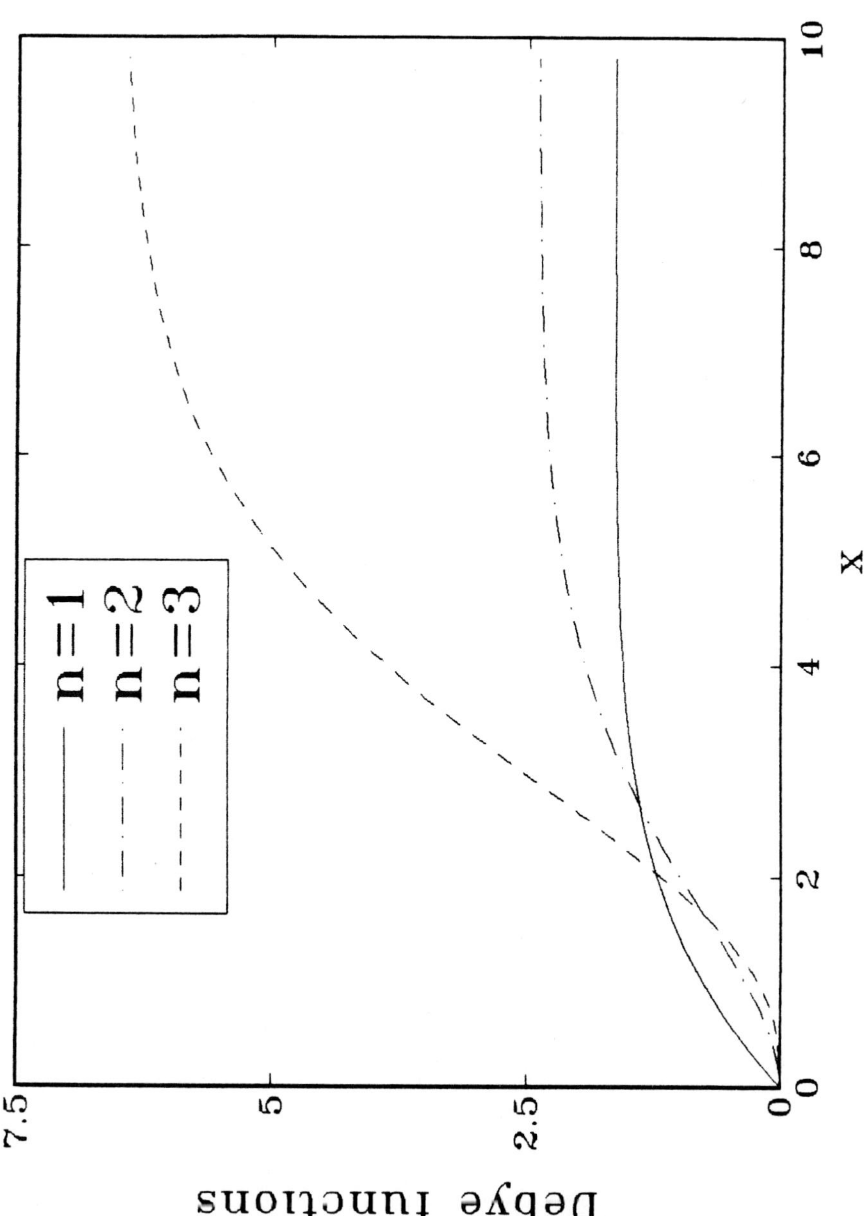

Fig. 27-1: Debye Functions.

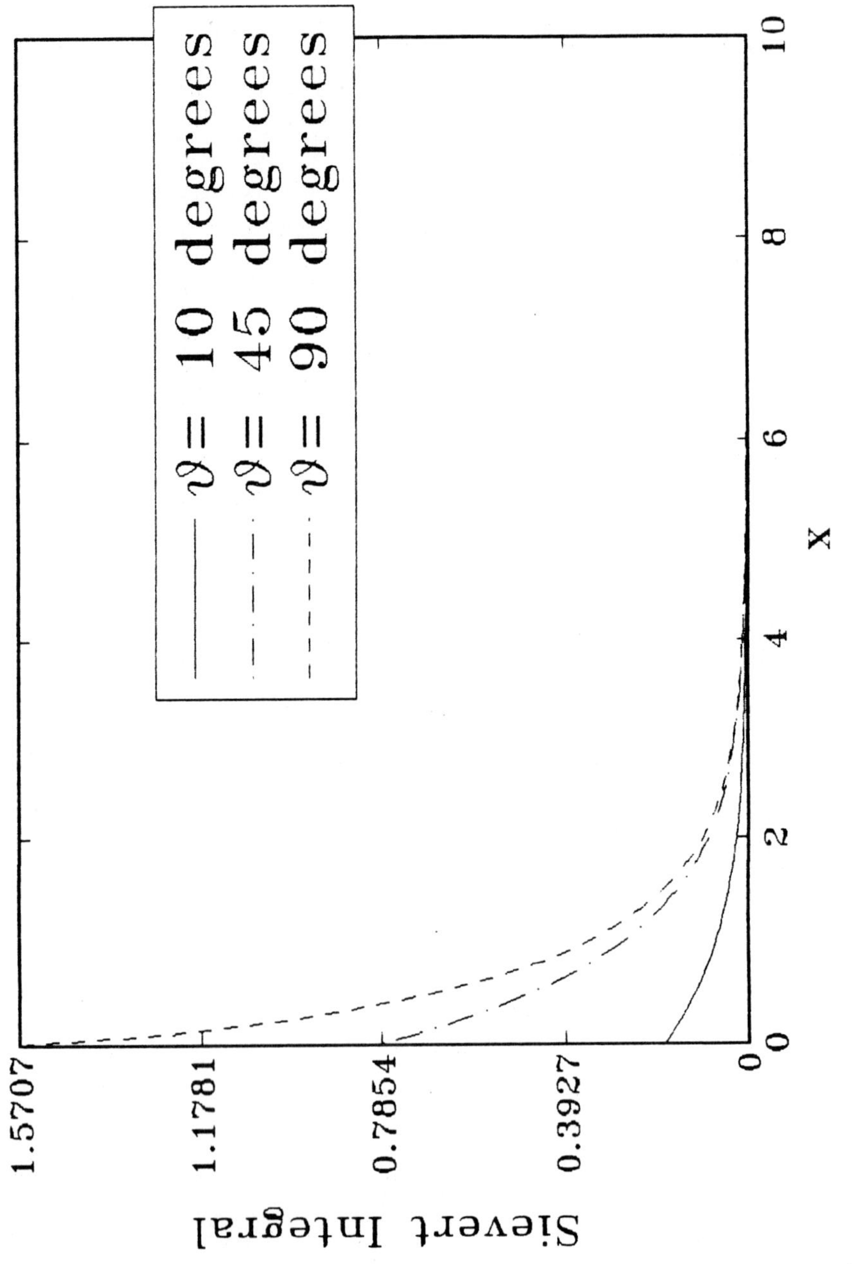

Fig. 27-2: Sievert Functions.

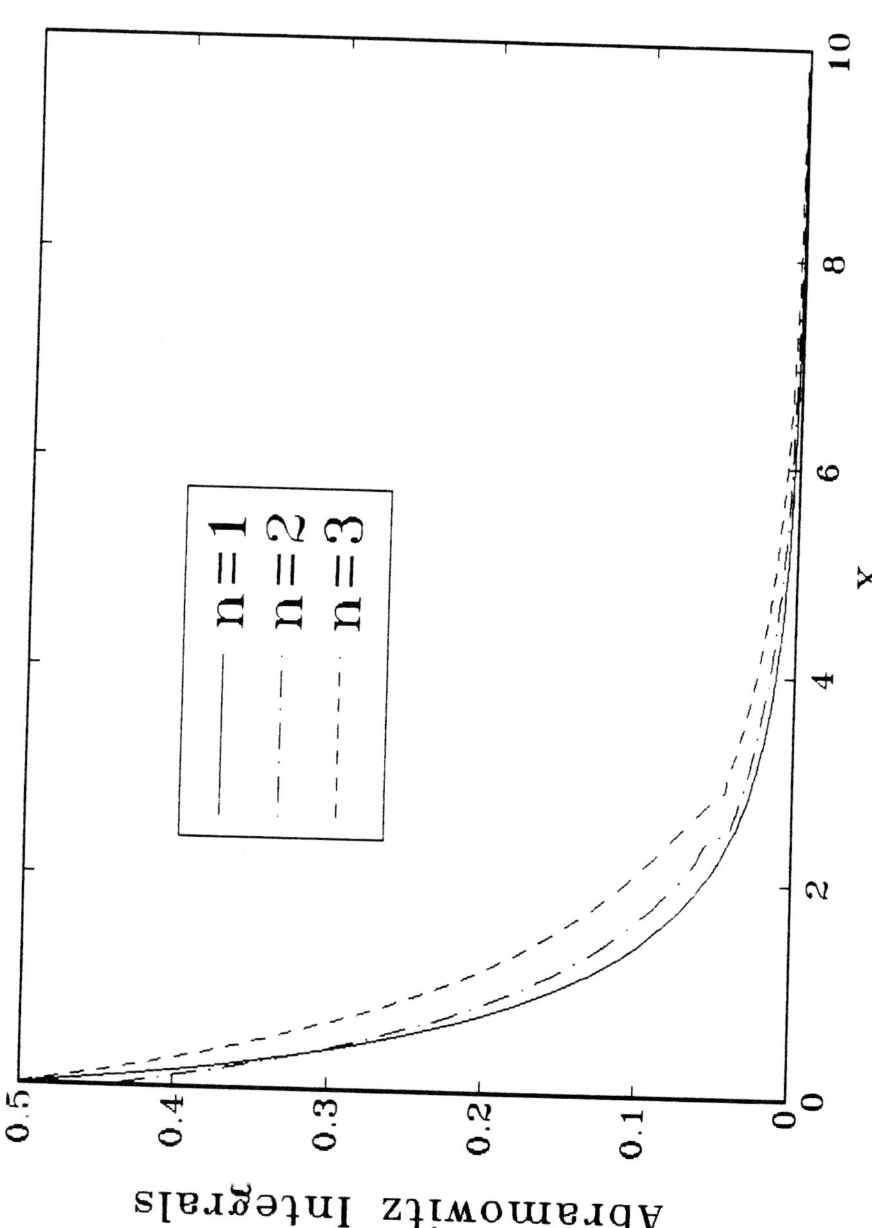

Fig. 27-3: Abramowitz Functions.

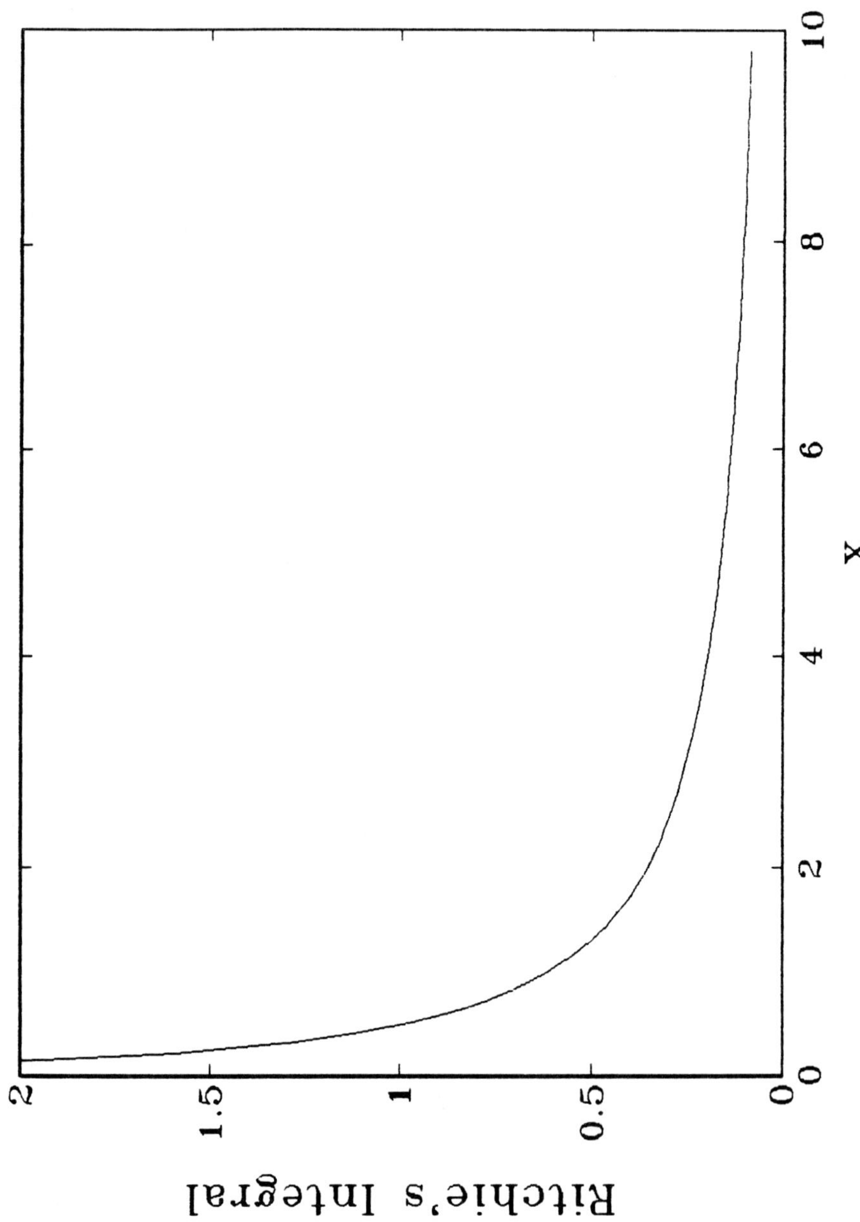

Fig. 27-4: Ritchie's Integral.

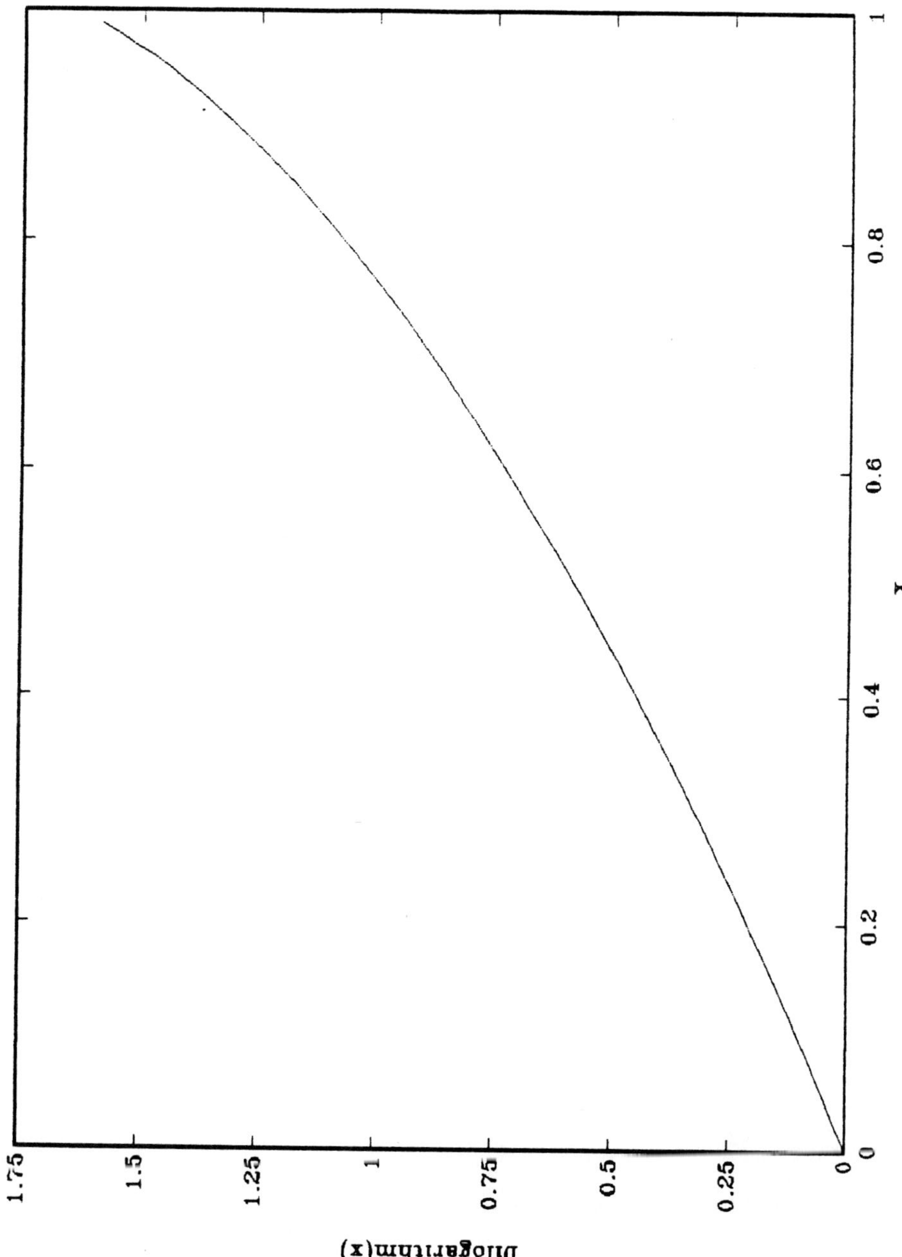

Fig. 27-5: Dilogarithm. This is the conventional (Euler definition) dilogarithm, not Spence's as in Abramowitz and Stegun. See text.

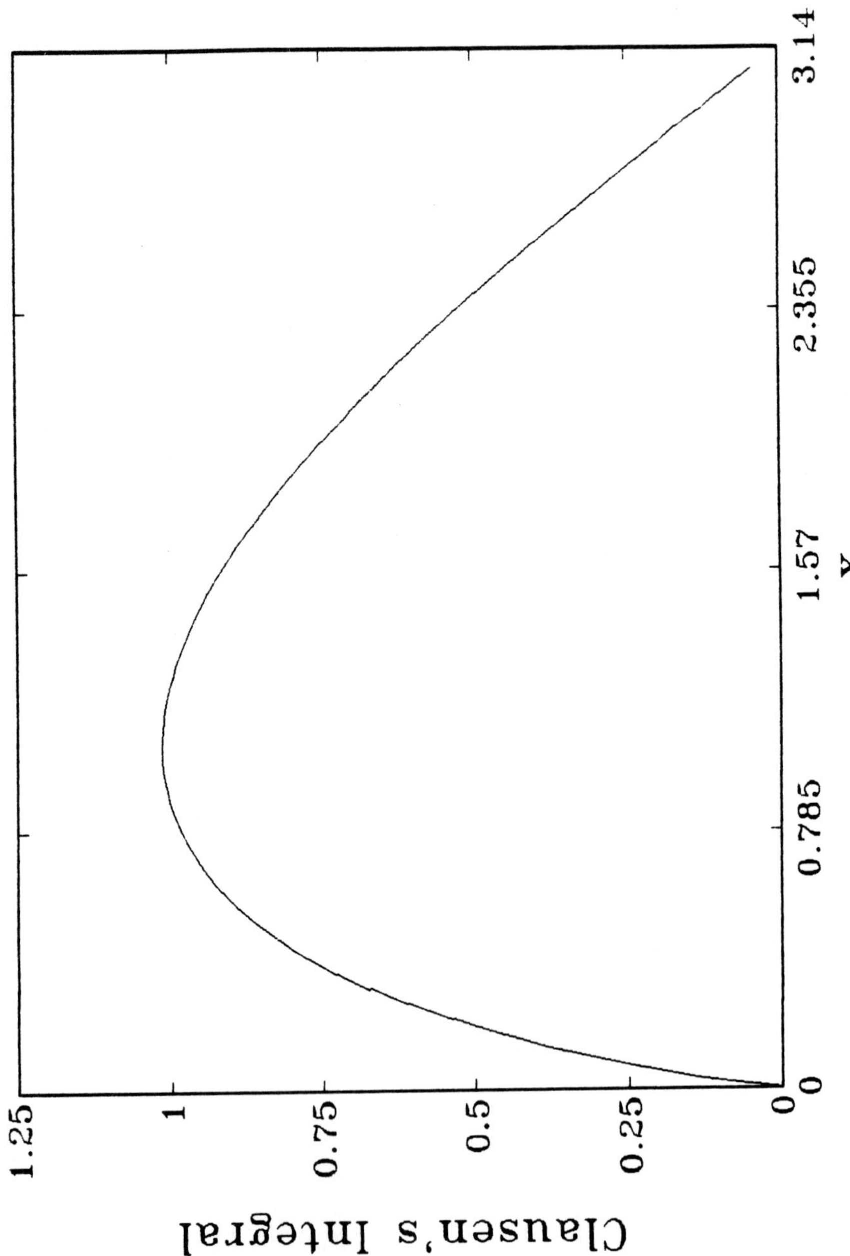

Fig. 27-6: Clausen's Integral.

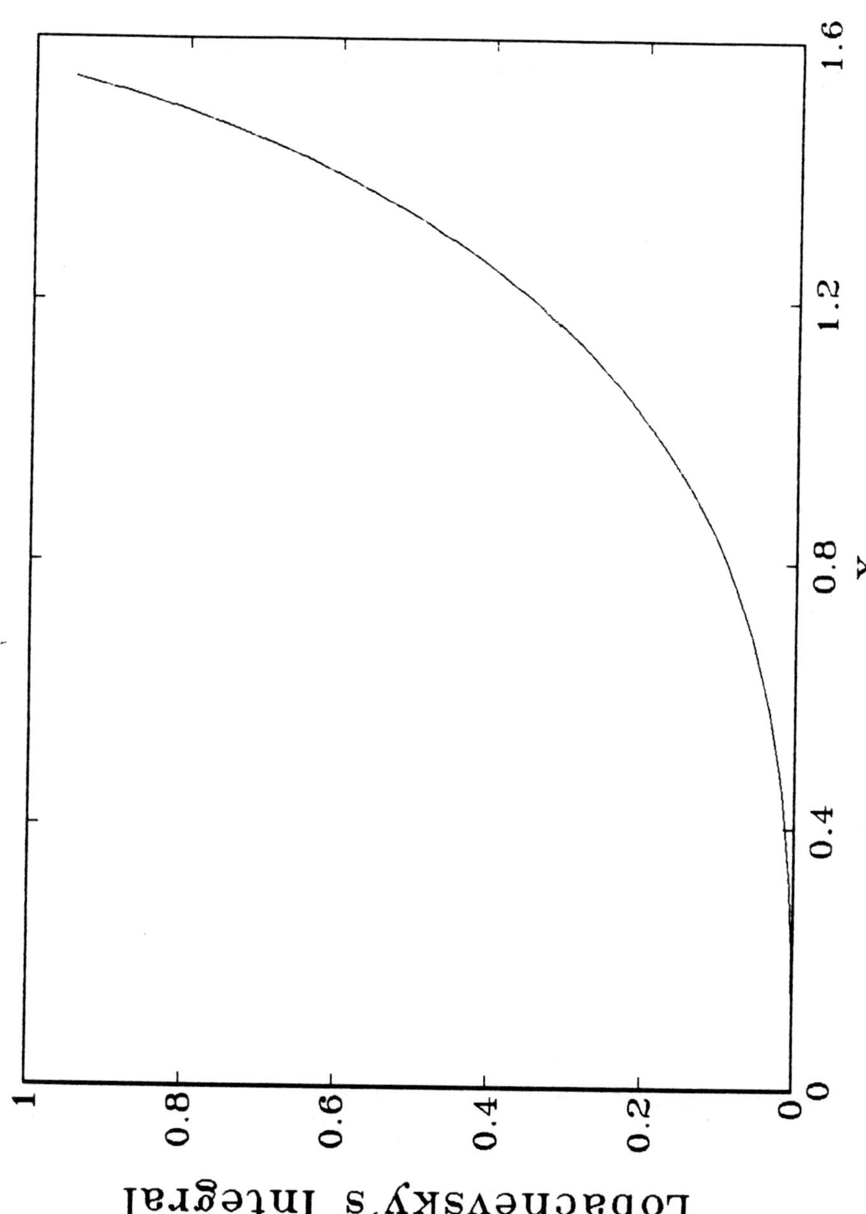

Fig. 27-7: Lobachevsky's Integral.

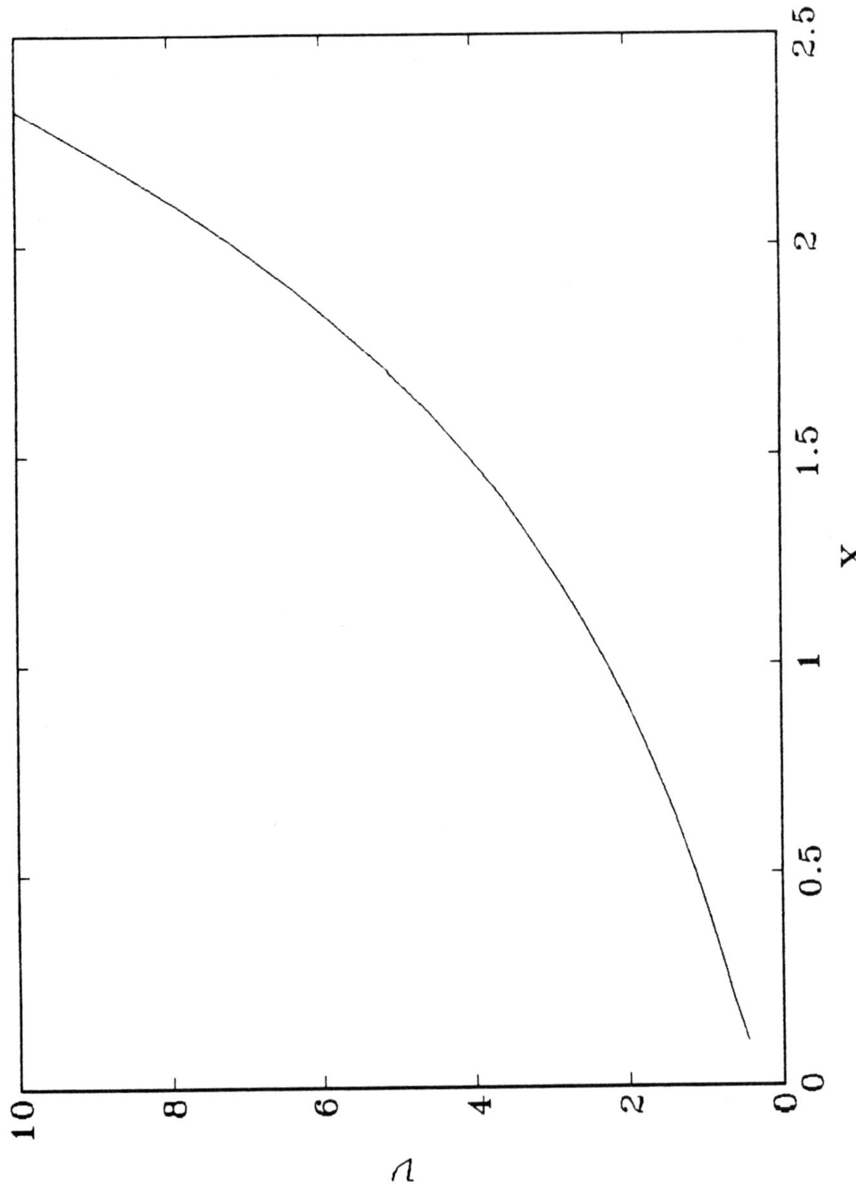

Fig. 27-8: ν Integral.

```
/*
sievert integral Ch27
from C Mathematical Function Handbook by Louis Baker
Copyright 1991 by Louis Baker. All rights reserved.
*/

#include <stdio.h>
#include "cmlib.h"
#include "protom.h"

extern int itkt,itmax;

double sievert(x,theta) double x,theta;
{
double sum,term,sq,en(),cos(),tt,y,z,kii();
int k,itmax=40;
z=cos(theta);
sq=z*z;
if(z!=0.) y=x/z;
else return errorcode;
sum=0.;
term=z;
for(k=0;k<itmax;k++)
   {
   tt=term*en(y,(double)((k+1)<<1) );
   sum+=tt;
   if(!k)term*=.5;
   else term*=((double)(2*k+1))/((double)((2*k+2)));
   term*=sq;
   if( abs(tt)<1.e-6 || abs(tt)<abs(sum)*5.e-7)break;
   }
z=kii(x);
/*printf(" sum=%e kii=%e\n",sum,z);*/
return z-sum;
}
```

```
/*
Dilogarithm
Dlog differs from Spences's integral for n=2 given by dilog
in that Dlog(x)=dilog(1-x)

from C Mathematical Function Handbook by Louis Baker
Copyright 1991 by Louis Baker. All rights reserved.
*/

#include <stdio.h>
#include "cmlib.h"
#include "protom.h"

#define dl1 1.644934066848226
static double dcoef[17]=
{.005047192127203,.005300972587634,.004091615355944,.00481549
0327461,
.005966509196748,.006980881130380,.008260083434161,.009997129
506220,
.012345919431569,.015625134938703,.020408155605916,.027777774
308288,
.040000000124677,.062500000040762,.111111111110322,.249999999
999859,1.};

double Dlog(x) double x;
{/* alternate version of Dilog- -Int from 0 to x of ln|1-
y|/y*/
double f,u,y,z,log();int i;
if(x==1.)return dl1;
if(x==0.0)return 0.;
if(x>=2.)
   {z=1./x;f=-1.;u=log(x);u=-.5*u*u+3.289868133696453;}
else if(x>1.)
   {z=(x-1.)/x;f=1.;u=-.5*log(x)*log(z*x-z)+dl1;}
else if(x>.5)
   {z=1.-x;f=-1.;u=-log(z)*log(x)+dl1;}
else if(x>0.)
   {z=x;u=0.;f=1.;}
else if(x>=-1.)
   {z=x/(x-1.);f=-1.;u=log(1.-x);u=-.5*u*u;}
else
   {z=1./(1-x);f=1.;u=.5*log(z)*log(x*x*z)-dl1;}
y=.008048124718341*z+.008288074835108;
y=y*z-.001481786416153;
y=y*z-.000912777413024;
for(i=0;i<=16;i++)y=y*z+dcoef[i];
return f*y*z+u;
}
```

```
/*
Polylogarithm function

CAVEAT: DO NOT USE FOR DILOGARITHMS! WILL BE INACCURATE!
use Dlog or dilog instead.
(We do not automatically substitute a call for these when
n==1. to provide a crude cross-check on each)
Note also that n is not constrained to be an integer.

from C Mathematical Function Handbook by Louis Baker
Copyright 1991 by Louis Baker. All rights reserved.
*/

#include <stdio.h>
#include "cmlib.h"
#include "protom.h"

#define abs(x) ((x)<0.?-(x):(x))
extern int itkt;
#define tol 1.e-7

double polylog(x,n) double x,n;
{
int k,itmax=500;
double sum,term,newt,pow();
if(x< 0.) return errorcode;
sum=0.;
term=x;
for(k=1;k<itmax;k++)
   {
   newt= term/pow( (double)k,n);
   sum+=newt;
   /*printf(" k=%d newterm=%le sum=%le\n",k,newt,sum);*/
   if( abs(newt)< tol || abs(newt)< tol*sum)goto done;
   term*=x;
   }
itkt=itmax;
done:
itkt=k;
return sum;
}
```

```
/*
"Abramowitz" functions f1, f2, f3 from Ch.27

from C Mathematical Function Handbook by Louis Baker
Copyright 1991 by Louis Baker. All rights reserved.
*/

#include <stdio.h>
#include "cmlib.h"
#include "protom.h"
extern int itkt;


double af2s(x) double x;
{
double log(),ln,sqrt(),sp,sq,sum1,sum2;
sp=sqrt(pi);
if(x>0.)ln=log(x);
else ln=0.;
sq=x*x;
sum2=.3333333+sq*(.000198*sq-.01667);
sum1= sp*.5*(1.+sq)+x*(sq*(-.3225+x*(-.1477
+x*(.03195+x*(.00328+x*(-.000491-.0000235*x)))))-1.);
/*sum1= .5*sp-x+.5*sp*sq-.3225*cube-.1477*sq*sq
+.03195*cube*sq+.00328*cube*cube-.000491*cube*cube*x
-.0000235*cube*cube*sq;*/

return .5*(ln*x*sq*sum2+sum1);
}

double af3s(x) double x;
{
double log(),ln,sqrt(),sp,sq,sum1,sum2;
sp=sqrt(pi);
if(x>0.)ln=log(x);
else ln=0.;
sq=x*x;
sum2=.0833+sq*(-.00278+.000025*sq);
/*sum1= 1.-.5*sp*x+.5*sq-.2954*cube+.1014*sq*sq
+.02954*cube*sq-.00578*cube*cube-.00047*cube*cube*x
+.000064*four*four;*/
sum1= 1.+x*(-.5*sp+x*(.5+x*(-.2954+x*(.1014+x*(
.02954+x*(-.00578+x*(-.00047+.000064*x)))))));

return .5*(sum1-ln*sq*sq*sum2);
}

double af1s(x) double x;
{
```

```
int k,itmax=400,in;
double
log(),sqrt(),sp,sq,ln,sum,term,coef,a,b,aa[2],bb[2],t;
sp=sqrt(pi);
sq=x*x;
if(x>0.)ln=log(x);
else ln=0.;
sum=0.;
term=1.;
in=0;
aa[0]=0.;aa[1]=-1.;
bb[0]=-sp;bb[1]=1.5*(1.-.57721556649);
a=0.;b=1.;
for(k=0;k<itmax;k++)
    {
    coef= a*ln+b;
    t=coef*term;
    sum+=t;
/*printf(" k in %d %d a,b %e %e s t %e %e
c=%e\n",k,in,a,b,sum,t,coef);*/
    if( abs(t)<1.e-6 || abs(t)<1.e-5*abs(sum))break;
    term*=x;
    itkt=k;
    if(k>1)
        {
        coef=1./((k+1)*(k-1)*k);
        aa[in]= -2.*aa[in]*coef ;
        bb[in]= (-2.*bb[in]-(3*k*k-1)*aa[in])*coef;
        }
    a=aa[in];b=bb[in];
    in++;
    if(in>1)in=0;
    }
return .5*sum;
}


double afa(x,n) double x,n;
{
int i,itmax=30,k;
double
sqrt(),exp(),pow(),y,z,sum,term,v,vi,a,old,older,t,oldt;
if(x<=1.)return -1.;
v= 3.*pow(.5*x,.666666);vi=1./v;
sum-0.;
term=1.;a=1.;old=0.;t=1.e10;
for(i=0;i<itmax;i++)
    {
    oldt=t;
```

```
   t=term*a;
   if( abs(t)>abs(oldt)) break;
   sum+=t;
   term*=vi;
   older=old;
   old=a;
   if(!i) a=(3.*n*n+3.*n-1.)/12.;
   else
      {
      k=i+1;
      a=(.5*(n-2*k)*(2*k+3-n)*(2*k+3+2*n)*older
         -(12*k*k+36*k-3*n*n-3*n+25)*old)/(12*(k+2));
      }
   if(abs(t)<1.e-6|| abs(t)<1.e-5*abs(sum))break;
   itkt=i;
   }
return sqrt(pi/3.)*pow(v/3.,.5*n)*exp(-v)*sum;
}

double af1(x) double x;
{
if(x<3.)return af1s(x);
return afa(x,1.);
}
double af2(x) double x;
{
if(x<2.25)return af2s(x);
return afa(x,2.);
}
double af3(x) double x;
{
if(x<3.)return af3s(x);
return afa(x,3.);
}

double af(x,n) int n; double x;
{
int m;
double new,old,older,oldest;
if(n==1)return af1(x);
if(n==2)return af2(x);
if(n==3)return af3(x);
oldest=af3(x);older=af2(x);old=af1(x);

for(m=4;m<=n;m++)
   {
   new=.5*( (m-1)*older+x*oldest);
   oldest=older;older=old;old=new;
   }
```

```
return new;

}
```

```
/*
nu and mu integrals of Erdelyi Vol III p.217
mu(x,alpha,beta) --caveat: Erdelyi has mu(x,beta,alpha)
nu=mu(x,alpha,0) or mu(x,0,0)

from C Mathematical Function Handbook by Louis Baker
Copyright 1991 by Louis Baker. All rights reserved.
*/

#include "cmlib.h"
#include "protom.h"

#define max(a,b) ((a)>(b)?(a):(b))

static double z,co,alphan,betan;
extern int level,maxlev,feval,levmax;
int lim1,lim2,lim3;

double nui(t) double t;
{double ans;

ans=pow(z,t)/gamma(1.+t+alphan);
if(betan!=0.)ans*=pow(t,betan);
return ans;
}


#define toll 1.e-10

double mu(double x,double ain,double bin)
{
double a,b,ans,dx,cutoff,print;int i,lim;
if(x<=0.)return errorcode;
/*printf(" in mu %le %le %le %d\n",x,ain,bin,lim1);*/
co=-1.;lim1=max(lim1,1);
z=x; maxlev= 6;cutoff=co;
if(co<=0.)
   {/*automatic selection of co. note bi>0 x>0.*/
   a=max(1.,nui(0.));cutoff=4.;
   infinite_loop
      {
      dx=nui(cutoff);
      if( dx< toll*a)break;
      cutoff*=2.;
      }
   }
co=cutoff;
/*printf(" cutoff=%le\n",cutoff);*/
a=0.;ans=0.; alphan=ain;betan=bin;
```

```
lim=lim1;dx= cutoff/lim;b=a+dx;
for(i=0;i<lim;i++,a+=dx,b+=dx)
   {
   /*printf(" a,b %le %le ans=%le now\n",a,b,ans);*/
   ans+=/* print=*/adsimp(a,b,1.e-7,nui);
   /*printf(" a,b,dans=%le %le %le now\n",a,b,print);*/
   }
/*printf(" ans after 1- %le\n",ans);*/
if(ain!=0.)ans*=pow(x,ain);
if(bin!=0.)ans/=gamma(1.+bin);
return ans;
}

double nu(double x)
{return mu(x,0.,0.);}

double Nu(double x,double a)
{return mu(x,a,0.);}
```

```
/*
Lobachevsky function

from C Mathematical Function Handbook by Louis Baker
Copyright 1991 by Louis Baker. All rights reserved.
*/

#include <stdio.h>
#include "cmlib.h"
#include "protom.h"

static double
   lcoef[25]= {-1./6.,  -1./60.,  -1./315.,  -17./22680.,  -
31./155925.,
   -691./12162150.,  -10922./638512875.,  -
929569./173675502000.,
   -3202291./1856156927625.,  -221930581./389792954801250.,
   -9444233042./49308808782358125.,  -
56963745931./870155449100437500.,
   -29435334228302./1298054391195577640625.,
   -2093660879252671./26350504141270226104687 5.,
   -344502690252804724./122529844256906551386796875.,
   -129848163681107301953./129391515535293318264457500000.,
   -
868320396104950823611./240587349198436013647975664062 5.,
   -
209390615747646519456961./160231174566158385089551792265625 0.
,
   -
28259319101491102261334882./593656501767616816756789390344140
625.,
   -
16103843159579478297227731./923715998955305103872044212679687
500.,
   -7051057469144926141380249173 42./
    10989472332471238703393306799355559179687 5.,
   -12902452085992622837883723891345 1./
    543978880457326315817968686568100179394531 25.,
   -51768752002756374733644471311053204./
    58804116977436974739922415018011629392548828125.,
   -22680552792491997823522126468923904459./
    691536415654658822941487600611816761656374218750 00.,
   -43588258945274750397872591971875276602./
    355527794338584677117095439830671923835434326171875.};


/* for x near pi/2, accuracy of sum is only about .001*/
/* should do expansion abt x=pi/2, where L(pi/2)= ln2*/
double Lob(double x)
```

```
{int k,mult=0;double y,sum,l1,l2;
if(x==0.)return 0.;
if(x==pi*.5)return pi*.5*log(2.);
if(x>pi)return pi*log(2.)+Lob(x-pi);
if(x<0.){x=-x;mult=1;}
if(x>pi*.25 && x<pi*.5)/* pi/4<x<pi/2*/
   {y=pi*.5-x;/*   0< y < pi*.25 */
   sum=pi*.5-2.*y;/*  0 <sum <pi*.5 */
   if(sum<=0. || y<= 0.){printf(" bad Lob %le
%le\n",sum,y);
               return errorcode;}
   l1=Lob(y);
   l2=Lob(sum);
   sum= l1+.5*l2-(pi*.25-x)*log(2.);
   return mult?-sum:sum;
   }
if(x>pi*.5 && x<=pi)
   {return pi*log(2.)-Lob(pi-x);}
/* at this point, 0<x<pi/4*/
y=x*x;sum=lcoef[24];
for(k=23;k>=0;k--){sum= sum*y+lcoef[k];    }
sum*=x*y;
return mult? sum:-sum;
}
```

```
/*
Test Driver Misc. functions
from C Mathematical Function Handbook by Louis Baker
Copyright 1991 by Louis Baker. All rights reserved.
*/

#include <stdio.h>
#include "cmlib.h"
#include "protom.h"

extern int lim1,itkt;
FILE *osiev,*oclaus,*of123,*odeb,*omu,*olob,*odi;

main()
{double p,q,x,y,z,d,r;int n,j,i;
osiev=fopen("sievert.out","w");
oclaus=fopen("clausen.out","w");
of123=fopen("f123.out","w");
odeb=fopen("debye.out","w");
omu=fopen("mu.out","w");
olob=fopen("lob.out","w");
odi=fopen("dilog.out","w");
fprintf(of123," 4\n");
   for(i=0;i<100;i++)
      {
      x= .1*i;
      fprintf(of123,"%le %le %le %le\n",x, af(x,1),
       af(x,2),af(x,3));
      }
 fprintf(osiev," 4\n");
   q= pi/180.;
   for(i=0;i<100;i++)
      {
      x= .1*i;
      fprintf(osiev,"%le %le %le %le\n",x,
 sievert(x,10.*q),
       sievert(x,45.*q),     sievert(x,90.*q));
      }

 fprintf(oclaus," 1\n");
   for(i=0;i<100;i++)
      {
      x= pi*i/100.;
      fprintf(oclaus,"%le %le\n",x, clausen(x));
      }
 fprintf(odi," 1\n");
   for(i=0;i<100;i++)
      {
      x= 1.*(i)/100.;
```

```
       fprintf(odi,"%le %le\n",x, Dlog(x));
       }
fprintf(odeb," 4\n");
   for(i=0;i<100;i++)
       {
       x= .1*i;
       fprintf(odeb,"%le %le %le %le\n",x, debye(x,1),
        debye(x,2),debye(x,3));
       }
fprintf(olob," 1\n");
   for(i=0;i<100;i++)
       {
       x= pi*.5*i/100.;
       fprintf(olob,"%le %le\n",x, Lob(x));
       }
fprintf(omu," 1\n");
printf(" enter p, q for mu(x,p,q)
plots\n");scanf("%le%le",&p,&q);
   for(i=1;i<100;i++)
       {
       x= i/10.;
       fprintf(omu,"%le %le\n",x, mu(x,p,q));
       }
printf(" for z=0 dilog=%le %le\n",dilog(0.), Dlog(0.));
printf(" for z=1 dilog=%le %le\n",dilog(1.), Dlog(1.));


infinite_loop
   {
   printf(" for mu:enter x=0,alpha,beta,lim1\n");
   scanf("%le%le%le%d",&x,&p,&q,&lim1);
   printf(" x etc %le %le %le %d\n",x,p,q,lim1);
   if(x<0. || lim1 <1)break;
   printf("mu(%le,%le,%le)=%le\n",x,p,q,mu(x,p,q));
   }
infinite_loop
   {printf(" for Clausen integral enter theta de-
gree\n");scanf("%le",&x);
   if(x<=0.)break;
   y= x*pi/180.;
   printf("clausen=%le %le %le\n",x,y,clausen(y) );
   }
printf(" sievert:\n");
for(i=0;i<10;i++)
   {
   x=i*2.;
   for(j=1;j<9;j++)
       {
       if(j<7)d=j*10.;
```

```
      else if(j==7)d=75.;
      else d=90.;
      r=d*pi/180.;
      printf(" sievert x=%f theta=%f
%e\n",x,d,sievert(x,r));
      }
   }

infinite_loop
   {printf(" for Debye enter x,n\n");scanf("%le%d",&x,&n);
   if(n<=0)break;
   printf(" %le", debye(x,n) );
   }
infinite_loop
   {printf(" for Abramowitz f enter
x,n\n");scanf("%le%d",&x,&n);
   if(n<=0)break;
   printf(" %le", af(x,n) );
   }
infinite_loop
      {printf("enter x for Lobachevsky\n");scanf("%le",&x);
      if(x==0.)break;
      printf(" Lob=%le\n",Lob(x));
      }
for (i=1;i<50;i++)
   { x= i*.02;y=1.-x;printf(" x=%f 1-x=%f Dilog=%le %le\n"
      ,x,y,Dlog(x),dilog(y));
   }
infinite_loop
   {
   printf(" enter z, n for polylog\n");
   scanf("%le%d",&x,&n);
   if(x<=0.||n<=0)break;
   z=x;
   printf(" x=%f n=%d polylog=%le \n"
      ,x,n,polylog(z,(double)n));
   printf("   iterations used=%d\n",itkt);
   }
return 0;
}
```

```
/*
test driver Ritchie's integral
from C Mathematical Function Handbook by Louis Baker
Copyright 1991 by Louis Baker. All rights reserved.
*/

#include <stdio.h>
#include "cmlib.h"
#include "protom.h"

FILE *out;

main()
{double x;int i;
out=fopen("rich.out","w");
fprintf(out," 1\n");
for(i=1;i<100;i++)
   {
   x=i*.1;
   fprintf(out,"%le %le\n",x,ritchie(x));
   }
infinite_loop
   {
   printf(" enter x for Ritchie integral\n");
   scanf("%le",&x);printf("
ritchie(%le)=%le\n",x,ritchie(x));
   }
}
```

Test Output: Misc. functions

```
 enter p, q for mu(x,p,q) plots
.5 .5
 for z=0 dilog=1.644934e+00 0.000000e+00
 for z=1 dilog=0.000000e+00 1.644934e+00
 for mu:enter x=0,alpha,beta,lim1
-1 0 0 0
 x etc -1.000000e+00 0.000000e+00 0.000000e+00 0
 for Clausen integral enter theta degree
45
clausen=4.500000e+01 7.853982e-01 9.818721e-01
 for Clausen integral enter theta degree
0
 sievert:
 sievert x=0.000000 theta=10.000000 1.801855e-01
 sievert x=0.000000 theta=20.000000 3.491149e-01
 sievert x=0.000000 theta=30.000000 5.236006e-01
 sievert x=0.000000 theta=40.000000 6.981325e-01
 sievert x=0.000000 theta=50.000000 8.726651e-01
 sievert x=0.000000 theta=60.000000 1.047198e+00
 sievert x=0.000000 theta=75.000000 1.308997e+00
 sievert x=0.000000 theta=90.000000 1.570796e+00
 sievert x=2.000000 theta=10.000000 2.412761e-02
 sievert x=2.000000 theta=20.000000 4.535912e-02
 sievert x=2.000000 theta=30.000000 6.451260e-02
 sievert x=2.000000 theta=40.000000 7.966355e-02
 sievert x=2.000000 theta=50.000000 8.997316e-02
 sievert x=2.000000 theta=60.000000 9.536114e-02
 sievert x=2.000000 theta=75.000000 9.712683e-02
 sievert x=2.000000 theta=90.000000 9.713910e-02
 sievert x=4.000000 theta=10.000000 3.227588e-03
 sievert x=4.000000 theta=20.000000 5.902053e-03
 sievert x=4.000000 theta=30.000000 8.008082e-03
 sievert x=4.000000 theta=40.000000 9.331648e-03
 sievert x=4.000000 theta=50.000000 9.952711e-03
 sievert x=4.000000 theta=60.000000 1.012892e-02
 sievert x=4.000000 theta=75.000000 1.014806e-02
 sievert x=4.000000 theta=90.000000 1.014807e-02
 sievert x=6.000000 theta=10.000000 4.352361e-04
 sievert x=6.000000 theta=20.000000 7.725998e-04
 sievert x=6.000000 theta=30.000000 1.002209e-03
 sievert x=6.000000 theta=40.000000 1.118105e-03
 sievert x=6.000000 theta=50.000000 1.156068e-03
 sievert x=6.000000 theta=60.000000 1.161823e-03
 sievert x=6.000000 theta=75.000000 1.162045e-03
 sievert x=6.000000 theta=90.000000 1.162045e-03
 sievert x=8.000000 theta=10.000000 6.624449e-05
 sievert x=8.000000 theta=20.000000 1.034543e-04
 sievert x=8.000000 theta=30.000000 1.269426e-04
```

```
 sievert x=8.000000 theta=40.000000 1.365651e-04
 sievert x=8.000000 theta=50.000000 1.386650e-04
 sievert x=8.000000 theta=60.000000 1.388385e-04
 sievert x=8.000000 theta=75.000000 1.388416e-04
 sievert x=8.000000 theta=90.000000 1.388416e-04
 sievert x=10.000000 theta=10.000000 1.163239e-05
 sievert x=10.000000 theta=20.000000 1.453015e-05
 sievert x=10.000000 theta=30.000000 1.639127e-05
 sievert x=10.000000 theta=40.000000 1.690535e-05
 sievert x=10.000000 theta=50.000000 1.700873e-05
 sievert x=10.000000 theta=60.000000 1.701514e-05
 sievert x=10.000000 theta=75.000000 1.701519e-05
 sievert x=10.000000 theta=90.000000 1.701519e-05
 sievert x=12.000000 theta=10.000000 1.762489e-06
 sievert x=12.000000 theta=20.000000 1.937677e-06
 sievert x=12.000000 theta=30.000000 2.067341e-06
 sievert x=12.000000 theta=40.000000 2.113286e-06
 sievert x=12.000000 theta=50.000000 2.119905e-06
 sievert x=12.000000 theta=60.000000 2.120148e-06
 sievert x=12.000000 theta=75.000000 2.120149e-06
 sievert x=12.000000 theta=90.000000 2.120149e-06
 sievert x=14.000000 theta=10.000000 2.263440e-07
 sievert x=14.000000 theta=20.000000 2.483677e-07
 sievert x=14.000000 theta=30.000000 2.627458e-07
 sievert x=14.000000 theta=40.000000 2.668776e-07
 sievert x=14.000000 theta=50.000000 2.673069e-07
 sievert x=14.000000 theta=60.000000 2.673163e-07
 sievert x=14.000000 theta=75.000000 2.673164e-07
 sievert x=14.000000 theta=90.000000 2.673164e-07
 sievert x=16.000000 theta=10.000000 2.923209e-08
 sievert x=16.000000 theta=20.000000 3.200291e-08
 sievert x=16.000000 theta=30.000000 3.360122e-08
 sievert x=16.000000 theta=40.000000 3.397498e-08
 sievert x=16.000000 theta=50.000000 3.400314e-08
 sievert x=16.000000 theta=60.000000 3.400351e-08
 sievert x=16.000000 theta=75.000000 3.400351e-08
 sievert x=16.000000 theta=90.000000 3.400351e-08
 sievert x=18.000000 theta=10.000000 3.792324e-09
 sievert x=18.000000 theta=20.000000 4.141190e-09
 sievert x=18.000000 theta=30.000000 4.319291e-09
 sievert x=18.000000 theta=40.000000 4.353287e-09
 sievert x=18.000000 theta=50.000000 4.355152e-09
 sievert x=18.000000 theta=60.000000 4.355167e-09
 sievert x=18.000000 theta=75.000000 4.355167e-09
 sievert x=18.000000 theta=90.000000 4.355167e-09
 for Debye enter x,n
1 1
 7.775071e-01 for Debye enter x,n
1 3
```

```
 2.248338e-01 for Debye enter x,n
0 0
 for Abramowitz f enter x,n
.5 3
 3.278535e-01 for Abramowitz f enter x,n
.5 2
 2.653823e-01 for Abramowitz f enter x,n
.5 1
 2.531762e-01 for Abramowitz f enter x,n
0 0
enter x for Lobachevsky
1
 Lob=1.875382e-01
enter x for Lobachevsky
2
 Lob=1.885436e+00
enter x for Lobachevsky
3
 Lob=2.177112e+00
enter x for Lobachevsky
0
 x=0.020000 1-x=0.980000 Dilog=2.010090e-02 2.010113e-02
 x=0.040000 1-x=0.960000 Dilog=4.040728e-02 4.040916e-02
 x=0.060000 1-x=0.940000 Dilog=6.092484e-02 6.093142e-02
 x=0.080000 1-x=0.920000 Dilog=8.165959e-02 8.167569e-02
 x=0.100000 1-x=0.900000 Dilog=1.026178e-01 1.026503e-01
 x=0.120000 1-x=0.880000 Dilog=1.238060e-01 1.238641e-01
 x=0.140000 1-x=0.860000 Dilog=1.452313e-01 1.452967e-01
 x=0.160000 1-x=0.840000 Dilog=1.669008e-01 1.669585e-01
 x=0.180000 1-x=0.820000 Dilog=1.888223e-01 1.888708e-01
 x=0.200000 1-x=0.800000 Dilog=2.110038e-01 2.110506e-01
 x=0.220000 1-x=0.780000 Dilog=2.334539e-01 2.334930e-01
 x=0.240000 1-x=0.760000 Dilog=2.561817e-01 2.562173e-01
 x=0.260000 1-x=0.740000 Dilog=2.791967e-01 2.792221e-01
 x=0.280000 1-x=0.720000 Dilog=3.025090e-01 3.025363e-01
 x=0.300000 1-x=0.700000 Dilog=3.261295e-01 3.261511e-01
 x=0.320000 1-x=0.680000 Dilog=3.500696e-01 3.500874e-01
 x=0.340000 1-x=0.660000 Dilog=3.743415e-01 3.743569e-01
 x=0.360000 1-x=0.640000 Dilog=3.989583e-01 3.989722e-01
 x=0.380000 1-x=0.620000 Dilog=4.239338e-01 4.239469e-01
 x=0.400000 1-x=0.600000 Dilog=4.492830e-01 4.492960e-01
 x=0.420000 1-x=0.580000 Dilog=4.750219e-01 4.750356e-01
 x=0.440000 1-x=0.560000 Dilog=5.011677e-01 5.011756e-01
 x=0.460000 1-x=0.540000 Dilog=5.277391e-01 5.277480e-01
 x=0.480000 1-x=0.520000 Dilog=5.547561e-01 5.547612e-01
 x=0.500000 1-x=0.500000 Dilog=5.822405e-01 5.822468e-01
 x=0.520000 1-x=0.480000 Dilog=6.102161e-01 6.102242e-01
 x=0.540000 1-x=0.460000 Dilog=6.387087e-01 6.387134e-01
 x=0.560000 1-x=0.440000 Dilog=6.677466e-01 6.677533e-01
```

```
 x=0.580000 1-x=0.420000 Dilog=6.973611e-01 6.973650e-01
 x=0.600000 1-x=0.400000 Dilog=7.275863e-01 7.275885e-01
 x=0.620000 1-x=0.380000 Dilog=7.584605e-01 7.584640e-01
 x=0.640000 1-x=0.360000 Dilog=7.900260e-01 7.900280e-01
 x=0.660000 1-x=0.340000 Dilog=8.223305e-01 8.223340e-01
 x=0.680000 1-x=0.320000 Dilog=8.554274e-01 8.554294e-01
 x=0.700000 1-x=0.300000 Dilog=8.893776e-01 8.893787e-01
 x=0.720000 1-x=0.280000 Dilog=9.242507e-01 9.242528e-01
 x=0.740000 1-x=0.260000 Dilog=9.601267e-01 9.601278e-01
 x=0.760000 1-x=0.240000 Dilog=9.970991e-01 9.970997e-01
 x=0.780000 1-x=0.220000 Dilog=1.035278e+00 1.035279e+00
 x=0.800000 1-x=0.200000 Dilog=1.074795e+00 1.074795e+00
 x=0.820000 1-x=0.180000 Dilog=1.115808e+00 1.115809e+00
 x=0.840000 1-x=0.160000 Dilog=1.158516e+00 1.158517e+00
 x=0.860000 1-x=0.140000 Dilog=1.203168e+00 1.203168e+00
 x=0.880000 1-x=0.120000 Dilog=1.250088e+00 1.250088e+00
 x=0.900000 1-x=0.100000 Dilog=1.299715e+00 1.299715e+00
 x=0.920000 1-x=0.080000 Dilog=1.352675e+00 1.352675e+00
 x=0.940000 1-x=0.060000 Dilog=1.409928e+00 1.409929e+00
 x=0.960000 1-x=0.040000 Dilog=1.473126e+00 1.473126e+00
 x=0.980000 1-x=0.020000 Dilog=1.545800e+00 1.545800e+00
 enter z, n for polylog
.5 1
 x=0.500000 n=1 polylog=6.931471e-01
   iterations used=20
 enter z, n for polylog
.5 2
 x=0.500000 n=2 polylog=5.822405e-01
   iterations used=16
 enter z, n for polylog
.5 3
 x=0.500000 n=3 polylog=5.372132e-01
   iterations used=13
 enter z, n for polylog
0 0

C:\CMATHLIB\CMATH\S91 endpr
```

Test Output: Ritchie's Integral

```
 enter x for Ritchie integral
1
 ritchie(1.000000e+00)=6.051337e-01
 enter x for Ritchie integral
2
 ritchie(2.000000e+00)=3.543361e-01
 enter x for Ritchie integral
.5
 ritchie(5.000000e-01)=9.635605e-01
 enter x for Ritchie integral
.1
 ritchie(1.000000e-01)=2.165044e+00
 enter x for Ritchie integral
```

```
/*
Clebsh-Gordon, Wigner, related coefficients
from C Mathematical Function Handbook by Louis Baker
Copyright 1991 by Louis Baker. All rights reserved.

triangle   tests triangle inequality
DELTA      delta function (inline)
isint,notint   is the (type double) an integer?
m1e      -1^x

wigner()   wigner coef. efficient
      (minimal calls to gamma function)
Clebsh-Gordon   Clebsh-Gordon coef. calls wigner
wigner3j   3j symbol calls wigner.
wigner6j   wigner 6j calls racah.
Wigner6j   wigner 6j calls racah. more natural order of arg.
racah      W of Racah
V      V of Racah
X      X of Racah =Wigner9j
CG      Clebsh-Gordon calls V
Wigner9j   9j symbol uses Wigner6j

based upon: Racach Phys Rev 62 438 (1942) (W,V,X)
Angular Momentum, Brink & Satchler, Oxford U Press 1968 9j
Bethe & Jackwicz, Intermediate Quant. Mech &
Abramowitz&Stegun, wigner
Mizushima, Theor. Phys. Wiley,1972. 9j,special values
 */
#include "cmlib.h"
#include "protom.h"
#include <stdio.h>

#define ab(x) ((x)>0. ? (x):0.)
#define min(a,b) ((a)<(b)? (a):(b))
#define max(a,b) ((a)>(b)? (a):(b))
#define DELTA(a,b) ((a)==(b)?1.:0.)
#define tol  3.e-7
#define gamret 1.e60

int notint(x) double x;
{ double y;
y=x-((int)x);
return y==0.?0:1;
}
/* check if multiple of 1/2 ideally,use to chk all argu-
ments*/
int nothint(x) double x;
{ double y;
y=2.*x;
```

```
y=y-((int)y);
return abs(y)<tol?0:1;
}

double gam(x) double x;
{
int y;
y=x; if(!y)return gamret;
if( abs(x-(double)y)< tol && y<0)return gamret;
return gamma(x);
}

int triangle(j1,j2,j) double j1,j2,j;
{ if( abs(j1-j2)<=j && j<=(j1+j2))return 1;
return 0;
}

double m1e(x)double x;
{int j;
j=x;
if(x!=(double)j){fprintf(stderr," -1 to non-in-
teger=%f\n",x);return 0.;}
return (j%2)?-1.:1.;
}

/* Wigner or Clebsh-Gordon coef.*/
double wigner(j,j1,j2,m,m1,m2) double j,j1,j2,m,m1,m2;
{double coef,arg1,arg2,arg3,arg4,arg5,sum,term;
int k,kmin,kmax;
if(abs(m-m1-m2)>1.e-8) return 0.;
if(j2==0. && m2==0.) return  (j==j1 && m==m1)? 1.: 0.;
if( abs(m1)>j1 || abs(m2)>j2 || abs(m)>j ||
 j1+j2-j<0. || j1-j2+j <0. || j+j2-j1<0.) return 0.;
coef= sqrt((2.*j+1.)*gam(j1+m1+1.)*gam(j1-
m1+1.)*gam(j2+m2+1.)
 *gam(j2-m2+1.)*gam(j+m+1.)*gam(j-m+1.)
 *gam(j1+j2-j+1.)*gam(j+j1-j2+1.)*gam(j+j2-
j1+1.)/gam(j+j1+j2+2.));

 kmin=max(0,max(j2-j-m1,j1-j+m2));
 arg1=gam(j1+j2-j+1.-kmin);
 arg2=gam(j1-m1+1.-kmin);
 arg3=gam(j2+m2+1.-kmin);
 arg4=gam(j-j2+m1+1.+kmin);
 arg5=gam(j-j1-m2+1.+kmin);
 if(arg1==errorcode ||arg2==errorcode||arg3==error-
code||arg4==errorcode
 || arg5==errorcode) sum=0.;
 else sum= m1e((double)kmin)/(arg1*arg2*arg3*arg4*arg5);
```

```
/*printf(" coef=%e\n",coef);
printf(" k=0 sum=%e\n",sum);*/
if(sum!=0.)term=sum;
else {term=1.;
   if(arg1!=errorcode) term*=arg1;
   if(arg2!=errorcode) term*=arg2;
   if(arg3!=errorcode) term*=arg3;
   if(arg4!=errorcode) term*=arg4;
   if(arg5!=errorcode) term*=arg5;
/*printf(" arg %e %e %e %e
%e\n",arg1,arg2,arg3,arg4,arg5);*/
   term=1./term;
   }
/*printf(" term=%e\n",term);*/
kmax=min(j2+m2+1,min(j1+j2-j+1, j1+1-m1));
/*printf("kmin, kmax %d %d\n",kmin,kmax);*/
kmin++;
for(k=kmin;k<kmax;k++)
{
   arg1=(j-j2+m1+k);
   arg2=(j-j1-m2+k);
   if(arg1<=0.)arg1=1.;
   if(arg2<=0.)arg2=1.;
   term=-term*(j1+j2-j-k+1)*(j1-m1-k+1)*(j2+m2-
k+1)/(arg1*arg2*k);
/*printf(" arg1,2=%e %e term=%e sum=%e
\n",arg1,arg2,term,sum);*/

   sum+=term;
/*printf(" sum, term now %e %e\n",sum,term);*/
   if(abs(term)<=abs(sum)*tol)break;
   }
return sum*coef;
}

double ClebshGordon(j1,m1,j2,m2,j,m)double j,m,j1,m1,j2,m2;
{return wigner(j,j1,j2,m,m1,m2);}


/*wigner 3j coefficients*/
double wigner3j(j,j1,j2,m,m1,m2) double j,j1,j2,m,m1,m2;
{
if((m1+m2+m)!=0. || !triangle(j1,j2,j))return 0.;
return wigner(j,j1,j2,-m,m1,m2)/sqrt(2.*j+1.)*m1e(j1-j2-m);
}

double delta(a,b,c)double a,b,c;
{double value;
value= sqrt(ab(gam(a+b-c+1.)*gam(b+c-a+1.)*gam(a+c-b+1.)
```

```
   /gam(a+b+c+2.)));
return value;
}

double gammn(x) double x;
{if(x>0.)return gamma(x);return 0.;}

/* Racah W(abcd;ef)*/
double racah(a,b,c,d,e,f) double a,b,c,d,e,f;
{/* arguments:j1 j2 j3 j j12 j23 */
double coef,sum,sign;int k;
double z,zmin,zmax,q;
/* See Racah Phys. Rev 62 eqn 39 p.444 for triad sum condi-
tion*/

if(nothint(a)||nothint(b)||nothint(c)||nothint(d)|nothint(e)|
|nothint(f))
   {fprintf(stderr," Racah W:argument not n/2 \n");return
0.;}
if(notint(a+b+e)
||notint(c+d+e)||notint(a+c+f)||notint(b+d+f))
   {fprintf(stderr," Racah W: nonintegral triaad
sum\n");return 0.;}
if(!triangle(a,b,e) ||!triangle(c,d,e)||!tri-
angle(b,d,f)||!triangle(a,c,f))
   return 0.;
coef=delta(a,b,e)*delta(a,c,f)*delta(b,d,f)*delta(c,d,e);
/*printf(" coef %e\n",coef);*/
if(coef==0.)return 0.;
sum=0.;
zmax=min( a+b+c+d+1.,min(c+d-e,min(a+b-e,min(a+c-f,(b+d-
f)))))+1.;
/*zmin=  -max(e+f-a-d,e+f-b-c);*/
zmin=0.;
k=zmin;
sign= k%2?-1.:1.;
if( zmin==(double)k && zmin<0.){zmin=0.;sign=1.;}
/*printf(" zmin, zmax %e %e sign %e\n",zmin,zmax,sign);*/
for(z=zmin;z<=zmax;z+=1.)
   {sum+=q=sign*gammn(a+b+c+d+2.-z)/
      (gam(z+1.)*gam(e+f-a-d+z+1.)*gam(e+f-b-c+z+1.)
      *gam(a+b-e-z+1.)
      *gam(c+d-e-z+1.)*gam(a+c-f-z+1.)*gam(b+d-f-z+1.));
   if(abs(sum)<1.e-20 && zmin<0.)sum=0.;
   else sign=-sign;
   /*printf(" sum now %e z was %e term %e\n",sum,z,q);*/
   }

/*printf(" coef, sum %le %le\n",coef,sum);*/
```

```
return coef*sum;
}


/*  form of wigner 6-j symbol {  a b e  }
             c d f          */
double wigner6j(a,b,c,d,e,f) double a,b,c,d,e,f;
{return (((int)(a+b+c+d))%2?-1.:1.)*racah(a,b,d,c,e,f);}


/*  form of Wigner 6-j symbol {  a b c  }
             d e f
*/
double Wigner6j(a,b,c,d,e,f) double a,b,c,d,e,f;
{return (((int)(a+b+e+d))%2?-1.:1.)*racah(a,b,e,d,c,f);}

/* form of Wigner 9-j: { a b c }
          d e f
          g h i
*/
double Wigner9j(a,b,c,d,e,f,g,h,i)double a,b,c,d,e,f,g,h,i;
{double sum,k,coef,kmin,kmax,kinc,q;
sum=0.;
kmax=
abs(a)+abs(b)+abs(c)+abs(d)+abs(e)+abs(f)+abs(g)+abs(h)+abs(i
);
kmin=0.;kinc=1.;
for(k=kmin;k<=kmax;k+=kinc)/*increment k by one? kmin =0,1,
or smth else?*/
   {
   coef=1.;if((2.*k-((int)(2.*k)))!=0.)coef=-1.;
   sum+=q=(2.*k+1.)*coef*Wigner6j(a,b,c,f,i,k)
   *Wigner6j(d,e,f,b,k,h)*Wigner6j(g,h,i,k,a,d);
   }
return sum;
}

/* X should be Wigner9j*/
double X(a,b,c,d,e,f,g,h,i)double a,b,c,d,e,f,g,h,i;
{double sum,k,coef,kmin,kmax,kinc,q;
sum=0.;
kmax=
abs(a)+abs(b)+abs(c)+abs(d)+abs(e)+abs(f)+abs(g)+abs(h)+abs(i
);
/*kmax*=3.;*/
kmin=0.;/* was -kmax*/
kinc=1.;
for(k=kmin;k<=kmax;k+=kinc)
   {
```

```
   if(!triangle(k,a,i)||!triangle(k,d,h)||!tri-
angle(k,b,f))continue;
   sum+=q=(2.*k+1.)*racah(a,i,d,h,k,g)
   *racah(b,f,h,d,k,e)*racah(a,i,b,f,k,c);
   /*printf(" X k,q sum %le %le %le\n",k,q,sum);*/
   }
return sum;
}

/* V, CG based on Racah method in Bethe & Jacwitz*/
/* Racach V(a,b,c;A,B,C) */
double V(a,b,c,A,B,C) double a,b,c,A,B,C;
{double term,coef,sum,factor,p,q;int k;
if(notint(a+A)||notint(a-A)||notint(b+B)||notint(b-B)||
   notint(c+C)||notint(c-C)||
   notint(a+b-c)||notint(a+c-b)||notint(b+c-a))
   {fprintf(stderr," nontinegral sums in Racah V\n");return
0.;}
if((a+A)<0.||(a-A)<0.||(b+B)<0.||(b-B)<0.||
   (c+C)<0.||(c-C)<0.||
   (a+b-c)<0.||(a+c-b)<0.||(b+c-a)<0.){return 0.;}
/*if(abs(A)>a||abs(B)>b||abs(C)>c)return 0.;*/
coef= gam(a+b-c+1.)*gam(a-b+c+1.)*gam(b+c-
a+1.)/gam(a+b+c+2.)
   *gam(a+A+1.)*gam(a-A+1.)*gam(b+B+1.)*gam(b-B+1.)
   *gam(c+C+1.)*gam(c-C+1.);
sum=0.;factor=1.;
for(k=0;k<1000;k++)
   {
   p=1.+k;q=1.-k;
   term=factor/(gam(p)*gam(a+b-c+q)*gam(a-A+q)
   *gam(b+B+q)*gam(c-b+A+p)*gam(c-a-B+p));
   sum+=term;factor=-factor;
   if(abs(term)< 1.e-6*abs(sum))break;
   }
return sqrt(coef)*sum;
}

double CG(j1,j2,j,m1,m2,m)double j1,j2,j,m1,m2,m;
{
if(m!=(m1+m2)) return 0.;
return sqrt(2.*j+1.)*V(j1,j2,j,m1,m2,m);
}
```

```
/*
test driver wigner
from C Mathematical Function Handbook by Louis Baker
Copyright 1991 by Louis Baker. All rights reserved.
*/

#include <stdio.h>
#include "cmlib.h"
#include "protom.h"

#define ab(x) ((x)>0. ? (x):0.)
#define min(a,b) ((a)<(b)? (a):(b))
#define max(a,b) ((a)>(b)? (a):(b))
#define DELTA(a,b) ((a)==(b)?1.:0.)
#define tol  3.e-7

void main()
{double j,j1,j2,m,m1,m2; double sqrt();
double a,b,c,d,e,f,g,h,i;
while(1)
{
printf(" for Wigner enter j j1 j2 m m1 m2 j to break\n");
scanf("%le%le%le%le%le%le",&j,&j1,&j2,&m,&m1,&m2);
if(j<0.)break;
printf(" wigner=%e %e\n",wigner(j,j1,j2,m,m1,m2),wig-
ner3j(j,j1,j2,-m,m1,m2));
}
while(1)
{
printf(" for Clebsh j1 m1 j2 m2 j m j to break\n");
scanf("%le%le%le%le%le%le",&j1,&m1,&j2,&m2,&j,&m);
if(j<0.)break;
printf(" CG=%le %le\n",Clebsh-
Gordon(j1,m1,j2,m2,j,m),CG(j1,j2,j,m1,m2,m));
if(j==2.)
   {
   h=0.e20;
   if(j==.5 && m==.5 && j2==j1-.5&& m2==-.5-m1)
      h= m1e(j2-m1-.5)*sqrt((j2-
m1+.5)/((j2+1.)*(2.*j2+1.)));


   if(m==2.&&j2==j1-1.&& m2==2.-m1)
   h=m1e(j2+m1+1.)*sqrt(20.*(j2-1.+m1)*(j2
m1)*(j2+m1+1.)*(j2+m1+2.)/
   (2.*j2*(2.*j2+1.)*(2.*j2+2.)*(2.*j2+3.)*(2.*j2+4.)));
   else if(m==1.&&j2==j1-1. && m2==1.-m1)
      h=m1e(j2+m1)*2.*(j2+2.-2.*m1)*
      sqrt(5.*(j2+m1)*(m1+j2+1.)/
```

```
    (2.*j2*(2.*j2+1.)*(2.*j2+2.)*(2.*j2+3.)*(2.*j2+4.)));
   else if(m==0.&&j2==j1-1.&& m2==-m1)
   h=m1e(j2+m1)*2.*m1*sqrt(30.*abs(j2-m1+1.)

*(j2+m1+1.)/(2.*j2*(2.*j2+1.)*(2.*j2+2.)*(2.*j2+3.)*(2.*j2+4.
)));
   printf(" should be=%le\n",h);
   }
}
while(1)
{printf(" for racah enter a b c d e f a100 to break\n");
 scanf("%le%le%le%le%le%le",&a,&b,&c,&d,&e,&f);
 if(a<-100.)break;
printf(" racah %le 6j %le\n",racah(a,b,c,d,e,f),Wig-
ner6j(a,b,e,d,c,f));
printf(" a+c-f=%le\n",a+c-f);
if(e==.5)
   {if((b==a+.5)&&(d==c-.5))
      {printf("W=%le\n",m1e(a+c-f)*
         sqrt(ab((a-c+f+1.)*(f-a+c)
         /((2.*a+1.)*(2.*a+2.)*(2.*c)*(2.*c+1.)))));
      }
   if((b==a+.5)&&(d==c+.5))
      {printf("W=%le\n",m1e(a+c-f)*
         sqrt(ab((a+c+f+2.)*(a+c-f+1.)
         /((2.*a+1.)*(2.*a+2.)*(2.*c+2.)*(2.*c+1.)))));
      }


   }
if(e==1.)
   {if(b==a && c==d)
      {printf("W=%le\n",m1e(a+c+f-1.)*
         (a*(a+1.)+c*(c+1.)-f*(f+1.))

/sqrt(ab(4.*a*(a+1.)*(2.*a+1.)*c*(c+1.)*(2.*c+1.))));
      }
   if(b==a+1. && d==c-1.)
      {printf("W=%le\n",m1e(a+c-f)*
         sqrt(ab((f-a+c)*(f-a+c-1.)*(a-c+f+2.)*(a-c+f+1.)
         /(4.*(a+1.)*(2.*a+3.)*(2.*a+1.)*c*(2.*c-
1.)*(2.*c+1.)))));
      }
   if(b==a+1. && c==d)
      {printf("W=%le\n",m1e(a+c-f)*
         sqrt(ab((a+c+f+2.)*(a-c+f+1.)*(a+c-f+1.)*(c+f-a)

/(4.*(a+1.)*(2.*a+3.)*(2.*a+1.)*(c)*(2.*c+1.)*(c+1.)))));
      }
   if(b==a+1. && d==c+1.)
```

```
      {printf("W=%le\n",m1e(a+c-f)*
         sqrt(ab((a+c+f+3.)*(a+c+f+2.)*(a+c-f+2.)*(a+c-f+1.)

/(4.*(a+1.)*(2.*a+3.)*(2.*a+1.)*(2.*c+3.)*(2.*c+1.)*(c+1.))))
);
      }
   }
if(e==0.)
   {printf("W=%le\n",m1e(a+c-f)*
        (a==b?1.:0.)*(c==d?
1.:0.)/sqrt((2.*a+1.)*(2.*c+1.)));
   }
if(e==a+b)
   {printf("sb=%le
\n",sqrt(ab(gamma(2.*a+1.)*gamma(2.*b+1.)*gamma(a+b+c+d+2.)
   *gamma(a+b+c-d+1.)*gamma(a+b+d-c+1.)*gamma(c+f-
a+1.)*gamma(d+f-b+1.)/(
   gamma(2.*(a+b)+2.)*gamma(c+d-a-b+1.)*gamma(a+c-
f+1.)*gamma(a+f-c+1.)
   *gamma(a+c+f+2.)*gamma(b+d-f+1.)*gamma(b+f-
d+1.)*gamma(b+f+d+2.)
   ))));
   }
}

while(1)
   {printf(" enter abcde for Wigner6j ab0/cde a to
break\n");
   scanf("%le%le%le%le%le",&a,&b,&c,&d,&e);
   if(a<0.)break;
   printf("6j=%le ab0/cde=%le\n",Wigner6j(a,b,0.,c,d,e),

m1e(a+e+c)*DELTA(a,b)*DELTA(c,d)/sqrt((2.*a+1.)*(2.*c+1.)));
   g=a*(a+1.)+b*(b+1.)-c*(c+1.);
   printf(" 6j=%le aa1bbc=%le\n",Wigner6j(a,a,1.,b,b,c),
   -
g*m1e(a+b+c)/sqrt(a*(2.*a+1.)*(2.*a+2.)*b*(2.*b+1.)*(2.*b+2.)
));
   h=(2.*a-1.)*a*4.*(2.*a+1.)*(2.*a+2.)*(2.*a+3.)
   *(2.*b-1.)*b*(2.*b+1.)*(2.*b+2.)*(2.*b+3.);
   if(h>0.)h=m1e(a+b+c)*2.*(3.*g*(g-1.)-
4.*a*(a+1.)*b*(b+1.))/sqrt(h);
   else h=0.;
   printf("6j=%le aa2bbc=%le\n",Wigner6j(a,a,2.,b,b,c),h);
   }
while(1)
   {printf(" enter abcdefghi for Wigner9j  a to break\n");
   scanf("%le%le%le%le%le%le %le %le
%le",&a,&b,&c,&d,&e,&f,&g,&h,&i);
```

```
    if(a<0.)break;
    printf(" 9j=%le %le\n",
       Wigner9j(a,b,c,d,e,f,g,h,i),X(a,b,c,d,e,f,g,h,i));
    if(i==0.)
       {printf("=%le\n",Wig-
ner6j(a,b,c,e,d,g)/sqrt((2.*c+1.)*(2.*g+1.))
        *DELTA(g,h)*DELTA(f,c)*m1e(b+d+c+g));
       }
    }

}
```

```
Wigner sample output:
 for Wigner enter j j1 j2 m m1 m2 j to break
1.5 1 1.5 .5 -1 1.5
 wigner=-6.324555e-01 -3.162278e-01
 for Wigner enter j j1 j2 m m1 m2 j to break
-1 0 0 0 0 0
 for Clebsh j1 m1 j2 m2 j m j to break
1 -1 1.5 1.5 1.5 .5
 CG=-6.324555e-01 -6.324555e-01
 for Clebsh j1 m1 j2 m2 j m j to break
0 0 0 0  -1 0
 for racah enter a b c d e f a100 to break
1 1 1 1 1 1
 racah 1.666667e-01 6j 1.666667e-01
 a+c-f=1.000000e+00
W=1.666667e-01
 for racah enter a b c d e f a100 to break
-200 0 0 0 0 0
 enter abcde for Wigner6j ab0/cde a to break
1 1 1 1 1
6j=-3.333333e-01 ab0/cde=-3.333333e-01
 6j=1.666667e-01 aa1bbc=1.666667e-01
6j=1.666667e-01 aa2bbc=1.666667e-01
 enter abcde for Wigner6j ab0/cde a to break
2 1 1 1 1
6j=-0.000000e+00 ab0/cde=0.000000e+00
 6j=-2.236068e-01 aa1bbc=-2.236068e-01
6j=1.527525e-01 aa2bbc=1.527525e-01
 enter abcde for Wigner6j ab0/cde a to break
-1 0 0 0 0
 enter abcdefghi for Wigner9j  a to break
1 1 1 1 1 1 1 1 - 0
 9j=5.555555e-02 5.555555e-02
=5.555556e-02
 enter abcdefghi for Wigner9j  a to break
2 1 1 1 1 1 1 1 0
 9j=5.555555e-02 5.555555e-02
=5.555555e-02
 enter abcdefghi for Wigner9j  a to break
-1 0 0 0 0 0 0 0 0
```

Chapter 28

Scales of Notation

There is nothing in this chapter of Abramowitz and Stegun relevant to a mathematical function library. There are numerous packages of programs to calculate with arbitrary precision integer, rational, and real numbers, often to a variety of bases. There is a public domain, multiple precision package for the IBM-PC family, called UMBASIC, which is available on many bulletin boards. It is coded in assembly language, so it is not portable. *Mathematica*®, of course, will do arbitrary precision operations but it is neither public domain nor portable to arbitrary systems, although it is coded in C and available for a number of popular platforms. Dagonet software offers a package of C routines for such purposes. Write for details.

Chapter 29

C++ Programs

Chapter 29 of Abramowitz and Stegun dealt with Laplace transforms, which are of no interest here. Instead, we include a number of C++ packages. Operator overloading in C++ allows complex variables to be dealt with in a much simpler fashion than with the macros in file **complex.h.** Here, a class of complex numbers is defined in **complex.hpp**. This is used to write a number of packages for complex functions. One uses the arithmetic-geometric mean (AGM) method to evaluate elliptic functions for complex arguments and moduli. Others provide for the Hurwitz zeta function, the Lerch Phi Transcendent, the Meijer G function, and the generalized Hypergeometric function. A number of different implementations are given for the generalized Hypergeometric function, based upon a direct summation of the series and a summation method, based upon Pade or rational approximation. The Pade method is based on that discussed in Spanier and Oldham, and is used for the Hurwitz Zeta and Lerch Phi functions. It runs into problems for large numbers of terms, with the limit of 80 terms having been determined empirically on an 80387-based system. Other systems may have other limit values. The series method does not have the same difficulty, but is generally slower for similar parameters. Convergence is of course not guaranteed for all arguments for either implementation. See Erdelyi or Andrews for more discussion of the Meijer G function. The MacRobert E function is a special case of the Meijer G function. Spanier and Oldham discuss, in a section (Chapter 18) named Pochhammer's symbol, a vast number of functions that can be expressed as generalized Hypergeometric functions. They denote by the parameters K and L the number of Pochhammer symbols in the numerator and denominator, respectively. Each term in the series is similar to that of the generalized hypergeometric series, except that the factor of $n!$ is missing from the denominator. Because $n!=(1)_n$, we can easily convert between the two. Denoting their function by ${}_K G_L$, if we are given a formula for ${}_m F_n$ we may easily convert it to the form ${}_m G_{n+1}$ by adding the additional parameter 1 to the list of elements in the denominator. Conversely, we can convert ${}_K G_L$ to ${}_K F_{L-1}$ if one of the parameters in the list of L parameters is 1, or to ${}_{K+1} F_L$ if it is not by adding the parameter 1 to the list of parameters in the numerator. We include the Arithmetic-Geometric Mean method for application to Elliptic functions with complex modulus and argument. Finally, we include programs for Fock functions.

It is not our intention to teach coding in C++ in this chapter. The class definitions and associated headers for complex numbers, vectors, and matrices and the associated methods are described in my article in *C User's Journal.*

Hurwitz Zeta and Lerch Phi Transcendent

These are defined as in Chapter 23.

Methods

We provide two methods. A direct summation of the defining series is used. In addition, a modification of a method described in Spanier and Oldham and applied to a number of functions, including the Riemann zeta function, is provided as well. Their method forms a Pade or rational approximation to the sum. Note that, as remarked previously, difficulties were encountered due to overflows when more than a number of terms (approx. 80 on a PC with an 80387) were used. The principal modification to their method is to check for convergence and stop when the desired accuracy has been achieved.

Meijer G and Generalized Hypergeometric Functions

The generalized Hypergeometric function ${}_nF_m$ is defined as above. The other functions arise from attempts to generalize such functions meaningfully to cases in which $n > m + 1$. C. S. Meijer introduced the function

$$G^{m,n}_{p,q}\left(x\middle|\begin{matrix}a_1,a_2,\ldots\\c_1,c_2,\ldots\end{matrix}\right)=$$

$$\sum_{k=1}^{m} P\ {}_pF_{q-1}\,(1+c_k-a_1,\ldots,1+c_k-a_p\,;1+c_k-c_1,\ldots,1+c_k-c_q\,;(-1)^{p-m-n}x)$$

where :$1 \le m \le q$, no two of the c_k's differ by an integer (including zero), none of $a_k - c_k$ are positive integers, if $p = q$ we further require $|x| < 1$, and $P = \dfrac{\prod\limits_{j=1}^{m}{}'(c_j - c_k)\prod\limits_{j=1}^{n}(1 + c_k - a_j)}{\prod\limits_{j=m+1}^{p}(a_j - c_k)\prod\limits_{j=n+1}^{q}(1 + c_k - c_j)} x^{c_k}$, where the prime denotes that in the first product in the numerator the term for j = k is omitted.

The MacRobert E function, developed earlier than the G functions, has been generally superceded by it since it is a special case, $E(c_1,c_2,...c_q : a_1,...a_p : x) = G^{p,1}_{q+1,p}\left(x \middle| \begin{matrix} 1,a_1,a_2... \\ c_1,c_2... \end{matrix}\right)$

Methods

Series are used for the generalized Hypergeometric functions. The definitions of the G and E functions are used, along with the relation $G^{m,n}_{p,q}\left(1/x \middle| \begin{matrix} a_1,a_2,... \\ c_1,c_2,... \end{matrix}\right) = G^{n,m}_{q,p}\left(x \middle| \begin{matrix} 1-c_1,1-c_2,... \\ 1-a_1,1-a_2,... \end{matrix}\right)$, which may be used to transform a G function for p > q to one for which the opposite is true.

Elliptic Functions

We present here complex-arithmetic versions of the elliptic functions. This includes the functions of Chapters 16-18 as well as the Elliptic Exponential and its inverse, the Elliptic Logarithm. The latter is defined by $EL(a,b,x) = \int_{\infty}^{x} \frac{dt}{\sqrt{x^3 + ax^2 + bx}}$ and is therefore seen to be an elliptic integral. Note that one of the roots of the cubic is zero, and the other two may therefore be found by solving a quadratic.

Applications

See Chapters 16-18. The only functionality which the C routines of that chapter lack and the C++ routines possess is the ability to handle arbitrary, complex modulus *m*. Specifically, for the incomplete elliptic integral of the second kind, $E(\varphi,m)$, it is possible to handle negative *m*.

Methods

The AGM (see Chapter 16) is used. It was not possible to check the elliptic exponential and logarithm as desired (see Chapter 17), but the functions do appear to be inverses of one another. One should, nevertheless, proceed with caution in their application. In calculating the Jacobian Elliptic functions, it was found necessary to split the argument into its real and imaginary parts and use 16.21-1.-16.21.4 of Abramowitz and Stegun. Otherwise, overflows would quickly result in applying the AGM due to exponentials of arguments with positive real parts.

Note that we had to request more stack size than the default value (4K for TurboC). Obviously, whether or not this happens for this or other programs, and how one enlarges the stack area if necessary, are compiler- and machine-specific. Testing for stack overflow is a good idea on any machine.

Fock Functions

These functions are of interest in diffraction and scattering problems, including radar cross section work. They were developed by V. A. Fock in connection with the scattering of high-frequency electromagnetic radiation by convex bodies without sharp edges. Here, high-frequency means that the wavelength is small compared to the curvature of the body. In this regime, Fock showed that scattering can be analyzed "locally."

Recall from Chapter 10 that the Fock-type Airy functions are w_1 and w_2, which may be defined in terms of the more conventional Airy functions or as $w_1(\tau) = \frac{1}{\sqrt{\pi}} \int_{\infty e^{-2\pi/3\, i}}^{\infty} e^{\tau t - t^3/3}\, dt$, and $w_2(\tau) = \frac{1}{\sqrt{\pi}} \int_{\infty e^{2\pi/3\, i}}^{\infty} e^{\tau t - t^3/3}\, dt$. These functions are complex conjugates. Call the path of the first integral Γ_1 and that of the second Γ_2. Among the integrals of these functions of interest in scattering theory are:

$$u(\tau) = \frac{e^{i 3\pi/4}}{\sqrt{\pi}} \tau^{3/4} \int_{\Gamma_1} \frac{w'_2(t)}{w_2(t)} e^{-i\tau t}\, dt,$$

$$v(\tau) = \frac{e^{i\pi/4}}{2\sqrt{\pi}} \sqrt{\tau} \int_{\Gamma_1} \frac{w_2(t)}{w'_2(t)} e^{-i\tau t}\, dt$$

$$v_1(\tau) = \frac{e^{i 3\pi/4}}{\sqrt{\pi}} \tau^{3/4} \int_{\Gamma_1} \frac{w_2(t)}{w'_2(t)} e^{-i\tau t}\, t\, dt,$$

$$f(\tau) = \frac{1}{\sqrt{\pi}} \int_{\Gamma_1} \frac{1}{w_1(t)} e^{i\tau t}\, dt, \quad g(\tau) = \frac{1}{\sqrt{\pi}} \int_{\Gamma_1} \frac{1}{w'_1(t)} e^{i\tau t}\, dt,$$

$$\hat{p}(\tau) = \frac{1}{\sqrt{\pi}} \int_{-\infty}^{\infty} \frac{Ai(t)}{Bi(t) + i\,Ai(t)} \; e^{i \tau t} \, dt \,, \quad \hat{q}(\tau) = \frac{1}{\sqrt{\pi}} \int_{-\infty}^{\infty} \frac{Ai'(t)}{Bi'(t) + i\,Ai'(t)} \; e^{i \tau t} \, dt.$$

Note that some authors use capital letters for some of the functions. Some use definitions involving exp(i τ t) instead of exp(- i τ t), due to a different assumption concerning the time dependence of the incident fields. Be careful of such differences when applying these functions! For example, $\tilde{f}(\tau) = \frac{1}{\sqrt{\pi}} \int_{\Gamma_1} \frac{1}{w_2(t)} \; e^{-i \tau t} dt$ would be the complex conjugate of $f(\tau)$ and would be the function specified in treatments that assume an $e^{-i\omega t}$ behavior for the incident wave. Additionally, functions such as $p^*(x) = \hat{p}(x) + \frac{1}{2\sqrt{\pi x}}$, $q^*(x) = \hat{q}(x) + \frac{1}{2\sqrt{\pi x}}$, and

$$G(x) = \begin{cases} e^{-i x^3/3} \, \tilde{g}(x) & x \le 0 \\ \tilde{g}(x) & x > 0 \end{cases} , \quad \tilde{G}(x) = \begin{cases} e^{-i x^3/3} \, \tilde{f}(x) & x \le 0 \\ \tilde{f}(x) & x > 0 \end{cases}$$

are encountered. There do not seem to be standard names for these functions, although McNamara et al. suggest some. As noted in Chapter 10 concerning the applications to Airy functions near caustics, the approximations which underlie the Fock theory also apply only in the immediate vicinity of the shadow boundary. For details on the applications of these functions, see the references given below in the Methods section.

Methods

The fits and approximations in Lee and Safavi-Naini (for v_1) , Ruck, Barrick, Stuart and Kirchbaum, McNamara et al., are all used. See these books, and those by Fock and edited by Bowman et al., for discussions of the applications of these functions.

References

L. C. Andrews, *Special Functions for Engineers and Applied Mathematicians* (N. Y.: Macmillan, 1985).

L. Baker, "Complex Arithmetic and Matrices in C++," *C User's Journal*, **9**, 2, p.147, Feb. 1991.

Electromagnetic and Acoustic Scattering by Simple Shapes, (J. J. Bowman, T. B. A. Senior, P. L. E. Uslenghi, ed.), (N. Y.: Hemisphere Publishing Corp., 1987).

V. A. Fock, *Electromagntic Diffration and Propagation Problems* (N. Y.: Pergamon Press, 1965).

Higher Transcendental Functions, Vol. I, Bateman Manuscript Project (A. Erdelyi, ed.), (N. Y.: McGraw-Hill, 1953. Reprinted by R. E. Krieger, Malabar, FL, 1981).

S.-W. Lee, S. Safavi-Naini, *IEEE Trans. Antennas & Prop.*, **AP-26**, p.593, 1978.

D. A. McNamara, C. W. I. Pistorius, J. A. G. Malherbe, *Introduction to the Uniform Geometrical Theory of Diffraction* (Boston: Artech House, 1990).

G. T. Ruck, d. E. Barrick, W. D. Stuart, C. K. Kirchbaum, *Radar Cross Section Handbook* (N. Y.: Plenum Press, 1970).

J. Spanier and K. B. Oldham, *An Atlas of Functions* (N. Y.: Hemisphere Press, 1987).

```
// complex.hpp
#include <math.h>
#include <stdio.h>

class complex {
   protected:
      double x,y;
   public:
//       complex( double xx = 0., double yy = 0.) //create
//          { x=xx;y=yy;}
         complex( double xx , double yy = 0.) //create
          { x=xx;y=yy;}
         complex( ) //create
          { x=0.;y=0.;}
      inline void operator=(complex rvalue)
         {x=rvalue.x;y=rvalue.y;}
      inline void operator-=(complex rvalue)
         {x-=rvalue.x;y-=rvalue.y;}
      inline void operator+=(complex rvalue)
         {x+=rvalue.x;y+=rvalue.y;}
      inline void operator*=(complex rvalue)
         {
          *this=complex(rvalue.x*x-rvalue.y*y,
            rvalue.x*y+rvalue.y*x);
          //return *this;
         }
      inline void operator*=(double rvalue)
         {
         *this=complex(rvalue*x, rvalue*y);
         //return *this;
         }
      inline complex operator+(complex rvalue)
         {return complex(x+rvalue.x,y+rvalue.y);}
      inline complex operator-(complex rvalue)
         {return complex(x-rvalue.x,y-rvalue.y);}
      inline complex operator-() //unary minus
         {return complex(-x,-y);}
      inline complex operator*(complex rvalue)
         {return complex(
          rvalue.x*x-rvalue.y*y,
          rvalue.x*y+rvalue.y*x);}
      inline friend complex operator/(double dividend,
          complex divisor)
        { double temp;
        temp=1./(divisor.x*divisor.x+divisor.y*divisor.y);
       return complex((dividend*divisor.x)*temp,
             (-dividend*divisor.y)*temp);
       }
      inline complex operator/(complex divisor)
```

```
{
double temp;
temp=1./(divisor.x*divisor.x+divisor.y*divisor.y);
return
    complex((divisor.x*x+divisor.y*y)*temp,
    (divisor.x*y-divisor.y*x)*temp);
  }
inline int operator==(complex rvalue)
   {return (x==rvalue.x && y==rvalue.y);}
inline double real() {return x;}
inline double imaginary() {return y;}
inline complex conjugate()
   {return complex(x,-y);}
inline friend complex operator*
   (complex num,double real)
   {return complex(num.x*real,num.y*real);}
inline friend complex operator*(double real,complex
num)
   {return complex(num.x*real,num.y*real);}
inline friend complex operator+
   (complex num,double real)
   {return complex(num.x+real,num.y);}
inline friend complex operator+
   (double real,complex num)
   {return complex(num.x+real,num.y);}
inline complex operator+=(double real)
   {return complex(x+=real,y);}
inline complex operator-=(double real)
   {
   return complex(x-=real,y);}
inline complex operator++()
   {x+=1.;return *this;}
inline friend complex operator/
   (complex num,double real)
   {return complex(num.x/real,num.y/real);}
inline friend complex operator-
   (complex num,double real)
   {return complex(num.x-real,num.y);}
inline friend complex operator-
   (double real,complex num)
   {return complex(real-num.x,-num.y);}
double abs();
complex cexp();
complex clog();
complex csin(); complex ccos();
complex operator^(double expon);
complex operator^(complex expon);
friend complex operator^(double base,
  complex expon);
```

```
   void print( char *ahead="",char *behind="");
   complex hurwitz(complex );
};
```

```
/*
Elliptic functions
of Complex argument and modulus, using
Arithmetic-Geometric Mean (AGM)
from C Mathematical Function Handbook by Louis Baker
Copyright 1991 by Louis Baker. All rights reserved.

K,E : complete integrals of 1st, 2nd kind
F,E : same, of second kind,incomplete
Z Jacobi Zeta
scdn  Jacobian elliptic functions sn,cn,dn
heuman lambda
jacobi theta functions
neville theta functions

for scdn, the modulus m is given; in all other cases k
(m=k^2) is given
the angle phi in radians is first argument of the incom-
plete integrals and Z

*/
#include "Cmatrix.hpp"

#define maxterm 100
#define abstol 1.e-10
#define reltol 1.e-7
#define zerotol 1.e-14
#define tolphi 1.e-6
#define errorcode -1.e60
#define pi 3.14159265358979323846264338279
#define lim 15.
#define max(a,b) ((a)>(b)?(a):(b))
#define infinite_loop for(;;)
#define rabs(x) ((x)<0.? -(x):(x))

complex tangent ( complex& x);
complex tanh(complex& x);
complex sinh(complex& x);
complex asin(complex&x);
complex acos(complex&x);
complex arctan(complex&x);

complex csum;// used for E
complex Zsum;
//int incomplete;

complex agm( complex& a0,complex& b0,complex& c0)
{complex a,b,c,d;double p2=2.;
a=a0;b=b0;csum = c0*c0;
```

```
infinite_loop
   { c=(a-b)*.5;
   //b.print(" b=","\n");
   d=(a+b)*.5;b= (a*b)^.5 ;a=d;
   if ( c.abs() < abstol ) return a;
   // next two lines for computation of E(k) only
   csum += c*c*p2;
   p2*=2.;
   }
}

complex K(complex& k)
{
// k= sin alpha
complex a,b,c;
if( (k-pi*.5).abs() < zerotol ) return -errorcode;
a=1.;c=k; b= ( 1.- k*k) ^ .5 ;
return pi/(2.*agm( a,b,c));
}

complex E(complex& k)
{
// k= sin alpha
complex a,b,c,d;
a=1.;c=k; b= ( 1.- k*k) ^ .5 ;
d=K(k);
return  d*(1.-.5*csum );
}

int cutphipm=1;

complex F( complex& phi0,complex& k)
{complex
a,b,c,d,phi,dphi,pr,dphip,m,add,mult(1.,0.),m2(1.,0.);
double p2=2.,dif,newdif;
 int m2p=0,ins;//nq=0,ios=1,i4=0;
 complex or; double reler=1.e20;//oreler=1.e20;
m=k*k;
if(phi0.real()>=0.)
   {
   phi=phi0;
   m2=1.;
   }
else
   {
   phi=-phi0;m2=-1.;
   }
dif=phi.real();
// reduce phi
```

```
if(cutphipm)
   {
   ins= (dif/pi);
   dif -= ins*pi;
   if(dif>  .5*pi) {ins++;dif-=pi;}
   if(dif< -.5*pi) {ins--;dif+=pi;}
   if( rabs(dif)> .5*pi)
      fprintf(stderr," F wrong phi reduction %le\n",dif);
   add=2.*ins*K(k);
   }
if( dif<0.)
   {
   dif=-dif;mult=-1.;
   }
phi=complex( dif, phi.imaginary());
// PBLM  if phi0= pi/2. use complete integral
if(phi.abs() < zerotol ) return complex(0.,0.);
if((phi- .5*pi).abs() < zerotol)
      {
      Zsum= 0.;
      return K(k);
      }
// reduce m
// Zsum will not be computed for the given phi and m
// hence cannot allow m reduction for cases where Z or E
needed
/*
if(cutphipm)
   {
   a= 1.+m;
   if( (m).abs() > 1.)
      {
      b= 1./k;
      c=k;//c=sqrt(m);
      a= asin( c * phi0.csin() );
      // Zsum will be modified
      return F(a,b)/c;
      }

   if( m.real() <0.)
      {
      a= 1.-m;//(1+m) if arg -m
      b= -m/a; m/(1+m)
      c= 1./(a^.5);
      d=b^.5;
      //Zsum will be modified
      return c*(K(d)-F( pi*.5-phi0,d) );
      }
   }
```

```
*/
a=1.; b= ( 1.- m ) ^ .5 ;Zsum= 0.;//c0 irrelevant;
//m.print(" m for F=","\n");
//k.print(" k for F=","\n");phi.print(" phi for F=","\n");
infinite_loop
   { c=(a-b)*.5;
//b.print(" b=","\n");
   dphi=    arctan(b/a* tangent(phi));
//dphi.print(" dphi=","\n");
//phi.print(" phi=","\n");
dphip=dphi;

//dphip.print("before while dphi=","\n");
while ( dphip.real()<(phi.real()-2.*pi)){m2p++;dphip +=
2.*pi;}
//dphip.print("after while dphi=","\n");
if( dphip.real()<(phi.real()-pi)){dphip += pi;}
//dphip.print("after if1 dphi=","\n");
dif= rabs(phi.real()-dphip.real() );
newdif= rabs(phi.real()-dphip.real()-pi );
if( newdif<dif) dphip +=pi;
//dphip.print(" actual dphi used=","\n");
   phi +=dphip;
   or=pr;//oreler=reler;

   d=(a+b)*.5;b= (a*b)^.5 ;a=d;
   reler=(phi-2.*dphip).abs();
   //if ( (c.abs()  abstol) && reler  tolphi ) break;
   if ( (c.abs() < abstol) ) break;
   //for E
   Zsum += c * phi.csin();
//c.print(" c=","\n");
//phi.print(" phi=","\n");
//Zsum.print(" zsum now=","\n");
   p2*=2.;

   }
// Z= Zsum  = E- (E/K)*F .  E= csum+ (E/K) F () are complete
reler=(phi-2.*dphip).abs();
if( reler > 1.e-4)
   fprintf(stderr,"F:poor convergence of phi %le\n",reler);
Zsum= (m2*mult)*Zsum;
return  m2*(phi/(p2*a)*mult+add);
}

complex Z(complex& phi,complex& k)
{complex dum;int savpm;
savpm=cutphipm;
cutphipm=0;
```

```
dum= F(phi,k);
cutphipm=savpm;
return Zsum;
}

/* we overload the name E*/

complex E(complex& phi,complex& k)
{complex f,term,total;int savpm;
savpm=cutphipm;
cutphipm=0;
f= F(phi,k);
//f.print(" F again"," ");phi.print(" for phi="," ");
//k.print(" k=","\n");
term=f*E(k)/K(k);
total=Zsum+term;
cutphipm=savpm;
return total;
}

complex jtheta,amplitude;

complex argm( complex& u, complex& m)
{
double bigk,q,p;complex bk; int n;
// would it be safe to do this kind of reduction for other
m?
//also, desirable to do split sn(x+iy), etc.
// to avoid u.cexp() blowing up
if( rabs(m.imaginary()) < zerotol && rabs(m.real())<1.)
   {
   bk=(1.-m)^.5;
   bk=K(bk);
   bigk=bk.real()*4.;
   q=u.imaginary();
   n= q/bigk;
   q-=n*bigk;
   p=u.real();
   bk=K(m^.5);
   bigk=bk.real()*4.;
   n= p/bigk;
   p-= n*bigk;
   bk=(1.-m)^.5;
   bk= K( bk);
   if( (u-bk*complex(0.,1.)).abs()< zerotol)
      return errorcode;
   return complex(p,q);
   }
else return u;
```

```
}


#define NAGM 40

void scdns( complex& u,complex& m,complex& sn,complex&
cn,complex& dn)
{
int i,l,n;
complex a[ NAGM ],c[ NAGM ],phi[ NAGM ],v,am,am1,b,argu,t;
double tol=1.e-7;
/* Jacobian theta function valid for all real m<=1 */
double twon; complex term,k,sum,lou,sqrtm1;
//printf(" entered scnd\n");
//if(m)
//                  {/* A&S 16.10.1-4*/
//                  t=-m;mu= t/(1.+t);mu1=1./(1.+t);
                k=sqrt(mu1);v=u/k;
//                  jef(v,mu,&term,&sum,&lou);
//                  *dn= 1./lou;
//                  *sn= k* term* *dn;
//                  *cn= sum* *dn;
//                  return;
//                  }
//if(m1.)
//                  { /* A&S 16.11.1-4*/
//                  mu=1./m; k=sqrt(mu);v=u/k;
//                  jef(v,mu,&term,&sum,&lou);
//                  *sn=k*term;
//                  *cn=lou;
//                  *dn=sum;
//                  return;
//                  }
//v=argm(u,m);
v=u;
if ( v.real()==errorcode)
   {sn=errorcode; cn=sn; dn=sn;
   jtheta=errorcode;
   return ;
   }
am=m;
if(m.abs()==0.)
   {
   sn=v.csin();
   cn=v.ccos();
   dn=complex(1.,0.);
   jtheta=0.;//q=1.
   fprintf(stderr," m==0 return\n");
   return;
```

```
    }
else if(m.real()==1. && m.imaginary() == 0.)
    {
    sn=tanh(v);
    cn=1./  sinh(v);
    dn=cn;
    jtheta=0.;
//q=1 using 1+2 sum from 1 to inf -1^k coskz,z=2theta
// Jolley 429
    fprintf(stderr," m==1 return\n");
    return;
    }
am1=1.-am;
a[0]=1.;
sqrtm1=(am1)^.5;
b=sqrtm1;
/*c[0]=sqrt(m);not used anywhere*/
for(i=1;i< NAGM;i++)
    {
    a[i]=.5*(a[i-1]+b);
     if( (a[i]).abs()< zerotol)
        {
        fprintf(stderr," scdn: a[i] vanishing for i=%d\n",i);
        break;
        }
    c[i]=.5*(a[i-1]-b);
    if((c[i]).abs()<tol)break;
    b=(b*a[i-1])^.5;
    }
n=i;
//printf("scdn: n=%d\n",n);
twon=pow(2., (double)(n));

phi[n]=a[n]*v* twon;
sum=0.;
term= .5/twon;
//term.print(" first term","\n");
for(i=n;i>0;i--)
    {
    if( (a[i]).abs()<zerotol)
        {
        //printf(" scdn a[%d]=0\n",i);
        }
//(a[i]).print(" a=","\n");
//(c[i]).print(" c=","\n");
//(phi[i]).print(" phi=","\n");
//((phi[i]).csin()).print(" csin=","\n");
    argu=c[i]*(phi[i]).csin()/a[i];
//argu.print(" argu=","\n");
```

```
   t= asin(argu);
   phi[i-1]=.5*(t+phi[i]);
   sum-= term* ((2.*phi[i-1]-phi[i]).ccos()).clog();
   term*=2.;
//sum.print(" sum=","\n");
   }

argu=phi[0]; amplitude=argu;
//argu.print(" amplitude(argu)=","\n");
sn=argu.csin();
cn=argu.ccos();
lou= (phi[1]-argu).ccos();
//lou.print(" lou=","\n");
if( lou.abs() < zerotol)
   dn= errorcode;
else dn= cn/lou;
//tek(0,m,&k,&term);
k= K( m^.5 );
term= argu.ccos();
//term.print(" term now=","\n");
if( term.abs() < zerotol)
   {
   jtheta=errorcode;
   }
else
   {
   jtheta=sum+.5* (2.*sqrtm1/pi*k * lou/ (term)).clog();
   jtheta=jtheta.cexp();
   }
//jtheta.print(" scdn: returning jtheta","\n");
}

void scdn( complex& u,complex& m,complex& sn,complex&
cn,complex& dn)
{
complex s1,c1,d1,s,c,d,x,y,dnom,i(0.,1.),amps;
x= u.real();
y=complex(u.imaginary(),0.);
scdns(x,m,s,c,d);amps=amplitude;
dnom= 1.-m;
scdns(y,dnom,s1,c1,d1);
if( rabs(u.real())<zerotol)amps=i*amplitude;
dnom=1./( c1*c1+m*s*s*s1*s1);
sn= dnom*( s*d1+i*c*d*s1*c1);
cn= dnom*( c*c1-i*s*d*s1*d1);
dn= dnom*( d*c1*d1-i*m*s*c*s1);
// cannot return amps for complex argument! jtheta also not
reliable
```

```
if( rabs(u.real())>zerotol && rabs(u.imagi-
nary())>zerotol)amps=errorcode;
return ;
}

complex heuman(complex& phi,complex& k)
{
complex m,e,ff,ee,kk,kp,m1; m=k*k;m1=1.-m;kp=m1^.5;
kk=K(k);e=E(k);
ff=F(phi, kp);
ee=E(phi, kp);
return 2./pi*(kk*ee-(kk-e)*ff);
}

void theta(complex& v,complex& m,
complex& t1,complex& t2,complex& t3,complex& t4)
{
complex sn,cn,dn,bigk,k,kp,u,srk,srkp;
k=m^.5;
bigk=K(k);
u=2.*bigk*v/pi;
scdns(u,m,sn,cn,dn);
if (jtheta.real()==errorcode)
   {
   t1=complex(errorcode,errorcode);
   t2=t1;t3=t1;t4=t1;
   return;
   }
kp=(1.-m)^.5;srk=(k)^.5;srkp=(kp)^.5;
t1= sn*srk*jtheta;
t2=cn*srk/srkp*jtheta;
t3=dn/srkp*jtheta;
t4=jtheta;
}

void neville(complex& u,complex& m,
complex& ts,complex& tc,complex& td,complex& tn)
{
complex v,bigk,t1,t2,t3,t4,t10,t20,t30,t40,k;
k=m^.5;
bigk=K(k);
v=u*pi/(2.*bigk);
theta(v,m,t1,t2,t3,t4);
if (t1.real()==errorcode)
   {
   ts=complex(errorcode,errorcode);
   tc=ts;td=ts;tn=ts;
   return;
   }
```

```
theta(complex(0.,0.),m,t10,t20,t30,t40);
ts=t1*bigk*2./(pi*t20*t30*t40);
tc=t2/t20;
td=t3/t30;
tn=t4/t40;
}
```

```
/*
Elliptic functions of Complex argument and modulus, using
Arithmetic-Geometric Mean (AGM)- Supplemental

from C Mathematical Function Handbook by Louis Baker
Copyright 1991 by Louis Baker. All rights reserved.

Weiererstrass
InvWeier
ElExp
ElLog

*/
#include "Cmatrix.hpp"
#include <stdio.h>

#define maxterm 100
#define abstol 1.e-10
#define reltol 1.e-5
#define zerotol 1.e-14
#define errorcode -1.e60
#define pi 3.141592653589793238462643383279
#define lim 15.
#define max(a,b) ((a)>(b)?(a):(b))
#define infinite_loop for(;;)
#define rabs(x) ((x)<0.? -(x):(x))

complex tangent ( complex& x);
complex tanh(complex& x);
complex sinh(complex& x);
complex asin(complex&x);
complex acos(complex&x);
complex arctan(complex&x);
complex F( complex& phi0,complex& k);
void scdn( complex& ui,complex& m,complex& sn,complex&
cn,complex& dn);

struct cmplx { double x,y;};
extern "C" ccubic(struct cmplx *,struct cmplx *,struct
cmplx *,
   struct cmplx *,struct cmplx *,struct cmplx *);
extern "C" solvq(struct cmplx *,struct cmplx *,
      struct cmplx *,struct cmplx *);

void croots(complex& a,complex& b, complex& c,
   complex& b1, complex& b2, complex& b3)
   {
   struct cmplx a1,a2,a3,r1,r2, r3;
   a1.x=a.real();a1.y=a.imaginary();
```

```
   a2.x=b.real();a2.y=b.imaginary();
   a3.x=c.real();a3.y=c.imaginary();
   ccubic(&a1,&a2,&a3,&r1,&r2,&r3);
   b1=complex(r1.x,r1.y);
   b2=complex(r2.x,r2.y);
   b3=complex(r3.x,r3.y);
   }

void qroots(complex& a,complex& b,
   complex& b1, complex& b2)
   {
   struct cmplx a1,a2,r1,r2;
   a1.x=a.real();a1.y=a.imaginary();
   a2.x=b.real();a2.y=b.imaginary();
   solvq(&a1,&a2,&r1,&r2);
   b1=complex(r1.x,r1.y);
   b2=complex(r2.x,r2.y);
   }

//

complex Weierstrass(complex& x, complex& g2, complex& g3)
{
complex r1,r2,r3,a1,a2,a3,lambda,m,phi,k,beta,sn,cn,dn;
int rr=0;
a1=0.;a2=-.25*g2;a3=-.25*g3;
croots(a1,a2,a3,r1,r2,r3);
//r1.print("r1=","\n");r2.print("r2=","\n");r3.print("r3=","\
n");
if( rabs(r2.imaginary()) < zerotol )
   {
   rr++;
   }
if( rabs(r1.imaginary()) < zerotol )
   {
   beta=r2; r2=r1;r1=beta;rr++;
   }
if( rabs(r3.imaginary()) < zerotol )
   {
   beta=r3; r3=r2;r2=beta;rr++;
   }
// below real m 1 real, 2 conj. roots r2=real root
//printf(" %d real roots\n",rr);
if(rr!= 1) goto alt;
beta=r2;
phi=( a2+(beta*(a1*2.+3.*beta) ))^.5;
lambda= phi^.5;
if(phi.abs() > zerotol )
   {
```

```
   m=(.5-.125*(6.*beta+2.*a1)/phi);
   if( rabs(m.imaginary()) < abstol ) m=complex(
m.real(),0.);
   //m.print("m=","\n");
   x= -2.* x*lambda;
   //x.print("x=","\n");
   scdn(x,m,sn,cn,dn);
   // cn= cos phi. want x
   //cn.print(" cn=","\n");
   return (beta + phi*(1.+cn)/(1.-cn));
   }
alt:
//below real m  for 3 real roots or none
if( (x-r3).abs() > zerotol && (r1-r3).abs()>zerotol)
 goto   ok;
else
   {
   lambda=r1;r1=r3;r3=lambda;
   }
if( (x-r3).abs() > zerotol && (r1-r3).abs()>zerotol)
 goto ok;
else
   {
   lambda=r2;r2=r3;r3=lambda;
   }
if( (x-r3).abs() > zerotol && (r1-r3).abs()>zerotol)
 goto ok;
fprintf(stderr, " trouble in Weierstrass\n");
return complex(errorcode,errorcode);

ok:
// (for all real roots) r1r2r3
r1.print("r1=","\n");
r2.print("r2=","\n");
r3.print("r3=","\n");
if( r1.real()<r2.real())
   {lambda=r1;r1=r2;r2=lambda;}
if( r2.real()<r3.real())
   {lambda=r2;r2=r3;r3=lambda;}
if( r1.real()<r2.real())
   {lambda=r1;r1=r2;r2=lambda;}
//printf(" alternative method Weierstrass\n");
//r1.print("r1=","\n");
//r2.print("r2=","\n");
//r3.print("r3=","\n");
lambda= ((r1-r3)^.5) *.5;
//lambda.print(" lambda=","\n");
m= (r2-r3)/(r1-r3);
//m.print("alternative m=","\n");
```

```
k=m^.5;
phi= -x*lambda*2.;
scdn(phi,m,sn,cn,dn);
//k= beta + phi*(1.+cn)/(1.-cn);
lambda= r3+(r1-r3)/(sn*sn);//byrd and friedman 238
return lambda;
}

complex ElLog(complex& x, complex& a, complex& b)
{
complex r1,r2,r3,a1,a2,a3,lambda,m,phi,k;
a1=a;a2=b;a3=0.;
//croots(a1,a2,a3,r1,r2,r3);
r3=complex(0.,0.);
qroots(a,b,r1,r2);
if( (x-r3).abs() > zerotol && (r1-r3).abs()>zerotol)
 goto ok;
else
   {
   lambda=r1;r1=r3;r3=lambda;
   }

if( (x-r3).abs() > zerotol && (r1-r3).abs()>zerotol)
 goto ok;
else
   {
   lambda=r2;r2=r3;r3=lambda;
   }
if( (x-r3).abs() > zerotol && (r1-r3).abs()>zerotol)
 goto ok;
fprintf(stderr, " trouble in ElLog\n");
return complex(errorcode,errorcode);
ok:
phi= ((x-r1)/(x-r3))^.5;// cos phi
phi= acos(phi);
lambda= ((r1-r3)^.5) *.5;
m= (r2-r3)/(r1-r3); k= m^.5;
return (- F(phi,k)/lambda);
}


complex InvWeier(complex& x, complex& g2, complex& g3)
{
complex r1,r2,r3,a1,a2,a3,lambda,m,phi,beta,k,lou;

a1=0.;a2=-.25*g2;a3=-.25*g3;
croots(a1,a2,a3,r1,r2,r3);
//r1.print("r1=","\n");r2.print("r2=","\n");
//r3.print("r3=","\n");
```

```
if( (x-r3).abs() > 1.e-20) goto ok;
else
   {
   lambda=r1;r1=r3;r3=lambda;
   }

if( (x-r3).abs() > 1.e-20) goto ok;
else
   {
   lambda=r2;r2=r3;r3=lambda;
   }
if( (x-r3).abs() > 1.e-20) goto ok;
fprintf(stderr, " trouble in InvWeierstrass\n");
return complex(errorcode,errorcode);
ok:
//phi= ((x-r1)/(x-r3))^.5;// cos phi
//phi= acos(phi);
//lambda= ((r1-r3)^.5) *.5;
//m= (r2-r3)/(r1-r3);
beta=r2;
phi=( a2+(beta*(a1*2.+3.*beta) ))^.5;
//phi.print(" lambda^2=phi=","\n");
lambda= phi^.5;
m=(.5-.125*(6.*beta+2.*a1)/phi);
if( rabs(m.imaginary()) < abstol )
   m=complex( m.real(),0.);
//m.print("m=","\n");
lou=(x-beta+phi);
//lou.print(" denom=","\n");
if( lou.abs()<zerotol)
   {
   return errorcode;
   }
phi= acos( (x-beta-phi)/lou);
//phi.print("phi=","\n");
k=m^.5;
return (.5* F(phi,k)/lambda);
}

complex ElExp(complex& Q, complex& a, complex& b)
{
complex r1,r2,r3,a1,a2,a3,lambda,m,x,sn,cn,dn;
a1=a;a2=b;a3=0.;
//croots(a1,a2,a3,r1,r2,r3);
r3=complex(0.,0.);
qroots(a,b,r1,r2);
if( (x-r3).abs() > 1.e-20) goto ok;
else
   {
```

```
    lambda=r1;r1=r3;r3=lambda;
    }

if( (x-r3).abs() > 1.e-20) goto ok;
else
    {
    lambda=r2;r2=r3;r3=lambda;
    }
if( (x-r3).abs() > 1.e-20) goto ok;
fprintf(stderr, " trouble in ElExp\n");
return complex(errorcode,errorcode);
ok:
//phi= ((r2-r1)/(x-r3))^.5;// cos phi
//phi= acos(phi);
lambda= ((r1-r3)^.5) *.5;
m= (r2-r3)/(r1-r3);
x= -Q*lambda;
scdn(x,m,sn,cn,dn);
//x= beta + phi*(1.+cn)/(1.-cn);
x= r3+(r1-r3)/(sn*sn);
return x;
}
```

```
/*
Test driver for: Elliptic functions
of Complex argument and modulus, using
Arithmetic-Geometric Mean (AGM)

from C Mathematical Function Handbook by Louis Baker
Copyright 1991 by Louis Baker. All rights reserved.

*/
#include "Cmatrix.hpp"

#define maxterm 100
#define abstol 1.e-10
#define reltol 1.e-5
#define errorcode -1.e60
#define pi 3.141592653589793238462643383279
#define lim 15.
#define max(a,b) ((a)>(b)?(a):(b))
#define infinite_loop for(;;)

extern unsigned _stklen= 54321U;

extern complex csum;// used for E
extern complex Zsum;
//int incomplete;
complex agm( complex& ,complex& ,complex& );
complex F( complex& ,complex& );
complex K(complex& );
complex E(complex& );
complex Z(complex& ,complex& );
complex E(complex& ,complex& );
extern complex jtheta,amplitude;
void scdn( complex& ,complex& ,complex& ,complex& ,
complex& );

complex heuman(complex& phi,complex& m);
void theta(complex& v,complex& m,
complex& t1,complex& t2,complex& t3,complex& t4);

void neville(complex& u,complex& m,
complex& ts,complex& tc,complex& td,complex& tn) ;

complex Weierstrass( complex&, complex&, complex&);
complex InvWeier( complex&, complex&, complex&);
complex ElLog( complex&, complex&, complex&);
complex ElExp( complex&, complex&, complex&);

main()
{  complex z,phi,s,c,d,t1,t2,t3,t4;double x,y;
```

```
   complex u;

infinite_loop
   {printf(" K&E,etc.:enter complex k");
   scanf("%le%le",&x,&y);z=complex(x,y);
   if(x==0. && y==0.)break;
   K(z).print(" K=","\n");
   E(z).print(" E=","\n");
   printf(" enter complex
phi");scanf("%le%le",&x,&y);phi=complex(x,y);
   F(phi,z).print(" F=","----------------------\n");
   printf(" 2nd; incomplete\n");
   E(phi,z).print(" E(phi,k)=","-----------------\n");
   //phi.print(" Z for phi=","\n");
   Z(phi,z).print(" Z=","------------------\n");
   //z.print(" z for heuman lambda=\n","--------------\n");
   //phi.print(" phi for heuman lambda=\n","--------------
\n");
   heuman(phi,z).print(" heuman lambda=","\n");
   }
infinite_loop
   {printf(" Jacobi:enter complex m (not k)");
   scanf("%le%le",&x,&y);z=complex(x,y);
   if(x==0. && y==0.)break;
   printf(" enter complex u");scanf("%le%le",&x,&y);phi=com-
plex(x,y);
   phi.print(" phi=","\n");
   scdn(phi,z,s,c,d);
   s.print(" sn=","\n");
   c.print(" cn=","\n");
   d.print(" dn=","\n");
   jtheta.print(" jtheta=","\n");
   amplitude.print(" amplitude=","\n");
   }
infinite_loop
   {printf(" theta functions:enter complex k");
   scanf("%le%le",&x,&y);z=complex(x,y);
   if(x==0. && y==0.)break;
   printf(" enter complex v
");scanf("%le%le",&x,&y);phi=complex(x,y);
   phi.print(" phi=","\n");
   theta(phi,z,t1,t2,t3,t4);
   t1.print(" t1=","\n");
   t2.print(" t2=","\n");
   t3.print(" t3=","\n");
   t4.print(" t4=","\n");
   u=z*z;//m=k^2
   phi.print(" phi=","\n");
   u.print(" m=","\n");
```

```
   neville(phi,u,t1,t2,t3,t4);
   t1.print(" neville t1=","\n");
   t2.print(" neville t2=","\n");
   t3.print(" neville t3=","\n");
   t4.print(" neville t4=","\n");
   }

infinite_loop
   {printf(" Weierstrass: enter complex g2 g3 x");
   scanf("%le%le",&x,&y);
   t2=complex(x,y);
   scanf("%le%le",&x,&y);
   t3=complex(x,y);
   scanf("%le%le",&x,&y);
   z=complex(x,y);
   if(x==0. && y==0.)break;
   u=Weierstrass(z,t2,t3);
   u.print("Weierstrass=","\n");
   z=InvWeier(u,t2,t3);
   z.print(" Inverse Weierstrass=","\n");
   //u=ElLog(z,t2,t3);
   //u.print("EllipticLogarithm=","\n");
   //z=ElExp(u,t2,t3);
   //z.print("EllipticExponential=","\n");
   }
infinite_loop
   {
   printf(" EllipticLog/Exp: enter complex a,b,x");
   scanf("%le%le",&x,&y);
   t2=complex(x,y);
   scanf("%le%le",&x,&y);
   t3=complex(x,y);
   scanf("%le%le",&x,&y);
   z=complex(x,y);
   if(x==0. && y==0.)break;
   u=ElLog(z,t2,t3);
   u.print("EllipticLogarithm=","\n");
   z=ElExp(u,t2,t3);
   z.print("EllipticExponential=","\n");
   }
}
```

```
// Cvector.hpp
#include <stdlib.h>
#include "Complex.hpp"
static complex *present;

class Cvector {
   protected:
   public:
      int size,base;
      complex *head;
Cvector::Cvector( int s=1 , int b=0 , complex initvalue=
(0.,0.) )
         //constructor
         {
         head= new complex[s];
         base=b;
           for(size=0,present=head;size<s;
            size++,present++) *present = initvalue;
           size=s;
//                   printf(" Cvector built\n");
         }
      Cvector( Cvector&);    //copy
      ~Cvector()//destructor
         {
         delete head; //printf(" Cvector axed\n");
         }
      void operator=( Cvector& rhs);
      complex operator*(Cvector& rvalue);//dot product
      inline int length()
         {return size;}
      inline complex& elemnt( int i)
         {return head[i-base];}
      inline void setelemnt( int i, complex& value)
         {head[i-base]=value;}
      void check(int);
      complex& element(int i);
      void setelement(int i, complex& value);
   };
```

```
//cmatrix.hpp

#include "cvector.hpp"

class Cmatrix  {

private:
   void init(int row=1,int col=1,int b=0);
public:
   complex** m;
   int rowkt,colkt,base;

   Cmatrix(int rowkt,int colkt,int b)
      { init( rowkt, colkt, b);} //constructor
   Cmatrix() {init();}        //  "
   Cmatrix( Cmatrix&);        // init
        ~Cmatrix();           // destructor
   void operator=(Cmatrix& );
   inline complex& elemnt(int i,int j)
      {return m[i-base][j-base];}
   void check(int,int);
   complex& element(int,int);
   inline void setelemnt(int i,int j,complex value)
      {m[i][j]=value;   }
   void setelement(int,int, complex);
   friend Cmatrix operator*(Cmatrix&,Cmatrix&);
//Mat*Mat
   friend Cvector operator*(Cmatrix&,Cvector&);
//Mat*Vector
};
```

Test Output: Elliptic functions

```
 K&E,etc.:enter complex k.9486883298 0
 K= 2.578137e+00+-0.000000e+00 i
 E= 1.104767e+00+-0.000000e+00 i
 enter complex phi1.8
0
 F= 3.255798e+00+0.000000e+00 i ---------------------
 2nd, incomplete
 E(phi,k)= 1.182555e+00-1.220060e-18 i -----------------
 Z= -2.125989e-01+0.000000e+00 i -----------------
 heuman lambda= 1.130833e+00+0.000000e+00 i
 K&E,etc.:enter complex k0 1.4142
 K= 1.171424e+00+-0.000000e+00 i
 E= 2.184428e+00+-0.000000e+00 i
 enter complex phi.5 0
 F= 4.669347e-01+0.000000e+00 i ---------------------
 2nd, incomplete
 E(phi,k)= 5.372349e-01+0.000000e+00 i -----------------
 Z= -3.334874e-01+0.000000e+00 i -----------------
 heuman lambda= 7.049803e-01+6.226463e-05 i
 K&E,etc.:enter complex k0 0
 Jacobi:enter complex m (not k).81
0
 enter complex u.2 0
 phi= 2.000000e-01+0.000000e+00 i
 sn= 1.976208e-01+0.000000e+00 i
 cn= 9.802785e-01+-0.000000e+00 i
 dn= 9.840560e-01+0.000000e+00 i
 jtheta= 9.736660e-01+0.000000e+00 i
 amplitude= 0.000000e+00+0.000000e+00 i
 Jacobi:enter complex m (not k)0 0
 theta functions:enter complex k.5 0
 enter complex v .5619166 0
 phi= 5.619166e-01+0.000000e+00 i
 t1= 4.841643e-01+0.000000e+00 i
 t2= 7.714667e-01+0.000000e+00 i
 t3= 1.037352e+00+0.000000e+00 i
 t4= 9.626390e-01+0.000000e+00 i
 phi= 5.619166e-01+0.000000e+00 i
 m= 2.500000e-01+0.000000e+00 i
 neville t1= 5.367643e-01+0.000000e+00 i
 neville t2= 8.657458e-01+0.000000e+00 i
 neville t3= 9.826509e-01+0.000000e+00 i
 neville t4= 1.018642e+00+0.000000e+00 i
 theta functions:enter complex k0 0
 Weierstrass: enter complex g2 g3 x-10 0 2 0 .1 .03
Weierstrass= 7.658833e+01-5.050379e+01 i
 Inverse Weierstrass= 1.000000e-01+3.000000e-02 i
 Weierstrass: enter complex g2 g3 x10 0 2 0 .07 .1
```

```
r1= -2.033642e-01+0.000000e+00 i
r2= -1.469617e+00+0.000000e+00 i
r3= 1.672982e+00+0.000000e+00 i
Weierstrass= -2.297450e+01-6.305323e+01 i
 Inverse Weierstrass= 7.000000e-02+1.000000e-01 i
 Weierstrass: enter complex g2 g3 x0 0 0 0 0 0
 EllipticLog/Exp: enter complex a,b,x1 0 2 0 3 0
EllipticLogarithm= -1.081060e+00-1.231250e-14 i
EllipticExponential= 3.000000e+00-5.351275e-14 i
 EllipticLog/Exp: enter complex a,b,x1 0 2 0 1 1
EllipticLogarithm= -1.452840e+00+4.178565e-01 i
EllipticExponential= 1.000000e+00+1.000000e+00 i
 EllipticLog/Exp: enter complex a,b,x0 0 0 0 0 00 0
```

```
/*
Complex C++ Utilities

from C Mathematical Function Handbook by Louis Baker
Copyright 1991 by Louis Baker. All rights reserved.

*/
#include "Cmatrix.hpp"

#define maxterm 100
#define abstol 1.e-10
#define reltol 1.e-5
#define zerotol 1.e-14
#define errorcode -1.e60
#define pi 3.141592653589793238462643383279
#define lim 15.
#define max(a,b) ((a)>(b)?(a):(b))
#define infinite_loop for(;;)
#define rabs(x) ((x)<0.? -(x):(x))
#define ABS(X) rabs(X)
#define topexp 350.

void complex::print( char *ahead,char *behind)
   {char *between="";
   if(y>=0.)between="+";
   printf("%s %e%s%e i %s",ahead,x,between,y,behind);}

double complex::abs()
   { return sqrt(x*x+y*y);}

complex complex::cexp()
   {double scale;
   scale= x;
   if( x> topexp) return complex( errorcode,0.);
   if( x<-topexp) return complex( 0.,0.);
   scale= exp((scale));
   return complex(scale*cos(y),scale*sin(y));
   }
complex complex::clog()
   {double mant,arg,mag;mag=(*this).abs();
   if( mag < zerotol ) return complex(errorcode,0.);
   mant = log(mag);
   arg= atan2(y,x);
   return complex(mant,arg);
   }

complex complex::operator^(double expon)
   {
   complex z;
```

```
   z= (*this).clog( ) * expon;
   return z.cexp();
   }

complex complex::operator^(complex expon)
   {
   complex z;
   z= (*this).clog( ) * expon;
   return z.cexp();
   }


complex complex::csin()
{double z,zi,sinh,cosh,real;real=x;
if( y> topexp) return complex( errorcode,0.);
if( y<-topexp) return complex( 0.,0.);
z=exp( y); zi=1./z; cosh=.5*(z+zi);sinh=.5*(z-zi);
//printf(" csin real imag arg %e %e\n",real,z);
return complex(cosh*sin(real),cos(real)*sinh);
}

complex complex::ccos()
{double z,zi,sinh,cosh,real;real=x;
if( y> topexp) return complex( errorcode,0.);
if( y<-topexp) return complex( 0.,0.);
z=exp(y); zi=1./z; cosh=.5*(z+zi);sinh=.5*(z-zi);
return complex(cosh*cos(real),-sin(real)*sinh);
}

complex tangent ( complex& x)
{
return x.csin()/x.ccos();
}

complex tanh(complex& x)
{complex i(0.,1.);
return -i*tangent( x*i);
}
complex sinh(complex& x)
{complex i(0.,1.);
return  -i* ( x*i).csin();
}

complex asin(complex&x)
{complex i(0.,1.);
return      -i * (i*x+ ((1.-x*x)^.5)).clog();
}
complex acos(complex&x)
{complex i(0.,1.);
```

```
return      -i * (x+ i*((1.-x*x)^.5)).clog();
}

complex arctan( complex& x)
{complex i(0.,1.),a;
 a= ( i+x )/(i-x);
 return .5 * i * a.clog();
}


complex cgamma( complex& xin)
{complex xi,factor(1.,0.),g,lg,x;
//reflect
x=xin;
if(x.real()<0.)
   {return pi/(cgamma(1.-x)*(pi*x).csin());
   }
while(x.abs()< lim){factor=factor/x;x++;}xi=1./x;
g= factor*((-x).cexp())*((x)^(x-.5))*sqrt(2.*pi)*
(1.+xi*(1./(12.)+xi*(1./(288)-
xi*(139./(51840)+571./(2488320.*x)))));
lg=g.clog();
//lg.print(" log gamma=","\n");
return g;
}


double loggam(x) double x;
{
int i;
double z,tmp,ser,*coeff;
static double logsr2pi=.918938533;
static double b[9]={.035868343,-.193527818,
.482199394,-.756704078,
.918206857,-.897056937,.988205891,-.577191652,1.0};

if(x<=0. &&  !((int)((((int)x)-x))) )return errorcode;
/*if( x<0.&& x> -1. )
   {
   return((loggam(1.+x)-log(-x)));
   }
else requires two levels of recursion and  log call,not sin
*/
if (x<-0.) /*was x< -1. when above implemented */
      {/*transform to x>0. will blow up if x integer, as it
should*/
      z=1.-x;/* z>2. */
      return(log(pi/ABS(sin(pi*z)))-loggam(z) );
      }
```

```
else
   if (x<=1.)/* 0<=x<1 */
       {
       /*z=1.-x*/;/*  0<=z<1*/
       /*return( log(z*pi/sin(pi*z))-loggam(1.+z));*/
       /* Ab& Stegun-takes less than half the time*/
       if(x==0.)return 0.;
       tmp=b[0];
       coeff=&(b[1]);
       for(i=1;i<9;i++)tmp= tmp*x+ *(coeff++);
       return(log(tmp/x));
       }
/* use below for x>1.*/
else
   if(x<=2.)
       {
       tmp=b[0];
       coeff=&(b[1]);
       z=x-1.;
       for(i=1;i<9;i++)tmp= tmp*z+ *(coeff++);
       return(log(tmp));
       }
z=1./x;
tmp=z*z;
/*ser= (1./12.+tmp*(-1./360.+tmp*(1/1260.-tmp/1680.)
))/x;*/
ser= (.08333333333333+tmp*(tmp*
    (0.000793650793-.000595238095*tmp)
   -.002777777777))*z;
return (logsr2pi-x+(x-.5)*log(x)+ser);
}

double gamma(x) double x;
{
double y,z;
if(x<=0. &&  !((int)(((int)x)-x)) )return errorcode;
y=exp(loggam(x));
if(x>=0.)return(y);
z=  2*(((int)(-x))%2) -1;
return(y*z);
}

double bernoulli(n) int n;/* n even 0<=n*/
{
double r,sum,term,x,y,b0=1.,b1=-
.5,b2=.166666666,g,gamma(double );
int i,itmax=50;
if(n==0)return b0;
if(n==2)return b2;
```

```
if(n==1)return b1;
if(n%2==1)return 0.;
r=(double) n;
if(n>3)
    {
    sum=0;
    for(i=1;i<itmax;i++)
        {
        term= pow( (double)(i) ,-r);
        sum+=term;
        if(ABS(term)<5.e-7 || ABS(term/sum)<5.e-7)break;
        }
    g=pow(2.*pi,r);
    x=1.;
    if((n>>1)%2 ==0)x=-1.;
    return 2.*sum*gamma(r+1.)/g*x;
    }
return 0.;
}
```

```
/*
Fock Functions
from C Mathematical Function Handbook by Louis Baker
Copyright 1991 by Louis Baker. All rights reserved.
*/

#include "complex.hpp"

#define pi 3.141592653589793238462643383279
#define errorcode -1.e60
#define ABS(x)  ((x)>0.?(x):-(x))

// -zeros of Ai
double
zai[10]={2.33810741,4.08794944,5.52055983,6.78670809,7.94413,
9.02265,
10.0402,11.0085,11.9300,12.8288};
// - zeros of Ai'
double
zaip[10]={1.01879,3.24820,4.82009,6.16330,7.37217,8.48849,9.5
3545,
10.5277,11.4751,12.3848};
// values of Ai' at zeros of Ai
double aiz[10]={.70121,-.80311,.86520,-.91085,.94734,
-.97792281,1.00437012,-1.05776869,1.04872065,-1.06779386};
// values of Ai at zeros of Ai'
double aipz[10]={.53566,-.41902,.38041,-.35791,.34230,
-.33047623,.32102229,-.31318539,.30651729,-.30073083};

// w1= sqrt(pi)*(Bi+Ai) w2= sqrt(pi)*(Bi-Ai) v=-2j(w1-
w2)=sqrt(pi)Ai w1=w2*

static double
ga[28]={1.861,1.833,1.802,1.766,1.726,1.682,1.633,1.58,
1.523,1.463,1.399,1.344,1.266,1.197,1.113,1.059,.991,.925,.85
9,.797,.738,
.488,.315,.203,.13,.054,.022,.009};

static double
gp[28]={15.43,10.07,5.78,2.47,0.07,358.49,357.63,357.42,
357.79,358.67,360.,1.71,3.75,6.07,8.62,11.36,14.24,17.24,
20.32,
23.46,26.64,42.56,57.98,72.9,87.57,116.75,145.93,175.12};

static double
fa[25]={2.160,1.992,1.829,1.672,1.521,1.377,1.241,1.112,
.992,.879,.776,.681,.594,.516,.446,.383,.327,.279,.236,.199,.
167,.0665,.025,.0091,.0033};
```

```
static double
fp[25]={295.88,291.82,288.97,287.25,286.57,286.85,288.01,
289.98,292.68,296.04,300.,304.99,309.46,314.83,320.58,326.63,
332.95,
339.49,346.22,353.09,.08,35.88,71.61,106.51,140.67};

int fockfg(double t, complex& f, complex& g)
{int i;double z,eps,mag,phase; complex factor,iu(0.,1.),sum;
if( t < -1.)
   {
   // asymptotic result for large negative t.
   // nothing better for range -1 to -2 available
   z=t*t*t;
   f= iu*2.*t* (-iu*z/3.).cexp()*(1.-iu*.25/z+.5/(z*z) );
   g= 2.* (-iu*z/3.).cexp()*(1.+iu*.25/z-1./(z*z) );
   mag= f.abs();phase= atan2( f.imaginary(),f.real());
   printf(" f mag=%le phase(rad)=%le\n",mag,phase);
   mag= g.abs();phase= atan2( g.imaginary(),g.real());
   printf(" g mag=%le phase(rad)=%le\n",mag,phase);
   return 1;
   }
eps=.00001;
if(t<=1.)
   {
   i= (t+1.+eps)/.1; z= (t-i*.1)+1.;
   }
else if(t<=3.)
   {i= 20+(t-1.+eps)/.5; z= t-(i-20)*.5-1.;
   }
else
   {i=24+(t-3.+eps);z=t-(i-24)-3.;
   }
//{printf("  z=%le t=%le i=%d\n",z,t,i);}
mag= ga[i]*(1.-z)+z*ga[i+1];
phase= pi/180.*(gp[i]*(1.-z)+z*gp[i+1]);
factor= complex(cos(phase),sin(phase));
g= mag*factor;
printf(" g magnitude, phase(rad) %le %le\n",mag,phase);
if(t>3.)// asymptotic results
   {
   sum=0.;
   for(i=0;i<10;i++) sum += (-.5*(sqrt(3.)-iu)
                         *t*zai[i] ).cexp() /aiz[i];
   f= sum*(-iu*pi/3.).cexp();
   for(i=0;i<10;i++) sum += (-.5*(sqrt(3.)
                -iu)*t*zaip[i]).cexp()/(zaip[i]*aipz[i]);
   g= sum;
   f.print(" f asymptotic=","");g.print(" g=","\n");
   mag= f.abs();phase= atan2( f.imaginary(),f.real());
```

```
   printf(" f mag=%le phase(rad)=%le\n",mag,phase);
   mag= g.abs();phase= atan2( g.imaginary(),g.real());
   printf(" g mag=%le phase(rad)=%le\n",mag,phase);
   return 2;
   }
else
   {
   mag= fa[i]*(1.-z)+z*fa[i+1];
   phase= pi/180.*(fp[i]*(1.-z)+z*fp[i+1]);
   factor= complex(cos(phase),sin(phase));
printf(" f magnitude, phase(rad) %le %le\n",mag,phase);
   f= mag*factor;
   }
return 0;
}


static double pr[51]={.04,.221,.377,.503,.602,.674,.723,
.754,.768,.771,.766,.756,.742,.726,.712,.699,.689,.682,
.679,
.682,.69,.707,.732,.77,.827,.911,1.043,1.27,1.732,3.135,0.,
-2.522,-1.119,-.657,-.429,-.297,-.211,-.152,-.11,-.08,
-.058,-.041,
-.029,-.019,-.012,-.008,-.004,-.001,.001,.002,.003};
static double
pip[51]={.879,.84,.769,.678,.577,.469,.354,.265,.173,.091,.01
9,
-.043,-.113,-.139,-.174,-.202,-.224,-.24,-.251,-.257,-.260,
-.26,-.256,-.252,
-.244,-.236,-.225,-.214,-.202,-.19,-.177,-.164,-.151,-.138,
-.125,-.113,
-.101,-.09,-.08,-.07,-.061,-.053,-.045,-.039,-.032,-.027,
-.023,-.018,-.014,
-.011,-.01};
static double qr[61]={-.135,-.314,-.458,-.568,-.646,-.694,
-.717,-.718,
-.703,-.676,-.639,-.596,-.548,-.499,-.449,-.399,-.35,-.3,
-.251,-.201,

-.15,-.096,-.035,.034,.119,.229,.385,.634,1.118,2.542,0.,
-3.074,-1.65,
-1.166,-.918,-.762,-.654,-.573,-.508,-.454,-.409,-.369,
-.333,-.301,-.273,
-.246,-.222,-.2,-.18,-.161,-.144,-.128,-.113,-.1,-.088,
-.077,-.067,
-.058,-.05,-.042,-.033};
static double qi[61]={-.838,-.771,-.676,-.562,-.44,-.317,
-.199,-.09,-.008
,-.094,-.166,-.226,-.274,-.311,-.338,-.357,-.368,-.372,
```

```
-.371,-.365,
-.356,-.342,-.327,-.309,-.289,-.268,-.246,-.223,-.2,-.177,
-.154,-.131,-.109,
-.088,-.067,-.048,-.031,-.014,-.0013,-.015,-.027,-.038,
-.048,-.056,-.062,
-.068,-.072,-.075,-.078,-.079,-.079,-.079,-.078,-.077,
-.075,-.072,-.070,
-.067,-.064,-.061,-.059};



// called p,q  or phat,qhat. various authors

int fockpq(double t, complex& p, complex& q)
{int i;double z,eps; complex factor,iu(0.,1.),sump,sumq;

if( t<= -3.)
   {
   z=t*t*t;factor=(-iu*(pi*.25+z/12.)).cexp();
   p= factor*(1.-iu*2./z+20./(z*z));
   q=-factor*(1.+iu*2./z-28./(z*z));
   return 1;
   }
if(  t >= 2.)
   {
   sump=0.; sumq=0.;
   for(i=0;i<10;i++)
      {
      sump += (-.5*(sqrt(3.)-iu)*t*zai[i]).cexp()
      /(aiz[i]*aiz[i]);
      sumq +=  (-.5*(sqrt(3.)-iu)*t*zaip[i]).cexp()
      /(zaip[i]*aipz[i]*aipz[i]);
      }
   factor=-(-iu*pi/6.).cexp()/(2.*sqrt(pi));
   p= sump*factor;
   q= sump*factor;
   if(t>3.)return 1;
   }
eps=.00001;
i= (t+3.+eps)/.1; z= (t-i*.1)+3.;
//{printf("  z=%le t=%le i=%d\n",z,t,i);}
if(z<0.)z=0.;

if(t> -.1 && t< .1)
   {
   p=complex( .3-.5/(sqrt(pi)*t),pip[i]*(1.-z)+z*pip[i+1]);
   q=complex( -.25-.5/(sqrt(pi)*t),qi[i]*(1.-z)+z*qi[i+1]);
   }
```

```
if(t<=2.)p= complex(pr[i]*(1.-z)+z*pr[i+1],pip[i]*(1.-
z)+z*pip[i+1]);
q= complex(qr[i]*(1.-z)+z*qr[i+1],qi[i]*(1.-z)+z*qi[i+1]);
return 0;
}
```

```
// lower case p*,q* scattering functions

int fockscat(double t, complex& p, complex& q)
{
double spi,spii,sqta,d;complex term,sum1,sum2,ee;int i;
spi=1./sqrt(pi);spii=spi*.5/t;
if(t>2.)//deep shadow
   {
   ee=(complex(0.,-5.*pi/6.)).cexp();
   for(i=0;i<5;i++)
      {
      d=aiz[i];
      term= (ee*t*zai[i]).cexp()/(d*d);
      sum1+=term;
      d=aipz[i];
      term=(ee*t*zaip[i]).cexp()/(d*d*zaip[i]);
      sum2+=term;
      }
   term= spi*(complex(0.,pi/6.)).cexp();
   p=spii-sum1*term;
   q=spii-sum2*term;
   }
else if(t<-3.) //brightly lit
   {
   sqta= sqrt( ABS(t) );
   term=((complex(0.,pi*.25)+com-
plex(0.,1./12.)*t*t*t).cexp())*.5*sqta;
   p= spii +term*(1.+complex(0.,2.)/(t*t*t));
   q= spii -term*(1.-complex(0.,2.)/(t*t*t));
   }
else// interpolate -3
   {
    fockpq(t,p,q);
    d = .5/(sqrt(pi)*t);
    q+= d;
    if(abs(t)>=.1) p+=d;
    else { spi= .314-.015*(t+.1)/.2;
         p=complex(spi,p.imaginary());
         spi= -.279+.026*(t+.1)/.2;
         q=complex(spi,q.imaginary());
```

```
        }/* interpolate real part p */
   }
return 0;
}

//radiation functions
// very crude- do not use if possible to avoid!!!!!!
int fockrad(double t, complex& G, complex& Gtwiddle)
{
if(t>3.)
   {G=1.8325*((complex(-.8823*t,-.5094*t)).cexp());
//best t4
    Gtwiddle=complex(0.,0.);
   }
else if(t<-2.)
   {G=complex(2.,-.5/(t*t*t));// good for t2.5
   Gtwiddle=complex(2.,.5/(t*t*t)) *complex(0,-t);
//best t4.
   }
else//interpolate-
   //G plot only from -2 to 3
   // f,g plots -3 to 4 still need -4 to -3 for Gtwiddle
use above for G
   {
   G= complex( 2./( 1.+ .43* exp(t*1.65)), -t/(1.+2.*t*t));
   Gtwiddle=complex( .5/(1.+t*t) , 4.*exp( -.87*(t+2.)));

   }
return 0;
}


//coupling functions
// u=  x^1.5  exp 3ipi/4 integral  (w2'/w2)exp-jxt dt
// v= .5 x^.5 exp ipi/4  integral  (w2/w2')exp-jxt dt
// v1= x^1.5 exp 3ipi/4 integral t(w2/w2')exp-jxt dt

fockc(double t, complex& u, complex& v, complex& v1)
{double sp,st,y;complex i,q,sum1,sum2,sum3,p;int k;
if(t<0.){q=complex(0.,0.);u=q;v=q;return 0;}
i=complex(0.,1.);
q=(complex(0.,pi*.25)).cexp();
p=(complex(0.,-pi/3.)).cexp();
sp=sqrt(pi);
st=sqrt(t);
y=t*st;
if(t<.6)
   {
   u= 1.+y*(-sp*.5*q+y*(5./12.*i+y*(sp*5./64./q
```

```
      -3.701e-3*y)));
   v= 1.+y*(-sp*.25*q+y*(7./60.*i+y*(sp*7./512./q
      -4.141e-3*y)));
   v1= 1.+y*(sp*.5*q+y*(-7./12.*i+y*(-sp*7./64.
      +4.555e-3*y)));
   }
else          //t=.6
   {
   for(k=0;k<10;k++)
      {
//sum1.print(" sum1=","");
//sum2.print(" sum2=","\n");
      sum1+= (-i*t*p*zai[k]).cexp();
      sum3+= (-i*t*p*zaip[k]).cexp();
      sum2+= (-i*t*p*zaip[k]).cexp()/(p*zaip[k]);
      }
   u= q*sp*2.*sum1*y;
   v=sp*sum2/q*st;
   v1= q*sp*2.*sum3*y;
   }
return 0;
}


main()
{int i;double d;complex p,q,g,gt,u,v;
for (i=0;i<51;i++)
   {d= -3.+(i)*(6./50.);
   fockpq(d,u,v);
   printf(" x=%le\n",d);
   u.print(" phat=","");
   v.print(" qhat=","\n");
   }
u= complex(0.,-pi/4.); u=u.cexp();
for (i=0;i<51;i++)
   {d= -6.+(i)*(12./50.);
   fockscat(d,p,q);
   printf(" x=%le\n",d);
   p.print(" p= ","");
   q.print(" q=","\n");
   p*=u;q*=(u);
   p.print(" e*p= ","");
  (q).print(" e*q=","\n");
   }
for (i=0;i<21;i++)
   {d= -4.+(i)*(8./20.);
   printf(" x=%le ",d);
   fockfg(d,p,q);
   p.print(" f=","");
```

```
    q.print(" g=","\n");
    }


for (i=0;i<=20;i++)
    {d= +(i)*(.6/20.);
    printf(" x=%le\n",d);
    fockc(d,u,v,g);
    u.print("  u=","");
    v.print("  v=","\n");
    g.print("  v1=","\n");
    }
// x=.6 and x=.65 both will be sum not series
    {d= .65;
    printf(" x=%le ",d);
    fockc(d,u,v,g);
    u.print("  u=","");
    v.print("  v=","\n");
    g.print("  v1=","\n");
    }

for (i=0;i<20;i++)
    {d=.5 +(i)*((5.-.5)/20.);
    printf(" x=%le\n",d);
    fockc(d,u,v,g);
    u.print("  u=","");
    v.print("  v=","\n");
    g.print("  v1=","\n");
    }
/*
for (i=0;i<20;i++)
    {d= -6.+(i)*(12./20.);
    printf(" x=%le ",d);
    fockrad(d,g,gt);
    g.print(" G=","");
    gt.print(" Gt=","\n");
    }
*/
}
```

Test Output: Fock functions

```
 x=-3.000000e+00
 phat= 3.524617e-02+1.029498e+00 i  qhat= -1.755807e-01-
9.483228e-01 i
 x=-2.880000e+00
 phat= 2.241200e-01+8.385800e-01 i  qhat= -3.168800e-01-
7.691000e-01 i
 x=-2.760000e+00
 phat= 3.820400e-01+7.653600e-01 i  qhat= -4.624000e-01-
6.714400e-01 i
 x=-2.640000e+00
 phat= 5.089400e-01+6.719400e-01 i  qhat= -5.726800e-01-
5.546800e-01 i
 x=-2.520000e+00
 phat= 6.077600e-01+5.683600e-01 i  qhat= -6.498400e-01-
4.301600e-01 i
 x=-2.400000e+00
 phat= 7.230000e-01+3.540000e-01 i  qhat= -7.170000e-01-
1.990000e-01 i
 x=-2.280000e+00
 phat= 7.542800e-01+2.631600e-01 i  qhat= -7.177000e-01-
8.836000e-02 i
 x=-2.160000e+00
 phat= 7.681200e-01+1.697200e-01 i  qhat= -7.019200e-01-
1.144000e-02 i
 x=-2.040000e+00
 phat= 7.707000e-01+8.668000e-02 i  qhat= -6.737800e-01-
9.832000e-02 i
 x=-1.920000e+00
 phat= 7.652000e-01+1.404000e-02 i  qhat= -6.355600e-01-
1.708000e-01 i
 x=-1.800000e+00
 phat= 7.420000e-01-1.130000e-01 i  qhat= -5.480000e-01-
2.740000e-01 i
 x=-1.680000e+00
 phat= 7.257200e-01-1.397000e-01 i  qhat= -4.980000e-01-
3.115400e-01 i
 x=-1.560000e+00
 phat= 7.114800e-01-1.751200e-01 i  qhat= -4.470000e-01-
3.387600e-01 i
 x=-1.440000e+00
 phat= 6.984000e-01-2.033200e-01 i  qhat= -3.960600e-01-
3.576600e-01 i
 x=-1.320000e+00
 phat= 6.884400e-01-2.252800e-01 i  qhat= -3.460000e-01-
3.683200e-01 i
 x=-1.200000e+00
 phat= 6.790000e-01-2.510000e-01 i  qhat= -2.510000e-01-
3.710000e-01 i
```

```
 x=-1.080000e+00
 phat= 6.821600e-01-2.570600e-01 i  qhat= -1.999800e-01-
3.648200e-01 i
 x=-9.600000e-01
 phat= 6.906800e-01-2.600000e-01 i  qhat= -1.478400e-01-
3.554400e-01 i
 x=-8.400000e-01
 phat= 7.085000e-01-2.597600e-01 i  qhat= -9.234000e-02-
3.411000e-01 i
 x=-7.200000e-01
 phat= 7.350400e-01-2.556800e-01 i  qhat= -2.948000e-02-
3.255600e-01 i
 x=-6.000000e-01
 phat= 8.270000e-01-2.440000e-01 i  qhat= 1.190000e-01-
2.890000e-01 i
 x=-4.800000e-01
 phat= 9.136400e-01-2.357800e-01 i  qhat= 2.321200e-01-
2.675600e-01 i
 x=-3.600000e-01
 phat= 1.052080e+00-2.245600e-01 i  qhat= 3.949600e-01-
2.450800e-01 i
 x=-2.400000e-01
 phat= 1.297720e+00-2.132800e-01 i  qhat= 6.630400e-01-
2.216200e-01 i
 x=-1.200000e-01
 phat= 1.844240e+00-2.010400e-01 i  qhat= 1.231920e+00-
1.981600e-01 i
 x=-1.110223e-16
 phat= 0.000000e+00-1.770000e-01 i  qhat= 0.000000e+00-
1.540000e-01 i
 x=1.200000e-01
 phat= -2.493940e+00-1.637400e-01 i  qhat= -3.045520e+00-
1.305600e-01 i
 x=2.400000e-01
 phat= -1.100520e+00-1.504800e-01 i  qhat= -1.630640e+00-
1.081600e-01 i
 x=3.600000e-01
 phat= -6.433200e-01-1.372200e-01 i  qhat= -1.151120e+00-
8.674000e-02 i
 x=4.800000e-01
 phat= -4.184400e-01-1.240400e-01 i  qhat= -9.055200e-01-
6.548000e-02 i
 x=6.000000e-01
 phat= -2.110000e-01-1.010000e-01 i  qhat= -6.540000e-01-
3.100000e-02 i
 x=7.200000e-01
 phat= -1.511600e-01-8.980000e-02 i  qhat= -5.717000e-01-
1.374600e-02 i
 x=8.400000e-01
```

```
 phat= -1.088000e-01-7.960000e-02 i  qhat= -5.058400e-01-
1.848000e-03 i
 x=9.600000e-01
 phat= -7.868000e-02-6.946000e-02 i  qhat= -4.513000e-01-
1.572000e-02 i
 x=1.080000e+00
 phat= -5.664000e-02-6.036000e-02 i  qhat= -4.058000e-01-
2.788000e-02 i
 x=1.200000e+00
 phat= -2.900000e-02-4.500000e-02 i  qhat= -3.330000e-01-
4.800000e-02 i
 x=1.320000e+00
 phat= -1.886000e-02-3.886000e-02 i  qhat= -3.004400e-01-
5.612000e-02 i
 x=1.440000e+00
 phat= -1.184000e-02-3.180000e-02 i  qhat= -2.719200e-01-
6.224000e-02 i
 x=1.560000e+00
 phat= -7.760000e-03-2.676000e-02 i  qhat= -2.445600e-01-
6.824000e-02 i
 x=1.680000e+00
 phat= -3.760000e-03-2.260000e-02 i  qhat= -2.202400e-01-
7.224000e-02 i
 x=1.800000e+00
 phat= 1.000000e-03-1.400000e-02 i  qhat= -1.800000e-01-
7.800000e-02 i
 x=1.920000e+00
 phat= 2.020000e-03-1.098000e-02 i  qhat= -1.606600e-01-
7.900000e-02 i
 x=2.040000e+00
 phat= 2.909827e-03-8.660098e-03 i  qhat= -1.433600e-01-
7.900000e-02 i
 x=2.160000e+00
 phat= 3.163356e-03-6.419935e-03 i  qhat= -1.271000e-01-
7.894000e-02 i
 x=2.280000e+00
 phat= 3.133550e-03-4.654143e-03 i  qhat= -1.119600e-01-
7.792000e-02 i
 x=2.400000e+00
 phat= 2.928990e-03-3.284475e-03 i  qhat= -8.800000e-02-
7.500000e-02 i
 x=2.520000e+00
 phat= 2.627433e-03-2.240422e-03 i  qhat= -7.680000e-02-
7.196000e-02 i
 x=2.640000e+00
 phat= 2.283098e-03-1.459803e-03 i  qhat= -6.664000e-02-
6.988000e-02 i
 x=2.760000e+00
```

```
 phat= 1.932413e-03-8.888628e-04 i  qhat= -5.752000e-02-
6.682000e-02 i
 x=2.880000e+00
 phat= 1.598571e-03-4.820084e-04 i  qhat= -4.936000e-02-
6.376000e-02 i
 x=3.000000e+00
 phat= 1.295107e-03-2.012684e-04 i  qhat= -3.300000e-02-
5.900000e-02 i
 x=-6.000000e+00
 p=  -1.142219e-01+1.222952e+00 i  q= 4.282409e-02-
1.221498e+00 i
 e*p=  7.839907e-01+9.455248e-01 i  e*q= -8.334483e-01-
8.940107e-01 i
 x=-5.760000e+00
 p=  -1.067233e+00-6.350654e-01 i  q= 9.557691e-
01+6.562373e-01 i
 e*p=  -1.203707e+00+3.055886e-01 i  e*q= 1.139861e+00-
2.118010e-01 i
 x=-5.520000e+00
 p=  8.649774e-01-7.355200e-01 i  q= -9.844161e-
01+7.135292e-01 i
 e*p=  9.154020e-02-1.131723e+00 i  e*q= -1.915460e-
01+1.200629e+00 i
 x=-5.280000e+00
 p=  4.965440e-01+1.008849e+00 i  q= -5.757854e-01-
1.023419e+00 i
 e*p=  1.064473e+00+3.622541e-01 i  e*q= -1.130808e+00-
3.165244e-01 i
 x=-5.040000e+00
 p=  -1.054775e+00+5.125417e-01 i  q= 9.583550e-01-
4.810925e-01 i
 e*p=  -3.834167e-01+1.108260e+00 i  e*q= 3.374756e-01-
1.017843e+00 i
 x=-4.800000e+00
 p=  -6.726070e-01-9.075221e-01 i  q= 5.218527e-
01+9.291233e-01 i
 e*p=  -1.117320e+00-1.661101e-01 i  e*q=
1.025995e+00+2.879838e-01 i
 x=-4.560000e+00
 p=  6.396883e-01-8.051914e-01 i  q= -7.967426e-
01+7.748929e-01 i
 e*p=  -1.170284e-01-1.021684e+00 i  e*q= -1.545003e-
02+1.111314e+00 i
 x=-4.320000e+00
 p=  9.197254e-01+3.322501e-01 i  q= -1.032639e+00-
3.806829e-01 i
 e*p=  8.852804e-01-4.154078e-01 i  e*q= -9.993694e-
01+4.610026e-01 i
 x=-4.080000e+00
```

```
 p=  1.230965e-01+9.919321e-01 i  q= -2.026758e-01-
1.001525e+00 i
 e*p=  7.884443e-01+6.143595e-01 i  e*q= -8.514988e-01-
5.648719e-01 i
 x=-3.840000e+00
 p=  -7.373490e-01+7.214236e-01 i  q= 6.396699e-01-
6.727855e-01 i
 e*p=  -1.126098e-02+1.031508e+00 i  e*q= -2.341629e-02-
9.280461e-01 i
 x=-3.600000e+00
 p=  -1.027907e+00+3.655677e-03 i  q= 8.680173e-
01+7.761681e-02 i
 e*p=  -7.242552e-01+7.294251e-01 i  e*q= 6.686643e-01-
5.588976e-01 i
 x=-3.360000e+00
 p=  -7.780381e-01-6.004883e-01 i  q= 5.431310e-
01+6.701463e-01 i
 e*p=  -9.747654e-01+1.255466e-01 i  e*q= 8.579166e-
01+8.981335e-02 i
 x=-3.120000e+00
 p=  -3.012381e-01-8.596139e-01 i  q= 5.862498e-
03+8.798370e-01 i
 e*p=  -8.208463e-01-3.948313e-01 i  e*q= 6.262841e-
01+6.179933e-01 i
 x=-2.880000e+00
 p=  1.261704e-01+8.385800e-01 i  q= -4.148296e-01-
7.691000e-01 i
 e*p=  6.821816e-01+5.037496e-01 i  e*q= -8.371646e-01-
2.505070e-01 i
 x=-2.640000e+00
 p=  4.020859e-01+6.719400e-01 i  q= -6.795341e-01-
5.546800e-01 i
 e*p=  7.594510e-01+1.908157e-01 i  e*q= -8.727212e-
01+8.828517e-02 i
 x=-2.400000e+00
 p=  6.054605e-01+3.540000e-01 i  q= -8.345395e-01-
1.990000e-01 i
 e*p=  6.784410e-01-1.778094e-01 i  e*q= -7.308228e-
01+4.493943e-01 i
 x=-2.160000e+00
 p=  6.375206e-01+1.697200e-01 i  q= -8.325194e-01-
1.144000e-02 i
 e*p=  5.708053e-01-3.307849e-01 i  e*q= -5.967694e-
01+5.805908e-01 i
 x=-1.920000e+00
 p=  6.182756e-01+1.404000e-02 i  q= -7.824844e-01-
1.708000e-01 i
 e*p=  4.471147e-01-4.272591e-01 i  e*q= -6.740738e-
01+4.325262e-01 i
```

```
 x=-1.680000e+00
 p=  5.578064e-01-1.397000e-01 i  q= -6.659136e-01-
3.115400e-01 i
 e*p=  2.956459e-01-4.932115e-01 i  e*q= -6.911640e-
01+2.505800e-01 i
 x=-1.440000e+00
 p=  5.025008e-01-2.033200e-01 i  q= -5.919592e-01-
3.576600e-01 i
 e*p=  2.115528e-01-4.990907e-01 i  e*q= -6.714821e-
01+1.656745e-01 i
 x=-1.200000e+00
 p=  4.439210e-01-2.510000e-01 i  q= -4.860790e-01-
3.710000e-01 i
 e*p=  1.364158e-01-4.913834e-01 i  e*q= -6.060464e-
01+8.137314e-02 i
 x=-9.600000e-01
 p=  3.785000e-01-2.600000e-01 i  q= -3.908000e-01-
3.554400e-01 i
 e*p=  8.379215e-02-4.514877e-01 i  e*q= -5.276714e-
01+2.500330e-02 i
 x=-7.200000e-01
 p=  3.605000e-01-2.556800e-01 i  q= -3.596000e-01-
3.255600e-01 i
 e*p=  7.411893e-02-4.357051e-01 i  e*q= -4.844813e-
01+2.406991e-02 i
 x=-4.800000e-01
 p=  3.425000e-01-2.357800e-01 i  q= -3.284000e-01-
2.675600e-01 i
 e*p=  7.546244e-02-4.089057e-01 i  e*q= -4.214074e-
01+4.302038e-02 i
 x=-2.400000e-01
 p=  3.245000e-01-2.132800e-01 i  q= -2.972000e-01-
2.216200e-01 i
 e*p=  7.864442e-02-3.802679e-01 i  e*q= -3.668611e-
01+5.344313e-02 i
 x=-2.220446e-16
 p=  3.065000e-01-1.770000e-01 i  q= -2.660000e-01-
1.540000e-01 i
 e*p=  9.157033e-02-3.418861e-01 i  e*q= -2.969848e-
01+7.919596e-02 i
 x=2.400000e-01
 p=  2.885000e-01-1.504800e-01 i  q= -2.348000e-01-
1.081600e-01 i
 e*p=  9.759488e-02-3.104057e-01 i  e*q= -2.425093e-
01+8.954800e-02 i
 x=4.800000e-01
 p=  2.705000e-01-1.240400e-01 i  q= -2.036000e-01-
6.548000e-02 i
```

```
 e*p=  1.035629e-01-2.789819e-01 i  e*q= -1.902683e-
01+9.766559e-02 i
 x=7.200000e-01
 p=  2.525000e-01-8.980000e-02 i  q= -1.724000e-01-
1.374600e-02 i
 e*p=  1.150463e-01-2.420427e-01 i  e*q= -1.316251e-
01+1.121853e-01 i
 x=9.600000e-01
 p=  2.345000e-01-6.946000e-02 i  q= -1.412000e-01-
1.572000e-02 i
 e*p=  1.167009e-01-2.149322e-01 i  e*q= -1.109592e-
01+8.872776e-02 i
 x=1.200000e+00
 p=  2.060790e-01-4.500000e-02 i  q= -9.792101e-02-
4.800000e-02 i
 e*p=  1.139000e-01-1.775397e-01 i  e*q= -1.031817e-
01+3.529948e-02 i
 x=1.440000e+00
 p=  1.840592e-01-3.180000e-02 i  q= -7.602084e-02-
6.224000e-02 i
 e*p=  1.076635e-01-1.526355e-01 i  e*q= -9.776518e-
02+9.744525e-03 i
 x=1.680000e+00
 p=  1.641536e-01-2.260000e-02 i  q= -5.232643e-02-
7.224000e-02 i
 e*p=  1.000935e-01-1.320547e-01 i  e*q= -8.808177e-02-
1.408102e-02 i
 x=1.920000e+00
 p=  1.489444e-01-1.098000e-02 i  q= -1.373563e-02-
7.900000e-02 i
 e*p=  9.755554e-02-1.130836e-01 i  e*q= -6.557399e-02-
4.614888e-02 i
 x=2.160000e+00
 p=  1.369261e-01+1.283987e-02 i  q= -1.077534e-
01+1.567518e-01 i
 e*p=  1.059005e-01-8.774223e-02 i  e*q= 3.464705e-
02+1.870334e-01 i
 x=2.400000e+00
 p=  1.233975e-01+6.568953e-03 i  q= -5.913912e-
02+1.491300e-01 i
 e*p=  9.190014e-02-8.261024e-02 i  e*q= 6.363318e-
02+1.472685e-01 i
 x=2.640000e+00
 p=  1.114203e-01+2.919606e-03 i  q= -2.071732e-
02+1.372031e-01 i
 e*p=  8.085051e-02-7.672156e-02 i  e*q= 8.236785e-
02+1.116666e-01 i
 x=2.880000e+00
```

```
 p=  1.011467e-01+9.640169e-04 i  q= 8.846516e-03+1.228523e-
01 i
 e*p=  7.220320e-02-7.083987e-02 i  e*q= 9.312516e-
02+8.061430e-02 i
 x=3.120000e+00
 p=  9.247240e-02+3.116010e-05 i  q= 3.090236e-02+1.075280e-
01 i
 e*p=  6.540990e-02-6.536583e-02 i  e*q= 9.788502e-
02+5.418249e-02 i
 x=3.360000e+00
 p=  8.518064e-02-3.304563e-04 i  q= 4.674927e-02+9.227824e-
02 i
 e*p=  5.999814e-02-6.046547e-02 i  e*q= 9.830730e-
02+3.219384e-02 i
 x=3.600000e+00
 p=  7.902800e-02-4.036804e-04 i  q= 5.758180e-02+7.780916e-
02 i
 e*p=  5.559579e-02-5.616668e-02 i  e*q= 9.573586e-
02+1.430290e-02 i
 x=3.840000e+00
 p=  7.378895e-02-3.526497e-04 i  q= 6.445745e-02+6.455370e-
02 i
 e*p=  5.192730e-02-5.242603e-02 i  e*q= 9.122466e-
02+6.805449e-05 i
 x=4.080000e+00
 p=  6.927409e-02-2.642727e-04 i  q= 6.828356e-02+5.273852e-
02 i
 e*p=  4.879731e-02-4.917105e-02 i  e*q= 8.557554e-02-
1.099200e-02 i
 x=4.320000e+00
 p=  6.533346e-02-1.789863e-04 i  q= 6.981848e-02+4.244186e-
02 i
 e*p=  4.607117e-02-4.632430e-02 i  e*q= 7.938005e-02-
1.935820e-02 i
 x=4.560000e+00
 p=  6.185234e-02-1.115776e-04 i  q= 6.968191e-02+3.364039e-
02 i
 e*p=  4.365731e-02-4.381510e-02 i  e*q= 7.305990e-02-
2.548520e-02 i
 x=4.800000e+00
 p=  5.874449e-02-6.416278e-05 i  q= 6.836985e-02+2.624563e-
02 i
 e*p=  4.149326e-02-4.158400e-02 i  e*q= 6.690324e-02-
2.978632e-02 i
 x=5.040000e+00
 p=  5.594532e-02-3.362370e-05 i  q= 6.627150e-02+2.013093e-
02 i
 e*p=  3.953554e-02-3.958309e-02 i  e*q= 6.109575e-02-
3.262631e-02 i
```

```
 x=5.280000e+00
 p=  5.340603e-02-1.546725e-05 i  q= 6.368609e-02+1.515105e-
02 i
 e*p=  3.775283e-02-3.777470e-02 i  e*q= 5.574627e-02-
3.431945e-02 i
 x=5.520000e+00
 p=  5.108907e-02-5.561206e-06 i  q= 6.083852e-02+1.115574e-
02 i
 e*p=  3.612150e-02-3.612936e-02 i  e*q= 5.090763e-02-
3.513103e-02 i
 x=5.760000e+00
 p=  4.896494e-02-7.216400e-07 i  q= 5.789355e-02+7.998838e-
03 i
 e*p=  3.462293e-02-3.462395e-02 i  e*q= 4.659295e-02-
3.528089e-02 i
 x=6.000000e+00
 p=  4.700986e-02+1.251000e-06 i  q= 5.496798e-02+5.543967e-
03 i
 e*p=  3.324187e-02-3.324010e-02 i  e*q= 4.278841e-02-
3.494805e-02 i
 x=-4.000000e+00  f mag=8.001038e+00 phase(rad)=9.168868e-01
 g mag=1.999527e+00 phase(rad)=2.479870e+00
 f= 4.866984e+00+6.350518e+00 i  g= -
1.577497e+00+1.228663e+00 i
 x=-3.600000e+00  f mag=7.201757e+00 phase(rad)=1.420190e+00
 g mag=1.999110e+00 phase(rad)=2.980269e+00
 f= 1.080533e+00+7.120235e+00 i  g= -1.973152e+00+3.211074e-
01 i
 x=-3.200000e+00  f mag=6.403166e+00 phase(rad)=3.076311e+00
 g mag=1.998196e+00 phase(rad)=-1.651340e+00
 f= -6.389527e+00+4.177142e-01 i  g= -1.607687e-01-
1.991718e+00 i
 x=-2.800000e+00  f mag=5.606173e+00 phase(rad)=-5.252721e-
01
 g mag=1.995980e+00 phase(rad)=1.022736e+00
 f= 4.850391e+00-2.811207e+00 i  g=
1.039970e+00+1.703642e+00 i
 x=-2.400000e+00  f mag=4.813341e+00 phase(rad)=3.055239e+00
 g mag=1.989863e+00 phase(rad)=-1.693363e+00
 f= -4.795406e+00+4.151332e-01 i  g= -2.432806e-01-
1.974935e+00 i
 x=-2.000000e+00  f mag=4.033188e+00 phase(rad)=1.126868e+00
 g mag=1.969742e+00 phase(rad)=2.634931e+00
 f= 1.732214e+00+3.642257e+00 i  g= -1.722282e+00+9.558384e-
01 i
 x=-1.600000e+00  f mag=3.301150e+00 phase(rad)=-1.462634e-
01
 g mag=1.884748e+00 phase(rad)=1.300521e+00
```

```
 f= 3.265902e+00-4.811179e-01 i  g= 5.032225e-
01+1.816327e+00 i
 x=-1.200000e+00  f mag=2.823310e+00 phase(rad)=-8.715001e-
01
 g mag=1.361311e+00 phase(rad)=3.618122e-01
 f= 1.817306e+00-2.160666e+00 i  g= 1.273175e+00+4.818628e-
01 i
 x=-8.000000e-01  g magnitude, phase(rad) 1.802000e+00
1.008800e-01
 f magnitude, phase(rad) 1.829000e+00 5.043478e+00
 f= 5.945586e-01-1.729665e+00 i  g= 1.792838e+00+1.814776e-
01 i
 x=-4.000000e-01  g magnitude, phase(rad) 1.633000e+00
6.241821e+00
 f magnitude, phase(rad) 1.241000e+00 5.026723e+00
 f= 3.836961e-01-1.180194e+00 i  g= 1.631603e+00-6.752865e-
02 i
 x=2.220446e-16  g magnitude, phase(rad) 1.399000e+00
6.283185e+00
 f magnitude, phase(rad) 7.760000e-01 5.235988e+00
 f= 3.880000e-01-6.720357e-01 i  g= 1.399000e+00-1.585206e-
15 i
 x=4.000000e-01  g magnitude, phase(rad) 1.113000e+00
1.504474e-01
 f magnitude, phase(rad) 4.460000e-01 5.595177e+00
 f= 3.445403e-01-2.832101e-01 i  g= 1.100428e+00+1.668170e-
01 i
 x=8.000000e-01  g magnitude, phase(rad) 8.590000e-01
3.546509e-01
 f magnitude, phase(rad) 2.360000e-01 6.042679e+00
 f= 2.292073e-01-5.621389e-02 i  g= 8.055425e-01+2.982989e-
01 i
 x=1.200000e+00  g magnitude, phase(rad) 6.880000e-01
5.205270e-01
 f magnitude, phase(rad) 1.469000e-01 1.263618e-01
 f= 1.457288e-01+1.851319e-02 i  g= 5.968794e-01+3.421681e-
01 i
 x=1.600000e+00  g magnitude, phase(rad) 4.707000e-01
7.697251e-01
 f magnitude, phase(rad) 6.235000e-02 6.885847e-01
 f= 4.814331e-02+3.962000e-02 i  g= 3.380106e-01+3.275780e-
01 i
 x=2.000000e+00  g magnitude, phase(rad) 3.150000e-01
1.011942e+00
 f magnitude, phase(rad) 2.500000e-02 1.249830e+00
 f= 7.887086e-03+2.372328e-02 i  g= 1.670178e-01+2.670769e-
01 i
 x=2.400000e+00  g magnitude, phase(rad) 2.702000e-01
1.116103e+00
```

```
 f magnitude, phase(rad) 1.864000e-02 1.493478e+00
 f= 1.439774e-03+1.858431e-02 i  g= 1.186682e-01+2.427466e-
01 i
 x=2.800000e+00  g magnitude, phase(rad) 1.811000e-01
1.349157e+00
 f magnitude, phase(rad) 7.360000e-03 2.037812e+00
 f= -3.313642e-03+6.571862e-03 i  g= 3.981106e-02+1.766700e-
01 i
 x=3.200000e+00  g magnitude, phase(rad) 1.148000e-01
1.630242e+00
 f asymptotic= -1.983083e-03+9.584507e-04 i  g= -8.311593e-
03+1.075094e-01 i
 f mag=2.202554e-03 phase(rad)=2.691383e+00
 g mag=1.078302e-01 phase(rad)=1.647953e+00
 f= -1.983083e-03+9.584507e-04 i  g= -8.311593e-
03+1.075094e-01 i
 x=3.600000e+00  g magnitude, phase(rad) 8.440000e-02
1.833957e+00
 f asymptotic= -9.770347e-04-1.935927e-05 i  g= -2.038541e-
02+7.301327e-02 i
 f mag=9.772264e-04 phase(rad)=-3.121781e+00
 g mag=7.580569e-02 phase(rad)=1.843064e+00
 f= -9.770347e-04-1.935927e-05 i  g= -2.038541e-
02+7.301327e-02 i
 x=4.000000e+00  g magnitude, phase(rad) 5.400000e-02
2.037672e+00
 f asymptotic= -3.832700e-04-2.035156e-04 i  g= -2.420972e-
02+4.755740e-02 i
 f mag=4.339522e-04 phase(rad)=-2.653455e+00
 g mag=5.336494e-02 phase(rad)=2.041668e+00
 f= -3.832700e-04-2.035156e-04 i  g= -2.420972e-
02+4.755740e-02 i
 x=0.000000e+00
  u= 1.000000e+00+-0.000000e+00 i   v= 1.000000e+00+-
0.000000e+00 i
  v1= 1.000000e+00+0.000000e+00 i
 x=3.000000e-02
  u= 9.967438e-01-3.244969e-03 i   v= 9.983719e-01-
1.624955e-03 i
  v1= 1.003256e+00+3.240456e-03 i
 x=6.000000e-02
  u= 9.907904e-01-9.120251e-03 i   v= 9.953951e-01-
4.579825e-03 i
  v1= 1.009209e+00+9.083940e-03 i
 x=9.000000e-02
  u= 9.830822e-01-1.661792e-02 i   v= 9.915405e-01-
8.375158e-03 i
  v1= 1.016916e+00+1.649449e-02 i
 x=1.200000e-01
```

```
  u= 9.739574e-01-2.533668e-02 i    v= 9.869764e-01-
1.282445e-02 i
  v1= 1.026036e+00+2.504165e-02 i
 x=1.500000e-01
  u= 9.636137e-01-3.501843e-02 i    v= 9.818006e-01-
1.781235e-02 i
  v1= 1.036368e+00+3.443674e-02 i
 x=1.800000e-01
  u= 9.521872e-01-4.546986e-02 i    v= 9.760794e-01-
2.325536e-02 i
  v1= 1.047770e+00+4.445425e-02 i
 x=2.100000e-01
  u= 9.397812e-01-5.653429e-02 i    v= 9.698620e-01-
2.908771e-02 i
  v1= 1.060133e+00+5.490352e-02 i
 x=2.400000e-01
  u= 9.264789e-01-6.807867e-02 i    v= 9.631873e-01-
3.525481e-02 i
  v1= 1.073365e+00+6.561552e-02 i
 x=2.700000e-01
  u= 9.123514e-01-7.998669e-02 i    v= 9.560869e-01-
4.170974e-02 i
  v1= 1.087384e+00+7.643580e-02 i
 x=3.000000e-01
  u= 8.974614e-01-9.215467e-02 i    v= 9.485879e-01-
4.841115e-02 i
  v1= 1.102114e+00+8.722026e-02 i
 x=3.300000e-01
  u= 8.818665e-01-1.044890e-01 i    v= 9.407135e-01-
5.532195e-02 i
  v1= 1.117481e+00+9.783249e-02 i
 x=3.600000e-01
  u= 8.656208e-01-1.169047e-01 i    v= 9.324847e-01-
6.240845e-02 i
  v1= 1.133414e+00+1.081419e-01 i
 x=3.900000e-01
  u= 8.487762e-01-1.293238e-01 i    v= 9.239203e-01-
6.963972e-02 i
  v1= 1.149841e+00+1.180227e-01 i
 x=4.200000e-01
  u= 8.313838e-01-1.416750e-01 i    v= 9.150376e-01-
7.698719e-02 i
  v1= 1.166686e+00+1.273525e-01 i
 x=4.500000e-01
  u= 8.134942e-01-1.538931e-01 i    v= 9.058527e-01-
8.442433e-02 i
  v1= 1.183874e+00+1.360122e-01 i
 x=4.800000e-01
```

```
  u= 7.951587e-01-1.659183e-01 i    v= 8.963810e-01-
9.192637e-02 i
  v1= 1.201323e+00+1.438852e-01 i
 x=5.100000e-01
  u= 7.764289e-01-1.776959e-01 i    v= 8.866367e-01-
9.947018e-02 i
  v1= 1.218951e+00+1.508568e-01 i
 x=5.400000e-01
  u= 7.573580e-01-1.891766e-01 i    v= 8.766338e-01-
1.070341e-01 i
  v1= 1.236668e+00+1.568144e-01 i
 x=5.700000e-01
  u= 7.380006e-01-2.003157e-01 i    v= 8.663856e-01-
1.145977e-01 i
  v1= 1.254382e+00+1.616467e-01 i
 x=6.000000e-01
  u= 7.197698e-01-2.129194e-01 i    v= 8.560491e-01-
1.223308e-01 i
  v1= 1.283294e+00+1.769269e-01 i
 x=6.500000e-01    u= 6.843165e-01-2.294700e-01 i    v=
8.379984e-01-1.347359e-01 i
  v1= 1.313765e+00+1.858919e-01 i
 x=5.000000e-01
  u= 7.827127e-01-1.738007e-01 i    v= 8.899142e-01-
9.695231e-02 i
  v1= 1.213060e+00+1.486401e-01 i
 x=7.250000e-01
  u= 6.315013e-01-2.515312e-01 i    v= 8.100087e-01-
1.530083e-01 i
  v1= 1.361306e+00+1.951616e-01 i
 x=9.500000e-01
  u= 4.743770e-01-2.977273e-01 i    v= 7.205901e-01-
2.034144e-01 i
  v1= 1.502095e+00+1.850646e-01 i
 x=1.175000e+00
  u= 3.264998e-01-3.109774e-01 i    v= 6.264347e-01-
2.439125e-01 i
  v1= 1.619007e+00+1.178625e-01 i
 x=1.400000e+00
  u= 1.990801e-01-2.944071e-01 i    v= 5.318838e-01-
2.722997e-01 i
  v1= 1.694756e+00+2.475825e-03 i
 x=1.625000e+00
  u= 9.886023e-02-2.565045e-01 i    v= 4.406599e-01-
2.881881e-01 i
  v1= 1.719215e+00-1.458857e-01 i
 x=1.850000e+00
  u= 2.751647e-02-2.072471e-01 i    v= 3.556789e-01-
2.924606e-01 i
```

```
  v1= 1.689474e+00-3.092188e-01 i
 x=2.075000e+00
  u= -1.735795e-02-1.556391e-01 i   v= 2.789686e-01-
2.868017e-01 i
  v1= 1.609169e+00-4.702686e-01 i
 x=2.300000e+00
  u= -4.073382e-02-1.083114e-01 i   v= 2.116933e-01-
2.732903e-01 i
  v1= 1.486721e+00-6.149744e-01 i
 x=2.525000e+00
  u= -4.857045e-02-6.910618e-02 i   v= 1.542637e-01-
2.540821e-01 i
  v1= 1.333216e+00-7.336303e-01 i
 x=2.750000e+00
  u= -4.656383e-02-3.938490e-02 i   v= 1.064940e-01-
2.311897e-01 i
  v1= 1.160455e+00-8.209792e-01 i
 x=2.975000e+00
  u= -3.938535e-02-1.871651e-02 i   v= 6.777192e-02-
2.063541e-01 i
  v1= 9.794858e-01-8.756115e-01 i
 x=3.200000e+00
  u= -3.039143e-02-5.640541e-03 i   v= 3.721630e-02-
1.809883e-01 i
  v1= 7.997060e-01-8.990345e-01 i
 x=3.425000e+00
  u= -2.167745e-02+1.689263e-03 i   v= 1.380731e-02-
1.561732e-01 i
  v1= 6.284608e-01-8.946950e-01 i
 x=3.650000e+00
  u= -1.432209e-02+5.063513e-03 i   v= -3.514089e-03-
1.326836e-01 i
  v1= 4.710065e-01-8.671213e-01 i
 x=3.875000e+00
  u= -8.692264e-03+5.977304e-03 i   v= -1.577664e-02-
1.110311e-01 i
  v1= 3.306956e-01-8.212549e-01 i
 x=4.100000e+00
  u= -4.724833e-03+5.546986e-03 i   v= -2.393429e-02-
9.151265e-02 i
  v1= 2.092717e-01-7.619756e-01 i
 x=4.325000e+00
  u= -2.144750e-03+4.526563e-03 i   v= -2.884110e-02-
7.425672e-02 i
  v1= 1.071965e-01-6.937947e-01 i
 x=4.550000e+00
  u= -6.116183e-04+3.373666e-03 i   v= -3.124029e-02-
5.926612e-02 i
  v1= 2.396400e-02-6.206772e-01 i
```

```
 x=4.775000e+00
  u= 1.957540e-04+2.329762e-03 i    v= -3.176305e-02-
4.645383e-02 i
  v1= -4.161992e-02-5.459594e-01 i
```

```
/*
"Abramowitz" functions f1, f2, f3 from Ch.27
from C Mathematical Function Handbook by Louis Baker
Copyright 1991 by Louis Baker. All rights reserved.
*/

#include <stdio.h>
#include "complex.hpp"
int itkt;

#define pi 3.141592653589793238462643383279
#define errorcode -1.e60
#define ABS(x)  ((x)>0.?(x):-(x))


complex af2s(complex& z)
{
complex x,ln,sp,sq,sum1,sum2;
sp=sqrt(pi);
x=z;
if(x.abs()>0.)ln=x.clog();
else ln=0.;
sq=x*x;
sum1=(-.000491-.0000235*x);
sum1= x*(sq*(-.3225+x*(-.1477
+x*(.03195+x*(.00328+x*sum1))))-1.);
sum1+=sp*.5*(1.+sq);
sum2=.3333333+sq*(.000198*sq-.01667);
/*sum1= .5*sp-x+.5*sp*sq-.3225*cube-.1477*sq*sq
+.03195*cube*sq+.00328*cube*cube-.000491*cube*cube*x
-.0000235*cube*cube*sq;*/

return .5*(ln*x*sq*sum2+sum1);
}

complex af3s(complex& x)
{
complex ln,sp,sq,sum1,sum2;
sp=sqrt(pi);
if(x.abs()>0.)ln=x.clog();
else ln=0.;
sq=x*x;
sum2=.0833+sq*(-.00278+.000025*sq);
/*sum1= 1.-.5*sp*x+.5*sq-.2954*cube+.1014*sq*sq
+.02954*cube*sq-.00578*cube*cube-.00047*cube*cube*x
-.000064*four*four;*/
sum1=(-.00578+x*(-.00047+.000064*x));
sum1= 1.+x*(-.5*sp+x*(.5+x*(-.2954+x*(.1014+x*(
```

```
.02954+x*sum1)))));

return .5*(sum1-ln*sq*sq*sum2);
}

complex af1s(complex& x)
{
int k,itmax=400,in; double dk;
complex sp,sq,ln,sum,term,coef,a,b,aa[2],bb[2],t;
sp=sqrt(pi);
sq=x*x;
if(x.abs()>0.)ln=x.clog();
else ln=0.;
sum=0.;
term=1.;
in=0;
aa[0]=0.;aa[1]=-1.;
bb[0]=-sp;bb[1]=1.5*(1.-.57721556649);
a=0.;b=1.;
for(k=0;k<itmax;k++)
   {
   coef= a*ln+b;
   t=coef*term;
   sum+=t;
/*printf(" k in %d %d a,b %e %e s t %e %e
c=%e\n",k,in,a,b,sum,t,coef);*/
   if( t.abs()<1.e-8 || t.abs()<1.e-7*(sum.abs()))break;
   term*=x;
   itkt=k;
   if(k>1)
      {
      dk=k;
      coef=1./((dk+1)*(dk-1.)*dk);
      aa[in]= -2.*aa[in]*coef ;
      bb[in]= (-2.*bb[in]-(3.*dk*dk-1.)*aa[in])*coef;
      }
   a=aa[in];b=bb[in];
   in++;
   if(in>1)in=0;
   }
return .5*sum;
}


complex afa(complex& x,int& n)
{
int i,itmax=300; double k;
complex y,z,sum,term,v,vi,a,old,older,t,oldt;
/*if(x<=1.)return -1.;*/
```

```
v= 3.*((.5*x)^.666666);vi=1./v;
sum=0.;
term=1.;a=1.;old=0.;t=1.e10;
for(i=0;i<itmax;i++)
    {
    oldt=t;
    t=term*a;
    if( t.abs()>oldt.abs()) break;
    sum+=t;
    term*=vi;
    older=old;
    old=a;
    if(!i) a=(3.*n*n+3.*n-1.)/12.;
    else
        {
        k=i+1;
        a=(.5*(n-2*k)*(2*k+3-n)*((2*k+3+2*n)*older
            -(12*k*k+36*k-3*n*n-3*n+25)*old))/(12*(k+2));
        }
    if(t.abs()<1.e-8|| t.abs()<1.e-7*(sum.abs()))break;
    itkt=i;
    }
return sqrt(pi/3.)*((v/3.)^(.5*n))*((-v).cexp())*sum;
}

complex af1(complex& x)
{
if(x.abs()<3.)return af1s(x);
return afa(x,1.);
}
complex af2(complex& x)
{
if(x.abs()<2.25)return af2s(x);
return afa(x,2.);
}
complex af3(complex& x)
{
if(x.abs()<3.)return af3s(x);
return afa(x,3.);
}

complex af(complex& x, int n)
{
complex nn,old,older,oldest;
int m;
if(n==1)return af1(x);
if(n==2)return af2(x);
if(n==3)return af3(x);
oldest=af3(x);older=af2(x);old=af1(x);
```

```
for(m=4;m<=n;m++)
   {
   nn=.5*( (m-1)*older+x*oldest);
   oldest=older;older=old;old=nn;
   }
return nn;
}

main()
{int i,n;double d;complex u,v,w,z,x;
for (i=0;i<51;i++)
   {d=(i)*(10./50.);
   x=complex(d,0.);
   u=af(x,1);
   v=af(x,2);
   w=af(x,3);
   z=af(x,4);

   printf(" x=%le\n",d);
   u.print(" 1="," ");
   v.print(" 2=","\n");
   w.print(" 3="," ");
   z.print(" 4=","\n");
   }
for (i=0;i<51;i++)
   {d=(i)*(10./50.);
   x=complex(0.,d);
   u=af(x,1);
   v=af(x,2);
   w=af(x,3);
   z=af(x,4);

   printf(" x=%le\n",d);
   u.print(" 1="," ");
   v.print(" 2=","\n");
   w.print(" 3="," ");
   z.print(" 4=","\n");
   }
}
```

```
Test Output: Abramowitz Functions, complex arg.
 x=0.000000e+00
 1= 5.000000e-01+0.000000e+00 i   2= 4.431135e-
01+0.000000e+00 i
 3= 5.000000e-01+0.000000e+00 i   4= 6.646702e-
01+0.000000e+00 i
 x=2.000000e-01
 1= 3.697654e-01+0.000000e+00 i   2= 3.572934e-
01+0.000000e+00 i
 3= 4.203885e-01+0.000000e+00 i   4= 5.779790e-
01+0.000000e+00 i
 x=4.000000e-01
 1= 2.855520e-01+0.000000e+00 i   2= 2.922752e-
01+0.000000e+00 i
 3= 3.557106e-01+0.000000e+00 i   4= 5.095550e-
01+0.000000e+00 i
 x=6.000000e-01
 1= 2.254685e-01+0.000000e+00 i   2= 2.414850e-
01+0.000000e+00 i
 3= 3.025314e-01+0.000000e+00 i   4= 4.529869e-
01+0.000000e+00 i
 x=8.000000e-01
 1= 1.807463e-01+0.000000e+00 i   2= 2.010715e-
01+0.000000e+00 i
 3= 2.584178e-01+0.000000e+00 i   4= 4.049744e-
01+0.000000e+00 i
 x=1.000000e+00
 1= 1.465634e-01+0.000000e+00 i   2= 1.684847e-
01+0.000000e+00 i
 3= 2.215635e-01+0.000000e+00 i   4= 3.635088e-
01+0.000000e+00 i
 x=1.200000e+00
 1= 1.199378e-01+0.000000e+00 i   2= 1.419311e-
01+0.000000e+00 i
 3= 1.905890e-01+0.000000e+00 i   4= 3.272501e-
01+0.000000e+00 i
 x=1.400000e+00
 1= 9.889655e-02+0.000000e+00 i   2= 1.200960e-
01+0.000000e+00 i
 3= 1.644158e-01+0.000000e+00 i   4= 2.952351e-
01+0.000000e+00 i
 x=1.600000e+00
 1= 8.207459e-02+0.000000e+00 i   2= 1.019775e-
01+0.000000e+00 i
 3= 1.421788e-01+0.000000e+00 i   4= 2.667093e-
01+0.000000e+00 i
 x=1.800000e+00
 1= 6.849630e-02+0.000000e+00 i   2= 8.677440e-
02+0.000000e+00 i
```

```
 3= 1.231548e-01+0.000000e+00 i   4= 2.410010e-
01+0.000000e+00 i
 x=2.000000e+00
 1= 5.744682e-02+0.000000e+00 i   2= 7.379881e-
02+0.000000e+00 i
 3= 1.066961e-01+0.000000e+00 i   4= 2.173943e-
01+0.000000e+00 i
 x=2.200000e+00
 1= 4.839187e-02+0.000000e+00 i   2= 6.239657e-
02+0.000000e+00 i
 3= 9.215693e-02+0.000000e+00 i   4= 1.949675e-
01+0.000000e+00 i
 x=2.400000e+00
 1= 4.092569e-02+0.000000e+00 i   2= 5.536811e-
02+0.000000e+00 i
 3= 7.880488e-02+0.000000e+00 i   4= 1.776180e-
01+0.000000e+00 i
 x=2.600000e+00
 1= 3.473586e-02+0.000000e+00 i   2= 4.776243e-
02+0.000000e+00 i
 3= 6.570591e-02+0.000000e+00 i   4= 1.570613e-
01+0.000000e+00 i
 x=2.800000e+00
 1= 2.957908e-02+0.000000e+00 i   2= 4.130095e-
02+0.000000e+00 i
 3= 5.157321e-02+0.000000e+00 i   4= 1.341539e-
01+0.000000e+00 i
 x=3.000000e+00
 1= 2.542164e-02+0.000000e+00 i   2= 3.579370e-
02+0.000000e+00 i
 3= 5.246624e-02+0.000000e+00 i   4= 1.323899e-
01+0.000000e+00 i
 x=3.200000e+00
 1= 2.176361e-02+0.000000e+00 i   2= 3.108573e-
02+0.000000e+00 i
 3= 4.623691e-02+0.000000e+00 i   4= 1.206076e-
01+0.000000e+00 i
 x=3.400000e+00
 1= 1.868136e-02+0.000000e+00 i   2= 2.704993e-
02+0.000000e+00 i
 3= 4.079445e-02+0.000000e+00 i   4= 1.099255e-
01+0.000000e+00 i
 x=3.600000e+00
 1= 1.607518e-02+0.000000e+00 i   2= 2.358150e-
02+0.000000e+00 i
 3= 5.005312e-02+0.000000e+00 i   4= 1.254679e-
01+0.000000e+00 i
 x=3.800000e+00
```

```
 1= 1.386446e-02+0.000000e+00 i    2= 2.059354e-
02+0.000000e+00 i
 3= 4.356222e-02+0.000000e+00 i    4= 1.136585e-
01+0.000000e+00 i
 x=4.000000e+00
 1= 1.198359e-02+0.000000e+00 i    2= 1.801376e-
02+0.000000e+00 i
 3= 3.800507e-02+0.000000e+00 i    4= 1.030308e-
01+0.000000e+00 i
 x=4.200000e+00
 1= 1.037893e-02+0.000000e+00 i    2= 1.578172e-
02+0.000000e+00 i
 3= 3.323083e-02+0.000000e+00 i    4= 9.345733e-
02+0.000000e+00 i
 x=4.400000e+00
 1= 9.006372e-03+0.000000e+00 i    2= 1.384674e-
02+0.000000e+00 i
 3= 2.911628e-02+0.000000e+00 i    4= 8.482593e-
02+0.000000e+00 i
 x=4.600000e+00
 1= 7.829492e-03+0.000000e+00 i    2= 1.216615e-
02+0.000000e+00 i
 3= 2.556004e-02+0.000000e+00 i    4= 7.703731e-
02+0.000000e+00 i
 x=4.800000e+00
 1= 6.818093e-03+0.000000e+00 i    2= 1.070393e-
02+0.000000e+00 i
 3= 2.247820e-02+0.000000e+00 i    4= 7.000358e-
02+0.000000e+00 i
 x=5.000000e+00
 1= 5.947038e-03+0.000000e+00 i    2= 9.429567e-
03+0.000000e+00 i
 3= 1.980096e-02+0.000000e+00 i    4= 6.364675e-
02+0.000000e+00 i
 x=5.200000e+00
 1= 5.195329e-03+0.000000e+00 i    2= 8.317165e-
03+0.000000e+00 i
 3= 1.746992e-02+0.000000e+00 i    4= 5.789753e-
02+0.000000e+00 i
 x=5.400000e+00
 1= 4.545366e-03+0.000000e+00 i    2= 7.344662e-
03+0.000000e+00 i
 3= 1.543603e-02+0.000000e+00 i    4= 5.269428e-
02+0.000000e+00 i
 x=5.600000e+00
 1= 3.982350e-03+0.000000e+00 i    2= 6.493231e-
03+0.000000e+00 i
 3= 1.365793e-02+0.000000e+00 i    4= 4.798205e-
02+0.000000e+00 i
```

```
 x=5.800000e+00
 1= 3.493801e-03+0.000000e+00 i   2= 5.746766e-
03+0.000000e+00 i
 3= 1.210058e-02+0.000000e+00 i   4= 4.371182e-
02+0.000000e+00 i
 x=6.000000e+00
 1= 3.069170e-03+0.000000e+00 i   2= 5.091456e-
03+0.000000e+00 i
 3= 1.073421e-02+0.000000e+00 i   4= 3.983980e-
02+0.000000e+00 i
 x=6.200000e+00
 1= 2.699509e-03+0.000000e+00 i   2= 4.515439e-
03+0.000000e+00 i
 3= 9.533443e-03+0.000000e+00 i   4= 3.632683e-
02+0.000000e+00 i
 x=6.400000e+00
 1= 2.377216e-03+0.000000e+00 i   2= 4.008499e-
03+0.000000e+00 i
 3= 8.476592e-03+0.000000e+00 i   4= 3.313784e-
02+0.000000e+00 i
 x=6.600000e+00
 1= 2.095815e-03+0.000000e+00 i   2= 3.561830e-
03+0.000000e+00 i
 3= 7.545047e-03+0.000000e+00 i   4= 3.024140e-
02+0.000000e+00 i
 x=6.800000e+00
 1= 1.849777e-03+0.000000e+00 i   2= 3.167819e-
03+0.000000e+00 i
 3= 6.722819e-03+0.000000e+00 i   4= 2.760931e-
02+0.000000e+00 i
 x=7.000000e+00
 1= 1.634370e-03+0.000000e+00 i   2= 2.819880e-
03+0.000000e+00 i
 3= 5.996124e-03+0.000000e+00 i   4= 2.521625e-
02+0.000000e+00 i
 x=7.200000e+00
 1= 1.445539e-03+0.000000e+00 i   2= 2.512303e-
03+0.000000e+00 i
 3= 5.353059e-03+0.000000e+00 i   4= 2.303947e-
02+0.000000e+00 i
 x=7.400000e+00
 1= 1.279803e-03+0.000000e+00 i   2= 2.240127e-
03+0.000000e+00 i
 3= 4.783321e-03+0.000000e+00 i   4= 2.105848e-
02+0.000000e+00 i
 x=7.600000e+00
 1= 1.134163e-03+0.000000e+00 i   2= 1.999044e-
03+0.000000e+00 i
```

```
 3= 4.277972e-03+0.000000e+00 i    4= 1.925486e-
02+0.000000e+00 i
 x=7.800000e+00
 1= 1.006036e-03+0.000000e+00 i    2= 1.785297e-
03+0.000000e+00 i
 3= 3.829246e-03+0.000000e+00 i    4= 1.761200e-
02+0.000000e+00 i
 x=8.000000e+00
 1= 8.931910e-04+0.000000e+00 i    2= 1.595612e-
03+0.000000e+00 i
 3= 3.430381e-03+0.000000e+00 i    4= 1.611494e-
02+0.000000e+00 i
 x=8.200000e+00
 1= 7.936999e-04+0.000000e+00 i    2= 1.427132e-
03+0.000000e+00 i
 3= 3.075481e-03+0.000000e+00 i    4= 1.475017e-
02+0.000000e+00 i
 x=8.400000e+00
 1= 7.058914e-04+0.000000e+00 i    2= 1.277355e-
03+0.000000e+00 i
 3= 2.759394e-03+0.000000e+00 i    4= 1.350549e-
02+0.000000e+00 i
 x=8.600000e+00
 1= 6.283162e-04+0.000000e+00 i    2= 1.144094e-
03+0.000000e+00 i
 3= 2.477614e-03+0.000000e+00 i    4= 1.236988e-
02+0.000000e+00 i
 x=8.800000e+00
 1= 5.597154e-04+0.000000e+00 i    2= 1.025431e-
03+0.000000e+00 i
 3= 2.226193e-03+0.000000e+00 i    4= 1.133340e-
02+0.000000e+00 i
 x=9.000000e+00
 1= 4.989937e-04+0.000000e+00 i    2= 9.196833e-
04+0.000000e+00 i
 3= 2.001666e-03+0.000000e+00 i    4= 1.038702e-
02+0.000000e+00 i
 x=9.200000e+00
 1= 4.451972e-04+0.000000e+00 i    2= 8.253726e-
04+0.000000e+00 i
 3= 1.800988e-03+0.000000e+00 i    4= 9.522604e-
03+0.000000e+00 i
 x=9.400000e+00
 1= 3.974941e-04+0.000000e+00 i    2= 7.411988e-
04+0.000000e+00 i
 3= 1.621482e-03+0.000000e+00 i    4= 8.732765e-
03+0.000000e+00 i
 x=9.600000e+00
```

```
 1= 3.551577e-04+0.000000e+00 i   2= 6.660178e-
04+0.000000e+00 i
 3= 1.460789e-03+0.000000e+00 i   4= 8.010816e-
03+0.000000e+00 i
 x=9.800000e+00
 1= 3.175529e-04+0.000000e+00 i   2= 5.988209e-
04+0.000000e+00 i
 3= 1.316829e-03+0.000000e+00 i   4= 7.350694e-
03+0.000000e+00 i
 x=1.000000e+01
 1= 2.841238e-04+0.000000e+00 i   2= 5.387187e-
04+0.000000e+00 i
 3= 1.187764e-03+0.000000e+00 i   4= 6.746900e-
03+0.000000e+00 i
 x=0.000000e+00
 1= 5.000000e-01+0.000000e+00 i   2= 4.431135e-
01+0.000000e+00 i
 3= 5.000000e-01+0.000000e+00 i   4= 6.646702e-
01+0.000000e+00 i
 x=2.000000e-01
 1= 4.549057e-01-1.480911e-01 i   2= 4.273692e-01-9.655467e-
02 i
 3= 4.901887e-01-8.754118e-02 i   4= 6.498080e-01-9.581314e-
02 i
 x=4.000000e-01
 1= 3.731440e-01-2.461542e-01 i   2= 3.872075e-01-1.796639e-
01 i
 3= 4.622920e-01-1.693248e-01 i   4= 6.146762e-01-1.770374e-
01 i
 x=6.000000e-01
 1= 2.817742e-01-3.050362e-01 i   2= 3.315160e-01-2.451987e-
01 i
 3= 4.194967e-01-2.413909e-01 i   4= 5.696913e-01-2.419490e-
01 i
 x=8.000000e-01
 1= 1.920694e-01-3.337272e-01 i   2= 2.672041e-01-2.924982e-
01 i
 3= 3.654183e-01-3.013524e-01 i   4= 5.213471e-01-2.925799e-
01 i
 x=1.000000e+00
 1= 1.097163e-01-3.396317e-01 i   2= 1.995457e-01-3.225295e-
01 i
 3= 3.036220e-01-3.480352e-01 i   4= 4.733361e-01-3.319833e-
01 i
 x=1.200000e+00
 1= 3.751579e-02-3.288040e-01 i   2= 1.324722e-01-3.370841e-
01 i
 3= 2.373858e-01-3.811826e-01 i   4= 4.274179e-01-3.631946e-
01 i
```

```
 x=1.400000e+00
 1= -2.340341e-02-3.061532e-01 i   2= 6.881887e-02-
3.383391e-01 i
 3= 1.695817e-01-4.012176e-01 i   4= 3.840806e-01-3.888014e-
01 i
 x=1.600000e+00
 1= -7.292450e-02-2.756209e-01 i   2= 1.053067e-02-
3.286025e-01 i
 3= 1.026241e-01-4.090548e-01 i   4= 3.430398e-01-4.108044e-
01 i
 x=1.800000e+00
 1= -1.115456e-01-2.403345e-01 i   2= -4.116903e-02-
3.101664e-01 i
 3= 3.845653e-02-4.059592e-01 i   4= 3.036098e-01-4.306387e-
01 i
 x=2.000000e+00
 1= -1.401270e-01-2.027404e-01 i   2= -8.564557e-02-
2.852319e-01 i
 3= -2.144173e-02-3.934502e-01 i   4= 2.649818e-01-
4.492896e-01 i
 x=2.200000e+00
 1= -1.597249e-01-1.647176e-01 i   2= -1.227544e-01-
2.558859e-01 i
 3= -7.604076e-02-3.732491e-01 i   4= 2.264425e-01-
4.674737e-01 i
 x=2.400000e+00
 1= -1.714806e-01-1.276762e-01 i   2= -1.528941e-01-
2.202158e-01 i
 3= -1.247473e-01-3.472749e-01 i   4= 1.873887e-01-
4.800205e-01 i
 x=2.600000e+00
 1= -1.765464e-01-9.264058e-02 i   2= -1.745422e-01-
1.852185e-01 i
 3= -1.674021e-01-3.176895e-01 i   4= 1.511831e-01-
4.954504e-01 i
 x=2.800000e+00
 1= -1.760371e-01-6.032150e-02 i   2= -1.894881e-01-
1.498466e-01 i
 3= -2.042951e-01-2.870009e-01 i   4= 1.175691e-01-
5.107830e-01 i
 x=3.000000e+00
 1= -1.708276e-01-2.999222e-02 i   2= -1.983246e-01-
1.150920e-01 i
 3= -2.100070e-01-2.487606e-01 i   4= 7.565400e-02-
4.876485e-01 i
 x=3.200000e+00
 1= -1.620870e-01-4.473461e-03 i   2= -2.017130e-01-
8.174940e-02 i
```

```
 3= -2.329247e-01-2.092900e-01 i    4= 3.229459e-02-
4.953036e-01 i
 x=3.400000e+00
 1= -1.506849e-01+1.753618e-02 i    2= -2.003481e-01-
5.043446e-02 i
 3= -2.490269e-01-1.691248e-01 i    4= -1.300996e-02-
4.989975e-01 i
 x=3.600000e+00
 1= -1.373718e-01+3.606421e-02 i    2= -1.949307e-01-
2.160273e-02 i
 3= -3.023162e-01-7.805177e-03 i    4= -2.783468e-01-
5.765732e-01 i
 x=3.800000e+00
 1= -1.228010e-01+5.122910e-02 i    2= -1.861467e-
01+4.430519e-03 i
 3= -2.862291e-01+2.386909e-02 i    4= -3.245713e-01-
5.371896e-01 i
 x=4.000000e+00
 1= -1.075312e-01+6.321587e-02 i    2= -1.746510e-
01+2.747115e-02 i
 3= -2.681439e-01+5.213255e-02 i    4= -3.662417e-01-
4.950811e-01 i
 x=4.200000e+00
 1= -9.203252e-02+7.225591e-02 i    2= -1.610568e-
01+4.742781e-02 i
 3= -2.484282e-01+7.701850e-02 i    4= -4.033241e-01-
4.505574e-01 i
 x=4.400000e+00
 1= -7.669279e-02+7.861065e-02 i    2= -1.459277e-
01+6.429481e-02 i
 3= -2.274439e-01+9.857537e-02 i    4= -4.357574e-01-
4.039344e-01 i
 x=4.600000e+00
 1= -6.182498e-02+8.255825e-02 i    2= -1.297731e-
01+7.813643e-02 i
 3= -2.055436e-01+1.168724e-01 i    4= -4.634661e-01-
3.555456e-01 i
 x=4.800000e+00
 1= -4.767487e-02+8.438311e-02 i    2= -1.130460e-
01+8.907268e-02 i
 3= -1.830655e-01+1.320024e-01 i    4= -4.863747e-01-
3.057482e-01 i
 x=5.000000e+00
 1= -3.442872e-02+8.436762e-02 i    2= -9.614254e-
02+9.726667e-02 i
 3= -1.603298e-01+1.440825e-01 i    4= -5.044201e-01-
2.549246e-01 i
 x=5.200000e+00
```

```
 1= -2.222064e-02+8.278582e-02 i   2= -7.940334e-
02+1.029134e-01 i
 3= -1.376348e-01+1.532528e-01 i   4= -5.175624e-01-
2.034803e-01 i
 x=5.400000e+00
 1= -1.113972e-02+7.989872e-02 i   2= -6.311525e-
02+1.062301e-01 i
 3= -1.152538e-01+1.596747e-01 i   4= -5.257947e-01-
1.518400e-01 i
 x=5.600000e+00
 1= -1.236640e-03+7.595091e-02 i   2= -4.751458e-
02+1.074478e-01 i
 3= -9.343306e-02+1.635276e-01 i   4= -5.291492e-01-
1.004408e-01 i
 x=5.800000e+00
 1= 7.470242e-03+7.116833e-02 i   2= -3.279055e-
02+1.068045e-01 i
 3= -7.239031e-02+1.650057e-01 i   4= -5.277024e-01-
4.972514e-02 i
 x=6.000000e+00
 1= 1.498928e-02+6.575686e-02 i   2= -1.908919e-
02+1.045389e-01 i
 3= -5.231372e-02+1.643146e-01 i   4= -5.215776e-01-
1.327654e-04 i
 x=6.200000e+00
 1= 2.135055e-02+5.990169e-02 i   2= -6.517405e-
03+1.008860e-01 i
 3= -3.336190e-02+1.616675e-01 i   4= -5.109455e-
01+4.790709e-02 i
 x=6.400000e+00
 1= 2.660132e-02+5.376728e-02 i   2= 4.852853e-03+9.607275e-
02 i
 3= -1.566427e-02+1.572819e-01 i   4= -4.960229e-
01+9.398347e-02 i
 x=6.600000e+00
 1= 3.080214e-02+4.749772e-02 i   2= 1.498048e-02+9.031546e-
02 i
 3= 6.780480e-04+1.513762e-01 i   4= -4.770708e-
01+1.377107e-01 i
 x=6.800000e+00
 1= 3.402331e-02+4.121745e-02 i   2= 2.385121e-02+8.381721e-
02 i
 3= 1.559091e-02+1.441666e-01 i   4= -4.543897e-
01+1.787349e-01 i
 x=7.000000e+00
 1= 3.634196e-02+3.503230e-02 i   2= 3.147378e-02+7.676632e-
02 i
 3= 2.902556e-02+1.358647e-01 i   4= -4.283158e-
01+2.167389e-01 i
```

```
 x=7.200000e+00
 1= 3.783939e-02+2.903059e-02 i   2= 3.787634e-02+6.933519e-
02 i
 3= 4.095673e-02+1.266748e-01 i   4= -3.992148e-
01+2.514470e-01 i
 x=7.400000e+00
 1= 3.859895e-02+2.328448e-02 i   2= 4.310304e-02+6.167977e-
02 i
 3= 5.138060e-02+1.167922e-01 i   4= -3.674765e-
01+2.826279e-01 i
 x=7.600000e+00
 1= 3.870420e-02+1.785130e-02 i   2= 4.721098e-02+5.393925e-
02 i
 3= 6.031266e-02+1.064013e-01 i   4= -3.335083e-
01+3.100970e-01 i
 x=7.800000e+00
 1= 3.823743e-02+1.277494e-02 i   2= 5.026734e-02+4.623624e-
02 i
 3= 6.778547e-02+9.567431e-02 i   4= -2.977288e-
01+3.337177e-01 i
 x=8.000000e+00
 1= 3.727841e-02+8.087254e-03 i   2= 5.234685e-02+3.867712e-
02 i
 3= 7.384646e-02+8.477057e-02 i   4= -2.605620e-
01+3.534015e-01 i
 x=8.200000e+00
 1= 3.590349e-02+3.809416e-03 i   2= 5.352955e-02+3.135263e-
02 i
 3= 7.855570e-02+7.383545e-02 i   4= -2.224310e-
01+3.691073e-01 i
 x=8.400000e+00
 1= 3.418483e-02-4.677283e-05 i   2= 5.389872e-02+2.433866e-
02 i
 3= 8.198384e-02+6.300014e-02 i   4= -1.837525e-
01+3.808401e-01 i
 x=8.600000e+00
 1= 3.218991e-02-3.477630e-03 i   2= 5.353919e-02+1.769713e-
02 i
 3= 8.420999e-02+5.238145e-02 i   4= -1.449315e-
01+3.886487e-01 i
 x=8.800000e+00
 1= 2.998113e-02-6.486414e-03 i   2= 5.253580e-02+1.147697e-
02 i
 3= 8.531988e-02+4.208186e-02 i   4= -1.063565e-
01+3.926229e-01 i
 x=9.000000e+00
 1= 2.761558e-02-9.082230e-03 i   2= 5.097215e-02+5.715154e-
03 i
```

```
 3= 8.540399e-02+3.218973e-02 i    4= -6.839557e-
02+3.928907e-01 i
 x=9.200000e+00
 1= 2.514501e-02-1.127901e-02 i    2= 4.892951e-02+4.377629e-
04 i
 3= 8.455599e-02+2.277978e-02 i    4= -3.139272e-
02+3.896142e-01 i
 x=9.400000e+00
 1= 2.261576e-02-1.309461e-02 i    2= 4.648596e-02-4.338918e-
03 i
 3= 8.287116e-02+1.391354e-02 i    4= 4.335316e-03+3.829861e-
01 i
 x=9.600000e+00
 1= 2.006889e-02-1.454994e-02 i    2= 4.371569e-02-8.607346e-
03 i
 3= 8.044506e-02+5.640055e-03 i    4= 3.850127e-02+3.732253e-
01 i
 x=9.800000e+00
 1= 1.754032e-02-1.566824e-02 i    2= 4.068846e-02-1.236767e-
02 i
 3= 7.737236e-02-2.003373e-03 i    4= 7.084922e-02+3.605731e-
01 i
 x=1.000000e+01
 1= 1.506107e-02-1.647437e-02 i    2= 3.746921e-02-1.562675e-
02 i
 3= 7.374576e-02-8.990400e-03 i    4= 1.011558e-01+3.452887e-
01 i
```

```
/*
Riemann & Hurwitz
(generalized Riemann) Zeta Function
   series
from C Mathematical Function Handbook by Louis Baker
Copyright 1991 by Louis Baker. All rights reserved.
*/
#include "complex.hpp"
#define pi 3.14159265358979323
#define errorcode -1.e60
#define max(a,b) ((a)>(b)?(a):(b))
#define ABS(x) ((x)<0.?-(x):(x))

prep( complex& u, complex& v, complex& f)
{
f=0.;
do   {
   f+=u^(-v);u++;
   if(v.real()<1.)
      { while(u.real()>2.){u-=1.;f-=u^(-v);}}
   }while(u.real()<=v.real());
return 0;/* keep compiler happy*/
}

int j,k,kused,jused;

#define tolr 1.e-4
#define tola 1.e-10

complex complex::hurwitz(complex ain)
   {complex v,factor,sum1,sum2,a,b,c,ev,bi,term;
   // sum1,sum2 automatically zeroed to start
   int i;double z,bernoulli(int),scale;
   v=  *this;ev=-v;a=ain;
   prep( a,v,sum1);j=k=4;scale=.25;
   jused=j=max(j, (int)((v.abs()+.999)*scale));
   if(x<0.)jused=j=0;
   b=a+ ((double)j); c=a;
   bi= complex(1.,0.)/(b*b);
   for(i=0;i<j;i++){sum1+= c^ev;c=c+1.;}
   //sum1.print(" J sum=","\n");
   k= max((1.-x)*8.,k);
   z=2.;
   factor=(v-1.)*v*bi*.5;
   for(i=1;i<=k;i++)
      {
      term= factor*bernoulli(i<<1);sum2+=term;
      factor = factor*(v+z)*(v+z-1.)*bi/((z+2.)*(z+1.));
      if(factor== complex(0.,0.))break;
```

```
      if( term.abs() <sum2.abs() * tolr || term.abs()<tola)
break;
      z+=2.;kused=k;
      }
   //sum2.print(" k sum=","\n");
   sum1+=(b^ev)*.5;
   ev=1.-v;
   sum2= -(1.+sum2)/ev*(b^ev);
   return sum1+sum2;
   }

complex Riemann_zeta(complex& s)
{return s.hurwitz(complex(1.,0));}


#define lim 15.

complex cgamma( complex& );

complex xi( double t)
{ complex a(.5,t) ;complex b; b=.5*a;//b=.25+it/2
return -.5*(.25+t*t)*((complex(pi,0.))^(-b))
    *cgamma(b)*Riemann_zeta(a);
}

main()
{double x,y;
complex a,b(1.,0.),c(0.,1.);
printf(" size complex=%d\n",sizeof(complex));
a=b+c;
a.print("summand=","\n");
printf(" magnitude=%e\n", a.abs());
b=a/c;
b.print("quotient=","\n");
a=b.cexp();
a.print(" exponential=","\n");
b=a.clog();
b.print(" log of a=","\n");
a=complex(1.,0.);b=complex(4.,0.);
a.print(" a ","");b.print(" b ","\n");
b+=1.;b.print(" b after +=1. =","\n");
while(1)
   {
   printf(" enter x,y for s\n");scanf("%le%le",&x,&y);
   b=complex(x,y);
   printf(" enter x,y for a\n");scanf("%le%le",&x,&y);
   a=complex(x,y);// a=1 for Riemann Zeta function
   c=b.hurwitz(a);c.print(" zeta=","");
   b.print(" for z=","\n");
```

```
    printf("kused=%d jused=%d j,k %d %d\n",
      kused,jused,j,k);
    }
}
```

```
Test Output: Hurwitz Zeta
 size complex=16
summand= 1.000000e+00+1.000000e+00 i
 magnitude=1.414214e+00
quotient= 1.000000e+00-1.000000e+00 i
 exponential= 1.468694e+00-2.287355e+00 i
 log of a= 1.000000e+00-1.000000e+00 i
 a  1.000000e+00+0.000000e+00 i  b
4.000000e+00+0.000000e+00 i
 b after +=1. = 5.000000e+00+0.000000e+00 i
 enter x,y for s
2 0
 enter x,y for a
1 0
 zeta= 1.644934e+00+0.000000e+00 i  for z=
2.000000e+00+0.000000e+00 i
kused=4 jused=4 j,k 4 4
 enter x,y for s
3 0
 enter x,y for a
1 0
 zeta= 1.202057e+00+0.000000e+00 i  for z=
3.000000e+00+0.000000e+00 i
kused=4 jused=4 j,k 4 4
 enter x,y for s
0 0
 enter x,y for a
0 0
 zeta= 5.000000e-01+0.000000e+00 i  for z=
0.000000e+00+0.000000e+00 i
kused=4 jused=4 j,k 4 8
 enter x,y for s
```

```
/*
Riemann & Hurwitz
(generalized Riemann) Zeta Function
   Pade summation
from C Mathematical Function Handbook by Louis Baker
Copyright 1991 by Louis Baker. All rights reserved.
*/
//#include am.hpp    //for Zortech C++
#include <iostream.h> //for TURBO C++
#include <math.h>
#include "complex.hpp"
#define errorcode -1.e60
#define ABS(x)  ((x)>0.?(x):-(x))
#define max(a,b)  ((a)>(b)?(a):(b))
#define pi 3.14159265358979323846264338327 9

double Rzeta2( int k)
// Riemann Zeta function of 2*(k+1) returned
{double z[6]={1.64493406684822643647,1.08232323371113819152,
   1.01734306198444913971, 1.00407735619794433938,
   1.00099457512781808534,1.00024608655330804830};
if(k<6)return z[k];
// return 1+ 2^(-2k)+...+ 6^(-2k) in simplified form;
if(k>=30)return 1.;
double fk=-((k+1)<<1); double p2=pow(2.,fk);
return 1.+((p2+pow(3.,fk))*(1.+p2)+pow(5.,fk));
}

void prep( complex& u, complex& v, complex& f)
{
f=0.;
do    {
   f+=u^(-v);u++;
   if(v.real()<1.)
      { while(u.real()>2.){u-=1.;f-=u^(-v);}}
   }while(u.real()<=v.real());
}

#define tolabs 1.e-10
#define tolrel 1.e-5


int size=80,szused,jused;

complex complex::hurwitz(complex u)
{
complex b,c,f,t,p,q,*h,hold,tpu,ev;int i,j,k; double
diff,tk,z,scale;
if( *this==1. || ((u-*this+(*this).abs())==0.&&
```

```
  (*this).imaginary()==0.))return complex(errorcode,0.);
prep(u,*this,f);
//u.print("modified a=","");f.print(" modifed sum=","\n");
ev= -(*this);
j=4;scale=.25;
jused=j=max(j, (int)(((*this).abs()+.999)*scale));
if(x<0.)jused=j=0;
b=u+ ((double)j); c=u;
for(i=0;i<j;i++){f+= c^ev;c+=1.;}
//f.print(" modifed sum=","\n");
if( size%2)size++;//size must be even integer
h=new complex[size+1] ;
t=complex(-2.,0.);
h[0]=1.;k=0;
tpu=2.*pi*b;
tpu=1./(tpu*tpu);
while(k<size){
   tk=k<<1;
   t*=(*this+tk)*(1.-*this-tk)*tpu;
   z=Rzeta2(k);
   k++;
   h[k]=h[k-1]+t*z;
   q=0.;j=k;
   do   {
      p=h[j-1];
      if(h[j]==p)
         {
         h[j-1]=-errorcode;
         if(p==-errorcode)h[j-1]=q;
         }
      else h[j-1]= q+1./(h[j]-p);
      q=p;j--;
      }while(j);
   if(!(k%2))
      {
      diff=(hold-h[0]).abs();
      if(diff<tolabs || diff<tolrel * h[0].abs())break;
      hold=h[0];
      }
   };
 szused=k;
 ev= -(*this);
 tpu= 1.+ev;
 q=-h[0]*(b^tpu)/tpu;
 delete h;
 return f+.5*(b^ev)+q;
 }

 main()
```

```
{complex u,v,w;double a,b,c,d;

while(1)
   {
   cout << " enter v,u" ;
       //scanf("%le%le%le%le",&a,&b,&c,&d);
      cin >> a >> b >> c >> d ;
   if(a==0.&&b==0.&&c==0.&&d==0.)break;
      u=complex(c,d);v=complex(a,b);
      w=v.hurwitz(u);
       w.print(" Hurwitz=","\n");
   cout  << " max k used=" << szused << ", J used: " <<
jused << "\n" ;
   };
}
```

```
Test Output: Hurwitz Zeta
 enter v,u2 0
1 0
 Hurwitz= 1.644934e+00+0.000000e+00 i
 max k used=4, J used: 4
 enter v,u3 0 1 0
 Hurwitz= 1.202057e+00+0.000000e+00 i
 max k used=4, J used: 4
```

```
/*
Lerch Phi Transcendent
 (Generalized Riemann/Hurwitz Zeta)
from C Mathematical Function Handbook by Louis Baker
Copyright 1991 by Louis Baker. All rights reserved.
*/
#include "complex.hpp"
#define errorcode -1.e60
#define ABS(x) ((x)>0.?(x):-(x))
#define pi 3.14159265358979323846264338327 9

#define tolabs 1.e-8
#define tolrel 1.e-6
// were 1.e-5,1.e-3 respectively

int size=80,szused;

complex Lerch(complex z,complex a,complex xx)
{
complex f,t,p,q,*h,hold,tpu,ev;int j,k; double diff,tk;
if( size%2)size++;//size must be even integer
h=new complex[size+1] ;
// t=1.;
t= 1./(a^z);
h[0]=1.;k=0;tpu=xx; ev=complex(1.,0.);
while(k<size){
   k++;
//test t[n]=x^n geometric series 1+x+x^2+...=1/(1-x)
//                    t*=xx;
   f=ev+a;
   if(f.abs())t= tpu/(f^z);
   else t=0.;
   tpu*=xx;ev+=1.;
   h[k]=h[k-1]+t;
   q=0.;j=k;
   do    {
      p=h[j-1];
      if(h[j]==p)
         {
         h[j-1]=-errorcode;
         if(p==-errorcode)h[j-1]=q;
         }
      else h[j-1]= q+1./(h[j]-p);
      q=p;j--;
      }while(j);
   if(!(k%2))
      {
      diff=(hold-h[0]).abs();
      if(diff<tolabs || diff<tolrel * h[0].abs())break;
```

```
        hold=h[0];
        }
    };
szused=k;
hold=h[0];
delete h;
return  hold;
}

main()
{complex u,v,w,x;double a,b,c,d,e,f;
while(1)
    {
    printf(" enter v,u,x");
         scanf("%le%le%le%le%le%le",&a,&b,&c,&d,&e,&f);
    if(a==0.&&b==0.&&c==0.&&d==0.)break;
        u=complex(c,d);v=complex(a,b);w=complex(e,f);
        x=Lerch(v,u,w);
        //u= 1./(1.-w);
        x.print(" Lerch=","\n");
        //u.print(" 1/(1-x)=","\n");
    printf(" max k used=%d\n",szused);
    };
}
```

```
Test Output Lerch Phi Transcendent
 enter v,u,x2 0 1 0 1 0
 Lerch= 1.641276e+00+0.000000e+00 i
 max k used=44
 enter v,u,x2 0 1 0 .5 0
 Lerch= 1.164481e+00+0.000000e+00 i
 max k used=10
```

```
/*
Generalized Hypergeometric Function and Meijer G
   simple series used for former
from C Mathematical Function Handbook by Louis Baker
Copyright 1991 by Louis Baker. All rights reserved.
*/
#include "Cmatrix.hpp"

#define maxterm 100
#define abstol 1.e-8
#define reltol 1.e-5
#define errorcode -1.e60
#define pi 3.14159265358979323846264338327 9
#define lim 15.
#define max(a,b)  ((a)>(b)?(a):(b))

complex cgamma(complex&);

// generalized hypergeometric function pFq or pFq-1
// if 0<=k<=q then the k-th factor (c)k in denominator
omitted pFq-1
// if k=-1,say, then pFq= sum x^n/n!
(a[0])n..../{(c[0])n.....}

complex ghgF(int p,int q,complex x, Cvector& a, Cvector& c,
int k)
{complex sum(1.,0.),oldsum,power(1.,0.),btm;double
test,fact;
Cvector denom(max(q,1)),numer(max(p,1));
// use 2F1 if p=2,q=1
//x.print(" x in ghgf=","\n");
//printf(" in ghgF: p q %d %d k=%d\n",p,q,k);
fact=1.;
for(int j=0;j<p;j++)
   {
   //(a.element(j)).print(" a=","\n");
   numer.setelement(j,a.element(j));
   //(numer.element(j)).print(" numer=","\n");
   }
for( j=0;j<q;j++) {denom.setelement(j,c.element(j));
     //(denom.element(j)).print(" denom=","\n");
     //(c.element(j)).print(" a=","\n");
         }
//power.print(" power=","\n");
for(int i=0;i<maxterm;i++)
   {
   oldsum=sum;btm=1.;
   for(j=0;j<p;j++){power *= numer.element(j);
         //power.print(" power=","\n");
```

```
        numer.setelement(j,numer.element(j)+1.);}
    for(j=0;j<q;j++){if(j!=k)btm *=denom.element(j);
        denom.setelement(j,denom.element(j)+1.);}
    //btm.print(" btm=","\n");
    power *= (x/(btm*fact));
    //power.print(" power=","\n");
    sum+= power;fact+=1.;
    //printf(" fact=%e\n",fact);sum.print(" sum=","\n");
    test=(sum-oldsum).abs();
    if(test< abstol || test< reltol* sum.abs() )break;
    }
//sum.print(" ghgf=","\n");
return sum;
}

complex Gmeijer(int m, int n, int p, int q,Cvector& a,Cvec-
tor& c, complex& x)
{/* Meijer G function*/
complex coef,sum,denom,differ;double re;int j;
if(m<1 ||m>q){fprintf(stderr," Meijer:illegal m\n");return
errorcode;}
if(n<0 ||n>p){fprintf(stderr," Meijer:illegal n\n");return
errorcode;}
Cvector aa(max(1,q)),cc(max(1,p));
if(p>q)    /* p>q implies for pFq-1 as p'Fq' p'q'+1*/
    {
    //printf(" Meijer G: pq\n");
    for(j=0;j<q;j++) aa.setelement(j, 1.-c.element(j));
    for(j=0;j<p;j++) cc.setelement(j, 1.-a.element(j));
    sum=Gmeijer(n,m,q,p,aa,cc,1./x);
    return sum;
    }
else if(p==q)
    {if( x.abs()>=1.){//printf(" p=q Meijer\n");
      return complex(errorcode,0.);}
    }
for(int k=0;k<m;k++)//arrays based at zero(default)
    {
    coef=complex(1.,0.);
    denom=complex(1.,0.);

for(int j=0;j<p;j++)
    {cc.setelement(j,1.+c.element(k)-a.element(j));
    //(cc.element(j)).print(" numer=","\n");
    }
for( j=0;j<q;j++) {aa.setelement(j,1.+c.element(k)-c.ele-
ment(j));
      //(aa.element(j)).print(" denom=","\n");
        }
```

```
//coef.print(" coef=","\n");
   for( j=0;j<n;j++) if(j!=k)coef *= cgamma(1.-aa.ele-
ment(j));
//coef.print(" coef=","\n");
   for( j=0;j<n;j++) coef *= cgamma(cc.element(j));
//coef.print(" coef=","\n");
   for( j=n;j<p;j++)denom*= cgamma(1.-cc.element(j));
//denom.print(" denom=","\n");
   for( j=m;j<q;j++) denom *= cgamma(aa.element(j));
   coef *= (x^c.element(k))/denom;
//denom.print(" denom=","\n");
//printf(" before call ghgF ");coef.print(" coef=","\n");
//sum.print(" sum=","\n");
   sum += coef*ghgF(p,q,((p-m-n)%2?-1.:1.)*x,cc,aa,k);
//printf(" after call ");sum.print(" sum=","\n");
   }
return sum;
}

main()
{
complex a,b,c;double x,y;
/*
while(1)
   {printf(" enter complex x\n");scanf("%le%le",&x,&y);
   if(x==0. && y==0.)break;
   a=complex(x,y); (cgamma(a)).print(" gamma=","\n");
   }
*/
Cvector A(10),B(10);
while(1)
   {printf(" enter complex x\n");scanf("%le%le",&x,&y);
   if(x==0. && y==0.)break;a=complex(x,y);
   A.setelement(0,complex(3.,0.) );
   b=Gmeijer(1,0,0,1,B,A,a); b.print(" answer="," ");
   ((a^3.) * ((-a).cexp())).print("","\n");
   }
while(1)
   {printf(" 1F1: enter complex x\n");scanf("%le%le",&x,&y);
   if(x==0. && y==0.)break;b=complex(x,y);
   printf(" enter complex a\n");scanf("%le%le",&x,&y);a=com-
plex( x,y);
   printf(" enter complex c\n");scanf("%le%le",&x,&y);c=com-
plex( x,y);
   A.setelement(0,(1.-a));
   B.setelement(0,complex(0.,0.));
   B.setelement(1,(1.-c));
   b=Gmeijer(1,1,1,2,A,B,(-b))*cgamma(c)/cgamma(a);
```

```
   b.print(" 1F1(a,c,x) =","\n");
   }
}

error(char* msg,int index,int s)
   {
   printf("%s%d %d\n",msg,index,s);
   exit(1);
   return 0;/* keep compiler happy*/
   }

void Cvector::check( int index)
   {int loc;
   loc=index-(*this).base;
   if (loc<0)
      error(" Cvector error: index-
base",index,(*this).base);
   if (loc>= (*this).size)
      error(" Cvector error: index too
large",index,(*this).size);
   }

void Cmatrix::check( int i,int j)
   {int loc;
   loc=i-(*this).base;
   if (loc<0)
      error(" Cmatrix error: row index-
base",i,(*this).base);
   if (loc>= (*this).rowkt)
      error(" Cmatrix error: row index too
large",i,(*this).rowkt);

   loc=j-(*this).base;
   if (loc<0)
      error(" Cmatrix error: column index-
base",j,(*this).base);
   if (loc>= (*this).colkt)
      error(" Cmatrix error: column index too
large",j,(*this).colkt);

   }


void Cmatrix::init(int row, int col, int b)
   {
   if(row<1||col<1)error(" matrix needs at least one
row/col ",row,col);
   rowkt=row;colkt=col;base=b;
   m= new complex *[rowkt];
```

```
   for(int j=0;j<rowkt;j++)m[j]= new complex[colkt];
   complex zero;complex one(1.,0.);
   //initialize to identity matrix.
   for(int
i=0;i<rowkt;i++){for(j=0;j<colkt;j++)m[i][j]=zero;
      m[i][i]= one;// omit this line for init. to zero
matrix
      }
   }

Cmatrix::Cmatrix(Cmatrix& a)
   { init(a.rowkt,a.colkt,a.base);
    for(int i=0;i<a.rowkt;i++)for(int
j=0;j<a.colkt;j++)m[i][j]=a.m[i][j];
   }

Cmatrix::~Cmatrix()
   {for(int i=0;i<rowkt;i++)delete m[i];
   delete m;
   }


complex& Cvector::element(int i)
   {
   check(i);return head[i-base];
   }

void Cvector::setelement( int i, complex& value)
   {
   check(i);
   head[i]=value;
   }
complex& Cmatrix::element(int i,int j)
   {
   check(i,j);return m[i-base][j-base];
   }

void Cmatrix::setelement( int i, int j, complex value)
   {
   check(i,j);m[i][j]=value;
   }


void Cmatrix::operator=(Cmatrix& a)
   {
   if(this==&a)return;
   for(int i=0;i<rowkt;i++)delete m[i];
   delete m;
   init(a.rowkt,a.colkt,a.base);
```

```
   for(i=0;i<a.rowkt;i++)for(int
j=0;j<a.colkt;j++)m[i][j]=a.m[i][j];
   }

 Cvector::Cvector( Cvector& orig) //copy
   {
   size=orig.size;base=orig.base;head=new com-
plex[orig.size];
   for(int i=0;i<size;i++)head[i]=orig.head[i];
   }

Cmatrix operator*(Cmatrix&a, Cmatrix& b)
   {
   int i,j,k;complex zero;
   if(a.colkt!=b.rowkt)
      error(" cannot multiply matrices colkt,rowkt
",a.colkt,b.rowkt);
   Cmatrix prod(a.rowkt,b.colkt,a.base);
   for(i=0;i<a.rowkt;i++)for(j=0;j<b.colkt;j++)
      {prod.m[i][j]=zero;
      for(k=0;k<a.colkt;k++)prod.m[i][j] +=
a.m[i][k]*b.m[k][j];
      }
   return prod;
   }


Cvector operator*(Cmatrix& a, Cvector& b)
   {
   int k;complex zero;
   if(a.colkt!=b.size)error(" cannot mult. matrix,vector
",a.colkt,b.size);
   Cvector prod(b.size,b.base,zero);
   for(int i=0;i<a.rowkt;i++)
      {prod.head[i]=zero;
      for(k=0;k<a.colkt;k++)prod.head[i] +=
(a.m[i][k])*(b.head[k]);
      }
   return prod;
   }

complex Cvector::operator*(Cvector& rvalue) //dot product
   {int i; complex *element,*relement; complex
sum(0.,0.);// sum
   if(rvalue.size!= size)
      error(" dot product unequal length vectors
",size,rvalue.size);
   for(i=0,element=head,relement=rvalue.head;i< size;
      i++,element++,relement++)
```

```
      sum += *element * *relement;
   return sum;
   }

void Cvector::operator=(  Cvector& rhs)
   {
   if( this== &rhs)return;
   if(size!=rhs.size)
      {
      delete head;
      head= new complex[rhs.size];
      }
   for(int j=0;j<size;j++){head[j]=rhs.head[j];}
   }
```

Test Output: Meijer G

```
 enter complex x 2 0 answer= 1.082681e+00+0.000000e+00 i
1.082682e+00+0.000000e+00 i
enter complex x 0 0
1F1: enter complex x 1 0
enter complex a 1 0
enter complex c 1 0
1F1(a,c,x) = 2.718279e+00+0.000000e+00 i
1F1: enter complex x 0 0
```

```
/*
Generalized Hypergeometric Function and Meijer G
   Pade summation used for former
from C Mathematical Function Handbook by Louis Baker
Copyright 1991 by Louis Baker. All rights reserved.
*/
#include "Cmatrix.hpp"

#define maxterm 100
#define abstol 1.e-8
#define reltol 1.e-5
#define errorcode -1.e60
#define pi 3.14159265358979323846264338327 9
#define lim 15.
#define max(a,b) ((a)>(b)?(a):(b))
complex cgamma(complex&);

// generalized hypergeometric function pFq or pFq-1
// if 0<=k<=q then the k-th factor (c)k in denominator
omitted pFq-1
// if k=-1,say, then pFq= sum x^n/n!
(a[0])n..../{(c[0])n.....}
// pade approx. version
int szused,sizep=60;

complex ghgF(int p,int q,complex x, Cvector& a, Cvector& c,
int k)
{complex sum(1.,0.),oldsum,power(1.,0.),btm;double
test,fact;
complex f,t,pc,qc,*h,hold;int j,kk; double diff,tk,z;
if( sizep%2)sizep++;//size must be even integer
h=new complex[sizep+1] ;

Cvector denom(max(q,1)),numer(max(p,1));
// use 2F1 if p=2,q=1
//x.print(" x in ghgf=","\n");
//printf(" in ghgF: p q %d %d k=%d\n",p,q,k);
fact=1.;
for( j=0;j<p;j++)
   {
   //(a.element(j)).print(" a=","\n");
   numer.setelement(j,a.element(j));
   //(numer.element(j)).print(" numer=","\n");
   }
for( j=0;j<q;j++) {denom.setelement(j,c.element(j));
      //(denom.element(j)).print(" denom=","\n");
      //c.element(j)).print(" a=","\n");
         }
//power.print(" power=","\n");
```

```
h[0]=1.;kk=0;hold=1.;
while(kk<sizep){
   kk++;
//test t[n]=x^n geometric series 1+x+x^2+...=1/(1-x)
//                  t*=xx;
   btm=1.;
   for(j=0;j<p;j++){power *= numer.element(j);
         //power.print(" power=","\n");
         numer.setelement(j,numer.element(j)+1.);}
   for(j=0;j<q;j++){if(j!=k)btm *=denom.element(j);
         denom.setelement(j,denom.element(j)+1.);}
//btm.print(" btm=","\n");
power *= (x/(btm*fact));
//power.print(" power=","\n");
   t=power;
   h[kk]=h[kk-1]+t;
   fact+=1.;
   qc=0.;j=kk;
   do   {
      pc=h[j-1];
      if(h[j]==pc)
         {
         h[j-1]=-errorcode;
         if(pc==-errorcode)h[j-1]=qc;
         }
      else h[j-1]= qc+1./(h[j]-pc);
      qc=pc;j--;
      }while(j);
   if(!(kk%2))
      {
      diff=(hold-h[0]).abs();
      if(diff<abstol || diff<reltol * h[0].abs())break;
      hold=h[0];
      }
   }
szused=kk;
hold=h[0];
delete h;
return  hold;
}


complex Gmeijer(int m, int n, int p, int q,Cvector& a,Cvec-
tor& c, complex& x)
{/* Meijer G function*/
complex coef,sum,denom,differ;double re;int j;
```

```
if(m<1 ||m>q){fprintf(stderr," Meijer:illegal m\n");return
errorcode;}
if(n<0 ||n>p){fprintf(stderr," Meijer:illegal n\n");return
errorcode;}
Cvector aa(max(1,q)),cc(max(1,p));
if(p>q)    /* p>q implies for pFq-1 as p'Fq' p'q'+1*/
   {
   //printf(" Meijer G: pq\n");
   for(j=0;j<q;j++) aa.setelement(j, 1.-c.element(j));
   for(j=0;j<p;j++) cc.setelement(j, 1.-a.element(j));
   sum=Gmeijer(n,m,q,p,aa,cc,1./x);
   return sum;
   }
else if(p==q)
   {if( x.abs()>=1.){//printf(" p=q Meijer\n");
      return complex(errorcode,0.);}
   }
for(int k=0;k<m;k++)//arrays based at zero(default)
   {
   coef=complex(1.,0.);
   denom=complex(1.,0.);

for(int j=0;j<p;j++)
   {cc.setelement(j,1.+c.element(k)-a.element(j));
   //(cc.element(j)).print(" numer=","\n");
   }
for( j=0;j<q;j++) {aa.setelement(j,1.+c.element(k)-c.ele-
ment(j));
      //(aa.element(j)).print(" denom=","\n");
         }

//coef.print(" coef=","\n");
   for( j=0;j<n;j++) if(j!=k)coef *= cgamma(1.-aa.ele-
ment(j));
//coef.print(" coef=","\n");
   for( j=0;j<n;j++) coef *= cgamma(cc.element(j));
//coef.print(" coef=","\n");
   for( j=n;j<p;j++)denom*= cgamma(1.-cc.element(j));
//denom.print(" denom=","\n");
   for( j=m;j<q;j++) denom *= cgamma(aa.element(j));
   coef *= (x^c.element(k))/denom;
//denom.print(" denom=","\n");
//printf(" before call ghgF ");coef.print(" coef=","\n");
//sum.print(" sum=","\n");
   sum += coef*ghgF(p,q,((p-m-n)%2?-1.:1.)*x,cc,aa,k);
//printf(" after call ");sum.print(" sum=","\n");
   }
return sum;
}
```

```
main()
{
complex a,b,c;double x,y;
/*
while(1)
   {printf(" enter complex x\n");scanf("%le%le",&x,&y);
   if(x==0. && y==0.)break;
   a=complex(x,y); (cgamma(a)).print(" gamma=","\n");
   }
*/
Cvector A(10),B(10);
while(1)
   {printf(" enter complex x\n");scanf("%le%le",&x,&y);
   if(x==0. && y==0.)break;a=complex(x,y);
   A.setelement(0,complex(3.,0.) );
   b=Gmeijer(1,0,0,1,B,A,a); b.print(" answer="," ");
   ((a^3.) * ((-a).cexp())).print("","\n");
   }

while(1)
   {printf(" 1F1:enter complex x\n");scanf("%le%le",&x,&y);
   if(x==0. && y==0.)break;b=complex(x,y);
   printf(" enter complex a\n");scanf("%le%le",&x,&y);a=com-
plex( x,y);
   printf(" enter complex c\n");scanf("%le%le",&x,&y);c=com-
plex( x,y);
   A.setelement(0,(1.-a));
   B.setelement(0,complex(0.,0.));
   B.setelement(1,(1.-c));
   b=Gmeijer(1,1,1,2,A,B,(-b))*cgamma(c)/cgamma(a);
   b.print(" 1F1(a,c,x) =","\n");
   }
}

error(char* msg,int index,int s)
   {
   printf("%s%d %d\n",msg,index,s);
   exit(1);
   return 0;/* keep compiler happy*/
   }

void Cvector::check( int index)
   {int loc;
   loc=index-(*this).base;
   if (loc<0)
      error(" Cvector error: index-
base",index,(*this).base);
   if (loc>= (*this).size)
```

```
      error(" Cvector error: index too
large",index,(*this).size);
   }

void Cmatrix::check( int i,int j)
   {int loc;
   loc=i-(*this).base;
   if (loc<0)
      error(" Cmatrix error: row index-
base",i,(*this).base);
   if (loc>= (*this).rowkt)
      error(" Cmatrix error: row index too
large",i,(*this).rowkt);

   loc=j-(*this).base;
   if (loc<0)
      error(" Cmatrix error: column index-
base",j,(*this).base);
   if (loc>= (*this).colkt)
      error(" Cmatrix error: column index too
large",j,(*this).colkt);

   }


void Cmatrix::init(int row, int col, int b)
   {
   if(row<1||col<1)error(" matrix needs at least one
row/col ",row,col);
   rowkt=row;colkt=col;base=b;
   m= new complex *[rowkt];
   for(int j=0;j<rowkt;j++)m[j]= new complex[colkt];
   complex zero;complex one(1.,0.);
   //initialize to identity matrix.
   for(int
i=0;i<rowkt;i++){for(j=0;j<colkt;j++)m[i][j]=zero;
      m[i][i]= one;// omit this line for init. to zero
matrix
      }
   }

Cmatrix::Cmatrix(Cmatrix& a)
   { init(a.rowkt,a.colkt,a.base);
    for(int i=0;i<a.rowkt;i++)for(int
j=0;j<a.colkt;j++)m[i][j]=a.m[i][j];
   }

Cmatrix::~Cmatrix()
   {for(int i=0;i<rowkt;i++)delete m[i];
```

```
    delete m;
    }


complex& Cvector::element(int i)
    {
    check(i);return head[i-base];
    }

void Cvector::setelement( int i, complex& value)
    {
    check(i);
    head[i]=value;
    }
complex& Cmatrix::element(int i,int j)
    {
    check(i,j);return m[i-base][j-base];
    }

void Cmatrix::setelement( int i, int j, complex value)
    {
    check(i,j);m[i][j]=value;
    }


void Cmatrix::operator=(Cmatrix& a)
    {
    if(this==&a)return;
    for(int i=0;i<rowkt;i++)delete m[i];
    delete m;
    init(a.rowkt,a.colkt,a.base);
    for(i=0;i<a.rowkt;i++)for(int
j=0;j<a.colkt;j++)m[i][j]=a.m[i][j];
    }

 Cvector::Cvector( Cvector& orig) //copy
    {
    size=orig.size;base=orig.base;head=new com-
plex[orig.size];
    for(int i=0;i<size;i++)head[i]=orig.head[i];
    }

Cmatrix operator*(Cmatrix&a, Cmatrix& b)
    {
    int i,j,k;complex zero;
    if(a.colkt!=b.rowkt)
       error(" cannot multiply matrices colkt,rowkt
",a.colkt,b.rowkt);
    Cmatrix prod(a.rowkt,b.colkt,a.base);
```

```
   for(i=0;i<a.rowkt;i++)for(j=0;j<b.colkt;j++)
      {prod.m[i][j]=zero;
      for(k=0;k<a.colkt;k++)prod.m[i][j] +=
a.m[i][k]*b.m[k][j];
      }
   return prod;
   }


Cvector operator*(Cmatrix& a, Cvector& b)
   {
   int k;complex zero;
   if(a.colkt!=b.size)error(" cannot mult. matrix,vector
",a.colkt,b.size);
   Cvector prod(b.size,b.base,zero);
   for(int i=0;i<a.rowkt;i++)
      {prod.head[i]=zero;
      for(k=0;k<a.colkt;k++)prod.head[i] +=
(a.m[i][k])*(b.head[k]);
      }
   return prod;
   }

complex Cvector::operator*(Cvector& rvalue) //dot product
   {int i; complex *element,*relement; complex
sum(0.,0.);// sum
   if(rvalue.size!= size)
      error(" dot product unequal length vectors
",size,rvalue.size);
   for(i=0,element=head,relement=rvalue.head;i< size;
      i++,element++,relement++)
      sum += *element * *relement;
   return sum;
   }

void Cvector::operator=(  Cvector& rhs)
   {
   if( this== &rhs)return;
   if(size!=rhs.size)
      {
      delete head;
      head= new complex[rhs.size];
      }
   for(int j=0;j<size;j++){head[j]=rhs.head[j];}
   }
```

Test Output: Meijer G with Pade

```
 enter complex x 2 0 answer= 1.082682e+00+0.000000e+00 i
1.082682e+00+0.000000e+00 i
enter complex x 0 0
1F1:enter complex x 1 0 enter complex a 1 0
enter complex c 1 0
1F1(a,c,x) = 2.718282e+00+0.000000e+00 i
1F1:enter complex x 0 0
```

```
/*
MacRobert E function

from C Mathematical Function Handbook by Louis Baker
Copyright 1991 by Louis Baker. All rights reserved.
*/

#include "Cmatrix.hpp"

#define maxterm 100
#define abstol 1.e-8
#define reltol 1.e-5
#define errorcode -1.e60
#define pi 3.141592653589793238462643383279
#define lim 15.
#define max(a,b) ((a)>(b)?(a):(b))

complex Gmeijer(int m, int n, int p, int q,Cvector& a,Cvec-
tor& c, complex& x);

//MacRobert's E expressed in terms of Miejer's G:
// defining B locally produced a bug 50714 report by Zor-
tech ZTC2B
complex Emacrobert(int p,int q, Cvector& a, Cvector& b, com-
plex& x)
{
Cvector B((1+q));
B.setelement(0,complex(1.,0.));
for(int i=1;i<=q;i++)B.setelement(i, b.element(i-1));
return Gmeijer(p,1,q+1,p,B,a,x);
}
```

Chapter 30

Xref

I had intended to include a complete cross-reference for all of the functions of this book, showing both the callers and callees of each function. This would have taken a prohibitive amount of space, however. Because this book is being distributed with a diskette of programs, the obvious solution is to distribute the program I wrote to perform this task, and let the reader generate his own, customized cross reference.

The program is written in TurboC. It uses functions such as **findfirst()** and **findnext()** to search through a sequence of files matching a specification which may include wildcards, such as ***.c**. This function may not be available on all systems, but an equivalent should be.

The user can customize this program at will. It reads in a list of keywords and function names to ignore from file **keywd.dat**. It creates two separate lists (caller and called). You can customize the list of keywords (and others) to be ignored. Have fun! The applications of this program clearly go beyond a mathematical function library.

Taking a cue from the Free Software Foundation, I should copyleft[1] this program. Having difficulty with telling my right from my left, let me introduce the concept of **copysideways**. If you have read this far, you are deemed to have implicitly agreed to any licensing agreement I care to invent. (Just kidding. But remember, **all** of this book and the associated software is copyrighted.)

The listing of **protom.h** in Chapter 2 serves as a catalog of the available functions, their location by filename, arranged by relevant chapter. The **callers** and callees **files** are on the diskette included with this book.

1. If you are not familiar with this term, that is too bad. Ask R. Stollman.

```
/*
adaptive integration routine
uses Simpson's rule adaptively
(from "C Tools for  Scientists and Engineers" by L. Baker)

CONTENTS:

adsimp
   adaptively computes integral of function

simp
   recursively applies simpson's rule

main
   test driver

funct
   function to be integrated

DEPENDENCIES:
NONE
*/



/* maxlev = max. allowed level
   levmax = max. level used
   level  = current level
   feval  = number of function evaluations used*/

/*#include "libc.h"
#include "math.h"
*/
#define abs(x) ((x)?(x):-(x))
#define max(a,b) ((a)>(b)?(a):(b))
int level,maxlev,levmax,feval;

double adsimp(a,b,eps,f) double a,b,eps,(*f)();
{
double simp(),aa,epss,absarea,ans,fa,fb,fm,range,est;
levmax=1;
feval=3;
level=1;
/*maxlev=6;*/
aa=a;epss=eps;
absarea=1.;
est=1.;
/*printf(" in adsimp %le %le\n",a,b);*/
range=b-a;
fa=(*f)(a);
```

```
fb=(*f)(b);
fm=(*f)(.5*(a+b)) *4.;
/* printf(" intergrand fa,fb,fm %e %e %e\n",fa,fb,fm);*/
ans=simp(aa,range,fa,fm,fb,absarea,est,epss,f);
/*printf(" in adsimp simp=%le\n",ans);*/
return(ans);
}

double simp(a,da,fa,fm,fb,area,est,eps,f)
double a,da,fa,fm,fb,area,est,eps,(*f)();
{
double absarea;
double
dx,x1,x2,est1,est2,est3,f1,f2,f3,f4,sum,epss,norm=.588;
absarea=area;
/*printf("simp %e %e %e %e %e \n %e %e %e %d\n"
,a,da,fa,fm,fb,absarea,est,eps,level);*/
dx=.333333333*da;
epss=eps*norm;
x1=a+dx;
x2=x1+dx;
f1=4.*(*f)(a+.5*dx);
f2=(*f)(x1);
f3=(*f)(x2);
f4=4.*(*f)(a+2.5*dx);
/*
f1=4.*funct(a+.5*dx);
f2=funct(x1);
f3=funct(x2);
f4=4.*funct(a+2.5*dx);
*/
feval+=4;
est1=(fa+f1+f2)*dx*.166666666666;
est2=(f2+fm+f3)*dx*.166666666666;
est3=(f3+f4+fb)*dx*.166666666666;
absarea=area-abs(est)+abs(est1)+abs(est2)+abs(est3);
sum=est1+est2+est3;
level++;
levmax= max(level,levmax);
if ( ((abs(est-sum)> eps*absarea)||(est==1.))
                    && level<maxlev)
    sum= simp(a,dx,fa,f1,f2,absarea,est1,epss,f)
      +simp(x1,dx,f2,fm,f3,absarea,est2,epss,f)
      +simp(x2,dx,f3,f4,fb,absarea,est3,epss,f);

level--;
return(sum);
}
```

```
/*
test driver jacobian elliptic function and relatives

from C Mathematical Function Handbook by Louis Baker
Copyright 1991 by Louis Baker. All rights reserved.
*/

#include <stdio.h>
#include "cmlib.h"
#include "protom.h"


extern double jtheta, amplitude,kimag,eimag;

main()
{double a,b,c,d,x,y,m,k,e,omp,eh,eta,g2,g3;
struct complex z,p,pp,etap,ans;
struct complex v,qq,ans3,ans1,ans2;int i,j;double zz;
struct complex ee,f,g;
double r,s,t,sig=1.e-4;
double ts,tc,td,tn,u,alpha;
double eps,n,phi;

infinite_loop
   {
   printf(" E(u) enter mag u, theta(deg), m(==0. to
quit)\n");
   scanf("%le%le%le",&a,&b,&d);
   c= b*pi/180.;
   if(d==0.)break;
   else printf(" for m=%le theta(rad)=%le,|u|=%le\n",d,c,a);
   CMPLX(z,a*cos(c),a*sin(c));
   ce(&z,d,&p);printc(&p);
   }
infinite_loop
   {
   printf(" K,E(m) enter m(==0. to quit)\n");
   scanf("%le",&a);
   if(a==0.)break;
   tek(0,a,&c,&d);
   printf(" K,E= %le %le\n",c,d);
   if(kimag!=0.)printf(" imag parts %le %le\n",kimag,eimag);
   }

while(1)
   {
   a=0.;b=0.;
   printf(" for tef(incomplete): enter m (-1 to quit) ");
   scanf("%le",&x);m=x; if(m==-1.)break;
```

```
   printf("enter phi");scanf("%le",&alpha);
   /*if(alpha==0. && m==0.)break;*/
   tef(alpha,m,1.e-5,&a,&b);
   printf(" at phi=%le,m=%le,F=%le E=%le Z=%le\n"
      ,alpha,m,a,b,jzeta(alpha,m));
   }

while(1)
   {
   /*alpha= (j+1)*pi*15./180.; m=sin(alpha);m*=m;*/
   a=0.;b=0.;
   printf(" tef: enter m -1. to quit ");
   scanf("%le",&x);m=x;
   if( m==-1.)break;
   tef(pi/6.,m,1.e-3,&a,&b);printf(" at pi/6=30,m=%g,%le
%le\n",m,a,b);
   }
printf(" complete integrals\n");
for(j=0;j<16;j++)
   {
   m= (j+1)*.05;
   tek(0,m,&a,&b);printf(" %le %le %le\n",m,a,b);
   }
printf(" incomplete, 30deg \n");
for(j=0;j<4;j++)
   {
   alpha= (j+1)*pi*15./180.; m=sin(alpha);m*=m;a=0.;b=0.;
   printf(" alpha=%f %g ",alpha,m);
   tef(pi/6.,m,1.e-3,&a,&b);printf(" %le %le\n",a,b);
   }
printf(" jzeta\n");
printf(" %le \n",jzeta( pi/6.,.25));
printf(" jacobian elliptic\n");
jef(.2,.81,&a,&b,&alpha);
printf(" .2|.81 sn=%le cn=%le dn=%le
%le\n",a,b,alpha,jtheta);
jef(.2,.19,&a,&b,&alpha);
printf(" .2|.19 sn=%le cn=%le dn=%le
jtheta=%le\n",a,b,alpha,jtheta);
jef(.75342,.7,&a,&b,&alpha);
printf(" .75342|.7 sn=%le cn=%le dn=%le
%le\n",a,b,alpha,jtheta);
jef(.6,.36,&a,&b,&alpha);
printf(" .6|.36 sn=%le cn=%le dn=%le
%le\n",a,b,alpha,jtheta);
alpha=heuman(pi/6.,.25);
printf(" heuman=%le\n",alpha  );

eps=.3333333;/* 30 degrees */
```

```
u= eps*1.68575;
neville(u,.25,&ts,&tc,&td,&tn);
printf(" neville s,c,d,n %le %le %le %le\n",ts,tc,td,tn);



while(1){
printf(" e3: enter n phi m  all 0 to end.\n");
scanf("%le%le%le",&a,&b,&c);
n=a;phi=b;m=c;
if(a==0. && b==0. && c==0.)break;
printf(" %g %f %f %le\n",n,phi,m,e3(n,phi,m,1.e-4));
}




while(1)
   {
   printf(" Weierstrass:enter z=x+iy,g2,g3 quit z==0");
   scanf("%le%le%le%le",&a,&b,&c,&d);
   if(a==0.)break; z.x=a;z.y=b; x=c;y=d; g2=c;g3=d;
   weier(&z,x,y,&p,&pp,&m,&k,&e,&omp,&eta,&eh);
   printf(" P and P':");printc(&p);printf("
");printc(&pp);printf("\n");
   printf(" m= %le K=%le E=%le omega(2) %le e or h2
%le\n",m,k,e,omp,eh);
   sigma(&z,&ans,k,omp,eta,m,g2,g3);
   printf(" sigma= %le %le\n",ans.x,ans.y);
   zetaw(&z,&ans,k,omp,eta,m,g2,g3);
   printf("zetaw %le %le\n",ans.x,ans.y);
   }
printf(" m given q\n");
for(i=1;i<21;i++)
   {
   zz= i/20.;qq.y=0.;qq.x=zz;emf(&qq,&ans);
   printf(" q=%le m=%le or %le
%le\n",zz,mq(zz),ans.x,ans.y);
   }
for(i=1;i<21;i++)
   {
   zz= i/100.;
   printf(" q=%le m=%le %le\n",zz,mq(zz),mq(zz));
   }

printf(" q for .9997 %le\n",q(.9997));

while(1){
```

```
printf(" theta:enter v,q both com-
plex");scanf("%le%le%le%le",&a,&b,&c,&d);
if(a==0. && b==0. && c==0. && d==0.)break;
CMPLX(v,a,b);
CMPLX(qq,c,d);ctheta(&v,&qq,&ans1,&ans2,&ans3,&ans);
printf(" ans=%le %le %le %le %le %le %le %le\n"
,ans.x,ans.y,ans3.x,ans3.y,ans1.x,ans1.y,ans2.x,ans2.y);
}

quartic(0.,0.,0.,-1.,&z,&ee,&f,&g);
printf(" quartic %le %le %le %le %le %le %le %le\n"
   ,z.x,z.y,ee.x,ee.y,f.x,f.y,g.x,g.y);
while(1)
{
printf(" enter real m, complex z for
cef");scanf("%le%le%le",&a,&b,&c);
if(a==0.&& b==0. &&c==0.)break;
m=a;z.x=b;z.y=c; cef(m,&z,&ee,&f,sig);
printf(" e %le %le f %le %le\n",ee.x,ee.y,f.x,f.y);
}
while(1)
{printf(" enter complex z, real g2 g3 for invw test\n");
scanf("%le%le%le%le",&a,&b,&c,&d);
g2=c;g3=d; z.x=a;z.y=b;
invp(g2,g3,&z,&f);
printf(" answer %le %le\n",f.x,f.y);
}
}
```

C Functions Index

Index

ABOUT THE AUTHOR

Louis Baker, Ph.D., is a senior researcher at Mission Research Corporation in Albuquerque, New Mexico. Prior to this, he held positions at Sandia National Laboratories and the Naval Research Laboratory in Washington, D.C. Dr. Baker has written numerous articles on electromagnetic field propagation, computer interfacing, artificial intelligence, and computer simulation.